KNOWLEDGE, NATURE, AND THE GOOD

KNOWLEDGE, NATURE, AND THE GOOD

ESSAYS ON ANCIENT PHILOSOPHY

John M. Cooper

PRINCETON UNIVERSITY PRESS

PRINCETON AND OXFORD

COPYRIGHT © 2004 BY PRINCETON UNIVERSITY PRESS

PUBLISHED BY PRINCETON UNIVERSITY PRESS,

41 WILLIAM STREET, PRINCETON, NEW JERSEY 08540

IN THE UNITED KINGDOM: PRINCETON UNIVERSITY PRESS,

3 MARKET PLACE, WOODSTOCK, OXFORDSHIRE OX20 1SY

ALL RIGHTS RESERVED

LIBRARY OF CONGRESS CATALOGING-IN-PUBLICATION DATA

COOPER, JOHN M. (JOHN MADISON), 1939–

KNOWLEDGE, NATURE AND THE GOOD:

ESSAYS ON ANCIENT PHILOSOPHY / JOHN M. COOPER

P.   CM.

INCLUDES BIBLIOGRAPHICAL REFERENCES AND INDEX.

ISBN 0-691-11723-3 (ALK. PAPER)—ISBN 0-691-11724 (PBK. : ALK. PAPER)

1. PHILOSOPHY, ANCIENT. I. TITLE.

B171.C684 2004

180—DC22   2003065498

BRITISH LIBRARY CATALOGING-IN-PUBLICATION DATA IS AVAILABLE

THIS BOOK HAS BEEN COMPOSED IN SABON

PRINTED ON ACID-FREE PAPER. ∞

PUP.PRINCETON.EDU

PRINTED IN THE UNITED STATES OF AMERICA

1   3   5   7   9   10   8   6   4   2

CONTENTS

THE GOOD

PREFACE

IN REASON AND EMOTION (Princeton, 1999) I collected most of the papers on ancient ethics and moral psychology that I had written up to that time. By then I had also published a number of essays on other aspects of ancient philosophy. In the meantime I have written further essays both on ancient moral philosophy and on ancient epistemology, metaphysics and physics, and philosophy of mind. Since these have appeared in a widely dispersed set of journals, proceedings, and specialist collections, and even though several of them have been reprinted in anthologies, friends and colleagues have urged me to bring them together in this second volume of essays. By doing so, I hope to give readers easier access to the older papers, which continue to be read in courses and seminars, and which are reprinted here with no substantial changes. But I also include revised and expanded final versions of four of the most recent papers (chapters 1, 7, 9, and 11). One paper, chapter 13, appears here for the first time.

These thirteen essays are on diverse topics from different periods of ancient philosophy. The topics range from Hippocratic medical theory and Plato's epistemology and moral philosophy to Aristotle's physics and metaphysics, Academic skepticism, and the cosmology, moral psychology, and ethical theory of the ancient Stoics. They are unified only insofar as, throughout, I have attempted, whatever the particular topic being pursued, to understand and appreciate the ancient philosophers' views in philosophical terms drawn from the ancient philosophical tradition itself (rather than by bringing to them, and interpreting them in terms of, contemporary philosophical concepts and debates). Through engaging creatively and philosophically with the ancient philosophers' views, these essays aim to make ancient philosophical perspectives available in all their freshness, originality, and deep, continuing, philosophical interest to philosophers and philosophy students of the current day. I am certainly not alone nowadays in adopting such a personal point of view in my writing about ancient philosophy. I am pleased to think that by presenting these papers to a wider public than the specialist audiences to which they were addressed in their original places of publication, I can hope to help both to propagate this approach to the study of ancient philosophy and to gain appreciation for its fruits among the philosophical community in general.

These essays are the product of more than thirty-five years' work on problems of ancient logic, metaphysics, physics, moral psychology, and ethical and political theory. I owe too much to too many people over these years—for instruction, advice, assistance, encouragement, and (not least) intellectual companionship—to be able to thank them all. But, though by now the debt is an old one, I cannot fail to mention my teacher and then colleague in the 1960s, G.E.L. Owen, who was an inspiration to me both in my early days and ever since. My Princeton (earlier, Pittsburgh) colleague, Alexander Nehamas, read and commented on almost all these essays, in many cases at more than one stage of preparation. His friendship and support have been indispensable.

I incurred several specific debts in the final preparation of the book. I owe thanks, once again, to Donald Morrison for his help in selecting the art for the book's cover, and to Christopher Noble for his help with the bibliography. I thank Princeton University for granting me leave, and the American Council of Learned Societies for its fellowship support, during academic year 2002–03, when much of my time was spent finishing up several of the essays and putting the book together. I owe thanks also for Molan Goldstein's assistance, at a later stage, in copyediting a bunch of very disparate essays, most of them published according to very different editorial standards, into a uniform, attractively presented book; and to Carol Roberts for preparing the indexes.

Finally, I thank my wife Marcia—for everything.

One editorial note: I have collected in the bibliography full bibliographical information for both secondary articles and books that I cite, and for editions and translations of the primary sources. In footnote citations, I give the author's name, title of the work, and, where relevant, editor's or translator's name, together with an abbreviated title that I hope will be easily recognized by readers familiar with the literature in the specific area covered. Others need only turn to the bibliography under the name in question in order to obtain full information.

Princeton University

ACKNOWLEDGMENTS

CHAPTERS 1–6 and 8–12 appeared in their original form, or are to appear, in the following publications; chapters 1, 9, and 11 have been expanded and extensively revised for inclusion here. The second half of chapter 7 was previously published, as noted below. Chapter 13 has been written especially for this volume.

1. "Method and Science in *On Ancient Medicine*," in Helmut Linneweber-Lammerskitten and Georg Mohr, eds., *Interpretation und Argument* (Würzburg: Königshausen & Neumann, 2002), 25–57. With permission of the publisher.

2. "Plato on Sense-Perception and Knowledge (*Theaetetus* 184–186)," *Phronesis* XV (1970), 123–146. With permission of Koninklijke Brill NV, Leiden, The Netherlands.

3. "Plato, Isocrates and Cicero on the Independence of Oratory from Philosophy," in J. J. Cleary, ed., *Proceedings of the Boston Area Colloquium in Ancient Philosophy*, vol. 1 (1985) (Lanham, Md.: University Press of America, 1986), 77–96. With permission of the publisher.

4. "Arcesilaus: Socratic and Sceptic," in V. Karasmanis, ed., *Year of Socrates 2001—Proceedings* (Athens: European Cultural Center of Delphi, 2004). With permission of Prof. Karasmanis and the European Cultural Center of Delphi.

5. "Aristotle on Natural Teleology," in M. Schofield and M. C. Nussbaum, eds., *Language and Logos* (Cambridge: Cambridge University Press, 1982), 197–222. With permission of the publisher.

6. "Hypothetical Necessity," in A. Gotthelf, ed., *Aristotle on Nature and Living Things* (Pittsburgh: Mathesis Publications, 1986), 151–167. With permission of the publisher.

7. "A Note on Aristotle on Mixture," in J. Mansfeld and F. de Haas, eds., *Aristotle: On Generation and Corruption I* Proceedings of Symposium Aristotelicum XV (Oxford: Oxford University Press, 2004), 315–326.

8. "Metaphysics in Aristotle's Embryology," *Proceedings of the Cambridge Philological Society* no. 214 (1988), 14–41.

9. "Stoic Autonomy," *Social Philosophy and Policy* 20 (2003), 1–29. With permission of Cambridge University Press.

10. "Two Theories of Justice," *Proceedings and Addresses of the American Philosophical Association* 74:2 (2000), 5–27. With permission of the American Philosophical Association.

11. "Plato and Aristotle on 'Finality' and '(Self-)Sufficiency,'" in R. Heinaman, ed., *Plato and Aristotle's Ethics* (London: Ashgate, 2003), 117–147. With permission of Ashgate Publishing, Ltd.

12. "Moral Theory and Moral Improvement: Seneca," forthcoming in J. J. Cleary and Gary Gurtler, eds., *Proceedings of the Boston Area Colloquium in Ancient Philosophy*, vol. 19 (Leiden: Brill, 2004). With permission of Koninklijke Brill NV, Leiden, The Netherlands.

KNOWLEDGE

CHAPTER 1

METHOD AND SCIENCE IN

ON ANCIENT MEDICINE

I

THE TREATISE *On Ancient Medicine* is nowadays one of the most admired, and most studied, of those making up the Hippocratic Corpus. Surprisingly, perhaps, this favored position is a distinctly modern phenomenon, one not found among the ancients. In the mid-second century A.D., Galen knew the work,[1] but he did not devote a commentary to it, as he did to many others in the Hippocratic Corpus that he thought most important and worthwhile. He even wrote commentaries on some he thought entirely or largely "spurious," that is, not by the "great" Hippocrates.[2] But he almost totally ignored *On Ancient Medicine*—according to him also a "spurious" work. He seems never to refer to it by name in any of his works surviving in Greek. So far as I can determine he refers to it only once in his surviving works altogether—namely, in the commentary on *Epidemics II* that survives in the Arabic of Hunain Ibn-Ishaq, which was itself translated into German in 1934 by Franz Pfaff[3] (I come back to this passage shortly). Galen seems nowhere to discuss any of its main claims or themes, either to reject them as "un-Hippocratic" (as he certainly must have thought many of them; I return to this below) or to congratulate the author for having gotten something right. (As usual with Galen, that would mean something in agreement with Galen's own views but not nearly as well expressed.) Likewise, the opinions in this treatise apparently did not figure in any positive way in the work of those of Galen's more immediate predecessors from whose views, as well of course as his own extensive independent reading, Galen formed his

---

[1] In his Hippocratic Glossary he explains some words that appear in the corpus only in *On Ancient Medicine* (hereafter *AM*)—though without naming the work. See J. Jouanna, ed., *De L'Ancienne médicine*, 97–99.

[2] For example, the commentary on *Prorrhetic I* and the part of the commentary on *Regimen in Acute Diseases* dealing with the "spurious" appendix.

[3] *Corpus Medicorum Graecorum* (hereafter CMG) 5.10.1, *In Hippocratis Epidemiarum Librum I Commentaria*, ed. Ernst Wenkebach, and *In Hippocratis Epidemiarum Librum II Commentaria ex Versione Arabica*, ed. Franz Pfaff.

own conception of Hippocrates and Hippocratic medicine.[4] Otherwise he would have attacked them for their error, and thus been drawn into some discussion of the work itself.

Thus the evidence suggests that by about the end of the first century A.D.—the time when, according to Wesley Smith, Hippocrates and the Hippocratic Corpus were being canonized as ultimate authorities in medical research—*On Ancient Medicine* was ignored or even dismissed by leading medical theorists. Interestingly, however, it seems that the treatise had earlier figured quite prominently in the establishment of the Empiric school of medicine. Galen mentions that Heraclides of Tarentum and Zeuxis, two prominent Empirics respectively of the early and late first century B.C., wrote commentaries on "all the books of Hippocrates."[5] But it is quite unclear what he thought that meant; in any event we seem to have no record of any commentary by either of them on *On Ancient Medicine*. Still, Smith draws attention to a passage of Galen—the one I referred to above, from the Arabic text of the commentary on *Epidemics II*—and one of Celsus, as supporting his own suggestion that the original Empiric writers of the third century B.C., or at any rate such later adherents of the sect as Heraclides and Zeuxis, made a special point of appealing to the treatise to authorize their own anti-rationalist methods.[6] (I come back below to the question of proto-Empiric method in *On Ancient*

---

[4] On these see Wesley D. Smith, *The Hippocratic Tradition.* 64–74.

[5] See the introductory remarks to his commentary on *In the Surgery* (κατ᾽ ἰητρεῖον, *De Officina Medici*), Kühn XVIII B, 631. The remark is repeated in the introduction to the commentary on *Humors* in the Galenic corpus, which is a Renaissance forgery (Kühn XVI 1).

[6] See Smith, *Hippocratic Tradition,* 208–10. The Galen passage comes in his comment on *Epidemics* (hereafter *Ep.*) 2.2.12: "One must say that in hemorrhage, patients develop a greenish color (ἐκχλοιοῦνται), and one can find many other such things related to wetness and dryness, to hotness and coldness" (Smith trans. in the Loeb edition of *Hippocrates,* vol. VII). Galen, referring to *Ep.* 2.1.10, interprets the text as relying on the following explanation: the loss of blood brings about coldness in the liver, which in turn weakens it so that the blood it produces from the juices coming from the nutriment in the stomach is "unfinished"; this results in the discoloration of the skin referred to. He points out that this passage confirms his attribution to Hippocrates, in his own work *On the Elements, from Hippocrates,* of the view (it is his own as well) that cold, heat, wetness, and dryness are fundamental properties and constituents of the body, any significant excess or deficiency of which is deleterious to health and needs to be corrected by redressing the balance. He cites (*CMG* 5.10.1, p. 220) unnamed others who interpret this text (he does not tell us just how they managed that) as holding the same view as the "work entitled *On Ancient Medicine,*" namely that cold, hot, wet, and dry are not fundamental for curing diseases, and offering further evidence for it. That is ridiculous, says Galen, given that in *On the Nature of Humans, Aphorisms,* and "the other genuine writings" of Hippocrates—even elsewhere in *Ep. II* itself—it is so very clear that Hippocrates expresses the precisely opposite view. Anyone should be able to see that he is saying the same thing here too. Galen does not assign these interpreters to any particular sect, but given the prevalence of Empiric writers among

Medicine: the method recommended is really, I argue, if we are to use these later terms at all, deeply "rationalist" and not "Empiric.") The Empirics seem to have inaugurated the practice of writing commentaries on Hippocrates (as opposed to mere glossaries explaining the meaning of odd or archaic or specifically Ionic forms in the works of the corpus; the latter seem to have begun, as the Empiric sect itself did, in and around the circle of Herophilus in mid-third century Alexandria). So it may well be that the Empirics did pay special attention to, and place special value on, our treatise—interpreted, of course, in their own ways. Even if that is so, the attention paid to *On Ancient Medicine* in antiquity was relatively short-lived: already by the end of the first century A.D., as I have noted, the treatise had effectively dropped out of sight, and Galen's influence in later antiquity and medieval and early modern times made it remain so.[7]

On Ancient Medicine was not regarded as one of the major works of the Hippocratic Corpus until in 1839, Littré, thinking that evidence in

---

the older commentators it is plausible to suppose, with Smith, that he is citing Empiric commentators.

Celsus, in his *Prooemium* 33–35, reports the Empirics as having traced the beginning of medicine to the observations of alert persons in noticing what happened when sick people in the early days of an illness did or did not take food, or took it before, or in the midst of, or just after an onset of acute fever, or ate a full or a reduced quantity. Accumulated experience of this sort led the first physicians to the position where they could accurately prescribe appropriate diets for people when ill, and specify occasions either to take or to omit food, all with beneficial results for their patients. This is very close in general outline to the much elaborated account of the origin of medical science that the author of *AM* gives in chaps. 5–7 (an account we find in no other early text). The similarity is striking and does, I think, lend support to Smith's suggestion. (See further below, section V, on "Empiric" methodology as prefigured in *AM*.)

[7] Jouanna in the *Notice* to his Budé edition (p. 8), reports that *AM* was not translated either into Latin or into Arabic in late ancient or medieval times. I should add that Celsus (early first century A.D.) does not refer to, and makes no use of, *AM* (which is perhaps not surprising, at least so far as books 3–8 are concerned, given their subject matters). In the introduction to his *Glossary of Hippocratic Terms* the grammarian and literary scholar Erotian, writing later in the first century, includes *AM* among the genuine works of Hippocrates "tending toward the theory of the (medical) art," along with *Oath*, *Law* and *On the Art*. See E. Nachmanson, ed., *Erotiani vocum Hippocraticarum collectio cum fragmentis*, 9. And in quite a few places the author of the little treatise *On Rabies* lifts clauses and phrases from *AM* chap. 20 (see M. Pohlenz, "Das zwanzigste Kapitel von Hippokrates *de Prisca Medicina*"), and also others from several other works. (*On Rabies* is preserved in one manuscript as the nineteenth so-called Letter of Hippocrates—the treatise is allegedly being sent by Democritus in a letter to Hippocrates. Hermann Diels edited it, dating it to early imperial times; see "Hippokratische Forschungen V"). It is curious that rabies is not discussed anywhere in the Hippocratic Corpus; indeed, its Greek name, λύσσα, occurs in the corpus only once, in fact in *AM* chap. 19, where it seems not to refer to the disease, but to frenzy or mad agitation in general. But in both these cases the interest in the work is purely literary, and no attention is paid to or use made of its theoretical ideas.

Plato's *Phaedrus* (270c–d) establishes it as a genuine work of the great Hippocrates himself, placed it first in his epoch-making edition of the corpus. For Littré, in *On Ancient Medicine* Hippocrates himself explains the methods proper to medical research (while vigorously rejecting new-fangled ones based on pre-Socratic philosophizing about nature), and sets out the basic principles underlying all medical knowledge. Littré's inference from the passage in Plato was not generally approved, but both the Teubner editor H. Kühlewein (1894) and W.H.S. Jones in the Loeb Classical Library (1923) nonetheless followed him in placing *On Ancient Medicine* at the head of their editions. The work has been the subject of a vast number of specialized studies in the past hundred and fifty years, and it must nowadays be among the most widely read and appreciated works in the corpus—even if current scholarship has renounced the attempt to assign the authorship of this or indeed any Hippocratic writing definitely to the physician of Cos. In what follows I explain and discuss the questions about the methods appropriate to the practice and theory of medicine, and indeed of natural science as a whole, to which this relatively short treatise is centrally devoted. My discussion will, I hope, provide new grounds for admiring its anonymous author's intellectual daring and his truly fascinating ideas about the proper bases for theory construction in the sciences of nature. At the same time, in both interpreting and assessing his views, we will need to attend closely to the questions I have raised about his position in the history of ancient medicine.

II

I begin by giving a heavily interpretative and in parts controversial summary of the work's main line of analysis and argument. In explicating and discussing the author's views in later sections of this essay, I draw attention to the controversial aspects of my interpretation, and attempt to defend them. Here, then, is the summary.

Our author insists that well before his own time (he was probably writing about 420–410 B.C.)[8] there already existed a true "art" of medicine—or, as we should rather translate the word τέχνη in this context, science (1.9, 12.10–16).[9] He insists that this traditional science of medicine, of

---

[8] This is the date accepted by Jouanna (Budé ed., 84–85), chiefly on the basis of the reference to Empedocles in chap. 20, and something close to a consensus seems to favor it nowadays.

[9] For convenience I cite here the lineation marked in the margins of the Loeb text; in subsequent references I add also the page and line of the Budé. (Except where something significant may turn on it, I ignore differences between these two texts: in general, Jouanna prefers

which he presents himself as a practitioner, had been from the very beginning established firmly and directly upon the actually existing, true foundations for any real knowledge of human health and illness—that is, for any real knowledge of their constitution and causes—and the means available to human invention for sustaining the one so far as possible and avoiding, moderating, and eliminating the other. A firm commitment to these foundations was involved in the method (ὁδός) for investigating medical questions that, from the beginning, traditional Greek medicine employed. If only investigators continue to use the same method—fortified by a knowledge of, and beginning their investigations from, the accumulated discoveries of their predecessors—the *whole* science (ἡ τέχνη πᾶσα ἡ ἰητρική, *AM* 8.18-20 = 127, 12–14; see also 2.1–5 = 119, 12–16) can without doubt one day actually be completed: the best physicians will then know everything that actually can be *known* about health and the various diseases, and about how to treat the latter (so far as the nature of things permits their knowledgeable treatment at all).

---

to follow the more challenging text of manuscript M, while Jones opts for the often smoother and easier text of A.) The two passages cited here are found respectively at p. 118, 8 and 132, 18–133, 7 of the Budé edition. To these references one might add 2.9–11 = 119, 19–120, 2—especially if, with the Budé, one reads ὅτι ἐστίν (A) (that the science exists) at 2.11 instead of the Loeb's ὅ τι ἐστίν (M) (what it is); in that case the author announces the whole subsequent discussion, from there until the end of chapter 12, as devoted to establishing the *existence* of this science. (Jones, the Loeb editor, also opted for A's text in his subsequent edition and retranslation, "Philosophy and Medicine in Ancient Greece.") In his note to 120, 2, Jouanna points to 12.10–16 = 132, 18–133, 6 as making A's text preferable, since it concludes the discussion here announced by saying explicitly that a certain consideration is not a good ground for denying the existence of the ancient science. However, that remark develops (and rebuts) a specific criticism of traditional medicine that arises somewhat coincidentally out of the author's argument in chaps. 9–11 and should not be taken as marking a return to the language of this initial statement of what is to be accomplished in chapters 2–12. In chaps. 9–11 the author shows, by examining what happens to certain people in health, that in cases of illness, overeating is in principle just as harmful as eating too little. Hence it is necessary to adopt a not precisely quantifiable regimen, more complex than that given by the simple rule to avoid all "strong" food and have recourse directly to the "weakest"—gruel. The discussion of these points has stimulated the admission on his part that medical science cannot attain to complete and full exactness in its dietary prescriptions, but must make do with a "rough" sort of precision that permits small errors. He mentions this point first at 9.13–22 = 128, 9–17, and he resumes it at 12.10 ff. = 132, 18 ff. (the passage to which Jouanna refers), at the conclusion of an intervening analysis of the effects on some healthy people of departures from their usual (beneficial) diets. There, he insists that the absence of "full exactness" is no ground for declaring medicine no science or its alleged discoveries no discoveries at all but due to mere chance: on the contrary, it is a great achievement to have come by way of reasoning "close to that which is most exact," and a proof that traditional medical inquiry has proceeded finely and correctly. Since the author addresses this objection in connection with his own developing account of traditional medicine, it seems inappropriate to cite this passage as evidence for the right textual

Recent theorists of medicine, however, our author complains—he does not name them, and it will not serve our purposes to speculate about whom he might have had in mind[10]—seemed to assume that traditional Greek medicine had not yet attained the status of a true science. According to them, it was neither a science itself nor based on any τέχνη (1.8–20 = 118, 7–119, 4). And that in turn was because, they thought, it had not yet reached the true foundations and correct first principles for the knowledge of health and illness. They held that the true first principles of medicine must be drawn from an investigation of the "nature of a human being," and that this can only be known by knowing general principles for nature as a whole (20.1–8 = 145, 17–146, 7). And, they thought, the correct method for obtaining such general natural knowledge, and the knowledge of human nature in particular—based on that general knowledge—is to lay down first as foundations (ὑπόθεσιν ὑποτίθεσθαι, 1.2 = 118, 2) a small number of a certain range of abstractly conceived natural powers. The next step would be to use those ultimate "powers" as explanatory principles to work out all the further details—including the specification of particular human diseases, their causes, and the proper therapies for them (1.1–6 = 118, 1–6; 13.3–7 = 133, 8–13). Thus these recent theorists thought that advances in philosophy of nature and in the grasp of the proper methods of scientific inquiry urgently demanded,

---

reading at 2.11 = 120, 2: the grounds on which the author's opponents actually denied to traditional medicine, or on which he considers that they denied, the status of a science, are to be grasped from what he says in chapter 1 (together with chaps. 13 and 20), and any failure of "full exactness" seems remotely connected at best to what he says there. For what this may be worth, one should note that the author of *On the Science of Medicine* (Περὶ τέχνης) does not include any such argument against the scientific status of traditional medicine among the many that he rebuts. As for the choice of textual reading at 2.11 = 120, 2, I cannot see any basis in the context for preferring A's text over M's: if (as in M) the author announces he is going to explain *what* medical science is, he is certainly going therein to explain and show *that* it is. Furthermore, the author has in fact already given arguments to establish that medical science exists: see 1.8–20 = 118, 7–119, 4. His proper next task is to explain *what* it is (and thereby confirm its existence). Hence M's text might seem preferable.
[10] The best discussion remains that of G.E.R. Lloyd, "Who Is Attacked in *On Ancient Medicine?*" Lloyd's intriguing suggestion that the doctrines attacked in *AM* are most closely exemplified, so far as our evidence allows us to say, by those of Philolaus has been taken up by Carl A. Huffman, whose study of Philolaus' theory of "ἀρχαί" and his methodology in general adds support to this suggestion (*Philolaus of Croton,* 78–92). Given, however, the paucity of our evidence about Philolaus' specifically medical theories, and the necessarily conjectural character of any reconstruction of them (even more is this so for other philosophers/physicians who have been canvassed in this connection), it would not help us much if we knew that Philolaus was our author's principal target. We would not be much aided thereby in attempting to work out our author's own views about proper procedure in medicine, or the bases for his objection to his opponent(s)' procedure; for all this, we must go to his own text.

and indeed also made possible, a reconstruction of traditional Greek medical practice in philosophically and scientifically more satisfactory terms. Or rather, what was demanded and possible now was its replacement by a new practice conducted in terms of these new abstract foundational principles (2.5–6 = 119, 16–18).

So much, then, for our author's introduction in the first two chapters of the issues he will be concerned with. He vigorously objects to this attack, as he regards it. His purpose in the treatise is to explain the traditional method (ὁδός, 2.2, 4.8, 8.20, 15.2 = 119, 13; 123, 16; 127, 14; 137, 13), its origin (ἀρχή, 2.2, 7.15 = 119, 13; 126, 16), and its principles, and to show its superiority, both in actually dealing with patients and in the theory of medicine, to that of the newfangled philosophical medicine (chaps. 3–12). In both practice and theory, the purely abstract principles of natural philosophy, he argues (mentioning the hot and the cold, the wet and the dry), are inappropriate to medicine (chaps. 2, 13–14). The powers at work in the human body, of which medical science must have a thorough knowledge and to which it must appeal both in theory and in practice, are fundamentally and irreducibly many, specific, and concrete. They must be understood in differential, concrete terms if either practice or theory is to sustain itself in the face of the observed facts: many *different* physical substances are hot or cold or wet or dry, and they have different effects depending on their *other* ingredients and the way those are combined, much more than they depend on the warmth or coldness, wetness or dryness, in them. In fact, these abstract powers made so much of by the philosophers have little lasting effect on the condition of the human body. Indeed, he argues, the hot and the cold are demonstrably the *least* powerful of all the powers, so far as human nature, health, and disease are concerned (chaps. 16–19). In denying all real efficacy in particular to the hot and the cold (and backing this up with detailed arguments drawn from medical experience) our author strikes a bold counterstroke, since from the beginning of his discussion (1.3–4 = 118, 3–4) he implies that the leading candidates for foundational principles proposed by newfangled medicine were precisely the hot and the cold.

But, on one possible interpretation, which I will defend later on (see note 47), he goes yet further in giving tit for tat. In chapter 20 he asserts that if anyone is ever to achieve a true grasp of the nature of a human being, and by implication a grasp of any of the principles constituting and governing nature itself as a whole, it will only be from the investigation, according to traditional methods of the science of medicine, of the human constitution and human health and disease (20.11–17 = 146, 9–15). In other words, whereas his opponents have asserted that one must begin from the knowledge of basic principles for the constitution of the world as a whole (the whole cosmos) and on that basis lay down principles for human nature, health, and disease, our author reverses this order. Yes, as the philosophers say (20.1–4 = 145, 17–146, 3), you cannot really know medicine without knowing the nature of human beings, and so also without knowing nature itself as a whole, but that is because in *first* knowing medicine—and only so—will you have what you need in order *then* to understand human nature and nature overall as well. The correct procedure for coming to know nature itself as a whole—for grasping the general principles for understanding the cosmos—is to study human nature, health, and disease according to the traditional method of Greek medicine. Natural knowledge in general (and not just medical science) begins from and is grounded in the investigation of the concrete facts at the bottom, so to speak. It is not suspended, as the philosophers asserted, from abstract principles developed first at the top and applied there first.

III

So much, then, for my summary. I have represented our author throughout as directing his explication and defense of traditional Greek medicine against a single, coherent opponent—newfangled philosophical medicine, I called it. I have drawn my account of philosophical medicine entirely from what the author says about it (see note 10). He introduces certain opponents explicitly in the first words of chapter 1 as some "people who have undertaken to speak or write about medicine while themselves laying down for their account an underlying principle." (The Greek of the participial phrase here is ὑπόθεσιν αὐτοὶ αὐτοῖς ὑποθέμενοι τῷ λόγῳ;[11] I discuss below in section IV my rendering of ὑπόθεσις as "underlying principle.") Soon thereafter he characterizes them as proposing "new methods" for medical research (2.7 = 119, 17),[12] and he explicitly returns to them in chapter 13. I assume that these are the same people referred to and argued against in chapter 20, even though the language with which the author brings them on there is neither the same nor closely related; it could certainly be interpreted as marking some specifically different, further set of opponents. First, then, let me defend this assumption.

At the beginning of chapter 20, in a somewhat abrupt transition, our author begins to address the views of "certain physicians and wise (or clever) men" (τινες ἰητροὶ καὶ σοφισταί):[13] they held that you cannot

---

[11] The Budé text differs slightly but, for present purposes, not significantly.

[12] See also 15.1–3 = 137, 12–13.

[13] I have cited the Loeb text, which follows manuscript A at this point; according to Jouanna's apparatus, the other manuscripts have τινες καὶ ἰητροὶ καὶ σοφισταί, which he

know medicine without knowing "what a human being is." Notice, first, that he employs the old term σοφισταί here, not φιλόσοφοι. This perhaps indicates that about 420–410 B.C., when I am assuming our author wrote, the latter noun was not yet firmly established, at least not as a quasi-technical designation of any special group of thinkers, as it certainly was by Plato's time not long afterward. However, he does go on to say that their views go in the direction of philosophy—and now he uses the term φιλοσοφίη, in what seems to be one of the earliest, and perhaps *the* earliest, occurrence of this word in surviving Greek literature. The opponents in chapter 1, however, are initially described simply as "speakers and writers on medicine." But though they are not specifically described as philosophers there (whether σοφισταί or adherents of φιλοσοφίη), it is clear from the nature of the underlying principles they lay down that in fact they are either philosophers of nature themselves or physicians influenced by natural philosophy. The passage quoted above referring to their use of an underlying principle specifies this as "hot or cold or wet or dry, or whatever other thing they may choose." Hot, cold, wet, dry, and so on, are pre-Socratic cosmological and physical principles par excellence. The author goes on to say that these "speakers and writers" choose "one or two" such underlying principles and reduce "the beginning of the causation of the diseases and death of human beings" all to this or these same source(s) (1.4–6 = 118, 4–6); on this basis, they "cast aside and reject as unworthy" both the traditional method of Greek medicine and all its discoveries, and follow a new method of their own (2.6–7 = 119, 16–18), namely the method of laying down underlying principles drawn from physics and cosmology. It is this laying down first of an underlying principle or principles in physics and cosmology, and then proceeding to employ it or them to explain diseases and death that he succinctly refers to at the beginning of chapter 13, when he describes his opponents as "those who do research in the science [of medicine] in the newfangled way, from an underlying principle" (13.1–2 = 133, 6–7). He claims there (he does not say this explicitly, but he clearly assumes it) that it is because in physical theory, hot and cold, or wet and dry, being opposites, are fundamentally at odds with each other, that when one of these theorists says that the hot is responsible for someone's disease he *must* recommend

---

also prints. That would yield a more distinct separation of the personages referred to into two groups: "certain physicians and certain wise or clever men," i.e., philosophers. M's and the other manuscripts' reading is perhaps supported by the fact that just below, at 20.9 = 146, 7–8, when our author rejects as less appropriate to medicine than to the art of painting what "any wise man *or* any physician" (τινὶ ἢ σοφιστῇ ἢ ἰηρῷ) has said or written "about nature": there he speaks separately about two groups, philosophers and physicians. But the effective difference between the two texts is slight.

treating it with an application of the cold, and mutatis mutandis for the dry and the wet (13.5–7 = 133, 10–13)—which is absurd, as our author then argues.[14]

Thus, even though he does not use any such descriptions, our author clearly identifies his opponents in the opening two chapters, and in the further discussion of their views in chapter 13 and following, as natural philosophers and physicians influenced by such philosophers' theories and methods. He is clearly understanding them in those terms, and attacking them for it. When we turn to chapter 20, we see him describing the λόγος of the "certain physicians and wise men" (that is, their theories or arguments) likewise as "tending toward philosophy" in their way of explaining their view that one must have complete knowledge (κατα-μαθεῖν) of what a human being is in order to correctly treat human beings medically (20.3–5 = 146, 2–4). He compares them with "Empedocles and others" who wrote "on nature" (περὶ φύσιος)—that is, who engaged in pre-Socratic natural philosophical and cosmological theorizing. In the course of writing about nature, he implies, Empedocles and these others wrote about "what man is from the beginning [or, perhaps: from a first principle],[15] and how he first came to be and from what things he was put

---

[14] It is important to notice that the author, whose own physiology is also based on a series of qualities that include opposites like sweet and bitter, does not think he has to, and indeed he does not, base his therapy on bringing to bear somehow an opposite or oppositely qualified substance to counteract whichever one is prominently involved in a disorder. His own theory holds that you must reduce or transform the offending substance by bringing it back into a state of being blended and tempered together with the *totality* of the other constituent substances of the body—it is its isolation that causes the trouble, and to introduce into the body some other, opposite substance in equally isolated form would only make things vastly worse. There is no reason at all to suppose that doing so would help with restoring the blended, tempered condition of the originally offending substance.

[15] It is not clear whether ἐξ ἀρχῆς at 20.7 = 146, 5 goes with γεγράφασιν or ἐστιν, a question on which commentators and translators have divided: its placement would make it go grammatically most naturally with γεγράφασιν, where that has as its complement ὅ τί ἐστιν ἄνθρωπος. But in either case (all the more if it is taken with both verbs), I wonder whether it means "from a beginning, i.e., a principle" of their own devising (compare 13.2 = 133, 8: ζητεύντων ἐξ ὑποθέσιος), rather than, as some commentators say, either "from the beginning of their books" or "from (man's) origin." Elsewhere in the treatise it does seem that ἀρχή means beginning or starting point in a literal, temporal sense, and not in the metaphorical one of a "first principle." That would not, of course, absolutely rule out an interpretation of this passage along these latter lines. In any event, the phrase if taken in the temporal sense does not yield an entirely satisfactory sense. It would imply something clearly incorrect if it means "from the beginning of their books"—Empedocles' poem seems clearly not to have begun with a discussion of human physiology, anatomy, and so on, but rather with the general principles governing reality as a whole, and before that with remarks on the senses vs. reason as the authoritative source of information about reality (see M. R. Wright, *Empedocles: The Extant Fragments*), if not actually with a prelude on spiritual purification (as the new Strassburg fragments suggest, see below, note 18). But if the

together" (20.6–8 = 146, 4–7).[16] And indeed, if we have in mind his earlier complaints against the speakers and writers who use hot and cold or
wet and dry as their underlying principle, we can readily see the force of
this comparison by considering the fragments of Empedocles' poem on
nature. Starting from his four "roots" (earth, air, fire, and water) plus Love
and Strife as "underlying principles," Empedocles describes a cosmic cycle
in which human beings and other animals come into being at a certain
point, with their specific natural constitutions determined by the ways
those "roots" mix together in the given case. Ancient tradition describes

---

meaning is "wrote about what a human being is from the time when humans first originated," that pointlessly and awkwardly anticipates what the author goes on to say immediately after: "*and* how he first came to be and from what things he was put together" (my
italics). The author seems to be marking two topics—connected, to be sure, but distinct—
that his opponents discussed: human nature itself, what it is; and how human beings originally came into being, what elements and the like they were put together from. Just below,
in stating his own contrary views, he again separates the question about human nature from
that about origins: except by following traditional methods of medical research one cannot
know "what a human being is and through what causes humans come to be" (20.16–17 =
146, 13–15).

[16] The received text at 20.6 = 146, 5 is mildly ungrammatical: the καθάπερ clause lacks a
main verb. It does seem clear that the phrase Ἐμπεδοκλῆς ἢ ἄλλοι οἳ περὶ φύσιος γεγράφασιν was intended to mean "Empedocles or others who have written about Nature"—i.e.,
authors of philosophical books of the sort that went, at least later on, under the title Περὶ
φύσεως (On Nature). Empedocles' own physical poem was given this name in the doxo-
graphical tradition, and though we do not know whether it went under that name in his
own lifetime it must have done so shortly afterward. This is how Festugière translates the
phrase (*L'Ancienne médecine*, 58–60 nn. 69–70). Thus we can begin from the firm basis
that here, at its first occurrence in the context, the phrase περὶ φύσιος means "about nature
as a whole." However, in the received text this phrase does not stand alone as complement
to the verb γεγράφασιν: the latter is qualified also by ὅ τί ἐστιν ἄνθρωπος κτλ., so that
the clause as a whole reads: "who have written about nature, [viz.] what man is. . . ." That
may make it look instead as if with this phrase our author is not taking note of philosophers
of nature as such (and assigning Empedocles and others to that classification)—as on my interpretation he is doing. Instead, it may seem, he is speaking of a group of persons who, he
says, wrote *specifically* on the nature of humans. In fact, as we can see from the instance of
Empedocles, these may be writers of works "On Nature," though on this alternative reading that is not how our author is referring to them. On this interpretation our author takes
no notice of the fact that Empedocles et al. wrote on the nature of humans as a subordinate
and applied part of an overall theory of nature as a whole; he is thinking of them solely as
writers on the nature of humans. That is how Jouanna translates in the Budé, and in a note
on the passage (p. 208) he insists that all the occurrences of the phrase περὶ φύσιος in this
chapter, following along with this reference for the first occurrence here, have to do specifically with human nature, never (even in part) with nature in general. The result would be
that here in chapter 20 our author is objecting simply to the view of these "physicians and
wise men" that one cannot know medicine without first knowing "what a human being
is"—without implying anything at all about a connection between the desiderated knowledge of human nature and pre-Socratic cosmology. We can avoid any temptation to accept
this bizarre result and preserve the natural meaning of οἳ περὶ φύσιος γεγράφασιν as re-

Empedocles as a physician[17] as well as a natural philosopher, perhaps partly on the basis of more extensive medical applications of his cosmological and overall physical theory than now survive in the poem itself.[18] At any rate, we can readily see that the initial opponents and the thinkers of chapter 20 at least belong to the same intellectual milieu: the latter, too, make claims about the source of true medical knowledge as lying in pre-Socratic cosmological theorizing like that of Empedocles, in which postulated "underlying principles" are made the basis for explaining everything. Our author admittedly does not, however, explicitly identify

---

ferring to a recognized category of writers of works "On Nature," if we simply permit the author (writing informally and with directness and vigor as he does throughout) to have intended the verb γεγράφασιν to be heard twice: once in the relative clause ("who have written about Nature") and then again as verb of the καθάπερ clause ("as for example those who have written about Nature have written what man is from a (or the) beginning [or: from a first principle] . . ."). This way of completing the syntax of the καθάπερ clause is easier and makes for a much better sense than Jouanna's own proposal (p. 207) that we complete it by understanding (from the verb τείνει of the main clause) τείνουσι ἐς φιλοσοφίην. Jouanna's proposal makes the author say that Empedocles et al. *tend* toward philosophy, just as do our "physicians and wise men" when they insist that in order to treat patients scientifically you have to know "what a human being is"—when in fact his point is plainly to assimilate his opponents (who write directly and specifically only about medicine) with such professed and recognized specialists in philosophy as Empedocles. Empedocles does much more than merely *tend* toward philosophy, and the author's point is spoiled if we do not see him exploiting that fact!

The ungrammaticality discussed in this note would disappear if, with A. Dihle ("Kritisch-exegetische Bemerkungen zur Schrift Über die Alte Heilkunst," 135–50), we regarded the words at 20.3–7 = 146, 2–5 (ἀλλὰ τοῦτο . . . ἐστιν ἄνθρωπος), which are dropped out in manuscripts written later than A and M (both dating from the 11th c.), as actually signaling an *interpolation* in A and M (see ibid., 145–46): in that case, all reference to Empedocles as an author who wrote on Nature and on the origin, etc., of human beings in particular would drop out of our text, as an intrusion from a marginal note in some archetype of A and M, while the later mss. would in this place reflect an independent tradition that preserved a text uncontaminated by this interpolation. However, there seems no reason to think the later manuscripts are, or derive from, anything but sometimes faulty copies of either A or M, and it seems impossible not to see in the omission the fault of a copyist whose eye skipped down from ὅ τί ἐστιν ἄνθρωπος in line 3 to the same words in line 7. On this see Jouanna in the Budé, 93–94.

[17] See, e.g., Diogenes Laertius, *Lives of Eminent Philosophers*, 8. 58, Celsus, *De medicina* prooemium 7 (which lists Empedocles along with Pythagoras and Democritus as early philosophers who thought medicine necessarily came within the scope of the philosophical knowledge of nature which they sought); Galen, *De methodo medendi* I 1. Diog. Laert. 8.77 actually attributes to Empedocles a work (of 600 lines) with the title *Medical Theory* (Ἰατρικὸς λόγος), but most scholars do not accept his evidence. Wright, *Empedocles*, 9–14, 19–20, surveys this and the other evidence about Empedocles' connections to medical science.

[18] Later ancient authors cite Empedocles' poetry under two different titles (and Diog. Laert. 8.77 gives these titles in such a way as to suggest there were two poems), leading most

these people as the same ones as before. Moreover, the earlier ones are said to apply cosmological notions specifically in their theories of the causes of human diseases and death, and nothing is said explicitly about the later ones' views on the causation of diseases. Contrariwise, the author does not describe the earlier opponents, as he does the later ones, as holding some general theory drawn from natural philosophy and cosmology specifically about the nature of human beings.

However, what he does say about the opinions of the opponents in each context (chapters 1 and 13 versus chapter 20) coheres closely with, and indeed naturally supplements, what he says in the other. This makes it most satisfactory to treat our author in chapter 20, as I have done, as expanding upon and telling us more about the views of the initial opponents. The theorists of chapter 1 surely had to have a theory of the nature of human beings that permitted or required, in their eyes, the postulation of the hot or the cold or whatever as causes of *diseases*. And the theorists of chapter 20 surely thought that by deriving a theory of *human nature* from natural philosophy and cosmology, they could then go further to develop on that basis a theory of disease and its causes: otherwise, how could they say, as our author reports them, that "Whoever does not know what a human being is cannot know the science of medicine—no, anyone who is going to *give correct medical treatment* to human beings must have a complete knowledge of that" (20.1–4 = 146, 1–3)? Obviously, they were claiming that knowing human nature would tell you the causes of diseases and therefore lead you to the correct therapy for them.

---

scholars to think he wrote two—one a cosmological poem, *On Nature,* and the other, *Purifications,* containing admonitions against eating meat (on the ground that all living things are akin to one another) together with eschatological ideas (presented in intensely personal terms) about embodied human life as a punishment for sinful acts in prior embodiments. But there are significant dissenters who argue for a single poem unifying and connecting cosmology and "purification" (see C. Osborne, *Rethinking Early Greek Philosophy,* 24–31, 108–31). The recent discovery in Strassburg of additional papyrus fragments of Empedocles' work is reported to include some already known *Purifications* lines (DK B139) within a context of lines belonging to *On Nature,* and this might suggest that there was only one poem after all, with two distinguishable parts (but does not necessarily do so: the lines in question might be repeated from one poem to the other). See Alain Martin and Oliver Primavesi, *L'Empédocle de Strasbourg.* Certainly, we can accept M. R. Wright's argument that the theory of the *Purifications,* if it was a separate poem, was in accord with and indeed applied that of *On Nature,* while supplementing it on certain key points; *Empedocles,* 57 ff. Whether there were two Empedoclean poems or one, setting out his cosmology and its applications, we are struck by the fact that in Plato's *Timaeus* we find Timaeus's speech developing, and concluding with, a theory of human diseases and their remedies based upon the cosmology and general theory of physics presented in the earlier parts of his speech. In this, Plato can be seen to be carrying on the pre-Socratic, or specifically Empedoclean, tradition to which our author so strenuously objects.

Presumably he supposes that what you would "learn" from general philosophy of nature about human nature in particular that would permit you then to deal with human illnesses is simply that the dominant agencies in any human body are the same principles, whichever those might be, that you have already laid down as the basis of your cosmological theories.[19] Just as when the weather is unduly hot, the cure is an onrush of the cold to drive out or mix with the hot, so too in the ill human body. This is the same therapeutic principle that, as we have already seen, our author attributes in chapter 13 to the people who used hot and cold, dry and wet, as their underlying principles.

Nonetheless, in chapter 20 and following he does not say that this is how the philosophical knowledge of human nature was supposed to be used in treating patients, and he does not repeat his criticisms of the therapy via opposite powers (given in chapter 15) or his refutation of the view that abstract powers cause diseases. However, he does clearly imply that on his opponents' theory you would have to say that all the *same* substances are good or bad equally for all human beings (anyhow all those in good health) since, after all, on their theory treatment derives from knowing the *single* nature of all human beings (20.23–25 = 147, 1–3). And in his own riposte he insists that the effects on different people of consuming the same foods show clearly that in fact different persons have *different* natures (διαφέρουσιν οὖν τούτων αἱ φύσιες, 20.40–41 = 147, 16–17). (Cheese is his example: eating a lot of it causes stomach pains in some, but wonderfully strengthens others.) Thus *before* (in chapters 14–15), he argued that you could not understand and treat diseases if you failed to observe the differential effects on a human body of a large number of concrete powers when they become isolated within the body and are no longer mixed and compounded with the other constituents into the unified mass of a given organ or other component of the body (see ὅτι . . . ὅλον ἕν τε γέγονε καὶ ἁπλοῦν, 14.55–57 = 137, 9–11). The abstract powers of heat and cold and wetness and dryness really don't have anything to do with diseases (14.20–23 = 135, 17–136, 2), and cer-

---

[19] A good example of just how this might go is provided by *On Breaths*, whose author thinks air/wind dominates the world as a whole, and therefore also both dominates the constitution of a human being and is responsible for any disorders that may affect that constitution. See *Breaths*, chaps. 2–5. It does seem clear, however (see Lloyd, "Who Is Attacked?" 114–15), that the specific theories of *Breaths* are not our author's main target: there is no special mention in *Breaths* of the cosmic opposites or of treatment by appeal to the offending agency's opposite, and for all we know *Breaths* may have been written after *AM*. *Breaths*'s theories do nonetheless provide a brilliantly clear example, indeed the best available to us, of what our author had in mind when he wrote both of philosophical medicine and of its scientific defects.

tainly the evidence shows that no single one or pair of such substances can be *the* cause. *Now* (in chapter 20), he makes the related point that abstract knowledge of human nature will not suffice for treatment of diseases. The physician has to know (and he can learn this only if he keeps to the methods and results of traditional Greek medicine) "both what a human being is in relation to what he eats and what he drinks, and what in relation to his other practices [e.g., baths, exercise, rubdowns], and what will result from each of these for each [type of] person" (20.20–23 = 146, 17–147, 1). In other words, you have to know the particular constitutions of the different types of patient, as those constitutions relate to the particular ingredients of particular foods and drinks and to the particular effects of baths, exercise and so on. The two accounts cohere closely together and indeed supplement one another in desirable ways.

Thus it does appear that we have a single doctrine under attack throughout, from appropriately different sides in the earlier and the later passages. The opponents hold there is a single power, or pair of opposite powers (active also in the cosmos at large), that causes human diseases; they hold that knowing this is part of knowing what human nature is; and accordingly they hold (or must hold, according to our author) that you treat every patient in the same way, by administering the same opposite antidote to whatever power you judge is causing the disturbance. The author replies first that the causes of diseases are not one or two simple, abstract powers, but many complex, concrete ones, and then that physical constitutions (φύσιες) differ too and these differences must be known if one is to treat patients correctly. Thus his criticisms in the first fifteen chapters or so of the "speakers and writers on medicine" who proceed "on the basis of an underlying principle" fit together with those in chapters 20 and following of the "physicians and wise men" who insist that no one can know medicine who does not *first* know nature as a whole—and human nature as part of that. They are two connected parts of a single attack by our author on a single doctrine.

I began this section by speaking of the somewhat abrupt transition by which our author turns in chapter 20 to discuss these questions about human nature and how one can properly come to know it. This abruptness has encouraged the idea, which I have argued is mistaken, that the author has completed his discussion of his original opponents by the end of chapter 19 and is now going on to discuss some additional ones. It is true that the sentence immediately preceding the beginning of chapter 20 reads (in the best text) as follows: "About these matters, then, I think I have given a sufficient explication."[20] Thus we are given a formal announcement

[20] I translate the Budé, which along with most editors (including Jones in his 1946 text) follows manuscript M. In the Loeb, Jones follows A in omitting the words translated "then"

that a certain stage of the discussion has now been completed, so that a new one is about to be embarked upon (or a prior one returned to). However, it seems quite clear on examination that the sufficiently explained matters intended are not the errors, taken altogether, of those who do medicine on the basis of ὑποθέσεις. The reference is, more specifically, to the account given in chapters 18 and 19 (or perhaps the author envisages this account as beginning already as far back chapter as 14) to the effect that imbalances of heat and cold within the body are never what causes diseases; rather, the cause is some failure in the coction, or mixture, or compounding of the constituents of the body, resulting in the display within the body of some specific one of its many ingredients in an isolated, most powerful form. (See the immediately preceding sentence, 19.54–56 = 145, 14–16, which draws the discussion on this point to a decisive close.) Thus Jouanna in his introduction in the Budé edition (p. 20) is quite wrong to suppose that the author means to say that he has completed his discussion of his initially announced opponents and that he is now launching an independent criticism of philosophical medicine in general—as if the discussion that follows, on "certain physicians' and wise men's" views about how to know the nature of a human being, has no essential connection to the initial opponents' method of drawing on underlying principles developed in natural philosophy. If that were the case, the earlier opponents would be included within the scope of the new discussion, if at all, only by way of a quite different and independent aspect of their theory from the one previously focused upon. But this is not so. In fact, having concluded at the end of chapter 19 his discussion of the true (and the false) physiologies and nosologies proposed respectively by himself and the opponents, the author now turns in chapter 20, as I have argued, to discuss a different, but closely connected, aspect of these same opponents' overall theoretical stance.[21]

---

and "sufficient"—which permits him to take the sentence as a concluding clause to the preceding one, thus eliminating any formal announcement here of a major shift in topic.

[21] It is sometimes wrongly suggested that the very words λέγουσι δέ τινες ἰητροὶ καὶ σοφισταί ("but certain physicians and wise men say") with which chapter 20 begins already show that the author has now turned to discuss a new and different group of opponents; see, e.g., Pohlenz, "Zwanzigste Kapitel," 405. It is certainly true that, unlike the form of words in chap. 13 with which the author takes up fresh objections against the opponents first introduced in chap. 1, this one does not indicate explicitly that this is what he is doing here too. Perhaps the choice of this vaguer characterization indicates the author's intention to include within the range of his reference now all medical writers who have made medicine dependent on philosophy of nature, even those who may not specifically have made the cosmological opposites the basis of their theories. The author of On Breaths is an example of such a writer. But in the context of this discussion, that is a relatively minor distinction, and nothing specific is made of it in what follows. In any event, this form of words certainly

IV

I would like to explain now, and defend, my use of the ideas of "foundations" and "underlying principles" in my account of the opponents' views. I rely here on the language of the opening sentences of the treatise, which speak of the opponents as laying down a ὑπόθεσις for themselves for their argument. (In what follows, I use this Greek noun without translating it.) The question is, what does our author understand by this word (and its associated verb, which he also uses here)? What is included, for him, in the idea of arguing "from a ὑπόθεσις" that one "lays down"? People have long noticed that the use of these words here has some affinity to the uses Plato makes of them—especially in *Meno, Phaedo, Republic,* and *Parmenides*—in connection, most prominently, with geometry and the mathematical sciences generally. In some contexts Plato describes special cases where a problem in geometry is approached ἐξ ὑποθέσεως, that is, by supposing some condition fulfilled rather than by deduction from anything already established. Elsewhere he downgrades mathematicians in general because they are necessarily condemned to arguing from ὑποθέσεις (axioms and definitions) that they simply take for granted as obvious without inquiring into or attempting somehow to establish them as correct. Plato also, sometimes as an extension of one sort or another from the mathematical case, uses the same language in application to philosophical logic and methodology—the "hypothetical method" of analysis and argument that he employs in the second half of *Meno*, in *Republic*, and (differently) in *Parmenides*.[22] So striking has the connection between

---

does not announce the "certain physicians and wise men" as an altogether new group. An author can always write, "but some people say," where the context shows that he is referring to views of people he has earlier identified more precisely.

[22] It is important to see clearly how different some of Plato's uses of the term ὑπόθεσις are from others. When Socrates introduces the notion of an investigation ἐξ ὑποθέσεως into the teachability of virtue in *Meno* 86e–87c, and explains what he has in mind by reference to a practice of geometers, he means—this much is clear, despite the difficulty of working out exactly what mathematical problem he has in mind—the statement of a *condition*, which if it can be established will allow us to bring our investigation to a determinate conclusion. Here ἐξ ὑποθέσεως means *on a condition*. It does not mean *on an assumption* (if that entails something not explicitly conditional, but a basic commitment of the one making it), much less *from an axiom* or some sort of basic and unquestioned principle in a science. In the *Phaedo* (at 92d6 and 101d2 ff.) Socrates refers to two ideas as ὑποθέσεις: first, the idea that the soul exists before it comes into a person's body, just as the Forms that it can come to know do; and second, the idea that Forms exist (or perhaps that by being participated in they are causes). In both cases he clearly envisages argument for and indeed the establishment of these ὑποθέσεις. He actually argued at length earlier in the dialogue that the soul exists before it comes into the body: that is the conclusion of the "argument from recollection" (see 76c11–13); and while he has not formally argued that Forms exist, he

our author's language and Plato's texts seemed that in 1952 the respected scholar Hans Diller argued in significant part on the basis of this usage that our treatise must postdate at least some and maybe even all of the works of Plato, thus pushing the date of composition down to perhaps as late as 350 B.C.[23]

In fact, however, in part on the basis of evidence from Plato himself, to which I will turn shortly, in interpreting *On Ancient Medicine* we should leave aside all comparison between its conception of arguing "from a ὑπόθεσις" and Plato's uses of the term for geometrical and related styles of argumentation. Instead, we should keep closely to the basic meaning of the verb from which this noun is derived: ὑποτίθεσθαι, lit. 'to place underneath,' to lay something down as a basis of further development of some sort. For our author, this carries a strong negative connotation of arbitrary, out-of-the-blue invention (at least in relation to medical facts), or at best mere and pure plausibility, where accurate knowledge based on detailed information would be far preferable; on this, see below, section VI. But the basic meaning is clear enough: in his usage a ὑπόθεσις is an underlying idea or fundamental conception to which one pays intellectual allegiance, and which one puts forward as a basis for developing an explanatory theory in some realm. We should not inflate his meaning by importing overtones of the axiomatic method in mathematics, or of the testing of hypotheses by examining their consequences.

We should bear in mind that our author was very probably writing about 420–410 B.C., as the reference to Empedocles in chapter 20 that we have just been considering strongly suggests: it seems to imply a date dur-

---

clearly *envisages* that being done (see 101d5–e1). So these ὑποθέσεις are not assumptions so much as basic conceptions that are supposed to clarify, and make possible some satisfactory understanding of, many otherwise puzzling phenomena. In *Parmenides* the items called ὑποθέσεις seem to acquire this designation because they are the contents of "if" clauses, to which then are appended by deductive argument various consequences, presented for scrutiny and reflection as one decides what, finally, to maintain as one's own view on some important matter (see 127d6–e2, 128d5–6, 135e8–136a2, and esp. 136a4–c5)— whether to maintain the original ὑπόθεσις or not, and if so on what understanding. Only in the *Republic* (VI 510b4–d3, 511a3–8) does Plato use the term in reference to the way that, in geometry and the rest of mathematics, scientists lay down definitions and axioms. He says they do this as if the things they lay down are clear to everyone, and clearly acceptable, and do not need any account or explication; instead, holding to these axioms and definitions as unquestioned assumptions, they simply deduce theorems from them—as if such a deduction establishes the theorems as true. Thus there are references in the *Meno* and *Republic* contexts, but not in either *Phaedo* or *Parmenides*, to ὑποθέσεις in mathematics—and even then the specific mathematical usages are quite distinct. Especially in the *Phaedo* this leaves open the question whether Plato's usage involves any sort of conscious application of mathematical terminology for philosophical purposes. (On this see in my text, below.)

[23] Hans Diller, "Hippokratische Medizin und attische Philosophie."

ing the period of maximum currency for Empedocles' theories, thus not more than a decade or two after Empedocles' death. If so, the author's use of the noun ὑπόθεσις (with its related verb ὑποτίθεσθαι) here and elsewhere in the treatise is very probably the first recorded use of those words to indicate a ὑπόθεσις of some sort in any context of logical argument, theoretical analysis, or explanation.[24] Apart from one isolated instance in the Hippocratic treatise whose title is usually but misleadingly translated as *On Breaths* (see note 24), we have no evidence at all of anyone in the fifth century B.C. (or even in the fourth) "undertaking to speak or write on medicine" (1.1–2 = 118, 1–2) using this terminology of ὑποθέσεις, and it is important to see that our author's words do not imply that anyone before him did speak or write in these terms in a medical context.[25] It is *he* who says that his opponents have "laid down a ὑπόθεσις for their argument"; he clearly implies that each of them spoke of some among hot and cold, wet and dry, or other abstract properties as the causes of all diseases, but, to judge simply from what he himself writes, it is perfectly possible that the characterization of their methods in terms of ὑποθέσεις is our author's own original contribution—original at

---

[24] There is one occurrence of the noun ὑπόθεσις elsewhere in the Hippocratic Corpus, in the last chapter of *On Breaths* (Περὶ φυσῶν—i.e., on air inside the body, in particular that which the author assumes comes in with our food and drink when they are consumed, and not merely that which is breathed in). Coming at the very end of the work (15.9 Loeb), it provides a retrospective reference to the author's governing theory, introduced at the outset (chap. 3), without this or any other quasi-technical terminology—the theory that the element air or wind (ἀήρ, πνεῦμα) controls everything and so is the cause in particular of diseases (as it is of life itself and health too). On this basis the author (evidently a "sophist" rather than a serious physician) has in the interim offered explanations one by one of the symptoms and constitutions of various recognized diseases. This treatise is presumably roughly contemporary with *AM*; nothing permits us to say more than that about the relative dates of the two works. So it could be that not *AM* but *On Breaths* has the earliest occurrence of ὑπόθεσις in this use. (Ms. A gives ὑπόσχεσις instead of ὑπόθεσις at 15.9. But though that follows nicely on the verb ὑπεσχόμην at 15.5, it gives the wrong sense: it is not the author's "promise" to declare the cause of diseases that he should now say has been shown "true" but his theory about air *as* that cause. See J. Jouanna, *Des vents* and *De L'art* 150–51.)

The verb ὑποθέσθαι occurs in the first sentence of *On Fleshes*, where the author remarks that if he is to write a treatise on medicine he needs to "lay down" opinions held in common by himself and his predecessors as a common starting point. He goes on to give an account of the origin and formation of the various fleshy parts of the human body, citing heat and cold as the basic "meteorological" principles for this account. This treatise, too, so far as we can tell, seems to be roughly contemporary with *AM* (see K. Deichgräber, *Hippocrates: Über Entstehung und Aufbau des menschlichen Körpers* [περὶ σαρκῶν]; and the introduction to R. Joly's Budé text and translation, *Hippocrate*, 13: 182–83.

[25] Contrast Lloyd, "Who Is Attacked?" 109: "the writer clearly assumes that his readers are familiar with these terms and with their use in the context of medical theories in particular."

least within the medical realm.[26] In addition, our knowledge of fifth-century mathematics (for example, the work of Hippocrates of Chios) gives no evidence that any use of these terms was an established part of geometrical theory at the time our author wrote—either for the sort of "conditional" analysis of a problem that Plato signals in *Meno* or for the axioms and definitions of an *Elements* of geometry to which Plato might seem to allude in *Republic* VI (see above, note 22). So though it is *possible* that our author was importing into the discussion of medical theory terminology already in place in theorizing about geometry, as commentators have assumed—we have no actual evidence that that might be so.

And in fact, among the uses of the term ὑπόθεσις in Plato the one to which our author's use is closest is that in the *Phaedo,* where there is no clear indication at all of indebtedness to mathematical theory. There, a ὑπόθεσις is simply a basic conception that is supposed to clarify, and make possible some satisfactory understanding of, many otherwise puzzling phenomena—for example, the ὑπόθεσις of the soul as preexisting its embodiment while in an intellectually active state, or the ὑπόθεσις of Forms of Beauty and so on, in which sensible beautiful things participate.[27] There is no suggestion that this understanding is to be derived by a process of "deduction" from the given ὑπόθεσις similar to argument in geometry from axioms and definitions; and argument for and indeed establishment of these ὑποθέσεις on some basis or other is explicitly envisaged (see above, note 22). Similarly, in *On Ancient Medicine* the philosophical medical theorists propose the hot and the cold or the wet and the dry as forces at work in a human body and then offer such an ὑπόθεσις as a basis on which to work out an account of the constitution of diseases and the explanation of their symptoms—not by anything like *deduction,* but by offering an illuminating and unifying set of ideas for working through and organizing the phenomena in a satisfying way. And, of course, they might well have had a lot to say about just why some one such ὑπόθεσις recommended itself—they could point to various indications in the world at large of the primacy of whatever forces they set-

[26] If we could know that *On Fleshes* or *On Breaths* was written before *AM* (see above, note 24) we might conclude that the author of one of those works was the innovator. Given the casual way in which the author of *On Breaths* introduces the term ὑπόθεσις at the end of his exposition, we might perhaps rather conclude that he was adopting a usage already established in medical writings familiar to him but now lost.

[27] See also *Sophist* 244c4–5, where, referring to Parmenides, the Visitor from Elea speaks of "the one who lays down this [viz., that being is one] as his foundational principle" (τῷ ταύτην τὴν ὑπόθεσιν ὑποθεμένῳ). This passage of the *Sophist* provides in fact a beautiful and perfect parallel to our author's usage when at the beginning of the work he writes about people ὑπόθεσιν αὐτοὶ αὑτοῖς ὑποθέμενοι τῷ λόγῳ.

tled upon.[28] Here, as I have said, in accordance with the fundamental meaning of the verb ὑποτίθεσθαι, a ὑπόθεσις is an underlying idea or basic conception or foundational notion that one puts forward, and on which one can then construct a body of explanatory theory in some area. For all we know, then, our author may be the first to exploit this verb and its noun to characterize the procedures of philosophers in approaching questions of human health and disease, as well as in approaching questions on their home ground of "things in the heavens and beneath the earth" (1.23–24 = 119, 6–7).[29] Perhaps the related, but much more restricted, uses drawn from mathematics that we find elsewhere in Plato are a separate development. In any event, we can understand perfectly well our author's use of these terms, as we can Plato's in the *Phaedo,* without reliance on any presumed use of them in mathematics, simply by looking to the basic meaning of the verb: to lay something down as a basis for further development of some sort. (I postpone to section VI below discussion of why our author does not similarly count his own theoretical ideas about human health and the causes of diseases as ὑποθέσεις laid down by himself.)

V

I turn now to the first of three large issues in the interpretation of our author's own views. He begins his defense of traditional Greek medicine by mentioning two sorts of "discoveries" that medicine has long had to its

---

[28] Hence I disagree with Lloyd when he says ("Who Is Attacked?" 110 n. 2) that the use of the word ὑπόθεσις in *On Breaths* is distinct from that in *AM.* An author can perfectly well put forward a foundational idea, such as that in *On Breaths*—that air/breath controls the universe and so is the cause of diseases—as a basis for understanding the symptoms of the recognized diseases (and so as a competitor with *AM*'s opponents' hot and cold or wet and dry), and yet still wish to give it confirmation, both through confrontation with the facts about the various symptoms of diseases and through some more general justifying rationale. This is what the author of *On Breaths* does, and the fact that he devotes his efforts to illustrating the power and acceptability of his ὑπόθεσις, whereas the theorists of *AM* are described simply as laying down their ὑποθέσεις and proceeding to work out their explanations on that basis, does not at all show that he means by the term something different from what the author of *AM* does, or that he conceives the function of such a ὑπόθεσις differently. If he were a practicing physician or a seriously committed medical writer, rather than the sophist he seems to be, he might, having now presented and argued for *his* ὑπόθεσις in this work, go on to write other strictly didactic medical works on the character and treatment (on that basis) of specific diseases.

[29] Or, if *On Breaths* or *On Fleshes* was written first, then the suggestion would be this: its author, or, more probably, other medical writers whose works he knew, introduced this usage on the basis I have indicated, calling their own controlling basic principles for diseases or other medical phenomena ὑποθέσεις.

credit (2.1–3 = 119, 12–14). First, the initial step (ἀρχή) was discovered (εὑρημένη) long ago[30] that allowed the establishment of a science of medicine, and along with it medicine's proper path or method (ὁδός). Then, as a result, and over a long period of time, many excellent discoveries (ἐξευρημένα, 12.15 = 133, 5) were accumulated by the continued application of this method, taking always into account earlier such discoveries. It is obvious what this second set of discoveries encompasses. These are all the specific rules of diet and specific foods both for ordinary daily use and for the treatment of specific maladies, all the accepted accounts of specific diseases and their appropriate treatment, and the like, that make up the body of practically applicable theory used by traditional medicine of the time. The author indicates this when he mentions the "further discoveries" about healthy diet that were still being made by gymnastics-masters at his own time, using, he writes, the time-honored medical method (προσεξευρίσκουσιν κατὰ τὴν αὐτὴν ὁδὸν ζητέοντες, 4.7–8 = 123, 15–16).

His views on the discovery of the initial step or "starting point" and the "method" are more challenging, however. Assuming that in the original dispensation of nature, human beings ate uncooked, unprepared, raw fruit, bushes, leaves, and grass, he traces the discovery of the "starting point" (ἀρχή) to that time in the distant past when, due to the many terrible sufferings people must have experienced while eating such a diet, certain people[31] undertook investigations in order to find nourishment

---

[30] I understand ἀρχή in ἀρχὴ καὶ ὁδός (2.1–2 = 119, 12–13) by reference to the same word at 7.15 = 126, 16, where it refers to the early attention certain smart people gave to human beings' needs as regards a "civilized" daily diet to replace the rough, uncooked, and otherwise unprepared food humans began by eating in the fields and off the trees, in the way that wild animals do. At 3.1 = 120, 16, again with the use of this word, the author locates the "initial step" later on in history, with the observation by further smart people that sick people do not profit from the same dietary regimen as ones in good health. This mild inconsistency reflects the distinction between medicine in a strict sense (the science of treating sick people) and medicine in a broader sense that includes the knowledge and skill, by the author's time widely spread in Greek culture, involved in selecting and preparing the ordinary foods people eat: this too, he says, rests on the same basic knowledge of our nature and physiology and of the powers of the various nutriments that medicine in the strict sense also rests upon. See chaps. 4 and 7.

[31] οὗτοι, 3.34 = 122, 6: here the author seems to assign this achievement to "the people of that time" as a whole, but that is just laxity of expression. Later, at 7.1–7 = 126, 3–8, in comparing the skill needed by "the physician," as discoverer of the mode of life and nourishment suitable for the sick, with the skill needed to take this first step—the skill of "the one" who discovered our current ordinary foods—he indicates clearly that he thinks this latter skill was the possession of a specially intelligent group of people, who specially applied themselves on behalf of the community to solving these problems. At 14.18 = 135, 16 he groups together (see 14.13–14 = 135, 11–13) the first physicians with these first preparers of food as οἱ πρῶτοι εὑρόντες (the first discoverers) of "the science."

that would suit the human natural constitution, as this old one manifestly did not. As a result, they discovered the different types of food that we still use in our ordinary diet—bread, barley cake, wine, boiled meat, and so on (3.10–54 = 121, 5–123, 8).[32] (He does not mention the domestication of wild plants over time through the development of new and more palatable strains, but focuses on methods of preparing foods from plants like wheat and barley such as by straining, grinding, or pounding the grains and then mixing, kneading, and then cooking the results.) Scientific medicine, strictly speaking, got its start only later, when it became clear that even with this improved food, not all was well with human beings: when people fell ill it was observed that they are not benefited by the same improved regimen as those who are well, so some new one needed to be devised. Following the same methods as the earlier discoverers of the healthy daily diet and building on what they had already learned about the properties of foods and about human digestion and physiology, the first physicians (that is, the first persons actually called by the name ἰητροί—as the earlier "dieticians" were not) devoted themselves to figuring out what dietary and other practices would help people when ill to recover their health (chapters 5–6).

The "starting point," then, was the observation by certain smart people that our initial natural diet was unsuitable for us, and the associated observation developed over time that we can do better by coordinating our diet in relation to the constitution of our bodies. What, however, was this ancient method of investigation in medicine, used by these smart people to devise an appropriate diet, that our author praises so highly? Commentators customarily characterize this as the or an "empirical" method, and if one bears in mind the contrast our author himself draws between this method and the rejected one of the philosophers (the method from underlying principles), then that is an apt description. The author emphasizes the need for careful and detailed observation of the various foods and drinks (and baths and so on) and their effects when taken by different people (well or ill) under different circumstances; and he contrasts this aspect of the method sharply with the "philosophical" writers' attempt to impose from above some abstract principles that are not arrived at from consideraton of such details. But when one speaks in the context of Greek medicine of an "empirical" method the term runs a great risk of

---

[32] He leaves it implicit here and for the most part elsewhere that from "our diet" today (ταύτην ᾗ νῦν χρεώμεθα, 3.35–6 = 122, 7–8), which these first scientists discovered, are to be excluded the highly spiced, gourmet dishes that some people eat (see 14.45–51 = 136, 21–137, 6): these foods, unlike the ordinary ones such as bread and cake and wine and well-boiled meat, are not in fact free from the sort of uncompounded ingredient that causes trouble if consumed by a healthy person.

being understood specifically in reference to the methods of the ancient Empiric school of medicine, or at least to the general approach to medical research and practice espoused by the members of that school.

I cited evidence above (section I) that Empirics of the first century B.C., and perhaps even the school's originators in the third century, appealed to *On Ancient Medicine* in defending their own modest methodology and in attacking the elaborate theorizing of Herophilus and other physicians whom they dubbed "rationalists" (λογικοί). It is easy to guess what they must have found particularly congenial in the treatise. First, there is the author's claim, in explaining the origin and progress of medical knowledge (chapters 3–8), that "necessity itself" (the fact that sick people were not benefited by the same regimen as healthy ones, 3.6–10 = 121, 2–5) caused the "initial step" toward the establishment of medicine. (This might be linked to the later Empirics' idea that medical remedies are often discovered "by luck" or happenstance; see below.) Second, we could point to his emphasis (see above, note 6) on the subsequent gradual accumulation of observations over time, leading to the establishment of a generally beneficial regimen and of specific remedies for specific diseases. (This could be accommodated with a little forcing under the Empirics' view that experience all by itself, without the aid of any sort of theorizing, could constitute medical knowledge.) Third, as we have seen, he emphasizes the importance of always beginning one's own further research by taking carefully into account the "discoveries" of one's scientific predecessors. This must have sounded like a prefiguring of the "ἱστορία" (the study of previous physicians' reports of their observations) that Empirics made a crucial element in their account of how medical knowledge was really just a matter of "experience."[33] It is clear, however, that the medical method, as our author conceives it, is deeply and fundamentally committed to precisely the use of reason for the discovery of hidden, theoretical causes that the *main* plank of the ancient Empiric sect's platform dismissed as impossible and pointless to attempt. When this is taken properly into account, the similarities that must have attracted the early Empirics to our treatise look very much less significant. The evidence on this point is worth careful scrutiny.

---

[33] On the Empiric school see M. Frede, "The Ancient Empiricists." Frede gives a good and useful account, so far as it goes, of the similarities and dissimilarities between Empiric medicine and the program outlined in *AM*, 246–48, as well as a good account of the Empiric school itself and its doctrinal development. Given the fairly precise doctrinal commitments of the Empirics—going very far beyond anything that we might normally understand by the simple term "empiricist" or "empirical," and quite different from the doctrines of the modern philosophical "empiricists"—I favor translating the Greek ἐμπειρικοί in this context, not with the rather misleading "empiricist," now the usual term employed by scholars, but with the older term "empiric," which was formerly used. I follow that practice in this essay.

Twice our author asserts, with sharp emphasis, that medical discoveries have come about through *reasoning* (λογισμός), and in the first of these passages (as also elsewhere)[34] he contrasts medical knowledge and practice through "reasoning" with anything achieved "by chance." Chance (τύχη), he assumes, is the very antithesis of science (τέχνη). In chapter 12 (10–16 = 132, 18–133, 6) he says:

> I maintain that one ought not on this ground to reject the ancient science as nonexistent or as not being finely researched, namely if it has not attained precision about all matters, but much rather, because it has been able through reasoning to get away from deep ignorance and come close, I should think, to that which is most exact, one ought to marvel at its discoveries, as products of a fine and correct method and not of chance.

And in chapter 14 (16–20 = 135, 14–17):

> And as it was by researching in a fine way, with a kind of reasoning appropriate to [the study of] the nature of human beings, that the first discoverers made these discoveries, they actually thought the science worthy to be ascribed to a god, as in fact it popularly is.[35]

Now the Hellenistic Empiric physicians made a point of insisting that many medical discoveries were really just due to luck: by chance a sick person ate something or did something that turned out to help, and doctors, noticing this, tried it in subsequent cases, with good results. In that way it came to be adopted into medical practice. According to the first Empirics, the only thing one might call reasoning that was needed or that could achieve any sound results was careful observation—including such chance ones—together with memory (of one's own observations and the reports of others).[36] Our author, however, gives no role at all in the science, not even in its earliest history, to chance observations. It is true that in

---

[34] See 1.15 = 118, 14; 21.5 = 148, 7.

[35] I follow the punctuation in the Budé here. When the author speaks of reasoning appropriate for the nature of human beings I take him to mean reasoning that is appropriate to use in investigating human nature, not reasoning that suits human beings in particular to employ—in other words, *not* the sort of reasoning the philosophers of chapter 20 are said to engage in on the same subject. The author would attribute to the earliest physicians an incoherent thought if he held that, according to them, a god possessed the science first and handed it on to them because the reasonings in traditional Greek medicine are just the right sort for human beings to *use*: that would immediately suggest that perhaps other rational beings (gods) would have used other methods (and so could not have handed *those* down). The author's idea rather is that, according to the first physicians, the gods were the first to know the right way to investigate human nature, and the physicians learned it from them.

[36] For later Empirics (especially those of the early second century A.D., Menodotus and Theodas), as we can see from Galen's account in *An Outline of Empiricism*, in M. Frede,

disparaging luck in another passage (1.11–16 = 118, 10–119, 1) his main point seems to be merely that good physicians' diagnoses and prescriptions are based on solid knowledge, so that their successes are not due to chance: such solid knowledge might have been built up in part from chance observations, for all our author says there. But in the passage just quoted from chapter 12 he seems to go further and to insist that *all* the discoveries of the science were based on solid reasoning, not on lucky guesses or random observations that proved out on further testing. Moreover, even to his original investigators, the ones who established a scheme of daily nourishment suited to our natures, he assigns the kind of reasoning about causes (what was later called αἰτιολογία) that the Empirics later on abhorred. In fact, close attention to his historical account of the origins of medical science shows that central to the very method (ὁδός) that he touts so highly is a commitment to a specific proto-theory of human physiology and of the characteristics of nutriments in relation to that physiology. This theory is much more prominent in his account of the traditional method than is any reference to observation and memory. In fact, he takes observation and memory very much for granted (as one might expect, given that only later debates brought them specifically to the fore). In explaining the "method," beginning with its origins in the work of the "first discoverers," he devotes his principal energy and philosophical ingenuity to explaining this proto-theory as it was adopted on the basis of reasoning—inferential, causal reasoning—by the earliest researchers and developed by their successors. As he explains it, the "method" seems actually to *consist* of adherence to this combined physiological theory and theory of nutriments as the basis for evaluating and building on observations—and not any reliance on observation, or observation and memory, itself.

According to our author, the earliest researchers held the view (ἡγεύμενοι) that from foods that are "too strong" (ἰσχυρόν) for the human constitution (φύσις) to "master" (κρατεῖν) come "pains, diseases, and deaths," while "nourishment, growth and health" come from those it can "conquer" (ἐπικρατεῖν)—namely, ones in which the harmful "strong and

---

trans. *Galen: Three Treatises on the Nature of Science* chap. 3, the correct method included not only a physician's own observations and the reports of other physicians' observations but also "transition to the similar"—a method of dealing with previously unobserved sorts of diseases by using observational knowledge of allegedly similar diseases or syndromes to figure out how to deal with these new ones. But (as, e.g., Galen himself indicates in chap. 4) the original Empirics in the third century B.C., or at any rate the principal theoretician among them, Serapion, seem not to have recognized this third procedure. See Frede, "Ancient Empiricists," 249–51. For basic information about the Empirics mentioned in this note, see the collection of testimonia and fragments in K. Deichgräber, *Die Griechische Empirikerschule.*

uncompounded" ingredients have been tempered with the aid of "weaker" ones, and molded and shaped with reference to the nature and strength of a human being (3.41–48 = 122, 13–123, 3). Hence they devoted much effort (πρηγματευσάμενοι, 3.40 = 122, 12) to grinding grains, blending them, watering them, kneading the dough, boiling or baking the products, and so on, all with a view to preparing foods that would be compounded and tempered in character, and not strong and raw, as was the case previously with the human diet.[37] This effort and the discoveries to which it led (this ζήτημα and this εὕρημα, 3.49 = 123, 3–4), he says, deserve the name "medicine" even if we do not normally think of such routine dietetics in those terms. The method that shaped the efforts and made the beneficial discoveries possible is nothing else than the application to the problems of nutrition (and, more generally, of ways of life) of the general idea—the brainchild of these first discoverers—that before eating the things that grow naturally in fields and on trees, we need to make them suitable as foods for us by transforming them in such a way as to remove from them their excessive "strength." We need to temper them by blending, mixing, cooking, and so on, so that the moderated strength that they thereby come to possess is amenable to our own physiological nature's powers of mastering and dominating and so assimilating what we consume. Immediately after the passages in chapter 3 that I have just been commenting on, the author speaks, in a passage I have alluded to in passing (4.6–10 = 123, 14–17), of further such discoveries made in his own day by gymnastics masters who applied "the same method." There is nothing in the preceding account except this general background idea about the excessive "strengths" of some foods in relation to our physiology, and its application by the first discoverers in their research, that he could be calling a "method" here. Thus the "same method" used by the gymnasts is simply the original theoretical insight into the excessive "strength" of uncompounded food and the importance of "tempering" these excesses by blending, mixing, and so on. It was these ideas that they applied so as to discover new and better nutriments.

The "method," then, established at the very beginning, was not merely of observing the effects of one or another diet on a human being's life and health. It was a method of such observation *guided* by a specific proto-theory about foods in relation to the physiology of the human body.

[37] Jones, in both the Loeb and his 1946 translation, incorrectly introduces the notion of experimentation into the author's history at this point. But πρηγματευσάμενοι does not at all mean "experimenting," but only expending much effort. No doubt the author is assuming that this effort involved noticing the results of one or another procedure in preparing the needed food, and being guided by those results in adjusting subsequent practice, but there is no explicit idea here or anywhere in his account of trying any *experiments*.

According to this theory, what was harmful to humans was *strong* foods, or foodstuffs in their strong form, namely, when their constituents were separated from one another and not blended together so as to reduce their different powers to affect the human body to levels the body was naturally constituted to control and profit from. It was through their initial insight that it is the excessive *strength* of wild and untreated food that has to be avoided, where strength is understood according to this idea of the separation as against the blending of ingredients, that the originators of medical science were able to devise our now normal daily diet. The same insight guided all their observations and led to all the further knowledge, both about human physiology and about the dietary needs of sick people, that subsequent generations of experts were able to achieve by further observations of their own. Here "strength," "separation," and "blending" are all theoretical ideas, certainly not things that could be directly observed.

Once actual physicians were on the cultural scene, this method underwent significant development, with greatly increased appeal to hidden theoretical entities as causes. (Perhaps some of these developments would better be included instead among the discoveries that were made *using* the method, but for our purposes we can leave any such refinement aside.) The first physicians, strictly speaking, our author tells us, held the view (ἡγησάμενοι) that it is not the bare hot, or cold, or wet, or dry that might injure a person, so that to restore him or her a dose of its opposite would be needed. No: they held (ἡγήσαντο) that it is the "strong" (ἰσχυρόν) instance of any of the large number of powerful qualities or stuffs that make up the human body which, when it is present in the food, is too great for the human natural constitution to master: this is what does harm (14.20–26 = 135, 17–136, 5). The powerful qualities or stuffs in question include the sweet, the bitter, the acid, the salty, the astringent, the flaccid, and "thousands of others" (ἄλλα μύρια)—but the natural philosophers' hot, cold, wet, and dry are not among them. The strong versions of these qualities or stuffs in food are the cases where the quality or stuff is found in the food in an uncompounded state, that is to say, when it is not worked into a single substance and blended together with others of these same stuffs or qualities (14.41–42 = 136, 19–20): such strong bitterness or saltiness or sweetness will wreak havoc on us. In the same way, we are also harmed when any of the previously blended, compounded, and tempered versions of these qualities or stuffs already worked into our bodily constitution separates out and collects somewhere within the body, all apart and on its own.[38]

---

[38] I speak vaguely here of "qualities or stuffs" because our author generally uses just the Greek article and neuter adjective to refer to what he also calls these "powers" (δυνάμιες)—

Indeed, it appears, the theory holds that at least one way that strong food harms us when whatever ingredient is uncompounded in it causes the body to secrete from its own bodily mass, in a separated and strong condition, more of the same stuff. When that interior separation has already happened, and we then eat a strong food having the same ingredient in isolated form, disaster can strike—a serious illness. Furthermore, different ones among us have stronger or weaker natures, and the stronger can put up greater resistance to strong foods, through their greater innate power to master the food; they can blend even a strong bitterness into the compounded and unified substance of their flesh or bone or specific organs. Or again, some people's constitution is such that they can easily assimilate, and indeed be strengthened by, for example, cheese, while others have something in their bodily constitutions that is aroused by something in the cheese and brought out from its previous mixed and tempered condition into a separated state—whence trouble befalls them (flatulence, indigestion, heartburn, constipation, and so on) (20.41–46 = 147, 16–148, 1). And when someone is ill, their normal capacity to assimilate even well-compounded, relatively "weak" food is much reduced. The first physicians, having observed that sick people are not profited by the same diet as when in health—how they observed this we are not told—decided at first that patients should simply reduce their intake of food. Apparently they decided this by an intuitive application of their dietitian-predecessors' theory of strong and weak foods. Sick people, who must of course have a weakened physiology, should take none at all of certain solid foods—

---

the sweet, the bitter, etc.—both in the human body and in the food we eat. However, a number of times, beginning at 14.47 = 137, 2, he speaks instead of "juices" or humors (χυμοί), mostly or always, it seems, to indicate the isolated and separated condition of one of the qualities or stuffs: a bitter humor would thus be a bitter juice, whether in the body or in a foodstuff, which stands uncompounded within it, and so in its strongest state—and its most potentially harmful one (for us: wild, and even domesticated farm animals' constitutions are perfectly adapted to the assimilation of such uncompounded and untempered food, 3.16–18 = 121, 10–12). See also 18.22 = 143, 4; 19.43 = 145, 5; 20.44 = 147, 19; 22.4 = 149, 4; 24.1, 5, 9 = 153, 7, 10, 14. This account, especially in its recognition of a potentially unlimited range of such humors, is noteworthy for its failure to assign significance to the four humors made so much of by the author of the Hippocratic On the Nature of Humans (pt. 1: see esp. chaps. 4–5), one of Galen's favorite and most admired treatises. Once in passing (but only this once) does our author speak of any of the "official" four humors: "when there is an outpouring of some bitterness, of what we call yellow bile, terrible nausea, burning and weakness take hold" (19.29 = 144, 12). This neglect of the four humors must have been among the features of our treatise that caused Galen's dismissal and lack of interest in it—in addition, of course, to our author's contemptuous rejection of the role in the human constitution and in human health and sickness of hot, cold, wet, and dry (Galen's comments in CMG 5.10.1, 200, cited above, note 6, make it plain that this latter failure was a main ground for his rejection of the treatise as "ungenuine").

the ones that are the "strongest" among the foods we normally eat—and must in general consume less overall (5.12–16 = 124, 9–13). But they soon learned by experience that sometimes this will not suffice, and specially weak diets of gruel or even simply of liquids are needed. The already disordered state of the bodily constitution must not be exacerbated by the addition of qualities or stuffs in the nutriment that will increase or aggravate the quantities of harmful qualities or stuffs already isolated within the body.

We can leave aside further details of our author's physiological theories and his account of how the constituents of foodstuffs are physically related to and interact with people's physical constitutions. The foregoing discussion is sufficient to show how deeply involved he and the method he says was discovered at the very dawn of medicine's prehistory are in making inferences to theoretical explanations—in inferring, from observations of what happens to people (either in health or when ill), to physiological theories and theories about the components of our food that offer explanations of what we observe. These explanations deal with underlying and for the most part unobservable entities[39] and not with surface—manifest—objects and characteristics. In this respect, he (and his method) belong squarely in what was later described as the rationalist wing of Greek medicine, not in that of the Empirics. In saying this, I wish to emphasize that, unlike the Empirics, who were a self-designated group with well-established commitments on how medical knowledge was constituted, the rationalists constituted no "school" of medicine (except as a projection of the Empirics' own assimilating accounts of their opponents). From the third century B.C., when Empiric medicine established itself, down to the end of the Hellenistic period in the first century B.C., there were just the Empirics, on the one hand, and everyone else, on the other. Despite large disagreements and differences about other theoretical and practical matters, these others (like our author in the late fifth century and other Hippocratic authors, as well as their successors who were not bitten by the Empiric bug) all naturally and readily engaged in inquiry into causes. In the course of such inquiry they proposed theories of the constitution of the human body and its organs, and of various diseases, involving hidden theoretical entities and unobservable physiological processes—such as the separated "strong" ingredients of our foodstuffs and our bodily parts appealed to by our author. When I say that the au-

---

[39] At 14.35–39 = 136, 12–16 we are told that sometimes the sweet, the bitter, etc., become "manifest" (φανερά) but that mostly they are not. Even when allegedly manifest, however, they remain within the body where no one could actually *see* them: hence, by the later standards of the Empirics these qualities or powers would remain "hidden" and objectionably theoretical postulates.

thor of *On Ancient Medicine* belongs squarely to the rationalist wing of Greek medicine I mean merely that in this respect, as I have shown at length, his views belong to the main wing of the Greek medical tradition as it became bifurcated in the third century. And, as I have pointed out, it was the Empirics themselves who made the anathematizing of his sort of causal inquiry the main plank of their sect's platform. I have mentioned some of the principal aspects of our author's methodological commitments that the Empirics could have pointed to in claiming his authority in their dispute with Herophilus and other later theoreticians, but it requires very selective attention to those commitments to think that, overall, he is recommending anything like their conception of experience and its self-sufficient role in constituting medical knowledge.[40]

VI

A further aspect of our treatise that must have attracted the early Empirics' favorable attention is its vigorous rejection of the philosophers' ὑποθέσεις as completely useless in explaining any medical facts. We need, then, to return to the philosophical medical writers against whose theories our author is objecting, in order to sharpen our understanding of what he thought made his own theories acceptable and those of his opponents—equally rationalist, in the precise sense I have specified, because they were equally wedded to explanations via underlying and unobservable entities—unacceptable. In my summary in section II, I emphasized the abstractness of the supposedly explanatory principles of the philosophical writers, and our author's insistence, because of their abstractness, on their inefficacy in understanding and treating human illnesses. In speaking of abstractness here I employ a term of my own—nothing corresponds directly to it in our author's critique—intending to capture thereby the core of his objections to these alleged principles. Let me turn, then, to these objections.

Our author argues that observation of patients shows that cosmological powers or properties such as heat and cold belong to many distinct components of the human body, and that these components as a matter of observed fact have different causal powers. In virtually all cases, it is

---

[40] I am grateful to Katerina Ierodiakonou, one of my commentators at the Athens-Pittsburgh Symposium on the History and Philosophy of Greek Medical Traditions from Hippocrates to Harvey in Athens (May 1998), for causing me to discuss more fully both the aspects of *AM* that might have invited favorable attention by the early Empirics and my claim that really, nonetheless, our author defends a method that can fairly be classed, in later terms, as rationalist, not Empiric or even proto-Empiric.

the other characteristics of these components (their sweetness or bitterness, acidity or saline character, and so on), not their heat or coldness, that have effects for better or worse on a human being's bodily condition. As he puts it (at 15.16–18 = 138, 6–8), in addition to ones that are astringent, or flaccid, or flatulence-producing, which he has mentioned in the preceding context, "there are many other things that are hot and that have different and contrary powers to one another." These differences are explained by the specific powers of each of these other qualities, which are seen in all the "strong" instances, whether the materials in question are hot *or* cold (and, we could add, whether relatively wet or dry) (15.25–30 = 138, 14–139, 3).[41] In chapter 13 he poses a related challenge. The logic of the opponent's position requires him to hold that either excess heat or excess cold, or an excess of one of the other cosmological properties, is the cause of any given disease. Yet (as our author points out at 15.1–7 = 137, 12–17) the opponent cannot prescribe "some hot" or "some cold" (since there is no such thing actually in existence). There is no actual material that is just cold, all by itself, or hot: heat and cold are found bound up with other qualities in the constitution of materials. In fact, he has to prescribe the same ordinary foods or medicaments we are all familiar with—and in the constitution and preparation of these it is obvious that lots of heat *and* lots of cold are present. So how could he say, if his prescription proves effective, that it was because of the hot in it rather than the cold?

Our author seems to think these faults are due to the opponent's not using detailed information about the human body in particular, and about the relevant experiences of people when sick or when well, as his springboard for proposing unseen theoretical agencies that he can then use to understand diseases and devise treatments. Instead, he imports his theoretical idea from the study of a different subject. He imports it from

---

[41] One might wonder whether he, or anyone he knows of, has actually done systematic tests to confirm this statement. Presumably not; it's enough for him that it seems so very plausible. Compare the clever argument of chapter 8: if you gave a man sick with a moderately serious disease a diet identical with his ordinary one (except considerably reduced in quantity) he would experience just as much pain as a moderately strong person when healthy would who ate a diet of vetches and barley off the field the way a cow or horse does (except in small quantities). This is an argument to show that, since we have long ago devised the nearly perfect diet for a healthy human, it must be possible by continued application of the same methods to devise a nearly complete system of dietary prescriptions for people when ill: the distance to be traversed in both cases is pretty nearly the same. Who supposes that the author speaks with such confidence on the basis of actually trying this experiment? It seems rather that he is so impressed with the cleverness of the idea, and the very great plausibility of its main premise, that he just *knows* the argument must be sound. It does not occur to him to put it to the test. Here we see again the "rationalist" character of our author's conception of medical history and his own methods in medical science.

the study of the formation, structure, and basic constituents of the cosmos as a whole, and the bases of its orderly progression through the seasons. I detect no irony or disrespect when our author says that with any direct inquiry into the nature of the cosmos[42] one has no choice but to proceed on the basis of an ὑπόθεσις—and I see here no contemptuous dismissal of research into such questions. Plainly, we simply do not have sufficient up-close access to the detailed facts about "the things in the heavens and those below the earth" to enable us to mimic directly the methods of traditional Greek medicine in that case (1.20–27 = 119, 4–11).[43] Any Greek who wanted to make some sense of these "invisible and intractable" matters (ἀφανέα τε καὶ ἀπορεόμενα) must necessarily propose some sufficiently comprehensive, plausible-seeming principles devised by him- or herself that might allow some plausible explanations of at least the gross regularities and other prominent facts. These might include Empedocles' four roots and the powers of Love and Strife, for example. The fact that others (Anaxagoras, or Diogenes of Apollonia, or Philolaus, or even Heraclitus) might offer quite different theories, and that one cannot by inspection obtain data about the celestial or subterranean world that might more or less directly offer confirmation for one rather than the others of these theories—as our author puts it, the fact that "there is not anything by referring to which one must know with clarity" (1.27 = 119, 10–11)—does not render the enterprise valueless. Some theoretical frameworks may allow us to do a better job in various respects than others, and taken all together they help us to see the possibilities for an adequate ultimate understanding, if further data should ever make that available to us. Certainly, this kind of inquiry puts us in a better position than we are in if we allow traditional religion and its interpreters to handle them unchallenged.

The point, however, is that with the nature of human beings, their health, and their illnesses, we are not in the same situation. We *do* have something to refer to in order to know "with clarity" just what the real causes are. This, the author says by implication, is found in "the perception of

---

[42] As opposed to the indirect and derivative one that he may be proposing himself at 20.11–15 (see below, sec. VII).

[43] I think it is better to read (with A and the Budé) καινῆς (newfangled) at 1.20 = 119, 4, rather than M's κενῆς (empty), printed in the Loeb. In addition to the quasi-parallel at 13.1 = 133, 7 to which Jouanna points in his note on the passage, there seems no reason in what follows to think that the writer regards it as a fond and empty thing to go around proposing ὑποθέσεις in order to form some theories, based on purely natural principles, about how the world itself might work. To condemn out of hand as "empty" all the work of pre-Socratic natural philosophy would seem to leave that whole realm in the hands of diviners and other superstitious people; and our author does not seem like someone who would willingly do that.

the body" (τοῦ σώματος τὴν αἴσθησιν, 9.17–18 = 128, 13).[44] He means, perhaps, the patient's body's perceptions or, alternatively, the perception by the physician of the patient's body. In either case, of course, the physician will be the one to ask questions about what the patient is experiencing and to probe the patient's body to help him or her to perceive additional things, in order to generate observations on the basis of which he can then construct his etiological theory—or its application to the given case. So it is ultimately the perceptions or observations of the *physician* that will provide the basis for the clear knowledge of causes in the medical case. Starting with those "perceptions of the patient's body"— those observations of the intelligent physician, who knows how to reason in a way that is suitable for the study of human nature (14.16 = 135, 15–16)—the physician is able to see that "all the causes of pain lead back to the same thing, namely, that the strongest things hurt a person most and most obviously, both one who is well and one who is sick" (6.15–18 = 125, 17–126, 2). And he can proceed beyond that conclusion to reach the complete theory of the ingredients of the human body (and of foodstuffs suitable for humans) and of the best compounded and tempered mutual mixtures of those components. So we do not need to make do with any ὑπόθεσις in this case. We have a secure observational basis for determining with full clarity what the real causes are. So long, then, as inferences to hidden causes are controlled by and arise out of detailed study of the observable, concrete facts about human illnesses and the experiences of people when suffering from them, our author has no objection to theoretical, causal reasoning, or to the appeal to hidden theoretical entities, in his explanations. He balks only when, as with philosophical medicine, such detailed information is set to one side where it *is* available, and theorizing takes its start instead simply from plausible-looking ideas about the organization and life of the universe as a whole—that is, from mere ὑποθέσεις.

---

[44] The author mentions the perception of the body as what we may call the "criterion" in connection specifically with the question of the specific quantities of food—neither too much nor too little—that a person should consume, whether for a diseased condition or a healthy one. The "measure" (μέτρον) in such cases, he says, is the "perception of the body." However, on his own account it is the general theory of human physiology, in relation to the different qualities of the various foodstuffs, that determines the right amount of specific foods for people of the different types of bodily constitutions to take under the different conditions. So the "perception of the body" (as interpreted by the physician) is the ultimate basis, according to our author here, for the whole theory of physiology and of the qualities of foodstuffs that he relies on throughout. Physicians know that "strong" foods are bad because of the pains that certain foods cause people, which thereby reveal to the alert and intelligent physician the fact that they are too strong for the patient's constitution, or for his or her special conditions when subject to some illness.

VII

On this interpretation, our author respects and values (up to a point) the study and the explanation of facts about the cosmos at large by the method of ὑπόθεσις, unnecessary and useless though it is for studying human health and disease. But, however respectable (faute de mieux) that method may be in its proper context, he insists that it does not provide any clear knowledge (εἰδέναι τὸ σαφές, 1.27 = 119, 10–11)—that is, any *knowledge* at all—even of the causes of what goes on in the heavens or below the earth. We are still in the area of more or less plausible conjecture when we propose that it is the natures of hot, cold, wet, and dry in their mutual interactions that explain the phenomena there. Remarkably, in chapter 20 (20.11–15 = 146, 9–13), on what seems to me the best interpretation of his words,[45] our author takes the bold step of claiming that if anyone ever *did* achieve clear knowledge of these matters (γνῶναί τι σαφές, 20.12 = 146, 10; the recurrence of this closely related language may be significant), it would be by employing the methods of traditional Greek medicine—that is, by going from knowledge of human nature, health, and diseases, developed along the lines we have already examined, to knowledge of the nature of the cosmos and of the causes at work in its constitution and maintenance.[46] He does not explain how he thinks

---

[45] On an alternative interpretation, he speaks only about how one could achieve clear knowledge of *human* nature, not knowledge of nature in general—i.e., the nature of the cosmos overall, to which pre-Socratic natural philosophy was devoted. I argue however, in notes 16 and 47, that throughout this passage, and therefore at 20.11 = 146, 9 in particular, the author refers by the words περὶ φύσιος always to the nature of the whole (including, of course, human nature), not human nature in particular. If so, then my interpretation, which is that also of Festugière and Jones, among other translators and commentators, follows.

[46] He also says, in an obscure further criticism, that he considers that "whatever has been said or written about nature by any wise man (σοφιστής) or any physician pertains less to medical science than to that of painting"—ἧσσον . . . τῇ ἰητρικῇ τέχνῃ προσήκειν ἢ τῇ γραφικῇ, 20.8–11 = 146, 7–9. Unfortunately it is not perhaps absolutely certain that he does mean painting here by γραφικὴ τέχνη, nor do I have any confidence in any of my own or other writers' attempts to grasp his point, if he does intend, as seems most likely, to refer to expertise in, or about, painting. Very possibly he is making a snide comment on Empedocles' frg. B 23 (Diels), where Empedocles appeals to the ability of painters (γραφέες) to produce *images* of all kinds of objects simply from combining bits of a few well-chosen pigments as evidence in favor of his own theory that all kinds of *objects* can result from combinations of bits of his four "roots"—our author has referred by name to Empedocles only a few lines earlier; 20.6 = 146, 5. (On this fragment and a related fragment, see Wright, *Empedocles*, 38–39, 179–81, 221–22.) For an ingenious new proposal and an authoritative discussion of other interpretations that have been proposed, see Dihle, "Kritisch-exegetische Bemerkungen," 146–50; see also Jouanna's note ad loc., pp. 208–9, for further discussion and references. Fortunately it does not seem necessary to understand this negative criticism in order to grasp adequately the sense and bearing of the positive claim our author goes on to make about how clear knowledge about cosmology might be attained.

medical knowledge, and the medical method, might perform this function. But given what we have learned so far, we can work out with some assurance the main part of what he might have in mind—even if we conclude that he is not quite entitled to say that it is *only* from a completed knowledge of medicine that one can come to know the nature of the cosmos itself, or that that by itself would suffice (see below, note 49).

Before I quote the relevant passage, we should recall that in his preceding account of the method of traditional Greek medicine, the author has said plainly that it centrally involves reasoning about human nature (see 14.16–20 = 135, 14–17, discussed in above section V). He now draws attention to the fact (implicit in all that preceded, including the passage of chapter 14 just cited) that the relevant reasoning about human nature treats that nature (20.20–23 = 146, 17–147, 1) *in relation to* "what [humans] eat and drink" and to the "other practices" of human beings, and considers "what will result from each of these for each [type of] person." Here, then, is what he says (20.11–23 = 146, 9–147, 1):[47]

---

[47] I translate the Budé text, which for convenience I give here:

νομίζω δὲ περὶ φύσιος γνῶναί τι σαφὲς οὐδαμόθεν ἄλλοθεν εἶναι ἢ ἐξ
ἰητρικῆς. τοῦτο δὲ οἷόν τε καταμαθεῖν ὅταν αὐτήν τις τὴν ἰητρικὴν ὀρθῶς
πᾶσαν περιλάβῃ—μέχρι δὲ τοῦτο πολλοῦ μοι δοκεῖ δεῖν—, λέγω δὲ ταύτην
τὴν ἱστορίην, εἰδέναι ἄνθρωπος τί ἐστι καὶ δι᾽ οἵας αἰτίας γίνεται καὶ τἆλλα
ἀκριβέως. ἐπεὶ τοῦτό γέ μοι δοκεῖ ἀναγκαῖον εἶναι ἰητρῷ περὶ φύσιος εἰδέναι
καὶ πάνυ σπουδάσαι ὡς εἴσεται, εἴπερ τι μέλλει τῶν δεόντων ποιήσειν, ὅ τι
τέ ἐστιν ἄνθρωπος πρὸς τὰ ἐσθιόμενά τε καὶ πινόμενα καὶ ὅ τι πρὸς τὰ ἄλλα
ἐπιτηδεύματα καὶ ὅ τι ἀφ᾽ ἑκάστου ἑκάστῳ συμβήσεται.

Thus I accept πᾶσαν at 20.14 = 146, 12 with most manuscripts (it is omitted in A and in the Loeb); and I adopt the Budé's punctuation (it is also Heiberg's in H. L. Heiberg, *Hippocratis Opera*, vol. I 1, *CMG*; and Festugière's), with a comma after ἱστορίην instead of (so the Loeb) after the following word, εἰδέναι.

In note 16, above, I have argued, against Jouanna, that at 20.6 = 146, 5, οἱ περὶ φύσιος γεγράφασιν means those "who [like Empedocles] have written about Nature"—and not those who have written specifically about the nature of human beings; the author's reference is to writers on nature as a whole who, he goes on to say, have devoted attention (viz., by relying on their general cosmological principles) to the nature of human beings in particular. Thus περὶ φύσιος in this first occurrence in the passage means "about nature" (as a whole), not "about human nature" (specifically). The same phrase first recurs four lines later (20.10 = 146, 8), where it ought again to mean "about nature" (as a whole). Indeed, it has to mean that at 20.10 whatever may be the meaning at 20.6: the author says that "whatever has been said or written about nature by any wise man (σοφιστής) or any physician" does not pertain to medical science (see further note 46). He could not mean to say that whatever any physician has said or written merely about *human* nature has nothing to do with medical science: he is full of praise for what traditional medical science has said about that (see, e.g., 14.16–20 = 135, 14–17). He means, as before, whatever has been said or written about nature as a whole (and, as part of that, human nature), whether by a philosopher or a physician. The occurrence of the phrase περὶ φύσιος at the beginning of

I consider that any clear knowledge about nature cannot be acquired from any other source but medical science: it is possible to know this fully (κατα-μαθεῖν)[48] when one has correctly grasped medical science itself as a whole (but until then it is very far from possible)—I mean [when one has grasped] this subject of inquiry (ἱστορίη), to know (εἰδέναι) what a human being is,

---

the passage translated then follows: here again, then, the reference is to (clear knowledge about) nature as a whole, not merely specifically human nature (so Jouanna).

I take λέγω δὲ ταύτην τὴν ἱστορίην (lines 15–16 in the Loeb) to specify αὐτὴν . . . τὴν ἰητρικὴν (lines 13–14)—and not, with most translators, to carry forward περὶ φύσιος γνῶναί τι σαφές (line 12), i.e., τοῦτο (line 13), that is, to specify what the content of the "clear knowledge about nature" referred to itself will be (viz., as Jouanna would have it, medical science). Among the translations I have consulted (Jones in the Loeb and in his 1946 edition; Festugière; Diller in *Hippokrates Schriften*; and Jouanna in the Budé; the appalling translation by J. Chadwick and W. N. Mann in Lloyd, ed., *Hippocratic Writings*, makes it impossible even to conjecture how they construed the Greek at this point), only Diller's takes the Greek this way. But the nearest noun phrase for λέγω δὲ ταύτην τὴν ἱστορίην to be explicating (and so the one it would normally pick up, even though it comes in a subordinate clause) is in fact αὐτὴν τὴν ἰητρικήν. So Diller's construction makes for better Greek usage. And, so construed, the clause makes excellent sense. The author has said that it is not possible to get any clear knowledge about nature (i.e., cosmology) except by first obtaining a complete grasp of medical science (20.11–13 = 146, 9–11). He then begins (lines 15–17 in the Loeb, 13–15 in Budé), entirely appropriately, to say clearly what *he* holds medical science consists of: it consists of knowing "what a human being is, through what causes he comes into being, and all the rest with precision." (Here "all the rest with precision" is important: it would include everything about human physiology and the constituents of nutriments, as well as of harmful things to consume, and so on, that our author has included in the true medical method and the discoveries made using it; thus it would contrast sharply with the "knowledge" of human nature claimed by the philosophers, which he rejects at the beginning of the chapter.) He goes on, in the remainder of the passage quoted, to tell us more precisely what according to him is involved in this knowledge: it means knowing what a human being is *in relation to* what he eats, etc. (Apart from its less satisfactory construction of λέγω δὲ ταύτην τὴν ἱστορίην, Jouanna's interpretation gives a less satisfactory sense: having claimed that it's not possible to obtain clear knowledge about *human* nature except from a complete grasp of medical science, the author now specifies—surely unnecessarily, since it was plain already at the mention of "what a human being is" at line 3 and its replacement, on Jouanna's interpretation, with περὶ φύσιος at line 6—what he and presumably everyone understands by "knowledge of human nature," viz., the investigation and knowledge of what a human being is, etc. Only then, in the following sentence, would he get around to saying how, on his own particular views, this knowledge is to be accomplished.)

On my overall interpretation of this passage I follow Festugière (*L'Ancienne médecine*, 18, with nn.), who finds our author, as I do, claiming traditional medicine as the sole basis on which anyone can obtain clear knowledge about nature as a whole—about cosmology. On Jouanna's interpretation our author would be reduced to saying something much less striking and provocative (though admittedly still controversial): that only medical science (and not "natural philosophy") can give clear knowledge about human nature. Festugière's translation is marred, however, by his failure to see the correct construction (Diller's) of λέγω δὲ ταύτην τὴν ἱστορίην (line 15–16 in the Loeb).

[48] For this interpretation of καταμαθεῖν see H. W. Smyth, *Greek Grammar*, ¶ 1648.

through what causes he comes into being, and all the rest with precision.[49] For I think this at least about nature is necessary for a physician to know (εἰδέναι), and to bend every effort in order to know, if he is to perform any of his functions—both what a human being is in relation to what he eats and what he drinks, and what in relation to his other practices, and what will result from each of these for each [type of] person.

His argument (construing the Greek in the way I have done) is this: Physicians must know human nature not as an isolated single nature but in relation to the natures of the foodstuffs and potable liquids, and baths and exercises, and all the other parts of a normal set of practices conducive to health, as well as the natures of all those that harm it. We have seen already how the author thinks foods and drinks consist of the same ingredients as our bodies do, and how he thinks they act upon, and are acted upon by, our organs, tissues, etc. This means that once medical science is fully completed one will know in full detail both what a man is, including the causes of his coming into being (viz., those ingredients), and "all the rest with precision." Here, this "all the rest" will have to include quite a lot, in principle presumably virtually everything (knowable) about the natures (in the sense of the physical constitutions) of a pretty vast range of other natural entities: other animals, to the extent that we eat their meat, many kinds of plants and fruits, and so on. Plus, we must know the nature of water (for baths), and the nature of all kinds of natural products that we use for rub-downs, for medical applications of all sorts, and so on. The claim then is that, because all this detailed knowledge about the natures of all sorts of things is included centrally within

[49] In the opening lines of the chapter, the author has rejected the claim of his opponents that "it is not possible for anyone who does not know what a human being is to know medicine, but one who intends to treat human beings correctly must have a thorough knowledge of that"; and he has explicated their conception of the knowledge of human nature in terms of knowing "how he first came to be and from what things he was put together"—i.e., cosmological and cosmogonical processes. (See, e.g., *On Fleshes* 3 ff.) One might find it puzzling, then, that the author now, on his own account, includes the rejected knowledge of "what a human being is" and "through what causes he comes into being" as components of medical science. The author's point, however, is precisely that *true* knowledge of what a human being is and how he comes into being is achievable solely through the investigations of traditional medical science—not through philosophical cosmology. In fact, the knowledge the cosmologists were aspiring to is itself only achievable as an offshoot of medical science when that has been brought to final completion (N.B. "science itself as a whole," line 14 in Loeb). His objection is not so much to the opponents' claim about needing to know "what a human being is" if one is to know medicine, as it is to their idea of the means by which that knowledge is to be gained. As I put it above (pp. 9–10), he boldly reverses the order of priority between cosmological and medical knowledge. So the knowledge of "what a human being is" that he includes within medical science at lines 16–17 is not the same as the rejected knowledge of "what a human being is" at line 3.

the knowledge constituting the completed medical science (indeed, the author seems to think it actually exhausts it), it should be possible to extend this knowledge to a general knowledge of the cosmos as a whole. And since that understanding of the natures of all these varied things is hardly going to be available to us from any other source (apart from an interest in their effects for health and disease, no one, he seems to assume, studies them), he concludes that that general knowledge is only achievable through medical science.

As we have seen, he thinks of human nature as essentially the nature of a material object compounded out of thousands of ingredients that when in their isolated, strongest forms, appear as juices. Likewise the natures of foods, drinks, other animals, plants, and so on. A product of his own time, then, he is thinking of all natural objects as simply material compounds of some sort or other. In this respect, he shares the outlook of the pre-Socratic philosophers of nature such as Empedocles. In chapters 22–23, it is true—I have had little occasion to refer to these chapters, because they have little to contribute to the author's views on method and science—he notices that the structures (σχήματα) of the bodily parts, too (for example, the "broad and tapering" structure of the bladder), need to be taken into account in understanding diseases. But it is only what we would call their physical, not their biological, properties or (as Aristotle would put it) their "forms" that he attends to. Accordingly, he may think that once medical science is truly completed we will have such an extensive detailed knowledge of the materials at work in nature, and of their causal properties, that we might at last replace the pre-Socratic philosophers' ὑποθέσεις with a set of theoretical concepts for explaining cosmogony and cosmology that are actually based, in the same solid way that medical science is, on an adequate range of observational information *about* what the things in the heavens and below the earth can reasonably be believed to be like.[50] The result would remain a natural science conceived in the pre-Socratic spirit, to the extent that it would limit itself to considering the natures of the materials making up the cosmos and their natural interactions and transformations. But it would be built up from below, through patient examination of detailed types of

---

[50] It seems that he overreaches here. Presumably, in order fully to know the fundamental principles of *all* the world's material contents, and of the heavens and their movements, one would need to know also about various materials presumably not included in the human body or our foodstuffs—say granite, silver, or even tree bark or seashells. But even if additional observational sciences besides medicine would have an indispensable contribution to make, one has to grant that, understood our author's way, a completed theory of medicine would include a vast and quite comprehensive knowledge of the materials the world contains. His enthusiastic exaggeration is perhaps forgivable.

stuff and modest inferences from there regarding their natures and causal powers and their modes of exercising them, and not imposed from above on the basis of grand but merely plausible reasoning that is empiricially un- or under-informed. In the context of his own time, such a bold and exciting program should count as brilliant and revolutionary enough to win for him much more notice—even admiring notice—than, so far as we can tell, his ideas received, either then or later in antiquity.[51]

[51] I thank Katerina Ierodiakonou and Mary Louise Gill for their comments on the first version of this paper, delivered at the Athens-Pittsburgh Symposium on the History and Philosophy of Greek Medical Traditions (May 1998). I benefited from the discussion of the paper in Athens, and also from discussion of successively revised versions at Texas A and M University and the University of Texas at Austin in November 1999, and at the Center for Hellenic Studies in Washington, D.C., in March 2000. Shortly before final revision of the manuscript (September 2000) I received comments of Mark J. Schiefsky (especially on section VII), who also sent me a copy of his Harvard dissertation, "*Technê* and Method in the Hippocratic Treatise *On Ancient Medicine*" (1999), which deals with many of the issues addressed in this essay sometimes in complementary, but sometimes in divergent, ways. I have not been able to take full account here of Schiefsky's work.

CHAPTER 2

PLATO ON SENSE-PERCEPTION AND KNOWLEDGE

(*THEAETETUS* 184–186)

I

PLATO'S ARGUMENT in the *Theaetetus* (184b–186e) against the proposal that knowledge be defined as αἴσθησις[1] has, I think, not yet been fully understood or rightly appreciated. Existing interpretations fall into two groups. On the one hand, F. M. Cornford[2] and others think that Plato rejects the proposal on the ground that the objects which we perceive are not the sort of objects of which one could have knowledge: only the unchanging Forms can be known. On the other hand, there are those[3] who think Plato's argument has nothing to do with Forms but instead turns on a distinction between sensation and judgment which has the consequence that the thinking we do *about* the deliverances of the senses, and not the mere *use* of the senses, is the source of our knowledge. The interpretation which I advance in this paper belongs to the second of these two broad classes, but differs from others in providing a more careful account of the distinctions which Plato seems to be making in this passage. Much of the interest of the argument lies, I think, in the analysis of the process of perception which Plato produces by distinguishing carefully the contribution of the senses from that of the mind; but this analysis has not been given the attention it deserves.

The complexities of the argument can be usefully indicated by a brief examination of Cornford's interpretation. According to Cornford Plato's argument proceeds in two stages. In the first (184b–186a1) Plato concludes that there is knowledge which is not a matter of perception, i.e.,

---

[1] An expression that might be translated by either "perception" or "sensation." I shall mostly say "perception," but the other sense should constantly be borne in mind; the ambiguity becomes important below, p. 50ff.

[2] In his *Plato's Theory of Knowledge*, 102–109. Subsequent references to Cornford's views are to this book.

[3] Cf. G. Ryle, "Plato's *Parmenides*," 317, reprinted in *Studies in Plato's Metaphysics*, ed. R. E. Allen (hereafter abbreviated *SPM*) p. 136; I. M. Crombie, *An Examination of Plato's Doctrines*, 2:14.

that "percepts cannot be the only objects of knowledge" (p. 106). In the second (186a1–e12), it is further concluded that the additional objects of knowledge referred to in the first stage are in fact the *only* objects of true or real knowledge.

In the first stage Plato appeals to the distinction between, on the one hand, the use of the faculty of sensing as such, i.e., the mere presentation of an object in sensation, and, on the other hand, the making of judgments. The point of this appeal is not, however, to suggest that since only judgments are true, judging does, but mere sensing does not, exhibit a sufficient order of logical complexity to count as knowing. Rather, this distinction is introduced in order to bring out the fact that there are other objects besides sense-objects with which we are "acquainted" (p. 106). In judgments we use such words as "is" and "similar," and the thought that something we are sensing exists or is similar to something else is not an achievement of mere sensing; we must bring in, and apply, the notions of existence and similarity, as well as use our senses. From this it is inferred that even if the presentation of an object of sense in sensation is an instance of knowledge, our power of making judgments shows that there is another way of being presented with objects, namely the intuition of Forms, here instanced by Existence, Similarity and the other so-called κοινά ("commons"). We could not apply the notion of existence to anything if we were not acquainted with Existence; and the knowledge of these (and other) Forms is not acquired by using the senses but by thinking—by an activity of the soul "all by herself" (185e1), without reliance on sensation.

The argument of Cornford's second stage (186a2–e10) is apparently meant to run as follows. Existence (οὐσία) is one of the κοινά mentioned in stage one. Hence both our acquaintance with the Form Existence and our ability to formulate judgments with the help of this notion are functions of the mind independent of sensation. But it is only in attaining to existence that truth is reached; so that knowledge too first occurs at the level of the mind's independent activity, and there is no knowledge in the use of the senses at all. Cornford admits that given the context the most natural way of understanding this last point would be that sensing does not involve the use of "is" and therefore does not amount to judging or asserting anything, so that since knowledge is necessarily knowledge of truths, sensing is in no case knowing. On this view Plato denies that to use the senses is to know anything by arguing that knowledge is the achievement of the mind's capacity to formulate judgments, which is an activity which goes beyond sensing itself. But Cornford thinks that the real point being made here relies on the other "independent activity" of the mind referred to above—that by which it becomes *acquainted* with Forms. The Forms, taken as a group, constitute in Plato's metaphysics the realm of οὐσία and he elsewhere associates knowledge with these objects;

so here too he must be making the point that since no object of the senses is a Form, nothing the senses give us belongs to the realm of οὐσία. It follows that no activity of the senses, or of the mind through the medium of the senses, can amount to knowledge.

There are obvious difficulties with this interpretation. For example, οὐσία is interpreted in the first stage as naming just one Form among others, but in the second, without any textual warrant for the change,[4] it becomes the collective name of all the Forms or of the metaphysical status of the Forms as a group. Again, although Cornford finds in the passage a distinction between judging and sensing, he represses this distinction at every turn in favor of the distinction between objects we are acquainted with in sensation and objects grasped by intuitive thought: with good reason, since as Cornford admits, the former distinction points towards the activity of judging as the area where knowledge is to be found, while the Forms-sensibles dichotomy leads to the quite different, indeed incompatible, suggestion that knowledge is not a matter of judging truly, but of intuitive awareness of a certain kind of object. Cornford's attempt to combine his distinction between sensation and judgment with a reaffirmation of the doctrine that only the intuition of Forms deserves the name "knowledge" produces a confused and inadequate line of thought.

Nonetheless, Cornford's interpretation has met with approval in certain quarters just because it does yield the conclusion that perception cannot be knowledge because the objects of perception are not knowable. Thus H. F. Cherniss, so far as this general conclusion is concerned, enthusiastically adopts[5] Cornford's interpretation as supporting his view concerning the unity of Plato's thought. Cherniss, indeed, goes well beyond Cornford when he suggests[6] that not merely the general conclusion of the passage, but even the *argument* supporting it, is borrowed from the *Republic*. In Cherniss's view *Republic* 523–525 is "parallel" to

---

[4] No doubt Cornford thinks there is *some* warrant in the fact, as he thinks, that throughout this part of the dialogue Plato assumes that sense objects are in Heraclitean flux: Plato would seem, given this assumption, to invite the interpretation of οὐσία at 186d3 and e5 as indicating the realm of Being as opposed to that of Becoming. But nothing of the kind is being assumed here about the objects of the senses: Heracliteanism is defined at 156a ff. (cf. 157b1, τὸ δ'εἶναι πανταχόθεν ἐξαιρετέον) as involving the refusal to say of anything that it *exists*, but at 185a precisely this *is* said by Socrates (and accepted by Theaetetus) about the objects of the senses. Cf. G.E.L. Owen, "The Place of the *Timaeus* in Plato's Dialogues," 86 (= *SPM* p. 324). Cherniss's attempted rebuttal of this point in "The Relation of the *Timaeus* to Plato's Later Dialogues," 244 n. 71 (= *SPM* p. 357 n. 1), shows that he has understood neither Owen nor Plato: in saying that Plato "goes on to ascribe οὐσία to objects of perception," Owen obviously meant that Plato says about objects of perception that they exist, and (as just noted) Plato certainly does say this.

[5] *Aristotle's Criticism of Plato and the Academy*, 236 n. 141.

[6] *AJP* (1957), p. 244 n. 71 (= *SPM* p. 357 n. 1).

Theaetetus 184–186 in assigning to the senses the task of "stimulating" the mind to engage in pure thought by turning away from the sense-world toward that of the Forms. Later on I will comment briefly on the alleged parallelism of these two passages, but for the moment I want to concentrate on what Cornford's and Cherniss's interpretations have in common.

Both Cornford and Cherniss think (rightly) that the main point being argued is that knowledge is achieved by the mind operating somehow independently of the senses. But both interpreters think that the mind's independent activity, when it produces knowledge, consists in acquaintance with Forms. This latter point is however not to be found in Plato's text at all, as I shall show in the next section. The only independent activity of the mind discussed by Plato is that in which it applies the κοινά to the objects of the senses, judging that something seen exists, is self-identical, and so on. He never alludes to our mode of awareness of Existence, Sameness, and so on, and does not locate our knowledge in any such awareness. Cornford is right to emphasize the importance here of some distinction between sensation and judgment; he goes wrong when he brings in the intuition or contemplation of Forms in explicating what Plato says about "judgment."

II

The passage begins (184b4–185a3) with an account of what perception (αἴσθησις) actually is and how it comes about. If Plato is to refute the claim that perception is knowledge he must first mark off the activity of perception from other supposed "cognitive" activities, so that he can then inquire whether perception, so understood, amounts to knowledge. Earlier in the dialogue (156a ff.) the process of sense-perception was represented as something occurring between the sense-organ and the external object perceived, and no account was taken of the fact that a person's *mind,* and not merely his bodily organs, is active in perception. So Plato points out (184d1–5) that our sensations (αἰσθήσεις, d2) are referred to the mind (ψυχή), and that it is not the sense organs (or the sense faculties) which perceive colors and sounds but the mind itself, operating *through* the organs, or, as he also says (e8, 185b8, e7), through the senses. The organs are parts of the *body* (184e5–6, 185d3), and the power of sight, touch and the rest are capacities of the *body* (185e7). It is quite incorrect to say, as Plato himself had said in the *Republic,*[7] that the senses see this or that, or say or report this or that: it is the subject himself who perceives

---

[7] Cf. 523c δηλοῖ, d5 ἐσήμηνεν, e4 ὁρᾷ, 524a3 παραγγέλλει, a7 σημαίνει, a8 λέγει.

things *with* his mind *through* the organs and powers of the body, who says or thinks this or that on the basis of his sense-experience. In perception, then, the mind is active through the medium of the senses. Furthermore, though without arguing the point, Plato seems to limit perception to what may be called elementary sense-perception, i.e., the perception of the "proper objects" of the five senses: colors, sounds, tastes, smells, and a supposed analogue for touch. He does not indicate how he regards seeing or otherwise perceiving a physical object, but presumably he would wish to say that this is not perception, strictly conceived, but already involves some of those higher reflective activities of mind to be introduced in a moment.

There are problems of interpretation here (particularly concerning how Plato understands the use of the mind in perception) but they are best put off until after the next section of the argument has been outlined. Here (185a–186e) Plato contrasts with the perceptual use of the mind, in which it operates through the medium of the bodily senses, a further and higher use, in which the mind works independently of the body and its senses (αὐτὴ᾽ δι᾽ αὐτῆς, 185e1, 6). Socrates shows that such an independent use exists by reminding Theaetetus that in some cases we have one and the same thought about the objects of several senses. Thus we can think that a color, a sound, and a taste are each of them the same as itself and different from the others; *what* we think about each of these things, namely *that it is the same as itself* and *that it is different from the others,* is the same in each case. What we are doing here is thinking something common to the objects of several senses, and Plato calls the predicates of such judgments κοινά, "common terms."[8] Plato explicitly includes among the κοινά existence, identity, difference, similarity, dissimilarity, being one, odd and even, good and bad, beautiful and ugly; all of these are properties of the objects of several, perhaps all, of the senses. Plato argues that

---

[8] Cornford, at one place (p. 105), notices that the word κοινόν here is to be understood by contrast with what is peculiar to the objects of a single sense. Yet further down the page he says κοινόν is to be understood "in the sense in which a name is common to any number of individual things," and hence that the κοινά are "the meanings of common names," i.e., Forms. Κοινόν is fairly frequently used in this way in Aristotle (e.g., *EE* 1218a8, *Met.* Z 1040b25, *NE* 1180b15), where the contexts show that it is to be understood as meaning τὸ κοινῇ κατηγορούμενον or τὸ καθόλου. But it is obvious that this is not how Plato uses the word here: since the κοινά are predicates belonging to objects of more than one of the senses, such predicates as *white* or *hard* will not qualify as κοινά. Yet they are certainly κοινῇ κατηγορούμενα. I know of no place in Plato where κοινόν is used in this Aristotelian sense: strictly not *Tht.* 208d7–9 and 209a10–11, to which Cherniss (*ACP,* p. 236 n.) refers. By κοινόν in our passage Plato certainly does not mean to refer to Forms generally. The κοινά may be Forms, though Plato does not say so; but they do not include any predicates except those which are common to objects of *several* senses.

in applying common terms to the objects of the senses, the mind is not perceiving but doing something else, which we may call reflecting and comparing (a term which is meant to cover what the mind does when it is ἀναλογιζομένη, 186a10, ἐπανιοῦσα καὶ συμβάλλουσα, b8, and συλλογιζομένη, d3). His reason for saying this is that acts of perception are always performed through one sense or another, and what can be perceived through one sense cannot be perceived through any other. Thus only colors can be seen, and no color can be heard or tasted. Hence we cannot be merely perceiving in thinking that a sound and a color exist: what we are then noticing about the objects, their existence, cannot be either an auditory or a visual property, since it belongs equally to the sound and to the color, and it is obvious that there is no further sense through which we could perceive such common properties. Judgments of this kind are made by the mind by itself and without the aid of any sense or organ of sense.

It is important to realize that in his discussion of the higher, reflective employment of the mind Plato is exclusively alluding to the activity of judging *that* something exists, is self-identical, etc.; he nowhere raises the question of how we become acquainted with Existence and the other terms we apply to sense-objects in so judging. For the moment I will take this for granted, leaving the proof until later.

In the first part of our passage, then, Plato draws two distinctions. He distinguishes between the role played by the mind in perception and that played by the senses, and he contrasts this use of the mind with a higher reflective use in which it works independently of the body and its sense-faculties and judges that the objects of the senses exist and that they possess other κοινά. Several points call for comment.

First, it should be noticed that in distinguishing between the senses (αἰσθήσεις) as powers of the bodily organs and the mind as that which[9] perceives (αἰσθάνεται), Plato is in effect using the notion of αἴσθησις in two ways. For the perceptual acts of the mind—the acts of seeing, hearing, smelling, etc.—can be called αἰσθήσεις (cf. 186d10–e2), as can the powers of the body which Plato says make these acts possible. Αἴσθησις as act is located in the mind, but αἴσθησις as power is in the body. Now there is an awkwardness in saying that the *mind* sees, hears and so on, (ὁρᾶν, ἀκούειν, 184c6–7, etc.) while locating the *power* of hearing, sight, etc. (ἀκοή, ὄψις, 185a2, c1–2) in the body and its organs: if the mind sees and hears, and not any bodily part, then surely the mind and not any part of the body is the possessor of the power of sight and hearing. But the

[9] Plato finds it natural to shift from saying that the person perceives through the sensory powers of the bodily organs (184b9, c6–7, 8, etc.) to saying (185c8, e6–7, 186b3) that the mind perceives through the senses.

awkwardness is particularly acute because the thesis which Plato hopes to refute by the analysis of perception being carried out here is put as the identification of αἴσθησις and ἐπιστήμη (184b5). Since αἴσθησις, in the analysis, can refer either to a power of the body or to an action of the mind, there is an initial doubt as to what Plato is going to deny in denying that αἴσθησις is knowledge. It might be suggested, for example, that by emphasizing that the senses are powers of the body Plato means to be saying that the *senses* do not contain knowledge: they do no more than provide material for the mind to act upon. It is the mind that does the knowing, and the senses are altogether dumb and devoid of thinking: in using the senses we are not, *per se,* even thinking about anything, much less knowing anything. If this is going to be his argument, Plato will only be denying that knowledge lies in the sensory powers of the body; he will not be saying that perceptual acts of the mind are themselves not acts of knowledge. Yet, one might object, this last is precisely what ought to be proved. But owing to the vagueness of Theaetetus' original definition and to the use of the word αἴσθησις to stand for the body's powers of sensory affection, Plato might fairly claim to have shown that on one plausible interpretation of the thesis it is false. This possibility should certainly be borne in mind, although I think that in the end it is reasonably clear that Plato means to reject even the claim that perceptual acts of the mind are acts of knowledge.[10]

The second remark to be made at this point concerns the nature of perceptual acts, as Plato conceives them, and the distinction between these and the higher acts of reflective judgment. Perception, as something the mind does through the senses, is contrasted both with the sensory affection of the bodily organs and with the higher reflective use of the mind. On close examination of the text, however, it appears that the perceptual use of the mind is conceived of rather differently in the two contrasts. Plato does not seem to have made a clean decision whether by perception he means mere sensory awareness, which does not involve any application of concepts to the data of sense, or sensory awareness plus the restricted use of concepts which is involved in labelling the colors, sounds, etc., presented in sensation with their names—"red," "hard," "sweet," "loud," and so on. This indecision on his part is of the greatest importance for the interpretation of the argument, if, as I just remarked, Plato intends to reject the claim of perceptual acts to be instances of knowing. To the extent that Plato is unclear what he includes under the notion of perceptual acts, both what he is denying and perhaps also why he is denying

---

[10] This seems to follow, for example, from 186d2, where knowledge is said not to reside ἐν τοῖς παθήμασιν, which, as 186c1–2 shows, is to be understood as a reference to perceptual acts of the mind.

it will remain unclear. What he says about perceptual acts must therefore be very closely scrutinized.

In drawing the contrast between bodily affection and perception Plato is naturally interpreted as understanding by "perception" sensory awareness by itself. Though he limits the objects of awareness to the proper objects of the five senses, saying that we perceive warm, hard, light, and sweet things (184e4–5), and even the hardness of a hard thing (186b2), through our senses, this need not imply that perception involves the awareness *that* these things are hard, light, and so on. And at one place he seems very clearly to be thinking of perceptual acts as acts of awareness only; he says they are common to men and beasts and can be performed already at birth (186b11–c2).[11] Presumably he does not imagine that beasts and day-old babies are capable of using concepts. Now if "perception" is here sensory awareness, then one would expect the higher, independent activity of the mind to be the application of concepts to what we perceive. The line between "perception" and reflection would then separate simple sensory awareness from the thinking, of whatever complexity, that one does *about* whatever one is presented with in sensation. On this view, the application of the concept *red* to a perceived color would require some independent action of the mind quite as much as the application of the concept *existence*. In fact, the concepts of existence, identity, and so on (the κοινά), would be in no way specially associated with the mind's independent activity;[12] the κοινά would have to be interpreted as mere examples, whose place could be taken by any other terms of any other class or category.

The fact remains, however, that the independent use of the mind is illustrated *exclusively* by the application of concepts which are applicable to the objects of more than one sense. This suggests that the independent use does not include judgments applying concepts peculiar to the objects of a single sense. And in fact, in contrasting perception and the higher use of the mind Plato does seem to contrast the application of the κοινά to

---

[11] Cf. also 186d2–3: παθήματα here too is naturally interpreted to mean acts of (passive) awareness.

[12] It might be suggested that οὐσία, at any rate, does occupy a special position. For, one might say, it is the one concept that is employed on every occasion on which any other concept is applied: every judgment is of the form "A is (or is not) B." One might attempt to argue that all application of concepts involves the use of the other κοινά as well: this is plausible for identity, difference, similarity, and dissimilarity. But it is not plausible for "two," "good," and "beautiful." In fact, however, the principle of selection for the κοινά is not their implication in all judgments, but their applicability to objects of different senses. So the supposed special position of at least some of them as regards the power of judgment is not Plato's reason for illustrating the independent activity of the mind by judgments involving them.

objects of sensory awareness, not with sensory awareness itself but with the application of *other* concepts, namely the concepts required for the labeling of the data of sense. Not only does he not illustrate the reflective-judgmental use of the mind by the application of a concept which, like *red,* belongs to only one type of sense-object; he very clearly indicates that thinking with such concepts is not a matter of reflective judgment at all. He says (185b4–5) that we are capable of investigating (ἐπισκέψασθαι) and deciding (cf. κρίνειν, 186b8) whether a color and a sound are similar or not, and that we do so with our minds independently of any bodily power. The same point is put (185e4–7) by saying that the mind does not operate through any sense in applying the words (ἐπονομάζεις, c6) "exists" and "does not exist" to things. By contrast, Plato says (185b9–c3), we investigate whether a couple of things are bitter by means of a bodily power, namely the sense of taste. This clearly means that in operating through the senses the mind applies the words "bitter," "red," "hard," etc., to sense-objects: "investigation about existence" involves the applying of the words "exists" and "does not exist," so "investigation about bitterness" involves the application of the words "bitter" or "not bitter." That this is so is made certain by the remark with which Socrates concludes his exposition of the contrast between the perceptual and the reflective uses of the mind: φαίνεταί σοι τὰ μὲν αὐτὴ δι᾽ αὑτῆς ἡ ψυχὴ ἐπισκοπεῖν, τὰ δὲ διὰ τῶν τοῦ σώματος δυνάμεων (185e6–7). In order to decide whether something exists, is similar to something else, etc., one has to reflect; in order to decide whether something is red one does not need to reflect, but to use the mind at the perceptual level only.

There is thus good evidence for each of two different views as to what Plato thinks is involved in what I have called the perceptual use of the mind. He sometimes seems to have in mind sensory awareness without the application of concepts to what is perceived, but in contrasting the perceptual and the reflective uses he seems to think of the labeling of the data of sense with elementary color, taste, etc., descriptions as itself taking place at the perceptual and not the reflective level. I do not think the evidence on either side can be explained away; the most one can do is to try to render the inconsistency palatable. The difficulty arises because Plato tries to combine two rather different distinctions, and this can be made understandable by considering how closely these distinctions are related to one another. We may begin by asking why Plato thinks that different powers of the mind are called on in deciding whether a κοινόν such as self-identity belongs to a sensed color than are exercised in deciding whether the sensed color is, say, red. The latter operation, the classification or labeling of the data of sense, does not indeed involve the application of a concept which belongs to objects of different senses, but why should that make any difference? In labeling a color, surely, one is, implicitly at least, engaged in reflecting, remembering, and comparing—activities which Plato represents as distinctive of the "independent" use of the mind (186a9–b1, b6–9). Indeed, it might be said that labelling the seen color calls upon the power to apply some of the κοινά themselves: to recognize the color as red one has to remember past colors, both red and non-red, and think this one *similar* to some and *dissimilar* from others. How can Plato have thought that the application of the elementary perceptual concepts could proceed without this sort of associative activity? And even if this can be managed without the use of the κοινά, why did Plato think it involves quite a different power of the mind from that exercised in thinking about existence, similarity, and so on?

A partial answer can be found, I think, in the view of thinking (διανοεῖσθαι) which Plato puts forward just a few pages later in the *Theaetetus*. Here (189e4 ff.) Plato defines the process of thinking as discourse carried on by the mind with itself.[13] On this model one might think of perceptual thought as a matter of saying to oneself, as one experiences various sensations, "red," "warm," "sweet," and so on. And employing the κοινά in thought will be represented as saying to oneself "That (i.e., that color just labeled 'red') exists," or "that color is the same as itself and different from this one," and so on. Now even if recognizing a color as red requires comparison and involves the *implicit* use of various of the κοινά, it is clear that one need not *explicitly* say to oneself "This color is like such and such other colors I've seen and unlike such and such others, so it's red." Anyone who possesses the color concepts is (normally) able to apply them without any explicit process of reasoning at all. But it is an essential feature of Plato's model of what thinking is that only things which one explicitly says to oneself are counted as things that one thinks. Hence all such implicit mental activities must go unnoticed and unaccounted for so long as one retains this model. The contrast Plato draws is between labeling sense data and *explicitly* thinking that, e.g., some given color exists, is the same as itself, different from something else, like or unlike it, beautiful or ugly, and so forth. The point seems to be that the color of a thing can simply be, as it were, read off it once one has the color concept in question; whereas noticing the similarity of one thing to another requires explicit thinking about the other thing and overt comparison, just as in Plato's view judging that something is good requires sifting past and present against the probable future (186a1 ff.). These judgments, and all judgments involving κοινά, require that one engage in more or

---

[13] The same account appears in *Soph.* 264a–b, and the different image of writing in a mental book, which appears in the *Philebus* (38e–39a) alongside the idiom of discourse with oneself (38d1–2, 6, e1–4), is not significantly different from the present point of view.

less elaborate *explicit* reflection.[14] It is the immediacy of the labeling function that seems to have impressed Plato, and to have distinguished it in his mind from thought employing the κοινά.

But even if Plato can by some such reasoning as this be justified in his separation of labeling and reflective judgment, what can be said in defense of his assimilation of the labeling power to simple sensory awareness? To begin with, it should be noted that the immediacy of the labeling operation is a consequence of the fact that, as it seems, one has in sensory awareness itself all the evidence one needs to justify the application of the appropriate label: I know that the color I see is red just because I can see it. On the other hand, in order to judge that it is beautiful, just seeing it is not enough; as Plato implies, I need in addition to call to mind other objects seen on other occasions and conduct a comparison to see if this color measures up to the appropriate standard of beauty. This means that the exercise of the labeling capacity, though of course it is different from sensory awareness, is very closely related to it. By labeling the data, it is natural to think, one merely makes explicit what was already contained in sensation. But in judgments of existence, usefulness, and so on, one goes beyond the data of sense themselves to consider their relations to one another, their probable consequences, and so on. From this point of view, then, the labeling function goes together with sensory awareness and is reasonably grouped together with it in contrast with reflective judgment. And when one adds that one crucially important step in the advance of knowledge is that from the labeling of sense-contents to explicit comparative reflection about them, one sees even more clearly why Plato, with his interest in knowledge, should tend to assimilate or confuse with one another sensory awareness and the labeling of its objects.

Now Plato's ambivalence in his characterization of perception complicates the interpretation of the remainder of the passage. The reason he gives for making knowledge the outcome of acts of reflective judgment but not acts of perception turns out to lend itself to different interpretations depending on which view of perception is assumed.

But before showing how this is so, I must justify the assumption made in the preceding discussion that in discussing the higher reflective employment of the mind Plato has in view only the power of formulating

---

[14] Is this true of judgments of existence and self-identity? The case of existence is hard to decide because of the obscurity of Plato's examples. If "this color exists" means "this is the real color of something," then I suppose explicit reflection is required. The thought that something is identical with itself is such an unnatural thought that I have no confidence in any conjecture as to what Plato conceived was involved in thinking it: perhaps he is guided here by the thought that self-identity is not a feature of a thing that can simply be read off it in the way colors can.

judgments involving the κοινά and not also or instead the contemplation of the objects Existence, Identity, and so on. To do this will require a close analysis of the passage in which the reflective employment of the mind is contrasted with the perceptual.

The relevant section opens at 185b7 with the question, "Through what do you think all these [i.e., the common terms] about them [viz., about sound and color]?" As Socrates explains, he has in mind that if you perceive that something is red, or sweet-flavored, you perceive these things through the medium of a sense and a sense-organ; and he wants to know whether one perceives something's existence or self-identity or unity through any analogous organ. At c7–8, having given this explanation of his question he repeats it: τούτοις πᾶσι ποῖα ἀποδώσεις ὄργανα δι' ὧν αἰσθάνεται ἡμῶν τὸ αἰσθανόμενον ἕκαστα; ("What sort of organs do you assign for all of these, through which our sense-perceptory part perceives them?"). Here commentators begin to translate and comment as if what is in question were, "How do we become acquainted with the entities Existence, Identity, Unity, etc.?" But it is evident that the question in Plato's text merely restates the question at b7 and that therefore nothing is said about our becoming acquainted with Existence; the question concerns rather our perceiving or judging that a thing exists. This is overlooked only because the restatement omits the phrase περὶ αὐτοῖν from the earlier statement (b8), which would make it clear that it is not a question of becoming acquainted with the meanings of these common terms,[15] but rather one of perceiving or judging *that* they do or do not apply to something.

That the περί phrase is to be understood with the restatement at c7–8 is made certain by Theaetetus' reply. He adds in his answer the περὶ αὐτῶν (d1) which was only implicit in the question: "You mean *their* existence and nonexistence, similarity and dissimilarity, sameness and difference, unity and other number." But he then goes on to omit the phrase, in the same idiomatic way, later in his reply when he in turn reformulates the question: διὰ τίνος ποτὲ τῶν τοῦ σώματος τῇ ψυχῇ αἰσθανόμεθα [αὐτῶν]; (d 3–4) ("Through what bodily part do we perceive these with our minds?"). And here again translators unaccountably omit the περί phrase and misunderstand Theaetetus to be asking himself whether we become acquainted with Existence and the rest, in themselves, through any agency of the body. Cornford compounds this error by misconstruing in Theaetetus' next answer (d7–e2) the force of the phrase περὶ πάντων which he again reimports. Theaetetus says, "The

---

[15] So Cornford, p. 105.

mind itself through itself, as it appears to me, examines (ἐπισκοπεῖν)[16] for every object [whether it possesses] these common attributes" (αὐτὴ δι' αὐτῆς ἡ ψυχὴ τὰ κοινά μοι φαίνεται περὶ πάντων ἐπισκοπεῖν). But Cornford takes περὶ πάντων with τὰ κοινά, and translates "the common terms that apply to everything," presumably thinking the phrase a variation of τὸ ἐπὶ πᾶσι κοινόν above (c4–5); but even if this is possible Greek it is obvious that περὶ πάντων ἐπισκοπεῖν is parallel to περὶ αὐτοῖν διανοῇ in the original statement of the question (b7), so that we have once again the same question about the application of these words to things and not a new question about how we become acquainted with their meanings. Other translators (e.g., Diès) take περὶ πάντων here with the verb, as its position surely dictates, but they have not, I think, seen the consequence of so doing. The consequence, to repeat, is that Theaetetus says nothing about how we become acquainted with Existence and Sameness, but rather tells us that judgments of the existence and identity of a sense quality are not made by the mind through the agency of any sense but rather by the mind independently.

It is, then, quite clear that περὶ αὐτοῖν (185b7) is to be supplied right through to 185e whenever there is mention of grasping, thinking, or investigating κοινά. Plato himself repeats it (or a variant) as often as he decently can: the commentators' shift from the question whether we use a bodily organ in applying the κοινά to things, to the question how we become acquainted with Forms, is sheer invention.

Nor does Plato subsequently raise this other question. In what follows (186a–c) he consolidates his position by running through the list of κοινά, adding some new ones and obtaining Theaetetus' agreement that these are all applied to things by the mind independently of perception. Here again translators confuse the issue by taking Plato to be discussing how we arrive at our acquaintance with these common entities; and again there are very clear signs that nothing of the sort is in question.[17] Thus when Socrates inquires whether καλὸν καὶ αἰσχρὸν καὶ ἀγαθὸν καὶ κακόν are among the κοινά about the οὐσία (existence)[18] of which the mind judges all by itself, Theaetetus replies in the affirmative (186a9–b1).

---

[16] Ἐπισκοπεῖν need not mean "contemplate" (so Cornford; cf. Cherniss, *SPM*, p. 6, and W. G. Runciman, *Plato's Later Epistemology*, p. 15): cf. ἐπισκέψασθαι, which is the aorist used to meet the defect in ἐπισκοπεῖν, just above, 185b5. Cf. also 161d5, e7, where both ἐπισκέψασθαι and ἐπισκοπεῖν appear and neither means "contemplate."

[17] Only 186a4 even remotely imports an interest in how we become acquainted with the κοινά; and its immediate sequel is quite evidently concerned not with this but with how to employ them in making judgments about αἰσθητά.

[18] Throughout the passage οὐσία seems to mean (something like) the existence of this or that: cf. 186b6 where καὶ ὅτι ἐστόν is epexegetical of τὴν οὐσίαν. At any rate, it never means the *nature* of a thing (see below, p. 58 f. for a needed qualification).

But he goes on to add that when the mind judges about these matters it calculates within itself past and present against the future. Now this is a pretty good brief account of how one judges whether a particular person or action or situation is good or bad or honorable or disgraceful: one does have to weigh past experience and present circumstances in order to get a reasonable judgment as to a person's future behavior or the consequences of an action, and so on. But it is precisely the *wrong* sort of thing to do in order to become acquainted with the existence and nature of a Platonic Form. Consideration of phenomena and phenomenal events is notoriously the main *obstacle* to becoming acquainted with these. It seems clear, therefore, that Socrates and Theaetetus are not discussing the question how we arrive at our knowledge of the Forms Honorableness, Disgracefulness, and the like; they are, rather, inquiring how one goes about making particular judgments about the goodness or badness, etc., of particular things.

The general point is reaffirmed once more with complete clarity in the immediately following lines (186b2–10). You perceive the hardness of a hard thing, Socrates says, through the sense of touch, and likewise the softness of a soft thing. But the existence of this hardness and this softness (or perhaps of hardness and softness in general), and their opposition to one another, and the existence of this opposition, are not discoverable by the use of the senses. For these, the mind compares things together and keeps going back over them within itself to answer its questions. Once again it is obvious that what interests Plato is the contrast between two operations of the mind, perceiving through the senses, and reflection, comparison, prediction, and in general the interpretation of the *significance* of what one perceives. Neither here nor elsewhere does he raise the question how the mind acquires its knowledge of the common terms which it employs in its interpretative activity.

Thus the difficulty noticed above (p. 45) in the first stage of the argument as Cornford interprets it is eliminated. There is no longer a conflict between the obvious implication of the sensing-judging distinction to which he appeals and the contrast between the perception of sense-objects and the contemplation of thought-objects: the latter contrast is not drawn in the argument at all. The contrast, as I have argued above, is that between elementary sensory awareness together with the labeling of its objects, on the one hand, and the supposedly more sophisticated level of thought attained in thinking that sense-objects exist, are different from one another, and so on.

III

So far, then, I have argued that Plato draws two distinctions, that between the role of the senses and the role of the mind in perception, and that between the use of the mind in perception and its use in reflective judgment involving the notions of existence, identity, and so on. The material thus provided is the basis on which Plato relies in rejecting the definition of knowledge as αἴσθησις.

The refutation Plato produces (186c6–e10) is characteristically brief and cryptic. He points out that one cannot be knowing anything when he does not grasp οὐσία (being, existence?) and truth, and then relies on the preceding analysis to show that in αἴσθησις ones does not grasp οὐσία and truth. We have already seen that Cornford interprets this as meaning that it is not through the use of the senses that one becomes acquainted with the Forms, the only truly real and knowable entities. But since, as I have shown above, there is no reference in what precedes to Forms,[19] or to the process of becoming acquainted with Forms, there is absolutely no excuse for any interpretation of this kind. What Plato means by "grasping being and truth" must be gathered from the account he has just given of perception and the employment of the κοινά in thought.

Clearly, Plato means to argue that the mind in perception does not acquire knowledge or evince knowledge, on the ground that knowledge is attained only when οὐσία is grasped, and that it is only in reflective judgment that the power to judge about the οὐσία of anything is evinced. But, because of the uncertainty about what Plato understands by "perception," two different lines of thought, both, I think, plausible and interesting, may be proposed as interpretations of his argument here.

Let us assume first that "perception" means sensory awareness, without conceptualization. Then it is natural to interpret Plato as pointing out that knowing involves, at least, thinking *that* so-and-so is the case. Knowledge therefore involves the applying of concepts, and since sensory awareness is a mental power not involving conceptualization it must be wrong to equate knowledge with sensory awareness.

There are several points in favor of such an interpretation. Foremost is the fact that Plato says that knowledge involves "grasping truth." This is very naturally interpreted as meaning that there is no knowledge where there is no formulation of truths, i.e., where there is no thinking *that*, no conceptualization. Secondly, Socrates in stating the conclusion of the argument seems to suggest just this contrast between sensory awareness and

---

[19] Even if the κοινά are Forms, Plato does not say they are, and for the very good reason that it nowhere matters to his argument what their metaphysical status is. See note 8 above.

thinking that so-and-so is the case: he says, "So there is no knowledge in the experiences we undergo (παθήμασιν), but rather in the reasoning (συλλογισμῷ) we do concerning them" (186d2–3). Here nothing indicates that the reasoning envisaged is restricted to any particular subject matter (not, for example, to questions about the application of κοινά); there seems to be a blank contrast between bare seeing, hearing, etc., and thoughts, of whatever sort, about what one is seeing, hearing, and so on.

But if Plato means to say that αἴσθησις occurs without the formulation of judgments, this point must somehow be found in his assertion that in perception we do not "grasp οὐσία". What has the failure to grasp οὐσία to do with the nonjudgmental character of perception? Throughout the argument so far οὐσία seems to have meant existence:[20] at its first introduction in the context (185c9, cf. a9 and c5–6) it seems to mean this and it does not appear to alter in meaning thereafter. Perception's failure to grasp οὐσία should therefore mean that the thought that something exists is not an act of perception This is no doubt true, but how does this failure imply that perception is altogether nonjudgmental? Judgments of existence are just one class of judgments. Does Plato mean to suggest that somehow we must always be making existential judgments whenever we make judgments of any other type? Or does he mean that before we can make judgments of other types we must be able to make existential judgments? Neither of these alternatives is at all attractive; but the mention of οὐσία here certainly seems not to be an arbitrarily chosen example illustrating a thesis which any other concept would have illustrated equally well.

Is it however correct to insist that grasping οὐσία must mean thinking that something exists? Even although οὐσία (and its cognates) in its earlier appearances in the passage is naturally *translated* "existence," "exists," etc. (as in 185a9, ὅτι ἀμφοτέρω ἐστόν), it does not follow that this is what the word *means* there or elsewhere in the passage. English sharply distinguishes the "is" of existence from the copula, but Greek does not; and it is arguable, and has been argued,[21] that the Greek verb εἶναι does not have "senses" corresponding to this distinction. It represents rather an undifferentiated concept straddling this particular distinction. If this is so, one can easily see how Plato might have thought that thinking with the concept οὐσία has a position of priority vis-à-vis all other conceptual thinking, and that to fail to grasp οὐσία is to fail to formulate judgments altogether. To grasp the οὐσία of something is not necessarily to think

[20] So Lewis Campbell (*The Theaetetus of Plato*) insists: cf. his note *ad* 186c3, and p. liv n. Cf. also my note 18 above.
[21] Cf., e.g., C. H. Kahn, "The Greek Verb 'To Be' and the Concept of Being." Cf. also G.E.L. Owen, "Aristotle on the Snares of Ontology," 71 n., for salutary remarks on Plato's use of the notion of τὸ ὄν in the *Sophist*.

that it *exists*, but may be no more than to think that it *is* F for some predicate F.[22] In that case, to be deprived of the use of εἶναι would mean that one was incapable of predicating anything of anything else, since the copula, which is indispensable to predication, would be unavailable. Hence, without the use of εἶναι one could not have the power of judgment, and therefore one could not have the use of any concepts at all.

In this way, assuming that by "perception" Plato means just sensory awareness, a good and interesting argument can be found behind his assertion that since perception does not grasp οὐσία, it does not arrive at truth, and therefore cannot constitute knowledge. But although, as I have indicated, such an argument fits the text quite well in several respects, doubt must remain whether it expresses Plato's meaning. For, as I have argued in the preceding section, the neat distinction, on which this interpretation depends, between perception as sensory awareness and the higher conceptualizing power of the mind, is not everywhere in the context adhered to by Plato himself. The higher power of the mind is restricted to the application of only certain concepts, namely the κοινά (which includes, besides those mentioned, also all others which belong to objects of different senses or involve reference to objects of different senses); perception, then, includes sensory awareness and the minimum interpretation of its objects which is involved in labeling them "red," "sweet," and so on. The labeling process certainly amounts to using certain concepts, namely what might be called minimal perceptual concepts; and since this is envisaged as taking place without the use of εἶναι, which only comes in with the addition of the higher power of the mind, Plato cannot mean to suggest that all use of concepts requires the use of εἶναι. So one must look further to find an interpretation that will fit this way of understanding the distinction between perception and reflection.

If, then, "perception" means sensory awareness plus the supposedly immediate classification of its objects, what reason can Plato be understood to be giving against the claim of perception to be knowledge? On this view, what would it be to grasp οὐσία, and why would the failure to do this entail that perception is not knowledge? The refutation of Protagoras earlier in the dialogue seems to offer a clue. Plato argues (177c–179c) against Protagoras that thinking a thing does not make it so, at least whenever prediction is involved, because in such cases the truth or falsity of the thought depends on the event; and even if each man is his own infallible judge of how the event turns out, when it occurs, the prediction, once made, is true or not depending on how things turn out (or

---

[22] At 186a10, to consider the οὐσία of καλόν, etc., quite clearly means to consider whether some given thing *is* beautiful, good, etc. Here the being of a predicate is its attachment to a subject; likewise the being of a subject is (in part at least) its bearing of a predicate.

seem to have turned out) (cf. 178d4–6). In making predictions, then, there is room for mistakes; not everyone can claim to have *knowledge* of how things *will* turn out (or even how things will *seem* to himself to have turned out). It is the expert physician who knows whether I will come down with a fever tomorrow (178c); the expert musician, and not just any layman, knows whether a lyre will be put in tune by loosening its strings (178d); and in general when one man can claim to *know* better than others how things will turn out, this claim must be based on his possession of an expertise which makes him wiser and more skilled than others in his particular subject area (179a10–b5). His prediction is not then a mere guess, as the layman's would have to be; it is founded on objectively valid principles of science or art and constitutes knowledge precisely because it is supported by such principles.[23]

This argument against Protagoras is recalled in our passage when Socrates adds καλὸν καὶ αἰσχρὸν καὶ ἀγαθὸν καὶ κακόν to the list of subject matters about which perception is incompetent to judge (186a8–b1). Judging here involves prediction, Socrates says; and in so saying he clearly refers back to what was said against Protagoras. In the argument against Protagoras, special emphasis was placed on the fact that questions of ὠφέλεια involve prediction, so that some πόλεις are wiser and more expert than others (172a, 179a5 ff., etc.); and in our passage Socrates joins ὠφέλεια with οὐσία as the two most significant matters in thinking about which we employ the higher reflective power of the mind—those of us, at any rate, who are capable of having thoughts on such subjects at all (186c2–5). The suggestion is that Plato bases his rejection of perception's claim to be knowledge on the ground that knowledge implies expertise and the appeal to objectively valid principles and standards, while perception does not go beyond subjective reports of the contents of sensory experience and therefore makes no judgments to which such standards and principles are relevant. There are no experts at perception; no one can claim that his perceptual reports, as such, are more true than anyone else's; no one subjects his own or anyone else's reports to criticism by appeal to the sort of standards Plato implies are operative in the doctor's prediction of fever and the pastry cook's of pleasure to the palate. Precisely because perception is purely subjective, because it is not open to criticism or correction (cf. ἀνάλωτοι, 179c5), perception cannot claim to be knowledge. Knowledge is always the result of directing one's thoughts in accordance with principles and standards; hence any claim to knowledge must be open to criticism by appeal to the ap-

---

[23] Compare Socrates' refutation of Thrasymachus's claim that ἀδικία—and not δικαιοσύνη—is a virtue and a sign of intelligence, *Rep.* 350a–c.

propriate standards. Because in perception there is no room for such criticism, perception cannot constitute knowledge.

On this interpretation the failure of perception to grasp the οὐσία of its objects would be taken to mean that in perception one notices only the color (etc.) a thing appears to have and says nothing about what its real color is. As I remarked above, οὐσία is an undifferentiated concept of being; but it seems naturally interpreted in this passage (at, e.g., 185a9) as expressing existence. To judge that a color exists one must engage in the kind of calculation of past and present perceptions with a view to the future which Theaetetus mentions in connection with judgments of value; and just as Plato insists that judgments of value imply the existence of objective standards which experts constantly use to guide their thought, so one must be guided by objective standards in saying how things in the world *are*. This is the work not of perception but of reflective judgment.

But if perception fails to attain to objectivity it also fails to "hit the truth" (186c9). A thought is pronounced true or false by appeal to the standards valid for the subject matter. Hence perception, as something altogether subjective and unguided by standards, yields neither truths nor falsehoods. Knowledge, then, must lie elsewhere; in fact, it is to be looked for in reflective judgment, where the notions of existence, identity, similarity, and so on, with their associated objective standards, enter for the first time.

I think this interpretation has much in its favor. The fact that it reads quite a lot into Plato's remark that perception fails to grasp οὐσία, and therefore misses truth too, is no objection against it; any interpretation must do the same. What matters is how one brings the context to bear on the interpretation of this final argument. In appealing to the notions of expertise and objective standards this interpretation makes good use of undoubtedly Platonic doctrines undoubtedly expressed in the context; and in understanding perception to include the classification of the contents of sensory experience it adopts what appears to be the correct interpretation of the contrast between αἴσθησις and the independent employment of the mind. And in bringing these two views together it provides a reasonable sense for the final argument.

Crombie[24] appears to reject an interpretation rather close to this one on the ground that it cannot accommodate the examples Plato gives of judgments involving κοινά other than οὐσία. Crombie thinks that on this view the "contribution which the mind makes" consists in "referring our sense-data to the external world"; and the difficulty then arises that one contribution of the mind mentioned by Plato is to notice that a color and

---

[24] *An Examination*, 15–16.

a sound are different, a contribution not plausibly interpreted as consisting in the referral of "sense-data" to the external world. On the view I have been expounding, however, the contribution of the mind is not limited in this way. Its contribution is the appeal to objective standards, and it is only in connection with the existence of the objects of sensory awareness that the appropriate objective standards involve the referral of "sense-data" to the external world. In other cases, e.g., those of self-identity and unity and the difference of a sound from a color, it would seem to be a law of logic that the mind invokes, and the fact that it is *applied* to objects of sensory awareness does not make it any the less something objectively valid. One cannot (let us suppose) dispute a man's report that what he sees in his visual field is a red color and what he hears is a bang. But if he goes on to say about the color and the noise that they are the same thing he's enunciating a falsehood; what he says at this level is subject to criticism.

Thus the upshot of the argument, on this second interpretation, is that knowledge brings with it objectivity and appeal to the sort of standards which experts employ. "Perception" fails to be knowledge because one need not be an expert in any sense or have the use of objective standards of any kind in order to be as good at perceiving as anyone else. On this reading, Plato arrives, by way of his assimilation of knowledge to expertise, at a position which gives to empirical knowledge the honorific title of ἐπιστήμη; and the emphasis which he places in this connection on objectivity has the very interesting consequence that Plato's conception of empirical knowledge has a definite Kantian flavor.

Plato, therefore, rejects the claim of "perception" (αἴσθησις) to constitute knowledge on one of two grounds, depending on which of two understandings of "perception" is adopted. If "perception" means mere sensory awareness, then it cannot be knowledge because knowledge involves discursive thought while "perception" is at a lower level of logical complexity. If "perception" means awareness of "sense-contents," explicitly labeled, then it fails to be knowledge because it makes no claims to objective validity. As I have already indicated, each of these interpretations is plausible, and neither, I think, can be definitely ruled out. But on the whole I prefer the second interpretation, because it accounts better for Plato's emphasis on thought about κοινά in particular as marking an advance beyond "perceptual" thinking and into the area where we can first speak of knowledge.

IV

But whichever of these interpretations is correct, the *Theaetetus* turns out to contain points of great originality—points completely ignored by interpretations which, like Cornford's and Cherniss's, attempt to make the *Theaetetus* merely repeat things already said in the *Republic*. The distinction between the senses as bodily powers and perception as a power of the mind, and the identification of what is known with some subclass of judgments, constitute noteworthy philosophical achievements. They also mark distinct advances over Plato's way of thinking about perception and knowledge in the *Republic*. Cherniss's claim that *Republic* 522–525 is parallel in argument to *Theaetetus* 184–186 can now be seen to be an entirely superficial view. The *Republic* passage is so far from being parallel that it actually makes mistakes which the *Theaetetus*' analysis is intended to show up. These are: (1) The *Republic* passage constantly speaks of the *senses* as saying this or that, whereas (as noted above) the *Theaetetus* scotches this misleading inaccuracy. (2) The *Republic* allows as judgments of perception things which the *Theaetetus*, in distinguishing perception from the mind's power of independent thought, insists belong to a level of intellectual activity entirely beyond perception. Thus at 523a3 Plato speaks of the perception that the same thing is both hard and soft, which seems to involve a judgment of identity and so cannot be a matter of perception in the *Theaetetus*' scheme; cf. also 523c11 ff. (perceiving a finger), 524d9–e6 (perceiving something as a unit). Further important differences between the two passages include: (3) The *Republic* counts both the question whether something is hard or soft, light or heavy (524a) and the question whether it is one (524b) as forcing the mind up to its highest level of operation: on either subject the senses are untrustworthy witnesses (523b3–4). But the *Theaetetus* distinguishes between the two cases, and actually allows that the mind operating through the senses does judge without recourse as to hard and soft, light and heavy and the other elementary perceptual properties (185b9 ff.; 186b). It is only with respect to *other* questions than these that the mind's higher capacities are called into play. Hence (4) there is no resemblance at all between the function of the senses as stimulative of thought (*Republic*) and the *Theaetetus*' distinction between perception and the higher functions of the mind. Finally, of course, (5) these higher functions of the mind have nothing to do with the contemplation of Forms, as νόησις in the *Republic* does.

Furthermore, and importantly, the *Theaetetus* avoids altogether the *Republic*'s misleading analysis of knowledge by reference to the objects to which it is directed; the objects about which Plato assumes we have knowledge in the *Theaetetus* include αἰσϑητά,[25] and knowledge is distinguished from other states of mind not by its objects but by how the knower is related to them. Plato's views on perception and knowledge in the *Theaetetus* are fortunately much more sophisticated than traditional interpretations make them appear. Scholars do Plato no service by trying to read into the *Theaetetus* epistemological doctrines they think they find in the *Republic*.[26]

---

[25] This assumption is not abandoned subsequently in the *Theaetetus*; it is very clearly reaffirmed in 201a–c (cf. Runciman, *Plato's Later Epistemology*, 37).

[26] The novelty of the *Theaetetus* is made to seem greater than it probably is by those who, like Cornford and Cherniss, think that Plato in the *Republic* and other middle period dialogues firmly denies that one can *know* anything about anything in this imperfect world. It is true that certain arguments and ways of speaking of the *Republic* imply that the things we perceive or have beliefs about are different things from those we can have knowledge about. But Plato certainly thinks that after undergoing the education he outlines, his rulers will be able to govern with knowledge, and this surely means that they will *know*, e.g., that a proposed course of action is right or wrong. The difference between the man who has δόξα and the man of ἐπιστήμη must, despite appearances, not entail a total difference of objects thought about. A more plausible view is that the ἐπιστήμων, because of his acquaintance with the Forms, is in a position to know things about the same objects about which the man of δόξα, because of his ignorance of the Forms, can only have beliefs. This view is in accord with the distinction between ἐπιστήμη and ἀληϑὴς δόξα in *Meno* 98 a, and has much else to be said for it. If this is the substance of Plato's position in the *Republic*, then the *Theaetetus* in allowing knowledge of αἰσϑητά does not subvert anything but unwanted implications of misleading arguments in the *Republic*; the *Theaetetus* can then be seen as offering a corrected and more adequate attempt to say some of the things Plato wished to say in the *Republic*.

CHAPTER 3

PLATO, ISOCRATES, AND CICERO ON THE
INDEPENDENCE OF ORATORY FROM PHILOSOPHY

I

ONE SOMETIMES hears it said that the ancient rhetorical tradition—the orators and teachers of oratory descending from the fifth century B.C. Sophists—had a distinctive, reasonably well developed theory of what constitutes sound argument on the subjects on which orators were expected to speak—justice, human private and communal good, excellence of mind and character, and so on. The suggestion is that in the oratorical tradition one can find a powerful alternative to the ideas developed in the philosophical tradition on this same subject, ideas that involve a commitment to concepts of justice, goodness, excellence, and so on, that are supposed to derive their credentials from a relation in which they were thought to stand to the actual nature of things, to which philosophical reflection (and only philosophical reflection) could in principle lead us. Writers in the oratorical tradition are, by contrast, supposed to eschew any appeal to concepts of justice and the rest, access to which requires special philosophical insights, in favor of argument based on nothing more fancy than ordinary, everyday, traditional ideas on the subjects in question. Now there is I assume no doubt at all that the ancient orators and theoreticians of oratory did proceed in this way: when they argue about justice or the community's good they develop their arguments by marshaling ordinary, everyday, traditional ideas about what something has to be like in order to be just or to be good for the community, etc. What is not so obvious is whether they (or any of them) ever elaborated any theory to explain and, according to some appropriate standard, justify this procedure. If they thought that sound argument on these subjects should proceed in this, rather than the philosophers', way, what basis, if any, did they actually give for so thinking? I believe that an examination of the evidence that is available to us does not support the conclusion that the orators did have any such theory. They argued exclusively by appeal to ordinary, traditional, common opinions, and they rejected the idea that there was any higher truth of such matters available to philosophers. But I do not find any good evidence at all that they developed a theoretical account of what constitutes sound argument on these topics to which they could appeal in defense of their procedures and against the claims of the philosophers. In this paper I will offer evidence for this conclusion drawn from an examination of Isocrates and Cicero, two of the most theoretically inclined writers in the tradition and so especially promising authors to consult to discover what foundations for oratorical argument their tradition developed.

Someone once asked Antisthenes, Plato's older contemporary and by tradition the immediate intellectual ancestor of the Greek Cynics, how he should educate his son. Antisthenes replied that if the son was going to live with gods the father should make him a philosopher, but if with men an orator.[1] As usual with such anecdotes, we are given no context or any indication how, if at all, Antisthenes went on to develop this thought, or what theoretical or practical conclusions he drew from it. It seems likely, however, that it owes something to a striking passage of Plato's *Phaedrus* (273e4–274a5). There Socrates says that philosophical knowledge is worth acquiring because it enables one to speak and act in a way pleasing to the gods, though, as a side benefit, it also makes one able to speak and act effectively in the eyes of human beings. Socrates' idea, as the preceding context shows, is that oratorical skill (what one needs in order to speak and act effectively in the eyes of human beings) is an offshoot and side benefit of philosophical study, which is itself properly pursued not for the sake of that benefit but because it makes it possible for a man to think and speak the language of the gods. Antisthenes, denying the dependence of rhetorical skill on philosophical knowledge of the puffed-up Platonic type, would then be forcing a choice between rhetoric and philosophy and implying that, if forced to choose, one had better train one's sons in rhetoric. It is obviously futile to prepare a boy to live among the gods, beings whose society he will in any event never share; and since rhetoric is what one needs to live satisfactorily among human beings, it is a nonphilosophical rhetoric that one should instruct him in.

If I am right to read this anecdote against the background of the *Phaedrus* one can see implicit in it an early (possibly the earliest) and quite telling response on behalf of oratory to Plato's preemptive moves in the *Phaedrus* against the traditional oratory of Greece. In what follows I want to trace, selectively but I hope not too selectively, other such responses. I focus on the *Phaedrus* for two reasons: first, because the *Phaedrus* contains the technical philosophers' most profound attack on oratory as it was actually practiced and taught (more profound than the flashier *Gorgias,* and more profound than Aristotle's theory in the *Rhetoric*), and secondly, because the view Plato takes of the relation of philosophy to rhetoric was adopted by the Stoics and thereby came to be

---

[1] Frg. 125 Mullach, 173 Caizzi (Stobaeus, *Eclogae* II 31, 76, 215.1–3 Wachsmuth).

the most influential view on this subject current among the Greek philosophers for the next several centuries. By considering the *Phaedrus'* theory and discussing how the orators did respond, or might have responded, to it we will be exploring central questions about the intellectual foundations of the Greek oratorical tradition.

Some pages before the passage of the *Phaedrus* I referred to a moment ago, Socrates introduces and briefly explains (259e–262c) his theory that real oratorical skill depends upon and is simply an application of philosophical knowledge of the actual nature of things—that is, of the knowledge, available to us human beings only by the methods of philosophical argument and analysis, of what (for example) justice and goodness in themselves are, independently and so to speak in advance of the accretion in human cultures of various more or less authoritative conventional ideas on these topics. I can bring out the force of his analysis best, however, by turning first to a later passage, immediately preceding the one already cited, in which he restates his earlier analysis. Here (272c–e) Socrates pauses to reconsider the traditional orator's claim, which he traces back to Tisias, one of the two traditionally recognized originators of self-consciously theoretical oratory, that in preparing speeches and conducting his professional affairs an orator has no need to consult the truth about what is just or good. He must, as everyone recognizes, pay attention to plausibility (τὸ πιθανόν, d8), that is, Socrates says, to likelihood (τὸ εἰκός, e1) (even truths must be made plausible if his speech is to succeed), and Tisias claimed that concern for plausibility was not just necessary but sufficient for the orator as well. He illustrated this (273b–c) by the example of a scrawny but spirited malefactor who assaulted and robbed a hefty but timid man, who then instituted a suit against him. Tisias insisted that neither party in his argument in court should tell the truth about the event and its circumstances: the jury would not believe either one if they did. Instead, the injured party should assert that the robber was not alone but had help. The robber should deny (if, presumably, though this is not said explicitly, the other evidence presented makes this plausible) that he was accompanied and insist that he could not have done what he is accused of, because little fellows like himself do not attack big ones like the victim. Thus the skilled orator will seek out the most plausible, i.e., Socrates says, the most likely, account of the disputed events. Oratorical skill consists simply in knowledge of plausibility and likelihood; it has nothing to do with figuring out and presenting the truth about the matters on which orators have to speak.

Now of course, as this example shows, by contrasting the true with the plausible Tisias had in mind truth about particular matters of fact over which disputes in law courts may arise. And Socrates has himself granted earlier in the discussion that oratorical skill does not involve any commitment to seeking out and presenting the truth about such matters of fact. He has said (261c10–d1) the skilled orator will be able to make the same things appear (e.g.) just and then again, if there should be call to do so, unjust to the same persons, and on this ground he has included Zeno of Elea, with his paired arguments on both sides of a question (moving or resting? similar or dissimilar?), as a consummately skilled orator (d6–e4). Oratory, on Socrates' own account, is the disciplined ability to argue with plausibility on either or both sides of a disputed question; the orator's skill is in itself indifferent to the facts. He is neither limited to arguing for what is in *fact* true nor, in case the conclusion he is arguing for happens to be true, does he have to argue it (as in Tisias' example) by appeal to an accurate statement of the actual circumstances. Socrates' claim is that even this neutral ability to argue both sides, if it is truly based in some form of disciplined knowledge—if it is a τέχνη and not an ἄτεχνος τριβή, 260e4–5, that is, if the skilled orator actually *understands* how and why he succeeds in being persuasive to the extent he does succeed— it requires knowledge of the truth about, so to speak, the *subjects* over which the dispute takes place. Suppose, for example, the dispute is over whether some act was right or wrong. Here the subject of dispute is rightness and wrongness. Then, Socrates claims, if the orator is to construct his argument, no matter which side he argues, on the basis of a genuine understanding of *how* this case *ought* to be argued, he must have a firm grasp on the actual natures of rightness and wrongness. He must, in other words, know what it is that he is setting out to get the people he is addressing to believe is exemplified in the case at hand. If he is arguing that the act was *wrong*, his task is to assemble some plausible grounds that might persuade his audience that the act possessed that property. But, Socrates holds, he won't *know* how to do that (though superficial, blind experience might have taught him the knack of doing it) unless he knows which among the things that are open to him to say about the act in question are, in the minds of his hearers, closely enough connected to wrongness so that they will accept them as sufficient reasons to conclude that the act was wrong. And, Socrates thinks, he won't know *that* unless he knows, first of all, what features of actions *really are* such as to be connected to wrongness. (In addition, Socrates adds at 271c10–272b2, he must know which kinds of person will find which ones of these features most indicative of wrongness, and why they will do so; finally, he must be able to tell to what kind of persons those whom he is addressing belong.)

Socrates' position, thus briefly summarized, is therefore the following. Even if, as Tisias and other authoritative rhetoricians maintain, the orator only has to concern himself with what is a *plausible ground* for accepting the particular factual conclusion for which he is arguing, and not with whether it is actually true, that does not absolve him altogether from concern for the truth. There is also the more fundamental truth of what it *is* for something—an act, a person, a thing—to have the property which the desired conclusion attributes to it. Without a concern for that, Socrates holds, one cannot come to know what to put forward as a ground for believing the conclusion. Thus the very knowledge of the plausible thing to say—which is what the expert orator *claims* to have— itself presuppose knowing the sort of truth—truth about the natures of things like justice, goodness, and the other disputable terms which the or- ator's speeches are always concerned with—that in fact philosophical methods and only philosophical methods are designed to bring to light.

But why is that? Why could not knowledge about plausibility dispense with this philosophical truth, this "nature" of rightness and wrongness, etc., altogether? Why could it not base itself simply and directly upon what people (more particularly, the people to be addressed) actually in fact *think* about rightness and wrongness? Surely, if one could get a firm and accurate grasp on that, it would suffice to enable one to find the most plausible available argument. Why does one need to go behind what people actually think to some essence or nature of rightness and wrongness, etc.? To this question Socrates has quite a telling answer. As I noted above, in his response to Tisias, Socrates mentions first plausibility (τὸ πιϑανόν) as what the orator has to be concerned with, and then glosses it by like- lihood (τὸ εἰκός). He explains Tisias' view as follows (272d7–e2): "In the law courts no one has any concern at all for the truth about these matters [viz., justice and goodness], but only for what is plausible. And that is the same as what is likely: one who intends to speak in a truly artful way must pay attention to what is likely." A little later, again claiming Tisias' agreement, he identifies τὸ εἰκός with the other common way of stating the orator's point of reference, τὸ τῷ πλήϑει δοκοῦν (273b1, cf. 260a2), "what the group [being addressed] thinks." Thus according to Socrates' account of the orators, they say what is plausible = what is likely = what the group being addressed thinks. But if that is right Socrates is in a strong position to insist that the orator cannot reliably carry out his task without knowing the truth about goodness, rightness, and so on. For what after all makes something a likely (εἰκός) ground on which to argue (e.g.) an action's wrongness? The English word "likely," like the Greek εἰκός, originally means "resembling." Unfortunately, though the English "likely" visibly bears the marks of this origin, it has come more often than not to be tied to frequence of occurrence in a way that seems not to rely at all on the root idea of resemblance; likelihood often amounts to no more than probability in the usual modern and contemporary sense that gets analyzed by the mathematical theory of chances. But the idea of re- semblance is central to the meaning of the Greek εἰκός, and it is almost ir- resistible to think that what an εἰκός thing to say (e.g.) about wrongness resembles is the full truth about what wrongness is. Socrates at any rate confidently insists that "in fact there comes to be this likelihood [of which Tisias makes so much] in the minds of the many as a result of resemblance to the truth" (273d3–4): what makes some fact seem to the many a likely basis for concluding that an action was wrong is that actions so characterized actually do resemble, more or less closely, wrong actions. And, Socrates adds, the person who knows the truth about wrongness will obviously be in the best position to assess which features that might be claimed for the actual case do resemble wrongness most closely, in the right sort of way, etc., to be found by those being addressed a plausible basis for arguing that it was a case of wrong action. Hence it does, after all, look as if knowledge about plausibility cannot be acquired without knowledge of the philosophical truth about the natures of wrongness and the other matters about which orators attempt to be persuasive.

This Platonic view of rhetoric has special attractions even from the orators' own point of view. On the Platonic theory, goodness, rightness, etc., are realities, existing with their own essences in the nature of things. Most people have no explicit knowledge of them, not even of their existence. Nonetheless goodness and rightness, etc., are at work in the actual world, obscured though their effects are by various empirical conditions of their realization. Most importantly, one effect they have, completely unknown to ourselves, is to influence the selection of those ideas about goodness, rightness, etc., that we individually and communally have formed over the years. The ideas that strike us as correct on these matters so strike us because they are partially adequate reflections—i.e., resemblances—of those real essences. Now no doubt a champion of the traditional oratory might find it awkward to accept this account of the origins of the popular ideas about justice and so on, on which in his oratory he must base his arguments. But it is a great strength of Plato's account that he both raises the question where the conventional ideas do come from and is in a position to give a quite reasonable answer to it. And if one accepts Plato's view one will have a natural and easy basis on which to defend one central claim that traditional oratory made for itself, the claim that oratorical skill gives one the power to shape public opinion, to lead people to adopt the views and attitudes the orator recommends, even if these should be very much at variance with those they brought to the discussion. For if the orator knows what on Plato's theory he must, he can introduce even quite new ideas on whatever topic, ideas that, however original, will have the power to persuade his hearers just because they more nearly resemble the actual truth about the terms under dispute than any of the grounds on which their prior opinions rested. By knowing the natures of justice and goodness and all the rest, the Platonic orator will also know quite accurately which among the things that might believably be said in any given case will be a persuasive characterization of it for the given purpose, whether these are the accepted and standard things to say in such cases or not. He will not be limited to saying things about it that are already self-consciously thought by his hearers to count in favor of the conclusions for which he is working, but can, as appropriate, use his superior knowledge of the truth and what resembles it to expand the stock of ideas his hearers have on the topic in question. Because he knows how to introduce striking ideas that persuade because they express something that closely resembles the truth, however novel they may be, he possesses in his own mind the resources to persuade the crowds he addresses, and is not disgracefully dependent (in the way, say, Socrates in the *Gorgias* argued Gorgias was) upon knowing what ideas his hearers already accept as the means by which to persuade them.

II

Rhetoric continued to be taught during and after Plato's time, as it had been before, without relying on, or granting the logical and practical priority of, this kind of specialized philosophical knowledge. How far did these rhetoricians develop an alternative, intellectually respectable account of what it was that they were teaching and themselves practicing in their speeches? If the Platonic account was rejected or ignored (as it was), what did the rhetoricians have to say in defense of their claim to possess a λόγων τέχνη, that is a systematic knowledge of something or other which would enable them to know what to say and how best to say it, in discoursing on the topics that orators regularly have to address? In what follows I concentrate on Isocrates and Cicero. My question is not whether Isocrates and Cicero specifically take account of Plato's arguments and attempt to answer them (Isocrates never betrays knowledge of the *Phaedrus,* as he does, for example, of Plato's *Apology,* and while Cicero claims to have read the *Phaedrus* he nowhere discusses its arguments). Rather, I want to know how far, whether or not by way of self-conscious response to Plato's claims for philosophy, these defenders of the autonomy of oratory develop intellectual foundations for rhetoric that can be regarded as worthy competitors of the Platonic view.

In no fewer than six of his extant speeches, as well as in several of the nine surviving letters, Isocrates takes the opportunity to comment at some length on his own endeavors as a teacher, to contrast his ideas about what an orator must know and how he should be trained with those of others, including Plato and Aristotle (though he does not refer to them by name), and to defend his own claims, as writer and teacher, to intellectual leadership among those in Greece who concerned themselves seriously with morals and politics. Isocrates frequently refers to the education he provided as ἡ περὶ τοὺς λόγους παιδεία, literally "education in speeches (or speaking)" (see, e.g., *Letter to Alexander* 4, *Antidosis* 168). The tendency of translators to render this Greek phrase simply as education in oratory or rhetoric rather obscures the scope and ambition of the training Isocrates offered. He points out more than once (*Nicocles or the Cyprians* 5–9, *Antid.* 249–50, *To Demonicus* 12, *Panegyricus* 48–50) that the human capacity to speak is the essential and necessary mark of that power of thought that makes us superior to other animals; in general, as Isocrates thinks, an effective education in speaking is nothing less than the development and training of the fundamental human ability to think, and it is that that Isocrates means to offer. That is why he also frequently describes the instruction he offers and the studies which for his own part he is constantly engaged in as φιλοσοφία (philosophy). Modern readers, prejudiced by Plato's account of the nature of philosophy in the *Republic* and elsewhere, are often shocked when they confront for the first time Isocrates' use of the word and his claim to be a philosopher just as much as (even, as we will see shortly, much more than) Plato or any other Socratic. Given what we know Plato made philosophy become there is a tendency to think that Isocrates in professing to be a philosopher was audaciously (not to say impertinently) laying claim to a higher status than any he had a right to claim and than mid-fourth-century usage would naturally permit him. This is certainly a mistake, as Isocrates' own completely unselfconscious way of using the word is itself enough to show. (See also Thucydides 2.40.) In effect, as anyone would grant, wisdom is the perfection of the human power to reason, so that philosophy, being the pursuit of wisdom, is simply the effort to perfect that power (cf. *Antid.* 271). It would be a gross anachronism to take the fact that Plato and those of his successors whom we are accustomed to call philosophers had special views about how that perfection was to be achieved (views that Isocrates did not share) as a ground for finding anything at all peculiar in Isocrates' use of the word φιλοσοφία. He claims, and very plausibly too, to be engaged in the effort to perfect his own and his students' power to reason well, and it simply follows from that that he is a philosopher.

Isocrates goes further, however. Though he does once, in passing, characterize philosophy as involving "the power not only to establish laws but also to investigate the nature of the universe" (τὴν φύσιν τῶν ὄντων, *Busiris* 22, tr. van Hook), he is elsewhere openly dismissive of efforts in the second of these two directions. In one place he refers (*Antid.* 268–9) to the cosmological theories of Empedocles, Ion of Chios, Alcmaeon, Parmenides, Melissus, and Gorgias (in the περὶ τοῦ μὴ ὄντος) (elsewhere *Helen* 3, he throws Zeno into this group too) as no doubt mind-catching (cf. περιττολογίαι, *Antid.* 269) but perfectly pointless and profitless speculations, and he advises those who want a real education to keep away from all such empty talk. In this passage (see *Antid.* 261) he classes together with these "ancient sophists" those of his contemporaries whom he elsewhere describes as "devoting themselves to disputations" (περὶ τοὺς ἔριδας διατρίβοντες, *Against the Sophists* 1, *Hel.* 1), and subjects them to the same condemnation. Now these so-called eristics, about whom Isocrates complains in this vein as early as 391 B.C. (*Ag. Soph.* 1) and as late as 342 (*Letter to Alexander* 3–4) and 339 (*Panathenaicus* 26–29), is a somewhat fluid group, but there can be no doubt that he always means some or other of those successors of Socrates who in their different ways developed Socratic dialectic (the question-and-answer examination of people's opinions) into the method of philosophy par excellence. Thus in 391 (before Plato himself has come on the scene) Isocrates' target is presumably Antisthenes and Megarians like Euboulides and Euclides; by about 370 (the presumptive date of the *Helen*) they clearly included Plato as well; and in the *Letter to Alexander* (342 B.C.) he is obviously referring especially to Aristotle, who took up his appointment as Alexander's tutor about that time. Besides pre-Socratic cosmology, then, Isocrates rejects also the teaching and writing of all the dialectical philosophers of his time, including most prominently Plato and Aristotle, as not worth bothering with. He gives his reason quite clearly in the *Antidosis* (261–9; cf. *Hel.* 5, *Panath.* 27–28, *Ag. Soph.* 7–8, 20): the practice of philosophical dialectic in the manner of Socrates and Plato, he claims, like the cosmological theories of the "ancient sophists," does not and cannot provide one with ideas that are of any use whatsoever in reasoning about or deciding any of the practical questions arising in private or communal life (262–3). For that reason it is not even entitled to the name "philosophy" (266, cf. 285). Only that pursuit can properly be called the pursuit of wisdom which already *gives* its devotees effective and valuable ideas about those matters that wisdom itself concerns, namely the conduct of human private and communal life. And this, Isocrates asserts, dialectic does not do, any more than geometry, astronomy, and other "exact sciences" do. He concedes that dialectic, like these sciences, is educationally useful, but that is only because it forces the pupil to apply his mind to intricate and difficult problems, so that those trained in it gain a superior power to grasp and learn the truly serious and worthwhile matters one must devote oneself to in actually acquiring the ability to think and speak well on practical questions affecting the conduct of human life. But it is only a "gymnastic of the mind and a preparation for philosophy" (266), no part of philosophy itself—no part of the study of those matters knowing about which constitutes the ability to think and speak well on the difficult practical questions that human beings constantly face.

Now notoriously Plato, and Socrates in Plato's dialogues, strenuously maintain that dialectic *does* give one precisely what Isocrates here denies it can, namely the insight into human nature, the human good, justice and virtue in general, and so on, that are the core of the ability to think and speak well on the very practical questions that the Isocratean writer and speaker intends to address. If "speaking well" means discovering the truth in some such matter and showing that it is true, Plato equips himself in the *Republic* with an elaborate theory claiming that that cannot be done without philosophical insight into the nature of certain "forms," and that that insight cannot be acquired except precisely in the processes of dialectic that Isocrates deprecates. And if "speaking well" means speaking so as to persuade others, who are not philosophically trained, that some decision or action is the right or the best one to take in their private or the communal life, then we have seen that Plato has in the *Phaedrus* an impressive theory maintaining that this too depends essentially on the kind of knowledge of good and bad, right and wrong, that only dialectic can provide. Maybe some of the topics debated in the process of a dialectical education seem unconnected to the grand themes on which the wise man must speak, and maybe in any event, as Isocrates says (*Antid.* 84), the conceptions of temperance, justice, and so on, which the dialectician develops and urges his pupils to follow are unheard of by the rest of the world; but Plato has arguments in support of a well-articulated view according to which these are nonetheless the correct conceptions and moreover the only ones that are serviceable for anyone who wishes to speak well, in either sense, on these topics. In the passages I have just summarized Isocrates has begun promisingly, but to sustain his position he needs to do two further things. First he must do something to undercut the dialecticians' claims to open up for us a superior, and the only *true*, knowledge about what he and they agree are those important matters that philosophy deals with. Secondly he must say something about the alternative sources of this knowledge that he offers his pupils: What are they? How are they to be tapped? On what basis does he claim that his instruction and his writing are in communication with them? In short, what intellectual foundations, alternative to Plato's, does he provide for philosophy or (equivalently for Isocrates) oratory?

To these foundational questions Isocrates' responses are regrettably weak, so weak as to suggest that he did not see clearly, or take seriously, the need to provide answers to them at all. To Plato's claims to have opened up the means by which to arrive at true and unshakable knowledge of justice, goodness, etc., Isocrates seems to make two ill-sorted responses. The net effect is neither clearly to deny that Platonic knowledge is possible nor to show that, even if it is possible, it is of no use either in practical life or for oratory. In a passage of the *Antidosis* where he is clearly speaking against philosophers like Plato Isocrates affirms his own view that "it is not in the nature of human beings to acquire a knowledge (ἐπιστήμη) by possessing which we actually know what we ought to do or what we ought to say"; the most we humans can hope for is to be able "most of the time to hit upon what is best by means of our opinions (δόξαι)" about what to do or say (271). Evidently Isocrates means to deny the possibility for human beings of the kind of knowledge the Platonists were talking about. But does he really do so? Under the umbrella of a putative "knowledge what we ought to do or say" might be included any of three separate things. First there might be knowledge of some principles or standards of what is right or wrong, good or bad, etc.— knowledge of which features of situations as they arise for evaluative judgment count one way or the other, how these are to be ranked and weighed against one another, and so on, leading to a definitive judgment, for each situation whose actual relevant features are completely and authoritatively known, as to what is right or wrong to do in that situation. Secondly there might be the further knowledge, about any given situation, whether or not it actually exemplifies each of the relevant features. And thirdly (since action and speech are constantly oriented to the future, as one tries to affect the subsequent course of events), there might be knowledge of what will or would happen if various available options were taken in the situation. When Isocrates denies there is any knowledge available to human beings by which to really *know* what to do or say, what knowledge does he mean to deny? Obviously Plato does not suppose that by dialectical study one can come to possess the ability infallibly to predict the future (so he does not claim that it can impart the third of these kinds of knowledge of what to do). Furthermore, Plato himself maintains that empirical things and events are often unclear, perhaps irredeemably so, so that one must rely on fallible judgment and opinion (δόξα), not knowledge (ἐπιστήμη), to decide what features a situation actually does exhibit. So he doesn't think knowledge of the second kind is provided by philosophical study. It is only knowledge of principles and standards of justice, goodness, etc., that he maintains dialectic can give us. Does Isocrates understand this? Is this the kind of knowledge he means to deny human beings can acquire?

It is a curious but I think important fact about Isocrates' attitude to the dialecticians that he never shows any clear awareness that their (or at any rate Plato's) position is what I have just described, and accordingly he never clearly rejects precisely the kind of knowledge through dialectic that Plato defended. Quite to the contrary: at one place or another in denying human beings can get "*knowledge* of what one ought to do or say" he does clearly deny that we can have knowledge of either of the two kinds Plato did *not* suppose we could have, but he nowhere clearly denies the possibility of precisely that knowledge of principles and standards Plato thought dialectic *could* give us. Thus in *Against the Sophists* (where although, as noted, chronology shows he can hardly be directing himself specifically against Plato) he attacks Socratic dialecticians who, like Plato later on, held that through dialectic one could acquire strict knowledge of how to act and through that achieve *eudaimonia* (3), and does so by insisting that not even the Homeric gods knew what the future would bring, so that all the more must human beings be denied such foreknowledge (2, 7–8). And in the *Antidosis* he insists that there can be no precise knowledge about the character of the occasions (καιρούς) to which one must apply one's general principles about what to do and say, that one can at best conjecture whether it has the features that make it amenable, according to one's general principles, to treatment in one way rather than another (184). In both cases the clear implication is that in Isocrates' view the dialecticians had implied that the kind of knowledge being rejected was possible, and offered to impart it to their pupils. And there is no passage where Isocrates specifically rejects dialectically derived knowledge of principles and standards of justice, goodness, etc. This evidence suggests, therefore, that Isocrates did not clearly understand what kind of knowledge dialecticians like Plato claimed their methods could yield, and was content to cast irrelevant aspersions on kinds of knowledge they did not in fact claim, in the belief that he could thereby impress the Athenian reading public with the superior soundness of his own methods of thought and instruction. If this is so, one seems forced to conclude that Isocrates was not interested enough in the foundational questions Plato and other dialecticians were concerning themselves with even to reject clearly the claims they were actually making.

This impression is confirmed if one asks what Isocrates thinks are the nature and sources of the sound "opinions" (δόξαι) about what to do or say that he claims are the most that human beings can hope for. One might expect him to come forward with a theory to the general effect that in ordinary life, judgments (say) about the justice of an action as a matter of fact, when rationally based at all, are always rendered by appeal to some or other of the opinions that have won acceptance among human beings (however that may have happened) about which features of actions count in favor of an action's justice. *Sound* judgments of justice will then be those that are based on an unusually wide and careful survey of such opinions and are supported by a large number of the relevant opinions that are generally regarded as being the weightiest. Or something like that. One will search Isocrates' works in vain for even a hint in such a direction. In the *Antidosis* (272–3) he offers to explain the studies by which a person might gain the kind of φρόνησις which would enable him regularly to have sound δόξαι on this kind of question. But among various irrelevancies the *only* concrete suggestion he goes on to make is that he will study "from all the actions of men which bear upon his subject those examples which are the most illustrious and the most edifying; and, habituating himself to contemplate and appraise such examples, he will feel their influence not only in the preparation of a given speech but in all the actions of his life" (277, tr. Norlin). A nice sentiment, but hardly sharp enough to count as an informative answer to the question Isocrates has asked himself! And it is virtually the only indication anywhere in his works of just how he thought sound opinions were to be arrived at and what made the ones so arrived at *sound*.

I conclude that a patient and sympathetic reading of Isocrates' speeches shows him to be a philosophical writer in one important sense (and it was presumably in recognition of this that Plato in the *Phaedrus*, 279a, has Socrates say that there is φιλοσοφία τις in his thinking). In his speeches he prominently appeals to general ideas the defense of which would call for what we along with Plato would recognize as philosophical argument. Some of these are in fact things that philosophers like Plato and Aristotle also maintain: for example, Isocrates says that a person's true advantage lies in living a life of justice devoted to promoting the common good as far as he can (*Antid.* 281, *On the Peace* 31–34, *Nicocles* 59, *To Demonicus* 38–9), and that "everyone does everything which he does for the sake of pleasure or gain or honor" (*Antid.* 217). But he does not develop even the beginnings of a theory about how such judgments are to be justified, or offer any coherent general explanation at all of what it is that his own recommendations on questions of public policy are based on. This total failure to explain the methodology of oratorical argument, the theoretical foundations of oratory, is presumably what Plato had in mind by saying Isocrates' mind exhibited only φιλοσοφία τις, and not φιλοσοφία *tout court*. For Plato, philosophical ideas without a philosophical methodology conferred only a limited and dubious title to the status of philosopher. The unfortunate fact seems to be that Isocrates' teaching was so spectacularly popular and so successful in producing recognized leaders in the political and intellectual life of fourth-century B.C. Greece that he felt no need to examine the theoretical foundations of his own brand of oratory or to attempt seriously to undermine those of his dialectical competitors. Ironically, Isocrates would have had to be more of a philosopher than in fact he was—one more impressed with the actual threat to his kind of oratory posed by the dialecticians, and more interested in questions of methodology—in order to give the kind of defense of oratory that his own claims for it demanded.

I have already hinted what Isocrates might have said, if he had taken seriously the dialecticians' challenge and attempted to answer those foundational questions that in the *Phaedrus* Plato answered to the disadvantage of the traditional oratory. (1) He might have denied, or claimed as insufficiently established, Plato's "absolute" knowledge of what justice and goodness and so on are. (2) Second, he might have worked out some rationale for holding that the only basis we have on which to judge the justice, advantage, etc., of courses of action is by appeal to the ideas about these matters that people actually find authoritative; the truth just is whatever, after careful and sensitive appeal to these authoritative ideas, ultimately recommends itself, and there is no need, and no possibility, of going behind these to some absolute or divine point of view from which to uncover the "real" truth of the matter. Now it is obvious that such a position is just what one might expect an ancient skeptic to take, and that suggests that for a thorough-going conception of oratory as uncommitted to and independent of any appeal to the philosophical *truth* about how to conduct human affairs one should consult the skeptical tradition. This encourages the thought that Cicero, an avowed philosophical skeptic, might have something better to say on behalf of oratory than we have found in Isocrates. For a link between the Greek skeptical tradition and the defense of rhetoric one must wait until the time of Cicero.

Cicero, of course, was an Academic, not a Pyrrhonian, skeptic, a follower of Carneades, whose philosophy he learned through the lectures of Philo of Larissa and Philo's pupil Antiochus of Ascalon. He maintained that his own oratorical skill owed its formation to his study of the skeptical philosophy of the Academy, not to any technical training in the oratorical "workshops" of his time (*Or.* 12), and his own account of the ideal orator is plainly based in his philosophical skepticism. But what kind of skeptic was Cicero? What did his philosophical skepticism amount to? He was a follower of the so-called "moderate skepticism" that his teacher Philo offered (incorrectly, as Cicero admitted) as an interpretation of the philosophy of Carneades. According to this conception, the skeptic was free to hold beliefs as to how things actually are in the world, even doctrinal beliefs of a philosophical and generally theoretical sort, so long as he was fully and constantly aware that in so believing he was not in possession of *knowledge* about anything, and therefore might after all be wrong. Philo's and Cicero's skepticism consisted in fact wholly in the *kind* of beliefs maintained (tentative, open-minded, undogmatic), not in *what* was believed, and certainly not in any forbearance or suspension of belief altogether. A good indication of the character of Cicero's skepticism is given by his *De Natura Deorum*, a dialogue in which representatives of the Epicurean view (Velleius) and the Stoic view (Balbus) on the gods expound their doctrines and present their arguments, which are then negatively criticized by a representative of the Carneadean Academy (Cotta). At the conclusion of it all Cicero pronounces his own view (*ND* III 95): he finds that the Stoic view has survived the Academic attack fairly well, and, as argued by Balbus, "seemed to him to incline more towards a resemblance to the truth" than did the Academic arguments against it (and a fortiori than the conflicting Epicurean view as argued by Velleius managed to do). Having carefully and fully examined all the arguments, *con* as well as *pro,* of the most distinguished thinkers on the subject of the nature and existence of gods and their relationship to the world and humankind, Cicero finds that, when all their arguments are weighed, one view, the Stoic, stands out in his mind as "more resembling the truth" (*ad veritatis similitudinem propensior*), that is, as having the quality and character of the truth to a higher degree than the Epicurean does. After examining this and many other matters carefully, Cicero concludes that one view *looks* like it is true, and so accepts (provisionally, "undogmatically," subject to reconsideration, etc.) that view (the Stoic one) as true. In this he shows that he agrees with Catulus' concluding remarks in the *Academica* (*Ac.* II 148): "A wise man . . . will hold an opinion, but . . . will understand that it is an opinion and that nothing can be comprehended and 'grasped' as being true. . . . I assent emphatically to the view that nothing can be 'grasped' as being true."

Now this is obviously a dangerous position for a skeptic to be in—to be agreeing with the leading dogmatic philosophers of his time both as to there *being* a final and absolute truth of the matter whether there are gods and how they relate to us, and as to what in all probability that truth is. As is well known, once Academic skepticism evolved to this position with Philo, educated people understandably ceased to see any significant difference between Academics and dogmatists or even, more particularly, Stoics at all. From the theoretical point of view what matters is what you believe, not how firmly established you think it is; and even dogmatic Stoics could admit the difficulty of arriving at the truth on such unobvious matters as the gods' nature and might accordingly hold to their view with caution and without arrogant assurance that they had everything figured out once and for all.

Correspondingly, Cicero's skepticism provides a very weak underpinning for oratory, if oratory is to stand on its own and not be subordinate to dogmatic philosophy. It offers an extremely weak basis for defending the intellectual independence and respectability of oratory. Cicero accepts the philosophers' notion of truth, and allows that there *is* an ultimate truth of things. It is only that we humans have not the means whereby to be certain when or if we ever attain to it. The most we are entitled to say is that one or another proposition about how things are has the *marks* of the truth, is *veri simile.* On Cicero's account, oratory, as the discipline whereby on certain matters we are enabled to argue effectively that some proposition *is veri simile,* has only a very precarious and provisional independence from dogmatic philosophy. Because Cicero accepts without question the *philosophers'* idea of the truth of things, he places oratory in bondage to any philosopher who may come along (and no skeptic, not even one of the relaxed Philonian-Ciceronian kind, can say this *won't* happen) who convinces us that he *can* establish the actual truth of things. And, more to the point, Cicero lays himself open to precisely the challenge that Socrates levels in the *Phaedrus* against the traditional orators of his time: if the orator, in order to conduct his argument, needs to know which opinions are most like the truth, or how to describe something so as to make it resemble what is *truly* just (and thereby convince his hearers that it *is* just), how can this knowledge be acquired unless by knowing what justice actually *does* amount to? In the end, Cicero seems to be caught in the toils of his own skepticism: by denying that he or anyone knows the truth about what justice is, he is not in a position to claim, as he needs to do to defend his oratorical practice, some systematic way of arriving at what most resembles the truth, and so what is the best thing to say as an orator arguing one's case.[2]

[2] I did the research for this essay while holding a Fellowship for Advanced Study and Research from the National Endowment for the Humanities.

CHAPTER 4

ARCESILAUS: SOCRATIC AND SKEPTIC

I

A T LEAST since the time of Cicero, the interpretation of what we call Academic skepticism has been uncertain and subject to dispute. For us today, the central disputed question, or related set of questions, concerns the relationship between the philosophical views of the Academics and their argumentative practices—from the time of Arcesilaus, when Plato's Academy first "went skeptical,"[1] down through his successors, Carneades and Clitomachus, in the late second century—to the self-styled Pyrrhonism inaugurated by Aenesidemus in the first half of the first century B.C. This is a question that Cicero never raises, and may not have been in a position to raise: he seems to have had no inkling of any such new Pyrrhoneans, though the first of them were his contemporaries.[2] But it was certainly raised by the new Pyrrhoneans themselves—by Aenesidemus, and by Sextus Empiricus, our principal exemplar, and

---

[1] This is Malcolm Schofield's phrase, in beginning "Academic Epistemology," his contribution to the *Cambridge History of Hellenistic Philosophy*, ed. K. Algra et al., 323–51.

[2] In his surviving works and letters Cicero never names Aenesidemus, or shows any knowledge of skepticism in his own time beyond the teaching of Philo (Clitomachus's successor as head of the Academy)—his own boyhood teacher at Rome. Nor does Cicero seem to know of Pyrrho himself (c. 365–275 B.C.) as any sort of skeptic. He never refers to Pyrrho in connection with doubts about the possibility of knowledge, the propriety of suspending judgment, or related issues—the staples for him of the Academic philosophy. Indeed Cicero never associates any epistemological views at all with Pyrrho's name. He assigns him only views in ethics: Pyrrho held that virtue is the only good, and that any other thing (such as the "preferred" and "counterpreferred" indifferents of the Stoics—health, wealth, pleasure or pain, and so on) is not only neither good nor bad, but there is nothing about any such thing that gives a reason or even, for the right-thinking person, so much as an *incentive*, for or against them. For Pyrrho, the wise man is unmoved, unaffected one way or another, by any of them, or the prospect of them—he is "apathetic" (see *Academica* 2.130). Now a modern reader may perhaps see lying behind this "apathy" a Pyrrhonian skeptical "life without belief," in which, never believing that things are any one way rather than some other, you only move, if at all, randomly or capriciously (some later testimony, e.g., Diogenes Laertius, *Lives of Eminent Philosophers*, 9.62, says this is the sort of life Pyrrho himself led); but Cicero clearly does not see that. For Cicero the apathy of Pyrrho's wise man rests specifically on the refusal to find any value in anything except virtue (and vice). Cicero associates Pyrrho repeatedly with Aristo and Herillus, early "unorthodox" Stoics who thought virtue the only good and refused to accept Zeno's distinction between preferred and counterpreferred indifferents. All three, he says, held long-exploded and disregardable theories about value (see *Tusc. Disp.* 2.15, 5.85; *de Off.* 1.6; *de Fin.* 2.35, 2.43, 3.11–12,

source of testimony, for the new school.[3] Recently a strong current of opinion (not unopposed, of course) has favored the view that these earlier and later ancient skeptical movements were in fact in agreement on all important matters of philosophical substance (relatively minor details aside). Thus, they should be treated as having put forward a single set of ideas, a single approach in philosophy, that we can call "ancient" or "classical" skepticism, and where necessary contrast with late Renaissance and modern skeptical thought—the skepticism developed by Montaigne and Descartes, presupposed by Locke and Berkeley and Hume and Kant, and made a standard topic in twentieth-century epistemology.[4]

4.43, 5.23). Thus, it appears, "Pyrrhonism" would not indicate to Cicero either a predecessor view or a successor view similar in any way to the Academics'.

[3] Aenesidemus notoriously said that the Academics of his own time held in a dogmatic way (as no proper skeptic should) that knowledge (i.e., knowledge as the Stoics defined it) was unattainable; they were no better than Stoics fighting Stoics (Photius, *Library*, 169b38–39, 170a14–17 Bekker). Sextus (*Pyrrhonian Sketches* [PH] 1.3) distinguishes his own Pyrrhonism from the Academic philosophy of "Clitomachus and Carneades and other Academics" by saying that the latter held that the matters investigated by philosophy are "ungraspable" or unknowable (ἀκατάληπτα), whereas the Pyrrhoneans keep on investigating so as to find out whether any such thing can be known (and do so without being convinced yet either that it can or that it cannot). It is noteworthy that Sextus does not name Arcesilaus here; on that, see below sect. V. He distinguishes (*PH* 1.220) between a "middle" Academy (Arcesilaus) and a "new" one (Carneades and Clitomachus) and makes only the "new" Academy just the sort of "negative dogmatists" that he describes in this passage of 1.3 (compare *PH* 1.232–33 vs. 226–30). I return to this distinction below, sect. V.

[4] See especially M. Frede, "The Sceptic's Two Kinds of Assent and the Question of the Possibility of Knowledge," *Philosophy In History*, ed. R. Rorty et al.; also G. Striker, "On the Difference between the Pyrrhonists and the Academics," in her *Essays on Hellenistic Epistemology and Ethics*. The differences that Striker does draw attention to are real and important, but as she says at pp. 147–48, the two schools "do not in fact seem very far apart from one another" and are "very close" "as far as skepticism itself is concerned." (She fails to see the very significant difference, precisely so far as skepticism itself goes, between Arcesilaus and Sextus that I develop below, sect. V: see her comments on "the skeptical Stoic," p. 141.) M. Burnyeat's "Can the Sceptic Live His Scepticism?" (*Doubt and Dogmatism*, ed. by M. Schofield et al., 20–53) begins with Hume's claim that the Pyrrhonian skeptic cannot live his skepticism, but proceeds to discuss ancient skepticism more generally (though with special reference to Pyrrhonism); he brings Academic "skeptics" frequently into his discussion, and applies to them the same analysis, concluding that ancient skeptics in general cannot live their skepticism. However, in "The Sceptic in His Place and Time" (in Burnyeat and Frede, eds., *The Original Sceptics*, 95 n. 7), Burnyeat registers the view, without explaining what he may have in mind, that there is a real and fundamental difference between Pyrrhonism and the "dialectical arguments for sceptical conclusions put forward by Arcesilaus and Carneades." In "Antipater and Self-Refutation" (in *Assent and Argument*, ed. B. Inwood and J. Mansfeld, n. 76), he suggests that there might be some difference between the way Academics and Pyrrhoneans understand the crucial idea of an "appearance"; if this is the basis for the real and fundamental difference he had in mind in the earlier article, it appears that Burnyeat too has not taken note of the crucial difference between Arcesilaus and Sextus that I develop below.

It is worth noting that it was apparently only the new Pyrrhoneans who called themselves skeptics—σκεπτικοί, lit. "searchers" or "inquirers"— and were so called by others in antiquity. Cicero, Sextus, and (so far as I know) all our other ancient sources never refer in that way to the Academic (as *we* say) "skeptics."[5] They always refer to the Academics only as Academics, and to their philosophy as the Academic one, not any sort of

---

[5] A potential exception is found in Aulus Gellius, *Attic Nights* 11.5.6 (late 2nd c. A.D.). In reference to the much-discussed question whether Pyrrhoneans and Academics really differ at all and if so in what way, Gellius says (perhaps on the authority of the second-century Academic Favorinus, whose *Tropes of Pyrrhonism* he has just cited), that Academics, just like Pyrrhoneans, are called (*dicuntur*) σκεπτικοί, ἐφεκτικοί, ἀπορητικοί (skeptics, or people who inquire; ephectics, or people who suspend; and aporetics, or people who raise difficulties). H. Tarrant, *Scepticism or Platonism?* 22, claims that this passage is evidence that "those descriptions were regularly used of Academics" in discussions about whether Academics differed from Pyrrhoneans at least as far back as the first century A.D. Two points should be noted, however. First, we have here a whole list of terms, in fact three of the four with which Sextus characterizes the Pyrrhoneans in his chapter on the names used for his school and its members (*PH* 1.7: Aulus Gellius omits only ζητητικοί)—not just "skeptics." Second, we should expect Favorinus, as an Academic concerned with preserving and winning adherents for his Philonian heritage against the upsurge of the new Pyrrhonism, to want to appropriate for the Academics as much as he could of the more attractive aspects of the new Pyrrhonism, and there is a very solid basis from what we know of Arcesilaus and Carneades for claiming that Academics are ephectics and aporetics (on Arcesilaus in this regard, see the heavy emphasis laid in Cicero's evidence about Arcesilaus's Socratic heritage on withholding assent and on raising questions about views positively put forward by others: below, sects. II and III). When he throws in "skeptics" as well, then, we should take this not as evidence of general philosophical and scholarly usage at the time but as part of Favorinus's own—motivated—back-appropriation for the Academics of attractive Pyrrhonian self-characterizations. When Gellius says that Academics, like Pyrrhoneans, "are called" by these names, we should understand that merely as reflecting Favorinus's insistence that they are equally entitled to them all. In fact, Gellius himself elsewhere uses the term σκεπτικός as a name specifically for the Pyrrhoneans (11.5.1). I do not know of any other ancient text that unambiguously refers to Academics as σκεπτικοί. (Numenius, as reported in Eusebius, *Praep. Evang.* 14.6.4–5, said that some earlier authors, including Timon, declared that Arcesilaus [alone among the Academics] was really a Pyrrhonist in all but name, and therefore deserved to be called a skeptic [σκεπτικός], rather than an Academic. Even if we take Numenius at his word, and Timon and other early writers did call Arcesilaus a skeptic, on these grounds, that does not amount to calling an Academic a skeptic [or a kind of skeptic], much less calling Academics in general by this name.)

It is noteworthy that even as late as in the *Anonymous Prolegomena to Platonic Philosophy* (ed. L. G. Westerink), which Westerink dates to the second half of the sixth century A.D., the author, in defending his characterization of Plato as a "dogmatic" philosopher and rejecting, for example, Arcesilaus's claim that in his dialogues Plato never advances any philosophical opinion as his own, five times uses the term ἐφεκτικός (never σκεπτικός) both to express the rejected alternative description of Plato and to characterize those skeptics who claim Plato as their model, whether these ἐφεκτικοί are to be distinguished from the Academics (7.10–14, 10.1–6) or the latter are to be included under the same heading (10.10, 11.20, 12.2). He felt quite comfortable describing Academics and Pyrrhoneans alike as ephectics; apparently not so for "skeptics."

"skeptical" philosophy. As Sextus makes clear,[6] to be a σκεπτικός philosopher (literally, one given to σκέψις, searching or inquiring) means to be one who constantly inquires about or considers questions of philosophy, and keeps on inquiring about and considering them. That is, a skeptic is one whose stock in trade is precisely that—taking philosophical questions up, inquiring into them, considering the matter at issue, without however ever coming to any conclusion, one way or the other—neither (1) by deciding that some given answer or theory is correct, nor even (2) by judging that one or more given proposed answers are definitely incorrect, nor, yet again, (3) by concluding that on the matter at hand there is no correct answer at all, either in the nature of things or anyhow available to us.[7] Of course, even though in antiquity the Academics were never called skeptics, it might still be that they were just as much entitled to this name—meaning by it, with Sextus, "ones who keep on inquiring, without reaching any conclusion"—as the official and self-proclaimed skeptics, the Pyrrhoneans, themselves were. In what follows I will pursue this question, so far simply as concerns Arcesilaus. I leave aside Carneades and other later Academics. My question, then, is whether Arcesilaus was a skeptic, where being a skeptic is understood Sextus's way: as one who keeps on inquiring into all sorts of philosophical matters, without reaching any conclusion of the sorts just specified on any of them.

II

Cicero in the *Academica* gives us by far the most extensive and detailed account of Arcesilaus as a philosopher that we have. In fact, each time through himself as speaker, Cicero presents two separate accounts of the

---

[6] See *PH* 1.7; see also Diogenes Laertius 9.70.

[7] One slender piece of possible evidence suggests that already Pyrrho might have been known during his lifetime or not long after for having given himself over to the activity of σκέψις. In his *Lampoons* (apparently in the second book, where he takes Xenophanes as his guide in pointing out the errors and arrogance of all other philosophers besides the modest, serene Pyrrho) Timon of Phlius, Pyrrho's pupil and publicist, has Xenophanes lament his own going off on treacherous dogmatizing ways, from age and lack of care for all σκεπτοσύνη (Sextus *PH* 1.224 = frg. 833, Lloyd-Jones/Parsons = 59 di Marco). Perhaps this archaic term indicates Xenophanes' own failure to philosophize in the way Pyrrho did. In that case, perhaps Aenesidemus, if he like Sextus called himself not only a Pyrrhonean but also a skeptic, affixed this name to his philosophical movement by way of reviving or anyhow drawing on a special emphasis on the importance of continued σκέψις in the reports about Pyrrho. However, Tarrant, *Scepticism or Platonism?* 23–24, points to Philo of Alexandria, writing in the first decades of the first century A.D., as the earliest author we know who used σκεπτικοί (sometimes) as a label specifically for Pyrrhoneans. From the fact that within his report of Aenesidemus's Ten Tropes, Philo uses this term in its broader meaning simply of

history of the Hellenistic Academy beginning with Arcesilaus but including its philosophical forebears. Cicero presents the first account in *Ac.* I
upon the invitation of Varro, who has just completed an exposition
(15–42) of Antiochus of Ascalon's view that the original Academic philosophy, beginning with Plato (but harking back to Socrates' discourses
praising virtue and exhorting men to its zealous pursuit), was a single,
complete, and comprehensive system, adhered to in all essentials by Aristotle, by Plato's immediate successors in the Academy down to Polemo
and Crantor, and again by Zeno the Stoic, whose many innovations did
not however make his Stoicism anything but the same "system" of philosophy as Plato introduced. It is then Cicero's turn, being as he and
Varro say (see 1.13–14) a pupil and adherent of Philo of Larissa, a recent
head of the Academy, to explain how and why, beginning with Arcesilaus, the Academy abandoned that philosophy for (what we call) skepticism. Cicero, of course, does not accept that Arcesilaus did abandon any
prior Academic system of philosophy, since on the view he presents both
Socrates and Plato were "skeptical" forerunners for Arcesilaus when he
rejected that "system" in its Zenonian version. Cicero's account (1.43–46)
starts with pre-Socratic alleged proto-skeptics, and proceeds to Socrates
and Plato and then to Arcesilaus, before our manuscripts break off in the
midst of a first mention of Carneades. Cicero's second account comes in
the *Lucullus* (*Ac.* 2), 72–78. Lucullus, in beginning his exposition of Antiochus's detailed objections to Arcesilaus's and Carneades' new philosophical opinions and practices, had himself objected strenuously to the
way the Academics, and Cicero in his first account (or rather its lost

---

"inquirer" (including those who, after inquiring, reached definite conclusions), Tarrant in-
fers that Aenesidemus must not in fact have used it himself as a label for himself and other
Pyrrhoneans. On the other hand, as Tarrant notes, Diogenes Laertius in the introduction to
his own exposition of the Ten Tropes, just after citing Aenesidemus's book as his source for
the tropes, mentions (9.78) as the goal of Pyrrhonian argumentation to bring out "the op-
positions inherent in inquiries" (τὰς ἐν ταῖς σκέψεσιν ἀντιθέσεις)—a conception of "inquiries" that reflects the more restricted, specifically skeptical, understanding of the term.
So even if Aenesidemus himself did not appropriate the term σκεπτικός in the way that Sextus does as a label for his own school, he seems to have laid the ground for that appropria-
tion by giving special emphasis to the centrality of ever-unfinished σκέψις in Pyrrhonian
philosophizing. That may be one, perhaps the principal, reason why (see note 5 above),
once the term σκεπτικός began to be used as a label for what we call skeptical philosophers,
it was reserved for Pyrrhoneans and was not applied equally to Academics: the latter could
easily be, and were, described as ephectics or aporetics (and even zetetics), but, it seems, the
associations of "skeptic" were too strongly with specifically Pyrrhonian constant inquiry.
(On the question when the term σκεπτικός came to be generally used as a label for
Pyrrhoneans, see also G. Striker, "Skeptical Strategies," in *Doubt and Dogmatism*, ed. M.
Schofield et al., n. 1.)

first-edition version), allegedly twist and misinterpret the views of various pre-Socratics, Socrates, and Plato in seeking to enlist respectable authorities to provide cover for Arcesilaus's sedition in departing from the "old system" so that his departure will look less vainglorious and less simply malicious (*Ac.* 2.13–15). Cicero's second account consists of his rebuttal of this charge of Lucullus.

The two accounts are in general, but not total, agreement.[8] In *Ac.* I, Cicero presents Arcesilaus as having been impressed, to begin with—just as Democritus, Anaxagoras, Empedocles, and "almost all the old philosophers," *and Socrates as well*, had been—with the insuperable obstacles that stand in the way of anyone's ever coming to know any truth ("limited senses, feeble minds, short lifespan, truth sunk in an abyss, . . . all things wrapped in darkness," 1.44).[9] On these grounds, says Cicero, all these predecessors of Arcesilaus had denied all possibility of cognizing, grasping, knowing anything. Arcesilaus reached this same conclusion from the same considerations: *on these grounds,* he denied that anything can be known (*negabat esse quicquam quod sciri posset,* 1.45)—but, taking his denial one step further, he went on to say that even that which Socrates had exempted (his own knowledge of this universal ignorance) was itself not knowable.[10] Thus, Cicero tells us in *Ac.* I, Arcesilaus, following Socrates, became persuaded by certain pre-Socratic arguments to accept the conclusion that nothing is either known or knowable, not even the truth of this conclusion itself. But that is not all. Cicero adds: *for these reasons (quibus de causis)* Arcesilaus further concluded that no one ought ever assent to any proposition. If nothing can be known it would be the most disgraceful thing you could do (something than which nothing is *turpius*)—in fact a disgraceful misuse of the mind—to affirm or deny anything at all. (Why so, we are not told.) Armed with these convictions, according to Cicero, Arcesilaus practiced the old Socratic method of arguing against other people's opinions, with a view to making the reasons against them equally weighty as those advanced by their

---

[8] Charles Brittain (*Philo of Larissa,* 175–78) usefully reviews the contents of the two passages; his purposes do not lead him to address the differences in the two accounts, as I do below.

[9] *angustos sensus, imbecillos animos, brevia curricula vitae, et . . . in profundo veritatem esse demersam.*

[10] Cicero's purpose in the *Ac.* II history (to rebut Lucullus's objections to the claims of Academics to find authoritative predecessors among pre-Socratics, Socrates, and Plato) does not lead him to reiterate Arcesilaus's second-order skepticism about knowledge that one does not know anything. However, Cicero adds a reference there (2.73) to Metrodorus of Chios, the fourth-century Democritean, quoting him as denying such knowledge. So if Arcesilaus did say what Cicero says in 1.45 he did, he was not the first to introduce this refinement. On Metrodorus, see Brunschwig, "Le Fragment DK 70 B 1 de Métrodore de Chio," in *Polyhistor,* ed. K. A. Algra et al.

proponents, so that his hearers might be persuaded to follow his advice and suspend judgment.

On this account, it seems clear that Arcesilaus cannot deserve the title of skeptic (σκεπτικός), if that is understood as one who inquires about everything and keeps on inquiring without reaching a conclusion, one way or another, on any question inquired into. Arcesilaus *has* inquired into the possibility of knowledge, and he has concluded that none is possible for a human being. (So that question is settled; it is not something open that is still being inquired into.) Even if he has further concluded that he does not *know* that knowledge is impossible, nonetheless, he has assented to the proposition that it is impossible. And his yet further conclusion, that it is a disgrace to assent to any proposition, is itself based on assent to a proposition—the proposition that it *is* a disgrace to assent to anything in the absence of knowledge. We must presume that Arcesilaus has inquired into what is and is not disgraceful to do with your mind, and has reached the conclusion, after inquiry, that it is a disgrace to assent if you don't actually *know* the truth of what you are assenting to. So on Cicero's account in *Ac.* 1.43–46, Arcesilaus is no skeptic.[11]

Cicero's second account, in *Ac.* 2.72–78, is not so forthright. Here he does not say that either Socrates or Arcesilaus based their idea that nothing can be known on pre-Socratic arguments about the weakness of the mind, the narrowness of the senses, truth's being sunk in the abyss, and so forth. About Socrates, Cicero says only that after reading so many Socratic discourses of Plato and others it is impossible for him to doubt that it appeared (*visum sit*) to Socrates that nothing is known by anybody (2.74). About Arcesilaus he says only that it appeared to Arcesilaus that

---

[11] As Cicero presents him, he also grossly contradicts himself. First, Cicero says that Arcesilaus reached the conclusion that nothing can be known, i.e., that he accepted and assented to the proposition that nothing can be known (but without thinking that he *knew* that to be true). Hence, he did not assent to this as to an item of knowledge: the result of his assent would have to stand, according to the universally employed Stoic terminology of Cicero's time, as a mere "opinion," understood as such. Then, Cicero says that Arcesilaus further concluded that, therefore, no one ought ever to assent to any proposition. Thus he assents (more than once) while holding that no one should ever assent to anything. Perhaps Cicero means (he says nothing about this) that Arcesilaus exempted from his condemnation of assents, first, the proposition that nothing can be known and, second, the proposition that it is a disgrace to assent to any (other) proposition (than these two). That would preserve logical consistency. But what possible principled ground could Arcesilaus, on Cicero's account in *Ac.* I, have offered for these exemptions? His general principle, which does I think have its attractions (I come back to this below, sect. III) is that the only ground on which one should ever assent is if you *know* the proposition that you are assenting to. So it is impossible to see how Arcesilaus could provide any decent basis that would license even these exceptions: he certainly did not think that either of these could be *known*. (See note 16 below on one possible revision to Cicero's account that would restore logical consistency.)

it was true that the wise person would not assent to anything not actually *known* by him (as, it is implied, it appeared to Arcesilaus that nothing would be), and that it is worthy of the wise person not to do so (2.77). This might seem to leave open the possibility that Socrates, and Arcesilaus mimicking him, did not base their ideas that no one knows anything and that no one ought to assent to any proposition, on the pre-Socratic considerations mentioned in 1.44 (and expanded upon in 2.72–74, with the addition of Xenophanes and Parmenides to the previous trio of Anaxagoras, Democritus, and Empedocles), but perhaps on something else.[12] Furthermore, it might leave open the possibility that they may not be correctly interpreted as holding these "views" on the basis of *any* inquiry that yielded these results as their reasoned conclusions, but on some other sort of basis altogether. In that case, one might still perhaps hold open the possibility that Arcesilaus (and Socrates, too, for that matter) was a skeptic.

Those are possibilities I do wish to hold open, and indeed to argue positively for as actualities. But it does not seem promising to argue for them (at all) on the basis of Cicero's account of Arcesilaus in *Ac.* 2.72–78. As I mentioned, Cicero's second account is a rebuttal of Lucullus's attack on his first one—a rebuttal that certainly gives no indication that it incorporates any alteration of the view there presented. Cicero seems clearly to intend just to restate and reinforce that earlier account.[13] So we should not take Cicero in 2.72–78, with his language of "appearance" and his neglecting to link these appearances to the pre-Socratic arguments as their grounds, to be giving a different account of the historical facts from that in 1.44–46. In fact, in both places, but most explicitly in the first book, he claims to be speaking for Philo, to be presenting Philo's account of the history of the Academy.[14] So we should interpret Cicero as having in mind in both accounts that it was on the basis of the pre-Socratic arguments he alludes to in both contexts that Arcesilaus had concluded that nothing is knowable.

However, the Philonian origin of this history should alert us to the need to tread carefully here. During the time when Cicero heard him at

[12] It is noteworthy that even in expanding the list of pre-Socratic proto-skeptics in 2.72–74 Cicero only claims to be arguing that Arcesilaus was perfectly entitled to point to these distinguished philosophers as predecessors in holding that nothing is or can be known. He does not repeat the earlier claim that either Socrates or Arcesilaus reached their own conclusion to this effect *through* the same considerations as led these predecessors to it.

[13] I think Brittain, *Philo of Larissa*, 175–78, is absolutely right about this.

[14] See *Ac.* 1.13–14, and the implications of 2.7–8, 2.17 (*Philo vester*), 2.66, 2.69, 2.73 (*atque hic [Democritus] non dicit quod nos [viz., Cicero and Philo], qui veri esse aliquid non negamus, percipi posse negamus*).

Rome, before the radical change of view recorded in his "Roman books" that gave rise to such outrage among Antiochus and others associated then with the Academy in Athens, Philo held that it was perfectly acceptable to conclude inquiries into philosophical matters with definite assertions— provided that one did not hold that such conclusions had been definitely, once for all, established as the truth, and that one only assented to them as opinions, not knowledge.[15] On such a view, it would be perfectly acceptable for Arcesilaus, and Socrates too for that matter, as a hero and presumed precursor of the later Academics, to have investigated along with the pre-Socratics into the possibility of knowledge (for humans) and to have concluded that it was not possible and also for Arcesilaus to have considered what a mind should do so far as assenting to propositions goes, if it could not reach knowledge, and to have concluded that it would be disgraceful to assent.[16] Thus, on Philo's and Cicero's views, it would make perfectly good sense to present both Socrates and Arcesilaus in the way that Cicero does present them: they inquired into the possibility of knowledge and concluded that it was not possible, and then Arcesilaus inquired into what a mind ought to do if it could not attain knowledge and concluded that then it would be a disgrace to assent to anything. Arcesilaus would not be a skeptic (on my understanding, derived from Sextus, of what that means), but he would be a bona fide Academic nonetheless, in Cicero's and Philo's view of the Academic philosophy. Cicero and Philo, then, are interpreting the origin, as well as the character, of Arcesilaus's "skepticism" through the lens of their own philosophical views.

Hence, it is reasonable to doubt the accuracy of Cicero's account in the *Academica*. It may quite well derive from back-reading intended to lend authority to Philo's own version of Academic skepticism. It may be, for all we can know, that in some way or other Arcesilaus himself did refer to pre-Socratic antecedents for his own skeptical doubts about knowledge in seeking validation, beyond his devotion to Socrates and Socratic methods of philosophizing, for his own position—thus giving Philo and

---

[15] See *Ac.* 2.18, and Brittain, *Philo*, 11–17.

[16] That Philo and Cicero themselves thought you *could* reasonably and not disgracefully assent without knowledge does not affect this point, except insofar as it might permit Arcesilaus as presented by Cicero to evade the obvious objection (see note 10 above) that on Cicero's own account he must be (disgracefully) assenting to the claim that it is disgraceful to assent to anything. This could now be interpreted as the thought that it is disgraceful to assent to anything *as known*, whereas a weaker and more tentative assent is rationally and morally acceptable. Thus on Philo's and Cicero's own philosophical principles there is a way of interpreting what Cicero says about Arcesilaus so that Arcesilaus comes out not self-contradictory after all. (That does not mean, of course, that it is at all a reasonable interpretation of Arcesilaus' views or of how he arrived at them.)

Cicero some basis in tradition for their self-serving story.[17] What one must question is that Arcesilaus ever suggested that his own doubts about knowledge were derived even in part from pre-Socratic considerations about the limitations of our senses, the feebleness of our minds, truth being sunk in the abyss, and so on.

III

But why should anyone think that Socrates, whatever might be true of Arcesilaus, reached the conclusion that no one knows or can know any-thing, in whatever sense and with whatever force (or qualifications) he did reach it, by arguing from those pre-Socratic considerations? The sug-gestion is perfectly fantastic, and no one nowadays would give it any cre-dence at all.[18] If we formed our ideas about Socrates from Plato's and others' dialogues, as Cicero at *Ac.* 2.74 suggests Arcesilaus did, we would never think that Socrates held that nothing can be known on *that* sort of basis. Rather, we would think, his ground was his own experience of ex-amining others who claimed or were reputed to have knowledge, who however always failed to stand up satisfactorily to his questioning of them on the subjects on which they were supposed to have it. The al-legedly wise could not explain their allegedly knowledgeable views, when questioned for the grounds of those views and about their consequences, without contradicting themselves or else having to assert quite implausi-ble things—without, again, being able to argue away the appearance of implausibility. And these were failings that, Socrates assumed, knowledge itself, if anyone actually possessed it, would necessarily preclude. If we go by the Socratic dialogues, these experiences, not the limitations of the senses or the feebleness of the mind (in some other respect) or the truth

---

[17] Having arrived at his doubts about knowledge by some other route (see sect. III below) he may then have pointed out that even other distinguished philosophers before Socrates had expressed, in some way or other, "skeptical" doubts. See C. Brittain and J. Palmer's in-teresting but speculative account, "The New Academy's Appeals to the Presocratics."

[18] Richard Bett (basing himself on the passage of Aristocles of Messene's work *On Philoso-phy* preserved in Eusebius *Praeparatio Evangelica* 14.18.1–5, which presents itself as re-porting what Timon of Phlius said about him) has argued that Pyrrho came to the conclusion that we cannot know anything, from considerations about how things them-selves are, viz., "equally indifferent and unstable and indeterminate" (*Pyrrho: His An-tecedents and His Legacy,* chap. 1). This looks very close to the sort of thing Cicero reports as having convinced various pre-Socratics (and Socrates) of the same conclusion. If this is right, one might suspect that Philo simply transferred to Socrates, as Arcesilaus's model for his own "skepticism," this basis for the early "skepticism" of Pyrrho. Or, conceivably, if in-deed Philo had read, remembered, and took seriously as historical truth, what Plato says at *Phaedo* 96a ff. about Socrates' early interest in pre-Socratic investigations into nature, and

being buried in the abyss, were Socrates' grounds for thinking that no one knows anything, and perhaps that no one can know. You might think, then, that if, as Cicero in *Academica* II says he did, Arcesilaus took up his stance as a philosophical questioner by following Socrates, with some sort of conviction of the impossibility of knowledge, and aiming at inducing in his hearers suspension of judgment, he would have done so on this sort of basis, not the one Cicero in fact attributes to him in *Ac.* I.

Now in fact in other works, where he is not bound to Philo's account of Arcesilaus's philosophical views or practices, Cicero does suggest just such a view. I have in mind particularly a passage of *On Ends* II, and one of *On Oratory* III. As he begins his criticism of Epicurean ethics in *On Ends* II, Cicero explains why he is not going to proceed as Torquatus had done in book I. Torquatus expounded and defended Epicurus through a single, long philosophical set piece, which, as Cicero says, even in the Academy of his own day (viz., that of Philo) would be the accepted way to proceed (*On Ends* 2.2). Cicero however wishes to preserve some of the virtues of Socrates' (and Arcesilaus') procedures by pausing at each juncture to see what in his counterargument an Epicurean would or would not be prepared to grant, and to argue accordingly. Socrates' way, Cicero says, was to

> use thorough inquiry and questioning to draw out their opinions from those with whom he was conversing, so that he could say anything that he thought in response to the answers they gave. This way was not held to by his successors, but Arcesilaus revived it, and made it a practice that those who wished to be his pupils should not inquire from him but should themselves say what they thought; when they had done so, he would argue against them. But his pupils defended their own opinion so far as they could,

in particular in pre-Socratic theories about the causes of things, Philo might have thought he had some basis therein for attributing the allegedly Pyrrhonian and pre-Socratic sort of view about the possibility of knowledge to Socrates too. However, the *Phaedo* passage only attests Socrates' early interest in the natural philosophy of the pre-Socratics, not at all anything to do with their only tenuously related epistemological views. The suggestion that Socrates reached his "skeptical" views by this route remains fantastic, and totally unsupported by our evidence from Plato and elsewhere about Socrates.

Surprisingly, Schofield, "Academic Epistemology," does however give it credence. He accepts Cicero's testimony in *Ac.* I as accurate for Arcesilaus. But since that evidence presents Arcesilaus as having followed Socrates in accepting the pre-Socratic arguments for the conclusion that nothing is known (while having gone further than Socrates did, in that Arcesilaus held that it was also not *known* that nothing is known), Schofield presumably accepts at least that *Arcesilaus* accepted the same story for Socrates. In fact, as I show below, as soon as one notices, as Schofield does not, and takes seriously, the fact that Cicero's history of the skeptical Academy in *Ac.* is a report of what he had heard from Philo, it becomes quite plain that this aspect of it is a fabrication, of no evidentiary value whatever, both as a report on Arcesilaus and as one on Socrates.

whereas with the rest of the philosophers the person who has asked some-thing then keeps silent.[19]

In *de Or.* 3.67 Cicero reiterates that Arcesilaus made it his practice (a pe-culiarly Socratic one) not to put on show any opinions of his own but to argue against what each person had said that *they* thought.[20] But before that he adds the very important information, or suggestion, that Arcesi-laus was the first to "absorb from various books of Plato and the Socratic discourses this point above all others: there is nothing certain that can be grasped either by the senses or by the mind."[21]

Here Cicero presents Arcesilaus as having reached his conviction that no certain knowledge can be attained (in whatever way it was a convic-tion) through his reading of Plato's and others' Socratic dialogues.[22] On this view, it had nothing to do with pre-Socratic worries about our sen-sory limitations, etc., but rather was the cumulative effect of full expo-sure to Socrates' practice of elenctic dialectic. It is easy to see how this might have happened. Socrates is such a skillful and resourceful dialecti-cian that you could easily get the impression that no matter what opinion anyone put forward on any matter of ethical theory or any other theo-retical question, even if it *were* quite true, Socrates could find something quite persuasive and unsettling to ask on the other side, which moreover the other person would not be quick or good enough at argument to find any means of disarming—or, if he was, Socrates could always find some-thing else relevant and unsettling to ask that *would* stymie the interlocu-tor in his effort to explain and defend it adequately, even to his own satisfaction. In displaying his talent, however, Socrates also holds up a certain ideal of what knowledge is and what it accomplishes for anyone who has it. It consists in the ability to stand up successfully to the most searching examination of the Socratic kind that the best dialectician (Socrates, in fact) could dish out—so that your announced opinion sur-

---

[19] *Is enim percontando atque interrogando elicere solebat eorum opiniones quibuscum dis-serebat, ut ad ea quae ii respondissent si quid videretur diceret. qui mos cum a posterioribus non esset retentus, Arcesilas eum revocavit instituitque ut ii qui se audire vellent non de se quaererent sed ipsi dicerent quid sentirent; quod cum dixissent, ille contra. sed eum qui au-diebant quoad poterant defendebant sententiam suam; apud ceteros autem philosophos qui quaesivit aliquid tacet.*

[20] See also *de Or.* 3.80; *Nature of the Gods* 1.11; *On Laws* 1.39.

[21] *Arcesilas primum . . . ex variis Platonis libris sermonibusque Socraticis hoc maxime ar-ripuit, nihil esse certi quod aut sensibus aut animo percipi possit.*

[22] I do not mean to suggest here that Arcesilaus made any distinction (of the sort that mod-ern scholars do) between "Socratic" dialogues of Plato (the "early" ones) and the rest (or, at any rate, the rest in which Socrates is the principal speaker). Still, it is reasonable to in-terpret Cicero in these passages as presumably having in mind principally such Platonic works as *Apology, Protagoras, Euthyphro, Laches, Charmides,* etc.

vives ultimately unscathed. If that is what knowledge really is, then what we see displayed in the Socratic discourses of Plato and others leaves the reader with a vivid and persuasive impression that no one has it, even that no mere human could possibly get it, so demanding are its standards.[23]

Now, if this is how Arcesilaus was affected by his reading of the Socratic discourses, then of course he did not arrive at a conviction of the impossibility of knowledge on the basis of any arguments at all to such a conclusion. After all, Socrates himself nowhere argues at all for any such conclusion.[24] Arcesilaus just got a deep foreboding and suspicion that no one has ever turned up, or will ever, who can pass Socrates' test: certainly not Socrates, as presented in the dialogues. Through his profession of ignorance, Socrates denies having the ability himself to stand up to the sort of searching examination on any question that he so expertly subjected others to. So it would be quite wrong to say that Arcesilaus learned or drew from the discourses any philosophical doctrine or opinion to that effect. Here it is important to recall the other main claim that Cicero makes in the passages from *On Ends* and *On Oratory* that we are examining. This is that Arcesilaus never taught, never argued for, anything at all on his own behalf: like Socrates, he listened to others and questioned

---

[23] Here we need to pay close attention to Socrates' exegesis of the poem of Simonides in the *Protagoras*. There Socrates argues (344b–c; cf. 341e) that when Simonides said that "God alone can have this privilege," viz., that of *being* good, he meant that the "best" human being there can be is one who at most sometimes "becomes" good by acting the way a being that *is* good would act (by default, this being would have to be a god), whereas inevitably such a one, like everyone else, will thereafter sometimes fail to do what is morally required and so, later, "become" bad again. It seems clear that this is just another case, of which there are several, where in interpreting the poem the character Socrates insinuates views of his own. Further, he himself has just before insisted (342a–343b) that the Dorians in general and the Spartans in particular were the greatest repository of ancient wisdom, and that this wisdom was in fact what lay behind their valorous and more generally all their virtuous actions. Socrates' moral, then, is that what the gods have, which makes them *be* good is wisdom (i.e., knowledge); that wisdom is denied to human beings, who even at their best (namely, according to Socrates' account, the Spartans) only can "become" good from time to time, by somehow or other doing good actions, i.e., the acts that wisdom, if you had it, would lead you to perform.

[24] The *Protagoras* passage cited in the previous note is perhaps the closest Socrates comes to arguing for this thesis. In reading that passage, one must bear in mind that if "wisdom" is unattainable except by a god, as Socrates proposes and more or less argues there, it follows that (Socratic) knowledge is also unattainable, since he treats those as the same thing. However, by formally attributing these views only to Simonides, Socrates preserves his stance of one who inquires only, and does not reach conclusions which he is then prepared and obligated to defend, if pressed. So Socrates does not put forward these views as his own philosophical conclusions, conclusions reached through philosophical argumentation, or ones that he is obligated to defend by argument if they are challenged.

them or their opinions, exclusively, and never entered the philosophical arena on the answerer's side on *any* point.[25] This means that in whatever way Arcesilaus did hold that knowledge is never attainable by human beings, this is nothing he would ever conceivably have enunciated as an opinion of his own. Indeed, if some pupil or opponent turned up who was clever enough to begin his conversation with Arcesilaus by announcing: "You know, I am convinced that no human being has ever known anything for certain," fully prepared to back this up with various reasons for so thinking—and surely that ploy must have occurred to *someone* during all the years that Arcesilaus was before the public—Arcesilaus would surely have argued against it. Cicero says that Arcesilaus always argued against *any* opinion that was announced to him. And it is not in the least difficult to think up lots of counterarguments he might have rolled out. After all, even in *Ac.* 1.44–46 Cicero says Arcesilaus did not think he *knew* it to be true that no one knew anything. Thus the view that no one knows or can know anything is with Arcesilaus a sort of heuristic

---

[25] If Cicero is right about this, and Arcesilaus never argued for, or presented as something that he would even consider arguing for, either his view that knowledge is not attainable by human beings or his view (see below) that it was a disgrace to assent to any proposition in the absence of knowledge, or indeed any other proposition, then G. Striker must be right in her analysis of Arcesilaus's "argumentative strategies" as always involving "dialectical" argument only. In philosophical argument he never reached conclusions to which he was himself committed on the basis of any commitment to the premises he used to reach them. (See her "Skeptical Strategies.") Striker does not refer to these passages of Cicero in support of her interpretation, so the success of her direct and independent account of Arcesilaus's reported arguments against the Stoics on how the wise man is rationally obligated to suspend on all questions (Cic. *Ac.* 2.77, Sextus Empiricus *M.* 7.155–57) and on how it is possible for a person to act even without assenting to anything (Sextus *M.* 7.158) can serve as strong confirmation of the correctness of Cicero's view (pp. 97, 100-101, respectively, in the reprint). In his account of Arcesilaus's views, Schofield pays no heed to these passages of Cicero (he does not refer at all to the relevant part of *de Or.* 3.67, and refers to *On Ends* 2.2 and *Nature of the Gods* 1.11 only in a grudging footnote, 325 n. 8). He also does not accept Striker's analysis of these Arcesilean arguments as wholly dialectical (but why not?—unfortunately the format of the *Cambridge History* does not allow authors to go into such details). As a result, Schofield gives a weakly defended and (in the light of *all* the evidence) entirely unacceptable account of Arcesilaus, as having been committed to accepting on his own behalf the proposition that the wise man will refuse assent to everything (326), and apparently also the proposition that one can act even without assenting to anything (333–34; Schofield's account of this argument is too filled with qualifications to allow the reader to be sure what his final position on this second "commitment" is)—as well as the proposition that no one knows anything (327). As I argue below, there *is* in fact a way that Arcesilaus is committed to the righteousness of suspension (but not to unknowability), but that way turns on implications of Arcesilaus's Socraticism, of which Schofield, like Striker, seems oblivious. So, ironically, Schofield's conclusions are half-right—not entirely mistaken, as you would have to conclude if you simply followed his own analysis and the grounds he actually gives in support of it.

principle, governing his practice, but laying no claim of its own to objec-tive truth. It stands inaccessible to critical evaluation because Arcesilaus never asserted it, and would indeed at any time have argued against it if anyone else had asserted it to him.

If, then, we remove from Cicero's account in the *Academica* all sugges-tion that Arcesilaus's (and Socrates') attitude to the unattainability of knowledge amounted to an opinion based on reasoned argument of any sort, it might begin to seem that, after all, Arcesilaus did deserve the title of skeptic—meaning by this term, an inquirer who keeps on inquiring and never reaches any conclusions *in* or *to* his inquiries. Cicero says in the *Academica* that Arcesilaus spent all his philosophical time presenting equally weighty considerations on the opposed side of any question, so as to induce suspension in his interlocutor. Is that not, essentially, to say, now that we have made that removal, that Arcesilaus constantly inquired into various questions on which others had opinions, always reaching a balance of reasons on both sides, and as a result suspending his own thought, while encouraging others to do the same? Does that not amount to inquiring and keeping on inquiring, without ever reaching any conclu-sion of whatever sort, on any question? So Arcesilaus would be a skeptic, according to Sextus's understanding of what being a skeptic means.

IV

Before we can accept that verdict we must attend to the second step in Cicero's argument in the *Academica*. Cicero argues that, from the premise that knowledge is unattainable by human beings, Arcesilaus used the further premise that it would be a great disgrace to assent to any proposition in the absence of knowledge of its truth to conclude that one ought never assent to anything. Where did this further premise come from? Cicero does not say. But now that we see the source of his first premise (the unattainability of knowledge), it should strike us that the same source, his reading of the Socratic discourses, must have provided him with the second as well. I mentioned above that in those discourses Socrates puts forward a certain ideal of knowledge. But no one who reads them could fail to see that Socrates also endorses this ideal, in that he passionately aspires to achieve knowledge, believes that human beings can only live their lives really well if they possess it, and holds that, by questioning and refuting others in reasoned argument, he comes progres-sively closer to that goal—even if he has not yet reached it, and presum-ably never will. His refusal to announce anything as his own opinion is plausibly thought to reflect his feeling that to do that is to betray your commitment to this goal and to settle for something less than knowledge as your guide in life—mere opinion. Right-thinking, morally serious persons will withhold assent until they have attained knowledge—knowledge being understood in Socrates' ideal way as the ability to undergo with success the most strenuous, most extended examination of whatever it is that you have asserted as your view. In short, Socrates shows himself to be a committed devotee of the life led according to reason: he withholds assent because reason itself demands him to withhold.

If these ideas of Socrates are the source of Arcesilaus's second premise, then we have to attribute to Arcesilaus a second idea derived from his devoted attention to Socratic discourses, besides the suspicion that knowledge is unattainable by human beings. Inspired by Socrates' fervor for reason's ideal of knowledge, he too accepts that reason should be our guide in life, and its perfection in knowledge our goal. When he always suspends, and thinks one *ought* to suspend, and encourages others to suspend, because considerations on the two sides of a given question are equally weighty, he thinks of himself simply as following reason where it leads. *It* leads to suspension, so *he* suspends—because reason says one *ought* to—and that is why he encourages others to do the same. It is, he thinks, a very great disgrace to assent without knowledge, because he follows Socrates' fervent example of a life devoted to reason. Socrates refused to assent to anything, that is to put anything forward as his own view, because he thought you should not do that unless you could back it up by the ability to withstand the most resourceful and unrelenting Socratic examination of it. And he had no assurance at all that *he* could withstand that test on any matter whatsoever. What, then, is the status in Arcesilaus's thought of this second idea—that you should never assent except with knowledge?[26]

---

[26] It is worth emphasizing that for Arcesilaus the ban on assent without knowledge has much stronger implications than the similar-sounding ban contained in Stoic doctrine about wise people. For the Stoics, wise persons' minds are so disposed that they will never assent except to an (allegedly) "cognitive impression" (καταληπτικὴ φαντασία), i.e., to one that is true and could not be false; "weak" assents, assents to impressions other than cognitive ones, yield only "opinions," and the wise never have any mere opinions. Whenever they do assent, the result is a "cognitive grasp" (κατάληψις) of the fact that is its content or object. According to a not unreasonable conception of knowledge, such a "grasp" would actually amount to knowledge; on such a view, the Stoics would be restricting the wise person's assents to impressions that when assented to do yield knowledge. However, in fact the Stoics (as part of their own Socratic heritage) agree with Arcesilaus in reserving the name "knowledge" (ἐπιστήμη) for a mental state that achieves the very demanding Socratic ideal I have been discussing: e.g., Sextus tells us that for the Stoics "knowledge is a cognitive grasp that is secure and firm and unalterable by (further) reasoning" (*Against the Theoreticians*, M 7.151). Thus when they permit and indeed insist on the propriety of assents to (mere) cognitive impressions, yielding true, 100 percent reliable "grasps" that, however, might or might not be thus "irreversible," they are permitting assents that might very well not con-

I suggested that the first idea is best regarded as a sort of heuristic principle, and certainly not a philosophical opinion for which Arcesilaus would ever agree to argue (or to accept examination on before he acted upon it). Likewise, it might seem, with this second one. It is not something which Arcesilaus arrived at as the conclusion of any arguments; he came to it through his fascination with Socratic discourses and by admiring Socrates and accepting him as his model. If some pupil or clever but malicious opponent came to him and announced, "It is my opinion that no one should ever assent to anything without being in the position to explain and defend his view successfully in the face of a Socratic examination—to do so would be the greatest disgrace for any rational being," Arcesilaus would surely argue on the other side, as he always did, seeking to balance whatever reasons the pupil or opponent could muster in support of their view with equally weighty ones against it. And again, it would not be difficult to think up arguments that Arcesilaus could roll out for this purpose. So Arcesilaus does not put this forward as a philosophical view of his own, for which he has to or intends to claim that there are good and sufficient, completely irreversible arguments to support it. Thus it might seem that it is just an idea (an inspiring one) that he has and follows in doing philosophy, as he just has the suspicion that no one knows anything or, it would seem, ever could—but does not *maintain* that that is so. If so, then, it continues to look as if Arcesilaus can legitimately be counted a skeptic in Sextus Empiricus's usage of that term: on any and all questions of philosophy he is an inquirer who keeps on inquiring and never reaches a conclusion in which he assents in any way on any side of those questions. Neither as to the nonexistence of knowledge nor as to the disgrace involved in assenting without it does Arcesilaus make any philosophical claim.

---

stitute knowledge. Cicero tells us (and all our other sources are in agreement with this, or anyhow in no way contradict it) that "it was against Zeno that Arcesilaus began his whole struggle" in (as Schofield puts it) "going skeptical" (*Ac.* 1.44). In the light of Arcesilaus's Socraticism as I explain it here, it seems right to understand his all-out attack on the very existence of cognitive impressions and cognitive grasps as motivated by a wish to defend the full-strength Socratic ideal. If there *are* no cognitive impressions then there can be no temptation (of the sort Zeno gave in to) to think that any lower standard for assent can be accepted than the original Socratic one—to assent only to propositions that are irreversible, because you could give a full and successful dialectical account of them. What must have outraged and offended Arcesilaus most in Zeno's proposals was the very idea that one could responsibly and respectably assent on the basis of anything less than full Socratic knowledge. In any event, when we read accounts in Cicero, or Sextus, or Plutarch, of Arcesilaus's insistence, in arguing against Stoics, that *on Stoic principles* one must never assent but must always suspend, it will follow a fortiori that on his own much stronger principles one must do the same. (Of course, as I am arguing, with Arcesilaus, this insistence is no philosophical doctrine, as it would be with Zeno, for which one might give philosophical arguments.)

But this second view functions for Arcesilaus as more than the mere suspicion that the first one is. He does not just have the idea (or suspicion) that when you do not know you should not assent; if Cicero's report is right he thinks it is a disgrace (indeed the greatest disgrace) to do that. So he is committed to a certain idea and ideal of reason—Socrates'—to violate which, he thinks, would be something really awful. In fact, his commitment to follow reason where it leads seems to be absolute, as it was with Socrates: he will suspend for just so long as reason does demand it (because there are equally weighty considerations on both sides of the question), but as soon as someone comes along to show, or he himself sees, that they are not equally weighty, and that every consideration on one side can be adequately dealt with and no longer stands against the opposed conclusion, he will follow reason in declaring that that is how things actually do stand. (He will then be in a position to *know* it, so he won't violate his principle about not assenting except with knowledge). In fact, he only suspends because reason, to which he adheres, keeps on indicating, inquiry after inquiry, that that is what he ought to do. And, it would seem, he recommends suspension to others on the same ground—as what reason, which should be the supreme guide in all our lives, tells them they ought to do.[27] The existence, and apparent depth, of this Socratic commitment to reason and to following wherever it leads must be taken into account when answering my guiding question: whether Arcesilaus should be counted a skeptic at all, in Sextus's sense of that term. This commitment is also a crucial distinguishing feature of Arcesilaus's philosophy as compared with Sextus's Pyrrhonism.

V

In fact, Sextus's comments on Arcesilaus's philosophy support in a very precise way the interpretation that I have been developing. As is well known, at the very beginning of the *Pyrrhonian Sketches,* Sextus decisively separates the "Academic" philosophy from any skeptical one, on the ground that the Academics have declared, after investigating philosophical questions for some time, that the answers to them are not graspable (by us). They have, in other words, brought their inquiries to a definite conclusion, rather than keeping them ongoing and open, as skeptics do. Although here the simple term "Academic" would surely be taken by any reader to include all the Academics, beginning with Arcesi-

---

[27] Or does he? Cicero cagily suggests in *Ac.* 1.45 that he thought it would simply be "easier" for people to suspend if they thought the considerations on each side were equally balanced—not that they would then be led by reason or reasoning to do so.

laus and going on down at least to Philo, it is noteworthy, though so far as I know scholars have not taken special notice of this, that in indicating whom he has in mind Sextus says simply "Clitomachus and Carneades and other [not: *the* other] Academics" (οἱ περὶ Κλειτόμαχον καὶ Καρνεάδην καὶ ἄλλοι Ἀκαδημάϊκοι), thus leaving open the question whether, in his opinion, this classification applies in fact to Arcesilaus and other Academics before Carneades. The possibility that it does not is confirmed when we read his treatment later in book I, first of Carneades' philosophy, and then of Arcesilaus's. The first thing he says (1.226) about what he calls the "new" Academy (that of Carneades and Clitomachus) is that, unlike the skeptics, its adherents firmly state as an established fact (διαβεβαιοῦνται) that all things are ungraspable. With Arcesilaus (the "middle" Academy, cf. 1.220), however, he says no such thing; indeed, the *first* thing he says (1.232) is that Arcesilaus does very much seem to have things in common with Pyrrhonian ways of arguing (πάνυ μοι δοκεῖ τοῖς Πυρρωνείοις κοινωνεῖν λόγοις). In fact, he adds, Arcesilaus does not make *any* assertions, but "suspends about everything," and even makes "the ultimate end" of his philosophizing to be suspension. This last point aligns Arcesilaus closely with what Sextus himself has said (1.25) about the Pyrrhonist's ultimate end.[28] Thus Sextus takes Arcesilaus,

[28] Sextus says the "end" for skeptics is "unperturbedness" (ἀταραξία)—not, as he reports for Arcesilaus, suspension. But he also says that on suspension, unperturbedness follows like a shadow on its body. David Sedley, "The Motivation of Greek Skepticism," in *The Skeptical Tradition*, ed. M. Burnyeat, 11–14, draws on Sextus's remark about Arcesilaus's "ultimate end" in weaving his account of the importance of the ideal of unperturbedness (through suspension) to Greek skepticism, allegedly including Arcesilaus. However, as I just noted, Sextus explicitly says that Arcesilaus made suspension itself, not unperturbedness, the "ultimate end." The Pyrrhoneans are firmly decided that unperturbedness is the end, and we have no evidence at all that Arcesilaus might have agreed—as if he was hinting that unperturbedness is the end while saying only that suspension is. I agree with Striker, "On the Difference," 148 n. 11, that for a Socratic the importance of not presuming to have knowledge when one does not have it is sufficient motivation for making suspension the ultimate end of one's philosophy (if one strongly suspects that no one can attain knowledge). In fact, it is quite easy to see how a report like Cicero's in *Ac.* 1.44–45, if corrected in the way I have corrected it in sect. IV above, could lead a later figure like Sextus to conclude that, in fact, the avoidance of assent, i.e., suspension, was the ultimate goal of all Arcesilaus's efforts in philosophy, both for himself and his interlocutors—not unperturbedness. I also agree with Sedley that Sextus's basis for attributing suspension to Arcesilaus as an ultimate end was not the mere fact (if this was a fact—we have no indication of any such thing) that somewhere or other in the reports of Arcesilaus's arguments he was found to have argued (perhaps from Stoic assumptions about ends; see Sedley, "Motivation of Greek Skepticism," 13) that suspension *is* the end. Suspension as the end was a further expression of his deep Socraticism. He did not need to come upon it through dialectical encounters with Stoics, and surely he did not do so: he got it from reading and reflecting on Plato's and other Socratic discourses.

as I have argued Arcesilaus in fact did, not to have adopted any philosophical views (views for which you are obliged, and prepared, to argue—views that you roundly assert as true, as things you believe), not even the views that nothing can be known or that it is a disgrace to assent when you do not know. As to unknowability, Sextus does not indicate how it is that he thinks (as presumably he does think) that Arcesilaus nonetheless maintains it. But it is noteworthy that he says that *Carneades* says that all things are nongraspable in a way that differs from the way skeptics say the same thing (1.226). So perhaps Sextus thinks Arcesilaus says all things are nongraspable in just the same way as Pyrrhonian skeptics do (i.e., as things they are inclined to think, that they have the impression may well be true, see 1.200). If so, I think Sextus has Arcesilaus exactly right on this point.

Where Arcesilaus differs from the Pyrrhoneans, however, according to Sextus, is in the *way* he suspended—the thoughts with which he suspended, and the motivations he had for doing so.[29] According to Sextus, Arcesilaus said that each act of suspension is really good in the nature of things, and each act of assent is really bad in the nature of things (1.233). For Pyrrhoneans, however, suspensions and assents are accepted as good and bad (things that you ought and ought not to do), respectively, only insofar as they appear that way to themselves (κατὰ τὸ φαινόμενον ἡμῖν)—Pyrrhoneans do not say firmly, as a matter of established fact (διαβεβαιωτικῶς), as Arcesilaus does, that suspensions are good and assents bad; they only have some impression of that sort. Now, as I will show, for this too we can find a solid basis in Arcesilaus's Socraticism as I have interpreted it. So, if my interpretation is correct, Sextus has Arcesilaus exactly right on this point too.

On my account, Arcesilaus is a Socratic in that like Socrates he is passionately devoted to reason; reason, he thinks, is our highest faculty, the one and only thing in us with which we should in the strongest and deepest sense identify ourselves.[30] This is not a philosophical doctrine for

---

[29] I leave aside the further and final point in Sextus's account of Arcesilaus (1.234), which in any event he introduces cautiously ("if we should trust the things that are said about him"; in the rest of his account he stands personally behind what he says, reporting straight out that Arcesilaus said or did this or that). This is that really Arcesilaus was a Platonic dogmatist all along, who merely used his method of arguing on the other side of his pupils' opinions in order to test their mettle, and if they seemed philosophically adept and capable enough, then he would drop the pretense and start teaching them the dogmas of Plato. Lucullus in Cicero, *Ac.* 2.60, makes what seems to be the same bizarre suggestion. See the same idea in Anonymous, *Comm. on Plato's Theaetetus* 54.14; Numenius *apud* Eusebius, *Praep. Evan.* 14.6.6; and Augustine, *Against the Academics* 3.38.

[30] This seems to me a much more central and important aspect of Arcesilaus's indebtedness to, and revival of, Socratic thought than (what is uniformly appealed to by scholars) his

Arcesilaus, in that he will never announce it as his opinion, and he does not hold it in a way that places a burden on him to defend it with arguments of his own or with rebuttals against its denial by anyone. Nonetheless this is a very deep conviction of his. His deep identification with reason is the ground for his thinking it the extreme of turpitude to assent when we don't have actual Socratic knowledge—to do so would abuse the very essence of our being. Hence it is a morally good act of the highest order not to assent but to suspend, just so long as we do *not* have that knowledge—suspending preserves and strengthens our very being. It is with that thought, and out of that motivation, that Arcesilaus suspends whenever he does, and stays away from assent. And, probably, that is why he recommends the same practice to others. In other words, his suspensions are themselves acts of reason, expressions of his passionate acceptance of reason as a guide to life and of reason's inherent standards, one of which (he thinks) is expressed in the principle that one should always suspend when one does not actually *know*. So, he supports suspension, as Sextus says he does, διαβεβαιωτικῶς—firmly, assertively, as something one *really* ought to do.

For Sextus, as he implies in distinguishing the Pyrrhonean's suspensions from the Arcesilean's, this is anathema. There is not room here to explain fully why that should be so for him. Briefly, however: almost the very goal of skepticism, for the Sextan Pyrrhonist, is to rid us totally of any such ideal, of the thought that reason, as a critical faculty with standards for judging truth and falsehood, and with self-recommending procedures for deciding what to think and what to do, has any authority whatsoever for our thought or for any of our actions. Getting rid of that ideal is the essential—both necessary and sufficient—condition for living an unperturbed life. For him, the fully fledged skeptic regularly suspends and thus lives an unperturbed life, simply by going by how things appear to him, not by following reason at all.[31] Such a person keeps on suspending each

---

adoption of Socrates' method of elenctic cross-questioning as the basis for his own philosophizing.

[31] I speak advisedly here only of the fully fledged Pyrrhonian skeptic: as Sextus explains (*PH* 1.12, 1.26 ff.), the skeptic starts out in philosophy with a committed belief in the power and value of reason as a faculty for critically deciding what to believe and how to act. His hope is to use rational scrutiny to discover what is true and what is false, so that he can then live his life on the basis of what reason decides. Hence, when during that phase he suspends (as, according to Sextus, he inevitably must—so equally balanced are considerations on both sides of all questions), those suspensions are undertaken through reason itself, because reason and its standards dictate them. It is only once he has unexpectedly found that unperturbedness follows on his regular and constant reason-directed suspensions, and he has formed the habit of expecting and welcoming suspension when he next inquires into something, that he is what I call a fully fledged skeptic. From then on he has (lightly, easily, unperturbedly) renounced reason and does not follow it any longer, even in his acts of

time, in recognition, to be sure, of the fact that critical reason, if it were to be followed, would demand this: after all, he suspends always after applying critical standards in evaluating the evidence on both sides, and so, after reaching the conclusion that, as it appears to him on that occasion, critical reason is incapable of deciding the question one way or the other. But he does not suspend *because* reason, if followed fully and correctly, does demand this. His suspensions are not faithful, devoted *acts* of critical reason. He suspends only (by now) because, happily, that is what he feels like doing.

So we can conclude that Arcesilaus does indeed deserve the title of skeptic, meaning by that a philosopher who inquires, and keeps on inquiring, into philosophical questions, but without ever reaching a reasoned conclusion of any sort on any of them. Every time he inquires into anything, he suspends. However, there is a very great difference between the skepticism of Arcesilaus and that of Sextus, precisely in regard to the role of reason in the acts of suspension that are common to the two. Both promote a life without assent, a life that renounces the typical Greek philosopher's ideal of knowledge as the basis for a well-lived human life. Arcesilaus, like Sextus, lives without knowledge and does so with satisfaction. As David Sedley has said, "What above all characterizes Hellenistic skepticism is . . . its abandonment of [the] desire [for knowledge]—its radical conviction that to suspend assent and to resign oneself to ignorance is not a bleak expedient but, on the contrary, a highly desirable intellectual achievement."[32] But for Arcesilaus this stems from a deep and abiding commitment to another ideal, one shared not with Sextus but rather with the mainstream of Greek philosophy—that of reason itself as our guide. Arcesilaus is satisfied, and feels fulfilled, by always suspending, just because reason, his guide, keeps on telling him to suspend. Sextus suspends because in his life he follows not reason but appearances—the way things strike him. So Arcesilaus suspends, while thinking διαβεβαιωτικῶς that suspension is good (that is the source of his self-satisfaction), while Sextus suspends expressing thereby no opinion at all about whether what he is doing is good or bad. *He* claims self-satisfaction from the fact that he has no such opinion, but only suspends because that is what he feels is appropriate, given his experiences. That difference seems to me more fundamental than anything the two skeptics have in common. So it is a mistake, I think, to speak of "ancient skepticism" as a single thing—as if

---

suspension. His suspensions from then on simply express how things appear to him. It then just keeps on appearing to him that suspension is the thing to do in the face of the balance of reasons, and he suspends following that appearance.

[32] "Motivation of Greek Skepticism," 10.

Pyrrhonian skepticism was in all major ways simply a revival and continuation of Academic skepticism under another name. Arcesilaus's skepticism is the expression of his Socratic commitment to living according to reason as our life's guide; Sextus's is the expression of a complete renunciation of reason altogether.

NATURE

CHAPTER 5

ARISTOTLE ON NATURAL TELEOLOGY

A RISTOTLE believed that many (not, of course, all) natural events and facts need to be explained by reference to natural goals. He understands by a goal (οὗ ἕνεκα), whether natural or not, something good (from some point of view) that something else causes or makes possible, where this other thing exists or happens (at least in part) because of that good.[1] So in holding that some natural events and facts have to be explained by reference to natural goals, he is holding that some things exist or happen in the course of nature because of some good that they do or make possible. Thus he holds that living things have many of the organic and other parts that they have because of the good it does them, so that these parts exist, and are formed, for the sake of the animal or plant itself whose good they subserve. To explain why they have them, and why as they are being formed they come to have them, one must refer to the whole animal or plant who needs them as the goal for which they exist. Aristotle gives or suggests, at one place or another, several arguments in favor of this thesis. Some of these press the analogy between artistic activity, which is admittedly goal-directed, and natural processes, thus extending explanation by appeal to goals from human action to nonhuman, even nonanimal nature. But these are not very good arguments and there are reasons for thinking that Aristotle did not think his view rested primarily on them.[2] So I will leave these arguments aside and

---

[1] See *Ph.* II 2, 194a32–3, II 3, 195a23–5, *Pol.* I 2, 1252b34–5, *EE* I 8, 1218b9–11, and the many passages where Aristotle routinely explicates "that for the sake of which" by linking it with the good, the fine, the better, etc. (e.g., *Metaph.* I 3, 983a31–2, *PA* I 1, 639b19–20). That the concept of a goal is the concept of something good is a view Aristotle inherited from Plato's *Phaedo* (cf., e.g., 97c6–d3, e1–4, 98a6–b3, 99a7–c7); unless one bears the connection between goal and good clearly in mind one will fail to understand much that Aristotle says about natural teleology and many applications he makes of it (see further n. 11 below). Andrew Woodfield (*Teleology,* 205–6), correctly notes that according to Aristotle all teleological explanations are claims that something happened *because it is good,* and makes this theme central to his own unifying account of teleological description.

[2] In *Ph.* II 8 the argument for natural teleology that Aristotle places first makes no appeal to the analogy between art and nature (198b32–199a8; see below, p. 116 ff.). Only then does he add, for good measure, the three arguments (199a8–15, 15–20, 20–30) which do develop this analogy. As early as Philoponus one can find cogent objections to Aristotle's

concentrate on two lines of thought that argue directly from considerations of physical theory to the conclusion that there are goals in nature. I first sketch Aristotle's theory that living things have two natures, a material and a formal nature, and explain how his belief in the goal-directedness of nature derives from this theory. Then I turn to consider his reasons for the doctrine that living things do have these two different natures, with its teleological implications.

I

Natural substances—and, in particular, living things—have, according to Aristotle, two natures, a formal nature and a material nature (*Physics* II 1, 193a28–31). A thing's nature is declared to be whatever, internal to it, is the source of (a) the changes it undergoes, under various circumstances, and (b) the ways it remains the same despite changing conditions (*Ph.* 192b13–14, 20–3). So according to Aristotle living things have within them two different such sources of change and/or continuity. Some of a living thing's behavior is due to the *matter* it is made of, but some is not due to that at all, but to its being the actual thing it is—a human being, or an elm tree, or whatever—that is, to its form. Thus that a certain thing has and maintains a certain size, shape, texture, etc., and grows and drops leaves of a certain character at certain times of the year, etc.—all this is due to its being, say, an apple tree. On the other hand, that any part of it yields to an axe or a saw and divides, ignites at a certain temperature and produces ashes of a certain kind and consistency, that it falls down under certain conditions, etc.—all this due to its being made of wood of a certain kind and consistency. Of course, it does not do or undergo any of these things entirely of its own accord; if there is no water and no sunlight it will not grow or maintain itself, if no fire is applied to it it will not turn to ashes. To account for its behavior one has to refer to things outside as well, and Aristotle is not denying this; but what it does when these outside things act upon it is determined also by what *it* is, and Aristotle holds that the contribution that the thing itself makes is to be traced not to one but to two sources, its matter (the particular wood it is made of) and its form (the particular kind of tree it is). It is the nature of that kind of wood to be hard but not too hard to cut with an axe, to burn in that kind of way, in the conditions specified, with just those results,

---

use of the analogy in at least the first two of these arguments (*CAG* XVI, 309.9–310.15 and 310.23–9). And since the first and most extensive argument Aristotle gives in this chapter is entirely independent of the art–nature analogy, one must reject the suggestion that is sometimes made that this analogy is central and fundamental to Aristotelian natural teleology.

and so on; and it is the nature of that kind of tree to have and maintain a certain size and shape, and grow leaves and fruit of just that kind, under normal favorable conditions.

Since, then, there actually exist in the world these two distinct kinds of natures, two kinds of source in natural things of their behaviors, explanation in the study of nature, if it is to be true to the facts, must correspondingly take place at two levels: the level of matter and its properties, and the level of form, that is, the level of the natural kinds and their properties. It is a fundamental principle of Aristotle's theory of nature that explanations of these two sorts are both of them basic to the understanding of natural phenomena generally, and equally so—they cannot be dispensed with in favor of anything more basic than they, nor can either be discarded in favor of the other. In particular, explanation by reference to form is not in the final analysis eliminable in favor of explanation by reference merely to matter. I will return to this point in the next section, once I have brought into my account the other two Aristotelian "causes" or bases for explaining things—the final cause (or end or goal) of something and the moving cause (or thing that set in motion the events leading up to it).[3] How does Aristotle connect these further two types of explanation with the two so far considered?

Let us begin with the "final" cause. Aristotle regularly identifies formal and final causes where natural substances are concerned (e.g., *Ph.* II 7, 198a25–6; *de An.* II 4, 415b10–12; *GA* I 1, 715a4–6, 8–9). In doing so, he has, I think, two points in mind. Consider first the process of formation by which a seed is developed into a mature living thing. If one inquires why at a certain stage in its growth the trunk divides in a certain way, the answer may be that what we have to deal with is an apple tree—if it had been a different sort of tree this division would not have taken place. This division occurs then because mature apple trees have a certain structure and shape, and this growing thing, being an apple tree, is taking on that shape and structure. And since each thing's nature, its mature natural condition, is a good for it, reference to the form here is reference

---

[3] I use the term "cause" here and in what immediately follows simply as conventional translation for Aristotle's αἰτία. I do not mean to prejudge thereby the question whether the explanations provided by reference to such "causes" are to be interpreted as causal explanations, rather than explanations of some other sort. In particular, in speaking of the irreducibility of formal and final "causes" to material and moving "causes" I want to leave open the question whether Aristotle means to be saying (a) that causal explanations (explanations by appeal to matter and motion) are not enough, and another sort of explanation is required as well (explanation by appeal to forms and natural outcomes), or (b) that in giving causal explanations of what happens in nature explanations by appeal to matter and motion do not suffice, and explanation by appeal to forms and outcomes is sometimes necessary as well. I return to this below, pp. 122–3.

also to the goal of the process of growth by relation to which, therefore, it is understood. Because the formal nature which the shoot has (that of an apple tree) is something it does not yet have fully, explaining what happens at such a stage by saying that it is an *apple* tree is at the same time to invoke a goal—the form of a natural kind is always defined by reference to the mature member of the species, and here that form is responsible for what happens only insofar as it is in prospect. Thus explanation by a thing's form is also explanation by its goal wherever one is attempting to account for some fact about the process whereby an immature or embryonic thing belonging to a certain species turns into a mature member of the kind. But formal explanation is also explanation by a goal even in the case where what one is explaining is the characteristic behavior of a mature specimen. The form of any natural living kind consists of an interlocking and mutually supportive set of capacities, so that to explain the exercise of any one of these capacities by reference to the form is to link it to the further exercise of some other capacity for which it provides a supporting condition. Thus when Aristotle says a tree puts out leaves of a certain sort because it is an apple tree this explanation will be expressed more fully by saying it does this in order to protect the fruit which, because it is an apple tree, will grow beneath the leaves. The reference to the tree's nature thus refers implicitly to a whole connected pattern of behaviors on its part, each one of which occurs in order to make possible later ones. Explanation by the formal cause thus involves explanation by final cause both in the formation and in the behavior of mature plant and animal specimens. The form that is appealed to in such explanations always functions partly as goal.

Final and formal explanation are, then, for Aristotle very closely linked, and jointly contrasted with explanation by the properties of matter. Where does the remaining kind of cause, the moving cause, stand in this contrast? Sometimes Aristotle connects the moving cause with the formal and final causes, but sometimes (particularly in the biological works) he associates it rather with the material. When he says at *Physics* II 7, 198a24–5, for example, that the formal, final, and moving causes often coincide he means that the immediate source of the motions that lead eventually to the existence of a living thing of a certain kind is always another living thing of precisely the same kind; and, furthermore, it is *qua* being a thing of that kind that the parent is the source of these particular motions. "A human being generates a human being," for example (*Ph.* 198a26–7). Thus where what you are explaining is the generation of a whole, fully formed living creature, the source of the motions must be a living creature of the same kind. But (and this is the level at which in the biological works he mostly invokes the moving cause) when one is explaining something that happens in the course of the formation of such a creature, then the moving cause will often be assigned not on the side of form and goal but on that of matter. Thus in a well-known passage of the *Generation of Animals* Aristotle says that "An eye is for some end, but a blue one is not . . . we must take it that these things [viz., eye color and other such features that serve no end] come about of necessity, and refer to the matter and the source of the movement as their causes" (V 1, 778a32–b1; cf. also 731b21–2, 789b7–8). That is, one can explain why an eye is blue on the basis of the characteristics of the particular matter from which it was made, together with the motions present in the matter as the process of formation took place. If, then, one thinks of moving causes not at the level of the end products of the processes but at that of the stage-by-stage development, there will often be two contrasting sets of explanatory factors. On the one side we have matter and moving cause (the nature of the materials together with the motions that arise in and around it); these are responsible for what happens, wherever and to whatever extent they are responsible at all, by being antecedent conditions from which what happens follows on what we may provisionally think of as mechanical principles. But on the other side we have form and goal, which are responsible not by being antecedent conditions but by being the end in view by which the earlier developments are, somehow or other, regulated.

II

There are then two distinct and independent levels of facts and correspondingly two levels of principles that Aristotle holds are responsible for what happens in the course of nature. There are facts about the various kinds of matter and principles of a mechanical sort governing their behavior in given conditions. And there are facts about the natural kinds of living thing and principles of a teleological sort governing their development and behavior. Aristotle's predecessors and contemporaries were all agreed, as we would also agree, that there are facts and principles of the first sort. This can be accepted as non-controversial. But what ground does Aristotle have for thinking there is, in addition to and independent of these, a second level of facts and principles such as he postulates?

In answering this question one must begin by taking note of certain assumptions Aristotle makes about the character of physical reality. The most important of these is his belief that the world—the whole ordered arrangement of things, from outer heavens right down to the earth and its animal and plant life—is eternal. That the heavens are eternal and move at a fixed rate in daily rotation by strict necessity is, of course, not a mere assumption of Aristotle's, it is in fact the conclusion of certain *a priori* arguments in *Physics* VIII. This does not, however, immediately imply that the sublunary world has forever been arranged as it now is. That there has always been and always will be an annual cycle of warm and cold periods, as the sun moves round the ecliptic, is perhaps arguable on this basis. But that the distribution of land and water and air, and the kinds of plant and animal life that now exist, should be permanent parts of the world order seems clearly to need further argument; these features are certainly not determined merely by the constancy of the movements of the heavenly bodies. Nonetheless, Aristotle did believe that the world's climate and the existence of the animal and plant life that depends on it were further permanent structural facts—as it were, part of the given framework of the world, over and above that provided by the celestial movements.[4] Partly, no doubt, he thought that even fairly cursory acquaintance with the basic facts about animal and plant life should convince anyone that our world is a self-maintaining system, with a built-in tendency to preserve fundamentally the same distribution of air, land, and water and the same balance of animal and plant populations as it had in his own time. The seasonal variation of hot and cold, wet and dry periods seems to have the effect that no permanent dislocation in the ecology takes place. Furthermore, every plant and animal species reproduces itself (or, in the case of spontaneously generated things, the conditions in which they are produced are regularly recurring); moreover, there appears to be an effective balance of nature, whereby no plant or animal is so constituted by its nature as to be permanently destructive of any other. Everything seems to fit together—the environment is permanently

---

[4] In *GA* II 1, 731b24–732a3 (cf. also *de An.* II 4, 415a25–b7) Aristotle appeals to the permanence of animal and plant life to explain why there is sexual differentiation and animal reproduction in general. Living things are better than nonliving and existence than nonexistence, so the continuous existence of living things is an important good; but since individual animals and plants are all perishable it is only by constant replenishment that this good can be achieved. Since there cannot be eternal individuals, there is instead "always a *genos* of human beings, of animals, and of plants" (b35 f.), and it is in order to sustain these genera in existence that reproduction through sexual differentiation takes place. It is true that in this argument Aristotle explicitly presupposes only that there are always plants and animals, not (except for human beings!) that there are always the *same* kinds. But the context shows that he is making this stronger assumption; for he goes on to speak of the arrangements which make possible the constant generation of the *existing* species. The stronger thesis is also found at *GA* II 6, 742b17–743a1, where Aristotle takes Democritus to task for saying that if something is always (ἀεί) so then that is sufficient explanation for it: what is *always* is infinite (τὸ δ' ἀεὶ ἄπειρον), i.e., lasts through infinite time, and there is no origin (ἀρχή) of the infinite, but to give an explanation of something is precisely to cite an origin (ἀρχή—but in another sense!) for it. If this were right, Aristotle says, we would be barred from seeking an explanation for why in animal generation we find just the organs and other parts we do find being formed in just the order in which they are actually formed. For the Democritean argument to be the threat he takes it to be Aristotle must be holding that the

such as is needed to support the kinds of plants and animals there actually are, and the natural processes of generation and growth seem to maintain permanently a fairly fixed population of those same plants and animals. One observes in the world itself, then, no internal disharmony or imbalance that could lead to its eventual destruction; and since there is nothing outside it that could attack it and cause its disintegration, it seems only reasonable to believe that in these respects no change is to be anticipated. And if none is to be anticipated in the future, there is *pari passu* no reason to believe that things were ever any different in the past.

Now for Aristotle the fact, as he thought it, that the species of living things are permanent features of the natural world has a very special significance. It is not simply as if nature, by some mechanism or other, managed to keep in existence a stock of arbitrarily shaped and structured, but complex, objects (specially shaped and colored stones, for example). For each plant and animal is structured in such a way that its parts *work together* to make possible the specific form of life characteristic of its species, and (in almost all cases) so that they make possible the continuation of the species by enabling some appropriate kind of reproduction. It is important to realize that things might not have been this way. The organs and other internal parts of animals and plants might not have been as highly adapted to one another as in fact they are. Empedocles hypothesized that during one stage of the world's history all manner of animals were constantly being formed by chance collocations of varied animal parts more or less like those of animals known to us; some of these individual animals, having the parts necessary to make a go of it, survived to old age, others only for a short time if at all. While this situation continued all kinds of odd creatures were constantly being produced which clung to life with difficulty or not at all, and the adaptedness for life of the animals and plants known to us would be distinctly the exception, by

---

existing species of animals, whose structure and generation he is investigating, are existent through infinite time. The strict interpretation required for "always" in this passage should put us on notice that when Aristotle speaks elsewhere of some arrangement as being so "always or for the most part" (ἀεὶ ἢ ὡς ἐπὶ τὸ πολύ) he means to say that that arrangement is found existing eternally or recurring regularly throughout all time, with only the occasional exceptions implied in the "for the most part" rider. Thus if he says that in some particular animal certain organic parts are formed always or for the most part in a certain way or order he does *not* just intend the hypothetical, "*if* or *when* these animals are formed, this is the way it always happens"; he means to assert the categorical conjunction, "these animals regularly are generated through all time, and this is the way it always happens." Some rare, fortuitous event that nonetheless happened in the same way every time would not be counted by Aristotle as something that happens "always or mostly" in a certain way; nor would he count animal generation as happening "always or mostly" in some particular way if animals were found in the universe only in a certain finite period of its existence, even though *when* they exist they are always or mostly generated in that way.

no means the rule. If the world were permanently that way, one could perhaps speak of the permanence of all those weird kinds of "animals," produced as they would continue to be by chance collocations of limbs springing up from the earth equally by chance, but in such a world the permanence of animal kinds would mean something very different from what it meant for Aristotle. For him, it meant the permanence of a set of well-adapted, well-functioning life forms. The preservation of the species of living things is therefore, as Aristotle understands it, the preservation of a fixed set of good things, things economically and efficiently organized so that they function in their environment for their own good.

The view that the world, together with its animal and plant life, is eternal was obviously quite a reasonable view in fourth-century Greece. But if it is *permanently* true that there *are* these given kinds of good, well-adapted plants and animals, and that the seasons follow upon each other in this given way, with those good effects, it becomes at once a condition of adequacy on any physical theory that it should be able to accommodate these facts. There are several possibilities. One might attempt to explain them by arguing, so to speak, from below: the materials of the world being what they are, and having the natures they do, the world naturally tends, by the operation of nothing but material principles, to produce and maintain just those kinds of living things that are actually observed. Or, one might attempt to explain them by arguing from above: for example, by claiming that it is a fundamental fact about nature, not to be further explained, that it tends toward maximal richness and variety, and then arguing that precisely the natural kinds that are actually observed, taken together with the environing inorganic stuffs, constitute the maximally rich and varied world. Thirdly, one might simply accept as a fundamental postulate of physical theory that the world *permanently has* whatever species it contains; that is, one might hold that it is an irreducible fact about the natural world, not further to be explained, that it so governs itself as to preserve in existence the species of well-adapted living thing that it actually contains. Of these alternatives Aristotle chose, and evidently thought one could not reasonably avoid, the last. He does not ever explicitly consider, so far as I can tell, a theory of the second sort. Perhaps he thought any such theory conflicts with well-established metaphysical principles, so that he could safely dismiss this alternative without discussion. For any such theory is committed to the idea that standards of goodness—in particular, of richness and variety—can be clearly conceived and specified in purely intellectual terms, in advance of study of the actual world, and that these standards can then be thought of as imposed on the world, as principles it must conform to, whether by its own inherent nature or by external compulsion. And Aristotle's metaphysics of the good rules out any such abstractly conceived standards. All our ideas about goodness, he thinks, are derived from familiarity with the actual world, and though we can extend these to conceive of possible arrangements that, if taken in isolation, might be better than the actual ones, there is no Idea of the Good to provide us with absolute standards worked out by the pure intellect on its own, by which one might securely judge that the actual world either is or is not the best possible. In fact the world may *be* maximally rich and varied, but we cannot argue that it is by appeal to self-justifying standards independent of and prior to the good things we find in the world as it is actually constituted. Our best *idea* of richness and variety is, as a matter of fact, probably given by the actual world: in any event, we have no independent idea of these things by which to judge the world, so there cannot be any such principle of physics as this second sort of theory demands.[5]

Whether for this reason or another, Aristotle does not consider the possibility of deriving the permanence of the species in this Platonic sort of way, from above. He does, however, argue against the first sort of theory. He represents his materialist predecessors as having favored this sort of view: they supposed one could explain why there are the species there are, why they are preserved, and why the seasons follow one another as they do, in terms of nothing but the natures of the various materials the world contains and the ways in which, given their distribution at any given time, they interact with one another. In other words, they thought that ultimately only the first of Aristotle's two levels of facts and principles ever needs to be appealed to in explaining anything. His second level they proposed to account for entirely in terms of material causes and moving causes involving nothing but the motions that arise in matter, given its nature, under given conditions.

One can distinguish two lines of argument in Aristotle against any such supposition. One of these, which I shall explore at some length below, consists in an outright denial of the materialists' claim that their principles enable them to explain the occurrence of living things with the organic parts we actually observe them to have. But first I want to discuss more briefly a weaker line of argument, weaker in the sense that in it Aristotle grants, for the sake of argument, this major claim of his materialist opponents: even granted this outrageous claim, Aristotle argues, the materialists cannot explain *everything* that the fact of the permanence of the species involves.

---

[5] This line of thought explains why Aristotle's teleology does not extend to arguing that the good of the world as a whole requires any particular species or any particular interlocking arrangements among whatever species are to exist. He consistently takes the existing species as given; *they* are the good things by reference to which to explain those features of reality that he thinks need to be explained teleologically. (The class of exceptions to this rule noted below, pp. 127–8, do not damage this point.)

This argument is found at *Physics* II 8, 198b32–199a8 (and see *Metaph.* I 3, 984b8–15). Interpreters have found this a difficult passage, but I believe the argument itself is rather straightforward. Without attempting a full-scale defense of my interpretation I shall simply state what I take the argument to be.

As I noted above, the animal and plant species we observe in nature are well-adapted. Their organs and other parts work together to promote their existence and functioning in their actual environments—a plant or animal's organs are, and do, *good* for it. Is there an explanation for this? The materialists argue that the various parts that are produced in the course of a creature's formation are produced by nothing but material necessity: the natures of the materials are such that *this* kind of tooth (a sharp one) necessarily comes up in the front of the mouth, and other material necessities result in *that* kind (a flat one) coming up in the back. But what explains the *fit* between these dental arrangements and the creature's need for food? The front ones, for example, are not just sharp, but useful for tearing food off, which is something the creature needs to do to survive and flourish. What account of *this* fact can the materialists give? Aristotle argues that the materialists' answer to this question is insupportable. (1) Where something occurs that in fact works to the advantage of someone or something, there are only two choices: either it is advantageous by coincidence or it happens for that reason, i.e., *because* of the good it does. If one admits that something is good, as the natural arrangements here in question indubitably are, one must either hold that this was a lucky coincidence, or grant that it happened that way (perhaps as a result of some agent's design, perhaps not) *for* the good of the person or thing in question. (2) Our materialists deny that in nature anything happens *for the sake of* any good that results, so they are forced to say, as Aristotle represents them as saying (198b16–32), that these good results are only coincidences: the teeth come up sharp in front by material necessity, but only *happen* to serve the creature's interests by doing so.[6] But, he argues, (3) a coincidence is necessarily an exceptional occurrence, and (4) animals' organs are *always* (with only occasional failures) formed in such a way as to serve the creature's needs. Hence it cannot be a coincidence, as the materialists say it is, that they do serve those needs. And if it is no coincidence, it must have the other explanation allowed: it happens that way *in order to* promote the creature's welfare.

---

[6] See 198b24–7; the sense of the ἐπεί clause in b27 is given by this expansion: ἐπεὶ οὐχ ἕνεκα τοῦ ἐπιτηδείους εἶναι, γενέσθαι τοὺς ὀδόντας ὀξεῖς, ἀλλὰ συμπεσεῖν τοῦτο ἐκείνῳ. It is essential for assessing this argument to notice that the opponents are represented as saying that the organs are *formed* as they are by necessity, but are *good* by coincidence. They do not claim they are *good* by necessity (whatever that would mean).

Aristotle's conclusion here does, clearly enough, follow from the premises he provides. Whether the opponents would have to grant all the premises is less clear. The premises about coincidences, (1) and (3), perhaps most often strike interpreters as questionable, though actually I believe each of them can be fairly vigorously defended.[7] What is quite certain, however, is that materialists like Democritus and Empedocles do not accept premise (4) in the sense in which Aristotle intends it (and the sense in which it must be taken to make the argument valid). It must be remembered (see n. 4 above) that when Aristotle says that the parts of animals and plants are *always* formed serviceably for the creature's needs he means that this has been going on *throughout all time*. And unless that is how (4) is taken the conclusion will not follow. If, for example, as Democritus is reported to have held, there have been infinitely many worlds (κόσμοι), some of them larger than others, some with no sun or moon, some without plants and animals or even water (Hippol. *Haer.* I 13 = DK 68A40), there have *not* always existed serviceably structured living things, reproducing themselves in the ways that now appear to be regular. And, as we have seen, according to Empedocles there are periods in the world's

---

[7] It might be objected, against (1), that while one may grant that any good outcome is either a coincidence or has *some* special explanation, this explanation *need* not be the teleological one asserted in (1). For if one has a run of heads in flipping a coin, and this is not a coincidence, it only follows that it has *some* cause (perhaps simply that the coin is untrue), not that it must have been produced for some purpose. But this reply overlooks that what premise (1) claims is not that *every* apparent coincidence that turns out not to be one must be explained teleologically, but only that when something *good* happens its being good must, if it is not a coincidence, have a teleological explanation. Thus the alleged counterexample must be expanded to make the run of heads a good thing for some reason (for example, because it means money for some particular person); but now we no longer have a counterexample, since this good that was done will remain a coincidence after the run of heads has itself been explained as due to the coin's weighting. Thus Aristotle's claim that if something good has an explanation and is no coincidence, the explanation must be teleological, is actually quite plausible. And even if it is not finally true, this will not give comfort to Aristotle's opponents. For certainly if some conjunction of phenomena is not a coincidence, it must at least have an explanation that connects the conjoined phenomena in a single, joint explanation (on this see Richard Sorabji, *Necessity, Cause and Blame* 10–11); and materialists driven to deny that the good done by the organs' arrangement is a coincidence surely cannot replace their separate explanations of how *each* organ is produced with a unified one claiming that the natures of the various materials in the world are in themselves such that this conjunction necessarily results every time.

The other premise, premise (3), can be seen to be perfectly unobjectionable if it is borne in mind that the criterion of the exceptional is defined against what happens throughout all time. For of course there is no assurance that any finite run of similar outcomes is not nonetheless a coincidence; but an *infinite* run with a preponderance of similar outcomes surely cannot be a coincidence but must have some special explanation. Strictly, perhaps, coincidences don't have to be exceptional, when taken in an infinite run, but they must not count for more than 50 percent of the cases, and that is good enough for the purposes of Aristotle's argument.

history during which all kinds of *un*serviceable combinations are produced (Simp. in *Ph*. 371.33–372. 9 = DK 31B61). On either of these views one could only hold the orderly and good arrangements presently prevailing to be an extended run of luck; viewed *sub specie aeternitatis* the good outcomes with which our experience makes us familiar are distinctly the exception, not the rule, and therefore the materialists' classification of them as coincidences would after all satisfy the requirements imposed by premises (1) and (3). Of course, Aristotle would insist that Democritus' theory of infinitely many world orders and Empedocles' story about the alternating epochs of control by Love and by Strife are nothing but unsupported fancies, and that his own theory of the eternity of the actual world is more reasonable. One can well sympathize with this contention, and it is worth emphasizing that if one does accept Aristotle's theory, and I am right that premises (1) and (3) are defensible, then this argument provides quite a good defense of Aristotle's teleological hypothesis. It must at least be granted that Aristotle was on stronger ground than his actual materialist opponents, even if we would ourselves, for different reasons from theirs, side rather with them in rejecting Aristotle's thesis of the eternity of the actual kinds of living things.

Aristotle's more thoroughgoing confrontation with the materialists is found in the following chapter of *Physics* II, chapter 9, where he explains and defends his claim that in the structure and formation of plants and animals and their functional parts the materials are not a necessitating factor in the way the materialists claim, but are only "hypothetically" necessary—necessary *if* the end result of a fully formed creature of the kind in question in any given case is to be attained.[8] The materialists, as

---

[8] Aristotle's doctrine of hypothetical necessity (*Ph*. II 9, *PA* I 1 639b21–640a10, 642a1–13, *GC* II 11, 337b14–33) is nowadays usually interpreted as maintaining the very implausible view that in natural processes *nothing* is necessitated except hypothetically: that, as Sorabji puts it (op. cit., 148), "in natural events" (not counting the motion of the stars and other such everlasting processes) there is no necessity other than "the merely hypothetical necessity of certain prerequisites, if a certain goal is to be achieved." (See also Ross, *Aristotle's Physics*, 43; and Balme, *Aristotle's De Partibus*, 76–7.) On this view, Aristotle is committed to denying all material necessities of a Democritean sort, things that happen because the materials present simply interact by their natures to cause them. One then faces the formidable task of understanding how if this is his theoretical position he nonetheless constantly invokes in his actual biological explanations material necessities that he sometimes explicitly *contrasts* with hypothetical ones; he does this even in *PA* I 1 less than twenty lines after the second of the two passages on hypothetical necessity cited above (642a31–b4, cf. esp. a32–5 ; for other similar passages see Balme, op. cit., 76–84). I believe Balme's attempt to accommodate these invocations of necessity to the prevailing interpretation of Aristotle's official position is quite unsatisfactory (Sorabji, op. cit., 149–50, 152–4, 162–3, gives a partial rebuttal of Balme's argument). But, more importantly, it is unnecessary; Aristotle's official position does not in fact deny *all* material necessity of an unhypothetical kind, and

we have seen, claim that the given natures of the materials making up the world are such that under the conditions prevailing in animal generation they necessarily interact in such a way as to produce the organs we actually observe the living things to have, and in that arrangement which constitutes the normal, fully formed specimen of the species in question. But Aristotle argues that as a matter of fact it is not possible to complete the project of derivation thus envisaged. Acquaintance with the various kinds of matter there are and the ways in which by their natures they behave under various conditions does not permit one to think that there *are* any true principles at this level sufficiently strong and comprehensive to make any such derivation possible. The Democritean hypothesis that there is a set of fixed, true principles specifying how material particles of different sizes and shapes behave under various conditions, and that everything that happens happens as a result of these principles ("by brute necessity") is mere fantasy. *Some* things do happen by this kind of necessity; but not very much does, and it is certainly not possible to start merely from a description in materialist terms of, say, a sperm and some female matter, together with a similiar description of the environing conditions, and build up, step by step, with appeal only to material necessity, the complex and highly organized newborn animal that *always*, unless

---

easily accommodates all the passages in the biological works where nonhypothetical necessities are invoked (if one discounts the occasional overgenerous concession to his materialist opponents, e.g. GA V 8, 789b2–5). What he denies is only that a natural *goal* (the whole living thing, with its fully formed organs) is ever produced by material necessity of a Democritean kind: that is, you cannot argue simply from the natures and powers of the materials present at the beginning of the process to their transformation into the fully formed living thing that eventually results. This is implied already by the way in expounding his view he makes comparisons to artifacts, e.g., walls and whole houses: the claim (see *PA* 639b27–30, *Ph.* 200a1–8, b1–4) is just that neither the whole artifact nor the whole animal is brought into being by material necessities. *Mete.* IV 12, 390b12–14 makes the point very clearly: "though cold and heat and their motion cause bronze or silver to come to be they do not cause a saw or a cup or a box to come to be; here craftsmanship is the cause, and in the other cases [the cases of natural generation] nature." If the passages about hypothetical necessity are read carefully and their contexts are borne in mind, I think the intended limitations emerge quite clearly enough: *some* things that happen in the course of formation of a living thing *do* happen by material necessity (e.g., GA II 4, 739b26–30, a membrane takes shape around the newly forming animal fetation by this kind of necessity—from one point of view, it's like any other thickish fluid, milk for example, acted on by heat), but, Aristotle insists, the *whole sequence* of events leading up to the fully formed creature does not. (Of course any talk in Aristotle of the necessity of events in the sublunary world must be understood not to apply strictly, since according to him such events only happen for the most part in any given way and never absolutely always so; strictly therefore Aristotle's material necessities do not conform to the Democritean idea of *absolute* necessity. But this difference must not be allowed to distract attention from the fact that Aristotle does allow significant scope to material necessity of essentially the type for which Democritus argued.)

something specifiable goes wrong, results. If one actually studies how matter, as such, behaves, instead of inventing theories about such things, Aristotle thought, one will see at once that this is so.

It is easy for us, with the hindsight made possible by post-Renaissance experimental physics and chemistry to suppose that Aristotle's atomist opponents had the better of this dispute. But such an attitude is quite unhistorical. The ancient atomists had no *empirical* reason to think that the powers attributable to matter of different kinds were sufficient to determine any of the actually observed outcomes. No Greek theorist had any conception of what controlled experiment might show about the powers of matter; insofar as empirical evidence bearing on this question was available either to Aristotle or to his opponents it amounted to no more than what ordinary observation could yield. And there is no doubt that ordinary observation, so far from suggesting any universal necessitation of such outcomes by the inherent properties of matter, leads to Aristotle's more modest estimate of what can be explained by reference to the material and moving causes. Who, having observed what happens when fire is applied to a stick of wood, would suppose that the material characteristics of that stick and that fire, together with the prevailing conditions of air-flow, and so on, dictate that just *so* much ash will result, and in just *that* arrangement? That the stick will be consumed, that it will be turned to ashes—that is clear; but ordinary observation does not license the belief that the outcome is in further particulars determined one way or the other. Similarly, when wet warm stuff, such as fourth-century scientists thought gave rise to an animal fetus, was affected by the watery, mobile stuff of the male semen, there might be grounds, taking into account only what follows from their constitution as stuffs of a certain consistency, etc., for thinking that some congealing and setting effect will result. But that the congealing and setting should be precisely that which constitutes an animal fetus? There was no reason at all to believe that *this* was determined on *that* sort of ground. So insofar as either Aristotle or the atomists had an empirical basis for their views about the powers of matter, Aristotle's position was far stronger. I do not mean to deny, of course, the inherent theoretical strengths of the atomists' "program"; but insofar as the dispute between them and Aristotle turned on actual evidence, Aristotle clearly had the better of this argument.

What then does account for the production of an animal fetus under the conditions in which we know such a fetus is produced? In his account in *Metaphysics* 1 of his predecessors' views on explanation, Aristotle remarks that some earlier philosophers (e.g., Anaxagoras) recognized that material necessity did not suffice, and also saw that one could not well say that there is no general explanation at all, that this outcome was due simply to chance—holding that *some* particular arrangement or other of the materials as they are congealed and set has to result, and that it just happens each time that what results is a properly constructed fetus of the appropriate kind (984b11–15). One might, I suppose, say that it is only a long run of luck that, so far as we know, has produced this regular-seeming result up to now, and that things may soon start turning out differently. But, as we have seen, Aristotle plausibly argued there was reason to believe that this is how things *always* have been and *always* will be. And if it *always* happens like this, throughout all time, some further explanation is required; it cannot be a matter of luck. So if this fact cannot be explained by deriving it from more basic natural facts about the material constitution of the world, then one must either invoke supernatural powers as responsible for it, or else posit as a second level of basic natural fact that the world permanently contains plants and animals (in addition to matter of various kinds), and indeed precisely the *same* plants and animals at all times. In other words: *if* one is determined to treat these regularities as a fact of nature, and they cannot be derived from other natural principles, one must take them as expressing a natural principle all on their own. Thus Aristotle's response, that it is an inherent, nonderivative fact about the natural world that it consists in part of the natural kinds and works to maintain them permanently in existence, is an eminently reasonable, even scientific, one.

But now—and this is the crucial point for our present discussion—by adopting the view that plants and animals are a basic, and not a derived, constituent of physical reality, one provides the theoretical background necessary to justify the appeal to goals in explaining the recurrent processes of animal and plant generation that we have been discussing. For, on this view, there is inherent in the world a fundamental tendency to preserve permanently the species of living things it contains. But the living things in question are so structured that each one's organs and other parts work together to make it possible for it to achieve to a rather high degree its own specific good, the full and active life characteristic of its kind, including the leaving of offspring behind; the actual plant and animal life that is preserved is all of it *good*. One can therefore claim to discover in any given process of animal generation one of those processes in which the tendency to preserve the species of living things is concretely realized. And because the regular outcome of each such process is something good, one is also entitled to interpret the process itself as directed at that outcome as its goal. For if it is a fundamental fact about the world, not derivable from other natural principles, that it maintains forever these good life-forms, then the processes by which it does so, being processes by which something good is achieved, are for the sake of the outcomes. Thus, for example, fetal materials coming from a female dog and acted upon by a male dog's sperm are transformed by certain definite stages into a puppy. This transformation cannot be explained by reference to the material constitution of these antecedent stuffs; left to themselves these materials would not, or would not certainly, have produced just those formations in which the features and organs that characterize a dog are developed. What happens in this case needs to be explained by referring to the fundamental tendency of the natural kinds of living things to be preserved in existence, and recognizing that this process is one of those by which a species, the dog, preserves itself by reproduction. This tendency, which is not ultimately reducible to the powers and properties of matter-kinds, is irreducibly teleological; it is the tendency of certain materials to interact, be formed and transformed in certain ways, *so as* to produce a well-formed, well-adapted, viable new specimen of the same species as the animals from which they came. So, given his view that living things are basic to the permanent structure of the world, Aristotle can argue that those stages in the formation of a fetus in which one can discern the development of the features and organs of the mature animal being produced are *for the sake of* that animal nature which is the final outcome of the process.

It is, then, by two related arguments professing to address observed natural facts and the need to explain them that Aristotle offers his best and most interesting reasons for accepting teleological explanations in the study of nature. In each of these the permanence of the natural kinds of living things figures prominently. In the first it is the fact that the permanent natural kinds are all of them well-adapted—that living things' organic and other parts serve their needs by enabling them to survive and flourish in their natural environments—that is said to demand teleological explanation, even if mechanical principles sufficed to explain everything else about them. In the argument just examined the focus is on the more elementary (alleged) fact that plants and animals are very complex objects whose regular and permanent production the natural powers of the matter-kinds are not sufficient to explain; that this nonetheless happens is only explicable, according to Aristotle, if we suppose the regular production of these objects is a fundamental goal (or rather, set of goals) in nature, so that the presence in nature of these goals is what makes the processes of animal and plant generation come about always in the way that they do.

It is worth emphasizing that, as I have just implied, the teleological explanations that these arguments of Aristotle's are meant to endorse are best construed as causal explanations of a certain kind, whatever one may think of them so construed. On Aristotle's view, certain goals *actually exist* in *rerum natura*; there *are* in reality those plants and animal forms that he argues are natural goals. Their existence there is what controls and directs those aspects of the processes of generation that need to be explained by reference to them, and that, indeed, is why they need to be so explained. Thus one could put Aristotle's view by saying that *one* kind of causal explanation refers to antecedent material conditions and powers: what *makes* wood burn when fire is applied to it is that fire is hot and so has the power to act in this way on wood. The given material natures of fire and wood are simply such that this happens. But similarly what *makes* a particular series of transformations take place in the generation of a dog is that it is a fundamental fact about nature that each kind of living thing reproduces so as to preserve itself. That series is made to happen *because* what is being formed is a dog, and it is a dog's nature to have certain particular organs and other features. Here what Aristotle thinks of as the cause of what happens is located not in the material nature of anything but in a certain formal nature, that of the dog. The recent tendency to explicate and defend Aristotelian teleology exclusively by appeal to essentially epistemological considerations leaves out of account this crucial fact about Aristotle's theory, that he grounds his teleological explanations thus in the very nature of things. It is quite true, and important, as for example Richard Sorabji says, that we will certainly always need teleological explanations, no matter how much we learn about causal mechanisms, because, among other reasons, our interests in asking "Why?" sometimes cannot be satisfied otherwise than by noticing some good that the thing inquired into does.[9] But it would be misleading to put such considerations forward as providing insight into Aristotle's theory or his reasons for holding it. For they leave out of account the fact that for Aristotle such explanations only *truly* explain where, and because, reality is *actually governed* in the ways the explanations claim; what our interests demand is only of significance where they may be satisfied by pointing to something about the actual workings of things. Here as elsewhere for Aristotle ontology takes precedence over epistemology. His commitment to teleological explanation is fundamentally misunderstood where this fact is not borne clearly in mind.[10]

[9] Sorabji, *Necessity*, 165–6. See the similar remarks of Martha Nussbaum, *Aristotle's "De Motu Animalium,"* 69–70, 78–80. Both authors record their indebtedness here to Charles Taylor's work on teleological explanation.

[10] This difference between Aristotle and contemporary defenders of teleological (or, as people now for no very good reason say, teleonomic) argument in biology is well brought out by a comment of David Hull. Focusing on the issue of reductionism Hull points out that the dispute nowadays is over "methodological reduction" and "theory reduction," not "ontological reduction." "Nowadays both scientists and philosophers take ontological reduction for granted. . . . Organisms are 'nothing but atoms, and that is that' (Hull, 2:281–316). "Philosophy and Biology," in Fløistad, ed., *Contemporary Philosophy: A Survey*. When Aristotle opposes the reduction of teleological explanation to mechanical-efficient causation he is opposing ontological reduction just as much as methodological (and theory) reduction.

III

We have now, I believe, uncovered the key to the interpretation of Aristotelian natural teleology: it is the alleged *fact* of the permanence of the species of living things, not explicable, as Aristotle plausibly thinks, on other natural principles, that constitutes the foundation and justification for all the types of teleological arguments he ever accepts in the natural sciences, with only one small class of exceptions. In my discussion so far I have emphasized the teleological explanation of processes of animal and plant generation. But it is easy to see that this same principle of the preservation of the species licenses other sorts of teleological explanation as well. Three of these are worth mentioning here because they are sorts of teleological explanation that Aristotle himself does, at one place or another and with apparent conviction, actually offer in his scientific writings. And since these three, together with the explanation of the processes of generation of living things, constitute all the principal kinds of teleological explanation to be found in Aristotle, one is entitled to conclude that it is on the principle of the permanence of the species that Aristotle ultimately rests his belief in the goal-directedness of nature in general.

To begin with, then, this principle allows full scope for functional analyses of living things, and for teleological arguments based upon them. Given Aristotle's assumption that natural kinds are preserved, the normal member of each kind must be viable in its natural habitat; it must grow to adulthood, preserve itself for some normal period, and arrange for the continuance of the species through successful reproductive activities. On this basis one can appeal, as Aristotle attempts to do *in extenso* in the *De Partibus,* to the contribution to a creature's life made by a given organ or other part as the explanation for its having that organ or part. Because every animal and plant must have a structure and organization that makes it a viable form of life, one is entitled to examine each species to see what in *its* organization contributes to viability; in discovering what each single organ or part does to this end (given what the others do), one discovers what makes the animal have that part.[11]

---

[11] In this summary I do not distinguish the several different ways in which Aristotle argues that an animal has an organ because it needs it. He says (e.g., at *PA* I 1, 640a33–b1, *GA* I 4, 717a15–16) that some organs are necessary for an animal (or a given animal) to have (all animals must have sense organs, blooded ones a heart, those that eat certain kinds of food multiple stomachs), while others that are not strictly necessary (the creature could survive without them) nonetheless do the animal good (flexible bone joints allow ease of movement, the kidney enables the bladder to do its job better, external testes free the animal from the need for urgent and violent sexual activity). It should be observed that despite these differences the patterns of argument here are basically the same: in both types of case an ani-

Secondly, Aristotle's assumption of the preservation of the species also licenses a wide variety of teleological explanations of facts about the physical environment. For if the species are to be preserved, the environment must both support the continued existence of the mature members of the species and provide the conditions under which new generations are produced and brought to maturity. So one is entitled, on Aristotle's assumption, to study the physical environment with a view to discovering the features of it that support the life cycles of the natural kinds the world contains. In discovering, for example, that heavy rain in winter and spring and warmth in summer and fall are necessary first to bring to life and then to promote the maturation of the world's plant life, one discovers why there is rain in winter and heat in summer.[12] So far as I am aware the frequency of rain in winter and heat in summer are the only features of the physical environment that Aristotle ever explicitly offers to explain teleologically: in the *Meteorologica* and other places where he discusses such matters he seems to concentrate on material and moving causes in explaining the phenomena. Perhaps he thought these processes were too remote for us to gain knowledge about how they operate sufficient to say what they were for; possibly with greater knowledge he would have begun to find a more extensive set of patterns of a teleological kind. In any event, it is clear both that his fundamental assumption about the preservation of the species makes teleological explanations possible here and that he himself, in the case of winter rain and summer heat, actually gives some.

---

mal is argued to have an organ because it is *good* for it to have it. In one case, having it is good because otherwise it would not exist or survive at all; in the other, having it is good because otherwise its existence would be encumbered in some respect. The difference is thus just that between two aspects of the single natural goal associated with each species; if nature makes animals viable because that is for their good, it is only to be expected that it advances their good in further ways, too. Sorabji in an interesting account of Aristotle's teleological analyses of animal organs (*Necessity*, ch. 10, esp. 155–60) neglects this common connection to the animal's good and as a result overemphasizes the differences between these two patterns of argument.

[12] See *Ph*. 198b36–199a5. It is sometimes overlooked that here, in preparing his defense against the anti-teleological argument stated just previously, Aristotle unequivocally endorses the teleological explanation of these meteorological regularities: these things, he says, do not happen by coincidence (ἀπὸ συμπτώματος), but must happen either in that way or for the sake of an end (ἕνεκά του), so that (199a5) they must be for the sake of an end (ἕνεκά του ἂν εἴη). The fact that he endorses the nonteleological view of these phenomena in giving his opponents' argument just before (198b18–23) is perfectly natural, since he is there speaking for them and not for himself. What his response shows is that he rejects both their premises and their conclusion. Nussbaum (*De Motu*, 94) is therefore wrong to cite 198b18–21 as evidence that Aristotle rejected such arguments as illegitimate.

Lastly, the account I have just given of the basis on which Aristotle explains the cycle of the seasons suggests the possibility of similar explanations of certain interactions among species. After all, an important part of the environmental needs of any species is the need for food of an appropriate sort, and this means that one should be in a position to say of some given plant and animal species, which serve as food for given other species, that the former exist *in part* for the sake of the latter. And there are other ways in which the species serve one another, e.g., the complementarity of plants and animals vis-à-vis carbon dioxide and oxygen. Where such adaptation exists Aristotle's principle of the preservation of the species will support the claim that the species which contributes to the continuance of another exists in part for the sake of the latter. And in a well-known passage of the *Politics* (I 8, 1256b15–22), Aristotle argues in precisely this way, though in considering primarily the relation of plants and animals to human needs he fails to represent accurately the full state of affairs.

> We must suppose that plants are for the sake of the animals and that the other animals are for the sake of the human beings—the domesticated ones both for their usefulness and for food, the wild ones (most of them, at any rate, if not all) for the sake of food and for support in other ways, to provide clothing and other instruments. If then nature makes nothing incomplete or without a point it is necessary that nature has made them all [i.e., I take it, all the other *animals*] for the sake of human beings.

Given the assumption of the permanence of the natural kinds what Aristotle says here seems perfectly justified (provided that one takes seriously his disclaimer that perhaps not *all* animals can be seen as supporting human life). Of course, he omits to mention either the ways in which animals serve plants, which support the reverse judgment that animals are for the sake of plants (think of bees), or the ways in which human beings serve the animals that they make use of and eat. (Presumably many domesticated species would long ago have passed out of existence if human beings had not protected them.) But though Aristotle's account is objectionably one-sided, the basic idea that plant and animal species exist for one another's sake is sound, if his general principle of the preservation of the kinds is true. It is worth noting that it also follows from this principle that any species that makes use of another for its own survival must not so reduce it that it fails to continue in existence. And that fact might be made the basis for a further application of teleology. In one passage (but, it seems, only one) Aristotle does argue in such a way. He mentions that some fish (dolphins, he wrongly says, and sharks) have their mouth underneath and therefore turn on their backs to get their food, and explains this as follows:

It looks as if nature does this not only for the sake of preserving other animals (for while they take time to turn on their backs the other animals save themselves—all the species in question feed on animals), but also to prevent them from indulging their insatiable appetite for food. For if they got food more easily they would quickly destroy themselves through overeating. (*PA* IV 13, 696b25–32)

Thus as a fourth class of teleological explanations, though it is one he almost entirely neglects in his biological writings, we can add explanation drawn from the adaptedness of plant and animal species to one another.[13]

In four contexts in nature, then, where Aristotle actually offers teleological explanations, such explanations are clearly authorized by the principle of the permanence of the species. There remains one class of cases that cannot be made to fit my account, because they appeal to a good that does not reduce to what some living thing needs to survive and flourish in its environment. In a number of places Aristotle appeals to a notion of fittingness derived from some conception of what is inherently well-ordered.[14] Thus he explains (*PA* II 14, 658a18–24) that in general

---

[13] There is no need to apologize as Nussbaum seeks to do (*De Motu*, 95–8) for Aristotle's occasional indulgence in this fourth kind of argument. The principles which support the other sorts of teleological argument, even those (the first two) which Nussbaum approves, equally support arguments of this fourth kind. She does not explain very clearly why she deprecates them, but I suspect that a certain looseness in her use of the expression "universal teleology of nature" leads her astray. Aristotle does indeed deny, what Plato is at least verbally committed to, that "the universe as a whole is an organism with its own *logos* and its own good" (p. 97), but that is perfectly compatible with holding that one species subserves the needs of another and exists partly for that reason. For here the good appealed to is not the proprietary good of the universe as a whole, but only that of that other species. I do not see why this should be described, as Nussbaum describes it, as a "universal teleology of nature": but if it *is* so described the expression is plainly being used in a sense different from the Platonic sense to which Nussbaum rightly objects on Aristotle's behalf. It is true that the good appealed to in this fourth class of explanations is not the good of the species whose characteristics are being explained, but I know of no passage in Aristotle which says or implies that teleological explanation in nature must appeal only to that kind of good. Certainly *Ph.* II 7, 198b7–8, to which Nussbaum refers, does not do so; it offers as an example the most common situation, where an organ or other part exists for the good of the creature itself which has it, but rules out only the Platonic kind of universal teleology. Our fourth kind of explanation introduces no new *goals* at all; only the good of living things is appealed to. It is just that there, as in the third kind of case, what contributes to the good of an animal kind is something that lies outside it.

[14] Aristotle's argument in these cases is that the arrangements in question are "for the better" (as he says explicitly at 658a24) but it is important not to confuse these cases with those cited above (n. 11) where, e.g., an animal is said to have a kidney because it is "for the better," i.e., better for *it*. The cases here in question are quite different, because the good in prospect is *not* the good of the species whose features are being explained. In fact, unlike all the teleological arguments so far considered, the good achieved in these cases is not the good of *any* animal or plant species at all.

body hair exists for the sake of protection, which is why quadrupeds have more hair on their backs than their undersides; but because human beings stand upright (so that they are equally exposed front and back) if this need alone were operative human beings would be equally hairy in back and front. Yet in fact men have more hair on their chests. Aristotle's explanation is that the front is nobler than the back—in this case, as always, nature uses the given conditions to make *what is better,* and it is better to devote scarce resources to protect the nobler parts. In several similar cases (*PA* 665a18–26, b18–21, 667b32–5, 672b19–24; *IA* 5, 705b3–16) Aristotle explains the location of an animal organ or other part by appeal to a general principle of "nobility" to the effect that front is better than back, above than below and right than left (stated at *PA* 665a22–6, *IA* 706b10–16); and in attributing to nature the tendency to favor the front, top, and right parts *where there is no reason not to,* he attributes to it goals that are quite independent of anything required by the preservation of the species. The good aimed at here is not any living thing's good, in the sense of its survival or well-functioning. In these passages Aristotle adopts a further fundamental principle about nature, that it tends to organize itself, subject to the prior satisfaction of the principle of the preservation of the species, so as to favor the front, top, and right parts over the rear, bottom, and left of anything. His motivation for accepting this principle certainly has the appearance of being somewhat pre-scientific, so there is on any interpretation no alternative but to treat it and the explanations it yields as separate from the explanations we have been concentrating on. The failure of my account to rank these further cases alongside the others and range them all under a single basic principle is no ground for objecting to the account I have given of the other cases; we have to do here with two separate aspects of Aristotle's philosophy of nature, and no unified account of them is presumably to be looked for.

IV

An attractive consequence of the account of Aristotle's commitment to natural teleology that I have given is that it explains one distinctive fact about his version of the teleological hypothesis. This is that Aristotle, unlike other teleologists of nature (Plato, the medievals, Leibniz), finds goal-directedness in natural processes without feeling any need at all to find intentions (whether God's or, somehow or other, nature itself's) lying behind and explaining it. In both the arguments we have examined in section II the central claim on which Aristotle rests his case, the principle of the permanence of the species, is offered as a *fact* about the natural world, his acceptance of which is based on ordinary observation and reasonable inference from it. And if that fact requires to be understood as the result of a tendency in nature *to* preserve these species, the goals thus postulated stand on their own without any need for support by thought processes whether in or antecedent to the arrangements of nature itself. In this crucial respect there is no difference for Aristotle between the existence of the goals of nature and the natural powers of the various kinds of matter one finds in the world. The teleological explanations based on the principle of the preservation of the species are no more mysteriously anthropomorphic and no more problematic than the mechanical explanations by reference to material and moving causes which invoke the natural powers of the various kinds of matter. Aristotle's theory that goals are at work in nature though without the support of thought processes of any kind turns out to be both coherent and philosophically well-motivated.[15]

[15] An early version of this chapter was read to audiences at the Catholic University of America, Yale University, and Rice University, and I profited greatly from the discussion on those occasions. In preparing the final version I benefited from comments by Jonathan Lear, James Lennox, Alexander Nehamas, and Malcolm Schofield on earlier efforts. My oldest debt goes much further back, however: to 1963, when in the course of his marvelous graduate class on Aristotle, in which over a two-year period Oxford students would read and discuss Aristotle's major philosophical works, G.E.L. Owen devoted several sessions to *Physics* II. Those discussions brought out how questionable Aristotle's arguments for teleology in nature are, but also made it clear that behind them lay something quite profound, if only one could put one's finger on it. Later, in the spring of 1971, in meetings of the monthly Ancient Philosophy Colloquium that Owen presided over in New York during his Harvard years, I enjoyed further stimulating discussion of these topics. Since Owen's enormous contributions to ancient philosophy through such discussions may tend to go unrecorded, I am specially pleased to be able to offer in his honor a paper whose seed was planted and nourished in that soil.

CHAPTER 6

HYPOTHETICAL NECESSITY

IN TWO PLACES in his extant works, in *Physics* II 9 and three connected passages of the *Parts of Animals* I 1 (639b21–640a10, 642a1–13, 31–b4), Aristotle introduces and explains his notion of "hypothetical necessity" (ἀνάγκη ἐξ ὑποθέσεως).[1] Judging from this terminology one might think a hypothetical necessity would be anything that is necessary given something else, or something else's being assumed to be so (cf. *APr.* I 10.30b32–40)—in effect, anything that follows necessarily from something else's being so, but that may not, taken in itself, be necessary at all. But this is not so; the necessity of New York's being north of Princeton given that it is north of New Brunswick and New Brunswick is north of Princeton, is not an example of what Aristotle calls a hypothetical necessity. This is because the hypothesis relatively to which a hypothetical necessity, in Aristotle's usage, is necessary is always a goal posited or set up (ὑποτεθέν) as something to be achieved.[2] Hence the necessity in question is always that of a means to some end. A hypothetical necessity, as Aristotle intends the term, is something necessary if some goal is to be attained. Thus, he says, a saw or an axe has to be hard in order to do its job of cutting or splitting, and in order to be hard it has

---

[1] See also *GC* II 11.337b9–338a3, where in discussing necessary coming-to-be (e.g., of the sun's biennial "turnings") he contrasts with such necessities the "hypothetical" necessities that characterize comings-to-be of things in the sublunary world. Aside from these three places the expression ἀνάγκη ἐξ ὑποθέσεως (and similar expressions) referring to a kind of necessity seems to occur in Aristotle only at *De somno* 455b25–27, where Aristotle describes the necessity that animals go periodically to sleep as a "hypothetical" one. There are further passages, especially in the *Organon*, where Aristotle refers to possibility or impossibility (or simple proof) ἐξ ὑποθέσεως (see *De caelo* I 11.281b2–9; *APr.* I 23.40b23–29, 41a23–30; 29.45b15–28; 44.50a16–38; *APo.* I 22.83b38–84a1, II 6.92a20–24), but it is only in the context of natural processes and natural phenomena that he treats hypothetical necessity as a philosophically important special *kind* of necessity.

[2] Thus Aristotle regularly expresses the hypothesis in relation to which something is hypothetically necessary in the future tense: "if this is to be" (see *PA* 642a32, ἡ δ᾿ ἀνάγκη ὁτὲ μὲν σημαίνει ὅτι εἰ ἐκεῖνο ἔσται τὸ οὗ ἕνεκα, ταῦτα ἀνάγκη ἐστὶν ἔχειν; similarly 639b27, 642a13, *Phys.* 200a12, 24, *De somno* 455b26–27). It is important to observe that "if this is to be" here refers not just to any potential event or outcome but (as τὸ οὗ ἕνεκα at 642a33 makes clear) only to events or outcomes that are goals of one sort or another. Obviously anything that exists or happens will generally have some conditions, not part of the thing's essence or nature, that must come about if it is to be, whether or not it is a goal of

to be made of bronze or iron (*PA* 642a9–11, *Phys.* 200a10–13):[3] hence it is necessary for a thing to be made of bronze or iron if it is to be a saw or an axe, and there must be bronze or iron to hand if one is to carry out the intention to make a saw or an axe.

Since, as Aristotle believes and argues in the *Physics* in the chapter immediately preceding the one on hypothetical necessity, nature, especially biological nature, acts for an end, the concept of hypothetical necessity will apply also to natural formations. Where one can identify and characterize in sufficient detail a natural end, for example the nature of a human being as an animal with certain particular capacities, one can ask, as with the saw and axe, what physical conditions must be realized—what a human body must be like—if an animal of that nature is to exist and exercise its natural capacities, that is, the capacities mentioned in characterizing its nature. In answering this question one will be specifying various hypothetical necessities that characterize the human body.

Just which features these might be according to Aristotle's view is something I will return to below, but it is important to notice here at the outset one exclusion. It is certainly true on Aristotle's view (cf. *PA* II 13) that human beings have to have both eyes and eyelids, but I take it that (he thinks) only the necessity for eyelids is or involves a hypothetical necessity. That is because hypothetical necessities are conditions *sine qua non* for ends (*Phys.* 200a5–6, *PA* 642a8), which is to say that they are things not already included in the end in view but rather things that are needed as external means to its realization. Aristotle warns in the *Eudemian Ethics* (1214b14–27) against the error of counting things, like breathing or being awake, that are merely conditions *sine qua non* for human flourishing as actual parts or constituents of the human good, and here the reverse error must be avoided, that of counting as merely a condition *sine qua non* what is in fact something essential to the animal nature in question. If for example it is part of human nature to have the

---

any sort. But (for good reasons) Aristotle does not speak of hypothetical necessity except where the outcome is also a goal: it may be true enough that my window would not have broken when it did if there had not been a heavy wind blowing, but the wind did not blow by (hypothetical) necessity. That is because the window's breaking was no natural (or other) goal: where something is being pursued as a goal there is *some* reason to think it will come about, and this gives point to saying about the conditions necessary for the outcome in these cases, but not the others, that they come about by necessity. Aristotelian hypothetical necessity is not simply the necessity of conditions necessary for some outcome, for something to happen.

[3] Here I run together two presentations of what Aristotle obviously thinks of as the same illustration. The *Physics* passage says, obviously incorrectly, that a saw requires to be made of *iron;* I take this to be venially approximate for what the *PA* says more fully (but not quite fully enough—presumably the necessity is not for bronze or iron, as the *PA* has it, but only for bronze or iron or some other similar material).

capacity to see then having eyes of *some* sort is necessary to a human being as part of his nature (see *GA* V 1.778b16–17), and is not a mere hypothetical necessity. It is, to be sure, not clear where to draw the line between what is actually part of human nature and what is not, but Aristotle's conception of hypothetical necessity depends upon observing the distinction at least in principle. He alludes to it at the end of *Phys.* II 9 (200b4–8)[4] and observes it near the beginning of *PA* I 1 in describing the procedure to be followed in explaining an animal's parts:

> Hence we should if possible say that because this is what it is to be a man (τοῦτ' ἦν τὸ ἀνθρώπῳ εἶναι), therefore he has these things; for he cannot be without these parts. Failing that, we should get as near as possible to it: we should either say altogether that it cannot be otherwise, or that it is at least good thus. (640a33–b1, trans. Balme 1972)

Following Balme,[5] I take it that the first necessity mentioned is the necessity of what follows directly from the human essence, as included in it, and it is only where, as Aristotle says, this kind of necessity cannot be claimed that the question of a hypothetical necessity arises.

The hypothetical necessity of certain animal parts is thus to be sharply distinguished from the necessity of those other parts the having of which is directly implied in the statement of the animal's essential nature.[6] What kind of necessity is this "hypothetical necessity"? Aristotle's answer lies in the fundamental association, explicit in the *Physics* account (200a14, 30–32) and implicit in the *Parts of Animals* (cf. 639b26–30), between hypothetical necessity and matter. For assuming, as Aristotle does, that the

[4] Commentators, beginning with Simplicius and Philoponus, miss this connection. They interpret this passage simply as making the point Aristotle spells out at length in *De an* I 1.403a29–b9 (see also *Meta.* 1025b34–1026a6), that a complete account of the essence of a natural thing will make reference to the matter of which it is composed (or in the case of an affection like anger, in which it is physically realized) (Philoponus *CAG* XVI 338.9–12, Simplicius IX 392.20–27; Ross, *Aristotle's "Physics,"* 533; Charlton, *Aristotle's "Physics,"* 128). But this overlooks the fact that here Aristotle argues not that matter must figure in the definition because these things' "being is not without matter" but because, and to the extent that, having certain *parts* is essential to them: it is because a saw must have teeth and these have to be iron to do their job that Aristotle says the definition will refer to matter. The matter of other, nonessential parts (say, the handle) will not, on Aristotle's argument here, find their way into the definition. His point is, therefore, not the general one about natural things having to have a material constitution that the commentators have seen in it.

[5] Balme, *Aristotle's "De partibus animalium" I and "De generatione animalium" I* (hereafter *Aristotle's "Part. an."*), 87.

[6] In his detailed discussions Aristotle only rarely refers to some part as essentially necessary; but see *GA* II 6.742a16–b17, esp. a34–35 and b1–3 (on why the heart is formed first) and V 1.778a34–35, b16–17.

various kinds of matter have their natures and properties independently at least of their role in constituting any *given* kind of living thing, it can reasonably be said that the actual physical features of any living thing will in very large part be the joint product of, on the one side, the creature's nature, specified in terms of capacities and functions, and on the other, the nature of the materials available to constitute a thing having that nature. That we have eyelids or eye coverings of some sort, is a hypothetical necessity because given the materials that are available for making eyes that see sharply and well as human eyes do, eyes must be fluid in character with only a thin and fine skin (to allow light to get through); but being fluid and thinly covered they are easily injured. Eyelids are thus necessary to protect the eyes (*PA* II 13.657a30–35). Here there are two successive appeals to the hypothetical necessity: first to the necessity for human eyes to be made mostly of fluid, and secondly to the necessity in that case for them to be covered with something solid and resistant to penetration, such as the skin that actually constitutes the eyelids. In such cases it is certain particular material that is necessitated: since different kinds of matter have different properties and behave in different ways by their natures, not just any matter *can* do what eye matter or eyelid matter must do. In the end it is the nature of the material elements the world is made up from and the natural facts about how they do and do not combine with one another to form materials with specific properties and powers that necessitates this particular material constitution and arrangement for the human eye. But though matter is thus the seat, as one could put it (cf. *Phys.* 200a14, ἐν τῇ ὕλῃ τὸ ἀναγκαῖον), of this necessity, its capacity to necessitate these arrangements is conditional on the production of human beings being something that occurs in nature. If this did not occur, then there would be none of these material formations that Aristotle says are necessary. Thus the *necessity* involved in hypothetical necessity is contributed by matter, and can therefore be called a material necessity; but this necessity only produces its effects given that there are to be the various kinds of living things that constitute the goals of natural production.

Aristotle's conception of hypothetical necessity thus unites two at first sight divergent ideas: the idea of matter as making some outcomes or arrangements necessary, and the idea of those outcomes and arrangements as nonetheless means to a natural goal. It is important to emphasize, however, that not every means actually employed in nature in the material constitution of a living thing, but only *necessary* ones, will count on Aristotle's view as hypothetically necessary. In the passage quoted above where he summarizes the procedures to be followed in the *PA*, Aristotle distinguishes between saying "altogether that it cannot be otherwise" and "that it is at least good thus" (640a36–b1): to survive at all and perform its essential functions a creature having the defining characteristics of a human being must have certain parts, e.g., a heart and a liver, but (Aristotle thinks) it does not have to have kidneys (the bladder being alone sufficient to dispose of the urine), nor does the male of the species have to have testicles in order to perform the reproductive function.[7] With a kidney and testicles things go better for such a creature, but they are not necessary. Here there is the same end in view in both classes of means—namely, the good which for human beings consists in living a human life—but only those means to this end that are also indispensable for its being achieved at all count as hypothetically necessitated. The others, which allow this goal to be achieved more efficiently or commodiously, though equally means to the end, are not indispensable for its being achieved, and so are not hypothetically necessitated. In short "hypothetical necessity" really is a kind of *necessity*.

Up to this point I have been summarizing and attempting to clarify the accounts Aristotle gives in *Physics* II 9 and *Parts of Animals* I 1 of what hypothetical necessity *is*. Summarily stated, an organ or feature of a living thing is and is formed by hypothetical necessity if, given the essence of the thing (specified in terms of capacities and functions) and given the natures of the materials available to constitute it, the organ or feature in question is a necessary means to the creature's constitution. Hence, if some feature of an animal body is explained as resulting from necessity hypothetically, it will be an essential component of the explanation that the feature subserves the good that is achieved by there being a well-formed animal of the kind in question. Explanation by appeal to hypothetical necessity is not an alternative to explanation by reference to goals. It is a *special case* of the latter kind of explanation, the case where the independently given nature of the materials available for use in realizing the goal makes precisely *one* possible means, or some narrowly circumscribed set of possible means, to the end in question mandatory. Now Aristotle does in his biological writings frequently enough offer to explain features of animal bodies in this way (e.g., the liquidity of the human eye and the possession of eyelids, mentioned above).[8] But in a large majority of the cases where he explains something as due to some necessity of or in the materials, the necessity invoked cannot be construed as a hypothetical one. I will cite some examples very shortly, but the general form of these explanations and the fact that they are to be sharply distinguished from appeals to hypothetical necessity is already made clear at the end of *Parts of Animals* I 1.

---

[7] I follow Balme's interpretation here (*Aristotle's "Part an.,"* 87). To the references given there add *GA* I 4.717a14–21 (on testicles).

[8] See also *PA* 665b12–14 (blood vessels), 668b33–36 (lungs), 671a7–8 (bladder), 672b22–24 (diaphragm, i.e., φρένες), 674a12–15 (stomach).

Here Aristotle gives a thumbnail account of the methods of argument to be employed in biology, using breathing as an example:

> Exposition should be as follows: for example, breathing exists for the sake of *this*, while *that* comes to be of necessity because of *those*. Necessity signifies sometimes that if there is to be *that* for the sake of which, *these* must necessarily be present; and sometimes that this is their state and nature. For the hot necessarily goes out and comes in again when it meets resistance, and the air must flow in; so much is already necessitated.[9] (642a31–37, trans. Balme 1972)

The first sentence here is admittedly not easy to understand, but that need not give us pause, since in the following sentences Aristotle states very clearly that while some material necessities are hypothetical ones—things that are necessary if an end is to be achieved—others are not, and the account he goes on to provide of the process of respiration illustrates this second kind of necessity. The nature of air and heat are such that when air gets heated it expands—their "state and nature" is such that this must happen. The air in the lung does get heated (he does not say how or why, and for purposes of the example it does not matter); so, expanding by necessity, it goes up the windpipe and out of the mouth. Again, the surrounding air, which is colder, by the same kind of necessity of its "state and nature," resists and (we are told) pursues the hot air back into the mouth and eventually down into the lung, where it gets heated, beginning the process all over again. I have filled out some details of this example, which Aristotle presents only sketchily, despite its telling a rather implausible story (it is not in fact the account of respiration Aristotle himself provides elsewhere), because it is important to see clearly how the explanation is suppose to work. It is plain that the behavior of hot air here claimed to be necessary is represented as resulting from the nature of heat and air in exactly the same way as Aristotle says his materialist predecessors had offered to derive everything from the nature of the materials making up the world. Compare how Aristotle in *Physics* II 8 characterizes their view: "since the hot is such and such by nature (τοιονδὶ πέφυκεν) ... these things are and happen by necessity" (198b12–14); *PA* 642a32–35, "necessity sometimes means that this is their state and nature (ὅτι ἔστιν οὕτως ἔχοντα καὶ πεφυκότα)." So according to him

---

[9] Peck (*Aristotle, "Parts of Animals,"* 78 note *b*) reasonably remarks that this passage looks like a displaced note, intended perhaps to follow 642a13 εἰ ἐκεῖνο ἔσται, somehow stuck on here at the end of the chapter. But there is no reason to doubt its authenticity. In fact the whole chapter seems to be composed of a series of disjoint discussions of points about methodology in biology, with little or no effort to impose a connected scheme of exposition on them.

in this *PA* passage, the hot air in the lung goes out by necessity, causing respiration. And since he here distinguishes this kind of necessity from what he elsewhere calls hypothetical necessity, in this passage Aristotle declares both that there is room in his own theory of natural explanation for appeal to material necessities of this pre-Socratic kind and that he does not construe them, or reconstrue them, as somehow hypothetical necessities after all.[10]

As I mentioned above there are many places in his biological works where Aristotle employs explanations parallel to that given here of respiration. The most fully elaborated case is that of the shedding of the front teeth and their replacement by new ones.[11] Aristotle says (*GA* V 8.789a8–b8, my translation),

> Once [the front teeth] are formed, they fall out on the one hand for the sake of the better, because what is sharp quickly gets blunted, so that [the animal] must get other new ones to do the work [of tearing food off]; . . . on the other hand they fall out from necessity, because the roots of the front teeth are in a thin part [of the jaw], so that they are weak and easily work loose. . . . Democritus, however, neglecting to mention that for the sake of which [things happen in the course of nature], refers to necessity all the things that nature uses—things that are indeed necessitated in that way, but that does not mean they are not for the sake of something, and for the sake of what is better in each case. So nothing prevents [the front teeth] from . . . falling out in the way he says, but it is not on account of those factors (διὰ ταῦτα) that they do, but on account of the end (διὰ τὸ τέλος): *they* are causes as sources of motion and instruments and matter.

In this passage Aristotle does two things that are of interest from the present point of view: first, he explicitly invokes material necessity of what he himself describes as the Democritean sort, while explicitly dissociating it from reference to natural goals. This shows that he accepts that there are material necessities of the Democritean kind, and that he is content to conceive them as operating simply alongside the kind of necessity that follows from the postulation of natural goals. But secondly, while admit-

---

[10] Contra Balme, *Aristotle's "Part. an.,"* 76–84. In "Teleology and Necessity" (Gotthelf and Lennox, *Philosophical Issues in Aristotle's Biology,* 275–85), Balme abandons this interpretation. On Balme's earlier view see further below pp. 138–39.

[11] Besides the passages cited in the text here and below, the following provide especially clear cases where Aristotle explains something as (materially) necessitated while distinguishing the necessitation in question from the "hypothetical" necessitation of certain means for the achievement of a natural goal: *PA* 658b2–7 (why human beings have so much hair on their heads), 663b12–14 (why deer shed their horns), 672a12–15 (lard about the kidneys), 694b2–5 (the webbed feet of water birds); *GA* 738a33–b4 (the formation of menstrual fluid), 767b8–15 (female births), 776b31–34 (the formation of mammaries), 778a29–b19 (eye color).

ting that both sorts of explanation for the falling out of the front teeth are correct—it happens both by necessity and for an end—he insists that the explanation by material necessity is nonetheless incomplete or defective in some respects not very fully specified: it is not διά the Democritean necessities referred to that the teeth fall out, but διά the end. Later on I will offer an interpretation of what Aristotle thinks justifies him in thus downgrading the Democritean explanation, even while accepting it.

Given the prominence and prevalence of appeals to what, following Aristotle's lead in this passage, I shall call Democritean necessity in Aristotle's biological writings, it is surprising that in his official expositions of hypothetical necessity he does not make it clear that in his own theory Democritean necessity continues to play a role. In fact in both expositions he contrasts the hypothetical kind of necessity which he champions with the kind of necessity invoked by his materialist predecessors in such a way as to give many interpreters the impression that he rejects the latter outright. Thus in *Parts of Animals,* while insisting (642a1–3) that many things in nature are formed by necessity, as indeed the materialists had maintained (639b22), he immediately adds:

> But perhaps one might raise the question what sort of necessity is referred to by those who say "by necessity." For of the kinds of necessity distinguished in our philosophical writings neither of the two can be present; but the third *is* found in things that have coming-to-be. For we say that food is something necessary according to neither of the first-mentioned kinds of necessity, but because it is impossible for it to be without it. And this is as it were by hypothesis. (642a3–9, my translation)

In his account of necessity in *Metaphysics* Δ 5, Aristotle does in fact distinguish three principal kinds of necessity (cf. also *Meta.* Λ 7.1072b11–13); and he illustrates one of these by the same example of food as here, saying that this kind of necessity is that of what a thing cannot live without (1015a20–21).[12] The other two kinds of necessity are that of what is forced against a thing's choice or nature, and the necessity of "what cannot be otherwise." This last kind of necessity applies primarily to eternal things (cf. *PA* 639b23–24), since it is absolutely impossible for these to be other in any respect than they are, but it is also sometimes made to cover the Democritean necessity by which physical materials act according to their natures: a thing of that nature cannot (at least, *usually* cannot) fail to act

---

[12] I believe Balme (*Aristotle's "Part. an.,"* 100) is wrong in suggesting *APo.* 94b36 as the probable reference of "in our philosophical writings" at *PA* 642a5–6. That passage mentions only the two rejected types of necessity, whereas Aristotle's mention of *the* third (ἡ τρίτη) is most plausibly taken as indicating that he has in mind a place where a threefold distinction is deployed. In his extant writings only *Metaphysics* Δ 5 fits this description.

in some given way in given circumstances if not interfered with.[13] The apparent implication of the passage quoted is, therefore, that of the three kinds of necessity that there are, only one, hypothetical necessity, can be correctly appealed to when one says that something is formed in nature by necessity. Admittedly, Democritean necessity is not explicitly alluded to in this passage, but since hypothetical necessity and Democritean necessity are different things, and since at least sometimes the latter is ranged under the rejected necessity of "what cannot be otherwise," it appears to be ruled out by implication.

The *Physics* chapter is more difficult to assess but it too seems, and has been thought, to deny the existence of Democritean necessity in the course of affirming that natural necessity is always ἐξ ὑποθέσεως. So it is small wonder that, faced with this apparent inconsistency between Aristotle's scientific practice and his theory of scientific method, David Balme in his commentary on *PA* I should have exerted himself to show that, properly understood, even such cases of necessity as that by which the front teeth fall out can be construed as reducing to hypothetical necessities after all. I will not review here Balme's very complicated argument (as noted above he later disclaimed it himself), but two brief comments may perhaps be ventured.

First, since Aristotle repeatedly contrasts these necessities with what is necessary as a means to some natural goal (see the passages cited in n. 11), it cannot in any event be said that Aristotle himself *classified* them as hypothetical necessities; Balme should rather be understood in his com-

---

[13] The *Metaphysics* chapter does not give examples of the necessity of "what cannot be otherwise," but three considerations suggest strongly that it is meant to include Democritean necessity. First, it would be surprising if *no* place were made in a chapter officially devoted to saying how many "senses" of "necessity" there are for this sense of necessity, and it cannot be accommodated under either of the other two principal senses, at least not as they are presented here. Secondly, this sense is made the basic one (1015a35–b6), from which the other two are treated as extensions, so one seems to be invited to regard it as having the flexibility needed to accommodate this case of necessity. And thirdly, as Ross no doubt rightly points out (*Aristotle, "Metaphysics,"* I 299), at *APo.* II 11.94b37, Aristotle himself marks a twofold distinction of types of necessity that must be taken as parallel to the second and third of the *Metaphysics'* three senses, and the examples there ranged under the necessity of "what cannot be otherwise" are the Democritean type (light particles passing through a lamp "by necessity," 94b27–30; thunder caused by quenching of fire "by necessity," b32–33). Thus it seems in any event certain that in *APo.* II 11 Aristotle makes the necessity of "what cannot be otherwise" (what the commentators refer to as "absolute" or "simple" necessity) cover material necessity of the Democritean sort. And if so, that is good reason to think the same classification is intended in *Meta.* Δ 5 as well. (It should be observed that Aristotle's way of describing "absolute" necessity at *APo.* 94b37–95a1, ἡ κατὰ φύσιν καὶ ὁρμήν, is very close to the characterization he gives at *PA* 642a34–35 of Democritean necessity: the inference to draw is that there too he means to classify Democritean necessity under the necessity of "what cannot be otherwise.")

mentary as attempting to show how, on Aristotle's own views about matter and its relationship to form, Aristotle could have and should have described those necessities as hypothetical ones. That is, though in these passages Aristotle contrasts Democritean material necessity with things that are necessary as means to natural goals, his own views allow him to maintain that these material necessities are actually themselves necessary only as means to natural goals. This fact, I believe, already makes Balme's enterprise seem rather ill conceived. But secondly, I doubt very much that Aristotle's views about matter and its relationship to form do imply, as Balme in his commentary on *Parts of Animals* maintained, that whatever given materials do by a necessity of their own nature turns out on examination to be hypothetically necessitated only. In so interpreting Aristotle, Balme based himself on passages in the *Meteorology* (IV 12) and *Parts of Animals* (II 1.646a12–b10: cf. also *GA* I 1.715a9–11) where Aristotle describes three stages in the constitution of a living thing: the non-uniform parts (organs) are the matter of the animal itself, the uniform parts (flesh, blood, bones, etc.) are matter for the organs, and, finally, the material elements (earth, air, fire, and water) are matter for the uniform parts. Balme correctly took Aristotle to hold that the items at each of these three levels have the character that they have for the sake of the items at the level next higher. But he thought that this implies, quite generally, that the material elements themselves have the natural properties they do for the sake of the animal forms which are going to be made out of them, so that if, say, fire by a necessity of its nature causes certain changes in certain liquids, that necessity itself can be seen as holding only because an element that has these powers is needed if there are to be living things. This seems to me a mistaken interpretation of what Aristotle is saying in these passages. He is not discussing the question why in general the elements have the natures they do, but only why a *particular* animal is made up of the certain *particular* elements, and in the certain particular amounts and ratios, that it is. His point is just that if an animal of a certain kind is to be constituted these certain amounts of certain elements must be present for use: in effect, for *this* creature *those* elements are hypothetically necessitated. But plainly that presupposes, and does nothing to explain, the natural powers of the elements concerned. For it is only because the elements antecedently *do* have the particular powers they have of combining with and affecting one another, that *this* elemental contribution (*so* much earth, *so* much air, and so on) rather than some other is necessitated in this case. When properly understood, then, it seems to me that the passages to which Balme appeals show Aristotle actually presupposing as simply given the material elements and their natures, and arguing from them to the necessity of certain particular elemental combinations in order to constitute particular animal natures.

So they tell against, rather than in favor of, Balme's thesis that for Aristotle the elements have the powers they do in order to make possible the world of living things.

It appears to me, therefore, that if the method Aristotle actually employs in studying biological entities and explaining their structure and development are after all consistent with his pronouncements on the methodology of biology, this can only be shown by interpreting the latter so that they do not conflict with the former. On examination I believe such an interpretation does turn out to be correct. Let us turn first to *Physics* II 9. The topic for discussion in this chapter is first stated at the beginning of chapter 8, which together with chapter 9 constitutes a connected account of the respective roles of final causes and necessity in the natural realm, i.e., the realm of living things. In introducing it there he makes it clear that in asking how "the necessary" operates in natural things (περὶ τοῦ ἀναγκαίου πῶς ἔχει ἐν τοῖς φυσικοῖς, 198b11–12), he means to ask on what basis matter of various kinds can by its nature be said to necessitate natural outcomes. For he explains what he means by "the necessary" here by referring to his predecessors' efforts to explain the formation of living things and their parts by appeal to the natural powers of matter-kinds as necessitating them (198b12–14). So when Aristotle returns to this question in chapter 9 and asks whether that which is by necessity (τὸ ἐξ ἀνάγκης, 199b34) is found in nature (only) on a hypothesis or (instead) without any such qualification (ἁπλῶς, b35), he is asking whether *in* necessitating natural outcomes, matter is to be thought of as doing so on a hypothesis, namely, given that some natural goal is to be produced, or simply on its own.[14] That is, I take the question from the outset to be not whether Democritean material necessity exists, but how it operates—on its own or rather within the context and against the controlling background of some presupposed natural goal.

Aristotle's predecessors, denying goals in nature, thought of material necessities as functioning entirely on their own to produce the observed natural, living things. This, as Aristotle says (199b35–200a5), is as if one thought to explain a wall as having been produced by rocks and dirt and sticks assembling themselves by nothing but their natural tendencies, as materials of those kinds, to move and interact with one another under given environing conditions. In fact, of course, the wall came about because someone wanted to cover and protect some possessions, so that the natural interactions and movements that the materials themselves con-

---

[14] On this way of taking the opening lines of the chapter see further below, pp. 143–44 and n. 19.

tributed only came into play because of the builder's intentions. Thus although the stones at the bottom of the wall hold up the superstructure and do so because, by a necessity of their nature as stones, they both stay put and do not contract under the weight as foam would, for example, this contribution they make to the being of the wall is only made by them because they have been placed there for the sake of the wall that the builder intends. In this case, then, stones or something very like them are necessary (i.e., hypothetically necessary) for the being of the wall (as Aristotle says, the wall could not have come to be without them, 200a5–6), but *that* is because these materials have, by their nature as the materials that they are, certain powers to act and react with other materials in certain fixed ways, by a necessity that is other than hypothetical: in general, he says at 200a7–10, where a thing has an end, it cannot be without certain things that have a "necessary nature," an ἀναγκαία φύσις, and by this he means things that by a necessity of their nature act and react in certain ways.[15] So, according to Aristotle in *Physics* II 9, Democritean necessity does play a role in nature, i.e., in the formation of natural, living things, but it does so only hypothetically—that is, only on the hypothesis that a living thing is to be produced. *Given* that a living thing is to be, certain materials are necessary (i.e., these materials are hypothetically necessary); this means that the presence of those materials is to be explained by reference to this goal. But once, for that reason, they *are* there, their nature, and the material necessity that belongs to it, will cause them to behave in various ways. They will act in those ways by necessity, and this necessity is not a hypothetical one.

An example may help to bring out the point. In *GA* II 4 Aristotle explains the fact that semen in congealing a portion of the menstrual fluid

---

[15] He certainly does not mean the tautology that it cannot be without what it cannot be without, i.e., without what has a nature that is *hypothetically* necessary for it to be. As *PA* III 2.663b23 shows (cf. b34), to have a "necessary nature" is to have a nature that necessitates certain modes of action and reaction in given conditions, without reference to any end that may be achieved by its so acting. The reference in our text (200a31–32) to "matter *and its movements*" as what in living things is necessary confirms that here too matter's necessity involves its behaving in certain ways by a necessity of *its* nature. Thus, in this chapter Aristotle applies the predicate "necessary" to the matter of a living thing in two senses: (a) it is hypothetically necessary for the being of the thing but (b) it is itself a necessary thing in the sense that it has a nature as a necessary result of which it behaves in certain more or less fixed ways. Perhaps one should take ἐξ ἀνάγκης at 200b2, 3, with the infinitives rather than with the main verb, δεῖ, as is grammatically certainly possible and as word order (especially in b3) rather suggests. In that case Aristotle will be saying here that in order for there to be health or a human being certain things must (δεῖ), i.e., by hypothetical necessity, happen and be present by necessity (ἐξ ἀνάγκης), i.e., by the *materially* necessary action of matter; the distinction between the two applications of necessity will then be explicitly marked by the two modal expressions δεῖ and ἐξ ἀνάγκης.

to form a fetus causes a membrane to form around its periphery as both due to necessity and happening for an end (739b26–30). It happens by necessity because, as can be observed when milk is heated, the surfaces of thickish fluids naturally do solidify when heated, and what the semen does is to heat up that portion of the catamenia. (It happens for an end because the forming creature needs a solid periphery to mark it off from the surrounding fluids—if it were not in a fluid environment things would be different.) Here the necessity is a Democritean, material necessity. But plainly there would be no congealing going on here even partly by that kind of necessity unless these materials (the semen, the catamenia) were there, and *they* are there because they are necessary (this time hypothetically) for the formation of a fetus, which is a natural goal. Thus, as I interpret Aristotle in *Physics* II 9, he wants to say that Democritean necessity does indeed exist and has a role to play in the formation of living things, but that where it does make a contribution it only does so because the materials whose necessary action is in question are themselves necessitated hypothetically. On this interpretation it could be said that Aristotle "subsumes" Democritean necessity under hypothetical necessity in the explanation of living things.[16] But that does not mean that he *reduces* it to hypothetical necessity. Plainly, as in the passage just cited about the congealing of the fetus, the Democritean necessity appealed to is contrasted with appeal to final causation, as no hypothetical necessity could correctly be. It is subsumed under hypothetical necessity only in the sense that its operation in the case of living things presupposes the need for materials of that kind; it is that need, and not the natural powers of material stuffs themselves acting by the necessities of their natures, still less by random chance, that explains their presence at the appropriate times and places. Nonetheless, *when* they are present they behave in certain ways by a necessity of their natures, and this necessity retains its character as nonhypothetical.

Aristotle's concern, then, is not to deny that some effects in the formation of living things are produced by Democritean material necessity, but to insist that the production of these effects by that necessity is contingent upon the forming plant's or animal's need for matter of the kind in question. But he insists on a second limitation as well. However much certain particular stages in the formation of a living thing may be materially necessitated, the end product, the finished living thing, is never the result of such necessitation: the end, he says (200a33–34), is the cause of the matter, but the matter is not reciprocally the cause of the end (nor does it ne-

[16] It is important to keep this restriction clearly in mind: I do not mean to suggest that outside this context Aristotle subsumes Democritean necessity under hypothetical necessity in even the attenuated sense argued for here. See further below p. 145.

cessitate it: 200a15–20). Democritean necessity does not suffice to explain the coming to be of any fully formed plant or animal: you cannot start from the presence of certain materials and trace a connected series of changes, resulting from nothing but necessities belonging to the natures and powers of the materials present, that leads up to the fully formed living thing as its outcome. Thus Aristotle's view, as he explains it in *Physics* II 9, involves two limitations on the operation of Democritean necessity, where living things are concerned. First, it is not by material necessity that the materials needed to form a living thing come to be present at its formation; that happens by hypothetical necessity only. And, secondly, the materials, whatever else they do necessitate, do not necessitate the end product of the process to which they contribute. In both these contentions, of course, Aristotle contradicts the determinist view of the materialist philosophers against whom his argument in the chapter is meant to be directed. But in neither of them does he deny that anything ever happens in the formation of living things by material necessity. Indeed, as I pointed out above, he approaches the discussion of hypothetical necessity in *Physics* II 9 after posing his question in such a way as to make clear his acceptance that Democritean necessity does play a role (198b11–16). His question is *how* this necessity figures, not whether it does; and the two limitations just discussed constitute the core of his answer to this question.

How, then, is it that so many readers come away from *Physics* II 9, as from *PA* I 1, thinking, even if unhappily, that Aristotle has rejected Democritean necessity altogether in favor of hypothetical? The chapter begins with a question, translated by Hardie and Gaye as follows: "As regards what is 'of necessity,' we must ask whether the necessity is 'hypothetical' or 'simple' as well."[17] Now this is usually read as referring to two different

---

[17] It is customary to take the καί (199b35), as Hardie and Gaye (*Aristotle: Physica*) do, as meaning "also," but there are good reasons to prefer the alternative "actually," "in fact" (cf. Denniston, *The Greek Particles*, 317). Read with "also" the Hardie and Gaye translation yields these two alternatives: (a) to suppose that only hypothetical necessities are to be found in nature and (b) to suppose that in addition to these there are also "simple" necessities. So the two alternatives share a commitment to hypothetical necessities, and so to teleological causation. In that case neither view represents the view of Aristotle's materialist opponents, as one might have expected. And it becomes hard to understand why in answering the question Aristotle spends so much time explaining and arguing for the presence of hypothetical necessity in nature, something the two views to be decided between share a commitment to, rather than simply discussing directly whether there are simple necessities in nature, the point over which the two alternatives differ. If καί is translated "actually," the second alternative will express the opponent's view, and then it will be quite natural that Aristotle exerts himself to argue that the necessity that matter contributes *is* hypothetical, with the natural implication that (however this is then to be interpreted) it is not a case of simple necessity.

kinds of necessity, Aristotle's hypothetical necessity (or necessity as a means to some goal) on the one hand, and the "simple" or "absolute" necessity of "what cannot be otherwise" on the other; it is to this latter kind of necessity that the materialists are thought to have wished to reduce all the behavior of material things. Since in what follows Aristotle plainly argues that the necessity in natural, living things is hypothetical, the inference seems forced that he proposes to do away with all talk of the other kind of necessitation, where "from certain conditions a certain result must follow."[18] That is, he rejects Democritean necessity altogether. Now on the interpretation I have presented there is no cause to reach this conclusion, since I have taken the opening question differently.[19] Instead of presenting as exclusive alternatives (explanation by) hypothetical necessity and (explanation by) material necessity, I take the contrast to be between two ways in which material necessity might be thought to operate. But, even if we adopt this interpretation in place of the usual one, we are not yet free of the difficulty. For we still face the fact that in *Parts of Animals* I (642a1–9, translated above) Aristotle insists that when things come about in living things and their formation by necessity this necessity is hypothetical, and refers to the other two kinds of necessity, including "absolute" necessity, only to deny that they apply in this context. What can be made of this? Must Aristotle here (and in *Physics* II 9 if its opening question is read in the usual way) be construed as denying altogether the operation of Democritean necessity?

I do not think so. In interpreting Aristotle's rejection of "absolute" necessity in the *Parts of Animals* passage, one must bear carefully in mind the two limitations on the operation of Democritean necessity that I have argued form the core of his positive doctrine in *Physics* II 9. First of all, the end product of a process of formation is never, according to Aristotle, materially necessitated. This means that so far as the *whole* living thing is concerned, the flat rejection of absolute necessitation does fully accord with Aristotle's position: anything necessary there may be in such outcomes really is, on his view, hypothetically necessary only. But, secondly, where material necessity does function—in forming the membrane round an animal fetus, in making an eye blue or brown, and so on—it is on Aristotle's view at best a *proximate* cause of the necessitated feature. That a blue eye is produced depends on the properties of the materials and their materially necessary interactions as the eye is being formed; but

---

[18] Ross 1936, 531.

[19] I take ἁπλῶς closely with ὑπάρχει and parallel to ἐξ ὑποθέσεως so that (as given above p. 140) the alternatives are (a) that the (material) necessity in natural things is present hypothetically and (b) that it is present without that qualification, i.e., that it operates on its own and without any dependence on natural goals.

it is not, on Aristotle's theory, by material necessity that those materials, with their necessitating properties, are present in the first place. To say, therefore, in the contexts of the discussion in *Physics* II 9 or *Parts of Animals* I 642a1–9, that it is even partly by "absolute" necessity that things happen in animate nature would be seriously misleading. Ultimately, on Aristotle's view, nothing that happens in the formation of a living thing *does* happen by "absolute" necessity; if you trace back its conditions beyond the first step or two you do not find this kind of necessity operating at all.

When, therefore, one bears in mind the two limitations on the operation of material necessity for which Aristotle argues in *Physics* II 9, it is not too surprising that in discussing in general terms the role of necessity in the operations of animate nature he should deny a place to "absolute" necessity, as he does in *PA* 642a1–9 and would do in *Phys.* II 9 on the usual translation of its opening sentence. But this does not mean that, even here, he denies to Democritean necessity the sort of role which he assigns to it at the end of *PA* I 1, and that he appeals to it for at many places in the biological works; on the contrary, as we have seen, he actually insists on the necessitating character of matter in the course of his discussion in the *Physics*. It is just that *ultimately* what happens by that necessity only happens because it is hypothetically necessitated. Properly interpreted, therefore, in neither exposition of his theory of hypothetical necessity (even if the opening question of *Phys.* II 9 is understood in the usual way) does Aristotle imply that hypothetical necessity is the only kind of necessity ever found in the workings of animate nature.

Before concluding, two points of clarification. First, as I noted in passing, Aristotle's discussions of hypothetical necessity in *Parts of Animals* and *Physics* only discuss the role of material necessity where animate nature is concerned. In the passages we have considered, he does not discuss at all the behavior of the material elements or other stuffs outside of this context. He holds, of course, that material necessity operates wherever matter is found, but his claim (as I have interpreted him) that it operates only against the background of hypothetical necessity is limited to the formation and behavior of living things. If, for example, ice forms on a pond as a result of material necessities attaching to the natures of cold air and water, nothing he says in these passages commits him to seek some hypothetical necessity to explain why the air and water in question became conjoined, with that result.[20]

---

[20] Still less is he committed to seek a hypothetical necessity to explain air and water's having these natures (see above pp. 138–39). Aristotle does indeed hold (see *Meteor.* IV 12) that even the simple physical elements have a formal as well as a material nature, and that the

Secondly, I am now in a position to explain why Aristotle, even while accepting some explanations by Democritean necessity, downgrades them—why he says, for example (*GA* 789b6–8), that even though the front teeth do fall out in the way Democritus says they do, it is not on account of (διά) the material factors he appeals to, but on account of the end, the good they do the creature whose teeth they are, that they do so.[21] For, as our discussion has brought to light, Aristotle holds that it is only because of this end that the initial teeth form where and as they do, with the result that the front ones are vulnerable to the material forces which result in their loosening and eventual loss. These material forces are, Aristotle says, instruments (ὄργανα, 789b8–9) that nature, i.e., the nature of the whole animal here being brought to perfection, uses, and on the interpretation I have presented this metaphor is quite apt as an expression of Aristotle's theory. If there had not been a need for front teeth, there would have been none there for the material forces to work upon. By placing them where it does the nature of the animal therefore also brings it about that they eventually fall out; so *that* nature (and not the nature of the materials) is ultimately responsible for this loss. And because the animal nature is responsible for what happens in the course of an animal's development by functioning as the end or final cause of what happens, it is the completed animal nature as end that bears the ultimate responsibility for the teeth falling out at a certain stage of development. So, on Aristotle's theory it is quite right to say, as he does, that though the teeth do indeed fall out by material necessity it is not *on account of* that necessity that they do, but *on account of* the end, i.e., on account of the completed animal nature that is being formed here.[22] Absent that, there would have been no teeth-falling-out-by-necessity to be explained; it is only *on account of* the fact that this end was being pursued that these teeth fall out by material necessity.[23]

It has frequently been remarked, and is obvious enough, that Aristotle developed the concept of hypothetical necessity in an effort to reconcile

---

formal nature is to be defined in terms of some natural function, some end the stuff in question naturally achieves (389b28–29, with 390a3–9; a16–20). But this just refers, e.g., to fire's tendency to heat things, and offers no ground for saying that fire has the nature it does (including the natural tendency to warm things up) for the *sake* of anything further.

[21] See above, pp. 135–36. Aristotle reiterates this complaint in *Physics* II 9, among other places: 200a6–7, 9–11, 26–27.

[22] For further explication and defense of this conception of how Aristotelian final causes function in biology, see chapter 5 above, esp. pp. 118–20.

[23] Thus I see no need to interpret Aristotle's preference for the teleological explanation over the material necessity one as based on the thought that teleological explanations, where available, do more of what we want explanations to do, that they better assuage the discomfort that leads us to ask "Why?" and so on, than the appeal to material necessity does.

necessity with teleology in the explanation of animate nature. On my interpretation this concept turns out to be both a coherent and, given the science of his time, a remarkably effective way of achieving this result. These are perhaps two good reasons for hoping my interpretation is correct.[24]

Resort to such epistemological considerations is anachronistic and betrays a fundamental misconception of the philosophical problems Aristotle faced and his way of addressing them.

[24] In working out my interpretation of Aristotle's views on hypothetical necessity, I have concentrated on *Phys.* II 9 and *PA* 642a1–13 together with the discussion of respiration as a sample case for biological explanation which follows only twenty lines later (642a31–b4). These passages, I have argued, express the same view about hypothetical necessity and its relations to Democritean necessity, but they seem clearly written in mutual independence. The same cannot be said for the third of the three passages of *PA* listed above (p. 130), 639b21–640a10, which is in fact just a shorter and less full summary of *Phys.* II 9 (to which it refers back at 640a3). For that reason I have made few detailed references to it: the interpretation I have given of *Phys.* II 9 applies *a fortiori* to this passage as well.

This chapter was originally prepared for presentation at a Conference on Philosophical Issues in Aristotle's Biology held at Marquette University in November 1981. In making revisions I have profited from discussions at the conference, and owe thanks also to Gail Fine, Allan Gotthelf, and Gisela Striker, who gave me helpful written comments on that first version. I am especially grateful to Striker, whose comments led me to make significant improvements in my interpretation of *Meta.* Δ 5 and its relation to the texts of *Phy.* and *PA* that have been my primary concern (see especially n. 13 above).

CHAPTER 7

TWO NOTES ON ARISTOTLE ON MIXTURE

I

ARISTOTLE SAYS that if (for example) some sugar is dissolved in some water, with the result that we now have a new homoeomerous or "like-parted" stuff, sugar water (and not merely some water with particles of sugar suspended in it), then the sugar and the water that we mixed together have nonetheless not been destroyed. By his account, sugar water does not result through the joint transformation of the two ingredients (and so their mutual destruction) into some new compound material, as it were with its own molecular structure distinct from those of the ingredients. Sugar water is what Aristotle calls a "mixture" (μίξις) of sugar and water, although these ingredients survive only in a very special way within it. The sugar water is not actually, but it *is* potentially, both (the) sugar and (the) water; *actually* it is (only) sugar water (GC I 10, 327b24–26). In the sugar water the δύναμις (= power? or = potentiality?) of the sugar and the δύναμις of the water are both preserved (327b30–31). In some sense, then, the water and the sugar that separately preexisted are both still there: they are there somehow "potentially," they are there so far as their "powers" or their "potentialities" are concerned. (For now I leave undecided how, more precisely, to understand δύναμις at 327b31.) Hence we could, in principle, undo the mixture and get back exactly the sugar and the water that we started with (327b28–29)—not merely some water and some sugar, or even water and sugar in precisely the initial quantities, but that very sugar and that very water.

How are we to understand this "power" or "potentiality" of water and of sugar that on Aristotle's account are preserved (or that *they* preserve) when they are ingredients in the sugar water? Apparently we have to understand the situation here differently from another case that Aristotle describes in which, as here, two substances interact to form a new substance. This is the case where (for example) some water and some fire reciprocally act on one another and together get turned into some air (II 4, 331b12 ff.). In this latter case, we have no mixture of fire and water from which we could recover the fire and the water that existed separately beforehand, and such that the new substance, the air in question, has in it, in some sort of potential form, both that fire and that water. For this case is, and Aristotle clearly describes it as, one in which air is *gener-*

ated from fire and water: hence, it is a case of the destruction of some fire and some water, in the interests of the generation from them of some air.[1] The air simply replaces the water and the fire. What happens in this case, on Aristotle's account, is this. Water is by nature wet and cold stuff (that is its definition, as a basic kind of matter), fire is by nature dry and hot stuff.[2] Here, then, the wet of the water defeats the dry of the fire, changing the fire so that the matter that underlies and constitutes it ceases to be dry and becomes wet, while—from the other side—the hot of the fire reciprocally and simultaneously defeats the cold of the water with the result that the water is changed so that its matter ceases to be cold and becomes hot.[3] So the underlying matter of the fire and the underlying matter of the water are each altered in a corresponding but different way, with the identical result. The matter of the fire remains hot, but becomes wet; the matter of the water remains wet, but becomes hot. Thus each is now hot and wet—and so each now underlies the same third stuff, namely air (since air by nature is hot and wet stuff). So we have now two quantities of air, joined together to form a single mass, whereas before we had two separate quantities, one a mass of fire and the other a mass of water side by side. Here, because the original fire and water have been destroyed in the course of the conversion of each by the other into air, there can be no thought of recovering *the* water and *the* fire we started with. It is true, of

---

[1] The γένεσις of the simple bodies from one another is announced at the beginning of the chapter (331a10–12) as the next topic; for its application to this specific case, see 331b36. For γένεσις as always involving destruction, see GC I 3, in particular 318a23–27: when anything comes into being, it does so from something else that thereby ceases altogether to be.

[2] See 330b3–7.

[3] See the talk of "overpowering" at 331a26–32: the wet that overpowers (κρατεῖν) the dry when, as is there discussed, air comes to be from fire is the wet belonging to some air which converts some fire into its own substance by overpowering the fire's dryness (and similarly for the other case there mentioned, of water's overpowering the heat of some air to convert it into water). In the more complex case discussed at 331b12–24, where water and fire act on each other so that each converts the other into a distinct *third* stuff, air (not into itself), though Aristotle does not use the language of "overpowering," he envisages the same process as taking place with respect not to the whole nature but, so to speak, to half of it in each case: each loses one of its natural properties, getting that replaced by its opposite, a different one in each case. (Aristotle speaks here simply of one quality of each substance being "destroyed," φθαρῇ b12, 15, 20: at II 7, 334b11–12 he makes it plain that what destroys the given quality is the other stuff's action on the stuff possessing that quality.) It is noteworthy that in the case of mixture Aristotle speaks of the two ingredients as also overpowering each other in some way (328a28–31), but in this case, he says, because they are equalized in their "powers" (ταῖς δυνάμεσιν ἰσάζῃ πως, a29), neither overpowers the other wholly, converting it into the same kind of stuff as itself (as happens in the contrasting case mentioned at a24–28), but each brings the other into some common intermediate state, something μεταξὺ καὶ κοινόν, a31).

course, that the reverse transformation might take place, a transformation of some of the air into fire and the rest into water—and even into the precise amounts of the two stuffs that were originally present. (Such a transformation would require the operation of some other, outside forces sufficient to work those respective conversions; the air, being a stable substance, does not have the power all by itself to work them.) But that would give us two new masses of water and fire, not the same old ones we started from. For the old fire and the old water were destroyed when the air came into being.

Nonetheless, on Aristotle's theory one can and must say in this case that, just as the water and the fire at the outset were each of them potentially air, so also the air that results is potentially both fire and water: see I 3, 317b13–18 and II 7, 334b9–10. So in this case, too, the new substance (air) is, in some way, potentially the two other substances from which it originated—just as the sugar-water mixture is potentially the sugar and the water that are its ingredients. But, for Aristotle, there is an important difference. Only with mixtures can one say that the new substance already has existing within it, in some way, the stuffs that it potentially is. Here, but not in the other case, the realization of that potentiality is also the recovery of the ingredients.

Aristotle has drawn attention to two importantly distinct phenomena: the mutual transformation of two stuffs into a third, new one, as against the mixture of two stuffs giving rise to a new one in which, in some way, the ingredients survive. But does his general theory of matter or stuffs in fact provide the conceptual resources he needs to keep these two phenomena distinct? How are we to distinguish the *special* way in which the mixture, though actually for example only sugar water, is potentially still both sugar and water, from the way that the resultant air in my example above is potentially both water and fire?

Evidently the difference is somehow to be located in what Aristotle says in the case of mixtures, and only in that case, about the preservation in the new substance of the δύναμις of each of the two ingredients (327b30–31). This term can of course simply mean "potentiality," but there are reasons for construing it here instead as meaning "power." First, if it means simply "potentiality," then the fact that Aristotle says about mixture but not about generation of a new substance through the destruction of its antecedents that the δύναμις of the stuffs from which the new substance comes to be survives within it would be of no significance: as we have seen, he could equally have said the same thing in the latter case too. If the air in his example in II 4 is both potentially fire and potentially water, we can certainly say that there exist in it those two potentialities. And then we would be at a loss as to how, in Aristotelian terms, to distinguish the two phenomena. More significantly, we find him saying later in his discussion, at 328a29, that when a mixture is to take place, the two ingredients-to-be are "pretty much equalized in their δυνάμεις"—whereas when this equality is lacking, what happens instead is that one of the two substances "overpowers" the other and simply increases its own size by converting the other into stuff of the same sort as itself, as happens when a drop of wine falls into 10,000 measures of water (328a23–28). In this last passage the term clearly means "powers" and not mere potentialities.[4] It seems, then, that we should interpret Aristotle's claim that the ingredients' δύναμις is preserved in the mixture (327b31) as referring not simply to their potentiality to be fully present but rather to the continued presence in the mixture of their inherent powers—a presence that grounds, in their case, that later possibility.[5] We can then use the survival of those δυνάμεις as the distinctive feature of mixtures that distinguishes *their* way of potentially being what they originated from, from the way that a substance generated from two others remains potentially them (merely because it can be changed back into them, and not because it retains any of their proprietary powers).

---

[4] Both Philoponus and Alexander of Aphrodisias clearly so understand the word in this context. For Philoponus, see *In Aristotelis Libros de Generatione et Corruptione Commentaria*, ed. H. Vitelli (*CAG*, vol. 14 pt. 2, Berlin: Reimer, 1897), e.g., at 198. 25–27. For Alexander, see *De Mixtione*, CAG, Supp. vol 2 pt. 2, 230. 26–34. *De Mixtione* has been translated into English in Todd, *Alexander of Aphrodisias on Stoic Physics*.

[5] It is crucial, then, to see that in the whole section 327b22–31 Aristotle first uses the word δύναμις twice in the dative (ἐστὶ τὰ μὲν δυνάμει . . . τῶν ὄντων, b23; ὄντος . . . δυνάμει . . . ἑκατέρου, b25) to mean "potentially" or "in potentiality," while later, at b31, using it in the nominative (σώζεται γὰρ ἡ δύναμις αὐτῶν, sc. τῶν μιγνυμένων) differently, in fact in just the sense he uses it a little later, at 328a29—to mean the ingredients' inherent powers. He means, in fact, to offer the retention of these powers as the ground, in this special case, of the potential existence of the ingredients in the mixture. One should notice that in between Aristotle has used the cognate verb (δυνάμενα χωρίζεσθαι πάλιν, b28) to refer to the ability or capacity of the ingredients to be separated out again from the mixture. So the sense of "potentiality" at b23 and 25 does not in any event extend to every occurrence of δύνασθαι/δύναμις in the passage. There is no good reason, then, to insist that it has to mean "potentiality" at b31. In his translation of 327b22–31 (in *Matter, Space and Motion*, 67, Richard Sorabji also renders δύναμις at line 31 as "power" while rendering it (correctly) at 23 and 25 as "potentiality." But he recognizes that it *might* be taken to refer simply to a merely potential existence in the mixture of its ingredients (p. 68), and he does not definitely opt for the other translation. H. H. Joachim in the Oxford translation understood the passage just as I do: he renders δύναμις at b31 as "power of action" (*The Works of Aristotle*, vol. 2, ed. W. D. Ross [1930]), but as "potentially" at b23 and 25; contrast C.J.F. Williams in the Clarendon Aristotle series (*Aristotle's "De Generatione et Corruptione,"* [1982], 34), who translates it throughout as "potentiality." J. Barnes in the revised Oxford translation, perhaps misled by the expectation that δύναμις should have the same sense at all three occurrences, has substituted "potentiality" for Joachim's "power of action" at b31 (*The Complete Works of Aristotle*, ed. J. Barnes, [1984], 1:536), thus obliterating Joachim's insight.

But in what way do these powers survive? And why, after all, should we suppose that they do? Here is a first (unsatisfactory, but instructive) stab at an answer. We should bear in mind that Aristotle thinks that in a mixture or blend (κρᾶσις, 328a8–9) all the perceptible properties of the resultant stuff, and all its dispositions for affecting other things, are directly determined by the antecedent properties of the original stuffs. In color, taste, hardness/softness, etc., as well as heat and moisture, the mixture or blend lies somewhere intermediate between the two original stuffs, and it does so because each of them has reciprocally been made by the other to shift to the same intermediate position with regard to all its perceptible qualities. The same is true of its dispositions for affecting other bodies.[6] Now, if one thinks, first of all, only about mixtures such as sugar water or wine diluted by water or other artificial mixtures, one might think of a mixture as inherently something temporary, something that would tend to come apart, with the ingredients naturally reverting to their independent, self-maintaining status, if the artificially imposed conditions of union were relaxed. That would provide some reason to think that the water and the sugar must retain within the mixture their individual identities and their independent existences in some way—in short, by preserving their distinctive "powers." Sugar water has no independent nature of its own (not even a derivative one), which, as such, would tend to make it persist stably. It continues to have its specific properties only through the continuing interaction between the two initial stuffs (whose powers are still present), which keeps the two of them "moderated" in this way. So it would readily come apart into its ingredients, simply because they do retain somehow their separate natures and their individual powers.

On this view, sugar and water continue to exist in the mixture (in some way) and to retain their separate identities, but due to the effects on each of the other ingredient each has departed temporarily from the unmitigated possession of its defining perceptible properties and its full natural powers for affecting other bodies. Each has come to possess instead some reduced or enhanced set of these "surface" properties, the same for each—and in fact the same as those that the mixture itself possesses throughout. Within the mixture, each of the ingredients actually possesses not its usual properties (of heat/cold, wet/dry, its consequent colors, etc.) but instead the "intermediate" properties of the mixture. However, each ingredient only manages to continuously possess these intermediate properties and to produce those intermediate effects on other bodies outside the mixture, because underneath its current appearances, it does retain its

[6] See I 10, 328a28–35.

own original powers. These powers are still at work, and if the conditions of the mixture were relaxed (so that each ingredient ceased to act on the other in this way), that would immediately have the effect that the separate ingredients would resume the natural and normal expression of that underlying nature and those underlying powers. They would immediately cease to have the "intermediate" properties that, in the mixture, they do have. They would revert to displaying also on their surface, so to speak, their normal distinctive perceptible properties and capacities for affecting other bodies.

Now, so far I have only considered artificial mixtures such as sugar water or wine water. For these, some such account looks plausible. However, in fact, for Aristotle the most important mixtures—and the ones for which he goes to the trouble to take up the question of the nature and possibility of mixtures—are the mixtures of the four simple bodies, earth, air, fire, and water, which constitute all the varied "like-parted" materials making up plants and animals (flesh, blood, bone, bark, vine, wood, and so on) plus the inorganic liquid and solid constituents of the sea, the earth, and the atmosphere. (See GC II 7–8.) Thus we learn in II 7 that flesh is a compound produced from the mixture in specific proportions of specific appropriate quantities of earth, air, fire, and water. Yet flesh and the rest, unlike sugar water, have their own quite determinate and self-sustaining natures: other describable potential mixtures of these ingredients don't "stick" and don't constitute continuing such "unions"[7] so as to count as mixtures of them. Such other conceivable mixtures just don't occur in nature at all (though from the chemical point of view they are perfectly respectable and perhaps even artificially producible). So Aristotle's idea cannot be that mixtures are inherently temporary and unstable stuffs, liable to fall apart if the ingredients did not dynamically keep interacting with one another inside them while continuing in some way to possess their original natures. All the ones that matter to Aristotle have their own forms, and are just as independently natured as earth, air, fire, and water themselves are (indeed, more so, given the greater complexity of their forms). A living animal's flesh is held together by the animal's form, and as part of that it is held together by its own form as the flesh that it is. It is not held together merely by the contingent fact that its ingredient earth, air, fire, and water are continuously working dynamically against one another in such a way as to sustain it as flesh.

---

[7] For this term as a description of what is involved in mixture, see the last words of GC I 10, at 328b22: "mixture is the union of the things mixed when they have undergone alteration" (ἡ δὲ μίξις τῶν μικτῶν ἀλλοιωθέντων ἕνωσις).

Thus, in interpreting Aristotle we cannot use the thought of mixtures as not independently natured entities whose continued existence, therefore, needs some dynamic and continuing expression of the natures and powers of the initial ingredients making them up. We must abandon this idea even for artificial mixtures like sugar water (not independently natured in some sense though they be). This thought is no part of his reason for saying that in mixtures the ingredients retain their inherent natural powers. Instead, it appears, Aristotle is simply assuming from his intuitive idea of mixtures as substances from which the ingredients can in principle be recovered (327b27–28) that therefore the ingredients must somehow (i.e., "potentially") be preserved in them—in the same way in both natural and artificial ones. And he offers the idea that their powers are retained (even if their normal "surface" properties have been altered) simply as a way of satisfying this requirement. Thus, according to him, the flesh or the sugar water (for example) is potentially earth, air, fire, and water or sugar and water, respectively, in a different way from that in which the simple body fire is potentially water, or fire and water together are potentially air. These latter potentialities hold simply in that the first-mentioned stuff(s) can be turned into the second by some naturally occurring process. Aristotle's way of putting the difference in the case of mixtures is to say that the flesh is potentially fire (and earth and water and air) in a special way, namely because the powers of each of these simple bodies are somehow at work within it. How, then, does Aristotle think these powers are at work? In order to answer this question we need to ask first, In what way of being something potentially is for example flesh potentially fire (and earth and water and air)?

Commentators have long noticed (as far back as Philoponus, at least) that this can be neither of the two connected cases of potentiality that Aristotle famously distinguishes in *de Anima* II 5, 417a22 ff. It is not a case of the sort of potentiality a young untaught person has for geometrizing (where he has the potential for this that all humans have got by their nature as rational beings—they can learn geometry and then use it). Nor is it that which an accomplished geometer, when he is not using his knowledge, has for geometrizing. The untaught person has not yet learned to geometrize, and so has not yet geometrized at all; however, on Aristotle's account, when some fire is an ingredient in some flesh it certainly has previously done all the things that fire does and it is not doing now because the flesh is only "potentially" fire. Yet the geometer who is not geometrizing retains his knowledge and ability (his ἕξις)—he is merely not using it—whereas fire in a mixture has actually been changed; the flesh it now helps to constitute is characterized differently from actually existing fire, and this certainly seems to mean that none of the flesh (nothing *actually* in it) has the ἕξις of fire at all any longer. It won't burn anything up, it doesn't flash and flame. Philoponus makes the interesting suggestion[8] that perhaps we should say that fire's condition in the mixture is comparable to that of the accomplished geometer who is drunk. The latter can exercise his ἕξις (which of course he retains), but in doing so he does not act in a way that truly reflects what that ἕξις is capable of. He follows a geometrical argument, or constructs one himself, but sloppily, or slowly, and with effort, or by fits and starts, and so on—in short, not "unadulteratedly" as Philoponus says (εἰλικρινῶς, 188. 22). So similarly, we might say that fire when it is an ingredient of flesh is affected by the other ingredients in such a way that, while remaining fire and retaining the nature and powers of fire—its full ἕξις—it only expresses those sluggishly or in a "diminished and tempered" degree.[9] Thus we could, following Philoponus, try to make sense of Aristotle's idea that fire and the other ingredients of flesh, or sugar and water in sugar water, are only "potentially" themselves, by supposing that they really *are* themselves (that is, they have the relevant ἕξεις) but that, due to the constant impinging of the ingredients on one another, they are able to exercise their natures only in a reduced or "restrained" way. Like a drunk geometer who is only "potentially" a functioning geometer because, given his condition, he functions only poorly, the fire in the flesh is only "potentially" fire because, under the conditions of mixture with the other simple bodies making up flesh, it is in fact less hot and dry, and less capable of burning, etc., than its actual nature, still preserved, would otherwise make it. On this suggestion, fire does in fact retain all its inherent powers (those of hotness and dryness), and uses them within the flesh, but their expression is restrained and diminished by the presence and mutual interaction of the other three bodies upon it.

Is this a coherent idea? Does Aristotle's physical (and metaphysical) theory actually support this way of thinking? In itself, so far as I can see, the idea is not incoherent, and Philoponus[10] deserves our admiration for

---

[8] *In GC*, 188. 14–26. Philoponus's suggestion is interestingly discussed by Frans A.J. de Haas in "Mixture in Philoponus: An Encounter with a Third Kind of Potentiality," in *The Commentary Tradition on De generatione et corruptione: Ancient, Medieval and Early Modern*, ed. J.M.M.H. Thijssen and H.A.G. Braakhuis, 21–46. For further discussion see the same author's "Recollection and Potentiality in Philoponus," in *The Winged Chariot: Collected Essays on Plato and Platonism in Honour of L. M. de Rijk*, ed. Maria Kardaun and Joke Spruijt, 165–84.

[9] As Joachim puts it (*Aristotle on Coming-to-be and Passing-away*, 181). Philoponus expresses the same point by the metaphor of being checked or restrained: in the mixture each ingredient acts κεκολασμένως (188. 23), not εἰλικρινῶς.

[10] Or Ammonius—Philoponus's commentary on GC is written partly from notes on his teacher Ammonius's lectures on the work.

thinking it up.[11] Indeed, it seems to me quite promising—provided that you can coherently explain what it is to be fire and to retain fire's powers even though they only express themselves in some restrained or diminished way. However, I do not think Aristotle's theories give him room to make coherent sense of this suggestion. For Aristotle the simple bodies' material nature is actually defined in *terms* of perceptible qualities, perceptible differences.[12] These qualities belong to those bodies essentially. Thus fire, on Aristotle's theory, is essentially both hot and dry. It possesses, of course, whatever other perceptible qualities follow for sublunary matter that has those two opposites—bright color, flamingness, lightness (κουφότης), etc.—but those perceptible qualities are not part of its definition or essence. Rather, they are consequential accidents. It might be that, under certain special conditions, some fire might not exhibit some or all of those secondary qualities, but so long as it is fire at all, it must remain hot and dry—*actually* hot and dry—because having those qualities is the essence of that particular material stuff, and a thing cannot survive the loss of its essence. If some matter that previously had those qualities loses them and takes on their opposites or even some intermediate condition, it must become another kind of stuff: what it was is destroyed, and the new kind of stuff takes its place. So it certainly seems that Aristotle cannot consistently say that some quantity of stuff is really fire—that is, that it retains, even in restrained or diminished circumstances, the δύναμις (powers) of fire, or the full ἕξις of fire that if unimpeded would express itself by burning and flickering and so on—while actually having lost those distinctive qualities and having assumed instead some intermediate temperature and intermediate position on the range wet/dry. So Aristotle's qualitative physical theory does seem to block him from saying (following Philoponus's proposal) that when it is ingredient in flesh, the simple body fire actually does remain fire. His physical theory does not leave him room to explain how it can remain fire

---

[11] It is notably absent from Alexander of Aphrodisias's exposition of the Aristotelian view in *Mixt.* chap. 13–15, pp. 228.5–233.14 Bruns.

[12] See *GC* II 3. Aristotle does not speak directly there of hot and dry, for example, being the "form" of fire or its essence (as Alexander of Aphrodisias does not hesitate to do in his exposition of Aristotle's view, see *Mixt.* 229.30–230.5); but he does speak of hot and dry being the differentiae for fire, i.e., what differentiates it from the other simple bodies (330b6). This presumably reflects the fact that in *GC* Aristotle discusses the simple bodies as (the basic) types of matter; in *De Caelo*, discussing them from a wider perspective as full substances, he seems to specify their forms (εἴδη) in terms of their natural places (see IV 3, 310a31–b1, b7–11; see also I 8, 276b21–25). Nonetheless, as Alexander's exposition makes clear, Aristotle's essential qualitative understanding of the natures of the simple bodies requires that their natures or essences be specified in such qualitative terms.

and preserve its essential powers as such while also occupying some non-hot, non-dry position on those scales.

However, Aristotle recaps his analysis of mixture in a remarkable passage of II 7, and there he does seem to claim that in the conditions of a mixture something can remain fire (i.e., be hot) even if it does have such an intermediate temperature. First he contrasts (334b4–7) the formation of a "mixed" body like flesh from earth, air, fire, and water with each of two alternative formations: the conversion of one simple body into another (for example, some fire overpowers some earth and converts it into fire), and a (notional) change where each of a pair of simple bodies that share one quality (dryness, say) simply loses its other defining property (fire and earth, say, interact so that fire simply *loses* its hotness and earth its coldness, with the result that all that is left is some unitary matter common to both, some stuff that was dry and nothing but dry). There exists a third possibility, he insists—in fact, the case where, as he explained in I 10, the simple bodies get mixed.[13] The fact, he now says, that bodies can have lesser or greater *degrees* of heat and cold, wetness and dryness, makes room for this as a further possibility in addition to the other two formations mentioned. When simple bodies interact neither of them has to *lose* any of its defining properties, as happens in those other cases (whether the property is just lost altogether or replaced by its opposite); they can retain them, but at a lesser degree. Aristotle has just been taking the hot dry stuff (fire) and the cold dry one (earth) as examples, and he continues to speak with those in mind.

> Is it like this then? A thing can be more and less hot or cold, so when it is without qualification and in actuality one of these it will be the other in potentiality; but when it is [these] not completely, but is cold for a hot thing and hot for a cold one because the mixed ingredients destroy one another's excesses, then it will be neither the [common] matter nor one or the other of those opposites without qualification and in actuality, but in between. . . . From these [that is, the simple bodies] flesh and bone and such things [come to be]: the hot thing becomes cold and the cold thing hot when it comes to the middle (for there it is neither [hot nor cold]). But the middle is of great extent and is not an indivisible [magnitude]. Similarly also dry and wet and suchlike things produce flesh and bone and all the rest, in accordance with a middle state.[14]

An example will help to clarify what Aristotle is saying. Consider some flesh, insofar as it is composed partly of fire and partly of earth, uniformly

---

[13] He has been discussing and criticizing Empedocles: this third possibility is one that Empedocles overlooked and could not in fact provide for.

[14] *GC* II 7, 334b8–30, omitting b14–25.

mixed together with one another throughout its extent. The flesh is of some medium temperature, neither hot nor cold "without qualification" (as pure, or separated, fire and earth respectively are). Insofar, then, Aristotle says, as fire is ingredient in flesh, flesh is "cold for a hot thing," while insofar as earth is ingredient in it, it is "hot for a cold thing." The clear implication is that the flesh, being composed of earth and fire in a thorough mixture, can be spoken of throughout its extent both as a hot thing (fire) and as a cold one (earth), each of which however, having had its excess destroyed by the other (it would have been better to say "abated"), is currently at a common intermediate temperature. That is, Aristotle is claiming that the fact that hotness and coldness (and wetness and dryness) come in degrees allows him to conceive of even the simple bodies, while remaining themselves, as taking on, in mixtures, diminished degrees of their respective essential perceptible qualities. In the flesh we have fire still existing, though it—the *fire* and not merely the flesh—is not now actually and completely hot at all. In effect, then, though Aristotle does not make this explicit, he is saying (to revert to the language of I 10) that the simple bodies retain their "powers" in mixtures—which is why, we can infer, the ingredients of a mixture can be recovered through its dissolution. This is a brilliant insight, and it is easy to see that it fits well with Philoponus's attempt to explain how fire can be "potentially" in a mixture in a way comparable to the drunk geometer whose drunken condition diminishes his ability to make use of his still-existing geometrical knowledge. Though Philoponus does not say so himself, what Aristotle says here in II 7 could be seen to support Philoponus's proposal as an interpretation of what Aristotle actually had in mind when he said the ingredients of a mixture retain their powers, and therefore are present "potentially" in the mixture.

However brilliant the suggestion, it is clear that in making it Aristotle exceeds the limits imposed by his own theory of the natures or essences of the simple bodies. It is true that the fire, in Aristotle's example, in getting mixed in with the earth, did not go all the way over to its opposite and become cold. This Aristotle insists would amount to its destruction and the coming into being of a different simple body. But it is not true in general that a thing, in order to be destroyed, has to be so completely undone as that. A corpse is not still a mass of flesh, despite the stuff that makes it up not being disposed totally oppositely to flesh; for the flesh to pass away it is not required that it have all its physical properties replaced by their extreme opposites. If heat is an essential characteristic of fire, then fire ought to be equally destroyed when the matter constituting it becomes at any rate a great deal *less* hot, as of course it does when it enters into the composition of some flesh. Some slight lessening in degree of its essential properties can be permitted in a simple body, to account for purer and less pure variations. But what Aristotle is envisaging here is a situation where something that allegedly remains fire is actually precisely as hot/cold and as wet/dry as some earth with which it has mixed! That thoroughly undermines any actual qualitative distinction between these two types of simple body. Nor, of course, in justification of the claim that, in the case in question, the ingredient fire does remain essentially hot in some underlying way, does it suffice to say that we can get back some pure and fully hot fire simply by separating it out from the flesh. The same is true in the case of a single mass of air that came into being when water and fire each converted a different one of the other's opposites so that both turned into air (II 4, 331b12 ff., discussed above pp. 148–50). Here, too, we can at least in principle "recover" fire and water, by transforming relevant parts of the air into water and fire respectively.[15]

What Aristotle seems to need in order to sustain his brilliant suggestion is some way of characterizing the simple bodies' essential nature in non-qualitative (or nonperceptible qualitative) terms: perhaps in terms of internal structure, or with some other way of identifying an indwelling nature that belongs to a thing whose matter is qualified, as the simple bodies are, by the "opposites."[16] He might then argue that that indwelling condition and the "powers" belonging to something possessing it, can be retained, even while its normal expression in terms of perceptible qualities was (abnormally) not present. If, for example, fire's nature were specified in such terms, we could make sense of the suggestion that some stuff in a mixture remained fire, even if restrained and diminished and not as hot or capable of burning as it would be outside a mixture.

[15] Alexander makes a big point of claiming that in mixtures only "slight assistance" (ὀλίγη βοήθεια) is required to separate out again the ingredients: they need "some addition in order to become completely themselves, but not total coming-to-be and total change" (Mixt., 231.19–22; see also 231.27–29, 232.20–31). One can grant that this change is easier than when, e.g., some air is changed back into some fire and some earth. But that does nothing to show that a total coming-to-be is not required in both cases. The fact that flesh is warm and moist (i.e., at an intermediate position on both the hot/cold and the wet/dry scales) is already, just by itself, sufficient to indicate the ease with which even a total transformation of some of it into water and some of the rest into fire (if that were required) might be effected. The distance to be gone in this case is not so great as with the generation of water and fire from air, since there change from polar opposites is required (to get water from air, the latter's dryness has to be replaced by wetness, and with fire a similarly polar change is needed).

[16] Such as Kit Fine proposes in "The Problem of Mixture," at pp. 307–14, 323–30. Fine suggests that the way in which, on an Aristotelian or quasi-Aristotelian theory, e.g., fire is essentially hot should be construed not in terms of anything about its perceptible characteristics (its "occurrent features") but rather in terms of its "latent" powers that are "qualifiedly present" when their operation is modified by the presence in their localities of other powers.

But so long as Aristotle defines the elemental bodies in the qualitative way that he does, namely in terms of basic perceptible qualities of heat, cold, and the like, I do not see how he can have such an option. For him, the fire that entered as an ingredient into the flesh or any other "like-parted" material has become, through mixture, warmish and moistish (and so, of course, have the other ingredients); it is no longer hot and dry. So Aristotle's theory of the nature of fire cannot sustain the claim that there survives in flesh something that has actually retained, even in a "diminished and tempered" degree or state, the ἕξις that something must have in order to be fire.

The upshot is that we cannot accept Aristotle's suggestion in his recap of his theory of mixture in II 7—that flesh, qua having fire as one of its ingredients, is "cold for a hot thing"—as providing the account we need of how in a mixture the "powers" of the ingredient simple bodies are retained. But if we have to reject that suggestion, on the grounds I have explained, we are at a loss to understand how otherwise those powers could possibly be present at all. How could fire's powers be present and somehow at work, if fire itself was not (except "potentially," and in no way actually)?

Aristotle has brilliantly and indeed accurately insisted that there must be a difference between mixtures—in which the ingredients remain what they were, without having been destroyed, while however having been altered—and those bodies that are produced by generation from previously existing but now destroyed bodies of other types (as described at II 4, 331b12). However, he has not succeeded in explaining, on his own account of the natures of the simple bodies, how it is that in mixtures these bodies are *only* qualitatively changed—that is, altered—not destroyed altogether. The "alteration" that takes place of the matter underlying and constituting them must, it seems, on his account, amount to no less than the destruction of the initial ingredient bodies. And without their continued presence (somehow) it seems impossible to sustain the thought that their *powers* are still present and at work in the mixture. At this point we see Aristotle reaching the limits of his own qualitative account of material bodies and failing to surmount the difficulties that his theory faces. Only, it seems, an account of the natures of elemental bodies in other than (perceptible) qualitative terms could get him past the requirements that he has himself brilliantly and accurately laid down for any correct account of the mechanics and chemistry of mixtures.

II

For Aristotle, mixtures are homoeomerous or "like-parted" stuffs, and their ingredients are physically more basic like-parted stuffs. According to his account of the nature and composition of flesh, for example, any quantity of flesh is divisible indefinitely into parts that have the same nature as each other and as any expanse of flesh of which they are parts. Further, flesh and all the other naturally occurring mixtures are composed of all the simple bodies (fire, air, water, and earth), and each of these ingredients is similarly like-parted. When the right proportions of some quantities of fire, air, water, and earth are mixed to form some flesh, he tells us, each of these acts on and is acted on by the others so that their differences in terms of what are for him the basic elements, namely the fundamental opposed material qualities of hot and cold, wet and dry, are brought into a specific unity characteristic of flesh, in particular.[17] Flesh has a particular, uniform, range of temperatures and locations on the scale of wetness/dryness, together with a consequent range of thickness or consistency, color, hardness/softness, weight, and so on. And similarly, mutatis mutandis, for all the other like-parted materials to which in the course of nature the simple bodies give rise.

Does Aristotle also hold that each and every part into which a mixture (a "chemical compound") like flesh might be divided has the same ingredients as the whole to which it belongs? On his view, is every part of such a stuff (however small) not only like every other part in its actual properties of wetness/dryness, hotness/coldness, color, consistency, etc., but also in the types of ingredients from which it originated? Does each part of flesh (and of all the other compounds) have inside it (in "potential" form) some earth, some air, some fire, and some water, in the same proportions as are in the whole of which it is a part, which could at least in principle be reconstituted by separation out from it? If so, then Aristotle adopts the view that in mixtures the ingredients are totally interfused with one another. Commentators often attribute this view to Aristotle (more on this below). But it is important to see that, if that is Aristotle's opinion, this is a further thesis, not one already implied by the two claims set out in the previous paragraph. Any quantity of flesh, for example, would still be perfectly homogeneous in all its actual qualities of temperature, texture, color, etc., all the way down into its parts, however small

---

[17] See GC II 3, 330a30, 33; Aristotle goes on to contrast his view with that of "those who make the simple bodies elements" (330b8). Cf. also Aristotle's frequent reference to the simple bodies as "the so-called elements" (322b2, 328b31, 329a16, 26), and the argument of II 1.

a particle of flesh you might imagine, even if at some stage in the division leading to those parts one reached particles whose materials were from not all four of the simple bodies but from three, or two, or even a single one. That is because, as we have seen, the key process involved in mixture, according to Aristotle, is the interaction of certain quantities of the simple bodies so as to "destroy one another's excesses" and to produce *in each simple body as it enters the mixture* a common, shared set of specific intermediate properties. Even if each largish mass of flesh has all four of the simple bodies as its ingredients (I discuss this requirement below), it does not follow that each tiny particle of flesh must likewise come from proportionate quantities of all four simple bodies. So long as each particle has the same relevant intermediate properties as each other particle and as the whole, flesh will remain a like-parted stuff. In order to sustain that result, a particle does not have to have its material origin in some quantities of all four of the simple bodies. Since each entering quantity, considered separately, has been altered so that it comes to possess the same set of qualities as every other entering quantity, nothing rules out the derivation of *some* very small portions of the material mass of the mixture simply from one, or two, or three, and not all four, of the entering ingredient bodies. In fact, careful attention to Aristotle's account, in the second part of *GC* I 10, of the processes by which mixtures are formed will reveal that his account exploits this possibility. Indeed, as we will see, the alternative view that commentators attribute to him is incompatible with his own (very reasonable) understanding of these processes. (On what grounds the commentators nonetheless attribute this view to him is a question to which I return below.)

Aristotle develops his account of mixtures in *GC* I 10 in four principal phases. Before beginning to argue for his own theory, he first sets out an argument alleging that mixture is impossible (327a34–b10). To dissolve this ἀπορία, or difficulty, one must obviously argue that a coherent account can be provided that satisfies two conditions: (1) none of the ingredients of any mixture is destroyed when they are combined to form the mixture, but all retain their identities and can in principle be retrieved, while (2) in being combined they undergo alterations so that while combined in the mixture they are not in every way the same as they are in their separated and uncombined state. In effect (see b6–9), these conditions, which Aristotle ultimately says his own account can satisfy, are the ones that together define mixture, as against other sorts of relationships among bodies from which other bodies or masses are derived. In the second phase, Aristotle presents the first part of his theory and disposes of one element in this ἀπορία (327b22–31). Here he explains that, thanks to the Aristotelian distinction between what a thing is actually (ἐνεργείᾳ) and what it is potentially (δυνάμει), we can say that a mixed stuff can perfectly well be actually (for example) flesh while potentially earth, air, fire, and water, the ingredients that were mixed together to form it: thus earth, air, fire, and water, flesh's ingredients, have not been destroyed when being combined in the flesh, since the flesh, though actually flesh and not actually any of these, is nonetheless potentially all of them. We have examined these claims above (sect. I). In the fourth and final phase, Aristotle explains the second part of his theory, in the last section of the chapter (328a17–b22). Here he takes up the question "how it is possible for this [that is, mixing so understood] to take place" (328a17–18). In doing so, he adds the remaining condition which, from the ἀπορία, we can see his account needs to satisfy: he shows how, though not actually destroyed in the mixture, the ingredients are in fact altered, so that they are not in all respects the same as they were before being combined together in the mixture. (This is the passage I want to focus on.)

But, third, before presenting this second part of his theory, Aristotle deals (327b31–328a17) with another ἀπόρημα, or difficult point, connected to or following on (συνεχές, 327b32) the preceding one. The preceding one concerned the nondestruction of the ingredients. The point of this second difficulty is, it seems, to propose an alternative response to the one Aristotle has just offered (via the distinction between being something actually and being it potentially) to the demand that in a mixture the ingredients not be destroyed. So, before proceeding to the second part of his own theory, Aristotle wishes to show that this alternative is unacceptable. Thus, he can say, only his theory can acceptably satisfy the demand that in a mixture the ingredients are not destroyed. We ourselves need to consider closely what Aristotle says against this alternative, before proceeding to examine the second part of his theory.

On the alternative suggestion, the ingredients remain fully actual in the mixture (and are not, after all, altered in any way from what they were when separate): what constitutes their being *mixed* is the additional fact that the ingredients, having been divided into small bits (and not destroyed), have then been distributed so that the bits of the one are among the bits of the other in such a way that neither of the ingredients is perceptible. The model here is grains of barley and wheat distributed among one another in some pile so that the pile doesn't look or taste like a pile of either barley or wheat.[18] The stuff looks, tastes, etc., throughout like a

---

[18] See 328a2–3. I take ἕκαστον at 327b35 to mean not "each of the bits" (so Williams in his translation, and also Joachim in his note to 327b33–35, p. 183), but "each of the ingredients," i.e., each of the μιγνύμενα just referred to, b34. This is not only the more natural way of taking the Greek, it is also the only way of taking it that really makes sense of the proposal. No one would think you had a *mixture* of, say, water and wine, if upon surveying the putative mixture you could see or otherwise perceive (e.g., in different parts of it)

single, new, and different kind of stuff—neither barley nor wheat. Or rather, Aristotle adds, we must impose as a further condition that the distribution of the bits should be made in such a way that any bit (μόριον, 328a1, 9–10) of the one ingredient should actually be alongside a bit of the other (ὁτιοῦν παρ' ὁτιοῦν, 328a4–5).[19] The motivation for this further requirement is clear enough. The simpler initial suggestion could be satisfied even if there were some bunching of bits (grains) of one or other of the ingredients, provided only that this did not produce a visible or otherwise perceptible irregularity in the overall expanse; yet it is counterintuitive to count such a case as one of thorough mixture, when, as would be so on that suggestion, a more thoroughly even distribution of the bits could be achieved. As Aristotle indeed immediately reminds us (328a2–3), appealing to what we would ordinarily say was really a mixture of barley grains and wheat grains, we do intuitively require, if something is to count as a (complete) mixture of bits of two sorts, that the bits be perfectly evenly distributed.[20]

---

any of the water or the wine in it—i.e., if what you were presented with had the full perceived character, in at least some parts of it, of one or the other of the separate ingredients. The relevant point is not that you must not see any bits that it has, but that you must not see the ingredient stuffs themselves. It's all right, according to this proposal, and reasonable enough in itself, that you should see that the stuff you are presented with is grainy and consists of assembled bits, just so long as the physical appearance is nowhere that of a lot of bits of the one ingredient or a lot of the other, as opposed to that of a *uniform* mass however grainy and however composed of bits.

[19] Following Christian Wildberg's suggestion in his Princeton seminar, April 1999, I read the manuscript text at 328a1, without Joachim's addition of <ὅτε>, and interpret as follows, drawing the elliptical material in my interposed parenthesis from 327b33–35, immediately preceding: ἢ οὔ, ἀλλ' ἔστιν <μίξις ὅταν οὕτως εἰς μικρὰ διαιρεθῇ . . . τῇ αἰσθήσει> ὥστε ὁτιοῦν . . . ("Or rather, there is mixture if the ingredients being mixed together have been so divided into small bits and placed among one another in this way, so that each ingredient is not obvious to perception, [and] so that any bit you like of [one of] the things that have been mixed is alongside a bit [of the other].") This makes good sense of the connection between the first and the second, corrected, suggestion, and it is acceptable in Aristotelian elliptical Greek for the ellipsis to be the whole of the relevant preceding text, as I propose. An alternative way of filling the ellipsis would be to take only the text from ὅταν to τρόπον, thus treating ὥστε ὁτιοῦν . . . as a *substitute* for the previous ὥστε clause. But in that case the second suggestion would not include the thought that it is crucial to mixture that the result should not allow us to perceive the separate ingredients anywhere across its extent; and in introducing this whole "difficulty" at 327b32–33 Aristotle seems clearly to envisage that all the suggestions to be considered will be ones according to which "mixture is something relative to perception."

[20] Thus I take ἐκείνως in 328a2 to refer back (as would be normal in contexts like this) to the simpler proposal (at 33–35): Aristotle is saying that we *do* say that barley and wheat grains have been mixed when the bits of the two sorts have been distributed among one another so that you cannot see wheat or barley anywhere (it nowhere looks like a pile of wheat or of barley grains, but has the uniform look of a different sort of pile altogether),

Before considering Aristotle's response to this suggestion (or these two suggestions, one weaker, the other stronger), I should point out that the interpretation I have proposed avoids the premature and confusing introduction into Aristotle's discussion here of ideas drawn from ancient atomism about how mixtures might be understood, which commentators beginning with Philoponus have regularly indulged in.[21] The suggestion Aristotle introduces here, in either of its versions, owes nothing to the idea of a division of apparently uniform, continuous stuffs into tiny indivisible and invisible corpuscles not possessed of any perceptible qualities whatsoever (apart from solidity, if that would count as perceptible in the relevant sense). On the contrary, his concern is with much more commonsensical ideas. His central thought is that in a mixture one ought not to be able to see or otherwise perceive the ingredients, but the whole should have its own distinct, uniform character. Ordinary division into ordinary bits is what he has in mind, not theoretical division into atoms.[22]

What, then, does Aristotle have to say against this alternative? The sponsors of the suggestion are depicted as accepting (328a4) that the ingredients that go into a mixture must be like-parted. In his reply Aristotle introduces the further claim ("but *we* say," 328a10–11) that the same is true of the resultant mixture: in both cases, all the parts must be like the parts of water, on the commonsense view of the latter and on Aristotle's own conception of it as a uniform material continuum. So the parts into which a mixture could be divided could not include any bits consisting simply of one of the ingredients, since such a part would differ in its qualities from at least some other parts of the same mixture (ones coming from the other ingredient): because a mixture is a like-parted stuff, each part has to be like every other part of that mixture, Aristotle insists. You could certainly have a combination or collection of such differing parts (a σύνθεσις, 328a6, 8), which could give rise to a mass with

---

but only provided that the grains are perfectly evenly distributed (i.e., when everywhere one grain of barley is next to one grain of wheat). (It is no obstacle to this interpretation that on Aristotle's own view of what counts as a mixture, solids like grains of wheat and barley cannot mix at all. He is speaking here simply of how we ordinarily speak; and we do speak of a mixture of grains under the conditions and with the restrictions he specifies.)

[21] See Philoponus *In GC*, 193. 1–9. See also Joachim, *Aristotle on "Coming-to-be"* and Williams, *Aristotle's De Generatione et Corruptione*, ad loc.

[22] Here I have learned from Wildberg's account in his seminar. Wildberg pointed out that if, as Joachim thinks, Aristotle in the stronger of the two proposals is discussing atomist division into bits, he must be very confused when he introduces as part of his exposition of the proposal (328a4) the assumption that when bodies are mixed with one another each is like-parted: obviously, the atoms of any body, which are its ultimate parts in atomic theory, are not of the same character as the whole, nor as parts of the whole that are themselves conglomerates of atoms.

perceptual characteristics of its own different from those of either ingredient, but that would not be a mixture or blend. This response applies
equally well to both the weaker and the stronger of the two versions of
the current suggestion, since it addresses the aspect of the overall view
that both have in common: that nonperceptibility of the ingredients is
sufficient to make a collection of intermingled bits of the ingredients into
a mixture of the ingredients.

Aristotle adds an independent objection specially tailored for the
stronger version alone. On that suggestion we were imagining any bit of
the one ingredient being alongside a corresponding bit of the other. He
now points out (328a15–16) that in fact that is in any case strictly impossible, since (as he has argued elsewhere) matter is indefinitely divisible: the smallest bit, however small, of an ingredient stuff is divisible into
further parts, and such parts of an undivided bit, when in the mixture,
are adjacent to (alongside) not any parts of another ingredient but ones
of the same ingredient of which they too are parts. You will in principle
never reach a point in the analysis of an ingredient into its parts where *all*
its parts ever could be aligned in the proposed way with the parts of another ingredient. Some parts will still remain inside undivided bits and so
alongside their congeners, not alongside bits of another ingredient.

So much, then, for a summary of Aristotle's response to this alternative
suggestion about how to understand the survival of the ingredients
within a mixture. Against both versions he has insisted that any mixture,
properly and narrowly speaking, is itself a like-parted stuff (so that the
model of the ingredients as like grains of barley shuffled through grains
of wheat does not apply, even if that were effected in such a way that the
whole had new and distinctive perceptual properties of its own: such
parts could not be parts *of a mixture*). And he has added that the stronger
version's idea that (all) the parts of the ingredients (however small) are
aligned alongside each other on a one-to-one basis is an impossibility.
Now, in both versions we are presented with stuffs which as ingredients
retain their original natures as separated stuffs, fully realized: the "bits"
are like grains of wheat and barley which all have the full nature of those
kinds of material. But notice that the objection added against the stronger
version clearly carries over also to stuffs formed from ingredients that in
the new substance retain not their full natures but only, as on Aristotle's
theory, some diminished or "restrained" version of those. In that case,
too, it cannot be that in the mixture all the bits of the materials coming
from any one of the ingredients are aligned alongside bits coming from
the others. Because of indefinite divisibility and like-partedness, there will
always be parts of the new substance that came, not from a different
source ingredient from that of their immediate neighbors, but from the
same ingredient.

Let us turn now to the second part of Aristotle's own theory of mixture (328a17–b22). Here, as I have said, he explains how it is that in being combined in the mixture the ingredients come to be altered in their perceptible properties (while somehow retaining their identities as distinct ingredients). Aristotle's central idea is the following. Sometimes, of two materials which are each easily divisible into their constituent parts, one (a larger quantity) overpowers the other through the action of its larger number of larger parts, so that, by acting on the fewer and smaller parts of the latter, it converts the other to its own nature (328a23–28). Thus a large fire converts a smaller quantity of wood to fire—the overpowering fire consumes the wood, growing larger through the addition to itself of the wood's substance (328a23–26).[23] This is a case, not of the alteration of materials that continue to exist, but rather of the destruction of one material, the wood, so as to increase the other by generating additional amounts of the latter. However, when two such materials are more or less equalized in their powers (ὅταν δὲ ταῖς δυνάμεσιν ἰσάζῃ πως, 328a28–29), then each makes the other shift in its qualities *toward* the one acting on it,[24] but neither converts the other to its own condition; instead, they jointly come to an intermediate state in common that differs from that of each of the agents themselves, as they were when the process began (328a28–31). Thus each of the ingredients comes to possess exactly the same perceptible qualities as the other then possesses, as a result of the mutual and equal acting-on and being-acted-on-by each other, a process which brings them into a common equilibrium state.[25] Thus, allegedly, as we have seen, the ingredients survive in the mixture while nonetheless having been altered in their perceptible characteristics of color, temperature, consistency, etc.—and having been altered in such a way that each of them then shares exactly the same such characteristics as the others. The effect is that what was earth, say, now comes to have just the same perceptible characteristics as the fire, or the air, or the water, that it has been mixed with also come to have. These characteristics are

---

[23] Aristotle's own example is a drop of wine poured into thousands of measures of water. On fire and wood see 327b10–13.

[24] See 328a29–30; I accept the manuscript reading εἰς τὸ κρατοῦν in a30 and interpret it as referring not to the resulting stuff (what "predominates" precisely by being the result), but rather to the one ingredient that is acting on the other. In this case it is true that the acting ingredient does not completely "overpower" the other one and so convert it into the same kind of stuff as itself (which is the sense of the verb κρατεῖν, e.g., at a26), but it does force the latter to lose its "extremeness" and move toward the agent's own quality.

[25] Aristotle points out that this happens mostly with liquid stuffs, or stuffs in a liquefied state, because they are in fact the ones that can be most easily divided into small parts and thus can act and be acted on in the way indicated (328a35–b4). I leave aside such further details of his account.

in fact the distinctive characteristics of the specific mixture—say, flesh or sugar water—that has resulted from this particular interaction.

As I have indicated, Aristotle speaks here of the materials that can undergo this joint mixture as ones that are easily divided into their parts while the parts remain marked off as separate bits, and that can therefore, by the many contacts with one another that such division makes possible, easily act on and be acted on by one another (328a35–b4). His implication is that large and undivided quantities of stuffs cannot mix with one another, or not easily, whereas such easily divided ones can. With many places of contact, the necessary pervasive mutual action and affection, leading to the common and intermediate qualitative characterization that constitutes the mixture, is made possible.[26]

Notice that Aristotle maintains that for a mixture to take place the ingredients must first divide each other into bits—small coherent masses of the same nature as the wholes. Then the small bits act on one another, each causing the other to shift in its perceptual characteristics of hotness/coldness and wetness/dryness so that they reach a new, common position on those scales. So his theory involves the inclusion in the mixture of bits of the ingredients, just as was the case on the rejected alternatives discussed in 327b32–328a17 (above, pp. 163–64). The important difference is that on his theory, but not on the alternatives, the bits do not remain possessed in full actuality of the defining perceptual qualities of the ingredients from which they came: they *each* shift, in the way we have seen, so that they lose those qualities which mark them off from one another and *each* gets in replacement a *common* new set of qualities that constitute the nature of the new substance itself. Hence the new substance comes out like-parted, as Aristotle insisted against the alternatives it had to do. Each of its parts comes to be characterized by the same set of new perceptual properties, those belonging to the whole as well. This applies to each of the interacting bits of the different ingredients from which it got constituted. For Aristotle's argument against the stronger version of the alternative view applies also to his own bits: it cannot be that *every* part of the new substance that comes from one ingredient is alongside a set of parts coming from the others, since the parts of each bit are alongside one another. And it is easy to see from his description of how the process of mutual "assimilation" of the bits of the ingredients works that his theory respects this requirement. Aristotle requires each finitely small bit of one ingredient to act on an adjacent finitely small bit of another ingredient *throughout* each of the small bits that are acted on. By acting at the points of contact along the common border, each of the

---

[26] See *GC* I 6, 322b25–29 on the necessity of contact for action and passion.

two contacting bits is assumed to be able to have its effects not just there, along that surface, but (given the unified condition of each of the bits), back into and all the way through the bit that it is acting on.

Thus Aristotle's theory denies, and his basic ideas are incompatible with, a complete interfusion of *all* the potentially infinitely many parts of the two ingredients as they engage in this process of mutual action and passion. And Aristotle's theory of how mixture comes about not only does not imply but in fact denies that the ingredients interpenetrate one another in such a way that any quantity of the resultant mixture has the same composition, in terms of the ingredients and their ratios to one another, as the whole mixture. Some parts (those deriving from the interacting bits of the ingredients) come from only a single ingredient and do not consist of some of each of the ingredients in potential form. Aristotle asserts that all the expanses of the resulting mixture have the same perceptible characteristics, but since he also claims that this results from the mutual interaction of finitely small bits of the separate ingredients acting on one another and converting each other into the same set of common characteristics, he implies that some expanses (small ones, no doubt, corresponding to the small size of the interacting bits) will come to have those common characteristics because they began as bits of one ingredient, while others will similarly come to have the same characteristics because they began as bits of another. In that case, although the whole resultant mixture will be completely uniform in its perceptual characteristics, this would be the result of a lot of separate bits of distinct ingredients coming to have those characteristics—and many parts of the like-parted mixture would not have in them, even in potential form, anything but the one ingredient from which they were produced by the mutual alteration that Aristotle's theory describes.

Thus Aristotle's theory in *GC* I 10 of how mixtures are created denies that each expanse within a mixture (however small, and all the way down through its potentially infinite divisions) must have originated from, and so preserves within it in potential form, a proportion of each of the ingredients of the mixture of which it is a part, equal to the proportion within the total mixture of those ingredients. His theory denies that when a mixture takes place the ingredients are totally interfused with one another.

Nonetheless, as I began this section by saying, commentators at least since Philoponus often attribute to Aristotle this "total interfusion" view of the ingredients in mixtures. Now, in II 8 Aristotle states and argues at length for the thesis (334b31–32) that "all the mixed bodies are put together from all the simple ones"—that is, that every mixed material (animal flesh and blood, tree bark, plant stems, rocks, veins of copper, etc.) is made of all four of the simple bodies. Each mixed body has in it (in merely potential form, of course) some earth, some air, some fire and some water (in differing proportions, of course). In beginning his commentary on II 8 Philoponus paraphrases this thesis as follows: "from every part of compounds (συνθέτων), such as flesh, every element is [that is, can be] separated out."[27] That is, Philoponus interprets Aristotle as holding in II 8 that every part of flesh, however small, comes from and has in it some of *each* of the simple bodies. But is that in fact Aristotle's thesis in this chapter? Aristotle seems to be envisaging whole, self-contained masses of these bodies—the flesh of my arm, the wood of a given tree, and so on. As we have seen, in his theory in I 10 of how mixtures take place Aristotle does of course assume that each of the ingredients will be preserved in certain proportions in the whole mass of any such self-contained mixture. But how about very small quantities within such self-contained mixtures? Does Aristotle's thesis here maintain about them too that they all have to have all four ingredients within them in Aristotle's potential way? If not, then, what Aristotle says here would not contradict his theory in I 10. So when he says "all the mixed bodies are put together from all the simple ones" perhaps he means to refer only to such self-contained instances—without specifically thinking of all their parts. On a strict interpretation, of course, the smallest bit of my flesh, on

---

[27] *In GC* 278. 7–8. Philoponus claims that Aristotle has assumed this thesis, so paraphrased, in his refutations of the views of "those who hold that the elements do not change into one another" (i.e., Empedocles), so that he is now, quite reasonably, going to give his arguments to establish something on which he has relied previously. I find no place where Aristotle has in fact relied on this assumption; certainly the argument of I 10, 328a5–17 (discussed above, pp. 163–64), which seems to be one of the places Philoponus must be referring to (even though in his comments there he does not mention Empedocles as one of Aristotle's opponents), does not rely on any such assumption. Indeed, as I have shown, it directly contradicts it. In his commentary on I 10, Joachim slips quite casually into describing Aristotle's theory in these terms without ever formally addressing the issue. Commenting on 328a9–10, he says "since the compound is ὁμοιομερές [homoeomerous], the constituents must be present in the same proportions in every part of it as in the whole." (Compare Williams in his comment on 327b31, offering to explicate what it means to say that a mixture is a like-parted stuff: "If the mixture as a whole is 55% B and 45% C each part must similarly be 55% B and 45% C: i.e., however small the parts into which you divide and subdivide A (the mixture), they will all be mixtures of B and C in this same ratio." I have shown above, paragraph 2 of this section, that this is a mistake; the like-partedness of mixtures definitely does not have this implication.) And at 327b33–328a17, explaining Aristotle's objections to the alternative views on mixture he there discusses, Joachim says: "According to both of them, μίξις is a mechanical mixing or shuffle, and not an interpenetration or a fusion, of the constituents"—as, he implies (but without saying why he thinks this), with suitable qualifications, Aristotle makes it to be. Kit Fine in his "Problem of Mixture" is only the latest in the long line of those who have interpreted Aristotle as holding the doctrine of total interfusion, without giving good, or even any, grounds for doing so. That interpretation seems simply to have become the received one by inadvertence.

Aristotle's theory, *is* flesh, just as much as is all the flesh in my arm, taken together; so, strictly interpreted, as Philoponus interprets it, the thesis that "all the mixed bodies are put together from all the simple ones" would imply or state that the smallest bit of my flesh is put together from all the simple bodies. But does Aristotle wish to be interpreted in that strict way when he states this thesis?

One of Aristotle's arguments for his thesis in II 8 might be thought to imply the stricter application. Aristotle claims (335a1–2) that without water in it something made from earth, as all the mixed bodies including flesh must be, would crumble and fall apart. It may seem that this ought to apply equally to any and every quantity of flesh—whether or not it is large enough to stand on its own as a self-contained expanse of flesh, such as that of a whole arm. You can't have your flesh crumbling apart even in very small volumes inside your arm or leg. So if, in general, flesh has to be composed of both earth and water in order not to crumble apart, then any bit of flesh, however small, must likewise be composed of both these ingredients—and, by extension, of all four. But perhaps we shouldn't fear that a small bit of flesh that did not derive from any water, but only from some earth, and was deeply imbedded in an expanse of flesh where there *was* lots of water, would fall apart. Maybe this fear would only be justified in relation to large quantities. So it is not so clear, after all, that this argument does require us to put the stricter construal on the thesis. The same applies, I think, to the other arguments too.[28] It seems to me, therefore,

---

[28] These are, of course, arguments for the general thesis announced at the beginning of the chapter: that each mixed body must be a mixture of all four of the simple bodies. None of these, as I say, requires that we understand this thesis in the strict way, as applying all the way down, to the smallest quantities of a stuff as well as to larger, self-contained ones. An argument directly in favor of this understanding might, however, be drawn from considering the form or essence of each mixed stuff, e.g., flesh. If the form of flesh is to be stated in terms of some specific proportion among ingredient earth, air, fire, and water, then it should follow that *any* quantity of flesh, however small, has to have some of each of those ingredients in it; otherwise it would by default lack the necessary form. It is not clear, however, that this is how Aristotle does understand the form of flesh: he may instead conceive of it as specified in terms, not of the ingredients and their ratio to one another, but of the resulting positions of the stuff on the ranges hot/cold, wet/dry, hard/soft, etc. Aristotle certainly speaks often of the λόγος (account, but the word also means "ratio" or "proportion") of flesh and so on, in addition to its material constitution, and in a famous passage of *Parts of Animals* I 1 (642a18–22) he praises Empedocles for having realized the importance of recognizing, in addition to matter, also "substance and nature" as bases for explanation—and he cites in illustration Empedocles' explaining what bone is in terms of "the ratio of the mixture" (λόγου τῆς μίξεως). Still, that is Empedocles, not Aristotle. Aristotle himself, in turning to say what, e.g., flesh is—λέγωμεν τί σάρξ, 389b23–4—in *Meteorologica* IV 12, emphasizes first of all the importance of the natural function of flesh, and he goes on to speak of the relevant (formal) bases for the differences of flesh from bone, hair, and so on,

an open question whether Aristotle's thesis in II 8 ought to be taken in the strict or the looser way. Only if it is taken in the strict way will a contradiction arise between II 8 and I 10, and only if it is so taken will Aristotle be committed in II 8 to a theory of total interfusion of the earth, air, fire, and water that make up any mixed body. The charitable interpretation, therefore, will take the thesis of II 8 in the looser way.

Despite the tenuous evidence, I suspect that commentators are so quick to attribute the total interfusion view to Aristotle because in interpreting him they have their eye surreptitiously on the Stoic doctrine of through and through "blends" due to Chrysippus. According to the Stoics a "blend" contains within itself in fully actualized form all of its ingredients.[29] The ingredients are spread through one another so that everywhere in such a mixture we would find, on analysis, each of them present in full actuality, all the way down through the indefinitely smaller successive divisions to which, as a continuum, the material in question is subject. In a water-wine blend both water and wine are everywhere to be found, in some specific proportions. On this theory there is a total interfusion of the ingredients, while they retain their full actualities. Now this theory obviously faces the apparently formidable difficulty of explaining how two or more ingredient bodies (actual wine and actual water, for example) can be in all the same places at the same time. That sounds like a conceptual impossibility: distinct actualized bodies need to be in separate places. Ancient critics were quick to press the objection. Aristotle's theory can seem to suggest the possibility of finessing this difficulty in a subtle and satisfying way: on his view, the distinct bodies (the ingredients) are not present in their full and actual condition, but only in some submerged or diminished potential form. On that view, it would be possible to maintain, with the Stoics, that everywhere within wine-water there is both wine and water—so there is total interfusion—*but* these ingredients are present not in their actualities but only in some sort of potential form. The objections against the Stoic view would thus fall to the wayside. No even apparent conceptual difficulty is involved if the material in a certain place is *separable* into two distinct bodies that are not present there except "potentially": each can then be present without needing to be in a separate location until actually separated. It is perhaps this thought that

---

not in terms of different proportions of the simple bodies but rather in differences in tension, ductility, hardness, softness, and so on (390b6–10), which result from the effects of heat and cold when the constituent bodies are set in motion so as to mix together and produce them. And, of course, Aristotle does hold that, all the way down through its indefinite divisibility, each part of flesh will exhibit all those same differentiating qualities.

[29] See the texts collected in A. A. Long and D. N. Sedley, *The Hellenistic Philosophers*, chap. 48.

has led commentators to find it so natural to understand Aristotle's theory in this way. However, it is well worth noting that this is not how Alexander of Aphrodisias interpreted it. In the exposition of Aristotle's view in his *On Mixture* XIII–XV Alexander nowhere supposes that Aristotle's theory does involve total interfusion. Since his treatise is aimed at criticizing and rejecting the Stoic theory, in favor of the Aristotelian one, he could hardly have failed to emphasize clearly the salutary difference between interfusion of potentially existing and actually existing ingredients, if he had thought of Aristotle's theory in those terms. Alexander's exposition coheres with my own interpretation, according to which interfusion, in whatever form or condition, is no part of Aristotle's view.[30]

Still, as I have granted, it may be that Aristotle does in the end (in II 8) commit himself to the total interfusion view of the composition of mixtures. If so, however, it is important to see that he does not show at all how to reconcile this idea with his account in I 10 of how the ingredients of a mixture can act on one another so as to produce the uniform stuff that results and that constitutes the given mixture. There, as we saw, he envisages a resultant that would as a whole have both (or all) of the ingredients within it somehow potentially, but in such a way that very small volumes of its total mass would not. Aristotle's theory of mixtures, as he sets it out in I 10, is among the cleverest and most fascinating contributions to physical theory in the whole of ancient scientific thought. Much of its novelty and distinctiveness is lost if it is read as anticipating and avoiding weaknesses in Chrysippus's theory—particularly since those weaknesses turn out on reflection to be more apparent than real.[31] Chrysippus's theory is itself a second among the cleverest and most fascinating pieces of ancient physical theory. We ought to appreciate each theory for its distinct contribution: for Chrysippus, total interfusion of bodies; for Aristotle, the possibility of a simple body continuing to exist though in a submerged and diminished condition.[32]

---

[30] See especially *Mixt.* 231.12–22, where Alexander discusses the role of small bits of the ingredients in effectuating their mixing. He says nothing at all there to suggest that he thinks the ingredients become totally interfused.

[31] Since, for Chrysippus as for Aristotle, bodies are material continua, subject to indefinite divisibility, there is no clear conceptual difficulty in two bodies being in the same place in the way his theory of blends requires. There would only be a difficulty if some smallest finite bit of a blended stuff were held to be everywhere both of two distinct stuffs, without separation. But, as I noted above, the theory of the material continuum precludes there being any such smallest bit: for Chrysippus, a water-wine blend is both (actual) water and (actual) wine all the way down, so to speak. You can always put off the question, addressed at any stage in the division: "*Where*, within this expanse, is the water and *where* the wine, if they are distinct, actually existing bodies?"

[32] I thank Christopher Bobonich for helpful comments and suggestions on the penultimate version of this chapter.

CHAPTER 8

METAPHYSICS IN ARISTOTLE'S EMBRYOLOGY

I

TRADITIONALLY, discussion of Aristotle's metaphysics, including his theory of form and the "what it is to be" any given substantial object, has dealt extensively with the relevant texts in the *Categories, Physics, De anima,* and, of course, the *Metaphysics* itself. But the biological works have been largely neglected as sources for knowledge about and insight into Aristotle's theory.[1] This seems to me unfortunate. In his biological works Aristotle invokes the form of an animal constantly and in interesting physical and, one would have said, metaphysical detail, as the explanation for much, and that the crucial part, of what happens to it as it develops to maturity and maintains and reproduces itself. One would expect these explanations to reveal something about the character of Aristotelian forms and perhaps even to help resolve some of the many questions not clearly settled by him in his metaphysical writings. It might, I suppose, be argued, on the contrary, that Aristotle thought that the notion of form needed for metaphysical purposes is quite distinct from that needed in order to explain the biological phenomena addressed in the *Parts* and the *Generation of Animals.* Conceivably there is no, or only a very loose, systematic connection between what is said about forms in the two sets of works, so that one is not entitled to infer metaphysical consequences—consequences for the nature of forms as they appear and are argued about on metaphysical terrain—from what forms are taken to be like in the biological context. I will not attempt to argue against this line of interpretation here. In the belief that the philosophical interest of doing so will be sufficient justification, I will simply proceed on the natural assumption that Aristotle did intend his biological theory of forms to be a continuous development and extension of whatever theory of substantial forms he meant to be the upshot of his discussion in the central books of the *Metaphysics.*[2]

---

[1] An important exception to this general rule are two papers by D. M. Balme, "Aristotle's biology was not essentialist"; and "The snub," revised and reprinted in A. Gotthelf and J. G. Lennox (eds.), *Philosophical Issues in Aristotle's Biology,* 291–312.

[2] It is a matter of indifference for my discussion what the order of composition of these works may have been.

I want to focus upon Aristotle's theory of animal reproduction and embryology in the *Generation of Animals* (*GA*)—his account of how an offspring is brought into being and made to resemble other members of its species in general, as well as its parents and various of its ancestors in particular. As is well known, Aristotle holds that it is a parent's form (more specifically, the father's form) that controls the offspring's formation as a member of the same species. But in that process, it also regularly happens that there come to be parental and more generally familial resemblances in the specific ways in which form becomes realized in the offspring. It is perhaps less well known that Aristotle holds that the parental form controls those resemblances, or some of them, as well. To the extent that the parental *form* is responsible for resemblances to parents and ancestors going beyond mere membership in the same species, and that these resemblances are not due instead to characteristics of the matter on which the form works, or to environmental conditions during or after gestation, one would apparently have to attribute to the parental form certain determinate powers that go beyond those that could belong to a form merely in virtue of the fact that it was a form of a member of that species. In that case the parent's form would have to be, not species-specific merely, but in some additional degree specific for particular further characteristics of bodily structure and organization—whichever ones require to be explained as deriving directly from the parent's formative role in generating the offspring.

Now this result does not sit well with either of the two currently most favored interpretations of the theory of substantial form to be found in Aristotle's metaphysical writings. Many who write on Aristotelian metaphysics seem almost to take it for granted that Aristotelian forms go with species, with natural kinds, one for each. Yet those who have recently revived the ancient interpretation according to which each individual substance has its own individual form have tended to hold that the features that distinguish one individual form from another, for members of the same species, lie outside the form itself as accidental properties of the substance whose form it is.[3] If I am right, neither of these interpretations can accommodate the evidence for his conception of forms provided by Aristotle's embryology. In order to show this it will be necessary first to consider that evidence in considerable detail.

---

[3] See Michael Frede, "Substance in Aristotle's *Metaphysics*," in his *Essays in Ancient Philosophy*, 72–80, and his and Günther Patzig's edition, German translation and commentary on *Metaphysics* Z.

II

In the discussions making up the first three books of the *GA* Aristotle's principal goal is to explain what Montgomery Furth has called the "whacking great a posteriori truth" that generation is normally reproduction, that animal offspring (occasional monstrous births aside) always belong to the same species as their two parents.[4] He explains this by the theory that the father's sperm, which is the causal agent active in generation, carries certain specific movements (κινήσεις) that are such as to shape the material that the mother provides in her womb into a member of the same species (and into nothing else that could survive). It does this by passing on to the offspring "the same movement with which it too is moved" (II, 3.737a20–1). For this movement in the father's sperm (or, more accurately, as we shall see, these movements) is derived from those that are present in his blood: it is from the further "concoction" and concentration of his blood that the sperm is produced. As the form that makes the father a human being is carried by these movements in his blood, it is easily understood that these same movements in the sperm are such as to make, if anything at all, another thing of the same species as the father. Now it is essential in understanding Aristotle's theory to make note of the fact that, on his account, what I have just said about the male sperm's relation to the father's blood holds equally of the female's menstrual fluid in relation to her blood. The menstrual fluid is also a "seminal residue" (σπερματικὸν περίττωμα), less concocted and less pure than sperm, and so not capable of generating anything, that is, not capable of coming alive by itself or making anything else come alive (I, 20.728a18, 26; II, 3.737a27–30; II, 7.746b26–9).[5] Both these seminal fluids are derived from that element in the adult's blood that "provides being both to the whole (animal) and to its parts," the kind of blood that Aristotle calls θρεπτικόν (and σπερματικόν) and distinguishes from the αὐξητικόν or growth-producing kind (II, 6.744b32–8). Accordingly, in both sexes the seminal fluid contains the full range of movements that the "nutritive" blood itself does, by which it was able to form all the bodily parts of the animal whose blood it is. It is this movement, as it occurs in the blood, that carries the "program" for all the specific tissues and or-

---

[4] See his *Substance, Form, and Psyche.*

[5] Although, as these passages witness, Aristotle often refers to both the menstrual fluid and the semen as *sperma*, he also often (most notably in *GA* I, 17, when raising the question whether both the male and female contribute something that then works to structure and form the embryo) uses this word more narrowly, to refer to what does do the work of structuring the embryo (and on his view, not the female fluid, but only the male does that).

gans that an animal of the kind in question has to have. That is why in the different, stronger form in which it occurs in the sperm, it carries this same "program," but in such a way as to pass it on to the fetus as that takes shape in the mother's womb. What, however, is the function of the menstrual fluids or καταμήνια and their movements in this process? At this stage (in books I and II) Aristotle says little about this, but the implications of his general theory of the formation of seminal fluids by further concoction of the θρεπτικόν or nutritive kind of blood, taken together with what little he does say about the role of the catamenia, make this clear enough. For Aristotle describes a progression in three distinct stages: from (1) the nutritive kind of blood to (2) the less pure, less fully concocted and "worked up" seminal fluid of the female (cf. δεόμενον ἐργασίας 728a27) to (3) the fully concocted, form-transmitting seminal fluid of the male. The female fluid is therefore somehow intermediate between nutritive blood and honest-to-god semen, and this intermediate status that Aristotle assigns it in books I and II has clear implications about its function in generation.

First of all, it must be remembered that nutritive blood is the *material* from which the tissues and organs are composed. As nutriment, it is absorbed by, it turns *into* those tissues and organs. The way in which this blood carries the "program" for the tissues and organs is as matter having a principle (in fact, presumably, the σύμφυτον πνεῦμα or "connatural breath") internal to it which causes it to take on the appropriate shapes and textures, etc., at the right places and times. Now one thing Aristotle says clearly and repeatedly about the catamenia is that they are material on which the male fluid works in order to form the fetation (= the proto-embryo—κύημα). And bearing in mind the catamenia's origin in nutritive blood, one can see why just this material is what is required. Presumably, only a material which already was such as to be formed into organs and tissues of the types required would be suitable. For example, human semen does nothing when juxtaposed with a female dog's catamenia, because a dog's catamenia are themselves definitely disposed to be made into a dog embryo or into nothing at all organic. Hence Aristotle says (II, 3.737a23–4) that the catamenia are potentially all the bodily parts of the creature that is to be constructed out of them, but actually none of them. The menstrual fluid *is* potentially all those parts, because it is derived from the nutritive blood of another member of the same species, and retains from that blood just those movements that are specific for those parts (cf. 738a37–b4: the menstrual fluid is suited to be turned into a new creature of the same species because it was already potentially material for the mother's body). Both in nutritive blood and in the catamenia these movements are movements of *matter;* they function as movements belonging to blood and to catamenia as *matter* for what is made out of them. Blood is matter for the animal itself whose blood it is; catamenia are matter for a new animal of the same species.

The seminal fluid of the male, however, has these same movements not as matter for a new animal, but as the source of its form (765b11). This means that it can make something formed from catamenia of the appropriate kind actually come alive, that is, come to possess an independent source of its own self-regulation, including most crucially the source of its own capacity to make its *own* nutritive blood (also its own auxetic blood).[6] The movements within the new creature's blood that are the physical realization of this capacity are given to it by the father, not by the mother, even though if the catamenia contributed by the mother did not have, as matter, the appropriate movements, the father using the instrument of *his* seminal fluid could not have caused it to come alive and so to come to possess that capacity.

III

So far I have limited myself to summarizing Aristotle's theory of reproduction as this is presented in the first two books of the *GA*. I have said nothing about particular or individual versus merely species-specific forms, because all that Aristotle is wanting to explain in these books is why offspring belong to the same species as their parents. It is only when in book IV he attempts to give detailed explanations of the processes by which female births and inherited resemblances to parents and grandparents occur that he reaches a level of fact to which this distinction might be relevant. I turn now to consider Aristotle's account of those processes.

Book IV opens by proposing for investigation (763b25 ff.) the question how sexual differentiation comes about. When, however, after discussing the views of some of his predecessors on this question, Aristotle presents his own account (765b6 to the end of chapter 1) he invokes principles that, as he remarks at the beginning of chapter 3 (αἱ δ᾽ αὐταὶ αἰτίαι καὶ τοῦ τὰ μὲν ἐοικότα γίγνεσθαι τοῖς τεκνώσασι τὰ δὲ μὴ ἐοικότα, 767a36–7), also provide the explanation for the fact that some offspring

---

[6] But only if there is a συμμετρία, a suitable balance or "symmetry" between its heat and movements and the wetness and quantities of the catamenia that it works upon. Aristotle emphasizes the need for this "symmetry" as early as I, 18.723a28–31: see also 729a16–19, 743a26–34, 772a10–22, 777b27–9, and especially 767a13–35, discussed below, p. 186. As Aristotle often makes explicit in these passages (729a17, 767a17–20, 772a11–12), this is a symmetry between an active factor in generation (the male) and a passive one (the material provided by the female). His talk of symmetry in this connection does not imply any kind of interaction between the two factors, in the sense of a joint working together by two independent but proportionately coordinated agents with a view to a common product.

resemble their fathers or their fathers' (male) ancestors, others their mothers or their mothers' (female) ancestors, either in overall structure and constitution and/or in that of certain bodily parts, while yet others show no particular resemblance to their forebears at all (767a36–b5).[7] And once he has discussed and offered his own explanation of the phenomena of inheritance, he summarizes his results by claiming that he has revealed a common cause for sexual differentiation together with these varied facts of inheritance (769a1–6). In order to understand fully what this common cause is, we need to begin by considering the passage of IV, 1 where it is first introduced, in connection (so far) only with sexual differentiation.

At 766a10–16 Aristotle lists some principles on which he says sexual differentiation depends, of which, however, only the last seems to play any significant role in the explanation he goes on to provide. This last principle runs as follows (a14–16): "Given that destruction [of a thing] is into [its] opposite, necessarily also what is not mastered by the agent that is working it up (τοῦ δημιουργοῦντος) changes into the opposite condition." Applied to the case of generation this means that if the male fluid and its movements fail to master the catamenial materials on which they are working to form the offspring, these materials will change (from being the male that they would have become if the male fluid had mastered them) to being the opposite of a male, viz. a female. What, however, is the cause of this failure by the male fluid to master the female? What in the nature of these fluids and the action of the one and reaction of the other causes this change in the materials? Aristotle gives a detailed answer to these questions only in chapter 3. There he introduces, for the first time in the whole treatise, (a) a differential account of the various movements that are to be found actually and potentially in the male's fluid, and (b) an *explicit* role for somehow corresponding movements in the female's fluid. Ultimately we will have to look closely at this account of the *several* male and female movements and their interactions in order to understand what Aristotle thinks causes this change. But already in chapter 1 two important points are clear.

First, the role of the female fluid remains, as in book II, wholly a role as matter. This is made explicit at 766b12–14, which (abstracting from textual difficulties which do not affect the main point) clearly says that it is only the male fluid that possesses a principle capable of setting in motion and shaping the female fluid into a fetus; the female's fluid is matter only. So when Aristotle says the male's fluid fails to master, or is defeated (ἡττηθῇ 766a20; cf. κρατηθέν b15, κρατηθέντος 768a34) in its efforts to master these materials, and so the materials are shaped into a female,

---

[7] He says also that the same principles explain monstrous births—offspring that are animals but not regular human beings at all. I do not discuss this extension of the theory.

he does not mean that some independent active, generative activity of the female materials takes over. The movements in the female materials are not a new, second set of movements, parallel to the movements in the male's fluid, that directly shape the fetus' bodily parts, as it were by default. Both before and after his discussion in IV of female births and inherited resemblances to ancestors Aristotle repeatedly emphasizes that only the male, through the movements in his semen, is capable in any way at all of fashioning (δημιουργεῖν) the materials provided by the female into a new animal (I, 22.730b4–32; II, 4.738b12–15, 20–3; IV, 4.771b21–4, 772b31–3), and three times in the course of this discussion he characterizes the male, by contrast with the female, as the δημιουργοῦν (766a15, 767a19, 768a16). So whatever the role of the female fluid's movements may be, it is not they, but the movements of the semen, that impose on the embryo its female soul and those specific movements in its body that are its soul's physical realization and that make it develop as a female.

Secondly, we already have in chapter 1 an important indication of what happens that causes the change of sex. In the passage already cited where he states his general principle about materials that are not mastered, Aristotle speaks, naturally enough (at 766a15–16) of these materials themselves changing into the opposite (of what they would have changed into if mastery had been achieved): they μεταβάλλειν εἰς τοὐναντίον. That, after all, is what has to be explained. But at 766b15–16, immediately after saying the female fluid is matter only and only the male's fluid is active and formative, he says this change in the materials is preceded and caused by a change in the male fluid itself: "so when it [the male fluid] has the mastery, it takes it [the female matter] over to itself, but when it is mastered, it [still the male fluid] changes to the opposite or else to extinction (εἰς τοὐναντίον μεταβάλλει ἢ εἰς φθοράν)." Indeed he had already said this at 766a18–21, where however it is possible not to catch the point. For the subject of μεταβάλλειν (change) there *could*, by a remote possibility, be the materials that are the understood object of the verb ἀγάγῃ in the previous clause (that is how Peck renders the lines) though by the rules of Greek grammar it ought to be the male ἀρχή, the subject of ἀγάγῃ.[8] But at the 766b15–16 this meaning is unmistakable: the defeat of the male fluid by the female fluid means that the *male fluid itself* in its working up of the materials is affected in such a way that *it* turns them into a female

---

[8] In both these passages I take it that μεταβάλλειν (change) is being used intransitively, as elsewhere in this context (766a16, 23–4; 768a14). A survey of Aristotle's usage shows that where he does use μεταβάλλειν transitively the object of the verb is almost always the respect in which the thing in question changes, almost never some other person or thing on which it effects a change. (The only clear instances of this latter kind that I have found are at *HA* 592a15 and *Poet.* 1459b29.) So Aristotle's words here do not mean that the male fluid "changes *the female fluid* to the opposite or to extinction."

(and see 767b22–3: the *male movements* brings about, ποιεῖν, this deficiency in the offspring). That is what it must mean to say that the male fluid "changes to the opposite" (on this, see further below): it changes so as to do the opposite of what it would otherwise have done.

IV

For the elaboration of this theory we have to turn to chapter 3. So far Aristotle has only said that sometimes the male fluid (or its movements— at 767b18–20 he says that it comes to the same thing whichever of these one says) fails to master the female fluid that serves as original matter for the fetus, and that when this happens a female birth results. This, however, as he now points out, is an over-general remark. For distinctions can be made among the movements of the sperm, and it is only when *certain* of these movements are mastered that a female birth results. There are, first of all, its actual movements, and then some that it has only potentially (767b35–37, 768a12): I will explain what this distinction comes to in a moment. Secondly, both the actual and the potential movements can be divided into movements at different levels. In explaining the different levels of the actual movements, Aristotle says the following.

The sperm of any individual male animal, say Coriscus or Socrates, has movements that belong to it (1) as movements of this particular individual qua father, (2) as movements of a male, (3) as movements of a human being, and (4) as movements of an animal (767b25–32; 768a12–13 says these are *actual* movements). So in the case of female birth, it is not the movements of the father's sperm, in general, that get mastered, but more precisely, those belonging to it as (2) movements of a male. It may happen that *these* movements are mastered (so that a female birth results) while nonetheless (1) the movements that it has as this particular individual qua father are not. When that happens, a female offspring results, but one resembling the father. In accordance with the general principle enunciated in chapter 1, when the father's fluid fails to master the mother's with respect to its movements (2), the material being worked on "goes over" (ἐξίσταται) to the opposite, that is, in this case, to being a female instead of a male (768a2–7)—because, not achieving mastery, the father's fluid "makes it deficient in that faculty in respect of which it failed to gain mastery" (767b22–3). But since the sperm masters the material with respect to the movements (1), there is no "going over" to an opposite in the relevant respect, and so we get an offspring (a female one) resembling the father.

Likewise, as Aristotle says is the more usual thing, it can happen that the sperm is defeated simultaneously with respect to both movements (1) and (2). The result is that it makes a female resembling her mother (768a24–6)—resemblance to her mother being the opposite of that resemblance to her father which is prevented when the movements (1) are defeated. By distinguishing movements (1) and (2) and allowing that the male fluid can achieve mastery, or not, with respect to these movements independently of one another, Aristotle can explain both how female births occur, and how a female may resemble either her mother or her father. Exactly similarly, he can also explain how a male child may resemble his mother, rather than his father: because the movements (1) are defeated he resembles his mother, the opposite of the resemblance to his father that the mastery of the movements (1) would have caused.

Before pursuing further elaborations, let us pause to note one crucial point. By saying that there are actually in any male animal's sperm movements belonging to it as that individual qua father Aristotle commits himself to at least the relative particularity of that animal's form. It is through the movements in its sperm, the same movements that were in its blood and conveyed its form to its own matter, that an animal conveys form to the offspring, and if these movements include ones that belong to it as an individual father (whatever exactly the extent of the individual features in question turns out to be), then the father's form is not one that could be shared by all other animals of the same species, or even all the males. Aristotle already makes this clear in book IV chapter 1, when he says that if all goes well the father, using the instrument of his sperm, brings the female matter over to his own peculiar form (εἰς τὸ ἴδιον εἶδος τὸ αὑτοῦ 766a19–20), that is, to possessing the capacity and tendency, as an independent living thing, to develop in such a way as to have those same features, whichever they are, that characterize the father as an individual and belong to him qua having that form.

So far I have discussed only the actual movements in the sperm. But there are potential ones as well, Aristotle says. First of all, an animal's sperm has potentially the movements of its πρόγονοι, i.e., its father, its father's father, and other male ancestors in the male line (767b37, 768a11, 16–18). It has these as potentialities of its movements (1), the movements that it possesses as being the sperm of this individual qua father. These potentialities can be realized when the sperm nonetheless achieves mastery with respect to the movements (1), and in fact only then. In that case one gets an offspring (whether male or female: sexual differentiation, as we have seen, is determined solely by whether mastery is achieved with respect to movements [2]) resembling *not* the father, but the father's father, or the father's father's father (and so on backward). This depends upon the phenomenon that Aristotle describes (first at 768a15) as the λύσις, the loosening or slackening, of the movements (1); a lesser λύσις means that the offspring comes to resemble an ancestor nearer the father, a greater one means resemblance to a more distant ancestor in this series (768b9–10).

But Aristotle seems to say that a male animal's sperm has potentially a second set of movements. At 768a14 he says it has potentially the movements of the female, by which I believe he refers to the *mother* of the prospective offspring.[9] That is, the sperm has in some sort of potential way the movements of the menstrual fluid of the female with which the male copulates. Now, as he goes on to say, the movements of the female animal's seminal fluid that belong to her fluid as that individual mother (i.e., its movements [1]) can also suffer loosening or slackening, just as the male's movements (1) can.[10] The result is parallel to what happens in the case of the slackening of the male's movements (1). When, but *only* when, the male's movements (1) are mastered (or, equivalently, fail to gain the mastery), instead of an offspring (whether male or female) resembling the mother being produced, it can happen that we get an offspring resembling the mother's mother, or the mother's mother's mother, instead. Here one gets a combination of both of the two basic processes that Aristotle postulates. First, the female fluid acts on the male fluid's movements (1) and defeats them so that they ἐξίστανται, depart from their own nature, and therefore make an offspring resembling not himself but the opposite of himself. But now, there is in addition a λύσις in the victorious female fluid, and so the potentiality in the male's sperm to make an offspring like the mother's *mother* (instead of like *her*) gets actualized. That is, it appears, Aristotle attributes to the male fluid, somehow in potentiality, all the movements that are in the female parent's seminal fluid—both those characteristic of her as an individual parent and those movements of all her female ancestors that she herself carries only potentially.

---

[9] Taken out of context "the movements of the female" might, I think, be given any of three interpretations: (1) the movements belonging to the menstrual fluid, (2) the movements (belonging to the semen) that are such as to fashion a female (compare 768a32, ἡ [κίνησις] τοῦ Σωκράτους and τὴν τοῦ πατρός), (3) the movements (belonging to the semen) that correspond to those both actually and potentially present in the mother's menstrual fluid. I argue in the next two paragraphs against opting for interpretation (1) in this context. I prefer (3) to (2) because I understand Aristotle's purpose in these lines (to 768a21) to be to explain how the semen can be responsible for fashioning not just a female (as [2] would permit) but one resembling her mother or any of her mother's forebears—the movements characteristic of whom are of course in the mother's menstrual fluid either actually or potentially. But on either of these two interpretations the basic principle is the same: Aristotle attributes to the semen, as a potential movement of its own, a movement it is going to put actually into the embryo in fashioning it.

[10] Since Aristotle only explicitly mentions movements in the catamenia while discussing the phenomenon he calls λύσις, which only operates on movements (1), he never has occasion to attribute to the female fluid movements (2), (3), and (4). On general grounds we can infer he must suppose these other movements are present too.

Now this is not as strange an idea as it may seem on first presentation. As we will see shortly, it has a deep rationale in Aristotle's theory of the role of the male as what alone fashions the offspring and gives it its soul or form. Moreover, it can be defended on the basis of general considerations about any process of fashioning something, whether by art or by nature. There is nothing outlandish or extravagant here at all, once Aristotle's idea is fully and properly understood.

V

But first I want to show through a detailed consideration of the text of *GA* IV, 3 that it really is Aristotle's view that the male animal's semen possesses somehow in potentiality the movements of the prospective mother of its offspring. In the penultimate paragraph above I cited 768a14 as explicitly affirming this view, but we will need to consider as a whole the long opening paragraph of the chapter (to 768a21), in which Aristotle formally sets out all the fundamental elements of his theory, this one included. The sentence at 768a11–14 reads: "Some of the movements [in the seminal fluid] are present in actuality, others in potentiality: in actuality, those of the male parent and of the universal, such as a human being and an animal; in potentiality, those of the female and of the ancestors." Now (I will return to this point below) the preceding context makes it overwhelmingly likely that the seminal fluid whose actual and potential movements Aristotle here means to be talking about is the male's fluid—the fluid that shapes and fashions the embryo, and that has clearly been the only subject of his discussion in the chapter up to this point. (That is why Peck does not go beyond what the Greek justifies when he translates "Some of the movements . . . are present in [the semen] *in actuality.* . . .")[11] If so, as I have claimed, Aristotle here explicitly states that the semen has, as a potentiality, the movements of the female, evidently (see n. 9 above) meaning those of the mother—the ones that, when actualized, will fashion an offspring resembling the mother or one of her ancestors. On the other hand, as I have also said, Aristotle clearly does introduce in this chapter, for the first time explicitly anywhere in the treatise, movements in the menstrual fluid that somehow correspond to the movements of the semen (though he continues to hold that only the male's movements are such as to fashion, shape, and constitute the offspring). Indeed he does this only four lines below (768a18–21), saying that just as

---

[11] The French translation of P. Louis agrees with Peck at this point.

the male parent's movements, when they relapse, relapse first into those of his father or, if not, into those of his grandfather, so the mother's relapse into those of her mother or, if not, into those of her grandmother. Perhaps then he already has this parallel between male and female movements in mind in what precedes. In that case one might suggest that the fluid whose movements Aristotle means to be discussing at 768a11–14 is not the male fluid only, as I have taken it, but seminal fluid in general—both the male's and the female's, together. Perhaps, then, in speaking of "the movements of the female" Aristotle here speaks not of movements even only potentially in the male fluid, but simply of the movements in the menstrual fluid itself.

On this suggestion, he will be saying that some movements in the generative fluids (in general) are present actually, others potentially only: actually present (viz., in the *male's* fluid) are the movements of the male parent and the universals, a human being and an animal, but potentially present (viz., in the *female's* fluid) are all those of the mother—those it has as movements of this particular individual qua mother, and as movements of a female, a human being, and an animal—*and also* (viz., in *both* fluids) those of the respective ancestors. This, however, makes little sense. (i) Exactly the same ground for saying, as Aristotle already explicitly did at 767b35–7, that the movements of the male parent as that parent, a male, a human being, and an animal are present *in actuality* in his semen, apply also to the corresponding movements of the female. So what possible reason could Aristotle have for saying that though the male's movements are present in actuality, the corresponding ones of the female are only there in potentiality? (ii) In any event, it is quite clear what the contrast between actuality and potentiality comes to in its present application. It is first introduced at 767b35–7, where the movements of his ancestors are said to be present in a male's semen potentially, by contrast with those actual ones belonging to it as himself, a male, etc. The thought clearly is that the potential ones are underlying movements that become active when, as with the postulated phenomenon of λύσις, the normally active ones give way. And that is certainly how it is to be taken in reference to the movements of the ancestors mentioned at the end of our sentence. But if in the female's fluid the movements of her ancestors are in this sense merely potential, that must be by contrast with the movements they replace if λύσις occurs, viz., the ones characteristic of her as an individual mother; and these ought therefore to be *actual* movements of the fluid, not a second set of potential ones instead, as they become on this interpretation of the sentence. One might try to find some other use of the word "potentially," according to which Aristotle might plausibly have thought that even the movements belonging to a woman's menstrual fluid

as that individual are present in it only potentially.[12] But that would require taking the single word δυνάμει (potentially) at 768a13–14 in two
different senses—one for the movements "of the female" and one for those
"of the ancestors," and one of these senses would have no warrant at all
in the evidently parallel uses of the term elsewhere in this chapter. It is impossible, then, to make good sense of this sentence on the supposition
that in it Aristotle is discussing movements in both the generative fluids.

In any event, the context makes it clear that at 768a11–14 Aristotle is
referring only to movements in the male's fluid, and that explicit reference to movements in the female fluid only occurs for the first time just
afterwards, at 768a19–21. In chapter 1, as I have explained, Aristotle introduces the central idea on which he will ground his detailed explanations—the idea that the male, active, fashioning agent in generation can
nonetheless fail to master the female, passive, material element (or, equivalently, be defeated by it). The reason he gives (at 766a19) for this defeat
is that the semen is deficient in heat and so cannot concoct the catamenia
to such an extent as to make them turn into another male (and, it is implied, one like the father, a19–21). In the next chapter he explains in more
detail that success or failure in mastery depends really on the συμμετρία
(balance, proportion) or its absence between the semen and the menstrual fluid (767a15 ff.). The heat of the semen must be in the right proportion to the moistness (and cold) of the menstrual fluid if there is to be
any "setting" of an embryo at all. If the particular semen is too hot for
the given catamenia, it will just boil them away and dry them up; if not
hot enough no congealing will take place at all. And likewise the exact
proportions in heat and wetness of the two seminal fluids will be responsible for whether a male or a female is produced. Both his talk of the semen
as sometimes mastering but sometimes being mastered by the catamenia,
and these comments on the need for "symmetry" between the two fluids,
make it clear already in chapters 1 and 2 that Aristotle is going to assign
an important role to the female fluid in determining the sex and (we may
add by anticipation) the inherited resemblances of the offspring. But although he has spoken repeatedly and from very early on in the treatise
about generative movements in the semen he has not yet openly mentioned movements in the menstrual fluid at all, much less any role they

---

[12] One might think, as Geoffrey Lloyd has suggested to me, of Aristotle's remarks at, e.g.,
737a22–34, 738b3–4, 740b18–20, to the effect that the material contributed by the female
is already potentially, though of course not actually, all the bodily parts that the male will
fashion it into. But these remarks hardly yield a sense in which the movements in the menstrual fluid, which are in fact Aristotle's grounds for saying that it *is* potentially all those
bodily parts, are not present in it actually, but only potentially; indeed, they imply precisely
the contrary.

might play in this connection. Indeed, his talk of a συμμετρία in the fluids' heat and wetness rather discourages the reader from thinking of corresponding, and somehow themselves operative, symmetrical *movements* on the female side: wetness, unlike heat, certainly does not connote movement in Aristotle's physical theory. It cannot be emphasized too strongly that, however much the theoretical basis for them has already been laid in book II, no actual mention of movements in the catamenia, much less of any role for them in sex determination and inherited bodily characteristics, has occurred before *GA* IV, 3.

Aristotle initiates the exposition of his own theory in *GA* IV, 3 by reminding the reader of the two principal things he has said already about the causes of female births. It is possible, he says (767b10–13), for the male sometimes not to master the female fluid, with a resulting female birth, through youth or old age or some such cause—youth and old age were mentioned at the beginning of chapter 2, 766b28–31, as being responsible for those deficiencies in the heat of the semen that at 766a19 he said explained its failure to concoct the catamenia sufficiently and so to "master" them. Thus he begins by continuing to focus exclusively on the semen and defects in it that lead to its failure to produce a male offspring. "For," he says (767b15–18), "when the spermatic residue [viz., the semen][13] in the catamenia is well-concocted [and so sufficiently hot] the movement of the male will make the [embryo's] shape like his own." He then makes the important generalizing remark I have quoted already, that when the semen *fails* to master the female fluid it is nonetheless the semen that

---

[13] The σπερματικὴ περίττωσις referred to here as being in the catamenia must be the semen, and not the female fluid itself, for two reasons. (i) This sentence supplements the statement at 767b10–13 just before about what causes a female birth, by stating the cause of the contrasting male birth. Since the female birth was said there to be caused by a defect in the hotness of the semen, we need a reference here to the well-concoctedness, and so hotness, of the semen as what causes the male birth. (ii) In the following sentence Aristotle makes a remark about the equivalency of speaking in such contexts of either the semen (γονή) or the movement (in it), and the relevance of that remark *here* is heightened by, if it does not actually require, a reference to the semen in the first part of this sentence. Read that way, Aristotle does precisely begin by speaking at 767b15 of the well-concoctedness of the *semen* only to conclude by saying (b17–18) what, when it is well-concocted, the *movement* of the male will effect; the remark at b18–20 is then fully in place, as indicating that no gap has in fact been left open in the explanation just given between the semen (and its features) and the formative movements. I have been unable to find any exact parallel for the expression ἡ περίττωσις ἐν τοῖς καταμηνίοις ἡ σπερματική (referring either to the semen or to the female generative residue), but Aristotle does of course speak frequently enough of a mixture of the two residues when conception occurs (e.g., 728a29–30), and he does occasionally mention semen being in the catamenia under such circumstances (e.g., 727a17–18). So neither Aristotle's usage nor his general theoretical position throws up any obstacle to finding here the reference to the semen that the surrounding context requires.

makes the embryo have a "deficiency" in precisely the respect that is controlled by the "capacity" in which it failed to master it—the *semen* fashions the offspring so that it is a female, or resembles its mother. He goes on to detail various "capacities" of the semen (767b23–35), adding at b35–7 that in addition to actual movements from its capacities for the individual characteristics of the father, a male, a human being, and an animal, the semen has present in it in a potential way the movements of his ancestors. There is no reference yet to movements in the catamenia, nor has Aristotle yet even opened up the theoretical space into which they might be fitted. After all, he posed the problem he is now solving in terms of how the semen produces the effects it is seen to produce (ποιήσει 767b17, 21; ποιεῖ 23), and it is only natural that he has gone on to explain them by telling us about the semen—about "capacities" and movements in it, such that it produces one result if they achieve mastery and the other if they do not. Up to this point it is exclusively the semen's capacities and movements that he has told us anything about.

The mention of the male's ancestors at 767b37 introduces the concept of potential movements, and with it the second of Aristotle's two postulated processes, that of the loosening or slackening of the movements. For the movements of the ancestors, which are potential movements, get progressively made actual (first those of the grandparent, then those of the great-grandparent, and so on) as the movements that are in the father's semen as that individual parent themselves undergo a lesser or a greater slackening or loosening (cf. 768a16–18, b8–10). It is only when he comes around to explaining this slackening of movements and consequent resemblance to ancestors, instead of to parents, that Aristotle opens up the theoretical space into which movements in the female matter might be placed. "And," he says (768a9–11), "similarly for the faculties next in line. For it [sc., the matter from which the offspring is being made] always tends to go over to that one of the ancestors that stands next in line, both on the father's side and on the mother's." In order to explain the offspring's "going over" to the mother's ancestors Aristotle proceeds to assign an explicit role to movements in the female residue. But first, in accordance with his general theory and in continuation of what he has been saying immediately before (768a2–9), where he has repeated his account of how the semen fashions the offspring into a female and/or a person resembling the mother, he points out that the semen itself contains, in potentiality if not actuality, all the movements that are necessary to it if it is to do all these jobs—the movements of the female, along with those of his own and her ancestors. This is our sentence at 768a11–14, quoted above: "Some of the movements [in the seminal fluid] are present in actuality, others in potentiality: in actuality, those of the male parent and of the universal, such as a human being and an animal; in potentiality, those of the female and of the ancestors."[14] Only then does he go on, in giving details of how resemblance to ancestors on either side is produced, to introduce into his explanation movements in the female residue itself.

> So then, when it [sc., the matter from which the offspring is being made] departs from its own nature, it changes over into the opposites. But the movements that are fashioning [the offspring] slacken into the nearby movements, for example if the movement of the male parent slackens, it goes over by the smallest variation to the movement of his father, or in the second place to that of his grandfather. And in this way too on the side of the females,[15] the movement of the female parent goes over to that of her mother, or if not to that, then to the movement of her grandmother. And similarly also for the more distant ancestors. (768a14–21)

Aristotle does not immediately explain (but see 768b15–25, and my comments below, pp. 194–95ff.) why he needs both the potential movements in the semen and these corresponding ones in the catamenia, but the reason is clear enough. On his view, reaffirmed in this chapter at 768b16 and 25–7, the semen is the active, formative agent, the catamenia the passive material in the generative process. As being the material from which the offspring is constructed, the catamenia cannot initiate any of the movements that fashion the offspring, or determine directly the course which any of these movements take. Aristotle points out two ways in which the catamenia can nonetheless affect these processes by affecting the semen itself, which is the source of them. First (see 768b25–7) it can be too cold or too great in amount for the semen to work it up fully

---

[14] Notice that the unexpressed dative with ἔνεισι at 768a11 ("the movements in . . . are present") is to be supplied from the dative at 767b35–6, ὑπάρχουσιν αἱ κινήσεις ἐν τοῖς σπέρμασιν, which in fact this sentence partially repeats. Since σπέρμασιν at 767b36 is the semen (only), so must the intended reference to seminal fluid at 768a11 be. This is added confirmation, if any were needed, for my interpretation of this sentence. (The fact that at 768b4 and 6 the implied dative with ἔνεισι includes both the semen and the female residue is irrelevant to the interpretation of ἔνεισι at 768a11. Once movements in the female fluid are introduced into Aristotle's account, at 768a18–21, they obviously fall within the scope of the general principles about actual and potential movements first set out for the male fluid alone at 767b35–7 and 768a11–14, and he simply takes note of this fact at 768b4 and 6).

[15] I translate Drossaart Lulofs's text. But I wonder whether one ought, instead of excising καὶ ἐπὶ τῶν ἀρρένων with Drossaart Lulofs, or excising this together with καὶ ἐπὶ τῶν θηλείων with other editors, to retain the manuscript reading, changing only the second καί of a18 to ὥσπερ, thus giving the sense: "And in this way too, on the side of the females as on that of the males. . . ." Our manuscripts might have resulted from a scribe's having been misled by καὶ ἐπὶ πατέρων καὶ ἐπὶ μητέρων at a11 to repeat that construction here by altering ὥσπερ to καί.

according to its natural tendencies (that is, it can cause the semen to fail to master it). One way this can happen is for the semen to be unable to make the offspring resemble the male whose semen it is, and then, as Aristotle has already explained, it makes the material go over to resembling the mother's side of the family. And here the second way Aristotle distinguishes in which the catamenia can affect the semen and its operations comes into play. Since any agent in acting on materials is itself reciprocally affected by them, the semen can be brought, in working on the catamenia, to be affected by them in such a way that its movements slacken, from being ones that would produce a resemblance to the mother to being ones that produce a resemblance to the mother's mother or another of her ancestors. The catamenia do this when their own movements (1) slacken into movements of the forebear in question; that alters the character of the catamenia as they reciprocally affect the semen, so that they induce its movements to slacken in just the way required. That is to say that one gets here a combination of both the two processes Aristotle postulates. The semen first fails to master the female fluid; the semen therefore departs from its nature and makes the offspring resemble not the father (as would be more natural) but the mother. But secondly (and this is where movements in the female fluid enter the theory explicitly) the movements of the female fluid themselves slacken, reciprocally affecting the semen as it acts on it, so that its potentiality to produce in the embryo movements for the mother's ancestors (instead for the mother herself) comes into play.

Now the sentence at 768a11–14 is the only explicit indication in his text that Aristotle postulated movements somehow potentially present in a male's fluid capable of imposing on an embryo bodily resemblances to its mother's side of the family. Regrettably, he does not pause to explain how we are to understand this "potential" presence (and how we are to relate it to the "potential" presence of the movements for resemblances to the male's own ancestors). Two possibilities suggest themselves. If one bears in mind simply the theoretical need that Aristotle has for such potential movements, the following, relatively vague conception may recommend itself. If there are to be resemblances to the mother or to any of her ancestors, then the embryo's own soul, through the formative movements in the blood its heart makes, must produce and maintain these. The material from which the embryo is itself originally constituted and by which it is nourished so long as it is in the womb, being provided by the mother, already carries, either actually or potentially (as an inheritance from her ancestors, through her own mother), all those movements—as movements of matter, however, not yet as formal movements (that is, movements of the *embryo*'s form). What the father's semen and its movements need to do, therefore, is selectively to elevate whichever of the movements belonging to the material provided by the mother will carry such resemblances to her side of the family as there are going to be, from being movements *of* matter to being formal movements *in* the matter. This suggests that we think of the potential presence of the female movements simply as the potentiality in a male's sperm to do this job: the power to work on the materials provided by the mother so as to elevate to the level of formal movements material movements already actually there (because they carried the instructions for the formation of her own bodily parts) or potentially present (as underlying traces inherited from her ancestors). On this conception, the semen would be said to have these movements potentially, just in virtue of the fact that it is capable of making the embryo have them as movements of its form—despite the fact that the semen does not impose them, in the sense of transferring from itself movements already actually or virtually existing in it, so much as simply work to strengthen movements provided by the mother in the catamenia.

On the other hand, Aristotle's mentioning together, and apparently without distinction, potential movements "of the female and of the [male's] ancestors" may suggest some more substantial way the semen might possess these movements. For it seems reasonable to think that an animal's semen has movements for his own ancestors (in respects in which he does not himself resemble them) in some underlying, non-actual, but nonetheless physically realized way. So perhaps Aristotle is thinking that there is in the semen some physically realized representation of the movements of the females he can copulate successfully with (and their ancestors). Obviously this will still be something vague and general, since it must cover so many distinct possibilities. But on this second conception, much more readily than on the first, it will be natural to speak of a male as having in a potential way the very movements by which the mother's blood and her catamenia are actually moved (and those that are potentially in them as inheritances from her ancestors)—and, as we have seen, that is how Aristotle puts his theory at 768a14. On this second conception, Aristotle will still be saying that the semen elevates the movements of the catamenia to the level of movements of the embryo's form, but he will be postulating some sort of physically realized representation of these movements in the semen as what makes it possible for it to do this. Aristotle's text does not allow us to decide between these two ways of construing the "potential" presence of the female movements in the semen.[16] In what follows, one should bear them both equally in mind.

---

[16] Since it says less about what in or about the semen enables it to do the required work, the first conception may seem less satisfactory than the second. On the other hand, it may be a virtue of the first conception that its commitments here are less substantial. At any rate, one might feel some discomfort with the second conception's idea that the semen has some sort,

VI

Thus, subject to clarification about how we are to conceive his own and the mother's ancestors' movements being potentially in the father's sperm in the first place, Aristotle has explained offspring, both male and female, resembling not the father or the mother, but any of his male ancestors in the male line or any of her female ancestors in the female line. Conspicuously, he has not yet explained, or even clearly allowed the possibility of, offspring of either sex resembling their father's mother or their mother's father, or any other female on the father's side or male on the mother's. I assume Aristotle intended to allow for these resemblances too, perhaps by simple extensions of his theory as so far expounded; but as I read him he does not mention such resemblances in this chapter or indicate how he would explain them.

We must take note of one last elaboration of the theory. So far I have spoken only of an offspring's inherited resemblance as a whole and overall to some single one of its forebears. But, as of course their nature as residues derived from nutritive blood already implies, both the male and female seminal fluids contain movements specific for each of the bodily tissues and organs, and specific for them with whatever special features of form and structure the parents' blood was so "programmed" to produce and maintain in them. (Obviously, though Aristotle does not say this explicitly, what are in question here are features of the movements [1].) So similarly for the potential movements in the fluids that, when the actual movements slacken, take over and in the way I have explained, produce resemblances in the offspring to the parents' parents and grandparents: potentially, movements specific for each of the tissues and organs of each of these forebears are also present in the seminal fluids. Accordingly (768b1–5) Aristotle can claim that his theory provides an easy explanation for all possible combinations of partial resemblances between offspring and either or both parents and any of these ancestors you like. Mastery and being mastered, and slackening of movements, can be partial and selective at every level.

Aristotle will not, of course, have given a complete explanation of these or any of the other phenomena of inheritance until he has said (i) what it *is* for a seminal fluid to have movements potentially and (ii) how the male's sperm, in particular, comes to have the movements potentially that Aristotle says it has. The answer to this second question will be par-

---

however general, of physically realized underlying movements *for* resemblances to any of the potential mothers' families. If that is the alternative, then perhaps the more noncommittal first conception is philosophically and scientifically preferable after all.

ticularly difficult, of course, for the movements of the female with whom the male happens at the moment to be copulating. For, as I have pointed out, Aristotle claims the male's sperm has in some sort of potential way the movements (1) of any female with whom it mates successfully. How does an animal's sperm come to have *those* movements, even potentially?

The answer to my first question is quite easy. What it is for a seminal fluid to have some movement *potentially* is for it to have that movement in such a way that an offspring it generates, or that is generated from it, comes, as a result of the generative activity, to have it *actually* in the blood that its heart makes. Or, to put the same point one stage further back in the process of explanation, it is to have those movements in such a way that the activity of generation makes the movements in the off-spring's body that depend on and express its form be in actuality the same as those merely potential movements in the seminal fluids. Aristotle obviously cannot think that under certain conditions the seminal fluid of an animal, while remaining that seminal fluid, comes itself actually to be moved by the movements specific for its parents' or grandparents' tissues and organs in those respects where the animal's own tissues and organs are significantly different. An animal's seminal fluid can only actually have whatever movements were actual in its nutritive blood, and these, ex hypothesi, were not actual there. The actualization of these potential-ities of movement cannot then be found in the semen or the catamenia themselves. But since the whole natural purpose of seminal fluid is to be the instrument or the material for reproduction, it seems acceptable to think of the realization of the potentials in those fluids as taking place outside them, in the offspring that comes into being. Anyhow, that is what Aristotle clearly intends.

For our inquiry this fact has particularly significant implications in the case of the male fluid. The female fluid has potentially the movements of her ancestors just as the male's does of his. But on Aristotle's theory the male fluid is the *sole* source, in the sense of the moving cause, of the off-spring's form and so of the movements in its body (in its heart, in the first instance, and derivatively from that in the blood that its heart manufac-tures) that express that form and convey it to its material constitution. When, therefore, Aristotle says that the male's sperm contains potentially both all the movements of its male forebears in the male line *and* all the movements of the female it copulates with, including those of all her cor-responding forebears, he is saying what he *must* say if he is to explain the phenomena about inherited characteristics while sticking to his basic theory of reproduction, as he has worked that out in *GA* I and II. If the offspring's metabolism regulates it in such a way as to fashion and main-tain certain specific shapes and organizations for its tissues and organs, these must be due to its form (unless there is some special other explanation of how this regularity is maintained). But on Aristotle's theory the male parent, and only it, causes, in the sense of being a moving, creative, shaping cause, the offspring to have just that form, whatever it turns out to be like, that it has. If some of what the offspring's form does is to make it like its mother and her family then the father's sperm, the instrument he uses to move, fashion, and shape the matter so as to have that form, simply has to have, in some way or other, those movements potentially in it. Otherwise it could not engender in the offspring all the movements that express and convey the offspring's form, and so we would have to look for a separate second source of some aspects of the offspring's form. It is clear, then, that so far from abandoning or incoherently contradicting his theory of reproduction by invoking movements in the female fluid to explain some of what happens, Aristotle goes to great lengths in *GA* IV, 3 to maintain it. By assigning the mother's movements to the father at the level of potentiality he insists, as he thinks one must, on the male's exclusive role as source of the offspring's form. Accordingly, in his theory of inherited resemblances Aristotle carefully denies any formative, active, creative role on the part of the female in bringing this form into existence. The contribution which it might appear she makes to that form, Aristotle insists, the father makes instead.

It should now be relatively easy to answer my second question, about how the male's sperm comes to have, even potentially, all these movements, both those of its male forebears and those of the prospective offspring's mother and her female forebears. About its having his forebears' movements I can be brief. (The explanation is parallel for a female's seminal fluid having in potentiality her female forebears' movements.) These the animal simply inherits. My form and the movements which express it in me derive from my father's form and the movements that express his in him, and his from his father, and so on backwards. There should be no difficulty, then, in seeing that all those movements may be retained in my sperm, the ones that are not there in actuality being retained in potentiality.

How the prospective mother's movements get into the sperm of the male she copulates with, in whatever way they do, is another question. We can best approach it by seeing how Aristotle accounts for the realization of these supposed potentialities. He appeals here to two connected ways in which in general when agents act on materials in an effort to shape and work them up, they in their turn are or may be affected by the materials (768b15–36; cf. 766a15–16, 18–21). First (b15–25) he explains the relapsing (λύεσθαι) of the male's movements[17]—into the move-

<hr/>

[17] It is noteworthy that though in the first words of this paragraph Aristotle offers to explain the slackening of movements in general (and so, among others the slackening of the movements in the catamenia mentioned at 768a18–21) in fact he goes on to discuss only the

ments of his own forebears, but also, as we have seen, into movements productive of resemblances to the mother and her forebears. This is a special case of the general phenomenon, discussed in *de Gen. et Corr.* I, 7.324a24 ff. to which he here (b23–4) refers, of an agent's being reciprocally affected by the patient on which it acts: "a thing which cuts gets blunted by the thing being cut, a thing which heats gets cooled by the thing being heated, . . . what pushes gets pushed in a way in return, what squeezes is squeezed back" (b16–20). These examples (especially the first) clearly suggest that Aristotle is thinking here primarily of such intermediate agents as the tools a primary agent uses to bring about its effects. And that is appropriate, since on his theory the semen is the instrument the father uses to set and shape the fetus, and it is something that sometimes happens to the semen, namely the λύσις of its movements, that he is trying to explain. Failure of mastery he explains (b25–36) as a case of an agent's being too weak or the materials being too formidable in some relevant respect for the agent to impose on them exactly what, given that it is that kind of agent, it has in it to do on suchlike materials—as for example happens with athletes in training, whose unusually large intake of food (he says, b29–33) overstrains their digestive systems' power to assimilate the nutrient and distribute it so as to maintain their normal proportions, with the resulting outsized and sometimes grotesquely misshapen musculature, etc., characteristic of athletes. Here, evidently and again appropriately, the semen's agency is being compared, if to that of a tool at all, at any rate to one (unlike, say, a doctor's knife) with its own inherent power to affect and shape the product.

Now for each of these general principles, but especially for the first, there are difficulties in understanding how Aristotle thinks its application to the semen produces the desired results. The reciprocal blunting of a knife and cooling of a hot object placed into contact with something colder than it are instances of an agent's undergoing the precisely opposite effect to what it does (both normally and in the given case) to the patient. But in λύσις the semen is affected by the catamenia so that what it then does to them is *different* from what Aristotle thinks should be normal, and moreover it is not easy to see how the change it undergoes (from exercising its actual to exercising one or more of its potential movements) can be construed as due to its undergoing the opposite of what it does (either normally or in the actual case) to the catamenia. According to

---

slackening of the movements in the semen—these are the only movements that are active, ποιοῦντα of anything. This confirms the secondary role assigned in his theory to movements in the catamenia. It also fits in well with the attribution to the semen of potential movements somehow corresponding to them: in effect, in discussing only the slackening of the semen's movements he will have covered the whole range of the phenomena.

Aristotle's account there is "going over to the opposite" in connection, not with the semen's λύσις, but with its being defeated by the catamenia. It appears that in these analogies Aristotle has somewhat run together his two processes of the defeat of the semen's movements by the catamenia and their slackening.

Perhaps the following analogy, a close relative of those Aristotle actually invokes, will help to resolve these difficulties, and to show why it seems to Aristotle to make good sense to attribute to the semen as potential movements the "movements of the female."[18] Consider a sculptor working on some soft stone. It turns out that his skills are not adequate to make this particular piece of stone have exactly the degree of surface finish that the statuary's art demands: he does not possess the lightness of touch necessary to achieve a greater degree of finish without chipping the stone. He might of course abandon the effort once the inadequacy of his skills becomes clear to him. But suppose he doesn't. Then whatever features of shape, surface texture, etc., the resulting statue has will have been the product of *his* art: his art will have been the originating source, and the only originating source, of these outcomes (assuming nothing pushes his hand or falls on the statue while he is working on it that affects these features). The stone itself contributes only as matter, not as a source of any of the changes it undergoes while these outcomes are being achieved. It is not as if there is a *nisus* in the stone for this kind of surface texture, etc. Yet the principles of the artisan's art, as they actually exist in him in whatever way principles of art do exist actually in an artisan, do not themselves explain these deviant features of the outcome. Still, even these features are not due, even in part, to any accident: the agent is the non-accidental moving cause of them, just as much as he is of the others. He at least settles for these outcomes, even though he does not set out to achieve them or intend them; on the contrary, he is aiming at as perfect a realization of the sculptor's art as he can achieve, not this defective one that he actually achieves. The skill within him is, however, such that this is the best that in these circumstances it is capable of producing. So we are led to recognize, in addition to the actual principles of the art in him, other somehow underlying and potential ones that suit him, precisely, to

---

[18] One should not object to this analogy on the ground that it compares the semen, which Aristotle treats as merely a tool used by the father (the actual "artisan"), to an artisan (the sculptor) rather than to his tools (chisel, etc.). For as I have pointed out Aristotle is evidently thinking of the semen as a highly refined, fully programmed, and self-starting tool not controlled by the father himself once it is set loose, and so, much more like the sculptor himself than his chisel (which is presumably why he refers to the movements in the semen as themselves δημιουργοῦσαι 768a16). It should also be borne in mind that Aristotle's doctrine in *Gen. et Corr.* I, 7 apparently includes reciprocal effects not just on the doctor's or the sculptor's tools, but also on these practitioners themselves: 324b3–13.

be the moving cause of these deviant features. What calls these "potential" principles into play are defects in the agent's manual abilities, or resistance in the materials, or both.

The father's sperm as moving cause of the offspring's form is a parallel case. Here too we find that sometimes, through no accidental interference of another moving cause, the materials do not come to have the movements that the principles for constructing the product that are actually present in the sperm dictate. The product comes to have female movements and/or movements that make it like its mother or her family. Yet it was nonetheless the sperm and not the materials themselves that put those movements there: there is no independent source of development to that end in the materials. The female seminal fluids are materials only; they make no motion toward coming alive unless and until they are moved about by the sperm. So, just as in the case of the statuary, we are justified in attributing to the sperm, somehow in potentiality, exactly those movements that *would* directly explain the presence of the same movements in the offspring.

This is obviously a very weak way of having movements or other principles potentially, on either of the two ways I have suggested we might construe this potential presence. And that is all to the good. One would not want it to turn out in any more robust sense that a male's sperm has in potentiality the movements in it of the females it happens to copulate successfully with. Still, the analogy with other artisans does support this weak way of having movements potentially, and that is what Aristotle needs in order to explain this part of the phenomena. For one must bear clearly in mind that though movements specific for a female, etc., are already present in the mother's seminal fluid, they are not present in the way they must come to be present in the offspring if it is to be a female and/or resemble the mother or her family. For the latter, they must be present as movements *of the form;* they must be movements deriving from its soul, not from its matter. And, on Aristotle's theory, only a form can make *such* movements come to be. Aristotle's claim is this: *because* those movements are present as movements of the matter, the male's form, in certain cases being reciprocally affected by them, produces the formal movements in the offspring that correspond to those movements in the matter and that make its body continue to have them after it becomes a self-regulating embryo. The formal movements imposed by the sperm enable the embryo itself to take over from its mother the capacity to maintain the existence of these movements in its material constitution.

Perhaps it is not going too far to suggest that this is Aristotle's intended explanation for how the male's sperm must have potentialities in it for a female birth and/or an offspring resembling the mother or her family, and how they get realized.

VII

It is clear from our study of *GA* IV, 1 and 3 that Aristotle holds a male animal's form directly responsible for details of its offspring's internal structure and organization that lie well below the level of its specific identity as a member of the lowest animal kind to which it belongs. In his discussion there Aristotle does not say *which* such details he thinks the form is responsible for. Presumably that is because his purpose is simply to show that and how his theory of reproduction is able to handle the kinds of births that are actually observed: both male and female, and males and females that resemble, both as a whole and/or with respect to various single bodily parts, one or more of their parents, parents' parents, etc. One may however appeal to other parts of the treatise to obtain light on this question. Aristotle pursues the general topic of resemblances of offspring to parents at some length in discussing the *panspermia* theory in I, 17 ff.—the theory held by some of his predecessors that the generative fluid is drawn from all parts of the body (and from both parents). At several places he mentions detailed types of resemblance, where he might be thought to be accepting that these are inherited through characteristics of the generative fluids. And in V, 1–4, he discusses, among other things, the causes of differences among human beings in eye color, the tendency to go gray or get bald as age advances, and the color and texture of the hair—all differences that *we* would count as at least partly genetic in origin. Does Aristotle, too, explain them as due to inheritance?

Aristotle cites four pieces of evidence (I, 17.721b12 ff.) as allegedly supporting the *panspermia* theory. The most important of these derives from the resemblances that offspring show to their parents (b20–4). But it must be carefully borne in mind in assessing this alleged evidence and Aristotle's response to it that, as Aristotle understands his opponents' argument, the resemblances in question are of two kinds.[19] First (see I, 18.723b3–9), there are resemblances that any member of the species shows to any other (of the same sex): the same organs and limbs distributed in the same manner and with more or less the same physical constitution (human flesh, hair, and toenails, say, as against canine). And secondly there are more specific resemblances in any of these respects to one or another of the parents in particular. Aristotle's *panspermia* opponents think that resemblances of both types require to be explained by

---

[19] In the Hippocratic treatise *On Generation* I can find no clear reference to the first type of resemblance. All the emphasis, at any rate, is on ways the offspring takes after one or the other parent in features distinctive of and more or less special to that parent. See sects. 8 and 9.

the supposition that, in general, each part of the body of each parent supplies some of the generative fluid from which the offspring derives. They find confirmation for their view in the alleged fact that mutilated parents produce offspring missing the same part (721b17–20) and that children resemble their parents even in acquired characteristics, such as brand marks on the father's arm that turn up also on the son's (b29–34).

Aristotle rejects this theory, of course, and he plainly does not feel obligated to accept that all the resemblances appealed to by its proponents (that brand mark, for example) have to be explained at all as due to features of the semen (let alone by the hypothesis that some of it comes from each part of the parent's body). For example, Aristotle himself denies that children with congenitally missing limbs, whether they share the mutilation with a parent or not, ever lack these limbs because of defects in the semen that fashioned them (IV, 4.772b35–773a3; cf. I, 18.724a3–7). But equally plainly he does accept that many of the resemblances his opponents had in mind are inherited, and will accordingly have to be explained as passed on from parent to child through the action of the semen: it's just that the *panspermia* theory is not the right explanation of how this happens. Unfortunately, however, it is not possible to infer anything from his discussion of this theory that helps answer our question about the extent of such resemblances.

To be sure, Aristotle says clearly that resemblances between child and parent are found in anhomoeomerous parts such as face, hands, and feet more than in the homoeomerous ones (tissues, etc.) (722a19–21), but this does not tell us which features of which of these parts he thinks are inheritable (for example, whether eye color is). Again, he objects that children resemble parents in many respects that his opponents will have to agree cannot be due to some of the semen's having been drawn from a corresponding part of the parent: voice, nails, hair, manner of movement, gray hair or beard (when the parent did not yet have these at the time of conception) (722a5–7)—indeed, he points out (723b30–2), a son who resembles his father tends to wear shoes that resemble his too. Given the variety of items in this list, and the nature of Aristotle's argument here, it would be hazardous to infer from these passages that he accepts even the resemblance in nails and hair between child and parents as explainable by inheritance. If one were nonetheless inclined to think he did mean to be granting his opponents that point (while denying that it could be due to some of the sperm being drawn from the parent's nails and hair), the possibility would remain open that he was granting only the general resemblance (human hair and nails, as against canine) and not a more particular resemblance to special features of the parent's nails and hair. And grayness in old age he definitely does not explain as inherited, in the sense of specifically provided for in the formative movements of the father's semen and/or the corresponding movements of the menstrual fluid; it is a side effect of the natural deterioration in the aging process (see *GA* V, 4).

David Balme has, however, attributed to Aristotle the view that "in a correct reproduction the offspring will be a replica of the sire," including even in nonessential details, such as eye color, type and color of the hair, and so on.[20] Balme seems to have been led to this interpretation by reflection on the significance of the priority for Aristotle of what I have been calling the movements (1) of the semen at *GA* IV, 3.767b26–35. Aristotle does indeed say there that the movements the semen has from the father as that individual, rather than as a male or a human being, come first and will control the formation of the offspring if nothing untoward happens. But Aristotle characterizes these movements not simply as movements of the individual father (in general) but of him καθὸ γεννητικόν (b28), "insofar as he is a procreator." In explaining this qualification he excludes from the scope of the movements "what he is incidentally, for example, if the male parent knows his letters or is someone's neighbor." Obviously he intends to exclude also even any congenital properties that may be similarly incidental, for example, if by some mishap in the womb the father were born with one leg shorter than the other. The semen only aims to reproduce in the offspring whatever properties of the father are relevant to his role as procreator, and while it is clear that this includes all his essential organs and limbs, and all their properties (even the individual ones) that are relevant to their correct functioning, there is a significant further question as to what these properties are. In general it is clear what Aristotle's answer is: whichever properties of the father's body the formative movements in his blood contain *specific information* for. What lies outside that, so that its presence in his body is, from this point of view, produced by the movements in the blood only incidentally or accidentally, it is not part of his procreator's role to pass on. This distinction, however it is worked out in detail, will determine, on Aristotle's view, in what respects the semen will see to it that the offspring resembles the father, and in what it may very well not resemble him, (even) if nothing untoward happens. A *replica* it certainly does not attempt to produce.

Does Aristotle, however, think eye color and the like are matters that the father's semen contains specific information for, and with respect to which it will cause a paternal resemblance in the offspring, if nothing untoward happens? If one consults Aristotle's discussion in *GA* V one can see that the answer is definitely in the negative. His explanation of eye color (V, 1.779a35–b1, b12–34), for example, is that it depends upon the amount of fluid that the eye happens to contain: people with more fluid in the eye than is ideal for seeing are dark-eyed (because large volumes of

[20] Balme, "The Snub," reprinted in Gotthelf and Lennox, *Philosophical Issues,* 292.

fluid are dark), those with less fluid than is ideal are blue-eyed (for the corresponding reason), those with just the right amount of fluid have eyes intermediate in color. The quantity of any person's eye liquid Aristotle treats as in effect an accident, the result of the amount of liquid that happened to be available for the semen when as moving cause it worked on that liquid to form the eye in the first place (778a35 ff.).[21] Likewise (V, 3) he explains differences in the condition of the hair, and hairiness itself, as due partly to accidental differences in the character of the skin and the amount and quality of the bodily fluids, and partly to environment: he explains the Scythians' and the Thracians' straight hair by the wateriness both of their constitution and of their climate, and the Ethiopians' curly hair by the dryness of both their brains and their climate (782b33–783a1).

It does not occur to him to explain any of these differences in constitution (not even these racial ones) by inheritance. Neither in connection with eye color nor with the hair does he anywhere employ the apparatus of mastery and being mastered and the slackening of movements that he has developed in book IV to explain characteristics inherited whether from the mother and her family or from the father and his. A sensitive reading of *GA* V shows, therefore, that Aristotle thinks the father's semen contains specific instructions for the formation in the child of an eye of the right type for human vision, but that what color it will be is determined by accidental features of the matter that the mother happens to provide for its formation on the occasion of the conception.

It follows that Aristotle does not think that the male parent's form is responsible for biologically superficial characteristics like eye color, pitch of voice, and coarseness or fineness, length, quantity, and natural straightness or curliness of the hair. These are material by-products, not anything the form's "program" contains a specification for. In our example from statuary they correspond to features that a statue has because the material it was made out of already had them too. These are accidents, not initially due to the parent's form and so not later on due to the offspring's own form, except incidentally, when that takes over from the parent responsibility for its growth and self-maintenance.

Taken altogether, then, Aristotle's various discussions of inherited resemblances between offspring and parents imply a less than fully determinate

---

[21] I mean only to be reporting Aristotle's view, not defending it. Since for most individual animals for most of their life spans, eye color remains the same, through growth, etc., it must continue to be true that the combination of the auxetic movements in the animal's blood and the availability of material for adding to and maintaining the eye has the effect of preserving this color. It is not clear that he has a good explanation for why this happens, if the form is not aiming at this result.

theory about what features of any animal its form is directly responsible for. Its form is not directly, but only incidentally, responsible for secondary, superficial, biologically insignificant characteristics, such as eye color. But it is directly responsible not only for its having all the tissues, organs, and limbs essential to a human being, but also for many individual features of the way these are found constituted and arranged in that particular animal. Roughly, these will be all those features that, as Aristotle thinks, cannot successfully be explained as due either to environmental influences or to incidental properties of the matter that goes to constitute and sustain them. The indeterminacy derives from the fact that Aristotle does not, and given the very incomplete information that research into animals had yet provided, presumably could not responsibly, draw this line at all sharply. But even with this limited degree of determinacy Aristotle's conception of animal forms in the *GA* has clear and significant consequences for his metaphysical theory of substantial form.

As I mentioned at the outset, some have thought from reading just the *Metaphysics* that Aristotelian form is a nonrepeatable instance of some general specific type, differing from other instances not internally (by reference to the *logos* of its being) but only by the accidental historical facts about the individual object whose form it is by which we mark that individual off from others of the same species. The *GA* makes it clear that, on the contrary, each form has in principle a full *logos* of its being as the form that it is that includes the specification of all those distinctive characteristics of structure and organization for which in the individual whose form it is it is directly responsible. In fact, *those* characteristics are not accidents at all, but precisely programmed for in the *logos* of the movements that the form imparts to the nutritive and auxetic blood from which the organs are originally formed and thereafter maintained. Thus Aristotelian forms are particular in that each form contains within itself the basis for its differentiation from (as well, of course, as its affiliation with) other forms of the same specific type. As Aristotle's theory of the different movements in the seminal fluid makes clear, the *logos* of the being of any form (say mine) when fully spelled out will contain a good deal of information (whatever is necessary and sufficient to determine that I am a human being) that is also contained in yours. But there will also be further information that determines those special ways I am a human being which mark me off from at least most other people by making me resemble my family and not theirs. Whether or not Aristotle thought these details sufficient in principle to describe me uniquely is unclear from anything he says or implies in the *GA*. But presumably he did not.

Two immediate consequences deserve emphasis. First, in the *GA* Aristotle makes no use of and has no need at all for those species forms—the form of a human being in general, for example, shared by all the human beings—that are the staple of much contemporary discussion of Aristotle's metaphysics. All the work such forms might be thought to do is already done by these more particular forms: my form makes me a human being, while also making me a human being with those particular further characteristics I inherited from my ancestors. But secondly, while such commitment to the detailed particularity of forms may seem to belong to the same movement of thought which, in the *Metaphysics,* at least pulls Aristotle toward a theory of forms as individual entities, one for each distinct individual substance, Aristotle's clear commitments in the *GA* do not extend that far. The decision whether Aristotelian forms are individual entities or in effect some sort of universals will have to be made on other grounds. But if they are universals they are universals of a much lower order of generality than has been thought; and if they are individuals they are individuals differentiated from one another not only by accidental historical facts about the material object whose form they are but, much more fundamentally, by the internal character of each individual form itself.[22]

[22] In revising this essay I have been aided by comments of Myles Burnyeat, Nicholas Denyer, Geoffrey Lloyd, and Robert Wardy when it was read to the Cambridge Philological Society. I have been greatly helped also by further written comments of Prof. Lloyd and by his paper "Aristotle's zoology and his metaphysics: the *status quaestionis.*" Finally, sharp questioning by Jonathan Barnes, David Charles, and Lindsay Judson when I read the paper at Balliol College, Oxford in May 1988 led to significant improvements in sections V and VI.

CHAPTER 9

STOIC AUTONOMY

A S IT IS CURRENTLY UNDERSTOOD, the notion of autonomy, both as something belonging to human beings and human nature, as such, and also as the source or basis of morality (moral duty), is bound up inextricably with the philosophy of Kant. The term "autonomy" itself derives from classical Greek, where (at least in surviving texts) it was applied primarily if not exclusively in a political context, namely, to certain civic communities possessing independent legislative and self-governing authority.[1] The term was taken up again in Renaissance and early modern times with similar political applications, but was applied also in ecclesiasti-

---

[1] Liddell, Scott, and Jones, *A Greek-English Lexicon* (hereafter *LSJ*), s.vv. αὐτονομία, αὐτόνομος. See also Martin Ostwald, *Autonomia: Its Genesis and Early History*; Ostwald, building upon E. J. Bickerman's demonstration ("Autonomia: Sur un passage de Thucydide [1,144,2]") that in the fifth and fourth centuries the term belongs to the vocabulary of interstate relations, argues persuasively that it was coined to help weaker states drawn into an orbit of dependence on a stronger one to assert and preserve their limited independence. (Such states included especially Athens's allies in the Delian League, which was initially established to combat the Persians, 478/7 B.C.) It was not applied in classical times to the stronger states themselves (though that application does occur in later Greek writers).

So far as I have been able to determine, there are just three places in surviving classical Greek literature (i.e., down to Roman imperial times) where the term is applied to individuals as such, and without immediate reference to political autonomy, so understood. (a) In one passage of Sophocles' *Antigone* (821, referred to in *LSJ*) the chorus, in a lyric exchange with Antigone about her already-decreed punishment, i.e., being deposited alive in a blocked-off cavern to make her own way to Hades, speaks of her as the only mortal to descend to Hades alive and "of her own law" (αὐτόνομος). The unusual choice of word here (where the basic meaning intended seems to be "of her own free will"—ἑκών—and the word is applied not in virtue of any political autonomy) must, however, have something to do with Antigone's own tragic insistence, which has led to her predicament, on following the higher religious law that requires burial for her traitorous brother in the face of directives of King Cleon forbidding it. If she does go down to Hades while still alive, and by her own act of defiance, that, too, will be a case of her following her own ideas of what law itself—religious and civic—requires in a case of such conflict with civic authority. In going down to Hades "of her own law" she is deciding for herself which law (or directive) to follow—with this consequence. So even here the context of civic law and political independence for the use of this term is not lacking, although it is a highly unusual case of it; there is no hint here of Kantian self-legislation of ends or of principles of self-criticism. (b) Somewhat similar is a passage of Xenophon's *Constitution of the Lacedaemonians* (3.1), where he praises Lycurgus's Spartan arrangements for teenage boys, contrasting them with customs

cal disputes about the independence of reformed churches from the former authority of the church of the Roman popes.[2] Kant's innovation consisted in conceiving of (finite) individual rational persons, as such, as law givers or legislators to themselves, and to all rational beings (or rather to all that are not perfect and holy wills), for their individual modes of behavior. For Kant, rational beings possess a power of legislating for themselves individually, according to which they each set their own personal ends and subject that selection, and their pursuit of the ends in question, to a universal principle, expressed in Kant's categorical imperative. The categorical imperative requires that one set one's own ends only within a framework that would warrant acceptance of them by all other such beings. For Kant, autonomy accompanies individual rationality, and has nothing to do with the political (or other organizational) circumstances of any specific community of agents, even though it understandably gave rise to his conception of a "kingdom" or "realm" of ends in which each (fully) rational end setter would cooperate with, and support, all other end setters in a harmonious pursuit by all of their individual self-set ends, under the umbrella of the commonly legislated categorical imperative.

---

in other cities, where boys upon reaching that age are freed from daily oversight by tutors (παιδαγωγοί) and left "to be their own law" (αὐτονόμους): the implied contrast here is with the laws (νόμοι) of Lycurgus (see the reference to those in 1.2, 8). Teenagers in other cities are not under special laws of good and modest behavior at all of the sort that Xenophon goes on to detail that were in force in Sparta (3.2–4); hence, they can be described as being "their own law"—they are allowed to do what they please (this is the meaning), since they are *not* subject to "youth laws" at all. (c) Isocrates turns the tables on Xenophon (whether the correction is intended or not) in the "epilogue" of the *Panathenaic Oration* (215). There, in seeking to draw favorable attention to his own allegedly balanced account, earlier in the speech, of Sparta's contributions to the values of Hellenism alongside those of Athens, Isocrates puts into the mouth of an unnamed former pupil, described as well known for his praise of Spartan practices, the word αὐτονομία, with strongly negative connotation, to describe one of the practices that Xenophon had praised so highly himself (2.6–9): that of encouraging young Spartans to steal food and other supplies from the non-Spartan country dwellers, provided that they could do so undetected. Thus, Isocrates seems to be saying, Xenophon was not right to count other Greeks' failure to have "youth laws" as granting the youths reckless "autonomy"; on the contrary, the Spartans are the ones who are guilty in this instance of making the boys and youths behave in recklessly "autonomous" ways that everyone else knows are disgraceful, despite their being demanded by Lycurgan laws.

Thus, even in these three apparently anomalous passages, personal "autonomy" carries with it a clear contrast with some existing legal provision with which it comes into conflict: Creon's directive, Lycurgus's "youth laws," normal rules of behavior forbidding stealing. (On the use of the terms αὐτόνομος and αὐτονομία in Dio Chrysostom's *80th Discourse* from the end of the first century A.D., see my subsequent discussion in the main text of this essay. On the various uses of the terms in later Greek, see n. 5 below.)

[2] Here I follow the summary provided in Schneewind, *The Invention of Autonomy,* 3 n. 2; and the full account in R. Pohlmann, "Autonomie," to which Schneewind refers.

Without making any reference to possible influences of Stoic ideas upon Kant—that would be beyond my competence, and would anyhow be work for a subsequent study—I shall explore here what I think are related, but interestingly different, ideas in ancient Stoicism.

I

In speaking of ancient Stoicism I have primarily in mind the work of the original Stoics of the third century B.C., and especially that of the great philosopher Chrysippus. However, in order to introduce the themes I want to discuss, I begin by citing a fascinating and, in this context, apparently overlooked oration of the late first-century A.D. popular philosopher, Dio of Prusa (also called Dio Chrysostom, "of the golden mouth," in recognition of his powerfully inspiring speechifying). Dio was not strictly a Stoic philosopher (he apparently did not teach or hold forth in any "school"), but he did study at Rome with the important Roman Stoic, Musonius Rufus (who taught in Greek, and who had among his other pupils Epictetus). During the middle decades of his life Dio was a wandering orator, in forced exile from both Rome and his home in Bithynia, in northwest Asia Minor. He was a popular proponent of salvation through "the philosophical life." His conception of what that life is like and the source of its value owes a very great deal to Stoic theory and example. The discourse I have in mind is the eightieth and last in the standard order, and bears the title "On Freedom" (Περὶ ἐλευθερίας).[3]

Dio opens the discourse with a conceit. He attributes to his audience bafflement at, and dismissal of, the odd behavior of self-professed philosophers, who wander about the town sporting beards, wearing torn cloaks reminiscent of Socrates, preferably walking barefoot, with no remunerative occupation or ordinary social connections, and paying no attention to the theatrical or other spectacles of Greek city life, or engaging at all in its political institutions. Rather, they attend individually to passersby on the street and engage them in conversation, or else just stand there in the middle of things thinking (80.2). Dio then turns the tables, by declaring that only such philosophers are, in fact, in the condition of freedom (ἐλευθερία), which was highly prized by all ordinary Greeks. Ordinary people, these critics of philosophers, are definitely not free: they are actually slaves. Indeed, Dio insists, only the philosopher is αὐτόνομος, living under his own law.[4] In contrast, all ordinary people

---

[3] *Dio Chrysostom*, trans. H. Lamar Crosby, Loeb Classical Library, vol. 5. In citing Dio, I follow the Loeb text.

[4] ἐγὼ δὲ τοῦτο μὲν λαμπρὸν ἡγοῦμαι καὶ μακάριον, εἴ τις ἐν οἰκέταις ἐλεύθερος εἶναι δύναται καὶ ἐν ὑπηκόοις αὐτόνομος (80.3).

are subject to direction by outside forces (80.3). (As he explains later, money, fame, or pleasures, with their alluring appeal, are their self-imposed mistresses, in fact their self-imposed fetters and enslavement, 80.7–14.)

Without immediately discussing or explaining this remarkable individual "autonomy" of philosophers, Dio goes on at once to explain (80.3–6) that the *political* autonomy that the cities and tribes have constantly fought for from time immemorial is worthless if, as in fact is the case, the people possessing it are themselves individually merely slaves.[5] Indeed, even the great lawgivers of the politically autonomous cities, such as

---

[5] This context makes it clear that Dio is claiming for philosophers self-rule under a law that is (in some sense) their own—one that he will specify in §5 as the law of nature or Zeus. It is worth bearing in mind, however, that the Greek compound αὐτόνομος (from the two stems αὐτο-, self, and νομο-, law) derives from the verbal root νεμ- (alt. νομ-) indicating distribution in the most generic sense, the dealing out of something. Already in Homer (*Od.* 9, 232–33) we find a special usage of the verb νέμω (active) meaning to pasture or graze animals—this is easily understood as implying the distribution or assignment specifically of some land to the animals in question for their nourishment—with a related use of the middle νέμομαι in connection with the animals' feeding themselves on the grass where they graze. (See Laroche, *Histoire de la racine NEM- en grec ancien*, 6–12, 115.) Some relatively late occurrences of the term αὐτόνομος seem clearly to reflect this usage (*LSJ* s.v. 3 cites already the second-century B.C. epigrammatist Antipater Sidonius for this sense): when for example Aelian says of the undomesticated sheep, dogs, goats, and cattle that allegedly inhabit certain parts of India that they roam "autonomous" and free and under no herder's rule (αὐτόνομά τε ἀλᾶσθαι καὶ ἐλεύθερα, ἀφιέμενα νομευτικῆς ἀρχῆς: *On the Characteristics of Animals* 16.20, ed. A. L. Scholfield, Loeb Classical Library), this "autonomous" plainly means not "under their own laws" but "self-grazing" (the recurrence of the root nom- in the word for the lacking herder is the giveaway). So, too, by an easy extension of the grazing-motif to birds, with Aesop's fable where a farmer rescues an eagle from the coils of a snake and lets it go off "autonomous," i.e., free to fly about as it pleases in search of its food: *Fabulae Aphthonii Rhetoris* 28 in *Corpus Fabularum Aesopicarum*, ed. A. Hausrath and H. Hunger, 2nd ed., vol. 1.2 (1959). We find a further, and remarkable, extension of the motif in Plutarch, *Dinner of the Seven Wise Men*, 155a–b, where Helios is said to be, among the gods, quite particularly "autonomous" because he roams the heavens in his chariot without a fixed residence (note the reference to the sun as ἄλλοτ' ἄλλην ἐπινεμόμενον τοῦ οὐρανοῦ χώραν just before he is called αὐτόνομος). One of the only two occurrences of αὐτόνομος in Epictetus (IV 1.27) seems best interpreted in the same way, with influence from the idea of grazing (as for the other, IV 1.56, later in the same discourse, see below, n. 13). The earliest surviving occurrences of the term (in the fifth and fourth centuries) do however all clearly involve a reference to law and government (see n. 1): Sophocles (1 occurrence), Herodotus (2), Thucydides (48), Isocrates (19), Xenophon (45), Demosthenic Corpus (9), minor Attic orators (9). It does not appear in Plato at all and appears only once in Aristotle (*Pol.* V, 1315a6). In later Greek, besides the senses of "self-grazing" and "following one's own laws," the term also occurs a number of times in connection with poetry (poetic license: see, e.g., Himerius (4th c. A.D., *Himerii Declamationes*, ed. A. Colonna, *Oration* 9 l. 5) and to denounce dogmatism or self-will in someone's

Solon in Athens, were not personally autonomous themselves (τούτων οὐδενὶ μετῆν αὐτονομίας), since the laws that they gave were not actually the laws that would have satisfied themselves, but rather only less satisfactory (indeed, bad) ones that were the best that their fellow-citizens could be persuaded to accept (80.4). Thus the law givers lacked autonomy, because the laws that they were famous for establishing were not ones that, if the law givers were left to themselves, they would have laid down for everyone, including themselves, to obey. The actual laws were not really *their* laws at all. In fact, autonomy—self-rule, or living under one's own laws—only comes when one obeys the law of nature (ὁ τῆς φύσεως νόμος), that is, the ordinance of Zeus (τὸν τοῦ Διὸς θεσμόν). This is the only law that is true, and that has any valid authority. Although it is open to view, people do not see it, and do not make *it* the leader of their lives.[6] This, however, is precisely what the philosopher does see, and what he does do. In living by the law of nature, the law of Zeus, he also lives by his *own* law and so obtains true autonomy—the only autonomy worth having.

In this short discourse Dio uses the Greek words for "autonomous" or "autonomy" repeatedly (four times in all),[7] always in a usage that he himself clearly grasps and, indeed, clearly explains, but in which the terms do not appear, except at best in very undeveloped form (see above, note 1), in Greek of the classical period. Classical Greek refers only glancingly to persons governing themselves individually on the basis of their own "laws" (laws if not necessarily self-imposed, then at least self-

---

statements or interpretations (e.g., Olympiodorus, *In Aristotelis "Meteora,"* ed. G. Stüve, *CAG*, vol. 12.2, p. 151.21); here it is the freedom of arbitrariness, not that of following one's own laws or rules, that is indicated. Once, in a passage of Clement of Alexandria (2nd–3rd c. A.D.), the νόμος in question seems to be, according to a very ancient special usage, a musical melody in general or a specially regimented musical form (the "nome"): at the beginning of his *Protrepticus*, Clement cites a Greek myth about a cicada at the Delphic games that by its singing helped the appropriately named Eunomos of Locri win the kithara competition. Clement remarks that the cicadas' song, sung in fact to God, is an αὐτόνομον one, i.e., "a melody all their own," better than the nomes (νόμοι) of Eunomus (on this see Merkelbach, "Un petit αἴνιγμα dans le prologue du *Protreptique*," in ΑΛΕΞΑΝΔΡΙΝΑ, 191–94). Thus the semantic richness of the νεμ- root provides Greek "autonomy" with a much wider background of connotations than the English term carries. These should always be borne in mind in reading the Greek texts, even those using the term in its political and moral applications.

[6] νόμον δὲ τὸν ἀληθῆ καὶ κύριον καὶ φανερὸν οὔτε ὁρῶσιν οὔτε ἡγεμόνα ποιοῦνται τοῦ βίου (80.5).

[7] Five, if one counts, as well, the very striking phrase that he substitutes once in explication or variation: τοῖς αὐτὸς αὑτοῦ χρῆσθαι νόμοις (80.3), "to use oneself one's own laws."

chosen or self-recognized). One striking feature of the text is that Dio first uses this terminology (80.3) before he introduces (in 80.5) any reference to laws of nature or of Zeus, which as I mentioned he eventually equates with the "laws" that a philosopher, in living according to his own laws, will obey. The idea of autonomy, as Dio uses the term from the outset, is simply that of living according to one's own "laws" of personal behavior. But what laws could these be? What justifies any claim, of the sort that Dio makes from the very beginning, and before making any reference to nature's law, that what the philosophers live according to are entitled to the name of *laws?* How is this to be understood?

It helps that Dio couples the term autonomy with freedom (ἐλευθερία) at its first occurrence, and slavery (ἐν οἰκέταις 80.3; cf. δουλεία 80.4) with the lack of autonomy, both in the personal and in the political spheres. Dio could confidently expect his readers to recall, immediately upon hearing philosophers described as the only free persons, the commonplace of Stoic theory, that only perfected human beings, "wise" people in Stoic terminology,[8] are free, while everyone else is both a fool and (therefore) a slave.[9] As Cicero explains the Stoic view (*Stoic Paradoxes* 5, §34), if freedom is the power to live as you will (*potestas vivendi ut velis*) then, in fact, only the wise are free.[10] Only the wise have a clearly conceived plan of life which they unwaveringly also follow; only they never do anything out of fear or through any threat or coercion; only they never regret anything that they have to do or anything that they have done. Everyone else acts in obedience to circumstances, acting as *circumstances* direct, so as to avoid pain, or monetary loss, or the like, and following opportunities for pleasure or gain as circumstances dictate. Such a person acts in the abject and broken spirit of a slave, as Cicero puts it, ordered about willy-nilly—as a person that has no will of its own (*arbitrio carentis suo*) (§35). Only wise people live as they themselves will. Even if they, too, vary their behavior to suit their circumstances, as everyone must, they do this not in pursuance of any fundamental attachment to anything that circumstances can control—any external object or condition, whether pleasant or painful or possessed of any other concrete characteristics. They act only out of a single, consistent desire, in every

---

[8] Σοφοί, traditionally rendered in English as "sages," but it is better to avoid that term nowadays, since it smacks of pretentiousness and obscurantism, and it was no part of Stoic theory that a wise person would have either of those qualities.

[9] See Diogenes Laertius, *Lives of Eminent Philosophers,* trans. R. D. Hicks, Loeb Classical Library, 7.121. For evidence that these claims were already, and offensively, made by Zeno, the Stoic founder, in his *Republic,* see 7.32–33.

[10] In Cicero, *De fato and Stoicorum paradoxa,* ed. and trans. H. Rackham, Loeb Classical Library.

circumstance, simply to "follow nature." (And, of course, their wisdom consists centrally in knowing what following nature means, in each circumstance that may arise.) Thus the wise, and only the wise, are free, according to well-known Stoic principles, because only they, in consistently "following nature" in all their actions, are acting on their *own* will—their will to follow nature. They are never led by the nose by particular, concretely characterized events that occur or that are in prospect. Diogenes Laertius, in setting out the Stoic view, speaks of this freedom as the "power of 'self-action,'" the power to do one's own actions (ἐξουσίαν αὐτοπραγίας, 7.121).[11]

Still, it is quite a step from freedom as self-action and acting according to one's own will (αὐτοπραγία) to autonomy or living according to one's own laws (αὐτονομία). As if to distract the listener from recoiling at his novel conception of autonomy as something that belongs to individuals as such (without reference to their political circumstances), Dio immediately follows up, as I said, by leaving aside freedom understood in Cicero's way, as an individual's "self-action," and pursues instead the implications of *political* freedom, and the autonomy that goes with that. It was for that sort of autonomy, he says, instead of this philosophical independence, that tribes and cities have always fought[12]—fruitlessly, he says, as the history of Solon's legislation shows. The laws of Athens that we know as Solon's were not "his own" laws: as Solon himself confessed in a famous poem, he was not (as Dio puts it) "autonomous" in laying down the political laws and social practices that he devised and imposed on everyone, himself included (once he returned from a voluntary ten-year exile). He imposed not the laws that he would have preferred, but the ones that he thought the citizens would accept. Under those laws the Athenians continued to be slaves in their dependence on external circumstances, even after achieving political self-rule under Solon's laws. Political autonomy was therefore useless to them, and so it is to all of us, as well. By contrast, Dio suggests, philosophers, however bizarre they might appear in the eyes of ordinary people and however unconventional their

---

[11] Plutarch quotes a passage of Chrysippus's lost work *On Lives* where Chrysippus equated the Platonic phrase, familiar from the *Republic* (and the *Charmides*), "to do one's own" (τὰ αὐτοῦ πράττειν, characteristic of virtuous people, e.g., just or temperate ones), with αὐτοπραγία or "self-action": *On Stoic Self-Contradictions* 1043b, ed. and trans. H. C. Cherniss, Loeb Classical Library, Plutarch, vol. 13, pt. 2.

[12] There is a problem with the text at this point; the manuscripts read in 80.3 something ungrammatical and unintelligible, ἀνόητοι εἴδους αὐτονομίας ἔρωτι ἔρωτες. I am not satisfied with the emendations that have been proposed by Post (printed, e.g., in the Loeb text and translated there) and others, but I believe that this issue does not affect what I say in my text.

way of life may be, have not only freedom but *true autonomy*—a life truly under their own rule, under their own laws.

It is only at this point (80.5–6), when he goes on to speak of the laws of nature and the laws of Zeus, that we hear from Dio any reason at all for thinking of the philosopher's or the wise person's life in that way, as one under "his own laws." Now, but not before, we can see that for the philosopher, living by his own will (freedom) is living by his own laws (autonomy), because his consistent will is not only to follow nature, or Zeus, but also in doing so, to obey nature's and Zeus's *law*. As Dio, and his audience, too, knew very well, it was a central tenet of Stoicism that this is what following nature means. As we hear from Diogenes Laertius (7.88), the Stoic "end," which is understood as living following nature (τὸ ἀκολούθως τῇ φύσει ζῆν), involves not doing anything that "the law common to all things" (ὁ νόμος ὁ κοινός) normally forbids; and, as Diogenes tells us, this law is equated with the correct reason (λόγος) that runs through everything and is the same as Zeus. So, in living following nature—that is, as we have seen from Cicero's explication, in living freely and by his own will—the Stoic philosopher also lives by Zeus's or nature's law, which thereby becomes his own law for himself.

It seems, then, that Dio felt the need to draw on both the Greeks' overriding goal of political autonomy and his claim that it fails to make people truly free (by the stringent, but well- and forcefully articulated, standards of Stoic philosophy), in order to prepare the way for, and to validate retrospectively, this conception of philosophical freedom as a more important, indeed the only true kind of, "autonomy." This seems to me to be some indication that the idea of personal, as against political, autonomy, which he introduces in this roundabout way, may have been Dio's invention. At the least, it does not seem that such use of the term was common coin by his time. (As I mentioned above, no earlier ancient author whose works have come down to us presents any such idea.)[13]

---

[13] Like Cicero in his *Paradoxa Stoicorum*, Philo Judaeus, who lived two to three generations earlier than Dio, wrote an essay in defense of the Stoic claim that only the wise person is free (*That Every Good Man Is Free*, ed. and trans. F. H. Colson, Loeb Classical Library). In one passage (sects. 45–47), he anticipates Dio in his comparison of the laws of Solon and Lycurgus, which established the political freedom of their cities, with the laws of god (and of right reason) which good people follow and which makes them free. Yet he does not, here or elsewhere, take Dio's step of describing the good people (or philosophers), on this ground, as autonomous. In fact, in the passage I have cited he does not even describe the free cities as autonomous. He merely says that they are free because they have laws and are not ruled by tyrants; and so likewise, or a fortiori, good persons, having right reason (the source of all other laws) as their law, are free, as well. (Philo uses the terms αὐτόνομος and αὐτονομία five times altogether in his writings and once in this essay, sect. 91; all these uses continue the focus in Greek of the classical period on the political or quasi-political autonomy of communities or groups of people, not the autonomy of individuals as such.)

Thus, it seems that Dio juxtaposed for the first time the standard Stoic idea of the philosopher's (or rather the wise person's) freedom with another standard Stoic idea, that the philosopher (or the wise person) always obeys nature's and Zeus's law. The result is a conception of the philosopher or the wise person as the only one who truly lives autonomously, that is, by his own law.[14]

II

Although they seem never to have used the term autonomy in this connection, I suggest that the classical Stoics did in fact conceive the lives of wise people in just the way that Dio does—as lives lived autonomously, under each individual's own law, where that law is also, and indeed by its origin, Zeus's or nature's law. The implication here—since the wise person is simply the perfected human being—is that Zeus's or nature's law is our law, too, the law of human beings as such. So it is only through accepting and implementing in one's life Zeus's law, that is, Stoic morality, that any human being achieves autonomy and lives autonomously. What, then, in Stoic theory grounds this idea? This question is the focus of my discussion. I will argue that for the Stoics the moral law or Zeus's and nature's law are not merely "ours" in the loose sense that they suit us somehow by nature or are proper to us (in Greek, that they are οἰκεῖον). Once we recognize and take seriously our own rationality, the Stoics think, we

---

[14] So far as I am aware, Dio's novelty was not matched (or followed) by later Stoic writers, with the sole and limited exception of one passage of Epictetus. In his discourse IV 1 (like Dio's, entitled "On Freedom"), in the course of arguing that we can only be free if we always will only what god wills and therefore only care about the character of our own προαίρεσις or power of choice, not about anything outside that, Epictetus refers (sect. 56) to freedom as something αὐτεξούσιον and αὐτόνομον, self-powered and self-governed. But he does not, as Dio does, go on to identify the laws of self-government with those of Zeus or nature. Similarly, when fourth-century Church Fathers speak of God's having given us free will (αὐτόνομος προαίρεσις: e.g., Gregory of Nyssa, De dominica orationes v, ed. F. Oehler, 274.32), the suggestion of self-governance through some *laws*, of God and of oneself, seems absent.

Conceivably, both earlier and later Stoic writers avoided the terminology of autonomy because they felt in it an unwanted implication, carried over from the original political context, where an autonomous state is one left free by a dominant power to decide certain things for itself, independently from the higher power's direction or preferences: namely, that an autonomous individual agent is free to decide certain matters with full authority even if the decision departs from or conflicts with the higher power's (Zeus's) wishes. The avoidance of the terminology of autonomy, explained Dio's way and in the way I develop it below, is, however, no proper indication that the Stoics in fact lacked the concept which *we* express in its terms, or that it did not play a significant role in their thought overall.

should see ourselves as bound by this law, reason's own law, which though it issues from Zeus's mind we also impose on ourselves in recognizing its authority for us. In short, in following this self-imposed law, we become autonomous agents—and the only way to live autonomously is to live that way.

The key point here is that, for the Stoics, only human beings, out of all nature's creations,[15] are rational—only they possess the power of reasoning. It is important, though, to attend closely to what this power consists in for the Stoics. We, with modern understandings of reason, might be inclined to think that it is simply the ability to tell what follows from what, or more generally to deal with given data so as to form some reasoned opinion about what to think, on the basis of them, about some question that might be asked. But that is not how the Stoics, or indeed ancient philosophers in general, think about rationality.[16] Rather, for them, reason is constituted, in the first instance (subject to further developments and perfections), by (the possession of) a somewhat open-ended set of particular *concepts,* which are themselves regarded as a body of basic knowledge, rationally articulated.[17] Human beings are not born rational,

[15] That is, its creations on or in the vicinity of the earth. The exception implied here is meant to cover the sun and moon and stars, which, according to the Stoics, were rational beings, too—I do not mean to suggest that the Stoics envisaged or accepted any such nonhuman rational beings as, e.g., creatures on alien planets, or creatures flying through the air as angels.

[16] On what follows see Frede, "The Stoic Conception of Reason" in *Hellenistic Philosophy,* ed. K. J. Boudouris, 2:50–61.

[17] The basic text here is one from Galen, who quotes Chrysippus in his book *On Reason* as saying that "reason is a collection of certain concepts or preconcepts" (ἐννοιῶν τέ τινων καὶ προλήψεων ἄθροισμα) (*On the Doctrines of Hippocrates and Plato* 5.3.1 = *Stoicorum Veterum Fragmenta* [hereafter SVF], ed. J. von Arnim, 2:228 = SVF 2.841). The required "collecting together" is completed, according to our sources, either at age seven or (more reasonably) at about age fourteen (Iamblichus in a passage selected by Stobaeus vs. Aëtius, SVF 1.149). (It seems likely that there is confusion in our sources between possessing λόγος in the sense of ability to speak a language and possessing it in the stronger sense of being directed by one's rational conceptions in all one's behavior, on which see below: the former could plausibly be thought to occur about age seven, the latter only later, say at age fourteen.) Further concepts can, of course, be formed after that, and refinements in the basic set can be effected (see elsewhere in the same Aëtius passage, SVF 2.83). If, as it seems, the Stoics held that we become rational all at once at that time (and were not rational until then), that is entirely compatible with their recognizing the necessity for a gradual, cumulative process leading up to the final transition. This case is precisely similar to that of virtue or the perfection of reason. Chrysippus notoriously insisted that there are no degrees in the possession of virtue—that either one had it (fully) or one didn't have it (at all, in which case one's condition was one of vice). But that did not prevent him from recognizing progressive steps toward the goal. One person could be in a condition closer to that of virtue than another. Such a person would be better in the sense of closer to being good. What Chrysippus refuses to allow is that anyone should be counted as better than anyone else in the sense of already being good, to a lower degree than the fully virtuous, but a higher degree than some

and no child before "the age of reason" (say, age fourteen) has any effective rational capacities at all.[18] As children we follow natural instincts, aided of course by parental guidance, in seeking our growth and survival in our environments and in engaging in our daily pursuits. In doing so, we come, through naturally imbued processes, to form original, "natural" concepts of all sorts of objects, and their properties, that we confront in our experience. We only become rational, possessed of reason, when, after a long period of such exposure to the world around us, we have accumulated this basic set of concepts. Thus, as we develop, we get an idea, or a concept, of human beings themselves (what it is to be a human being), of males and females, of mothers and fathers, of trees and plants that are of interest to us, of animals such as dogs or cats or cows or mice that are found in our environments and that make a difference to us. As we seek to survive and grow, we also form concepts of various foods, of utensils, and of course of all the colors and tastes, and sounds and textures, that matter to us in our daily lives. In addition to accumulating such basic knowledge as children, as we develop we also get the concepts of good and bad, and certain other evaluative notions.[19]

To say that we get these concepts "naturally" is to say that (still on the Stoic theory) we do not reach them by calculating or inferring anything in any way, for example, from our experiences; we just naturally, given our experiences of, and with, the world around us, form the relevant concepts.[20] You could say that this is how we are made, how we are constituted by nature when we are born into the world. We are born so as to develop in this way, and we do so develop unless some untoward cir-

---

others who have also reached a supposed threshold of virtue. See Plutarch, *Progress in Virtue* 75c, in *Plutarch's Moralia*, vol. 1, Loeb Classical Library; and *On Common Conceptions* 1063a–b, Loeb Classical Library, vol. 13, pt. 2.

[18] What I mean here by "effective" will become clear below.

[19] Obviously the formation of evaluative notions like that of goodness must follow different processes from that of concepts of objects like dogs or such properties as colors and textures (on how the concept of goodness is acquired, see Cicero, *De Finibus*, ed. H. Rackham, Loeb Classical Library, 3:20–21). For my purposes here, I can leave all such differences aside.

[20] It is presumably true that some of the concepts in question depend on other more basic ones, and have to be acquired after and through some use of the latter: that of an implement after those of this, that, and the other tool, say. So some sort of inference from the more basic ones may be needed in reaching the ones acquired later. I do not mean to be denying such "inferences" on the part of the Stoics. They hold, however, that reason is acquired all at once, at some certain age, when all the relevant concepts are simultaneously in place; so, during the earlier progressive acquisition of the individual concepts one cannot yet speak of reasoning (inference) as if that were a free, self-controlled process. Any preliminary use of some more basic concept in the acquisition of another one is itself something directed by nature (our nature), not by ourselves through our rational grasp of anything, or some alleged natural power of constructing or theorizing anything for ourselves from our experiences.

cumstance prevents it. In fact, because we do not reach these first and basic concepts by any sort of reasoning, but simply by a natural process of development, the Stoics think that these are guaranteed to be correct concepts: concepts such that their content is guaranteed to apply to, to be true of, some of what the world itself contains. The world contains things of which our basic natural concepts are true, just because those concepts have been reached in our development by these natural, non-inferential, and on our part totally nonvoluntary routes. We (our minds) have contributed nothing to the concepts' formation, so there is no possibility of distortion or mistake in them from our own minds. And what other source of mistake should anyone imagine there might be?

For a human to be a rational being, then, is, in the first instance, to possess this basic stock of totally natural, well-grounded, and correct concepts. These are concepts that all human beings, as such, will have, wherever and whenever they live, if they have not been specially prevented or deprived.[21] Thus, to be rational, for the Stoics, is first of all to possess a certain stock of basic knowledge: knowledge about the objects that a human being deals with in the ordinary course of living, and about the properties of those objects on the basis of which this ordinary interaction takes place. These objects and properties really are such as we conceive them, through our natural concepts. (Below I will consider some implications of this.) So far, I have said nothing about reasoning itself—that is, the power to draw inferences and to recognize logical consequence and incompatibility. These powers, it appears, are thought by the Stoics to be implicated in the possession of all concepts, including, of course, the concepts that constitute this basic stock.[22] To have the concept of a dog, for example, is (in part) to know that anything that *is* a dog has four legs (unless one has been removed, or the animal has suffered some horrendous birth defect), and that if a thing is not alive at all, or not made of flesh and hair (but rather, say, of metal) then it is not a dog. Thus, the Stoics' conception of reason does include the capacity to think logically (using, e.g., as in these illustrations, *modus ponens* and *modus tollens* as one applies concepts to things), but, in their view, that capacity is conceived as a component of natural conceptual knowledge, in the possession of which rationality basically consists. This is not some further capacity on its own, and, of course, it is not, by itself, the whole of rationality or even rationality's basic element.

---

[21] So the Stoics seem to have thought. But maybe this was intended to be subject to a certain amount of local or even temporal variation—the "natural" concepts for one group of humans living in one environment might differ in some particulars from the "natural" ones for another group.

[22] See the discussion in Frede, "Stoic Conception of Reason," 54–5.

Being rational does not, however, mean simply that one possesses basic knowledge and basic thinking capacities. When we reach the age of reason and become rational beings, instead of the nonrational, brute animal-like beings that children are even while undergoing the experiences from which they are arriving at the basic concepts, our nature now becomes such that we *use* our rationality in all our perceptual experiences, in everything we think, and in everything we do. Plutarch, in his essay *On Moral Virtue* (450d), quotes Chrysippus clearly to this effect: "[T]he rational animal is disposed naturally to use reason in all things and to be governed by it."[23] Before achieving the age of reason, as children of age three, five, nine, or twelve, we may, and will as we progress, have a limited ability to use such concepts as we have begun to acquire, and so to reason in ways that belong to them, but that is an on-and-off affair. The results of such conceptual thinking do not determine what we go on to think or what we do; natural instincts and inclinations continue to prevail with us, regardless of such episodes of reasoning. However, after we reach the age of reason, we use reason in all of our perceptions, all of our thoughts, and all of our actions, by a necessity of our nature. This means that when we see, say, a dog, and it looks to us like a dog, we are using our relevant concepts—thinking that, according to what we know a dog to be, this thing that we see *looks like that,* that is, it appears to have the properties that are contained in our dog concept. And we must either accept this impression and judge that it *is* a dog (i.e., that it actually instantiates the characteristics contained in the concept); or we must reject this impression (holding that, despite appearances, the thing that is seen does not instantiate those characteristics); or else we must suspend judgment either way, withholding any claim that it does or does not have the included properties. (I do not mean to say that any discursive process to such conclusions necessarily takes place, only that such is the content of the thought that one thinks.) Being rational means operating in this way, by a necessity of one's nature.

Now, in these acceptances and rejections, truth and falsehood play a directive role, again by virtue of what a rational nature itself includes. What one holds to be true is what one accepts (and to accept something is to accept that it is true), and what one holds to be false is what one rejects (and to reject it is to declare it false). Thus, Epictetus says (*Discourses* 3.3.2), "It is the nature of every soul [that is, every rational one]

[23] *Plutarch's Moralia,* ed. and trans. W. C. Helmbold, vol. 6, Loeb Classical Library (1939). The Greek text of the passage here translated is: τοῦ λογικοῦ ζῷου φύσιν ἔχοντος προσχρῆσθαι εἰς ἕκαστα τῷ λόγῳ καὶ ὑπὸ τούτου κυβερνᾶσθαι.

to nod yes to the true [i.e., what one takes to be true], to nod no to the false, and to suspend on the unclear."[24] Rational nature, simply being what it is, pursues the true and flees from the false. But equally, as Epictetus in this passage goes on to say, it also pursues the good (i.e., what it takes to be good) and avoids the bad. The rational soul's nature is "to be moved with desire for the good, with aversion from the bad, and in neither way to what is neither bad nor good."[25] Here we should recall that the concept of good (with, as its correlative, that of bad) is among the basic pieces of knowledge that Stoic theory claims all human beings acquire, by natural means, by the age of reason. Thus, once we are at, and past, that point in our lives, we are, as part of being rational, only ever moved toward action by the idea that something that is to be obtained (or avoided) by acting is either good or bad (and the rational desire for the good and aversion from the bad are what always motivate us).[26] In contrast, anything that we take to be neither good nor bad leaves us completely unmoved. It is, of course, quite possible, indeed quite normal, for human beings frequently to mistake what is false or unclear for what is true and vice versa, or to be moved to desire something that is not in fact good at all, or be averse from something that is not bad at all. Indeed, most human beings desire as good, and are repelled from as bad, only things that are actually neither bad nor good, according to Stoic theory. (I come back to this point below, in sect. V.) But in both sorts of cases, human beings are wielding correct concepts of the true and false, of good and bad; that is, they have an adequate basic knowledge of what it is to be true and what it is to be good (no doubt, however, it is not a completely developed knowledge). As Epictetus explains at length in one of his *Discourses,* their error lies in thinking that things that do not, in fact, instantiate the characteristics that are included in those concepts do instantiate them. But, no doubt, as Epictetus says, it also involves unclarity

[24] Epictetus, *The Discourses,* ed. and trans. by W. A. Oldfather, vol. 2, Loeb Classical Library. The Greek text of the passage here translated is: πέφυκεν δὲ πᾶσα ψυχὴ ὥσπερ τῷ ἀληθεῖ ἐπινεύειν, πρὸς τὸ ψεῦδος ἀνανεύειν, πρὸς τὸ ἄδηλον ἐπέχειν.

[25] πρὸς μὲν τὸ ἀγαθὸν ὀρεκτικῶς κινεῖσθαι, πρὸς δὲ τὸ κακὸν ἐκκλιτικῶς, πρὸς δὲ τὸ μήτε κακὸν μήτε ἀγαθὸν οὐδετέρως.

[26] Here we should recall that, for Stoics, even misguided and emotional desires, "appetites" and anger and so on, are functions of our reason. These may be irrational in the sense of being contrary to reason's proper standards for what should be desired, for what should be thought good or bad, or in what way one should desire something. But these desires are not irrational in the sense of being nonrational, that is, having some origin or seat in the human soul other than its rational nature. See, e.g., Plutarch, *On Moral Virtue,* 446f–447a, and the section "The Stoic Theory of the Emotions" in my introduction to Seneca's *On Anger,* in *Seneca: Moral and Political Essays,* ed. John M. Cooper and J. F. Procopé, 5–10.

and confusion in their minds about the content of the concept itself, as they in fact possess it.[27]

In fact, in rational nature itself, according to the Stoics, there are certain inherent standards for judging what is true, or false, or simply unclear. The rules of logic are among these. So if you accept some propositions as true, and they together imply some other proposition, then you ought to accept the latter as true as well (if you think of it at all), on the ground of that implication. Your rationality commits you to this, whether or not, in particular cases, you follow this rule when it applies. This rule is a norm of rational behavior inherent in rationality itself. Likewise Chrysippus notoriously insisted that some sensory impressions are such that when you experience them, as some later Stoics put it, they "all but seize you by the hair and drag you to assent."[28] These sensory impressions are so very obviously, manifestly, indisputably true that it would be deeply irrational not to accept them as such. The Stoics are not speaking here of any external compulsion, or any internal, merely psychological one, either, but rather of what you necessarily do simply because you are rational. You can see so *clearly*, when you have an impression of this kind, that the impression is true, that it could not possibly *not* be true. Your rational commitment to seeking the truth demands that you accept such an impression. While we do not find in our sources any special elaboration of such "rules" or "standards" of right reason, it is clear that the Stoics do suppose that rational nature presents itself to itself as answerable to such standards, even in cases where one might in fact be violating them. No doubt it is the task of philosophy to articulate the original and basic standards, and to expand their range by formulating new ones. But, in principle, all of these are standards to which rational beings, as such, are committed simply by their nature as rational. All anyone needs to do to recognize these standards is to think enough so as to see, on the basis of their own thought, that they are committed to them.

---

[27] See Epictetus, *Discourses*, vol. 1, II 17, esp. §§1–13. Epictetus maintains that we all have a "natural preconception" (φυσικὴ ἔννοια or πρόληψις, §7) of the good and the just, but that we can still disagree with one another in how to apply them—some apply the good preeminently to wealth, others pleasure or health—because we do not devote ourselves to giving proper articulation (διάρθρωσις) to our commonly possessed concept of good or just (§12–13). We ought to go to philosophers, in fact, precisely for help in giving our concepts that proper articulation (§3).

[28] As Sextus Empiricus reports: *Against the Theoreticians* (M.) 7.257. See *Sextus Empiricus*, trans. R. G. Bury, vol. 2, Loeb Classical Library (1935). The Greek text of the passage here translated is: αὕτη γὰρ ἐναργὴς οὖσα καὶ πληκτικὴ μόνον οὐχὶ τῶν τριχῶν, φασί, λαμβάνεται, κατασπῶσα ἡμᾶς εἰς συγκατάθεσιν.

III

In the preceding section I discussed what, according to Stoic theory, the power or capacity of reason (or reasoning) consists in. Before we can proceed to consider the implications of this for questions about human autonomy, we need to take into account that, for Stoics, the natural world as a whole, including not only our bodies but also our minds, is animated by a single mind, a single rational being and rational nature—Zeus. The natural world is a material world. Everywhere in it there is matter of one formation and complexity or another, and there are no gaps of emptiness.[29] However, Zeus is also everywhere in the world, and although he is a single body spread out everywhere, Zeus is not at all a *material* body.[30] Material bodies reduce ultimately to four basic material elements:

---

[29] See, e.g., Galen, *On the Differences in Pulses*, SVF 2.424, translated in part in Long and Sedley, *The Hellenistic Philosophers*, 1:293 (= LS 49D).

[30] Zeus is everywhere in the world: see Alexander of Aphrodisias *De Mixtione*, ed. I. Bruns, *Supplementum Aristotelicum*, 2.2.225, 1–2 (translated in LS 45H). Zeus, as the "active principle" (τὸ ποιοῦν), is not a material body, but rather something (reason, λόγος) that is *in* matter: see, in addition to Alexander just cited, Diogenes Laertius, *Lives*, 7.134 (translated in LS 44B, first part) together with Cicero, *Academica* 1. 39 (translated in LS 45A). The conception of body presupposed here (which permits there to be bodies that are nonmaterial), however odd when viewed from our own place in the history of philosophy, has a solid basis in Stoic thought, and in particular in what they derived from their study of Plato's *Sophist*. We can see *Sophist* 247d8–e4 (and its context: the Visitor's attempt to reach a defining account of what it is for anything to have being by finding a compromise between the views of the "materialist" Giants and the idealist "Friends of the Forms") lying behind the Stoic definition of body reported by Sextus Empiricus in *Pyrrhonian Sketches* 3.38. Obviously referring to the Stoics (see Cicero, *Academica* 1.39), Sextus reports that "some say that body (σῶμα) is what can act on or be acted upon (ποιεῖν ἢ πάσχειν)." (The Visitor offers this as a criterion of what has being rather than of body: Zeno and the other Stoics, in restricting what has being to bodies, adopt the Visitor's criterion as one for whatever is bodily in nature. They also divide the terms used by the Visitor in giving his criterion: for them, one sort of body—mind—has being by being active, the other—matter—by being acted upon.) Thus, for the Stoics, both the "active principle" (Zeus or λόγος) and the "passive principle" (matter) count as bodies. Sextus goes on in 3.39 to contrast this Stoic account with an Epicurean one, according to which being a body is associated with three-dimensionality plus posing resistance (ἀντιτυπία)—in effect, bulkiness. The Stoic position amounts to restricting bulkiness to material bodies, while permitting reason itself to count as a body, because it does have effects, can do things in the world, while not possessing any bulk. (When Diogenes Laertius and Galen cite Stoic "definitions" of body in the Epicurean terms of three-dimensionality and resistance, these are presumably to be understood as definitions specifically of *material* body: see LS 45E and F.) (I thank Andrea Falcon for help on the issues discussed in this note: see his *Corpi e Movimenti*, 57–66, and chap. 2 of his forthcoming English book, provisionally entitled *Bodies and Motions*.)

fire, air, water and earth.[31] But the body that is Zeus is not made of any
of these elements, not even elemental fire, taken on its own.[32] (Indeed, although this interpretation is controversial, I think that Zeus's body, as
understood by Chrysippus—not, however, it appears, by Zeno—is not

---

[31] See Diogenes Laertius, *Lives*, 7.135–36 and 7.142 (translated in *LS* 46B and 46C). When
I say that Zeus is not a material body, I mean that he is not in any way constituted from the
material elements, or any of them. In a different way, for the Stoics, Zeus or cosmic reason
does have a "material" basis, in that (when Zeus is "on his own" and before creation has
begun) this reason is "in," i.e., spread through, some qualityless stuff: reason is the "active"
principle, paired with a "passive" principle, the totally characterless "prime matter"
through which this reason spreads. See Diogenes Laertius, *Lives* 7.134, and above, n. 30.
[32] See Stobaeus *Selections*, ed. C. Wachsmuth and O. Hense (Berlin: Weidmann, 1884),
1:129–30 (= *SVF* 2.413, translated in part in *LS* 47A), a note on Chrysippus's account of
various uses of the word "element" (στοιχεῖον). Note that on this account, god is the "element" of all things in a very special sense (in effect, that of the originator of everything else).
God is what causes generation out of itself in a methodical way from a first beginning of
generation up to an end, in which everything previously generated is resolved finally back
into god. Fire is the basic element in a further special sense, as the first of the material elements to come into being by generation from god, while the other three elements (according to the common use of the term) are generated by god from that fire, by condensation of
it first into air and then successively into water and earth. Thus, god, on Chrysippus's account, is not to be identified in any way or sense with the material element fire. (Most commentators, including Long and Sedley, *Hellenistic Philosophers*, in their comments on the
passages collected in their chapters 46 and 47, fail to see this.) However, without naming
any particular one of them, or suggesting that there might have been any significant difference of view on this among them, Aëtius (in H. Diels, *Doxographi Graeci*, 1. 7. 33 = *LS*
46A) reports that for the Stoics, god is (among other things) "artistic" or "technically accomplished" fire that "proceeds methodically for the generation of the cosmos" (πῦρ
τεχνικόν; see Zeno in Stobaeus 1.213, 15–21 = *SVF* 1.120 = *LS* 46D for the distinction between this kind of fire and the more commonly recognized kind that just burns and consumes things, rather than crafting and working them up). The Greek I translate here is ὁδῷ
βαδίζον ἐπὶ γενέσει κόσμου; but some manuscripts of the pseudo-Plutarch *Placita* (but
none of Stobaeus *Eclogae* where the same passage from Aëtius appears) read instead ἐπὶ
γένεσιν, "to," instead of "for," generation, in close alignment with a related passage of Diogenes Laertius. There (7.156) Diogenes Laertius gives what seems intended as the same or
a closely related description, not of god, but rather of nature. He says: "Nature is, according to them, technically accomplished fire that proceeds to generation" (πῦρ τεχνικὸν ὁδῷ
βαδίζον εἰς γένεσιν); he does not say of what, and presumably we are to understand the
generation in question rather in relation to particular features of the natural world than to
the cosmos as a whole. It is clear here that "nature" is to be understood not as simply identical with god, since Diogenes Laertius explicitly glosses it as fire-like and artist-like
(πυροειδὲς καὶ τεχνοειδὲς) πνεῦμα or "breath"—that is, the god-pervaded πνεῦμα that is
god's constant and immediate tool for generation and direction of everything (else) material (see below, next note but one). Still, it does seem clear from the Aëtius passage cited
above that some Stoics (presumably Zeno) must have endorsed a use of "fire" (of the "technically accomplished" sort) to describe Zeus or god himself, as he exists in himself including before the beginning of creation—some sort of "pure" or pre-elemental version of fire.
(See further the following note.)

any form of fire at all, however "pure": Zeus is a body sui generis.)[33] Zeus is present everywhere—a body, but not a material one—completely intermixed with matter; through his contact everywhere with matter, all the way down through its indefinitely divisible substance, he can impose all the qualifications on matter that differentiate it into all its varied kinds. (Action from a distance is ruled out on Stoic physical principles.) By such contact, Zeus constitutes and sustains: first, the material elements themselves (with their specific differences); then particular, more complex types of different material stuffs; and, finally, the differentially

---

[33] See Philo, *On the Eternity [Indestructibility] of the World* 90 (*SVF* 1.511, *LS* 46M): "when the world has been conflagrated (τὸν κόσμον ἐκπυρωθέντα) . . . it must change either into a flame (φλόξ) as Cleanthes thought, or into a flash of light (αὐγή), as did Chrysippus." On Philo's account, both Cleanthes and Chrysippus thought it necessary to avoid saying that the world was consumed *into* a fire (as Zeno seems to have done—see Aristocles in Eusebius, *Preparation for the Gospel* 15.14.2 = *SVF* 1.98 = *LS* 46G, where, apparently on behalf of Zeno, Aristocles reports the workings of "the basic fire," τὸ πρῶτον πῦρ, in creating and ruling things), since no fire survives the loss of its fuel, whereas, *ex hypothesi*, at the conflagration all fuel (in fact all other bodies besides Zeus) is done away with. See the whole context, *Philo Judaeus*, trans. F. H. Colson, vol. 9, Loeb Classical Library (1941), sects. 85–93. Philo goes on to argue against both these views, more successfully against Cleanthes's suggestion than against Chrysippus's. On Chrysippus's view, what the world changes into when it gets conflagrated is the flash of light emitted by the fire of the conflagration itself: it is not in any strict sense a fire at all (see below in this note), as Cleanthes' proposal of a flame would make it, and it is certainly not the material on fire of the conflagration itself. A flash of light may last for only a second, but it does not simply cease once its source goes out, and it is not located simply at that source. If at (or rather, after) the conflagration, when he is by himself (see next note but one), Zeus is, or is like, a flash of light—in effect a concentration of energy—then, even when he is spread through all matter, it is as that concentration of energy that he is spread. Chrysippus's idea that Zeus is, or is like, a flash of light is quite a compelling way of developing the original Zenonian theory of the conflagration (and correcting it, though Chrysippus would never have admitted that, through distancing himself explicitly from any idea of Zeno's that Zeus should be conceived actually *as* fire of some specially pure or ethereal sort that survives the conflagration). Alexander of Aphrodisias repeatedly criticizes Chrysippus's view of light itself, φῶς, in several chapters of the so-called *Mantissa* to his work *On the Soul* (ed. I. Bruns, *CAG*, suppl. vol. 2); in one place he remarks, apparently appealing to a Stoic distinction, that if light is a body, as the Stoics think it is, it must either be fire or an "outflow" (ἀπορροή) from fire, "which they call a flash [αὐγή] and say is a third sort of fire" (138, 3–4; for the three sorts of fire according to the Stoics, see *Philo Judaeus* 86 = *SVF* 2.612). In calling a "flash" a third sort of fire, Chrysippus (if indeed he is in question) would seem to be self-consciously preserving a connection to Zeno's original claim that Zeus was a special sort of fire (see above in this note, and the previous note), but, as I have said, in fact he is correcting him by making Zeus to be, or comparing him with, something that within the physical world has its origin from fire but is nonetheless a self-subsistent something or other. (See further on the nature of light and flashes of it, the passages collected in *SVF* 2. 432.)

organized bodies of the different kinds of material objects, including the plants, animals, and human beings, that the world order contains.[34]

As a rational being or rational nature, this nonmaterial body, Zeus, is a reasoned understanding of, and basis for, everything that it creates and sustains. A particular plant is what it is, and bears all the conceptual and other relations that it bears to other things of its own, and of other types, because of Zeus's thought in constituting it. Likewise for everything else that the world contains—stuffs, individual objects, whatever. We can now see that the natural concepts that I mentioned above that humans acquire automatically are simply crude, basic versions of those with which Zeus has worked in forming the relevant objects and properties in the first place. That is why these natural concepts are correct concepts, why they constitute knowledge, albeit of a crude and rough-and-ready kind. To have these concepts is to possess a share of Zeus's own concepts, the ones that he used, and uses, in creating, constituting, and sustaining the world in which human beings live and operate. Zeus, of course, has a vaster conception of what he is doing in creating and sustaining these objects and properties than we do when we acquire our basic concepts of

---

[34] In doing all this, Zeus first has to constitute a special basic sort of material stuff, called by the Stoics "breath," or *pneuma*. This is made of fire *and* air (the hot and the cold elements, respectively), with the result that *pneuma*'s nature is simultaneously to contract (as cold) and to expand (as hot). It is thus suited to work on grosser kinds of material in such a way as to hold them together (by exercising its contractive, inward-turning, power). At the same time (by exercising its expansive, outward-reaching power), it makes these materials capable of affecting other material bodies through contact with them. And, depending on the degree of "tensility" in *pneuma* in its different locations (and/or at its different "levels" in some of the same locations), it can imbue things with their specific qualitative differentiations. Thus *pneuma* plays a very special role throughout Zeus's creative activity. It is important, however, not to confuse *pneuma* with Zeus himself. *Pneuma* is Zeus's essential, indispensable material tool. He remains a distinct body from, while spreading through, his tool, *pneuma*. Zeus and *pneuma* are both of them everywhere in the world, but only Zeus is the (ultimate) agent of what happens in the world. See the passages collected in Long and Sedley, *Hellenistic Philosophers*, 47B, D-I, O-Q. The Stoic theory of "through and through" mixture of distinct bodies (see ibid., chap. 48) was worked out so as to show how a body, such as Zeus, can be spread everywhere in some matter (in fact, in Zeus's case, in all of it), while *pneuma*, his material instrument, is equally spread everywhere through all the other forms of matter (and all material things). Since bodies are, all of them, divisible all the way down, there can be in every portion of any material body some of Zeus's body as well as some *pneuma* (indeed *pneuma* in any number of different degrees and kinds of tension, so as to enable the composition and different characteristics of the bodily thing in question). Note that Aëtius, in Diels, *Doxographi Graeci*, p. 310, = *SVF* 2.340, translated in Long and Sedley, *Hellenistic Philosophers*, 55G), says that for the Stoics, *all* causes are in fact "breaths" or *pneumata*. Thus causal agency (with the sole exception of Zeus's agency in creating the material elements and bringing *pneuma* itself into being) is always exercised through some *pneuma* belonging in one way or another to an agent.

them. His conception is even vaster than the much more sophisticated knowledge that we could develop by further investigation and thought of our own. He understands each thing, and each kind of thing, and each property of a thing, in relation to every other thing, and every other kind of thing, and every other property. As a single mind that is responsible for the *whole* world, Zeus understands everything he does at any one place, and over any one period of time, in relation to everything else that he does everywhere else and in all other periods.

Because Zeus is a rational being, he does everything that he does for the sake of the good (or to avoid the bad), precisely like adult humans. According to Stoic theory, our good is *in fact* (despite what most people may misguidedly think) entirely a matter of how our minds are conditioned and how, as a result, they work. All externals are neither good nor bad, but at best preferable or not. So also for Zeus. The good that he is constantly seeking in everything he does is the good that consists in the thoughts that he thinks in doing it, and in their relations both to the other thoughts that he is thinking at the same time and to the thoughts that preceded and those that are to follow. It is a mistake to think, as readers of the Stoics have sometimes thought, that this good that Zeus pursues is the beauty and order of the resulting *material* world, or of its progress through time. Zeus's thoughts are, indeed, all thoughts about how to constitute, sustain, alter over time, destroy, and create material things of an enormous and interlocking variety. But the *good* that is constantly aimed at in this process is the goodness of the ordered thoughts, absolutely nothing else. Ultimately, this good is the totality of the history of Zeus's thoughts in governing the world from its first formation right through to its final denouement in the so-called conflagration, when all matter is reabsorbed into Zeus's mind, and it or he is "all by himself"[35]— only then to restart the whole process, exactly as it happened before.

---

[35] See Diogenes Laertius, *Lives*, 7.136: κατ' ἀρχὰς μὲν οὖν καθ' αὑτὸν ὄντα. It should be observed that this passage, taken together with the Philo passage cited in note 33, shows that it is a mistake to say, as commentators often do (see, e.g., Long and Sedley, *Hellenistic Philosophers*, vol. 1:278–79), that, for the Stoics, Zeus cannot in fact be "abstracted" from matter but always exists as an internal principle within matter for forming it into material bodies. The sort of intelligent energy that Zeus is, in fact, is quite clearly conceived as being abstracted at the conflagration, or rather during the "time" between a conflagration (the end of the world) and the world's rebeginning. See also Diogenes Laertius, *Lives*, 7.137: "god . . . at certain cycles of time absorbing into himself the whole of material substance and again generating it from himself" (θεόν . . . ὃς . . . κατὰ χρόνων ποιὰς περιόδους ἀναλίσκων εἰς ἑαυτὸν τὴν ἅπασαν οὐσίαν καὶ πάλιν ἐξ ἑαυτοῦ γεννῶν). It is true that while he is "alone" Zeus pervades bare or prime matter, matter without any qualities; but he is abstracted from all material *bodies* of any and every sort. See above, note 31.

IV

According to Stoic theory, then, there are two kinds of rational beings—humans older than age fourteen, and Zeus or nature—each constituted, *qua* rational, in exactly the same way.[36] Zeus thinks at each moment one huge, single thought: a thought about everything that he is doing then everywhere in the material world, in constituting, sustaining, changing, moving from place to place, creating, or destroying things. Moreover, this thought is thought explicitly in relation to the preceding thoughts in progression, all the way from the beginning. It is also thought in relation to all of the succeeding thoughts that are going to come in succession, right up to the conflagration. So, in another way, this single thought, the overall thought that Zeus thinks at each moment, is much more immense than even that first hugeness might seem to imply. It is, all at once, the whole succession of thoughts that constitute Zeus's life history. The current thought is (so to speak) simply highlighted as the currently active and effective one in that series. Thus, Zeus's thought contains a correct, fully worked out concept of each and every kind of thing and each and every individual thing in the world. His thought also contains not only a correct account of what happens anywhere and to anything at any time in the world's history, but also a full knowledge of *why* it happens. The thought of whatever happens happening is needed as part of the overall history of thoughts constituting Zeus's history. Any such thought has its point in, and explanation by, that thought's relation to prior thoughts and subsequent ones, as well as to other thoughts about other things happening at the same time. It is the overwhelmingly good order of the whole series of thoughts, in all its internal relationships, that, on Stoic theory, is identical with the good, so this current thought's place in the series is explained by its contribution to that overall good. Thus, Zeus's thought constitutes the totality of the good, as well as that of truth. Anything true is true because it (or the concept or thought of it) has its place in Zeus's mind, in his mental history; and that history is the embodiment of goodness.

Different human beings, however, think special and different thoughts, depending upon the location of each one of them in the world, their particular experiences at the moment and before, or their expectations. Any human thought is always a local thought, sometimes one about or

---

[36] I leave out of the account here and in what follows the important difference between human rationality and Zeus's or nature's rationality, that (see note 35) Zeus brings matter into existence, and does not merely shape, characterize, move, and change it with his thoughts. However, this power of initial creation (and destruction) of matter aside, Zeus's rationality is, as I say in the text, constituted exactly in the same way as human rationality.

toward the whole world, perhaps, but always from a single, localized point of view. What, then, is any such individual to think, at any point in his or her history? Human thinking begins with an "impression" (a rational, that is, conceptual, one, since we are rational minds) to some effect: that so and so.[37] We are constantly bombarded with such impressions, not only through the senses, but also from memory, anticipation, habits of past thinking, and built-up concepts (whether they are concepts arrived at naturally or through voluntary thought). No doubt we are bombarded from other sources, too. Upon receiving these impressions, as I noted (sect. II), it is then up to each individual mind to exercise its judgment as to which of them to accept, to "assent" to, and which to reject, or to suspend judgment over. Some of these will be impressions about some apparent matter of fact (perhaps something theoretical, or, as we would say, something directly observational). Others will be about what is good or bad to pursue or to do. Because of reason's inherent natural inclination to seek what is true and to avoid anything false, and to pursue what is good and to avoid everything bad, the two key questions for judgment are as follows. Is this *in fact* true (as it appears to be, as I am inclined to think, given my current impression)? Or is this *in fact* good (as it appears to be, as I am inclined to think)? I mentioned above (at the end of sect. II) that there are standards and rules of "right reason" that we can invoke to help decide these questions. Ultimately, however, the standard is what Zeus himself thinks; he and the processes of his thought are definitive of what it is rational to think (that is, correct by the standards of reason itself). As Diogenes Laertius tells us (7.88), Zeus *is* right reason (ὁ ὀρθὸς λόγος).

In the passage where Diogenes Laertius tells us that Zeus is right reason, he also tells us that Zeus is "the law that is common to all things" (ὁ νόμος ὁ κοινός). Right reason, Diogenes says, is the same thing as this common law, Zeus being the "leader of the government of the things that have being" (καθηγεμόνι τούτῳ τῆς τῶν ὄντων διοικήσεως ὄντι), and the "things that have being" being all the bodies, material and nonmaterial, that make up the world. The law of Zeus, however, does not govern all of these bodies in exactly the same ways. The minds of rational beings are governed by Zeus differently from the way in which he governs everything else. Plants, nonrational animals, and all material stuffs, whether existing on their own or constituting a living thing, are wholly and directly governed by Zeus's own thoughts. He has a "plan," as we have seen, consisting in an ordered series of thoughts that he thinks (and

[37] See Diogenes Laertius, *Lives,* 7.49 (last sentence), 51 (last three sentences); Origen, *On Principles* 3.1.3 (*SVF* 2.988, translated in part in *LS* 53A[4–5]); and, in general, the materials collected in Long and Sedley, *Hellenistic Philosophers,* chaps. 39 and 53.

is going to think), and these thoughts produce and sustain all of the characteristics of those things, bring them into existence, remove them from it, alter and develop them, and move them from place to place, in ways that we can observe happening as well as in ways that we cannot. We can observe the effects of Zeus's "law," or nature's "law," in the behavior of the material bodies themselves. The nature of wood is such that when it comes into contact with a hot fire it burns, invariably, while the nature of stone is such that when it comes into contact with fire it merely (and invariably) heats up, even to a very high degree. The nature of the different metals is such that, depending on the specific metal and the size and intensity of the fire, in some cases a metal gets soft, or even actually melts, but in others it merely becomes heated up—but metals and stones never get burned up, as wood does. Similarly, mutatis mutandis, nature's "law" governs the behavior of the different nonrational animals: but in these cases the relevant "laws" are vastly more complex, encompassing as they do a variety of somewhat variable different behaviors, species by species, in response to different stimuli.

Nowadays, when we speak of laws of nature, we do so with reference to empirical generalizations like those about wood, stone, and metals that I have just mentioned, backed up, no doubt, by much theory about the behavior of molecules and particles; but that theory is itself based on further empirically supported hypotheses about how molecules and particles behave under varying conditions. It is of crucial importance in understanding the Stoic theory of natural law to realize that, for the Stoics, the law or laws of nature consist not in such empirical generalizations, or physical theory based on them, but rather in the thoughts of Zeus that lie behind and cause the behaviors of material things. It may be, and presumably is the case, that the best that we humans can do in order to grasp Zeus's law, so far as it applies to the things that I have so far been talking about, is by way of observation of the behavior of material bodies under different conditions and by the derivation by that means of empirical generalizations. However, even so, no statement about how material bodies behave, drawn up in that empirical way, in itself expresses any part of Zeus's or nature's law for them. That law consists in Zeus's or nature's rational determination to think whatever thought he or nature is going to think in causing the bodies to behave in the ways that we may (or may not) observe them to behave. And that determination is grounded in Zeus's or nature's conception of what thoughts, and what combination of thoughts, will constitute the best and most beautiful rational order of thoughts over the whole period of the world order's existence and development. The fact that, as it seems, we can observe many differences in the behavior of different sorts of things, and invariances in those behaviors, shows that one part of this self-determination on Zeus's part is a determination to operate in a vast and interlocking set of widely differentiated, but in each case universally applied and invariant, ways. To operate thus is part of the rational order that he or nature achieves; or, rather, it is its direct effect.

How, then, does Zeus's law govern rational beings and their minds? The first thing to notice is that, in many respects, the behaviors of our bodies (in the use of the term "body" that contrasts with "mind") are governed no differently from that of other material bodies. If rain falls on my head, then my hair and skin are affected in relevantly precisely similar ways to that of any animal or any nonanimate thing that is also rained on. Similarly if I eat something, the processes of digestion, etc., that then follow in my body proceed in ways similar to what follows when a nonrational animal eats something. Zeus's thought is just as directly responsible for all such processes in the human case as in the nonhuman, and in just the same ways. However, the second example, that of eating something, differs in the human case in one very important respect from the case of the nonrational animal: with the animal, Zeus's thought is directly the cause, and in precisely the same way, both of the animal's getting the sense impressions that it gets (the ones that lead it to obtain the item) and to its then eating it, as it is in causing the processes of digestion in the animal's body. As the Stoics put it, the animal's "impulse" to eat, which is triggered by the impression (together with its soul's nature and condition), is caused by Zeus's having a thought, following in due order on the thoughts of his that were involved in giving the animal the particular impression that it got. (So, too, and in exactly the same way, the impression itself, the nature of the animal's soul, and its condition at the time, are caused by Zeus's thoughts.) The "impulse" that is the animal's response to the impression, and the immediate cause of the animal's action of eating, follows automatically upon the receipt of the impression.[38] The human case is different.

---

[38] The sources leave it rather unclear in just what way an animal impulse does follow automatically upon receipt of the impression. Some sources speak of some counterpart in animals (at least, in some animals) of that "assent" which is necessary before a rational impulse (i.e., an adult human being's impulse) can be formed. See Alexander of Aphrodisias, *De Fato*, text, trans. and comm. R. W. Sharples, chap. 13–14 (relevant passages are collected in *SVF* 2.979–81, esp. p. 285 ll. 37–8, 286 ll. 7–8); see also Nemesius, *De natura hominis*, cited in *SVF* 2.991 and *LS* 53 passage O. This does seem to make sense of the fact that animals can learn to double-check something before proceeding to action; they do not always act immediately upon becoming aware of something that is apparently tasty to eat and within their range. In any case, with nonrational animals, the Stoics seem to have thought that, even if something like an assent to an impression is needed before an impulse can take shape in the animal's soul, the assent, too, is generated automatically (i.e., by a thought of Zeus), upon receipt of (the right sort of) impression. This is not so with rational animals, i.e., humans.

Human beings, when they act (act voluntarily, I mean), act because of reasons that they see for doing so. They may reach out and start to eat something immediately upon getting the impression of it as a good thing to eat, without any apparent process of thinking and deciding whether to eat it or what else to do instead. Nonetheless, it simply belongs to their nature as *rational* beings that they always act—even in such cases of un-reflective, virtually automatic, action—for what they take, at the time of acting, to be good reasons for doing what they do. It belongs to their nature to act always and only on some thought of their own (when they do really act, that is, act voluntarily) to the effect that this act is a good thing to do, that there is good reason to do it. Human beings cannot not do this, if they act in any way at all (even if they simply refrain from acting). If and when they have no thought at all of any reason to do anything, they merely stay inertly where they are, or get moved about by outside forces (or internal ones)—in either case, forces coming directly from Zeus's thoughts. Their thought is the direct and sole cause of their action, just as Zeus's thoughts are the direct and sole cause of the corresponding happenings in those other cases. So one way that Zeus governs human beings is by sustaining them in existence as rational beings, as beings that produce some of their behavior (that which is, as we put it, voluntary) from their own thoughts about what is best to do—not from *his,* as is the case with the behavior of animals and every other thing that the world contains. Zeus's intention in making rational beings part of his world—the world that he animates—is to make there be beings who are located in specific places and times, and who possess a localized outlook on the rest of the world, which will then act in accordance with their own rea-soned views of what to do (not necessarily with Zeus's). Accordingly, the causality of Zeus's thought in relation to them (insofar as they are be-having *qua* rational beings) is limited simply to making and sustaining them in existence as rational beings of this sort.

V

This, then, is one aspect of how Zeus's law applies to human beings, *qua* rational. It is by Zeus's law that we are created and sustained as rational beings, with this particular set of natural powers and under these partic-ular constraints. However, Zeus's law applies in a second way as well. In deciding what to think, and especially in deciding how to behave (volun-tarily), as, by Zeus's decision, our nature compels us to do, Zeus's law is *authoritative* for human beings. That is, it applies now in a second, purely normative way. Since this concerns specifically our voluntary be-havior, we need to take into account Stoic views on the scope and limitations of that behavior before we can turn to see what the content of this law might be, and how we can come to know it, as well as from what its authority for us derives.

Since any human being's reason is, of course, located entirely within his or her own body,[39] we can exercise our mind's powers, in the first instance and directly, only on our own bodies. Our mind has direct contact only with our own body,[40] and for anything to affect anything else, according to Stoic theory, direct contact is required.[41] In fact, strictly speaking, according to Chrysippus, the whole of any action (even one like walking) consists simply and entirely in that certain condition of the so-called leading or commanding part of the soul, the ἡγεμονικόν, that is, the mind (λόγος), which results when one decides to walk, or rather which is constituted by that decision.[42] What *follows*, however, upon a decision, for example to walk, if conditions are normal—for example,

[39] For Chrysippus and other Stoics, the human soul is a sort of high-quality breath (*pneuma*) spread throughout the body. Impulse, the direct cause of action, takes place in the "commanding part" of the soul, the part where reason is lodged or, anyhow, where acts of reasoning take place, i.e., in the heart. From there, the breath that is the first and immediate material body that reason uses as its tool spreads throughout the body—to all the sense organs, nerves, and muscles. (See Calcidius, *Commentary on the Timaeus*, cited in *SVF* 2.879 and trans. in part in *LS* 53G, quoting Chrysippus in Latin.) Thus, our reason can have its effects everywhere in us, even though it is concentrated in the "commanding part" residing in the heart.

[40] Indeed, strictly speaking, according to Stoic doctrine, it has contact only with our own soul, i.e., the *pneuma* or breath through which (in its seat in the heart) the mind is spread. That *pneuma*, the mind's instrument, by being in contact with the body and its organs then receives impressions from and in turn manipulates it. See the previous note.

[41] See Simplicius, *Commentary on Aristotle's Categories*, ed. K. Kalbfleisch, *CAG* vol. 8 (1907), 302.29–35 (= *SVF* 2.342, in part).

[42] See Seneca, *Moral Letters* 113.23, ed. and trans. R. M. Gummere, Loeb Classical Library (1925), vol. 3. Seneca reports that Cleanthes held a different view, viz., that the action (e.g.) of walking was the soul-breath extending from the commanding part out to where the bodily movement itself would begin, when that breath is in the condition for initiating that movement. It seems that Chrysippus intended to correct Cleanthes, in adopting the position that an action is strictly the commanding part itself, when in the relevant condition. Presumably, his reason was that our mind does not even control directly and without possibility of slipup or interference the state of the breath extending out from itself to the muscles and limbs. Hence Cleanthes' view would unacceptably deprive us of total causal responsibility for our own actions: in order to do what I have decided to do, Zeus himself, in sustaining our bodies and the breath spread through it from the commanding part out to the muscles, etc., would have to cooperate. The commanding part, like all the parts of the soul, is indeed a material body, some breath stationed in the heart, but our reason (itself a body, like Zeus himself, as noted above, but not a material one) is lodged in the breath of the commanding part in such a way as always to be able, immediately and without slip or any possible interference, to have the necessary effects on that breath for its decisions to count as precisely the decisions that they are (and not just some free-floating fantasies, unconnected to any possible results). Hence, given Chrysippus's understanding of what an action consists

the flexing of muscles and all the rest that goes on inside the body, and then the motions of the limbs and the progress of the whole body across some space—are not part of the action itself, of what we *do* when we decide. They are its consequences and effects (wholly intended, of course). For those things to take place, the body itself must be of a certain nature and condition; and for that Zeus is, at least primarily, himself responsible. (Some aspects of one's relevant bodily condition could have resulted from prior voluntary decisions and actions of one's own, not from Zeus's thoughts in constituting our bodies and in maintaining them, or causing them gradually to change or even to deteriorate. But, obviously, Zeus's direct causality is paramount, so far as the required condition of the relevant parts of our bodies is concerned.) This means that, in principle, I can only have any effects in the outer world, and indeed within my own body (except in my mind, that is, the commanding part of my soul), provided that Zeus does not block me. He could block me by changing my muscles and limbs, so that when I decide to walk (and, according to Chrysippus's stipulation, do walk), the muscles do not flex, or the limbs do not move, or whatever, and no movement across space takes place. In that case, my intentions would only get carried out so far as the action that consists in that decision itself goes. However, we know that Zeus cannot cause any such failure by any kind of simple fiat or miracle: the orderliness of his thought requires a regularity and invariance that would be grossly violated by any such interference on his part. So, normally, and absent some unexpected, but ultimately perfectly natural, sudden disability, I *can* control my muscles and limbs at will, and I *can* get myself to where I want to go (provided, again, that no outside force, whether another person's action and its consequences, or external natural events under the direct control of Zeus's lawlike thought, blocks me). Thus, it is part of what Zeus has done in creating us as rational animals that this degree of control normally does hold for us. His plan was to make there be rational beings who would take care of their own lives and their own affairs on the basis of their own rational understandings.[43]

---

in, we retain total causal responsibility for our actions. For your reason *not* to be able to cause these effects, perhaps because of some sudden defect in the breath of the commanding part, is for you literally to lose your mind—and so, to become incapable of voluntary action in the first place.

[43] See Diogenes Laertius, *Lives*, 7.86: nature regulates (οἰκονομεῖ) the lives of plants, the other animals, and human beings, as well, but in different ways. Animals have "impulse" added to plants' vegetative capacities, so as to be able to go on their own toward things that suit them (e.g., food), while "reason is given to rational animals by way of a more perfect kind of management . . .; for reason is added as the craftsman of impulse" (τοῦ δὲ λόγου τοῖς λογικοῖς κατὰ τελειοτέραν προστασίαν δεδομένου ... τεχνίτης γὰρ οὗτος ἐπιγίνεται τῆς ὁρμῆς).

In order to make possible such rational beings, it was necessary for Zeus to arrange the order of his own thoughts in such a way that this degree of control by agents, on the relevant movements of their internal organs and their outer limbs, is maintained (for the most part, in any event). It is at this point in our analysis that the second, or normative, aspect of Zeus's law for rational beings, which I mentioned at the beginning of this section, comes in. What does reason demand, or permit, of us in developing our own rational understandings of what to do, and in conducting our individual (and our communal) lives on that basis? As I mentioned above (sect. IV, first two paragraphs), the standards and norms of reason are directly exhibited in, indeed are ultimately constituted by, Zeus's or nature's own thinking. Zeus and nature *are* "right reason." One way of posing the question I just asked, therefore, is to ask, What does Zeus or universal reason think that we should do—what, in other words, does it wish us to do? This is what it is right for us to do, what reason (in us, too) declares that we ought to do, and what it is best for us to do. In general terms the answer is clear. Zeus and nature wish us to think, in each circumstance, whatever thought on our part would most perfectly cohere with all of the prior and all of the future thoughts that constitute the (rest of the) history of thoughts that is universal reason's, or Zeus's, own life. But these terms are too general to be of any use to us.[44]

More concretely—and this seems to be how the Stoics went about answering this question[45]—we can bear in mind that we are individual animals, living a special sort of life for an animal (one directed by our own individual powers of reasoning), but an *animal*'s life, nonetheless. So we can examine how nature or Zeus directly governs the lives of all of the vastly diverse creatures who, not being rational themselves, live by such

---

[44] Indeed, understood one way, this turns out to be a trivial and totally useless answer. If one takes into account (see sect. VI below) that human decisions and other thoughts are actually part of the history of Zeus's mind (since human minds are "disjoined portions" of Zeus's), whatever decision or other thought a person in fact does have at any moment is the one that most perfectly coheres with the rest of the series. Recall that, in Stoic theory, the total history of Zeus's thoughts is the most perfectly ordered one imaginable, or even conceivable. Understood in this way, this answer, therefore, would tell us simply to decide, do, and think on any occasion whatever we are in fact going to decide, do, or think. I intend the answer differently. We are to understand it as directing us to consider what action of our own would fit in best with the ways that Zeus or nature itself, in directing the progress of the parts of the world that are under its direct control (i.e., everything that is not the direct consequence of any human decision), does direct. We look to patterns or norms of rationality that are found in nature's own actions, in order to discover norms for our own human decision making: in making our own decisions, we will do our best to think thoughts that cohere with the rest of Zeus's thoughts, if we decide in our own case in accordance with such norms.

[45] See my exposition in Cooper and Procopé, *Seneca*, xxi–xxiv.

direct governance. If, once we reach the "age of reason," we are now to take over, with our own minds, our own governance, then surely we ought to follow the patterns of life that we see the nonrational animals following, so far as, given our differences from them, these patterns apply relevantly to us. Zeus's law for us must be some parallel to, or reasonable extension from, what we can observe as his law for other animals' lives. Consistency and coherence in Zeus's thinking about us, as animals, seems clearly to require this. In this way, the Stoics think, we can arrive at a large set of conditions and outcomes for ourselves that we can declare "preferred" ones, in that they give us good reason to pursue them, or to seek to maintain them so far as we can, and to avoid their "rejected" opposites. We have good reason to think that if we do make our decisions on this basis, we will be deciding in such a way as to make our thoughts cohere as well as possible with Zeus's or universal reason's thoughts. (We have and can have, normally, no better access to what Zeus or nature wishes us to do.) The preferred conditions and outcomes (or values) in question include health, continued life, all the attributes of a well-developed physical condition, warm and supportive relations in family life and with friends, loyalty, supportive social relations with all with whom we come in contact, the improvement of our own intellectual capacities generally, and the sense of ourselves as part of local, as well as wider, human communities, whose needs and interests thereby become needs and interests of our own.[46] It will be rational, as we are struck by various "impulsive" impressions during our daily lives, to evaluate these impressions, in deciding what to do, by appeal to these preferred values. In general, if you pursued these values, then the sort of life that you would want to, and try to, live would be a well-balanced and well-integrated one, with a full involvement in the life of the community and some appropriate productive work. So, part of Zeus's law for us is to live that way, to the extent that external circumstances can be made to permit us to do it.

Additional guides toward what it is rational to think and to do can be derived from the stock of natural concepts that all of us obtain during the time when we are growing up (see sect. II above). Most important here is the concept of goodness, since as I mentioned (end of sect. II), every action expresses an implicit or explicit decision to act that way, grounded in some thought that something or other is good, either to do or to get, or is bad and so is to be avoided. As I mentioned (sect. II next to last

---

[46] See Arius Didymus in Stobaeus, quoted in Long and Sedley, *Hellenistic Philosophers*, 58C–E, on "preferred" things or things in accord with nature (κατὰ φύσιν), and Diogenes Laertius, *Lives*, 7.108–9 on καθήκοντα (in Latin *officia*), variously translated "appropriate actions," "duties," or "proper functions," which are in fact actions aimed at obtaining or preserving "preferred" things or avoiding their opposites.

paragraph), most people spend their entire lives constantly misapplying and really grossly misunderstanding their own concept of the good, since according to that concept, what it is to be good is to be rationally well-ordered—something that ultimately can only apply to acts of thinking, or rather, to trains of thought.[47] Nonetheless, unless one does come to understand explicitly and self-consciously that this in fact is what goodness consists in, then one is failing to use one's naturally acquired rationality in a way that conforms correctly to its own inherent standards of thought. Thus, it is part of Zeus's law that we should understand goodness in this way, and therefore should never regard mere conditions of our bodies, passive states of our minds, or any external condition or outcome, whether of our action or produced in some other way, as either good or bad for us. Only our own thoughts, when they are appropriately well-ordered—and of course Zeus's thought, always and in general—are good things.

In this way, then, we can reason out for ourselves what individual actions we should undertake, under given circumstances, and what courses of action we should pursue—which ones we have the best reasons to decide on. If we think and act correctly (that is, as reason dictates), what we will do will be what is best for ourselves individually and personally—because it contributes to making the whole history of our own thoughts

---

[47] Chrysippus has views on how it comes about that so many of us do so constantly make such mistakes. See Diogenes Laertius, *Lives*, 7.89 (and cf. Galen, *On the Doctrines of Hippocrates and Plato* V 5. 14; Cicero, *On Laws* I 17. 47; and other testimonia collected in *SVF* 3.228–36). For Chrysippus, of course, to mistake the nature of the good and to regard having and using external objects, or enjoyment of them, as being good for us, is the root cause of vice. Vice arises, he says, on the one hand, from what we hear from our companions (including our parents as they raise us), who encourage us to think of the objects of pursuit and enjoyment to which they direct us, and to which by natural instinct we direct ourselves during our prerational years, as actually good. Such is the conventional view, and of course there are all kinds of pressures imposed on children as they grow up to accept conventional views of all sorts. On the other hand, and more fundamentally, vice arises from the persuasiveness of things themselves, especially pleasure. Here we can think of the fact that, as children, we are led in the first instance (and presumably we *need* to be so led, if we are to survive and grow) by experiences of pleasure and pain. In being led by them, we can hardly *not* come to think of those experiences themselves, as well as the objects with which they are most closely and constantly associated in our experience as being good and bad, respectively, once we come to develop and live by reasoned thoughts of our own. They are what we find ourselves led toward or away from, when we are beginning life and for our first fourteen years; in them our pursuits terminate. Hence, we very understandably, one could say *naturally*, come to regard pleasure and pain and what gives rise to them in us as ultimate ends, ends such that their very nature or essence make them pursuit- or avoidance-worthy. Though ancient opponents of the Stoics found much to object to in this account, I think myself that it is not at all unreasonable, or at odds in any way with basic Stoic commitments.

rationally best ordered and most coherent. We will not change our minds about what to do or what we should have done, or live in uncertainty, or suffer disappointment and regret; but all will proceed in our lives smoothly and harmoniously. In our thoughts, the past and present will fit together with each other, and with the future as we anticipate it. But what we do will also conform to Zeus's plan for how creatures like us should think and behave, and for how our thoughts would best combine with those of Zeus or nature itself in directing the rest of the world so as to constitute the best, most rationally ordered overall history of thought. Thus, we will follow Zeus's law, recognizing its authority as the embodiment of right reason, and in particular the source of right reason *for us*. And in doing so, we will adopt that law for ourselves, and impose it on ourselves, as our *own* law for living: we will see that this way of living and acting is most reasonable for us, in light of what we actually are, that is, in light of our natures as rational animals.

Now, according to Stoic theory, if we accept the norms for decision making and behavior adumbrated in the previous three paragraphs, and live fully according to them, then we will not only be living fully rationally. We will also be living as fully virtuous persons. We will govern our lives by the concrete values that were partially listed above: our own health, physical well-being, continued life, productive work, warm and supportive relations in family life and with friends, loyalty, cooperative social relations with all with whom we come in contact, a sense for the values of community, both immediate and wider, and so on. The Stoics argue, with considerable plausibility, that if we live like that, then we will be exhibiting, in our ways of thought and in our behavior, justice, temperance, loyalty, honesty, courage, industriousness, love and respect for humanity, and all the rest of those socially approved traits of character that are traditionally regarded as human virtues (however limited and inadequate traditional conceptions of their nature and requirements might be). However, we will also live with the full recognition that none of the preferred values listed above can correctly be thought of as anything good, nor are their opposites bad. The only good that is available in human life is the orderly thinking and deciding that occurs in the assiduous pursuit and maintenance of these values, while recognizing that their attainment, always and inevitably, also depends partly on what happens outside oneself and outside one's own control. In particular, their attainment depends on Zeus's own decisions in maintaining a course of external events (and, for that matter, events internal to our own bodies too) into which our own efforts fit, in such a way as to lead to our desired outcomes. These outcomes may be, and are, authorized by universal reason as the appropriate and correct ones for us to pursue, but this does not mean—and if we are virtuous, we will always bear this vividly in mind—

that Zeus's actual thoughts, in determining actual outcomes, will necessarily, on any particular occasion, lead to their fruition. If they do not eventuate, then we know (retrospectively, in the only way that with our limited knowledge we *can* know) not only that it was not meant to be, but also that it is in fact better that it did not happen. Its not happening, despite our legitimate efforts, was in fact the direct result of Zeus's maximally well-ordered, fully coherent thought history—the very embodiment of goodness.

VI

In sum, if we live in consistency with nature, that is to say, fully rationally, we will be living in accordance with norms, established by Zeus's law, of "preferability" and "rejectability," on the one hand, and goodness on the other. As a result, we will be living fully virtuous lives. I take it that when Dio of Prusa says in his oration *On Freedom* (§5, cited above, sect. I) that the law of nature or Zeus's law, though open to view (φανερόν), is neither seen by most people nor made by them the leader of their lives (οὔτε ὁρῶσιν οὔτε ἡγεμόνα ποιοῦνται τοῦ βίου), it is this second aspect of Zeus's law that Dio has in mind. This aspect concerns, specifically, the norms established in nature for our own decisions and actions, as I just explained. My analysis has now put us in a position to see why Dio is correct, as a matter of Stoic theory, even if not of standard or official Stoic terminology, to describe this law as *our* law, our law for ourselves, as well as Zeus's law for us. Hence, by following this law we achieve, as Dio says, autonomy. This law is Zeus's law for us only because it is reason's law: Zeus's law-giving authority is, or derives from, the authority of reason, which is identical, according to Stoic theory, to Zeus. And because, as I have explained, our own being as agents is wholly constituted by our rationality, this same law is thereby our own law, delivered by our own rational nature—by ourselves as we are in our essence—to ourselves as agents. Only if we live in full accordance with this law do we measure up to the law to which our own nature, as rational, makes us answerable. To the extent that we fail to measure up in our lives to this law—however much we are ourselves and, necessarily, the source of our interest in the modes of behavior or objects of pursuit that we adopt in lieu of the law's authority—we are living, as Dio puts it, in a self-inflicted, grievous slavery that is forbidden by the law (τῆς χαλεπῆς καὶ παρανόμου δουλείας ἐν ᾗ ζεύξαντες αὑτοὺς ἔχετε, §7). In this slavery, we misguidedly, arbitrarily, and pointlessly set up for ourselves interests and desires and whole ways of life that then dominate *us,* when we could and ought to be ruling ourselves by our own law—that is, when we could be living by reason's or Zeus's law for us, which we should recognize and follow, imposing it on ourselves as our own law too, our law as rational beings subject to reason's constraints.

It is obvious that this ancient conception of autonomy differs greatly from the familiar Kantian conception that has been, and still is, so influential in modern and contemporary thinking. The self-imposed law of Stoic autonomy is much more comprehensive in its requirements than the Kantian categorical imperative. The Stoic law gives directives for all kinds of personal and private matters, as well as for more public and communal ones. Furthermore, it makes no provision for finite rational beings as possessing the dignity of authoritative setters of their own ends (and derivatively also for others), within the limits of this basic categorical law. Under Stoic autonomy, ends are set for us by (universal) reason itself, never by the arbitrary pleasures and preferences of individuals among us. These and other differences, I think, all stem directly from the difference between Kant's and the Stoics' conceptions of the nature of reason and rationality itself. For Kant, reason is essentially something formal, a matter of logical consistency in one's reasoning from given premises to appropriate conclusions, and of the most abstract, universal principles for the organization of experience. For the Stoics, as I explained (sect. II), reason's formal aspects are, at most, the outer surface of something with a rich and deep substance of its own—it is a whole system of concepts that constitute a basic knowledge of the world and our place in it. This difference in the understanding of reason and rationality is, in fact, a central and fundamental difference between the whole tradition of ancient philosophy and that of modern, post-Renaissance thought.

Nonetheless, there are important resemblances and no doubt also historical connections between the two conceptions of autonomy, Kantian and Stoic. (As I indicated at the outset, however, I make no claims about, and will not explore here, any of the history that might connect them.) First of all, unlike many conceptions of autonomy current in contemporary usage, both Kant and Dio (on behalf of the Stoics) understand autonomy in strict accordance with its etymology, as involving being subject to and consistently following *law(s)* (νόμοι) of one's own making.[48] For Kant and Dio, autonomy is not mere self-direction or self-

---

[48] Dio (in his brief discourse) does not place as much emphasis as Kant does on autonomy's laws being laws of one's own making. As I noted above (sect. I), Dio identifies (*Discourses* 80.5–6) the only "true" and "valid" law simply as Zeus's or nature's, and he contrasts this with the law of men like Solon, which is wrongly held in such esteem in their respective cities. But when he goes on to conclude that philosophers, in following this law, undertake both to preserve it and to keep to what is *their own* (τοῦτον ἀνασώζειν . . . καὶ τό γε καθ᾽

governance, which might, of course, be quite arbitrary, unprincipled, and inconsistent. Secondly, in both theories the inner source of this law is conceived of as reason itself—in particular, reason as something with universal or universalizing scope. And thirdly, the law of autonomy in both cases is centrally conceived as the basis of morality (duty, virtue). To be sure, within each of these three common aspects of Stoic and Kantian autonomy, there are very important differences, as I have indicated; but these broad similarities are very striking.

Before concluding, I would like to make some brief comments on one difficulty that the Stoics faced if they were to develop and defend their conception of autonomy adequately—a difficulty with which, though again in different ways, Kant had to contend as well. In both theories, the freedom given by autonomy is not at all the same as the mere freedom of free choice—the freedom required by agents' responsibility as persons for their choices and actions. But it does seem a requirement on any acceptable conception of autonomy that autonomous agents also possess, and exercise in their autonomous acts, that lesser freedom, the freedom of personal responsibility. (Indeed, the term "autonomy" is often used loosely simply to denote this freedom.) As is well known, Kant struggled mightily in his works of moral philosophy subsequent to the *Groundwork of the Metaphysics of Morals* (1785) to work out theories of these two sorts of freedom that would allow not only autonomous agents, but also those who live "heteronomously" and flout the moral law, to retain the freedom of free choice and personal responsibility.[49] For the Stoics, the same difficulty arose in a very severe form because of their doctrine of *Fate*. This is the doctrine, roughly, that everything that happens at any time anywhere in the world happens through the determination of Zeus's thought, as part of his overall plan, and was conceived in some way or

---

αὐτὸν φυλάττειν, 80.6), and so to live autonomously, he is relying on claims he has made at some length, just before (§§3–4), about Solon. Solon, he says, was not "autonomous" in his law-giving, because, as I explained in section I, the laws he proposed were not "his own"—that is, ones he actually thought best—but instead those that the Athenian people would accept. Thus, in claiming that these philosophers are autonomous whereas Solon was not, Dio is implying that the law the philosophers follow is also their *own* law, in the way that Solon's laws were not his. That is, these laws are ones that they have devised for themselves by their own thought, as the best laws to live by. By implication, then, Dio's account of autonomy agrees with Kant's in this respect.

[49] There are many translations of the *Groundwork*; it is conveniently available in Immanuel Kant, *Practical Philosophy,* trans. and ed. Mary J. Gregor. In his effort in the *Groundwork* (chap. 3) to establish the authority for us of the categorical imperative, Kant developed an argument that had the implication that free will itself was only exercisable if one followed that imperative.

sense in advance of the coming to be of the world order—a plan that extends into the smallest detail, however trivial, of every circumstance and event.[50]

The Stoic theory of human action seems vulnerable, or worse, because of the way it attempts to combine freedom, and thus personal responsibility, with this global determinism by Fate. Critics of the Stoics, from ancient times onward, have found this a particularly difficult combination to sustain.[51] If Fate (equivalent to Zeus's thought) determines everything, does it not then determine our own thinking too in some way—however much the Stoics might have tried to deny it, in maintaining (as I have explained) our own responsibility for what we think and what we decide to do? Perhaps Fate does this by bringing us into existence, individual by individual, as persons who will, after they grow up, just *find* particular right or wrong courses of action persuasive—persons who, therefore, will take as good reasons certain particular considerations, whether or not they really are so. In that case, how can we be meaningfully held personally responsible for our own thought and action—to think and act freely—even if and when we act (allegedly) autonomously? On that understanding of Fate, it would be true, of course, that the actions themselves would have us—our thoughts about and decisions to do them—as

[50] Plutarch quotes from the first book of Chrysippus's *On Nature*: "For no particular thing, not even the least, can happen otherwise than in accordance with universal nature and its reason" (*On Stoic Self-Contradictions* 1050a). A little later he quotes him again: "For since universal nature reaches to all things, everything that happens in this or that way in the whole and in any of its parts happens in accordance with that nature and its reason, in unhindered sequence. Neither is there anything that could obstruct its regulation from outside, nor any way for any of its parts to undergo change or be in any condition except in accordance with universal nature" (1050c–d, quoted in *LS* 54T). (And, of course, we are among the parts here referred to.) Some of the most important ancient reports on the Stoic doctrine of Fate are collected in *LS* chap. 55, passages J–S.

[51] Thus, in introducing Chrysippus's effort to "mediate" between the old determinists (such as Democritus, allegedly) who simply, on the basis of fate, declared human actions to be necessitated and so not "free," and those who (such as Epicurus) exempted movements of the mind from control by fate in order to preserve freedom, Cicero says that although Chrysippus *wanted* to establish a view of human freedom that would make it compatible with universal determinism, he employed terminology of his own devising that got him into such difficulty that, against his will, he actually ended up lending support to the old determinists' position (*De Fato*, trans. H. Rackham, Loeb Classical Library, §39; see also §20). Alexander of Aphrodisias in his treatise *On Fate* (*De Fato*, ed. Sharples, chap. 27) argues at length that, in fact, people can be legitimately subject to praise or blame for their actions (i.e., are responsible for them as persons) only if—as the Stoics deny—they had the "liberty of indifference" in deciding to do them. In other words, they can be held personally responsible only if at that time they could either do or not do what they did.

their immediately determining and indispensable causes. So we would be *causally* responsible. But could we reasonably be held, or hold ourselves, responsible *as persons?* Could we deserve any credit or discredit for our decisions and our actions?

In the debates since antiquity over the relationship between Fate, as the Stoics understand it, and individuals' personal responsibility for their own thought and action, the Stoics have generally been interpreted as simply insisting that the sort of causal responsibility we undeniably do have (on their view) for our actions is all the responsibility we need, in order to be credited or discredited, as the case may be, for them—to be responsible for them as persons. Their Aristotelian opponent, Alexander of Aphrodisias, invented the notion of a "liberty of indifference," according to which right up to the time when the action is done both "it will happen" and "it won't happen" are open possibilities, and the decision could go either way. And late Aristotelians insisted that that liberty (something the Stoics with their theory of Fate cannot permit us) is in fact required if we are reasonably to be held responsible as persons. There, as it is usually presented, the ancient debate stalemated. But I think the Stoic view has been misunderstood. One crucial point seems to me to be overlooked—or at least its significance is missed. According to Stoic theory, our individual minds are held to be actual, disjoined *portions* of Zeus's mind.[52] Here, as it seems to me, we can find the best Stoic response—an

---

[52] "Disjoined portion" here translates ἀπόσπασμα, Diogenes Laertius, *Lives,* 7.143; see also Epictetus, *Discourses* 1.1.12. (Speaking in Zeus's voice, Epictetus says Zeus gives each of us μέρος τι ἡμέτερον, a part of himself; Seneca says less explicitly at *Letters to Lucilius* 92.1 that "our reason is the same as god's because it comes from it" (*ex illa est*), but in 66.12 he speaks of our reason as "a part of the divine spirit set in a human body," *pars divini spiritus.* The Greek word ἀπόσπασμα that Diogenes Laertius, *Lives,* uses here is often translated, e.g., by Long and Sedley, *Hellenistic Philosophers,* 1:319 (53 X), as "offshoot." But in the literal sense an offshoot can be a branch running off from a main stem to which it remains connected, while the Greek verb from which the noun is derived means to tear off or away, to detach. If we think of ourselves as "offshoots," it must be in the other meaning of the literal sense of this word, where "offshoot" refers to something cut off from a stem and planted on its own. Hence, to render this Stoic idea, I prefer the less elegant "disjoined portion" to the potentially misleading "offshoot." In his own account of "Freedom and Determinism in the Stoic Theory of Human Action" (*Problems in Stoicism,* ed. A. A. Long), Long mentions this aspect of Stoic doctrine (pp. 178–79) but without, so far as I can tell, seeing its full significance.

It is not quite clear how to reconcile the doctrine that all human minds are disjoined parts of Zeus's mind with the well-attested view of Chrysippus that only the souls of the wise survive right up to the end of the world (the conflagration), while others' souls survive for a time only (Cleanthes is reported to have assigned the greater privilege to all human souls, Diogenes Laertius, *Lives* 7.157). See Arius Didymus in Diels, *Doxographi Graeci* 471, 18

entirely adequate one—to the difficult questions about how Fate and personal responsibility can be combined.

Given that we are portions—albeit disjoined ones—of Zeus's mind, Zeus's universal causality (i.e., Fate), and his responsibility for everything through having planned it, cannot threaten to remove the possibility of either our own causality or our own personal responsibility for our acts. Our causality, and our personal responsibility, are in fact *part* of Zeus's. This causality is simply that which belongs to mind or minds (reason) as such: minds just *do* have the power to act on (suitable) materials with which they come into contact, and ultimately, as we have seen, only minds, through the *pneuma* with which they are mixed, have this power. Moreover, it is our privilege, as rational animals whose reason is a portion of Zeus's, to share with Zeus in the government of the world. Most of what happens he (or nature) causes directly through his own rational substance, and for his own reasons—or, rather, through the part of himself that is not separated off in the form of human minds. But the rest of what happens is caused by our own thoughts and decisions, undertaken for our own reasons. As I explained above (sect. IV), it is entirely up to us what we shall think, in reaction to the impressions that we receive. What we will think depends entirely on what we find it reasonable to think in the light of our impressions. Nor, as I understand Stoic theory, does Zeus play any role at all in determining what we *will* find reasonable to think. Through the natural processes I discussed in section II, we all are given minds that are adequate to the task of figuring out correctly what really *is* most reasonable, but it is then up to us to use that power as we think best—and we never lose this power, so long as we remain rational beings at all. So it is not true that Zeus has brought us into existence individually as persons who will inevitably grow up to take some particular sorts of considerations as providing good reasons. He has brought each and every one of us into existence (at the "age of reason") with rational powers that are adequate to the task of learning what sort of life is best, and leading that sort of life. It is then up to us what use we make of those powers.[53]

---

ff. (= *SVF* 3.809) and Aëtius IV 7 3 (= *SVF* 3.810). The reference in Diog. Laert. 7.143 to the doctrine of disjoined parts does, however, suggest that it was part of orthodox Stoicism, and not a late accretion from Imperial times.

[53] In attributing to Chrysippus this view of what is included in having a mind, in being rational, I am relying for the most part not on explicit statements of his or explicit ancient testimonies as to his views. It is indisputable that, on his view, Zeus or nature is responsible for our individual creation, including whatever specific characteristics and powers we are born with. Also, given his claim that the collection of concepts that constitute reason are instilled

Thus, since our minds are portions of Zeus's, the total history of the world's thoughts, which is the history of Zeus's thoughts, actually includes our thoughts, and thereby, of course, their effects, as part of its own course. The amazing thing is that even with all of our individual errors, the total ordered sequence of thoughts (our thoughts, plus Zeus's on

---

in us by natural processes (see sect. II above), he must hold that Zeus is responsible for giving us, at the age of reason when we change from animals of a nonrational nature to ones of a rational nature, all the additional characteristics and powers that belong to us *qua* rational. But if in doing that Zeus made some, or even almost all, of us prone to (what Chrysippus would regard as) one or another mental disorder (e.g., an entrenched inclination to think that bodily pleasure is a good, or the sort of feeling of inferiority or insecurity that makes one quick to find and flare up at any sign of belittlement, or any of the other characteristic attitudes that mark people as bad in one way or another), he would manifestly thereby stack the deck against us in our further self-development, growth to maturity, and subsequent lives. To do that cannot be part of Zeus's plan. The only way, so far as I can see, to understand how Chrysippus's Zeus might avoid doing this is for him to act as I say he does: to give each us at the age of reason (and preserve in us thereafter), as part of what it is to have a mind at all, the ability to figure out correctly, in our own reflections upon any impressions we receive, how to respond to them. So if we become pleasure lovers, or irascible and oversensitive honor lovers, or any other kind of bad person, that results from our own misuse of our reason—not from any initial endowment by Zeus, nor yet from Zeus's actions in giving us the impressions we actually receive over time. Cicero's account in *On Laws* I 21 ff. (*De legibus*, trans. C. W. Keyes, Loeb Classical Library) of reason as something common to all human beings (and to god), which obviously has Stoic roots, includes much that is suggestive of such a view: in sum, he says, human beings may differ in what they learn, but they have an equal capacity to learn, and all human beings have the rational power necessary to attain virtue (even if they might need some help along the way) (§30). In looking for contradictions in Chrysippus's views, between his claims for Zeus's providential concern for human beings and various ways in which he admits Zeus's role in the occurrence of things actually or apparently bad for us, Plutarch (*On Stoic Self-Contradictions*, chaps. 31–37) considers only "external" events (Zeus's giving us impressions that serve as pretexts for vice and wrongdoing, including the destruction of one another that we bring on through wars, or his causing illnesses and the like). Plutarch is concerned merely to show that, for Chrysippus, Zeus is an accessory (παραίτιον) in our vice, not that he is himself its direct cause. Again, when (chap. 47) he attempts to show that Chrysippus does make Zeus and Fate responsible for our bad actions, his arguments concern Zeus's responsibility for the impressions we receive that, when assented to by us, lead to vice or vicious action—or, loosely and unspecifically, Zeus's general responsibility for the government of the universe, of which we are parts. It seems not to occur to Plutarch to attribute to Chrysippus total responsibility of Fate in making us the kind of people we are in the first place. All this, too, coheres completely with my interpretation. (The same can be said for the related objections in *On Common Conceptions*, chaps. 13–20, 34.) Chrysippus's explanation of the origin of vice coheres with it, too: vice arises, on the one hand, from what we hear from our companions and, on the other, from the persuasiveness of things themselves, especially pleasure (Diogenes Liertius, *Lives*, 7.89; cf. Galen, *On the Doctrines of Hippocrates and Plato* V 5. 14, Cicero, *On Laws* I 17. 47). (See above, n. 47.)

his own) that cause all of the objects and happenings in the course of world history, displays the most perfect rational order that there could possibly be. (Of course, part of the beautiful orderliness of that history is due to, or consists in, the fact that it is the result of the contributions of a huge number of distinct minds, Zeus's plus each of our own. Each of us thinks according to our own ideas of what is best in light of the impressions that we receive.) This most perfect rational order happens, however, hardly at all through human effort to bring it about—most of us have no such intention, even no such idea at all. The rational order is brought about almost entirely by the power that Zeus has on his own, apart from human minds, to anticipate and plan the whole course of his own life, while allowing each of us at each moment to make up our own minds about what to think and what to do, and thus allowing *us* to contribute those parts of the sequence of *his* ideas. In planning his total life, he anticipates what each of us will think and decide at every moment in relation to the impressions that we will experience then, and in advance, as it were (from the very beginning), he adjusts the rest of his thoughts to accommodate our own into an overall magnificently well-ordered total history of thought—a history that is inconceivably beautiful and good.[54] Once the whole plan is fixed, of course, then all events are Fated, includ-

---

[54] In proposing this interpretation I am relying, first of all, on two quotations from Chrysippus in Plutarch's *On Stoic Self-Contradictions* 1050e–f (= *SVF* 2.1176, 1181). The first of these explains why Zeus causes various disagreeable things to befall human beings, claiming that, in part, they may come about "in consequence of [his] regulating things somehow in relation to the whole"; the second adds to these even vice itself (not that Zeus actually makes anyone be vicious or causes their vicious actions), saying that "it comes about not without some use in relation to the whole, since without it there would not be the good." Plutarch's discussion of the second passage in *On Common Conceptions* 1065b–66c is characteristically confusing for one attempting to recover Chrysippus's own thought and intentions, but I take it that the "use" Chrysippus envisages here for vice (or vicious actions) is in relation to what Zeus provides by way of context for it: Zeus adjusts events in the wider world of nature so as to make our own errors, when taken together with those, contribute to an overall beautiful outcome. This is a quite distinct point, I believe, from Chrysippus's claim, attested by Aulus Gellius (*Attic Nights*, ed. and trans. John C. Rolfe, Loeb Classical Library, VII 1.7–13 = *LS* 54Q), that since virtue and vice are opposites, each presupposes the other. That amounts to claiming only that the two concepts are interconnected, so that Zeus could not make the one a real possibility (that is, make it part of nature) without at the same time acting likewise for the other. Despite the implications of his initial objection (1065b), which does seem to conflate the two points, Plutarch develops criticisms of the second passage cited above that see the alleged usefulness of vice in relation to specific valuable outcomes, not the bare existence of virtue (see esp. 1066b–c). (If one could count Clement of Alexandria, *Miscellanies* I 86 = *SVF* 2.1184, as expressing Stoic views when he speaks of God's power and will to produce a good overall result out of human beings' self-chosen vicious deeds, one would find there an explicit indication that

ing the events consisting in our own thinkings and decidings: we do not have the late-Aristotelian liberty of indifference.[55] Nonetheless, in this way, whether or not we do follow Zeus's law in our own decisions, and so whether or not we live autonomously, we live with full personal responsibility for all of our own thoughts and all of our actions. We are exactly as responsible for our thoughts, and in exactly the same way, as Zeus himself is responsible for his own thoughts (or rather, again, for that part of his thoughts that he thinks in separation from us).[56]

---

some Stoics, at least, held the view I am attributing to Chrysippus. But I think the context makes it clear that Clement is speaking for himself, about the Christian god.)

Stephen Menn suggests to me that, on my interpretation, the Stoics adopted a view about Zeus's foreknowledge and planning that resembles that of Luis de Molina in the sixteenth century Christian debates about God's grace and human freedom (see Luis de Molina, *On Divine Foreknowledge: Part Four of the Concordia*, trans., intro. and notes Alfred J. Freddoso). Zeus's foreknowledge of what each of us will think and decide, according to what I have said, does seem quite close to Molina's conception of a third, "middle" kind of knowledge that, according to him, the Christian God has of human decisions. But there the similarity between the Stoics' and Molina's views ceases. No sixteenth-century Christian could think, in the way the Stoics did, of our minds as disjoined parts of God's, nor were the Stoics embroiled in any effort to make sense of the Christian doctrine of divine grace.

[55] Thus, the usual interpretation of the Stoic position is partly correct: Chrysippus was a compatibilist on the relationship of causal determinism to moral or personal responsibility. Given the nature and condition of my mind at any time, he thought, I cannot but do whatever it is that I (decide to do, and) do. But I remain, nonetheless, deserving of any credit or discredit, as the case may be. However, I deserve credit or discredit, not because my decision (an act of my own mind) is an indispensable cause of what I go on to do, but only because in possessing a mind I possess and never lose the power (so long as I do not lose my mind altogether) to recognize and grasp the *right* reasons for acting, and to see the *right* thing to do. To have a mind just is to have this power. It is only because, on his conception, having a mind does include that crucial feature that Chrysippus's compatibilism can, in fact, be sustained. We might have all kinds of other reasons, as has repeatedly been argued in the modern and contemporary literature of philosophy, for praising and blaming others and ourselves (thus, for holding people responsible), and we might, despite being clearheaded about the truth of determinism, continue to engage in these practices; we might even say that, as agents who *have* to decide what to do before we do anything, we cannot help but think of ourselves as subject to credit or discredit for our decisions, depending on how well we perform this task. But if the question of our personal (or "moral") responsibility or lack of it is a question—as, in fact, it is—of our *deserving* any credit or discredit we may get, the viability of the Stoics' answer depends crucially on the fact, central to the Stoic conception, that to have a mind really is to have this power.

[56] Here again I leave aside, as irrelevant to what I am saying, the fact that Zeus, in the portion of his thought that lies apart from what human minds contribute, possesses the power actually to bring matter into existence. Zeus's mind is, indeed, in this way as in others, vastly more powerful than our minds are, but in thinking whatever thoughts we do think, we are just as free, in the sense of personally responsible for what we do, as Zeus is in thinking his own thoughts.

Stoic autonomy, then, is a complex and, I think, deeply interesting conception of human nature, human rationality, and the basis of morality. In the similarities of autonomy as they conceive it to Kant's much more familiar conception, the Stoics deserve to be considered important forerunners of Kant—neglected though they are in this capacity. But, independently of historical comparison, the Stoic theory deserves to be studied and appreciated in its own right.[57]

[57] In revising this paper for publication in this book, I have taken into account helpful comments of Christopher Bobonich prepared for my presentation of it at a conference on Mind and Nature in ancient philosophy held at the University of California, Davis, in October 2002, and the subsequent discussion. I thank Victor Caston and the Department of Philosophy at Davis for the invitation and for providing an excellent forum for discussion of these issues. In addition, I have incorporated new material meant to respond to questions and comments of Myles Burnyeat, Margaret Graver, and Gisela Striker at two further presentations, at Boston and Florida State Universities, in March 2003. Finally, I owe a debt of thanks to the Philosophy Department at Stanford University for its invitation to deliver the Immanuel Kant Lectures, April 2003, for one of which I presented material from this paper. I have made further changes to take account of points made in the lively discussions at and after the lecture there. I also thank Michael Frede for discussion that led me to add last-minute clarifications to notes 31 and 52.

THE GOOD

CHAPTER 10

TWO THEORIES OF JUSTICE

IN LATER ANTIQUITY, Plato's *Republic* carried the secondary title "On Justice."[1] In fact, as befits a dialogue, it presents us with not one but two distinct—even opposed—theories of what justice is and what its functions are in the life of any just community. Plato's brothers Glaucon and Adeimantus set out one of these theories in book II, even though they profess to hope it is not true. Socrates develops the other one over the course of the remaining books. In pitting these two theories against one another, Plato articulated for the first time central issues about justice that remain very much alive in our own politics. They shape current debates in political philosophy, as well. We still have much of interest and value to learn from the study of Plato's *Republic*—and in particular from studying these two theories of justice. Or so I hope to show.

I

In his inconclusive debate with Thrasymachus in *Republic* book I, Socrates had insisted that justice really is a *virtue* of and for any human being (see 348c–352c). That is, it is a psychological characteristic, difficult to attain, that anyone who understood the relevant facts correctly would recognize that any and every human being needs, just as much as they need persistence and courage and self-control, if they are to lead satisfactory human lives. As such, justice is something to be prized, and a legitimate basis for satisfaction, even pride, for anyone who can attain it. At the beginning of book II (358b–362c), Glaucon challenges Socrates with a powerful and impressive account of the origin and function of justice which clearly implies that, on the contrary, justice is no virtue at all. It is only, for most of us, a regrettably necessary encumbrance in the living of our lives—while the naturally best-endowed, most capable human beings would be able (and right) to dispense with it altogether. In response, Socrates develops an account of his own—radically different

---

[1] See, e.g., Diogenes Laertius, *Lives of Eminent Philosophers* 3. 60, text and trans. by R. D. Hicks, Loeb Classical Library, 1:330–31).

from Glaucon's—of the origin of justice and of its functions in any human community. It is by examining in detail, and comparing with one another, the very different ethical and psychological underpinnings of justice presupposed respectively in Glaucon's and Socrates' accounts that I hope to bring to light insufficiently appreciated aspects of Plato's two theories of justice.

Despite their pious lack of confidence in it, Glaucon and Adeimantus set out with remarkable vigor and relish an impressive theory about what justice actually is. It is, Glaucon explains, an agreement or contract between each citizen and all the others that (in case they all *are* just people) each will leave all the rest unmolested, unharmed, and uninterfered with as they pursue their own interests as they individually see them. As he puts it, it is an agreement "neither to do injustice nor to have it done to one" (359a2): no invasion of people's property, no use of intimidation or force to prevent people from doing what they want, no lying or other trickery to wrest control of anyone's resources or otherwise take unfair advantage of them. As we could put it, for Glaucon, justice resides in an agreement of mutual forbearance: each is to leave the others alone to pursue their own interests, as they themselves see them, in return for the others leaving him or her similarly free and unmolested.

But what conception of these interests does Glaucon have? Glaucon sketches the behavior, if left free to do "whatever they wished," of people both just and unjust—that is, whether faithful observers in ordinary life of the terms of this agreement, or cheaters and freeloaders. In doing so, he speaks of them as motivated by appetite (ἐπιθυμία, 359c3): the sort of desire that later in the work Socrates correlates with the pursuit of bodily and sensory pleasure. And he adds that "everyone's nature naturally pursues πλεονεξία as good"—that is, "outdoing others and getting more and more."[2] Plainly, Glaucon thinks of each and every person as motivated, at the bottommost level, solely by desires for pleasurable gratification of various sorts. And he seems to think of this in an open-ended way: desires and gratifications can alter and ramify over time as one has new experiences and so learns of new and perhaps unexpected ways of getting pleasure. He thinks that people are driven by their basic desire for gratification to want as much and as great gratification as they can obtain— they want unlimited amounts of pleasure, on unlimited occasions. In this, of course, he is simply making more explicit the same assumption that underlay Thrasymachus's account of why justice was no sort of virtue at

[2] I cite here the translation by George Grube as revised by C.D.C. Reeve in Plato, *Complete Works*, ed. John M. Cooper and D. S. Hutchinson), p. 1000. Elsewhere I sometimes give translations of my own, sometimes follow Grube-Reeve strictly or with some variation, without notice as to which I am doing.

all. Clearly enough, Thrasymachus had assumed that all any human being ever wants, at the bottommost level, is pleasurable gratification, as much as possible.[3] On that assumption, justice and voluntary restraint would seem the height of folly, nothing at all to pride oneself on. Indeed, it would seem something to be ashamed of. We could put Thrasymachus and Glaucon's view of human psychology like this: proximately or immediately, everyone always desires the varied means by which pleasurable gratification can be achieved and ensured—that is, money, property, and power over others who might stand in the way or be needed when some gratification is being pursued—and as much of these things as one can manage to secure. It is these pursuits that, on Glaucon's account of justice, citizens agree to curtail in case, in order to achieve their immediate goal, they will have to inflict physical harm on or steal from, and so on, another person who is party to the agreement.

Now, on Glaucon's theory people in general agree to this contract simply because they know from experience, or can tell with a little imagination, how much worse off they are or would be in their prospects for gratifications without such a contract. Without the contract, all individuals, he assumes, would pursue the means of their own satisfaction without any such general restraint. And once the contract is in place, any single person, no matter how physically powerful or even already rich, can easily see that if the contract were suddenly abandoned by all he would be quite a bit worse off. Under the contract, though he does have to forgo some actions that would be beneficial to him in obtaining or securing greater means for gratification, he can count on others similarly to forgo when it comes to not attacking him or invading *his* possessions. Of course (and this is why Glaucon says that his theory of what justice is supports Thrasymachus's case against justice), so long as you could be reasonably sure that others will keep their part of the bargain even if you should not, you would have every reason to violate it. In other words, even if your interest in your own personal gratification might rationally lead you to agree to the contract and even keep to it, when the alternative would be everyone-for-themselves chaos, it also makes it rational for you to cheat when you can get away with it, or reasonably think you can. Nonetheless Glaucon can and does suggest—I think, reasonably so—

---

[3] Thrasymachus says a city's ruling group legislates as standards of justice for its citizens ones that will work to their own private advantage (συμφέρον, 338e2 and elsewhere), *and* to the disadvantage and harm of the citizens themselves (343c4–5). Being unjust, he says, the rulers seek always to "outdo" everyone else (πλεονεκτεῖν, first at 344a1)—he is thinking of them as engaged in a zero-sum game aimed at arrogating to themselves as great a quantity of the means of satisfaction for their desires as possible, and in that process depriving everyone else of the same to just that extent. It is on these clues to his underlying psychological assumptions that Glaucon follows up in the passages cited in the text above.

that, under the normal, actual conditions of uncertainty about whether they could get away with violating the agreement, most people may rationally keep the bargain.[4] Being strongly risk-averse where anything serious is at stake, he seems to be thinking, most people would prefer to hang on to the security they already know and reasonably value under the agreement, even at the possible cost of speculative and risky further gains they might potentially achieve by paying lip service to the contract, while breaking it when (they think) no one is looking.

But Glaucon goes further. Rationally keeping the bargain is compatible with a spirit of resentment, a sense of repression and irritation at the restrictions the contract imposes. Indeed, on the analysis so far, this is how you would expect people to feel who were motivated in Glaucon's way to keep to the terms of the agreement. Yet Glaucon says that most people would not merely keep to them, but would do so faithfully; and so they would be counted as genuinely just (according to his account of what justice is). Under a stable and convincing legal threat of retaliatory harm to violators, their nature's desire for their own maximal gratification would, he says, be *diverted* to respecting and honoring fairness or justice (παράγεται ἐπὶ τὴν τοῦ ἴσου τιμήν, 359c5–6).[5] They would be led to regard fairness and justice with respect, and to honor them on that basis. Thus they would keep to the terms of the contract out of a sense of justice, in addition to their rational pursuit of pleasurable gratification under these constraining conditions. Even if they did feel some of the resentment I just referred to, or at least a good deal of disappointment at having to forgo additional gratifications banned by the contract, this would be overlain and kept under control by this additional, and new, motivation— their sense of justice.

To be sure, Glaucon mimics Thrasymachus and calls such people "weak" and "no true men" (359b1–2)—if they were really strong and self-reliant, as true men should be, they would find the means to get away even with openly flaunting their disregard for the terms of the agreement, if their pursuit of their gratification made that necessary. In fact, he says, if you gave them Gyges' ring they'd at once cease to be faithful to the agreement. Of course, the fantasy is that having the ring would remove all the uncertainty about the consequences of violation and so also all the risk. With the ring, they could preserve the security of being thought to

---

[4] See 359a–b. He refers to such people as "ones who practice justice" (b6).

[5] The Greek παράγεται need not carry the implication, as (e.g.) Grube and Reeve translate it, of a diversion that constitutes a *perversion*. Glaucon is not saying that anything unnatural results from this development. To be sure, he does think that truly self-reliant and excellent human beings will resist all pressure toward developing any such respect. But they are the rare exceptions, and most people will duly and naturally acquire it.

be observers of the contract, while actually violating it with impunity when they saw an opening to do so. Readers sometimes take Glaucon to be saying that these conjectures about the behavior of the allegedly just man who possessed Gyges' ring show that, even as things are, no one at all actually *is* just: allegedly "just" people are all shamming.[6] However, he actually says only that anyone in ordinary circumstances who *is* just is so "by necessity" (or "compulsion," ἀναγκαζόμενος, 360c6).[7] What such a person recognizes as (for him) nonideal conditions of equality of power and so forth with others have put him in the position where, perforce, he does reasonably come to *be* just, that is, to respect and honor justice. The effect of possessing the ring is to remove the conditions in which that remains reasonable.

---

[6] This is the implication of Cicero's insistence (*On Duties* III 39; see *De Officiis*, ed. and trans. Walter Miller, Loeb Classical Library, 306–7), against Epicurean theorists of justice, that if they admit that in the Gyges' ring situation (however impossible its actual realization might be) they *would* seduce a man's wife and kill him (or whatever), that shows that *now* they are in fact iniquitous people.

[7] Read as an isolated sentence, what Glaucon says here—that a person "is just" only unwillingly and under compulsion—could mean merely that people only unwillingly and through compulsion ever do what justice, under the contract, requires; in that case, they might all the time be doing it in a spirit of resentment or irritation, without endorsing the contract and its requirements of them as fair, and without respecting it (in part) for that reason. They would not "be just" in the sense I have specified, but only in the weaker one of acting justly on a regular basis. But the passage cited in the last paragraph (359c5–6), which as I have argued recognizes a stronger sense of "being just," is only one of several in which Glaucon indicates that, on his view, people living in a society regulated by his contract will actually become just people in this stronger sense. Below, at 360d1–3, despite what he says at 360c6 about unwillingness and compulsion, he recognizes that some people might, even when possessed of Gyges' ring, refrain from acting unjustly—they would really *be* just in the strong sense, they would really respect these requirements, even beyond what Glaucon thinks reasonable. (They would be agreed by all to be "most wretched and stupid," of course.) A bit further on (361b6–7) in postulating a truly just man, to be compared for happiness with a truly unjust one, he calls the former "simple and high-minded" (ἁπλοῦν καὶ γενναῖον)—someone who wants really to "be good" (εἶναι ἀγαθόν) and not merely to be thought to be so. This too is a person who fits the stronger conception of "being just." Glaucon's language here picks up that of Thrasymachus at 348c11–12. There Thrasymachus, recalling his earlier description of people docilely obedient to their rulers' self-interested laws as "those who are truly naive and just" (τῶν ὡς ἀληθῶς εὐηθικῶν τε καὶ δικαίων, 343c6–7), describes justice as "just a very high-minded naïveté" (πάνυ γενναίαν εὐήθειαν). When one sees the links between these passages in book I and what Glaucon says at 360c6 (and 359c5–6), it seems right to interpret him even at 360c6 as referring to people who are faithful to the contract in a basically ungrudging spirit (despite their sense of compulsion). He is saying that they are faithful only because circumstances put them in the position where that attitude is imposed on them through the force of law referred to at 359c5–6: they would prefer that no contract was necessary, and that they could just go straight after their hearts' desires without the effects of this "diversion." Nonetheless, they do accept in a positive spirit, and honor, its requirements—they do not merely obey them.

Thus, Glaucon seems to be thinking that most people, situated as they actually are, would reasonably adopt a really firm policy of obeying the terms of the agreement. They would not allow themselves, at least in all ordinary circumstances, ever to think twice, ever to spend time considering whether in any particular case it actually might not pay to obey them. They would not stop to consider whether, just then, cheating would pay, but would rely instead on the well-established general presumption that keeping to the agreement was the right policy. Indeed, as we've seen, Glaucon thinks that they would acquire a firm habit of obedience that represented a second level of motivation, a sense of fairness, constructed out of or derived from the old interest in open-ended personal gratification that Glaucon sets at the base of all human motivation. They would come to think that adhering to the contract was a fair means of achieving the security from others that was so beneficial to them all. Thus they would adhere to it for that further reason. Others, of course, being less risk-averse or maybe just more fixated on possible further gains, could rationally refuse to be just (though they would still have an interest in seeming to be so). These people would rationally refuse altogether to faithfully keep the terms of the agreement, even if they only fairly rarely actually did violate it. They would always be ready to, and so they would actually be unjust people. They would have no, or only a weak and ineffective, sense of justice. Thus Glaucon's theory of what justice is and how it originates does provide for a corresponding sense of justice on the part of some or even most people: the sense that violating the agreement is bad and dishonorable. He insists that there is a good basis in human psychology, understood as involving at bottom nothing but the desire for unlimited pleasure, for expecting that some people raised in a city recognizing rules of justice defined by this theory will actually be just persons—where, again, what it is to be a just person is the condition, defined by this theory, of faithfully keeping to the agreement (in part) because it is a fair one, and out of respect for it because it *is* fair.

It might be helpful here to recall the "myth" in Protagoras's great speech in Plato's *Protagoras*. Zeus, says Protagoras (see 322c–d), gave to all human beings as part of basic, normal human nature a disposition for mutual respect and fair dealing (αἰδώς and δίκη). Hence they have a natural tendency to be forbearing and considerate of others, not to ride roughshod over one another or insist always on getting one's own way. Otherwise, Zeus saw, people would never be able to live together in communities and the human race would die out. Social life requires cooperation, and Zeus made it part of normal human nature that people should be able to, and should wish to, live with one another on some fair terms of cooperation. Glaucon appears to be assuming this much of Protagoras's account of normal human nature, without making it explicit. Glaucon's own theory of justice in terms of a mutual agreement not to harm and not to be harmed simply provides a specific set of ideas sufficient to give definite content to such an underlying, natural sense of justice or wish to live with others on fair terms. When he argues that most people motivated his way would come to honor the agreement if it was in place in their society, he seems to be appealing to Zeus's gift of a disposition for mutual respect as indeed part of human nature. In fact, if we do assume such a natural disposition, then it seems to me that this specific content for it really is one on which we should expect people with the basic motivations for gratification that Glaucon presupposes actually to converge. For normally risk-averse persons desiring maximum gratification for their appetites for pleasure, and wishing to live with one another on terms of fair cooperation, Glaucon's contract not to harm and not to be harmed does seem the right way to specify what fair cooperation requires. Or so I suggest.

II

When Socrates undertakes his response to Glaucon and Adeimantus's challenge, he does not, of course, agree to accept Glaucon's account of what justice is and how it arises. Nor does he suppose that the basic natural sense of fairness should or would lead most people to endorse the obligations of justice as defined by that theory. In fact, the first thing he does is to begin a prolonged investigation, *de novo*, into the true nature of justice. This investigation has at its foundation a flat rejection of the fundamental moral postulate that lies behind Glaucon's account. Socrates also rejects Glaucon's theory of human motivational psychology; I'll come back to that point shortly. For Glaucon, justice is a negative ideal: under justice as he conceives it, each person is to refrain from damaging the others (physically or in their property). There is no suggestion of any obligation of justice to aid another person. It is easy to see why for Glaucon this should seem the most that justice can legitimately demand. He assumes that people are motivated at bottom solely by their desires for personal gratification, and it can make excellent sense to such persons to accept a mutual-restraint pact, and so to develop a sense of fairness focused on the moral value of such restraint. Human beings individually or in league have obvious and significant powers to wreck and ruin another person's capacity to obtain or hang on to what interests him. Given this vulnerability, each of us has an urgent need to protect ourselves against harms that other persons can do us. This the contract provides. But a pact of that *plus* mutual aid might seem to such persons a very dubious proposition. Why encumber yourself with obligations to hold off from or forgo your own gratification while working to secure another person's means to his because that would aid *him*? Even if reciprocal obligations would thereby be won from the others, this seems to get deeper into the territory of speculative gains that, I suggested earlier, the typical risk-averse person with such motivations would want to keep out of. Where the pursuit of gratification is concerned, it seems better to let each person go their own way, and not include any such obligation to mutual assistance within the pact that establishes the content of justice. People are best left free to cater to their own positive interests as they see fit, without any obligations of justice on anyone else's part to help them. We generally don't need others to come to our aid in our pursuit of our own particular gratifications, certainly not in the way we need protection from attacks on our persons and property. Of course, under Glaucon's pact, private individuals could enter into private agreements of mutual assistance if they thought their and another person or persons' situation jointly favored this. Then, by making the agreement, they would voluntarily make it a harm to the other if they reneged. Thus, at the second level, obligations to aid specific others could be acquired: but no obligations to mutual aid, either general or specific, would be included in the basic pact itself.

Now just here is where Socrates' account of justice differs from Glaucon's. Just after Socrates begins his account (368c) he suggests (369a) that we need to start one step earlier, historically speaking, than Glaucon's account did. Glaucon postulated an agreement reached after people had already experienced the ill effects of living together in communities without the benefits of mutual restraint. But we need to ask: what ever led people in the first place to decide to live together in civic or protocivic social environments? Socrates' answer (midway through book II, at 369b) is the fundamental hypothesis of the whole positive construction in the remaining eight and a half books. Cities came into existence because people needed one another's help. None of us is self-sufficient—either in regard to the basic requirements of life (the original concern, Socrates supposes, of the first city dwellers) or in regard to further interests and needs that arise for the first time only within a civilized environment. All these further interests, regardless of their specific character and quality—even, it might be, their legitimate urgency for a civilized human being—Socrates designates as "luxuries," since they go beyond the simplest original needs necessary for continued life itself.[8]

What then, on this hypothesis, should we say about the essence of justice? What conception of fairness should we introduce to govern the interactions of persons who have come together because they need one

---

[8] See 372e3 with 373a4–6 and 373d10 (ὑπερβάντες τὸν τῶν ἀναγκαίων ὅρον).

another's assistance? Here Socrates makes a second assumption, or rather his initial hypothesis already included it implicitly. The basis of individual humans' lack of self-sufficiency lies, first, in the differential distribution among us of talents, capacities, and natural dispositions and, secondly, in the correlative inability of people singly to become as expert in everything that needs to be done to maintain their existence as they can in some of these (different ones for each). These points, together with the loss of efficiency if one spends less time at what one can do best and has to spend more at things one is not very good at, lead to Socrates' basic moral postulate: justice requires that the citizens shall individually each spend some of their time working for the good of their fellow citizens, in fair exchange for the similar work of each of the others for *their* good. More specifically, justice demands that people shall regularly devote their work time to making some one contribution each to the accumulation and maintenance of the common store of social goods in which all will then share—that is, to the means of meeting the needs for which people came together in the first place. Namely, they are each to make the one contribution that their own talents, abilities, and natural dispositions most suit them for.

We can see, then, that from the very outset Socrates' theory of justice is diametrically opposed to Glaucon's. Glaucon supposes justice is a matter of each person leaving the others alone—not harming them, not interfering with them, not preventing them from doing what they want. For Socrates, it consists in people's acting individually so as positively to *benefit* each of the others—in return, of course, for their own benefit from the others' reciprocal actions. Mutual aid, not mutual restraint, is the key to Socrates' notion of justice. But if that really is what justice fundamentally consists in, how are individual human beings to be brought to see that they should accept its demands? As we saw, on Glaucon's assumptions about human motivational psychology you could easily enough reach the conclusion that many or most human beings would have reason to accept and keep to a pact of mutual restraint (even if some of them would have reason to decide to be cheaters and freeloaders instead). But it seemed quite doubtful (given Glaucon's motivational assumptions) that they would see reason to accept a pact establishing the more extensive demands Socrates' theory would impose. Now, of course, it is Glaucon and not Socrates who wants to see justice as the result of a pact, entered into by people for reasons of their own. Nonetheless, it is still a legitimate question, and Socrates certainly is not going to reject it, what compelling reasons people can be given not only that mutual aid is what justice does demand, but that they should respect and observe that demand (even if it does not arise because of some pact). What, then, does Socrates think about the nature of human desires, that could lead him to think that (given their motivational psychology) people would be able to find good reasons for accepting his demands of justice as mutual aid, and not Glaucon's of mere mutual noninterference? How, on Socrates' theory, do we explain the possibility that people should come to have a corresponding *sense* of justice—a sense that acting against these demands is bad and dishonorable?

As I mentioned, when Socrates begins to describe the origin of cities, he speaks of the people forming a city as wanting to see that their *needs* are met; in particular, their needs for food, clothing, shelter, companions, and continued good health.[9] He does not speak of them at this stage as interested in their pleasures, much less as interested (as Glaucon had it) in some open-ended pursuit of maximum gratification via as large as possible a personal supply of money, property, clients, influence, and so forth. Needs (and the desire to fulfill one's needs) and pleasures (and the desire for pleasure) are importantly different, even if of course the two may coincide in many areas of life. What one needs no doubt includes pleasures of various sorts, and other things that one needs may very well carry pleasures with them. Still, needs as such are different from pleasures, and the desire to obtain what one needs is not the same as the desire for pleasure. For Socrates, people came together to form cities because they were motivated to seek as secure and efficient an arrangement as possible for the ongoing meeting of their basic needs. But anyone's needs are just what their good requires that they have. So Socrates' people, in being motivated to meet their basic needs, are motivated by a desire to secure their good. Thus it is the pursuit of their good that, on Socrates' postulate, leads people to form cities. Socrates, of course, does not put the matter in this explicit way himself. Plato leaves it for alert readers trying to think their own way through the argument to work that out for themselves.

Now, on this assumption about human motivation, it can, I think, seem reasonable to expect human beings—endowed by Zeus with the willingness to live with others on some fair terms of cooperation—to accept the dictates of Socratic justice. What, let us ask, would people motivated to secure their own good and endowed with a willingness to cooperate fairly with others also so motivated see as a rationally acceptable way to cooperate with others in city life? Each, I suggest, would willingly do the work that they can do best to contribute to an increased common stock of means for satisfying human needs of all sorts, in exchange for everyone else doing the same, with the understanding that then they would all mutually draw their personal share from that com-

---

[9] For food, shelter, and clothing, see 369d; good health and companionship enter obliquely at 372b–d (health at 372d2, and cf. 373d1–2, which implies that doctors were needed also, but much less so, in the minimal city).

mon stock. By accepting this, they each increase greatly their capacity to satisfy their individual needs—and the desire to do that is, ex hypothesi, what has been motivating them. Certainly, they can't expect others to take care of *their* needs unless they, too, make a contribution of their own to the needs of others. On the reasonable assumption of a sufficiently wide distribution of talents, capacities, and natural dispositions, Socrates' scheme of each doing what they are best at guarantees both that the others will also be making a maximum contribution and that the result will ensure a maximal stock out of which to supply everyone's needs—a very much greater stock than any single individual working on his own could expect to manage for himself.

So far, I have only argued that people with this Socratic motivation who were establishing a city for their mutual benefit would accept Socrates' principle of justice as a reasonable basis for regulating their common life. Another step is required, however, to show that once they lived in a society that was effectively structured so that people did work in Socrates' way for one another's mutual benefit they, or most of them, would acquire the corresponding sense of justice. To acquire such a sense of justice would mean that they would come to feel that it would be bad and dishonorable (because unfair) for them (or anyone) not to do their fair share, given their particular abilities and talents, to contribute to the common stock of means for satisfying the whole group's needs. Socrates' case here is made easier by the fact that he first considers a relatively simple social structure—Glaucon will call it a "city of pigs," but Socrates insists it is the "true" and "healthy" one (372d4, e6–7). Here, the only goods produced or imported are those needed to satisfy the people's minimum needs simply to maintain a comfortable but thoroughly unluxurious life. This is all the people actually want. That is because, as I mentioned, they are assumed not to be motivated at all by any of that open-ended desire for pleasurable gratification that was the hallmark of human life according to Glaucon's psychological principles. The effect of this exclusion is that these primitive people will experience no, or no effective, positive desire of any sort that might tempt them to cheat or freeload. They are not disposed to pamper themselves, or to go in for leisure-time activities of a pleasurable sort that would tempt them away from their work. They would be satisfied both with the work they are called to do and with the arrangements made in their city for meeting their needs. So, not seeing any reason to cheat or freeload—seeing nothing much to get out of behaving that way—they would surely come to feel that the equal cooperation of all that benefited them so greatly was proper and honorable. They would think, and feel, that those who shirked their duty out of momentary disinclination or tiredness, say, would be behaving badly and dishonorably. So, at any rate, Socrates seems to argue.

Thus, so long as we accept Socrates' idea that, apart from their Zeus-given willingness to live on fair terms of cooperation, all human beings are motivated exclusively by a desire for their own minimal good, we can see how that motivation might lead them not only to accept as reasonable the demands of justice understood as mutual aid, but also to acquire what would appear to be a sense of justice defined in those terms. Of course, as Glaucon and Thrasymachus have already shown, no one should believe that this is the only sort of motivation human beings have. The desire for gratification, for pleasure, as something quite open-ended (and not limited in its nature in the way that any set of true needs will be) is by itself a very powerful motivator too, for any human we know anything about. Socrates does not neglect this point. When Glaucon scornfully dismisses Socrates' minimal first city as suited only for pigs Socrates responds by expanding his city. He introduces what, as I mentioned, he calls "luxuries" of all sorts (372e ff.). In doing this, he is recognizing the presence in human beings, and the power, of desires for pleasures of all sorts (the sort of desires Glaucon and Thrasymachus thought exhausted human motivation), alongside the basic Socratic desire for one's own good. Interestingly, he suggests that accommodating this desire introduces into the city for the first time not only *in*justice but also justice (372e4–6). His thought seems to be that if people were motivated solely by the desire for their basic needs, their basic good, and accordingly never saw any positive inducement not to do their part by working in their own particular way for the common benefit, it would be wrong to say they were acting that way *because it was just*. Justice requires not merely fair taking of turns, so to speak, but doing so with some countervailing motivation *not* to do it, or at least while recognizing that one might get something quite nice if one shirked. So, for it to be appropriately said that they acted that way because it was just to do so, they would have to have overcome some tendency in themselves to act otherwise. In fact, Socrates thinks that it is only the powerful attraction of luxuries and the innate tendency of human beings to follow their open-ended capacity and desire for pleasure, even where it goes against their own good, that could lead them or tempt them to violate the principles of justice as mutual aid. So it is only when we take into account, in addition to people's desire for their own good, their desire for pleasurable gratification through luxuries that we can see justice, properly speaking, playing a role in human life. That being so, I spoke too soon when I said just now that in the primitive first city, people would be motivated by a sense of justice in sticking to their individual work for the common benefit. They might feel it to be dishonorable to shirk—out of tiredness or a temporary disinclination, as I suggested. But that feeling would not express a sense of justice. Really, the sense of justice only first arises when people in the luxurious city, motivated both by their desire for pleasure and their desire for their own good, are nonetheless dominated, as their predecessors in Socrates' story were, by their desire for their good. Here, but not really before, the psychological process described above, leading them to feel it was bad and dishonorable to cheat or freeload, would take the specific form of a sense of fairness or justice. Of course, this would only happen with some of the luxurious city's inhabitants—others, having their desires for pleasure less under the control of their desire for their good, could lack any sense of justice, or have one that was weak and often ineffective. They would be unjust people.

III

It is important to bear in mind that, on Socrates' theory, the dangerous—in principle limitless—desire for pleasure (for gratification) can cause people to act unjustly in either of two ways. It can work directly, leading them to act out of a felt attraction to pleasure, or to some particular pleasure, simply as such—because of the pleasure that it is. They would then find their attraction to pleasure too great to resist, even while recognizing their action as unjust and bad. On the other hand, the desire for pleasure can also affect people's actions more subtly, by causing them to get a distorted idea about where their good actually lies, about what they really need. They can get the idea (this is what happened to Thrasymachus) that, in fact, their own good simply consists in getting as much personal gratification as possible. In the latter case, they can pursue unlimited pleasure both for the pleasure that the pursuit promises, and also for the good that it (allegedly) brings or is. The Oligarchic, the Democratic, and the Tyrannical persons of *Republic* books VIII and IX are examples of this latter sort of case. They are people who have allowed their appetites (for pleasure of various sorts) to get the better of their own judgment about where their good lies. With them, this has happened to such an extent that (as Socrates picturesquely puts it) they force their Reason, the source of their concern for their own good, to sit beside the throne of dominant Appetite (or some particular appetites enthroned at the center of their souls) and think of nothing else as good except what will bring appetitive satisfaction (see 553c–d, 561a–c, 574d–e).

Thus, it seems obvious that what anyone and everyone needs more even than the basic goods provided in Socrates' first city—food, shelter, sex, and friendly companionship—are two things. First, they need some means by which to ensure that their ideas about where their good does lie (in the vast territory beyond the provision of those basic needs) are true and correct. In addition, they need some means to ensure that in their personal decisions and way of life overall, they keep a firm grasp on those ideas and do not fall victim, in either of the two ways just briefly canvassed, to distortions in their decisions and actions. For Socrates (and Plato) it is no easy matter to work out a correct or even halfway adequate understanding of human nature and the needs it gives us, and so of just what principles of living are the ones we should adopt if we are to achieve our good. It may be simple enough to figure out by observation and a little experimentation what the good of a given type of plant or an animal is and so what internal and external conditions such an animal or plant requires in order to live a flourishing and good life. But human nature is vastly more complex. It requires careful reflection and study, wide experience, an open-minded consideration of alternative possibilities, the evaluation of these in the light of possible objections, and so on, to come finally to a justified view on the corresponding questions for a human being.

How, then, are we, whether individually or as a political unit, to achieve a solid understanding of what sort of life would really be best for us? Since this is a question about objective facts, just as the corresponding question about a plant or an animal very obviously is, the answer to it has to be determined by investigation and study. What study is the one we need? It is plain to Socrates that only philosophy, in some version or other, enables us to argue such matters out, coolly and with an open and unprejudiced mind. Only philosophy reveals how to press objections and evaluate their force honestly and with as much human insight and independence of mind as can be mustered, how to think our way into unusual intellectual territory if reason leads us there, and how to keep on going unflinchingly in the face of difficulties as they arise. So if we are to have any chance of achieving our own good, we need philosophical reasoning and philosophical understanding—preferably our own individually. But since very obviously most of us are not up to the task of figuring out for ourselves what life *is* best for us, we need to have in our political community people who *are* up to it, whose lead we can follow. We should give them what they need by way of education and leisure so that they can do for the whole community what they can to help all of us to meet this very pressing need.

Now, the *Republic* is itself a work of philosophical argument on precisely these topics. So Socrates tells us a great deal, especially in book VII (and he at least sketches the philosophical grounds for his opinions), about how the philosophical investigation of these questions would have to proceed. For one thing, he thinks the study of what is truly good for a human being has to be devoted to the investigation of what he calls Forms—not physical objects or traditional ideas or customs or traditional institutions, not the ways things look or how they are represented in common thought and practice, but the full reality that lies behind those appearances. And he thinks that it is mathematical studies that give us the best preliminary grasp of the structures of reality that do lie behind the appearances—both the physical ones and the moral ones. He even gives a rather unclear and half-articulated idea of what the ultimate object of study in the realm of Forms will actually be like. The Form or Idea of the Good will be some paradigm of *rational order,* conceived in some sort of mathematical terms.[10] It is only by knowing all about goodness conceived in those terms, as rational order, that he thinks philosophers will actually be able to do for the rest of us the good that we need from them. So justice will demand that those with the talent for this sort of work actually do it on behalf of the rest of society and pass on the results to everyone else, for the guidance of their lives.

A philosopher, or at least professional teacher and writer of philosophy, might find all this rather gratifying. But no one could seriously think that justice demands that the contemporary philosophical profession be given any unique or even specially privileged place in investigating and directing social policy relating to these questions. Perhaps in ancient times that might have made some sense (or perhaps not), but, in any event, it would not do so today. Still, there is a serious point here of relevance to our own politics. This is that, as a matter of justice, our public institutions should underwrite and foster serious intellectual investigation (not necessarily and certainly not exclusively "academic," and including work in the literary and other arts) that aims at providing well-worked-out and seriously conceived ways of bringing rational order to human lives—with the conviction that this kind of order, together with the related discipline necessary for it, really do lie at the core of any truly good human life. Socrates' account implies that one thing that justice demands is that appropriately talented people should be educated to this task, and that so far as is feasible, given other constraints of justice, the models they create should be made available to and urged upon all, for the betterment of their own lives.

I mentioned just now a second most pressing need of each and every human being, beyond the means by which to obtain correct ideas about how best to live. We also need to ensure that we have the gumption to hold fast to the ideas about rational order that the philosophers and other intellectuals have worked out for us, and do not let our decisions and actions get distorted by our deeply and permanently established, open-ended desire for pleasurable gratification. Here Socrates introduces a third sort of motivation. In *Republic* book IV (435b–441c) Socrates

---

[10] See my discussion in "The Psychology of Justice in Plato," Cooper, *Reason and Emotion,* 142–44, and the passages cited there.

argues that human beings actually have three basic sorts of motivation—not just desires for pleasure and rational concern for our good. The third, which he calls "spirit" or "spirited desires," is the source of the aspiration, which he thinks belongs to every human being in some form or other, to distinguish themselves, to compete in worthwhile enterprises and by dint of hard work and discipline to hold through to the end—in other words, to make something of themselves. This grounds the powerful desire for self-esteem that he thinks every human being, by human nature, is endowed with.[11] With the help of our sense of self-esteem, we can hope to rise above the mere pursuit of pleasure and avoid either of the two sorts of distortions I mentioned. We can learn to bind our sense of self-esteem tightly to our ability to act on our reasoned ideas about our good (or, rather, for most of us, on the ideas we have acquired from what Socrates' philosophers truthfully tell us about it). Relying on those feelings of self-esteem, we can refuse to give in, in any way, to our simple desire for pleasure.

This takes us, at last, back to the topic of justice. Socrates argues in the latter half of book IV that justice really is, basically, just this sort of order within a person's soul as to the basic motivations that each of us by nature experiences. Suppose we have correct ideas, either from our own philosophical understanding of what goodness itself is or from others', plus a well-developed sense of self-esteem tied to our actually living according to those ideas, together with a love of pleasure that is basically in conformance with them. Then that is what it is to be a just person—one living in a properly ordered way. Of course, strictly speaking only someone capable of doing their own philosophical thinking could actually *be* just, since only such a person's reason would truly be in command in their soul, as rational order requires. But the rest of us can in some way approximate to that condition. We can dimly perceive that pleasure is not the good or even the most important type of good among the others. We can dimly perceive that exercising our human powers of control and organization in following a pattern of life that contributes to the common good satisfies our most important human needs. And for the rest we can confidently accept the judgment of others wiser than ourselves—if they truly do know what is best—as to what that pattern should be like. If we do, then we will live in such a way as to make the contribution that, given our individual capacities, talents, and natural dispositions, we can best make to help society as a whole satisfy the needs—both material and, more importantly, psychic—of everyone, ourselves included. That way of life will be a just one, both internally, because of how our souls are struc-

---

[11] See my discussion in "Plato's Theory of Human Motivation," chap. 4 of *Reason and Emotion*, 118–34.

tured, and externally because of what, given a soul so structured, we actually choose to do, and what we do do in our daily lives—namely, mutually look out for one another's good. We choose this life because we recognize that it is just, but even more because we see (even if only dimly) that it is the best life that, given our capacities, talents, and natural dispositions, we are capable of living.

IV

For Socrates, then, the just life led by all is at the same time the best, happiest life for each. At any rate, it is the best and happiest that their individual natural capabilities make possible for them.[12] There is a slight exception, or qualification, to be noted here. Socrates notoriously says in a famous passage near the beginning of book VII (519c–521b) that the philosopher-rulers of his just city will actually not live the best and happiest life *they* are capable of, if they do the just thing and live as rulers with a view to the good of the other citizens in common with their own, and do not lead a retired life aimed solely at their own philosophical fulfilment.[13]

---

[12] In saying this I gloss over important questions about Plato's views in the *Republic* concerning the capacity of ordinary people (indeed, of anyone except a committed and accomplished philosopher) to live happily at all—to any degree or at any level. In *Plato's Utopia Recast*, Christopher Bobonich argues that, on the *Republic*'s view, because no one but a philosopher has any inkling of what makes anything good (i.e., what the goodness of any good thing consists in), other people cannot obtain any value from anything they do or experience that might in fact, objectively speaking, really be good. Hence their life could not correctly be described as good at all (for them). (Bobonich argues that in the *Laws* and *Statesman*, in "recasting" his Utopia, Plato now recognizes that even without philosophy, people can come to understand enough about what goodness itself is so that they can come to live happily and well—even if not, of course, as happily and well as a fully accomplished philosopher.) Even on the *Republic*'s understanding, ordinary people's imitation of the truly just life of the philosophers would make their life, if not the best and happiest they were capable of, at any rate the least bad and least miserable possible for them. That will do for my purposes here.

[13] I have discussed this passage previously in "The Psychology of Justice in Plato" (1977), sect. III (see Cooper, *Reason and Emotion*, 144–49). In what follows I supplement what I said there in two ways. First, I bring into account Plato's explicitly political motivation in writing the *Republic*—his criticism of institutions and practices in the politics of the Greek cities at the time when he was writing. Secondly, I want to clarify the implications of my way of taking this passage for the question of Plato's eudaemonism (or lack of the same) in the theory of practical reason—whether Plato does, or does not, hold that rational pursuit of anything always involves pursuit of one's own good (one's *eudaimonia*) as one's (sole) ultimate end in that, or any, pursuit. In thinking through this passage again, and formulating this clarification, I have been helped by T. H. Irwin's "The Monism of Practical Reason," read

In addressing the questions this passage raises, I want to begin by saying something about Plato's project in the *Republic* as a whole, and about the orientation toward politics of its surface organization. Political discussions, about the best state and the details of its internal organization, occupy the foreground of a great deal of the work's argument—not the psychological and ethical questions I have been discussing so far. So Plato's principal objective, it might seem, is to establish the provocative thesis that democracy—which many then and now would think is the best, and certainly the most just, form of government—is in fact (almost) the worst, almost the most *un*just, of all political orders. There is only one exception, tyranny by one man and his henchmen over all the rest of the inhabitants of a state, whom these make their slaves—a sort of rule that no one except the tyrant himself or his henchmen could have a good word for, and even with the latter the good word would have to be uttered in irony. To be sure, the better order that Plato proposes as an antidote to the damage he thinks democracy does to the people living under it is not very much like any of the real-world alternatives known in any of the Greek cities (or today, either). It is fundamentally unlike rule by committees (elected or not) of the rich or the landed families, rule by committees drawn from the better educated, rule by absentee kings (or resident ones, either), rule by officials elected by the people, rule by the military. These were the principal alternatives, then as now. So it would be a serious mistake to count Plato in the *Republic* as taking sides in existing political debates at Athens, and favoring, for example, traditional oligarchic rule or the rule of the traditional landed families—rule by the traditional "elites" as against the mass of the people, to use Josh Ober's preferred terminology.[14] His allegedly better political order is a completely unheard-of type of rule, under the authority of philosophers who, as I have mentioned, have come to understand the allegedly true and sole adequate basis for judging anything at all to be good. As a result, these philosopher-rulers know what is good for individual persons (with their different capacities and tendencies) and for whole classes or orders of people (with their different contributions to make to the common good) who live together in a unified, politically independent community of the Greek sort. Plato's claim is that a rigidly hierarchical social and political order, under the direction of true philosophers, who really do know the ultimate basis on which anything at all is good for anyone, will give to the citizen population—all of it, it must be emphasized, with only a slight

---

to the Eastern Division meeting of the American Philosophical Association, Boston, December 1999. I thank Professor Irwin for making available to me a text of his presentation.
[14] See Josh Ober, *Political Dissent in Democratic Athens*.

question about themselves—the best life that they individually or corporately are capable of living.

In the passage of book VII (519c–521b) that I mentioned, Socrates concludes that what we can call the "complete" philosophers, who have finished the course of prescribed education and whose arduous dialectical training has brought them to a firm grasp of the nature of goodness itself, will be (and will have to be) "forced" to spend some of the rest of their days overseeing the government of their city. That suggests that the philosophers will have to sacrifice something, that they will live less well than they might have lived, if they do undertake this rule on behalf of the others (and themselves, too, of course, as citizens sharing in civic life). Socrates speaks of himself together with Glaucon and Adeimantus, the notional "founders" of the city, as the ones who will do the forcing (520a8–9). But, of course, he has to mean instead (as every reader is expected to see) that the complete philosophers (they, after all, are the sole rulers in the city) will maintain it as a practice for themselves, and so "force" *themselves,* to take turns in the political oversight of the guards and, through that, the lives of the rest of the people (while legitimately reserving to themselves ample leisure to continue, by turns, their philosophical pursuits). Well, then, what will the philosophers' reasons be for adhering to such a practice? Prompted by Socrates, Glaucon says they will do it because they are just people, and the founders' demand is a just one (520e1). Under the city's constitution the rest of the citizens have contributed, through the work they do, to the leisure and to the philosophical education of those destined to become complete philosophers, so it is only fair and just if the philosophers in return do their part in maintaining the constitution, with its benefits for the others (as well, of course, as for themselves and their successors).

Yes: the philosophers *are* just people. So they have a highly effective sense of justice which will lead them to accept this demand: it certainly does seem a just one, on Socrates' theory of justice as mutual aid. But the philosophers will certainly also adhere to Socrates' own principle (see 505d11–506b2) that one should do justice (like anything else truly worthwhile) also, and indeed first of all, because of the good that is in it—the "benefit" (ὄφελος) it gives you. For Socrates in the *Republic,* goodness *is* rational order. So the philosophers will adhere to this just requirement, in part, because in doing so they will advance, and virtually guarantee, the continuance of the beautiful order within the complex human life of the community brought about (or constituted) by people's living justly—the philosophers themselves, along with the members of the other two orders. Knowing the good as rational order in general, and because rational beings, simply as such, love and admire rational order, they will have a strong attachment to this specific instantiation, which they and only they can bring into existence. (Grander instantiations, such as that of the whole cosmic order, are obviously well beyond their reach. That goes on in its own way without any possible helpful input or interference from themselves.) With his rhetorical question at 520d6–7 ("they won't refuse, will they?") Socrates reasonably implies, therefore, that in adhering to this requirement they willingly choose this way of life over the life that he says they are required—and so, will require themselves—to renounce, namely "the life of genuine philosophy" (τὸν τῆς ἀληθινῆς φιλοσοφίας, 521b2).

In that renounced life one would spend all one's free time in philosophical reflection and in admiration of the final truths one has attained through Platonic dialectic. So the complete philosophers must hold that their pursuit, as rational beings, of the Good or rational order in general, and their firm decision to order their own lives in relation primarily to that pursuit, requires that they accept this life not only as the most just, but also as the best one for themselves—at any rate, it is, as they will clearly see, the best available to them—*given the circumstances*. If they make a sacrifice for the sake of justice and for the sake of their fellow citizens, this sacrifice is also made for the sake of their own self-enhancing pursuit of the good. Paradoxically, perhaps, but truly according to Socrates' theory, if, in deference to their passion for philosophical thinking, they refused to do the just thing, they would *miss* the value to themselves of that knowledge of the Forms and the Good that they would professedly be indulging exclusively in. That choice could only reflect a certain *dis*order in their own souls—the disorder in which injustice consists. On Socrates' theory of the virtues, being just and acting justly is also living well—living in accordance with what is personally and individually best for the just agent.

One could put Socrates' point as follows. The philosophers know in full detail what rational order is, in itself. As rational agents they love and admire rational order, wherever it is to be found, and have at least some positive interest in imposing it or bringing it about wherever they might be able to. Equally—indeed, even more—as rational agents they aim at the highest instantiation possible of rational order within their own souls and their own lives. And they see (given the external conditions provided by nature at large and by the natural capacities of the human beings they live with) that the most orderly way of life for them would be this one, which combines political rule with philosophical reflection. Thus the leading immediate aims of their actions are, respectively, the orderly life of the whole community (including the progress in philosophical understanding attained under their tutelage by the young philosophers-to-be) and the orderly abstract thinking inherent in their own philosophical contemplation. But they pursue these aims in this combined way because, as they can see, these really are the aims, in their circumstances, the pursuit of which will reflect and maintain the rational order within their own souls and their own lives. Thus only one of their underlying aims is the promotion or enjoyment of some state or activity private to themselves—their contemplation. The rest are good states or activities of other people. Nonetheless, their own good, as rational agents, consists in maintaining rational order in their souls and their lives through the pursuit of these aims in that combined way. It is this that Socrates means to say they would lose if, instead, they chose to drop these latter subordinate aims in favor of an exclusive concentration on the former.

Socrates does not clearly state these plain implications of his own previous argument. Instead he contents himself with the simple statement I have already mentioned: that the founders will require and "force" the philosophers to rule, even after they have become complete in philosophy, and to renounce the life of "genuine" philosophy. That is apparently because he wants to insist that no city can be well ruled if those in power have no conception of a way of life better than the "political life" (βίος πολιτικός, 521b9–10), the life whose focus and high point is the exercise of political power, through administering those "political offices" that philosophers themselves look down on (521b1–2). In all ordinary cities the unavoidable result is an unending contest, extremely harmful to the common good, among opposing political factions for what they regard as the privilege of rule. Socrates introduced this theme already in his debate with Thrasymachus (346e7–347d8). In returning to it now he runs the risk of leaving the reader with the impression that his philosophers will turn to rule only because they are forced to, perhaps by dislike of being ruled by their inferiors (see 347d1–2), and in any event with a sense of sacrificing their own good—and not because of their overriding devotion to the good order they can bring to their own and others' lives by such an undertaking. Indeed, the philosophers do know from their firsthand experience how much better and more satisfying the highest intellectual activities are. They know how much more satisfying would be a life focused, not at all on political power, but simply on philosophy, involving no activities of ruling, if only circumstances made it rational for them, individually and collectively, to choose it. In that important sense they do not choose political activities for their own sakes, or even as anything particularly good or worthwhile. They choose them as a second best, something forced on them by the circumstances of human life—specifically, by the need that even the best attainable human community has of their rule, if good order (something that, as rational beings, they care about very greatly) is to hold sway within it. However, the life they choose is not a "political life," but in fact a philosophical one after all: it may not be a "life of genuine philosophy" as that was specified at 521b2, but it *is* a philosophical life—one with a secondary commitment to political rule—not a "political life" in the sense given to that phrase at 521b9–10.

In fact, however, as I have said, in choosing this life over a life of pure ("genuine") philosophy, they do not sacrifice their own good. What they care most about is the rational order of the lives they lead in pursuing and enjoying rational order more generally. Given circumstances outside their control, the other choice would actually achieve less well what they most want. Socrates naturally neglects to spell all these complications out here. To do so would muddy, at least in the minds of many of Plato's readers, the important contrast that, given his heavy emphasis on political questions in writing the work, Plato wishes to insist on between the high-minded politics of his ideal city and the competitive, grasping politics of all existing ones. They might wrongly think that even in Plato's city the rulers act as rulers ultimately for their own private good or enjoyment. Plato's point is that if they *did* seek their own private good or enjoyment, the life they would choose would quite certainly not be the one they do choose, but rather the life of "genuine" philosophy. The careful reader should see that, nonetheless, this mixed intellectual-cum-political life *is* the best his philosophers can live, given what Socrates believes to be unavoidable and unalterable facts about the human beings making up any community. The difference, then, between the philosophers and the other citizens, which requires that slight exception or qualification to my claim that Socrates' city will give its citizens the best life that they individually or corporately are capable of living, amounts merely to the following. Extraneous circumstances prevent the city from giving the philosophers, but only them, the best life of which (if only circumstances were ideal) their natural disposition, talent, and self-education makes them capable. When that qualification is taken into account, it remains true on Socrates' theory that, because the human good is a corporate and never a merely individual accomplishment, the just life led by all is at the same time the best, happiest life for each.

V

Earlier, we saw that on Thrasymachus's and Glaucon's assumptions about human psychology, life is a zero-sum game. Through luck, or ingenuity, or greater power, some get more than others of the alleged goods of life—namely, the means for gratifying their limitless desires for pleasure. The others are correspondingly deprived of such goods. Given the limited quantity of means by which to develop and then satisfy such desires as they arise, each one's good is secured, to the extent that it actually can be, at others' expense. Since each wants to control as many as possible (ideally, all) of these means, any increase in any individual's good entails a decrease in all the others'. And, more important, each person's good is secured by the efforts and talent (or the sheer luck) of that single individual (plus any friends he or she might recruit). But on Socrates's theory of human motivation, and his theory of the human good, a common and joint enterprise of all is needed if the good of any of us is to be achieved to any worthwhile degree. We are none of us self-sufficient. None of us can achieve our good except by working together for our mutual assistance, as justice demands, in the pursuit of our good—each in the way that most suits his or her individual nature. On Socrates' account, the individual human good—a well-ordered life for each of us individually, which contributes to that larger well-ordering that constitutes our common life together in society—is a fundamentally social achievement, not one that any of us could manage on our own.

Where does Plato stand in this dispute about the human good and the nature of justice? Both the Glaucon and the Socrates of the *Republic*, together with their contrasted opinions on these questions, are *Plato's* creations. But the dialogue crowns Socrates with victory, not Glaucon (or Thrasymachus). So we can surely conclude that Plato stands, in the end, on Socrates' side. Socrates' views are, however, at best, more inspiring than they are satisfactorily worked out. The continued interplay throughout the work between Glaucon's negative, libertarian views and Socrates' positive, communitarian ones poses for us a challenge—as I think it did, and was meant to do, for Plato's contemporaries. How do we reconcile justice conceived as acting reciprocally for one another's good with the just demands of individuals for the free pursuit of their own gratifications—acting on their own ideas, if you like, of where their good lies? Plato's *Republic* introduced these questions into our philosophical, and our political, tradition. As we continue to wrestle with them today, its interest and value are by no means spent.[15]

---

[15] I thank Alexander Nehamas and Michael Frede for helpful discussions of an earlier version of this lecture, and an audience in Houston of Rice University and University of Houston faculty and students for their comments and questions when I read a paper there drawn from these materials. I have made many improvements as a result. I should acknowledge particularly Michael Frede's suggestion that Glaucon may be assuming Protagoras's view from the *Protagoras* about the natural disposition of human beings to want to live with one another on a basis of fair cooperation—though Glaucon might equally be reflecting similar ideas in tragic and other poetry of his own and earlier times.

CHAPTER 11

PLATO AND ARISTOTLE ON "FINALITY"

AND "(SELF-)SUFFICIENCY"

I

IN THE FIRST PART of chapter 7 of the first book of the *Nicomachean Ethics* (*NE*), Aristotle proposes two criteria for the specification of that good which he has been investigating since the first two introductory chapters of the work (i.e., τὸ ζητούμενον ἀγαθόν, I 7, 1097a15). This is the "end of action(s)" (τέλος τῶν πρακτῶν, I 2, 1094a18–19) or "the good and the best thing" (τἀγαθὸν καὶ τὸ ἄριστον, a22) or "the highest of all the goods achievable by action" (τὸ πάντων ἀκρότατον τῶν πρακτῶν ἀγαθῶν, I 4, 1095a16–17). Aristotle's proposed criteria are that this good should be one that is "unqualifiedly final" (alternatively, "unqualifiedly an end," ἁπλῶς τέλειον, I 7, 1097a33), and that it should be "self-sufficient" (αὔταρκες, b8). He takes care to explain what he means by these criterial terms, and to connect the two criteria together (I will come back in sect. III to these explanations: among other things of interest, they require that we present the first criterion in terms of "finality," as I have just done—not, as most often happens nowadays, completeness or perfection). Aristotle concludes the first part of the chapter by using these two criteria to argue that this good is in fact εὐδαιμονία (1097a34, b15–16)—I leave this Greek word untranslated (for reasons I will explain later, at the beginning of sect. IV). In the remainder of the chapter, Aristotle first gives an argument that *eudaimonia* itself is to be equated with exercise or activity of the soul that derives from and expresses the soul's excellence or virtue (ψυχῆς ἐνέργεια κατ' ἀρετήν)—or that, perhaps, it is activity deriving instead from the soul's "best and most final virtue" (κατὰ τὴν ἀρίστην καὶ τελειοτάτην) (1098a16–18). (Below I will have a good deal to say about this equation and the significance of his reference here to activity of the soul's best and most final virtue: see the last three paragraphs of sect. IV.) Then (a20 ff.) he comments on the limited informativeness of this equation while nonetheless emphasizing its importance, since for him it provides the basic principle (ἀρχή, b3, 7) for the philosophical understanding of how human life should be organized and led.

It has long been recognized that in proposing his two criteria for the specification of the highest good—finality and self-sufficiency, as I will call them—Aristotle is indebted to, and somehow follows, Socrates' discussion with Protarchus in Plato's *Philebus*, 20b–23b. There, using criteria quite similar to Aristotle's own, Socrates argues, and Protarchus is brought to agree, that neither pleasure (ἡδονή) nor mind or reason (νοῦς, φρόνησις) can be that by having which in it a life is made happy,[1] that is, that neither of these can be "*the* good" (τἀγαθόν, cf. 14b4, 22b4). Instead, Socrates argues and Protarchus agrees (eventually), only some or other so-called mixed life (mixed: συναμφότερος, 22a1; κοινός, a2, c7, d1; μεικτός, d7), one that has both pleasure and reason in it as ingredients or constituents, would be a, or the, life worth choosing. It follows, Socrates says, that the good would be whatever, belonging to the mixed life, is "sufficient" (ἱκανός, 22b1, 4) and makes it choiceworthy and good (αἱρετὸς ἅμα καὶ ἀγαθός, d7). Neither pleasure nor reason, then, is *the* good; *the* good is some third thing yet to be discovered. Only this third thing, being *the* good, can be what makes a life choiceworthy, good, and happy.

Socrates begins his argument for these conclusions (20d) by obtaining Protarchus's preliminary agreement on three apparently distinct, and perhaps even mutually independent and parallel, conditions on, or criteria for, what can count as *the* good: it is because both pleasure and reason fail these conditions that he will go on to argue that neither is the good. He says first, that the good must be τέλεον ("final" or "endlike"),[2] then

---

[1] See 11d4–6: Socrates announces at the outset that the debate concerns which "possession or disposition of the soul" (ἕξιν ψυχῆς καὶ διάθεσιν) can provide for all human beings a happy life, τὴν δυναμένην ἀνθρώποις πᾶσι τὸν βίον εὐδαίμονα παρέχειν. See also Protarchus's reformulation at 19c5–6: πρὸς τὸ διελέσθαι τί τῶν ἀνθρωπίνων κτημάτων ἄριστον.

[2] I translate Plato's τέλεον here as "final" or "endlike," rather than, e.g., "complete" or "perfect," partly in anticipation of Aristotle's understanding, which he carefully explains at *NE* I 7, 1097a25–34, of this same word (in a variant spelling) to express one of his own criteria for the highest good—a criterion obviously borrowed from Socrates in this passage. (See my discussion in sect. III, paragraph 2 ff., below.) But I also think, independently of Aristotle's apparent understanding of what the term means in Plato, that the translation "complete" would not convey correctly what Socrates has in mind (although, as I point out below, Socrates says nothing at all to explain what he understands by being τέλεον or why he thinks that it is a suitable criterion for the identification of the good). Socrates endorses these three criteria as guides in his own search for the good, after rejecting the claims of pleasure and reason, and the account he finally accepts (see below, sect. II, last paragraph) does not make the good some "complete" combination of lots of independently good things, with nothing missing—as the translation "complete" would necessarily imply. On the contrary, the closest Socrates can come to specifying the good is to name a value property that a life possesses because of the way the leading goods ingredient in it are combined together. To be sure, Socrates does insist that the good be "lacking in nothing," but that is the burden not of this criterion but of "sufficiency"—and the latter turns out also not to require that the good *be* some complete combination of good things. Thus if, as seems to be

that it must be "sufficient" (ἱκανόν), and thirdly that "anything that knows the good hunts and pursues it, wishing to choose it and possess it for its own, and does not bother about anything else except what is accomplished always together with things that are good."³ Socrates does not explain how he understands the first two criteria, those of finality, or end-likeness, and sufficiency. Nonetheless, despite the variation from Plato's ἱκανόν to his own αὔταρκες, to which I will return (pp. 283–84 below), it is plain that these requirements must correspond closely somehow to Aristotle's pair: Aristotle must have this passage in mind in *NE* I 7, and must somehow be following Socrates' example when he uses his criteria of finality and self-sufficiency to identify the highest good as *eudaimonia* and to specify it as activity deriving from and expressing the soul's virtue. However, as I will explain, the conclusion Aristotle reaches through the use of his two criteria is in fact very different from Socrates': it goes in a direction Socrates thought actually precluded by acceptance of his closely related triplet of criteria. In order to understand and assess Aristotle's conclusion, and his use of his criteria to reach it, it will be necessary to spend time first considering this passage of the *Philebus* quite closely.

II

I mentioned that Socrates presents his three criteria (20d) one after the other, as separate, parallel conditions. And later, in declaring his verdict that neither pleasure nor reason is the good, he clearly mentions each of the three. He clearly thinks he has shown that each of the candidates has failed each of the tests. In order to test the claims of pleasure and reason to be the good, he has discussed the life chockful of pleasure but totally lacking all functions of reason, and the life chockful of reason but devoid of pleasure. In declaring his verdict, he says (22b3–6): "So isn't it perfectly clear about these [lives], that neither of the two had in it the good? For it would have been sufficient, and final, and choiceworthy for all plants and animals, whichever ones were able to live in that way always throughout their life."⁴ In fact, however, he has argued in two steps, not

---

the case, in presenting his own criterion of being τέλειον in terms of finality, Aristotle is in effect offering an interpretation of what Socrates meant by his requirement that the good be τέλεον, I think he is offering the correct interpretation.

³ The Greek for the third condition is this: πᾶν τὸ γιγνῶσκον αὐτὸ θηρεύει καὶ ἐφίεται βουλόμενον ἑλεῖν καὶ περὶ αὐτὸ κτήσασθαι, καὶ τῶν ἄλλων οὐδὲν φροντίζει πλὴν τῶν ἀποτελουμένων ἅμα ἀγαθοῖς (20d8–10).

⁴ Μῶν οὖν οὐκ ἤδη τούτων γε πέρι δῆλον ὡς οὐδέτερος αὐτοῖν εἶχε τἀγαθόν; ἦν γὰρ ἂν ἱκανὸς καὶ τέλεος καὶ πᾶσι φυτοῖς καὶ ζῴοις αἱρετός, οἷσπερ δυνατὸν ἦν οὕτως ἀεὶ διὰ βίου ζῆν.

three: first, that each life needs (προσδεῖσθαι, 20e6; προσδεῖν, 21a11) something else beyond the pleasure or the reason that each respectively is fully supplied with, and then, in consequence, that neither life is choice-worthy. This is quite explicit in his examination of the life of pleasure (as I will explain just below), and it is plainly implied also for the life of reason.[5] Now, needing or not needing something further seems plainly linked to the sufficiency criterion; and the choiceworthiness or not of a life is plainly linked to the third criterion ("anything that knows the good wishes to choose it"). So Socrates argues from the insufficiency of these lives to their unchoiceworthiness—thus linking his criteria of sufficiency and choiceworthiness to each other. For Socrates, a life can be choiceworthy only if it is sufficient. But there is nothing in Socrates' argument that specifically draws on or relates to the good's being final or endlike. If nonetheless, as I have said, in giving his verdict Socrates thinks he has shown that neither pleasure nor reason satisfies the finality criterion any more than his other two, this is presumably because he silently presupposes that if some good is insufficient it is also not final. Any good that was insufficient, Socrates may think, would thereby show that there was some further end lying beyond or above it that was still unachieved when one possessed just it. (I return to this point below, pp. 282–83.)

Let us then consider Socrates' argument—his argument against the life of pleasure, since that is the only one he sets out in full. He imagines a person living his whole life through while experiencing *the greatest pleasures* at every moment but devoid of all rational capacities. Would Protarchus, an announced proponent of pleasure's claim to be the good, not think he needed anything further? Naturally enough, Protarchus at first replies that he would not (21a13): after all, having no deficiency of pleasure, what else could he need in order to be leading the best and the happy life,

---

[5] The examination of the life of reason, which follows immediately upon that of the life of pleasure, is abbreviated (21d6-e4). Socrates simply asks Protarchus whether anyone would "accept" that life (δέξαιτ' ἄν), and Protarchus answers "no" immediately in this second case, without further explanation. Socrates begins his examination of the life of pleasure (21a8) with the same question ("Would you accept ... ?"). But in that case Protarchus responds, "Why not?" So Socrates does not need to go through the details in the case of reason, as he has had to do for pleasure. However, he has indicated at 20e5–21a2, in announcing the tests to be administered to the two lives, that the question will be whether either "is in need at all of anything else" (besides its pleasures or reasonings respectively); and when Protarchus finally does (implicitly) agree that he would not, after all, "accept" the life of pleasure, he does so on the basis that that life is not choiceworthy, because something else is needed that it does not provide or contain (21d3–5). So both steps are implied also for the second examination too, that of the life of reason. Protarchus's rejection of that life is implied to be on the basis that because it needs something further, it is not choiceworthy. (As we will see, it is this inference that Aristotle disputes, and that his reformulation, and revision, of Socrates' criteria is aimed at avoiding.)

if indeed pleasure is the good—his announced position in the debate? Socrates points out, though, that if *ex hypothesi* he were devoid of all rational capacities, he would be unable, first, to realize that he was enjoying those pleasures at any moment when he was in fact enjoying them (that is, was enjoyably aware *of* them); also, second, he could not remember that he enjoyed the extreme pleasures of the past, since no memory would remain of any pleasure enjoyed in any present moment;[6] and, third, he could not figure out (and so anticipate) that he was going to enjoy great pleasures in the future (even if he was in fact going to). Present awareness *that,* memory, and calculation as to the future, are all functions of reason; so, lacking reason *ex hypothesi,* he would have no capacity for awareness *that,* memory, or calculation, not even in relation to these very great pleasures (the greatest, 21a9) that he would nonetheless be enjoying, that is, aware *of.* Could Protarchus really think he did not need these functions of reason, in addition to the greatest pleasures at every moment, in order to have an acceptable life?

Now, we need not, and certainly we should not, suppose that Socrates or Plato is cheating here, and that when Protarchus abandons his position in the face of these facts he does so simply because he thinks that having such awareness (awareness that), memory, and anticipatory powers would give him additional pleasures, very great ones. In that case, his devotion to pleasure as the good would itself require that he have these powers if in fact he is to live throughout his life enjoying the *greatest* pleasures (as Socrates hypothesizes he would in fact be doing in living the "life of pleasure"). If that is what he had in mind, then of course he ought never to have allowed Socrates to construe him as giving up the idea that

---

[6] Plato writes quite carefully here. The memory that Socrates says Protarchus would lack if he were deprived of reasoning "and everything related to it" (21b1) is memory-that, i.e., "that he had ever enjoyed himself." This memory is "propositional," just as the present awareness and anticipation of the future here referred to are. The Greek is: ἀνάγκη δήπου μηδ' ὅτι ποτὲ ἔχαιρες μεμνῆσθαι. However, Socrates immediately adds, as if in explanation: τῆς τ' ἐν τῷ παραχρῆμα ἡδονῆς προσπιπτούσης μηδ' ἡντινοῦν μνήμην ὑπομένειν, "and [it is necessary that] no memory at all would remain of the pleasure befalling you at the moment." If by this addition Socrates means to say that the reason why you would have no memory that you had enjoyed yourself when you did is that no trace of that pleasure survives in memory for you to recall at all, then Protarchus might well have objected. Presumably at least some irrational animals have memories, though they do not have memories-that; so, merely by being deprived of all reasoning power, Protarchus would not necessarily have lost all his memories of his experiences. However that may be, I take it that Protarchus has understood Socrates correctly about the principal point intended, viz., that he would lack all memory-that. He accepts that this, alongside failure to be aware-that and to anticipate-that, would be a very great loss; he values highly that kind of memory (in addition, perhaps, to its presupposition, bare event memory). This seems to me a reasonable admission on Protarchus's part.

pleasure is the good because of the admitted need for awareness that, memory, and calculation for the future. And Socrates should never have said that Protarchus's acceptance of these needs entailed the denial of his earlier position. No: in posing his hypothesis, Socrates is explicit that even without these powers a person might enjoy the *greatest* pleasures throughout his life, without remission (21a8–9). Therefore, if Protarchus understands the position, he does not accept the need for reasoning because without reasoning he cannot obtain the greatest pleasures, as it were in the first place. And even if Protarchus does value reasoning (as, presumably, he does) only insofar as it makes available to him the use of these rational powers *in relation to* present, past, and future enjoyments of pleasure, his response shows that he recognizes some extra and inherent value in reasoning itself (but only when so related), in addition to the value that, of course, he has accorded to the enjoyment of pleasure (including any pleasure he might get *in* using reason in these ways). Of course, it may be that Protarchus *is* too stupid to follow the argument, and only agrees that he would need reasoning in addition to pleasure if his life is to be happy, because he thinks that even having (or enjoying) all the greatest pleasures requires reasoning directed to present, past, or future states of pleasure. (How could we tell? He does not say anything about why he agrees; he just agrees.) Even so, no reader should suppose that that is what Socrates (or Plato) is arguing. Socrates is arguing that anyone who thinks about it (see the τις at 21d9, and similar language at e4, 22a5–6, b1–2), not just Protarchus in his presumed stupidity, will have to agree that reasoning does matter—that however much they might value pleasure, they also value reasoning (awareness that, memory, calculating anticipation) quite independently of any relation these may have to *getting* pleasure: reasoning powers are needed, in addition to pleasure, if any human being is to lead a happy life.[7]

---

[7] That this is what Socrates means to be arguing is placed beyond doubt toward the end of the dialogue (60d3–e7), when Socrates reviews his and Protarchus's discussion here and they both confirm its outcome: there, the question Protarchus answers no to is "whether he would want pleasure, as much and as intensive as it might be, without the true opinion that he enjoys it" (d7–9, trans. Frede).

As I mentioned, Protarchus presumably only concedes this need because he recognizes some added value in being aware that one is enjoying pleasure when one in fact is enjoying it, or in recalling it or reliably expecting it for the future—a value beyond that of any pleasure one takes in such acts of reasoning. Socrates goes on, as we will see, to speak as if some value has been conceded to reasoning without these limitations of subject matter. I think that is fair enough: once anyone sees the need, even on Protarchus's presumed ground, for the concession, it is clear enough that they have no good basis for insisting on the limitation. Whatever value there is inherent in any given acts of reasoning, qua acts of reasoning, must surely be replicable in some other acts with different contents or of different types.

To me, Socrates seems undoubtedly right in this claim. Protarchus was right to concede that more than pleasure is needed for any acceptable human life. Anyone who considers the matter must see this, even someone who loves pleasure with an overwhelming passion. In fact, Socrates says and Protarchus obviously agrees, the life chockful of pleasure but devoid of all reasoning is not a human life at all, but that perhaps of a sea-lung or oyster (21c6–8). When, having said this, Socrates asks (d3, invoking now his third criterion) whether such a life would be choiceworthy for us (αἱρετὸς ἡμῖν), Protarchus is stymied; he has nothing to reply. He sees clearly, or thinks he does, that it would not be. And this is to the detriment of his candidate for the good, since according to the third criterion anything that knows the good chooses it: if pleasure really were the good, then, we would have to choose it, and so also the life that contains it in abundance. Such a life would be among the things that are "accomplished always together with things that are good," and things so accomplished, according to the third criterion, are the sorts of things, and the only ones besides pleasures themselves, that we would have to concern ourselves for, if pleasure were the good. But it is not only for us that this life, chockful of pleasure, would not be choiceworthy, according to Socrates' argument. It would not be choiceworthy for *any* animal (not even the sea-lung or oyster who, if lucky, lived that way) or indeed for any plant, he says (22b5–6)—adding plants to what Protarchus himself claimed about all animals (22b1–2)! This too seems to me an entirely reasonable claim, when properly understood. Socrates' claim is that an oyster or plant whose natural capacities limited it so that the only good thing it can be aware of is pleasure would have nothing in its life that would make that life worth *choosing*. To be sure, one could prefer on its behalf, and hope, that it got a life of continuous extreme pleasure, and one could certainly rank such a life ahead of the alternatives available to it (ones with lots of pain, say). One could even, I would grant, count the life chockful of pleasure as a better, indeed a good life, for such a creature. But that would not make it one *worth choosing*: better still, perhaps, not to be born at all, or to die immediately after birth and not have to live a life— better than to be condemned by this "unhappy necessity" of your nature (cf. τινος ἀνάγκης οὐκ εὐδαίμονος, 22b6–7) to a life chockful of pleasure, but devoid of all functions of reason, as the best you can live. Of course, the plant or oyster does not have any choice in the matter; indeed, the very absence from its nature of all powers of reason carries with it the absence of the power of choice. So, it will live on, or not, helplessly— whether with a life of unending greatest pleasure, or one with some pain, or one with nothing but pain all the way through. But if it *did* have the power to survey lives beforehand and to make a choice, before losing the power to choose anything at all by coming to life, it could not choose *this* one, however good it might nonetheless recognize it to be for the one living it. To *choose* a life, it seems, implies that there is something in it so good that you would choose life itself, because of its presence in it, in preference to not coming to life at all—and pleasure is not a good of that kind. So anyhow Socrates seems to be thinking.[8] And very reasonably so, I should say.

Now, as I mentioned, Protarchus also thinks that the life chockful of reasoning is not choiceworthy (21e7–8). Pleasure, too, is needed in a choiceworthy life, he thinks, as well as the reasoning that he has already conceded is needed. Thus the life chockful of reasoning too, in his opinion, is lacking in something, and so (on both grounds) reason also— Socrates' initial candidate—cannot count as the good. However, the mixed life—that is, one chockful of both the greatest pleasures and all sorts of reasonings about everything (d9–10)[9]—seems to him choiceworthy, and the only one of the three that is. Socrates agrees (22b3–8).[10] If that is so, then, the good must be contained in some life that has both pleasure and reasoning in it: as the third criterion has made explicit, those who know the good choose it and so far as other things go (including lives) concern themselves solely with those that are accomplished with goods. What then can the good be—this thing that is in the mixed life and that by its presence makes that life a good and happy one? That is the main question with which Socrates' and Protarchus's discussion is occupied through the remainder of the dialogue.

[8] I should emphasize that the connection I have made here, and subsequently, between the choiceworthiness of a life and that life's being worth living at all is mine; Socrates himself does not explicitly draw it. Nonetheless, it seems to me the best way of understanding and making good sense of his repeated claim that a life chockful of pleasure but devoid of reasoning would not be choiceworthy—not even for an oyster or a blade of grass. See further n. 24 below.

[9] At 22a3 Socrates specifies the mixed life, upon his introduction of it, simply as mixed "from pleasure plus reason and reasoning" (νοῦ καὶ φρονήσεως), but I take it from the preceding context that when Protarchus agrees that the mixed life is choiceworthy we are to understand him as meaning one that merges the other two lives—and those were not merely lives of pleasure and reason, respectively, but of each at its highest and most complete level. As the dialogue proceeds, however, Socrates treats the mixed life more loosely, as simply one that has both pleasures and reasonings in it—leaving open for further consideration both which pleasures and which reasonings these will be, and how they are to be combined and mixed.

[10] A bit later Socrates seems to maintain that reason can be the good, after all, and so he confusingly appears to revoke his acceptance of Protarchus's judgment that the life of reason, too, is not choiceworthy (22c5). However, he restricts this claim to divine reason—human reason, the subject of the earlier discussion, he grants, is in a different condition. As reason exists *within* the physical world, reason and reasoning are not the good, then, Socrates continues to think. The conclusion of the preceding argument stands: a life that had the highest degree and extent of reasoning in it would still not be choiceworthy for us, or any other animal or plant that was naturally equipped to lead it, if it totally lacked pleasure.

Now, we can speak of the constituents of a life as all the activities and experiences, whether conscious or not, that make it up. So far, then, Socrates' argument has excluded the two principal constituents of the choiceworthy mixed life, at least if taken singly, from being the good: neither the reasonings nor the pleasures that this life contains can be counted as the good in it, by the presence of which it itself is a happy one. So it is no surprise eventually to learn that, on Socrates' view, not even the combination of these needed constituents—the reasonings and the pleasures taken together—are the good. Instead, he argues, the good in the mixed life derives from the *way* the two ingredients are combined. I will not go into his arguments, but his final view, set out at 64c–65a, is this: The good—or rather, that in the mixed life which is responsible for its being a good and happy one—is the beauty (κάλλος), harmony or proportionedment (συμμετρία), and truth or truthfulness (ἀλήθεια) of the mixture of pleasure and reasoning in the version of a mixed life that Socrates and Protarchus have constructed in the preceding discussion—these three properties being taken together as a single characteristic found in the mixture (65a1). Thus, for Socrates in the *Philebus*, the good is none of the good constituents of the happy life, not even some or all of the good constituents taken together. Rather, the good (or, at any rate, what stands at the threshold of its domicile, 64c1–3: in the *Philebus*, as in the *Republic*, Plato holds Socrates back from pronouncing on the actual nature of the good) is a certain complex single property of the happy life's constitution—namely, the way in which the included ingredients are beautifully and truthfully proportioned and harmonize with one another.

III

Now let us return to Aristotle in *NE* I 7. I said that by using his criteria of finality and self-sufficiency, Aristotle reaches quite a different conclusion from that of Socrates in the *Philebus* about the highest good—that is, about the source of the happiness of the best life.[11] Though we would need to consider many intricate detailed questions (some of which I address below) before we could claim properly to understand Aristotle's view about the highest good in the work as a whole, and his intentions for its

[11] I am greatly indebted to Gabriel Richardson for discussion on this point, and have learned a great deal from her own treatment in her Ph.D. dissertation (Princeton University, 2001) of the relation between Aristotle's discussion of finality and self-sufficiency in the first part of *NE* I 7 and Socrates' use of much the same criteria in the *Philebus*. (See her book, *Happy Lives and the Highest Good: Aristotle's Nicomachean Ethics*, a revision of the dissertation.) My discussion in this section is indebted to her account.

articulation, it cannot be doubted that beginning already in the second part of I 7 he identifies the highest good with some one or more constituents or ingredients of the best life. He does not at all think, as Socrates did, that the application of their closely similar criteria inexorably leads to the denial of that title to any constituent, and its reservation for some normative or evaluative feature of the choiceworthy life itself—for example, a feature of the way its constituents, or the good ones among them, are combined together. As I mentioned in my initial summary of the chapter (sect. I), Aristotle tells us in I 7 that *eudaimonia*, that is, the highest good, is a certain exercise or activity of the soul that derives from and expresses the soul's excellence or virtue (never mind for the moment whether he means an activity deriving from the sum of the virtues or from some particular one or ones). Any such activity is of course just one constituent or ingredient (maybe a vastly complicated and flexible one, varying to fit varied circumstances). It is neither the totality of the good ingredients (at any rate, pleasure is a further ingredient left out of account) nor yet any feature of a life as a whole, for example, of the way its ingredient activities and experiences are combined together to constitute it. In fact, Aristotle makes it clear that the activity he is referring to is an activity in one way or another of reason, using now neither of Socrates' terms for it (νοῦς and φρόνησις) but rather τὸ λόγον ἔχον, "what (in or of the soul) has reasoning" (1098a3–5):[12] it is an activity of the soul "in accordance with [that is, deriving from] reason or not without reason" (ψυχῆς ἐνέργεια κατὰ λόγον ἢ μὴ ἄνευ λόγου, a7–8; cf. ψυχῆς ἐνέργειαν καὶ πράξεις μετὰ λόγου, a13–14). So Aristotle's conclusion in I 7 simply flies in the face of Socrates' argument. According to Socrates, neither pleasure *nor* reason can be the good; a life chockful of reasonings still lacks something that is needed; such a life would not be choiceworthy. Aristotle plainly thinks that in fact, somehow or other, reason (maybe reason of some special restricted sort, or used in some particular way) *is* the good, the highest good, so that it makes any life that contains it choiceworthy. Our task will be, first, to see how Aristotle intends (and manages) to reach that conclusion from (essentially) the very criteria that Socrates in the *Philebus* had used to deny it. Once we have done that, we can go on to work out and discuss, in the light of his version of these criteria, Aristotle's own account of what the highest good *is*.

We can begin a closer examination of Aristotle's argument in I 7 by reverting to something I said in my opening summary. Unlike Socrates, Aristotle is careful to explicate his two criteria before applying them. To be

---

[12] Notice, however, that in the *Philebus* Socrates occasionally adds to his specifications of reason, besides νοῦς and φρόνησις, λογισμός and λογίζεσθαι (see 21a14, c5–6).

unqualifiedly "final" or τέλειον (which he and Socrates both agree any successful candidate for the good must be), Aristotle says (1097a33–34), is to be "choiceworthy for itself always and never because of anything else."[13] This amounts to saying that, as it were by definition of the term τέλειον as it is being used in this context, a good that is unqualifiedly τέλειον is such that it really is in the strongest possible way an *end* of action: it is always choiceworthy for itself, as ends must be, *and* in being choiceworthy it is never referred in any way to anything else—whether as a productive means to something further, or some sort of constituent in a larger whole, or in any other way owing any part of what is choiceworthy about it to any relationship it might bear to anything else. Indeed, upon introducing the word τέλειον in this context (1097a25–29), Aristotle clearly emphasizes its derivation from the word τέλος—"end."[14] For that reason, we must, if we are to be faithful to Aristotle's own explication of this criterial term, think of it not in terms of completeness or perfection but, indeed, as I have been doing, in terms of finality.

Having explained what he means by finality, Aristotle then claims that this requirement is fulfilled most notably (μάλιστα)—so anyhow we think (δοκεῖ)—by *eudaimonia*. Hence, he concludes that *eudaimonia,* as the unqualifiedly final good, is the highest good, *the* good.

I need to make two comments on this argument before proceeding to Aristotle's explication of the second criterion, that of self-sufficiency. First, before I 7, Aristotle has not yet given on his own account any characterization of *eudaimonia* at all, however vague.[15] He has mentioned (chaps. 4–5) that the vast majority of people agree in using this term to refer to "the highest of all goods achievable by action" (1095a18–20), and he has

---

[13] καὶ ἁπλῶς δὴ τέλειον τὸ καθ' αὑτὸ αἱρετὸν ἀεὶ καὶ μηδέποτε δι' ἄλλο, 1097a33–34.

[14] In his commentary on 1097a24–b6, Aspasius (*In Ethica Nicomachea,* ed. G. Heylbut, CAG 19.1) correctly emphasizes this fact. He says (15. 18–19) that Aristotle is going to show that "*eudaimonia* is an end, an end in the strict sense, and a most final end" (ὅτι ἡ εὐδαιμονία τέλος ἐστι καὶ κυρίως τέλος καὶ τελειότατον τέλος). It is a pity that recent translators and authors working on the *Nicomachean Ethics* have not followed Aspasius's lead here. (R. Gauthier and J. Y. Jolif, *Aristote: L'Éthique à Nicomaque,* 2d ed., are a partial exception; like me, they translate τέλειον as "final" in Aristotle's exposition of his criteria for the highest good. So does W. D. Ross in the original edition of his translation, in the Oxford translation of *The Works of Aristotle,* vol. 9 [1915]—unfortunately, J. Barnes has altered the translation to "complete" in his revision, *The Complete Works of Aristotle* [Princeton: Princeton University Press, 1984].) (I am grateful to Pierre Destrée for discussion on these matters.)

[15] In rejecting some of the popular conceptions of *eudaimonia* and the good in chapter 5, Aristotle does draw upon certain, as he thinks agreed, preconceptions about *eudaimonia,* e.g., that it cannot be easily taken away from one who has it, or that it cannot be something that would suit even farm animals. But he is not engaged there yet in any direct characterization on his own of *eudaimonia.*

mentioned pleasure, honor, virtue, wealth, and (by implication) the highest level of theoretical or philosophical knowledge as candidates that different people or groups of people have themselves shown in one way or another that they favor as being that highest of all goods, that is, *eudaimonia*. Presumably, then, when he says "we think" (δοκεῖ) that *eudaimonia* is "unqualifiedly final," choiceworthy always only for itself, he means merely that each of us thinks this, whatever candidate he or she may favor (if any). Despite the wide variation among specifications people make for *eudaimonia*, then, it is something that stands agreed on that *eudaimonia* is an "unqualifiedly final" good. Thus even if we think that lots of other things are choiceworthy in themselves, we also choose them for the sake of something else, in particular, for the sake of *eudaimonia*, whereas no one ever chooses *eudaimonia* for the sake of any of them, or indeed for anything else whatsoever (1097b1–6).[16]

My second comment concerns the form of Aristotle's argument. His argument goes like this: the best or the highest good is clearly something final (1097a28); *eudaimonia*, most notably, is thought to be something final, indeed unqualifiedly final (a35); therefore *eudaimonia* is the best or highest good. That is manifestly not a deductively valid argument: it only identifies *eudaimonia* as having a feature, or fulfilling a condition, that the highest good is admitted to require, without showing that nothing else does the same—something which, in that case, could dispute the claim of *eudaimonia* to *be* the highest good.[17] In fact, this is an argument

---

[16] Aristotle instances here "honor, pleasure, intelligence, and every virtue" (τιμὴν καὶ ἡδονὴν καὶ νοῦν καὶ πᾶσαν ἀρετήν, b2) as things we choose "for themselves" (we would choose them "even if nothing resulted from them") but also choose for the sake of *eudaimonia*. I take him to mean that we would choose these things even if no other good of their same order resulted (in particular, even when each did not result in any of the others, or when, e.g., no money, no "reward," as one might say, followed). As we will see later, *eudaimonia*, as something for the sake of which they are also chosen, is not in the relevant sense a "result" of them. (See sect. IV below.) Hence, in saying we would choose, e.g., pleasure even if nothing resulted from it, he is not implying that pleasure would still be choiceworthy apart from *eudaimonia*, i.e. (e.g.), in a life that was in no way or degree devoted to, or inclusive of, the highest good (whatever that turns out to be). This qualification is needed because, as I argue in sections IV–VI (see especially VI, second paragraph) Aristotle thinks that no good "subordinate" to *eudaimonia*, such as pleasure, is choiceworthy at all except when it is chosen for the sake of *eudaimonia*. (I thank Robert Heinaman for making me see the need to take note of this qualification here.)

[17] It is true that Aristotle immediately lists some good things that we choose for their own sakes, but also for the sake of *eudaimonia* (honor, pleasure, et al), which are therefore *not* unqualifiedly final. But that is not to say (and he does not add) that *every* other thing that we choose for its own sake we also choose for the sake of *eudaimonia*. If he had added that as a further premise, we would have a deductively valid argument to the desired conclusion. Perhaps that is what he intended (though the adverb μάλιστα, "most notably," seems in fact to envisage that perhaps some other good thing, though less obviously, might be thought

of the kind Aristotle refers to in the *Prior Analytics* and *Rhetoric* as being "from a sign" (ἐκ σημείου). He indicates in those contexts, quite rightly, that some such arguments are good ones even if they are not deductively valid.[18] This is plainly one of the good ones of that sort: *eudaimonia*'s being unqualifiedly final surely is a good indication, a good reason for thinking, that it is the highest good. Not a proof, but a solid indication. What else could anyone think of that might possibly give this same "sign," by being final in this unqualified way—namely, choiceworthy for itself always and never because of anything else?

In turning to his second criterion, of self-sufficiency, Aristotle proposes not to argue directly, as with finality, that *eudaimonia* is the highest good because it is a self-sufficient good; rather, he appeals to self-sufficiency to bolster his previously given reasons for thinking that *eudaimonia* is unqualifiedly final. He begins, "The same thing also clearly follows from self-sufficiency, since the final good is thought also to be self-sufficient" (1097b6–8).[19] Here the "same thing" that follows has to be the immediate conclusion for which he has just been arguing, namely that *eudaimonia* is an unqualifiedly final good.[20] Thus we get again an argument from a sign: the unqualifiedly final good is self-sufficient; but *eudaimonia* is self-sufficient; therefore *eudaimonia* is the unqualifiedly final good. I think that, in arguing so, Aristotle is intending to correct or clarify Socrates' ar-

---

also to satisfy the specified condition). As the text stands, however, the argument given is plainly invalid.

[18] See *Pr. An.* II 27; *Rhet.* I 2, 1357a33–b25; II 24, 1401a9–14; II 25, 1402b12–20, 1403a2–5; and the many places where Aristotle uses the term σημεῖον in particular contexts listed in the index to *Aristotelis Ars Rhetorica*, ed. R. Kassel, 244. See now James Allen, *Inference from Signs*, Study I, and pp. 8, 14–15, 29–38. See also M. F. Burnyeat, "Enthymeme: Aristotle on the Logic of Persuasion" in *Aristotle's Rhetoric: Philosophical Essays*, ed. D. J. Furley and A. Nehamas, 3–55, and "The Origins of Non-deductive Inference," in *Science and Speculation*, ed. J. Barnes et al., 193–238.

[19] φαίνεται δὲ καὶ ἐκ τῆς αὐταρκείας τὸ αὐτὸ συμβαίνειν· τὸ γὰρ τέλειον ἀγαθὸν αὔταρκες εἶναι δοκεῖ.

[20] J. A. Stewart (*Notes on the Nicomachean Ethics*), followed by F. Dirlmeier (*Aristoteles, "Nikomachische Ethik"*), in their notes ad loc. both mistakenly take "the same" to mean the further conclusion aimed at in the previous argument, namely that *eudaimonia* is the highest good. That cannot be right, however, because in that case the argument that Aristotle goes on to give (1097b8–16) would have to run differently from the way in fact it does. Aristotle uses as one premise in this argument (as is indicated in the passage just quoted, 1097b6–8) that "the final good is self-sufficient," but for the conclusion that *eudaimonia* is the highest good to follow, even by a deductively invalid sign argument, once one adds as a second premise (b15–16) that *eudaimonia* is self-sufficient, this first premise would have to be instead that the *highest* good is self-sufficient (not that the final good is). T. H. Irwin sees the logic here correctly: in his translation (*Aristotle: Nicomachean Ethics*, 2d ed. [1999]) he adds the correct supplement "[that happiness is complete]" to explicate "the same conclusion."

gument in the *Philebus* by explicitly establishing for self-sufficiency what Socrates merely assumed for sufficiency, namely that if some good is sufficient it is also final. As I pointed out (p. 273 above), Socrates does infer (but only implicitly) from the fact that pleasure is not sufficient, that it is also not final. Aristotle is explicit here in claiming that any final good *is* also (self-)sufficient (the presupposition of Socrates' inference):[21] he introduces that claim when he argues from the premise that the (unqualifiedly) final good is self-sufficient. The effect of Aristotle's argument is to relate the two criteria to each other in the following way. The highest good is (agreed to be) unqualifiedly final; and what is unqualifiedly final is (agreed to be) self-sufficient. Since it follows by valid deduction from those two claims that the highest good is self-sufficient, it is no error to speak, as I have been doing and as other commentators do, of self-sufficiency as a second criterion of the highest good for Aristotle, distinct from finality, as finality and sufficiency are of the good for Plato. Still, it is important to see that Aristotle explicitly subordinates self-sufficiency to finality, in making it a sign of the latter. For Aristotle, the criteria, though distinct, are explicitly made not parallel to each other. This is one revealing indication of the close attention Aristotle gave to Socrates' argument in the *Philebus* while working out his own views in the *NE*. In introducing his criteria Socrates had spoken as if they were separate and parallel, but in applying them he appeared to treat lack of sufficiency as implying lack of finality. Aristotle, by contrast, makes explicit the corresponding relationship between self-sufficiency and finality when introducing these criteria.

There is another indication. Before making his claim that *eudaimonia* is self-sufficient, Aristotle, as I remarked already, explains what he understands by self-sufficiency, just as he has also explained what he understands by finality: "that which is self-sufficient we put down as that which, isolated on its own, makes life choiceworthy and lacking in nothing."[22] It is noteworthy that in this account of self-sufficiency Aristotle combines the second with the third of Socrates' three criteria: for Socrates, not needing anything in addition was the mark of sufficiency (being ἱκανόν), while making the life that contains it choiceworthy was the burden of Socrates' separate third criterion. Thus, when Aristotle introduces his new term, αὐτάρκεια, it is not in fact a mere change of terminology, introducing a different term from Socrates' as a way of referring to Socrates'

[21] Socrates' assumption that anything that is not sufficient is also not final is logically equivalent to the claim that nothing can be both not sufficient and at the same time final. So it follows for Socrates that anything that *is* final has to be sufficient.

[22] τὸ δ' αὔταρκες τίθεμεν ὃ μονούμενον αἱρετὸν ποιεῖ τὸν βίον καὶ μηδενὸς ἐνδεᾶ, 1097b14–15.

second criterion (that is, not needing anything in addition). Rather, Aristotle uses this term to denote a new criterion, one that combines the idea of not needing anything in addition with the idea of making a life choice-worthy.[23] Thus, besides subordinating the criterion of (self-)sufficiency to the criterion of finality, Aristotle also eliminates Socrates' third separate and further criterion of making life choiceworthy. He incorporates it into a revised conception of sufficiency: namely, *self*-sufficiency, that is, making life choiceworthy *and* lacking in nothing.

It seems very probable that Aristotle took the trouble to find a different word (αὐτάρκεια, self-sufficiency, as I am translating it) to replace Socrates' sufficiency, precisely because he was acutely aware of the correction or clarification in Socrates' scheme that he was adopting. By announcing sufficiency and making life choiceworthy as two independent criteria, Socrates suggests that if anything is the good it must satisfy first the one condition and then, in addition, the other. This leaves open the thought that they might be separately satisfiable. Something might be such as to make a life choiceworthy by its presence, but nonetheless not be a sufficient good—in which case, by Socrates' argument, it could not be *the* good. For example, pleasure might indeed not be sufficient, as Socrates argues it is not: even if you have the fullest share possible of the greatest pleasures, you would still reasonably want something further; not all your wishes would be satisfied; you would prefer a life with pleasure if it were supplemented so as to satisfy those remaining wishes. But nonetheless, the life in question might be *choiceworthy*, despite containing the unmet need. (Or, less plausibly but still, I think, conceivably, vice versa: something might be sufficient to leave you desiring nothing further, but still not make your life choiceworthy.) In fact, however, in applying these criteria Socrates does not treat them as separately satisfiable. He begins his argument against the claim of pleasure to be the good by get-

---

[23] It is interesting to notice that the Aristotelian term, αὐτάρκεια, already appears once within the *Philebus* in, at any rate, close association with Socrates' criterion of sufficiency. Socrates is perfectly consistent throughout his discussion, both in 20–23 and again in the review of that argument and the further application of its conclusion in the 60s of the dialogue, in using the term ἱκανόν to express this criterion (see 60c4, c11, 61e6–7, 67a2–3, a7). However, at the very end, 67a5–8, in announcing one last time his conclusion that neither pleasure nor reason is the good, but some third thing distinct from either is better than they, he brings in the term αὐτάρκεια as, it would seem from the grammar, a way of referring together to Socrates' two first criteria, of sufficiency and finality. Reason and pleasure, he says, cannot be the good because "they lack 'self-sufficiency' and [i.e., that is?] the power of sufficiency and finality" (στερομένοιν αὐταρκείας καὶ τῆς τοῦ ἱκανοῦ καὶ τελέου δυνάμεως, a7). Even if Aristotle's adoption of the term may derive from this passage, it is clear that in distinguishing it from τὸ ἱκανόν in the way that he does, he gives to it a clearer, and better thought-through, significance than Plato did, whatever precisely Plato may have had in mind here. (I thank Sylvain Delcomminette for bringing this passage to my attention.)

ting Protarchus to see that even if he lived throughout his life with the fullest supply of pleasure, there would still be something he needed—articulate belief, memory, calculated anticipation, in short the power of reasoning. And Socrates goes immediately from that to the conclusion, which Protarchus himself accepts, that such a life would not be choice-worthy (not even choiceworthy for the luckiest possible oysters and sea-lungs, which would in fact lead it). But even if this conclusion about a life devoid of all reasoning is true, as I have suggested it is, and even if the premise is also true (that the life of pleasure *would* lack something needed), the inference is apparently not valid. For all we have been told to the contrary, there really might be an unmet need in a nonetheless choiceworthy life: you would be glad to be alive and to have a life to lead even with the lack, because of the value to you of other things the life brings. Why not? The effect of Aristotle's definition of αὐτάρκεια is to remove this gap in Socrates' argument against pleasure by making it clear that a choiceworthy life could still lack something needed—even though what the life of pleasure lacks (reasoning) is indeed something needed for choiceworthiness. On Aristotle's definition we are asked to read together the two conjoined conditions as constituting a single criterion: "makes a life choiceworthy and lacking in nothing." The result is that now Socrates' separate criterion of lacking in nothing is replaced by a narrower one: lacking in nothing *needed for choiceworthiness*.[24] Thus, some life might meet this condition even if it did lack something one would merely prefer to have in it, something one would miss if it were absent—so long as its absence did not make the life not choiceworthy, that is, not worth living.[25]

---

[24] In construing in this way the force of Aristotle's criterion of self-sufficiency I am guided by two considerations. First, there is no doubt that Aristotle means this criterion to differ from that of (mere) sufficiency as explained by Socrates in the *Philebus*. There would be no point in combining Socrates' language of "lacking in nothing" with his language of "choiceworthiness" in explaining this replacement criterion if the effect were simply to replicate Socrates' analysis, i.e., to propose that the self-sufficient good makes a life choiceworthy *and (so) lacking in nothing (at all)*. Second, we know that Aristotle is going to draw on these criteria so as to defend his conclusion that *eudaimonia* is in fact a single activity (excellent reasoning of some sort); but Socrates had used his criteria, apparently validly enough, to exclude any such ingredient of a life as constituting the good. Aristotle does not dispute Socrates' inference from his criteria, understood Socrates' way. And since one of the effects of adopting self-sufficiency understood in the way I suggest, in place of sufficiency, is that (see the next paragraph) it permits Aristotle to argue (as in fact he does) that a εὐδαίμων life might lack some goods that were still needed (i.e., might fail to satisfy Socrates' criterion of sufficiency), he *needs* to understand self-sufficiency in this way if he is to maintain consistency. When he says that the εὐδαίμων life might lack some needed or desirable goods, he will contradict his claim that *eudaimonia* is a self-sufficient good, if part of self-sufficiency is to lack nothing (at all) that is worth having.

[25] In glossing "not choiceworthy" here by "not worth living," I am relying loosely on Socrates' conception of the choiceworthiness of a life in *Philebus*, where his first use of the

To meet Aristotle's condition does not require making a life lacking in nothing, but only lacking in nothing needed for choiceworthiness.

This limitation is important in itself, as we will see, and it is needed if Aristotle is to complete successfully his own preliminary account of *eudaimonia* in *NE* I.[26] For he allows later on in his discussion (chap. 8) that in fact *eudaimonia* does "need in addition external goods" (τῶν ἐκτὸς ἀγαθῶν προσδεομένη, 1099a31–32), using the very verb that Socrates used in applying his criterion of sufficiency (20e6, 21a11): things like friends, wealth, political power, good looks or at least no really gross ugliness, good children or anyhow no scandalously awful ones. Aristotle does not mean here that you do not have *eudaimonia* without such goods, as if they were included as among its constituents or parts—he completed his preliminary specification of *eudaimonia* already in chapter 7, without mentioning any of these goods as included in it.[27] He means,

---

term (αἱρετός) expresses his recognition of the life of pleasure devoid of all reasoning as not a human life at all, but that of a "jellyfish or one of those shelled creatures living in the sea" (21c6–d3). I rely also on *Eudemian Ethics* I 5, where Aristotle raises the question, "What of all that is found in living is worthy of choosing?" (1215b17). In responding to this question, he repeatedly connects the idea of something in life worth choosing with whatever makes existence or life itself preferable to not having been born, or to nonexistence. See 1215b20–22, b26, b30.

[26] One should bear in mind, in considering Aristotle's difference from Plato over sufficiency versus self-sufficiency as a criterion, that Plato proposed criteria for the specification of the good (τἀγαθόν), whereas Aristotle speaks variously of "the good and the best" (τἀγαθὸν καὶ τὸ ἄριστον), "the end of actions" (τὸ τέλος τῶν πρακτῶν), and "the highest of all goods achievable by action" (τὸ ἀκρότατον τῶν πρακτῶν ἀγαθῶν). If one thinks of "*the* good," as presumably Plato did think in the *Philebus*, as referring to something that is the universal source of the goodness of anything and everything else that is good, it could seem quite plain, as Socrates maintains in proposing sufficiency as a criterion, that if anything good (i.e., anything one would need *as* a good) were lacking in a life that nonetheless possessed some candidate, then that candidate could not possibly be *the* good. If you already had in your life what makes anything that is good good, it might easily seem, how could you still have unmet needs for something good? If you did need to add something, surely you would have to say at the very least that, not the original candidate alone, but it plus this new thing was the sought-for good? Aristotle, of course, rejects any such conception of a universal single source of the goodness of anything good (see his arguments in *NE* I 6); so, for him, the target in seeking "the good" becomes a single organizing goal of life, which however cannot be presumed to be the metaphysical or even the moral source of the goodness of any and every other good thing a person might enjoy. So for him it seems obvious that even by achieving that goal in one's life one might still possibly have needs for additional goods. Hence Socrates' (mere) sufficiency cannot be a valid criterion for the (Aristotelian) good. (On this see further below in my text.)

[27] Hence one must understand "*eudaimonia* needs these goods in addition" at 1099a31–32 and b6–7 as indicating that it needs them not in addition to virtuous activity in order for *eudaimonia* to be achieved at all, but rather as a supplement to itself. This is, in the context, the most natural reading in any event. In the lines preceding, neither occurrence of "needs in addition" includes a reference to virtue as something *eudaimonia* needs in the first

rather, that even with *eudaimonia,* you need them too, if your *eudaimonia* is to be perfectly satisfactory—he says that *eudaimonia* needs them, implying, as I say, that even when you have *eudaimonia* these are further things you need.[28] Yet he has argued, in chapter 7, that *eudaimonia* does satisfy his criteria of finality and self-sufficiency, and so is the highest good. So, if self-sufficiency had been understood simply as Socrates' sufficiency, Aristotle could not say, as he does, that it satisfies that criterion: it would lack something, as Aristotle grants in chapter 8 that it does. On the other hand, with Aristotle's own understanding of this criterion, *eudaimonia* can satisfy the (revised) requirements for the highest good, because although indeed there are good things lacking in a life provided only that it has *eudaimonia* in it (lots of external goods, certainly many sorts of innocent pleasure, might be lacking), these missing goods, Aristotle can argue, are not ones that are needed *for the choiceworthiness* even of the resulting deprived life. The life of *eudaimonia* would be more satisfactory if it has them as well; they remain things to be wished and hoped for; they remain goods and every good is worth wanting and trying to get and concerning oneself over. But in a certain way they are not important: they are not make-or-break conditions for a life worth choosing, or worth living. Only *eudaimonia* is important in that way, for only it makes the life that has it worth choosing and worth living—and it does that all by itself, without needing the help of any other good to yield that result. It is *self*-sufficient, though not *sufficient*—if sufficiency is understood in Socrates' way.

Aristotle's limitation of Socrates' "lacking in nothing" to what is lacking in nothing needed for choiceworthiness of life is important for a second reason as well. In the *Philebus* Socrates argues, as we saw, not only that a life chockful of pleasure but lacking all use of reason would be unchoiceworthy but also, *pari passu,* that the life chockful of reason but lacking all pleasure would be so likewise. Although, as I pointed out above (sect. II), his argument about the life of reason is truncated, it certainly does appear that Socrates intends to argue for this parallel conclusion about reason on precisely the same ground as he argued for the conclusion about pleasure. That means that Socrates goes seamlessly from the premise that the life chockful of reason that lacks all pleasure lacks something needed if a life is to be satisfactory to the conclusion that

---

instance, for the additionally needed things to be added to, in order to constitute *eudaimonia* itself. That is, there is no reference to *virtue* as what *eudaimonia* needs these further things in addition to. Such a reference might support the other interpretation.

[28] For now, I do not go into the precise way that Aristotle thinks *eudaimonia* needs these external goods, whether as conditions needed before *eudaimonia* (some activity) can be fully present—i.e., engaged in fully—or as further goods needed even when *eudaimonia* is engaged in fully. See below, section V, beginning.

it is a life not worth choosing. As we saw, that inference is not obviously correct. Here is where Aristotle evidently objected. So long as lacking something means merely lacking something desirable, to be wished and hoped and striven for, needed if the life is to be fully satisfactory, there would be an important further question to consider: is the missing good of such a sort, or weight, that its absence does render the life not worth choosing, not worth living? Perhaps a missing good (for example, pleasure missing from the life of reason) is like wealth or other external goods, as Aristotle reasonably conceives them, in that it certainly is a good thing—worth desiring and worth being concerned for, worth regretting if it is absent—yet still, not really all that important. It might not be a make-or-break condition for a life worth choosing, or worth living.

It is at this point in his careful study of Socrates' argument in the *Philebus,* I suggest, that Aristotle saw the flaw that permitted Socrates to conclude—erroneously, we can now see—that not even reason can be *the* good. Even if, as we can agree, pleasure is not a good by having which in it a life is made choiceworthy (no matter whatever else is lacking, for example all reasoning), it need not follow, *pari passu,* that reasoning is not such a good. Yes, a life with lots of reasoning in it might lack things one would like to have, things one would miss if one didn't have them, but nonetheless it might still be *choiceworthy,* worth living. Once, with Aristotle, we abandon (mere) sufficiency as a criterion and combine sufficiency with making life choiceworthy into the more acceptable Aristotelian criterion of *self*-sufficiency (sufficiency *for* choiceworthiness), we open up the possibility of arguing (contrary to the *Philebus*) that excellent activity of reason (or, perhaps, some particular such activity) *is* the good. Such activity can be argued to be a good that is not only unqualifiedly final, but one that makes life worth living whether or not it is accompanied by any other goods—goods other than itself plus any consequences for the life that followed immediately and solely from its presence in it. If so, it would be *the* good, the good whose presence in a life makes it a happy one. Plato's error in the *Philebus,* as Aristotle sees it, then, was to suppose that simple sufficiency (sufficiency for a satisfactory or a fully satisfactory life) is a valid criterion for the identity and specification of the good. That is simply too strong a requirement. Why think that in order to be choiceworthy at all, or happy, a life has to have in it something that leaves *nothing* else to be even desired, nothing else needed at all? In fact, the relevant valid criterion is *self*-sufficiency—sufficiency for a life that is choiceworthy, one worth living (even if it might possibly lack some further good things).

In sum, then: Aristotle makes three major adjustments in taking up Plato's criteria for the good in the *Philebus* and reworking them for his own search for the identity and specification of the highest good. First, he does away firmly with any suggestion that his own criteria of finality and self-sufficiency are independently satisfiable: though they are distinct, self-sufficiency is subordinated to finality, as a sign of the latter. Second, he rectifies the unclarities in Socrates' application of his separate criteria of sufficiency and making life choiceworthy (why must something whose presence leaves a life insufficient also fail to make it choiceworthy?), and avoids the unsatisfactoriness of Socratic sufficiency as a criterion at all, by proposing his new criterion of self-sufficiency to replace both of these Platonic ones. Third, he carefully explains what he means not only by self-sufficiency but also by finality.

IV

With these innovations in the criteria for the highest good achieved in the first part of *NE* I 7, the way is open for Aristotle to think that perhaps, after all, the good might be some ingredient or constituent of the happy life—precisely what Plato had used his own criteria to rule out. *Eudaimonia,* as the highest good, must both be unqualifiedly final and self-sufficient, according to Aristotle's careful explanations of these two criteria. The question then becomes, What, then, *is eudaimonia?*

The first thing to notice is that in this context (as most often in Aristotle) the term *eudaimonia* refers not the happy life itself (the εὐδαίμων βίος), but rather to something in it that is responsible for the happy life's being happy (εὐδαίμων).[29] That is why I have left this term untranslated. First of all, if we gave "happiness" as our translation of *eudaimonia* into English here, that would probably be quite misleading. To say that happiness is what in a life makes it a happy one would inevitably invite the erroneous interpretation that what Aristotle is referring to by "happiness" is the quality, whatever one might then say about it, in having which a life is happy (εὐδαίμων): unperturbedness, we might think, or the smooth flow of one's life, as Epicureans or Pyrrhonean skeptics or Stoics might later have said. We ought then to be at a loss when we find him saying that *eudaimonia* is in fact an activity of reason. How could that be the quality by having which a life counts as happy? Second, however,

---

[29] See John Cooper, "Contemplation and Happiness: A Reconsideration" in *Reason and Emotion*, 219–20. In I 7 Aristotle is proposing some activity of reason as the correct answer to the question what *eudaimonia* is, where that competes with the answers canvassed in chapters 3 and 4—pleasure, honor or virtue, wealth, and so on. Manifestly Aristotle is not understanding that question as asking for a specification of the happy life itself—except insofar as opting for one of these candidates, or something else, would indicate, derivatively, that the life having it would be a happy one. See also S. Broadie, *Ethics with Aristotle* (New York: Oxford University Press, 1991), 26–27 and nn. 14, 15.

and much more decisively, in *NE* I Aristotle is clearly following Plato in the *Philebus,* so that he intends from the beginning to be proposing an answer to the question what *the good* is,—that is, what that particular good, among other goods, is that by having it a life is made happy (see *Philebus* 11d4–6)—and he is calling that good (as Plato does not) *eudaimonia.* Proposing such an answer presupposes acceptance of a substantive thesis, namely that there *is* something specifiable in a good and happy life (whether an ingredient or not) that gives it the quality of happiness (whatever that quality may be), and is the only thing that does convey that quality. Given the inadequacy of "happiness" and any other English term that comes to mind to convey this meaning, then, I will continue simply to use Aristotle's Greek word, with the insistence that it be understood in this way.[30]

Before proceeding to consider Aristotle's answer to the question what *eudaimonia* so understood in fact is, we need to bring into our discussion the brief passage, much discussed and disputed recently, which Aristotle appends to his argument, discussed above (sect. III), to show that *eudaimonia,* being the self-sufficient good, is the final good as well. This passage (1097b16–20), introduced by "And further . . ." (ἔτι δὲ . . .), is sometimes interpreted as introducing a third criterion for the good, alongside finality and self-sufficiency.[31] But that is clearly a mistake. Immediately after this passage Aristotle concludes the whole preceding discussion of the criteria by saying: "So *eudaimonia* appears to be [or: is clearly] something final and self-sufficient, being the end of things achievable by action."[32] Here he mentions only the two criteria of finality and self-sufficiency. So, it would seem, this appendage (1097b16–20) does not introduce a third criterion. In fact, this passage seems intended to tell us something about how Aristotle understands a certain requirement implied in the self-sufficiency criterion, as that has been explained just before, namely that the good (that is, *eudaimonia*) should itself be *most* choiceworthy (since, as

---

[30] Perhaps I should emphasize that this worry about "happiness" as a translation is unrelated to worries I expressed in *Reason and Human Good in Aristotle,* 89 n. 1. Even if, as I suggested there (not of course intending to say how any one offering a complete translation of the work should render the Greek term), "human flourishing" more accurately conveys the word's meaning (or Aristotle's understanding of it), that translation would be equally open to the concerns I have expressed here. If *eudaimonia* is (possibly) to designate some constituent activity or activities of a good and happy human life, neither "happiness" nor "flourishing" can well render the term in such a use.

[31] See Irwin's translation (1985 ed.), where it is set off with a special heading, coordinate with those for finality and self-sufficiency, "(5) The good is most choiceworthy; so is happiness."

[32] τέλειον δή τι φαίνεται καὶ αὔταρκες ἡ εὐδαιμονία, τῶν πρακτῶν οὖσα τέλος, 1097b20–21.

self-sufficient, it is what makes the life that has it a *choiceworthy* one, lacking in nothing that would be needed to make it worth choosing). His purpose, then, is to explain in just what way we are to understand the good's (*eudaimonia*'s) being most choiceworthy, inasmuch as it is the source of the choiceworthiness of any life that possesses it, and is thereby the self-sufficient good.[33] The passage reads as follows (in what I intend as an interpretatively neutral translation):

> And further, it [*eudaimonia*] is most choiceworthy of all things without being counted together—if counted together, it is clear that it is more choiceworthy taken along with the very least of goods, since that which is put together with it makes [lit., becomes] a larger quantity of goods, and of goods the greater is always more choiceworthy.[34]

In interpreting Aristotle's explanation here, it is important to bear clearly in mind that for him the superlative choiceworthiness of *eudaimonia* is a function of the role it plays *as an end,* indeed as an end in relation to anything and everything else in a properly conducted human

[33] That this is the right way to understand this passage is confirmed by a passage of *NE* X 2 discussed below, sect. V: 1172b26–35. Questions about the choiceworthiness of the good, and of other goods, are raised there with clear reference to Plato's discussion in *Philebus* 20–23, where, as we have seen, issues about the sufficiency of the good are at the forefront.

[34] ἔτι δὲ πάντων αἱρετωτάτην μὴ συναριθμουμένην—συναριθμουμένην δὲ δῆλον ὡς αἱρετωτέραν μετὰ τοῦ ἐλαχίστου τῶν ἀγαθῶν· ὑπεροχὴ γὰρ ἀγαθῶν γίνεται τὸ προστιθέμενον, ἀγαθῶν δὲ τὸ μεῖζον αἱρετώτερον ἀεί, 1097b16–20. I have translated with the intention to leave undecided which of two ways to take the participle συναριθμουμένην in its first occurrence: does μὴ συναριθμουμένην ("without being counted together") mean "because or in the sense that it is not the sort of thing to be counted together with other goods" or "under the condition that it is not counted together with other goods"? Depending on how you take it in its first occurrence, the second one will either express something counterfactual ("if it were the sort of thing to be added together with other goods, it would be more choiceworthy along with the least of goods, since that is how it always goes with goods that get counted together with one another") or something merely circumstantial ("but when it *is* counted together [as of course it can be] it is more choiceworthy along with the least of goods"). Aristotle's purpose here is to tell us in which sense or way the good *is* most choiceworthy, and he distinguishes from that way a different way that something might be most choiceworthy, namely in relation to other goods along with which it is being counted. It is not necessary for his purposes here to say whether the good is such (somehow) that it *cannot* be coherently counted together, or whether instead it can be so counted (in which case it is not most choiceworthy in the other sense or way). So long as he makes it clear in what way he understands that *eudaimonia*, or the good, *is* most choiceworthy, we do not need to know whether there is a different sense of "most choiceworthy" that coherently applies to it but that it does not satisfy, or none. So it would be a mistake to translate this passage in any way that made Aristotle opt for either of these understandings. His Greek is simply uncommitted either way on this question. (See further below, n. 52 and my discussion in the text there.)

life that is choiceworthy at all.[35] As I have explained, the passage to which these remarks are appended, and which they are intended to clarify, is an argument to show that *eudaimonia,* being a self-sufficient good, is also unqualifiedly final or "endlike"—that is, an end "choiceworthy for itself always and never because of anything else" (1097a33–34). Aristotle reminds us of this when he concludes the whole discussion of the criteria immediately afterward (1097b20–21) by putting forward the fact that *eudaimonia* is "the end of things achievable by action" in explication of its satisfying both of the two criteria, self-sufficiency as well as finality. Such an end is the constant and single source of the detailed organization of the way that people who make it their end live their lives. As such, then, it lies beyond all other goods, even all other ends, that are ingredient in their lives: for them, it is the focus for the choice and pursuit of all other goods, and all of those stand together as subordinate to it (however they may otherwise be differently related to one another). In this addendum Aristotle is saying that this good is most choiceworthy "without being counted together," and he contrasts this way with another way of being more or most choiceworthy, one that involves being counted together with other goods. Clearly enough, then, he is drawing attention to this categorial distinction between the way that this good is a good for the person and his life, and the way that all the subordinate goods are good. It is by relation to it that the latter are choiceworthy when, in the way, and to the extent that, they are. As such, in that relation, they can be compared with one another as better or less good, more or less choiceworthy. Likewise, they can be added together, in that considering some one of them and its value in relation to the single ultimate end permits rankings both with individual other goods and with combinations of them: one such good is improved (and more choiceworthy) if another such is added together with it. And there might be some one subordinate good that is most choiceworthy, in the sense that it, taken singly, is more choiceworthy than any other subordinate good also taken singly.

Aristotle's point, then, is that *eudaimonia, the* good, is "most choiceworthy" in a different way from this, that is, from the way that some single subordinate good might be most choiceworthy in relation to other subordinate goods. *It* is most choiceworthy in the way that an end is most choiceworthy in relation to anything whose value is subordinated to it, to anything that is in some way or other pursued for its sake. It is that for the sake of which, ultimately, any of them is ever chosen, or to be chosen, at all. It is the extreme, the final object of choice whenever any of them is chosen. *This* is the sense or way that it is most choiceworthy in

---

[35] Gabriel Richardson in discussion and in preliminary writing toward her dissertation (above, n. 11) has particularly, and particularly effectively, emphasized this point.

relation to them, and better than any or all of them—indeed, the absolutely best thing. It is not most choiceworthy or best in the way that some one among such subordinates might be ranked as most choiceworthy among them all.[36]

Further issues can be and have been raised in connection with this brief passage, but we can take this much as clearly established, I think—even though many who have written on the passage have not interpreted it in this way—and it suffices for my present purposes.[37] Aristotle envisages here some way that some single end might be the most choiceworthy of or for *all* things (all goods, all other ends), which could permit that end to be the (sole and self-sufficient) source of the choiceworthiness of any life in which it was achieved and present. From what Aristotle has said so

---

[36] Some light is cast on these issues by a passage of the *Magna Moralia* that also discusses *eudaimonia* and "counting together" (I 2, 1184a14–25). The example there of health in relation to healthy things (healthy foods, practices, etc., are presumably intended) in fact illustrates clearly and precisely the sort of orientation of some goods to an end that is the source of their value that, on my interpretation, Aristotle's account in *NE* I 7 of the "most choiceworthiness" of *eudaimonia* relies upon. So, in fact, the reason why, as the *MM* says, the way that *eudaimonia* is ἄριστον and most choiceworthy is not one that involves "counting together" is simply that no end is to be spoken of as most choiceworthy in relation to the things that are subordinate to it by being ranked as the best *among* them. As the *MM*'s author correctly says, to speak that way will result in the incoherence of its being better than itself—it as overarching end will be better than it as subordinate to that end. So far, then, this *MM* passage is illuminating. However, the author remarks that "we put *eudaimonia* together from many goods" (a19) and he seems to make that part-whole relationship what produces the incoherence when, as best, *eudaimonia* is "counted together"—confusingly, he does not focus clearly on the fact that then an end is being improperly counted together as far as goodness or choiceworthiness is concerned with its subordinates. But any part-whole incongruence is clearly not what Aristotle has in mind in *NE* I 7 in saying that *eudaimonia* is most choiceworthy without being counted together. Furthermore, appeal to the idea that *eudaimonia* is a whole of parts would seem to go counter to the very illustration via health of how *eudaimonia* stands in relation to its subordinates that the *MM* passage provides: health does not have healthy food, etc., as its *parts*. This difficulty would be removed if we could take the healthy things subordinate to health in the illustration as, e.g., the health of the foot, the health of the eyes, the health of the stomach, etc.—not foods, practices, etc.—so that health itself, the end, would simply be a whole put together from these "healthy things." (And then we could proceed to understand the *MM* as consistently and throughout deriving the incoherence of "counting *eudaimonia* together" with other goods from its character as a whole put together from them.) But that is an odd and nonstandard way of speaking of healthy things (ὑγιεινά) in relation to health (for the standard one, which I have adopted above, see, e.g., Aristotle, *Metaphysics* Γ2, 1003a33–37). Hence I think we have to regard the remark in *MM* 1184a19–20 that "we put *eudaimonia* together from many goods" as an excrescence, representing a misunderstanding of the view the author is presenting, and out of kilter even with the example he presents to illustrate the way the "most choiceworthiness" of *eudaimonia* is supposed to be understood. The view he is intending to present is in fact the one I have attributed to Aristotle in *NE* I 7.

[37] See further X 2, 1172b26–35, and my discussion below, sect. V.

far, the end that fulfills this role could even, in itself, be just one of the good ingredients or constituents of that life. Its special character as a good, even though there are other goods as well, subordinated to it, might be such that it and it alone rendered the life possessing it "choiceworthy and lacking in nothing." So what he says here fits together well, as it certainly ought to, with the conclusion he is going to argue for in the second section of the chapter, that the human good or *eudaimonia* is, quite simply, activity of the soul deriving from the excellent or virtuous condition of its reason-possessing part.[38] For that *is* a single activity (perhaps a complex or even variegated one) ingredient in the life, alongside others some of which, of course, are also, as ingredients, further goods. Nothing, in short, in his explication of how *eudaimonia* is most choiceworthy suggests or should be thought to suggest, that a "most choiceworthy" end as Aristotle understands that title would have to be some combination of all the intrinsic goods of life, or even any subset of them, aimed at as a sum total.[39]

Now in fact, as I indicated in my initial summary, in reaching his conclusion in the second section of the chapter, Aristotle actually adds "or, if there is a plurality of virtues, then it [*eudaimonia*] is activity deriving from the soul's best and most final (τελειοτάτην) virtue" (1098a16–18).[40] And of course, as he makes explicit already in the last chapter of book I, he

---

[38] Here and in the next section my attention focuses on questions about whether, and if so in what way, Aristotle's implicit claim that *eudaimonia*, as he specifies it in this conclusion, satisfies his two criteria for the highest good. I leave aside, as irrelevant to my concerns in this discussion, consideration of the argument itself by which he works out his specification (the so-called function argument).

[39] This was the view of J. L. Ackrill, most fully argued for in "Aristotle on *Eudaimonia*," *Proceedings of the British Academy* 60 (1974): 3–23. See also his *Aristotle's Ethics* (London: Faber, 1973), 243–44. Irwin, *Aristotle: Nicomachean Ethics*, 1st ed. (1985), 304, holds the same view (though in the second edition commentary [1999], 181–82, he proposes this only as one of two possible interpretations of the passage).

[40] He immediately adds, "in a complete life" (ἔτι δ' ἐν βίῳ τελείῳ). Here it seems clear that Aristotle is using his term τέλειον with its most common ordinary acceptation, not his specially explained one of "final or end-like:" he means a life that has had some normal human range of time, development, and experience over which to play itself out. I take it that this addition is intended to be part of the "definition" of *eudaimonia*, or the human good, that Aristotle adopts here in *NE* I 7, but for my purposes in this chapter I do not need to take it specially into account. In the formulation by which Aristotle specifies what *eudaimonia* is in *Eudemian Ethics* II 1 ("*eudaimonia* would be activity of a complete [τελείας] life deriving from complete [τελείαν] virtue," 1219a38–39), he includes reference to a complete life directly in the formal specification. It is noteworthy that in *EE*'s formulation the activity that is *eudaimonia* is given as that of all the virtues—i.e., virtue as a whole (cf. 1219a37)— with no suggestion that it might instead be simply that of some most final one among them. Nonetheless, if my interpretation below is correct, the *Eudemian* formulation does not differ from what Aristotle says here in *NE*, so far as concerns the happy life itself. On both for-

thinks there are indeed a plurality of virtues. On the one hand, there are moral or ethical virtues (many of those) and, on the other hand, intellectual ones (more than one of those too). Moreover, while he never explicitly ranks the virtues in terms of "finality," upon beginning his discussion of the life of contemplation in book X (promised already at 1096a4–5 in chapter 5 of book I), he does argue (1177a13–18) that the activity of νοῦς or intellect deriving from its proper virtue is "final" (τελεία) *eudaimonia*—and that this activity is "contemplative" (θεωρητική), that is, consists in the activity of theoretical thinking.[41] So, in book X, a specific virtuous activity—namely, excellent theoretical contemplation—is identified as "final" *eudaimonia*. Presumably, then, the virtue that gets exercised in this activity will itself be the most final of the virtues, the finality of the virtue being the basis for its activity's constituting final *eudaimonia*. This suggests pretty explicitly that the human good announced by Aristotle in I 7 is in fact already being conceived as (quite possibly) some single activity, a contemplative one, deriving from the one virtue (the "most final" of them) that constitutes the perfection of our ability to know, in a foundational way, or to contemplate, the fundamental principles on which the universe is grounded. I will say more about this conception in the next section; for now, it is enough to notice that it, too, could fit together well with Aristotle's explanation of how *eudaimonia* is "most choiceworthy." If excellent theoretical contemplation is the

---

mulations, the happy life will be devoted to the exercise of virtue as a whole—the moral as well as the intellectual virtues, including the one for "contemplation." See below, sect. VI.

[41] I am proposing here to understand the qualifier τελεία in application to *eudaimonia* in X 7 (as with τελειοτάτη ἀρετή at I 7, 1098a18) as meaning "final" or "endlike," in accordance with Aristotle's explicit statement (1097a33–34) of how the term is to be construed when proposed as a criterion for the highest good. It is certainly true that Aristotle also uses the term in the *NE* in its more ordinary acceptation of "complete" or "perfect" (as in his reference to a τέλειος βίος at 1098a18). In "Contemplation and Happiness" (n. 29 above), pp. 227–29, I translated τελεία εὐδαιμονία as "complete happiness" and explicated that by "perfect or fully realized happiness." My proposal here does not in fact depart in any essential way from my earlier understanding of the immediate significance of this phrase, since "final" *eudaimonia*, in being *eudaimonia* as the end or (most) endlike thing, and therefore the ultimate object of pursuit, is at the same time "perfect or fully realized" *eudaimonia* (in comparison with morally virtuous activity itself, pursued as an end). (I depart greatly, of course, from my earlier understanding of how to integrate Aristotle's reference to excellent contemplative activity as τελεία εὐδαιμονία into his overall theory of *eudaimonia* as the highest good.) However, I now think it plausible that Aristotle means, in speaking of τελεία εὐδαιμονία, as with τελειοτάτη ἀρετή, to be carrying over his criterial conception of a τέλειον ἀγαθόν as something "final" or "endlike" also to virtue and *eudaimonia* themselves, conceived as ultimate goods and ends. Coming squarely within the context of his discussion of the criteria for the highest good, and their application in identifying and specifying that good, these slightly extended uses of the term for finality are easy and natural.

unqualifiedly final and self-sufficient good, that would mean that it is the single highest end for the organization of a good and happy human life, an end whose character and value are such that simply achieving it would make one's life worth choosing, and lacking in nothing needed for it to be choiceworthy; other goods, of which of course there could be many, would find their place in the life under some controlling subordination to this good activity as final and highest end. Various detailed questions would need to be addressed, but this certainly sounds like a viable conception.

In the past I have resisted this interpretation and have proposed more than one way of reading Aristotle's texts so that they do not involve this idea. I did not see how to make good sense of his ethical theory (his theory of moral virtue and of the value of the moral life) on the basis of it.[42] Impressed by the evidence presented above that it *is* Aristotle's actual view, I now think that there might be hope of accepting it, without wreaking havoc on Aristotle's moral theory; and, besides, the philosophical view that emerges is of considerable interest. So without going (again) into the question whether this interpretation really is the correct or best available given all the evidence, let us see what we can do about Aristotle's moral theory if we are prepared at least to relax our resistance to it.

V

On the view that excellent contemplative activity is (all by itself) the good, Aristotle will be maintaining that this activity is the "end of things achievable by action," the end that is always somehow ultimately in view whenever those living a good human life do anything at all that they choose to do: it organizes and gives structure to the whole of their active, practical life. Further, its presence in their life is sufficient of itself to make it worth choosing, and so worth living. Absolutely nothing is lacking (nothing additional is *needed*) for the choiceworthiness of the life they lead. Thus, as Aristotle sees things, Socrates' mistake in the *Philebus* was to think that *no* ingredient activity or experience in life can be an adequate grounding for its choiceworthiness—that one must look instead to some principles of organization applied from outside, as it were, in combining into a life whatever principal ingredients there would be. No, says Aristotle: excellent contemplative activity itself, though an ingredient, can serve in all the ways that the good must function, given acceptable

---

[42] See *Reason and Human Good in Aristotle* (above, n. 30), 91–115; "Contemplation and Happiness" (above, n. 29).

criteria. It can serve both as an unqualifiedly final end that organizes and structures all other activities and (all by itself) as a self-sufficient good. We need next to consider how this might be so.

As I pointed out (sect. III), the self-sufficiency of the good leaves open that something else might still be needed from some other point of view than the choiceworthiness of the life led with ultimate reference to it. The first point to notice, then, is that in discussing the contemplative life in chapter 7 of book X Aristotle admits that even excellent contemplation still leaves one in need[43] of some other things (the necessities of life, as he calls them), just as morally excellent activity may do (except that the latter needs yet more, beyond the necessities).[44] Moreover, even the wise person (the σοφός), the one who possesses the virtue for contemplation, will find that his surpassingly excellent activity is better (βέλτιον) if he has fellow contemplators to share his thought-work with. In both these cases (the necessities alluded to, whatever exactly those are, and the fellow contemplators whose co-work will make one's own a better thing), Aristotle is clearly recognizing the additional value of something that improves your life with its presence—just, as we have seen (sect. III, fourth paragraph from the end), as with external goods like friends and good looks and good children in NE I 8. To say that you need these things (in addition), as he does, just means that your life will be improved if you have them—even if it is already a life of excellent contemplation.

In what way(s), then, are these additional things needed by persons devoted to the exercise of their virtues for contemplation? I take it that the need for co-workers is obvious enough. But how about the "necessities of life"? First of all, I assume that Aristotle is not referring here to anything that was needed simply in order to make possible virtuous activity—or indeed activity of any sort at all (something needed just for remaining alive and active, such as a minimum regular supply of food and water or air, or a climate at least minimally hospitable for human life, or those things plus being loved by some other people). Any such thing, though a necessity, would not be something beyond those activities, that was needed in addition to them, as providing some improvement in one's life. In fact, in the absence of those conditions there would be no activity, or no virtuous activity, at all. So I take it that by "necessities of life" here Aristotle is thinking of other things that we may think life needs, even if it can

---

[43] Aristotle's word for "need" here is δεῖσθαι. Socrates' term in applying his criterion of sufficiency in the *Philebus* is the same, but with the prefix προσ- ("in addition") (20e6, 21a11).

[44] Chap. 7, 1177a28–35: τῶν μὲν γὰρ πρὸς τὸ ζῆν ἀναγκαίων καὶ σοφὸς καὶ δίκαιος καὶ οἱ λοιποὶ δέονται, τοῖς δὲ τοιούτοις ἱκανῶς κεχορηγημένων ὁ μὲν δίκαιος δεῖται πρὸς οὓς δικαιοπραγήσει καὶ μεθ' ὧν, . . . ὁ δὲ σοφὸς καὶ καθ' αὑτὸν ὢν δύναται θεωρεῖν . . . βέλτιον δ' ἴσως συνεργοὺς ἔχων, ἀλλ' ὅμως αὐταρκέστατος.

be conducted without them—just as contemplation can be engaged in on one's own but goes better if pursued in association with co-workers. Hence, I suppose that, like Protarchus in the *Philebus*, Aristotle is thinking (at least principally) of the ordinary sorts of pleasures we all get and take an interest in while eating and drinking and otherwise engaging in our daily activities. He is thinking that if for some reason one did not enjoy these things one would lack something valuable: these pleasures, one could say, are themselves "necessities of life" (Plato calls some of them "necessary pleasures" in the *Republic*).[45] Aristotle's insistence is only that even without them a life that had excellent contemplation in it as an ingredient would still be choiceworthy: *any* life's choiceworthiness would be directly guaranteed by the presence in it of this activity (provided, of course, that any conditions actually necessary for engaging in it in the first place, and continuing to engage in it, are present).

Before proceeding to examine further how Aristotle's ethical theory fares if he holds that excellent contemplative activity is the human good (all by itself), we need to take into account one last passage, so far left aside, where Aristotle is responding to Socrates' argument in the *Philebus*. This comes in *NE* X 2, where Aristotle is reporting and commenting upon Eudoxus's defense of a hedonist theory of value.[46] Among other arguments for value hedonism, Eudoxus had argued, according to Aristotle, that pleasure must be the good, because pleasure, when added to other sorts of things that are good, makes those other goods more choiceworthy (that is, better), while "the good [or goodness] is increased [only] by itself" (1172b23–25).[47] Aristotle immediately objects (b26–27) that this

---

[45] See 554a, 559d ff. Plato speaks first of "necessary" and "unnecessary" kinds of desire or appetite, but he speaks also, by extension from those, of the corresponding pleasures as necessary or unnecessary, cf. 558d5, 561a3–4, 7, 581e3–4.

[46] I am indebted to Gavin Lawrence's discussion of this passage in "Nonaggregatability, Inclusiveness, and the Theory of Focal Value," at 58–64.

[47] προστιθεμένην τε ὁτῳοῦν τῶν ἀγαθῶν αἱρετώτερον ποιεῖν, οἷον τῷ δικαιοπραγεῖν καὶ σωφρονεῖν, αὔξεσθαι δὲ τὸ ἀγαθὸν αὐτῷ, 1172b23–5. Eudoxus's examples here of goods of another sort than pleasure are just actions and temperate ones. To be consistent with the hedonism he is here advancing we must suppose Eudoxus to have envisaged that just acts when no pleasure is taken in doing them are good because of future pleasure to which they will lead. (He cannot think just acts good in themselves, or for any other reason than some connection they have with pleasure.) So if we accept the general principle that "the good is increased [only] by itself," this will apply to such acts in the following way: these acts are good because of pleasure they involve (in the future); so when their goodness is increased (as everyone must admit) by pleasure in the acts themselves being added, that confirms that indeed pleasure, being the good, is increased by itself (= more of itself, further instances of itself). Thus anyone who grants that virtuous acts are improved if enjoyed in the doing is driven by Eudoxus's argument to identify the goodness of the acts insofar as not immediately enjoyed with some consequent pleasures. There is, thus, more of interest in this argument than Aristotle and Plato acknowledge, in making their criticisms of it.

argument can really only make the claim (ἀποφαίνειν) that pleasure is *among* the good things, no more a good than any other good. We can grant Eudoxus (this was his example) that an act of justice becomes more choiceworthy if the agent enjoys doing it, and we can grant that anything that increases anything's goodness has to be itself good. But from those premises it only follows that pleasure is *an* (intrinsic) good, one type perhaps among others. As Aristotle says (b27–28), the general principle Eudoxus is relying on in this argument, is that "every good is more choiceworthy together with another good than on its own (μονούμενον)," so that his example of just acts becoming more choiceworthy if enjoyed only shows that pleasure is one intrinsic good, one type of good (the just act itself being of another type, good independently of any relation it bears to pleasure).[48]

Aristotle adds (b28–31), plainly reporting the contents of *Philebus* 20–23, that Plato used this same argument (the one Aristotle himself has just set out in response to Eudoxus, using Eudoxus's premises to derive the conclusion that pleasure is merely one good among others) to *refute* the claim that pleasure is *the* good. Plato, Aristotle says, argued that the life of pleasure is more choiceworthy with reasoning than without it, so that if that mixture or combination is preferable (κρεῖττον), pleasure cannot be the good. For "the good does not become more choiceworthy by having anything added to it."[49] In fact Plato's argument in the *Philebus* does rely (in effect) on Eudoxus's general principle, that "every good is more choiceworthy together with another good than on its own." And it could very reasonably be interpreted, as Aristotle interprets it, as counting pleasure (along with reasoning, too, of course) among those goods

---

[48] Here it is important to see that Eudoxus is claiming that a just act itself is more choiceworthy when enjoyed, because of the addition to it of the pleasure. He is not saying merely that a just action plus the pleasure taken in doing it—that sum or package—is more choiceworthy than the act taken on its own. So the principle in quotation marks in my text makes the following claim: any good thing is *itself* made more choiceworthy when taken together with another good. (In Eudoxus's instance, a just act is made more choiceworthy by the addition of another good to it, the pleasure taken in it.) This principle is one that Aristotle, as we will see shortly, himself disputes (1172b32–35). If the good in question is *the* good, then it is not true that *that* good becomes more choiceworthy if some other good is added to it. So Aristotle accepts this principle in application only to goods other than the highest one.

[49] τοιούτῳ δὴ λόγῳ καὶ Πλάτων ἀναιρεῖ ὅτι οὐκ ἔστιν ἡδονὴ τἀγαθόν· αἱρετώτερον γὰρ εἶναι τὸν ἡδὺν βίον μετὰ φρονήσεως ἢ χωρίς, εἰ δὲ τὸ μικτὸν κρεῖττον, οὐκ εἶναι τὴν ἡδονὴν τἀγαθόν· οὐδενὸς γὰρ προστεθέντος αὐτῷ τἀγαθὸν αἱρετώτερον γίνεσθαι, 1172b28–31. In paraphrasing the first part of this passage as claiming that with this argument Plato "refutes the claim that pleasure is the good," I am taking the content of the ὅτι- or that-clause in the Greek ("pleasure is not the good") as expressing the conclusion of Plato's refutatory argument; that-clauses after verbs such as ἀναιρεῖν ("refutes") do not necessarily express instead the proposition refuted.

that become more choiceworthy when another good is added to it. I say only that Plato's argument could be so interpreted, because in fact Plato does not say anything at all in the *Philebus* passage about the choiceworthiness of goods such as pleasure, much less of the good itself: he only speaks of the choiceworthiness of the three lives he compares, those chockful of pleasure and of reason, plus the mixed life (21d3, 22a5, b1, 5, 7). However, it does seem not unreasonable to reconstrue Plato's argument as Aristotle does here, making it focus on the way that the good itself is and is not choiceworthy: as I have said (sect. IV) in discussing Aristotle's account of self-sufficiency in *NE* I 7, whatever makes lives choiceworthy by its presence is reasonably taken itself to be in some prior way choiceworthy, in fact the *most* choiceworthy thing.[50] Still, this is Aristotle's own gloss on Plato's argument, intended to show how Plato could be construed as responding to Eudoxus's claims on behalf of pleasure: if with Eudoxus "every good is more choiceworthy with another good than on its own," but the good itself is not made more choiceworthy by the addition to it of anything, then Plato's argument in the *Philebus* tells us, in effect, that pleasure cannot be the good because *it* is made more choiceworthy if reasoning is added to it.

At the end of the passage, Aristotle then adds, now in his own voice, the following remark (1172b32–35):

> And it is clear that [not only pleasure, but] nothing else could be the good that becomes more choiceworthy when together with any [other] thing that is intrinsically (καθ' αὐτό) good. What then is of this kind, that we can have a share in? *That* is what we are seeking.[51]

Now, of course, at this point in his discussion (X 2) Aristotle has not yet declared his discovery of what he says here he is seeking, namely the good that does not become more choiceworthy when together with any other intrinsic good. He will do so, however, only a few chapters farther on, in X 7. The highest good, or *eudaimonia*, he there declares, is the activity of excellent contemplative thought. So, in his view, excellent contemplative thought is a good that does *not* become more choiceworthy when taken together with any other good—not when taken together with ordinary

---

[50] One might point to ἑλεῖν (aorist of αἱρεῖν, the root verb in αἱρετόν, choiceworthy) at 20d9 (taken together with φροντίζει in 10) as having this implication (I quote this text above n. 3, and see my discussion in sect. II): Socrates might be thought to be saying here that nothing *else* is chosen (e.g., a life) except insofar as it is accomplished with *the* good, the latter being chosen in some prior way.

[51] δῆλον δ' ὡς οὐδ' ἄλλο οὐδὲν τἀγαθὸν ἂν εἴη, ὃ μετά τινος τῶν καθ' αὐτὸ ἀγαθῶν αἱρετώτερον γίνεται. τί οὖν ἐστὶ τοιοῦτον, οὗ καὶ ἡμεῖς κοινωνοῦμεν; τοιοῦτον γὰρ ἐπιζητεῖται, 1172b32–35.

pleasures, not when taken together with any other of the goods of life, not when taken together with good co-workers conducting their contemplative thought along with one's own and making it better.[52] Notice that this goes contrary to the Eudoxan assumption that "every good is more choiceworthy with another good than on its own," if that is taken without restriction, and made to apply not merely to subordinate goods (with that restriction Aristotle would endorse it) but also to the highest good itself. It also goes counter (as we have seen in sect. IV) to Plato's argument in the *Philebus,* that no particular good, no good kind of thing or kind of activity (neither pleasure nor reasoning) can be *the* good. Thus Aristotle accepts the principle that he says Plato used in order to refute Eudoxus— that "the good does not become more choiceworthy by having anything added to it"—but he disagrees with Plato's own conclusion drawn from it, that *the* good cannot be any *particular* good.

In the light of this passage of X 2, then, we see that Aristotle holds the following position. He holds that any life having excellent contemplative thought in it, as its ultimate and constantly organizing end, is good and choiceworthy—worth living—whatever else it has or lacks. It is worth living *because* that contemplation, appreciated for its intrinsic and overarching value, occupies this position in it (and because of nothing else, not even in part). He holds that some such lives are better—even, if you like, though Aristotle never quite says this, more choiceworthy—than others, because they have additional goods that are not present in the others. He holds, however, that when excellent contemplative thinking is ingredient as the organizing end in a life with such additional goods, that thinking is not *itself* more choiceworthy than when it is similarly ingredient in lives without them. Excellent contemplative thinking, we could say, is for Aristotle absolutely or unqualifiedly choiceworthy (ἁπλῶς αἱρετόν)— *nothing* can increase *its* choiceworthiness, even if the addition of further goods alongside it can increase the choiceworthiness of a life in which it is found.

---

[52] This shows that Aristotle's view that *eudaimonia* is most choiceworthy "without being counted together," as that notion is explained in I 7, 1097b16–20, does not include the thought that if or when it *is* counted together with other goods then it becomes more choiceworthy than it is without them. Thus the counterfactual reading of the participle συναριθμουμένην (see n. 34 above) gives a correct interpretation of Aristotle's actual view on the "most choiceworthiness" of *eudaimonia,* even though, as I argued above (sect. IV), it is not necessary—indeed, it is a mistake—to insist on understanding Aristotle's comments on the "most choiceworthiness" of *eudaimonia* in I 7 as excluding the thought that it is more choiceworthy when counted together.

VI

We can now return, in conclusion, to the difficulty I alluded to above (end of sect. IV) about moral virtue, if Aristotle does hold that excellent contemplative activity, all by itself, is the highest human good. What, then, are we to make of the value of morally good actions and of moral virtue itself? Precisely how do they relate to this highest good insofar as they are chosen and arranged or organized with a view to it—while it, all by itself, is the ultimate end of a good human life? We are left to a considerable degree to our own devices in attempting to answer this question on Aristotle's behalf, since it is a noteworthy (and, at least for us, a highly regrettable) fact that he nowhere takes this question up, nor does he even seem to feel that it poses any special problem. In the first chapter of book VI of the *NE* Aristotle raises the question of the ὅρος, or principle of delimitation for choosing the "mean" in ethical action and passion, but even if by the end of that book (see 1145a6–9) he has indicated that this principle is somehow to be equated with theoretical wisdom or its activity, he nowhere in book VI (or elsewhere) attempts to tell us anything directly and in detail about how this function of delimitation is supposed to be carried out. We can only attempt to construct an answer for ourselves, drawing on the somewhat scattered materials that Aristotle does provide us, together with other ideas that were available to him in his own intellectual milieu.

For present purposes, a brief sketch of how this might be done will suffice.[53] The first point to notice is that, as I interpret him, Aristotle recognizes a vast array of things that are, in a certain way, good independently of any orientation to the highest good. Bodily pleasure is good just because it satisfies natural desires of ours; food is good just because our bodily substance and the continuation of our physical lives, as well as other aspects of our lives, depend on it. Likewise, I would take it, companionship is good because again of complicated, and perhaps in some ways obscure, natural desires of ours. Similarly for all kinds of games and sports; fulfilling work; music and art and literature; perhaps even having power and control over others. All these things, and many others as well, answer to natural capacities and needs of human beings, as such. We need them; without some selection from among them, suitable to our individual personalities and situations, our lives are deprived. They remain good

[53] Gabriel Richardson has a great deal to say on this question in her dissertation (see n. 11 above). My own thinking has been very much improved by reading her work and discussing it with her, and my sketch draws on some of her ideas. I do not mean to suggest, however, that she would accept everything I say here.

for us whether or not we recognize moral or any other type of virtue as the highest good, or even as a good at all; they are good without reference to any other good, even the highest. Where, for Aristotle, the orientation to the highest good comes in, is with our *choosing* instances of such goods. When, and in what manner and way, shall we select and make use of such goods? Even if they are good independently of being oriented to the highest good, they are not *choiceworthy*, on Aristotle's conception, except when, and in ways that, such orientation provides. The orientation of these goods, in worthy choices, to the highest good seems to proceed, for Aristotle, in two stages, which we need to take up separately.

To begin with, to a very great extent moral virtue, as Aristotle conceives it, simply consists in molding our capacity for choosing in such a way that we do select such independent goods only on certain occasions or in certain circumstances, and only in certain particular ways and manners (and not others).[54] From the perspective of virtuous choosers the value of independent goods that they choose is subordinated to the values encapsulated in that correct choice, as such. The timing and the manner of the selection and use of these independent goods, deriving from the act of choice, are regarded as reflecting special values that are a level higher in worth than that of the independent goods themselves that are selected. The latter are choiceworthy only if chosen when and as they ought to be, and the inherent excellence of those acts of choice is seen by the choosing agent, and is to *be* seen, as ranking more highly in worth than any or all of the objects chosen. Thus, the way the independent goods are selected and used is of higher value than any value in the items selected themselves, or in the use and enjoyment of them. In that precise sense, moral action (and moral virtue, which expresses itself in moral action) constitutes a distinctly overarching end for the moral chooser. As such an end, controlling the choice and use of the independent goods, it constitutes a higher level of value than the value of those goods. The choice of such subordinate goods can never be made in a correct manner if this difference of level is not fully reflected in the very making of the choice. So, for Aristotle, moral action and moral virtue are important and higher-level ends to which any proper concern for these independent goods, as I am calling them, must be subordinated, as to an end that organizes and controls their pursuit.[55] The independent goods are and remain

---

[54] On this conception—common to all the Greek moral philosophers—the "moral" virtues are not limited to, and have no original connection to, serving the needs or interests of others besides the agent. They can encompass all kinds of personal and private concerns. Not only justice, but temperance and personal courage, too, count as virtues.

[55] I leave aside here all questions about what sort of considerations about action go into a moral choice, as Aristotle understands it. Even if it consisted entirely in some process of assessing, in their own terms, the independent values of the independent goods, and then

good for us, as I have indicated, simply because of the ways that they respond to needs (physical, psychological, social) that human beings, simply by their nature, all have. What moral virtue does is to direct our selection and use of them in such a way as to make us constantly aware of the higher value of our rationality itself—including our rationality in making orderly, suitable, overall coherent use of them.

However, according to Aristotle (if we accept the interpretation according to which excellent contemplation is, all by itself, our highest good), moral virtue itself is oriented toward excellent contemplative activity as to an end. So he also holds that the independent goods, being subordinated to the values of moral choice, are at the same time subordinated, through the subordination of the latter to the highest good or *eudaimonia*, to excellent contemplative activity as well—and indeed ultimately. But in what way are moral virtue and moral value oriented toward excellent contemplative activity as their end? One point to make right away is this. On this interpretation, Aristotle's view implies that just as in using the independent goods it is crucial, if that use is to be choiceworthy, for them to be chosen and used in the awareness that there is something better (so to speak, categorically better) than they are (namely, correct choice or, more generally, moral virtue); so, that choice, insofar as it is *moral* choice, must itself be aware that there is something better even than it—namely, excellent contemplative activity. Moreover (and this is my second point), moral virtue and moral choice are, of course, excellences of the reasoning part of the soul.[56] So one might expect to be able to work out some understanding of how excellent moral reasoning functions (for example with respect to its focus on truth, systematicity, coherence) that could make it mirror in some suitable way the excellent processes of excellent contemplative thinking. In other words, one might expect the two aspects of reason that Aristotle distinguishes, the practical and the theoretical, to be internally related in such a way that the moral excellences, those of practical reasoning, could be seen as lesser instantiations of the

---

figuring out some way of obtaining some maximum, or some satisfactory quantity, of the lower sort or level of value attaching to these goods, the level distinction I have insisted on would remain. The value of choosing well, and getting the choice right, would still function as an end to which the values of the independent goods would be subordinate in the way I have indicated.

[56] Strictly speaking, the moral virtues (temperance, courage, etc.) are, on Aristotle's view, conditions of the "desiderative" part or aspect of the soul, which is a reasoning part only in the extended sense that it can come, as it does when possessed of those virtues, to obey reason—i.e., practical reason—when the latter decides what is best. I leave aside here the details of Aristotle's views on the interplay between reason and feeling (nonrational desire) so as to concentrate on practical reason, conceived as the authoritative source of an agent's choices.

very same values fully instantiated in, and only in, theoretical thought. This would be a second way that the excellences of the practical use of the mind could be subordinated to the excellence of its theoretical use, precisely as to an end.

Thus one would be valuing the rational perfection present in practical thinking, when that is subject to the procedures and constraints of the moral virtues, as a subordinate end in two ways. (1) It would be subordinated as a value to the higher value of pure theoretical knowledge of the world order as a whole in its relation to the (rational) first principles on which it depends (a much larger and more complex system than the system of human life): in the very act of using reason to do morally virtuous actions for their own sakes, one would be deeply aware that there is a use of reason even better than that. And simultaneously (2) one would be recognizing the purer and more thoroughly reason-governed way of grasping the truth that is found in excellent theoretical thinking as a model for the less fully reasoned-out grasp of truth that moral understanding of human life can, at its best, achieve.[57] One would, as a result, be fairly described as pursuing even in one's moral actions the ultimate end of excellent theoretical thinking. That would always be in view, as a finally controlling value—controlling in that it was the highest and final perfection of reason, reference to which grounds, and is needed to ground, all worthy choices—both in choosing morally virtuous actions themselves and in one's selection, through moral virtue and its standards of evaluation, of independent goods to pursue and enjoy. On this interpretation, then, Aristotle would imply that morally virtuous persons who also grasped the true highest end, excellent contemplation, as the ultimate goal of human life, would be leading their moral and political life, too, constantly for the sake of such contemplation as their highest end.[58]

---

[57] In this connection one should take note of Aristotle's emphasis on the limitations of moral knowledge—its exceptionability, its reliance on perception for establishing some basic truths, etc. See *NE* I 4, 1094b22–1095a13; IV 5, 1126a31–b10.

[58] Here I intend to be describing the contemplative life (ὁ κατὰ τὸν νοῦν βίος, 1178a6–7); on the interpretation I am offering that will, of course, be a life of moral virtue too, since in such a life the values of moral choice will be fully present, supplemented however, in the way we have seen, by the goods of excellent contemplation. Aristotle contrasts this life with that of "the other virtue"—i.e., moral virtue (ὁ κατὰ τὴν ἄλλην ἀρετήν, 1178a9)—because, on this interpretation, it is perfectly possible to possess and practice the moral virtues without possessing or practicing the ones for contemplation. Though contemplation occupies no place in the activities making up such a life (the life of the excellent political leader, or the fine ordinary citizen), it will follow from the account I have given above of the moral virtues that in this life, too, contemplation will play a significant role nonetheless. One cannot be acting morally virtuously unless one has vividly in mind, as one makes one's moral choices among the independent goods, that there is something better—indeed, as I put it above, categorially better—than the goods involved in morally good choosing and action: viz., the

Much more, of course, would need to be looked into and thought about before an interpretation along these lines could be made finally acceptable. However, I think this sketch does show how we might understand Aristotle's idea that *eudaimonia,* or the highest good, is excellent contemplative thinking (all by itself), in such a way that it would not undermine the values of moral choice and moral action taken on their own as fundamental goods, and ends, for human life. It would not commit Aristotle to holding that the superior value of contemplation might in some circumstances so outrank moral values that one would, on his theory, be entitled simply to override the claims of morality and do something horrible in order to make room in one's life for some extra contemplation. And it would not commit him to any bizarre and unacceptable account of what actually is morally required, or permitted, of us: as if it could all of a sudden become an act of justice to do what in other circumstances would be a horrible violation, in consequence of the position at the top of the hierarchy of values assigned to excellent contemplation—because by doing it one could make possible some extra contemplative thinking.[59] On the view I have sketched, moral virtue and contemplative virtue, and the goods that I have been calling independent, are related to each other so to speak each *en bloc,* as values of different orders or at different levels. As I have explained, excellent contemplative activity, as the highest good, and the final and ultimate end of all choices and all actions, serves to organize and control the pursuit of these subordinate goods by being the fundamental type of value, the supreme value that must be recognized constantly, whenever any other good is chosen at all (if it is to be

---

good of excellent contemplative activity. Presumably because of limitations in their own natural capacities and talents, the people leading this life do not engage in contemplation, but they are nonetheless aware (vaguely, in the way someone who does not have actual experience of the thing they are missing might be aware) that there *is* something humanly better than moral action, and that this is a higher, philosophical, and contemplative use of the human rational powers. Reasonably, on my interpretation, Aristotle calls this life "happy in a secondary way" in comparison with the "happiest" life, the contemplative one (1178a7–9). It too is governed and controlled by the same ultimate end, that of excellent contemplation, even if the *activity* of contemplation plays no role in it. Though choiceworthy, however, because of the choiceworthiness of morally virtuous action, it is not self-sufficient—it is not "lacking in nothing" that contributes to choiceworthiness.

[59] To be sure, people devoted to excellent contemplative activity as the highest human good would presumably wish to limit in various ways their political, moral, and social connections and commitments, so as not to overvalue (as they would see it) the goods deriving from them. Part of what it is to see constantly that there is something of higher value than the goods of social, political, and moral life would be an effort to reserve one's time and energies so much as possible (given the requirements of morality) for the higher value of intellectually excellent work. If that led to a somewhat different conception of the extent of one's moral commitments from the traditional one among Greeks of his time, Aristotle could plausibly still claim that no violation of actual moral requirements would be entailed.

choice*worthy*). This is not a way of organizing one's choices that threatens to place contemplative activity in competition, as object of pursuit, with the other goods that are subordinate to it. Thus moral value is subordinated to contemplative activity as a kind of value, or in terms of the values that they are. Nonetheless, it is moral virtue, and only it, that tells us what is rationally required of us, or permitted, to *do*—what our choices among subordinate goods, and so our actions, should be. These choices are made in light of the totality of our human nature and our needs and interests as human beings—even if, as Aristotle recommends, we take our theoretical and contemplative powers as our most distinctive and highest capacities. We remain full human beings, with all the human needs, no matter what.

So there is no call (and, I think, in fact no room) to raise questions about what, given that excellent contemplation is the final and highest good, we should do if a requirement of moral virtue (say some duty of justice) should, as things have worked out willy nilly, force us to neglect an opportunity to do some heavy contemplating that without that requirement we would certainly give ourselves over to.[60] On the view I

---

[60] I take it that, on Aristotle's view of practical wisdom and moral virtue, it is part of the systematic, coherent, and true understanding of all the human needs, of which moral virtue oversees our pursuit, that there are relatively fixed, though flexible, standards of behavior that place a number of ordinary, natural human concerns ahead of any personal and private interests (even the interest in engaging in contemplative thought, for those capable of it). Temperance, for example, imposes a certain limit on our enjoyment of the pleasures of eating, drinking, and sex that would not permit our (say) engaging in them to excess (as judged correctly by that virtue) even if, in some circumstances (by some, perhaps fantastic, scenario), we could, by doing so (and only by so doing), increase our opportunities for excellent contemplative theorizing. Likewise, justice imposes limits on our pursuing our private interest even in contemplative activity, if that would require reneging on a promise, or abusing a trust, or otherwise inflicting grievous harm on another person, either by commission or omission. Given that assumption, those who, out of love of contemplation, should choose to spend extra time at contemplative work, at such costs, could not correctly expect to "gain" by getting the value of any extra period of contemplation (as if that "gain" would outweigh any loss of the less-valued moral good that would consist in doing the correct moral actions omitted). The cost to them would not just be the loss of time spent in doing the omitted morally virtuous acts. In fact, such action would prove that those agents had never, all along, understood correctly the standards of moral choice, in the first place. Thus, they would have missed completely *all* the value of morally virtuous choices and actions throughout all their previous actions. Such choices would reveal a deep error in their understanding of moral values, and so would indicate that, however often and however apparently correctly they had engaged in "moral action," they had never understood what it was and what it required. In this way, we can see that even if moral thinking and moral knowledge are lesser instantiations of the values of reason that are most fully and perfectly contained in excellent contemplation, the cost of choosing to pursue or engage in contemplative activity, even of a presumptively excellent character, at the cost of doing something morally bad, would be the total loss of *all* of the value of moral thought and action throughout one's life (or, anyhow,

have sketched, such a question would not arise, or it would be easily and immediately answered. On this view, a life is made choiceworthy simply by the presence in it of excellent contemplation as the good that is recognized as the highest.[61] As I have explained, that good is taken to be unqualifiedly choiceworthy: when carried out over a greater extension of time it does not become more choiceworthy than it would be over a lesser extent. So there would be no extra value achieved by the extra time contemplating that one could set against the values involved (both that of the independent goods and that of moral action itself) if one did the virtuous thing. So acting (see note 60) would entail the loss of the value not only of the omitted moral action, but of all "moral" actions one had done while harboring the misunderstanding of morality that allowing such "exceptions" would imply. In fact, on this view, the thing to do, clearly, is to meet all the legitimate requirements of morality first, including any that might take you away from contemplative thinking that without them you would have engaged in, and then give yourself over to such work when and as circumstances—including in the first instance various moral relationships and commitments—permit. So I do think that on the view I have been proposing, Aristotle's understanding of moral virtue, however unusual and indeed extraordinarily interesting it may be from other points of view, does not strain our credulity. The high appreciation of moral virtue as a fundamental human value, which so much of Aristotle's writing on ethical topics so clearly evinces, is not undermined if, in fact, Aristotle does hold that excellent contemplation is (all by itself) the highest human good and final end of human life, when properly conducted.[62]

---

for any period when one was prepared, explicitly or implicitly, to violate moral standards in favor of the self-indulgence of extra time at contemplating bought by such means). On Aristotle's theory of the special value of excellent contemplation, as I understand it, that could never be the right thing to do. (I thank Christopher Bobonich for raising questions about my interpretation to which these remarks are a response.)

[61] Of course a life devoted simply to moral virtue without contemplative understanding would also be for Aristotle a life worth living, and choiceworthy (see n. 58). I take Aristotle's view about the choiceworthiness of lives to be that any life in which rational functioning and its virtues (whether merely practical or theoretical too) are included as ends is worth living, and choiceworthy.

[62] In preparing this final version I have been assisted by valuable written criticisms and queries on an early draft by Robert Heinaman, T. H. Irwin, and my commentator at the Keeling Colloquium in London 2001, Anthony Kenny. I thank them and all the colloquium participants for a challenging and helpful discussion. Later versions benefited from discussion at the University of Delaware, where I presented the paper in December 2002, and Stanford University, where it formed the basis of one of my Immanuel Kant lectures, April 2003. I also have Pierre Destrée and Gerd van Riel to thank for their comments, of which I have tried to take account in this final version, when I delivered the paper in Leuven in May 2003.

CHAPTER 12

MORAL THEORY AND MORAL

IMPROVEMENT: SENECA

I

S ENECA'S STOIC WRITINGS show clearly that he had a complete and accurate, and also an admirably subtle, understanding of Stoic physical theory and Stoic epistemology and philosophy of language, as well as Stoic ethics—his constant primary concern. His understanding of these matters plainly conforms in all fundamentals to the "orthodox" Stoicism elaborately worked out by the end of the third century B.C. and set down in a multitude of philosophical treatises by Chrysippus, the greatest of the earlier Greek Stoics. This is so even if in points of detail and matters of emphasis Seneca's understanding also reflects the work of Greek writers of the second and first centuries B.C. (Panaetius and Posidonius, most notably). Chrysippus and these Greek writers expounded Stoic theory as experts not just in it, but also in philosophical truth. They were professional teachers of philosophy. They addressed their hearers and readers as possessors of the conclusive arguments that would establish, once and for all, all the truths of the Stoic philosophy—in philosophy of language and logic, in physics, in epistemology, as well as in all matters of ethical theory and the correct bases for living a human life. Their function in their writings was to establish, on the basis of philosophical argument and analysis, and to defend against the contrary views of other philosophers, or in response to their attacks, the positions on all these questions that marked Stoicism off as a single school of philosophy, with distinctive doctrines of its own.[1] They did not, of course, write as if they were complete "sages" themselves—that is, perfectly and completely developed instances of human nature, according to the Stoic account of such perfection. For the Stoics, that perfection requires much more than grasping, in some single writing or otherwise at some single time, the reasons that allegedly support, and conclusively support, particular points of Stoic doctrine. It requires such a grasp on these as leads one constantly,

---

[1] I do not mean to deny that there were differences of opinion on some matters among individual Stoic teachers, or developments over time in the doctrine of the school. Since my purpose in this general sketch is to mark Seneca's writings clearly off from those of these earlier Greek Stoics, such details matter little.

without any possibility of failure, to live the sort of life that the Stoic philosophy was intended to establish as the correct one for a human being. Such a grasp is one that cannot be shaken by any possible arguments later presented, or events in one's own or another's life, that might seem to cast doubt on them. That sort of grasp no Greek Stoic author professed to have. Nonetheless, they did write as philosophical experts, experts in the truth, expounding and defending Stoic doctrines on the basis of philosophical considerations which they argued did establish them as true.

In two important respects, Seneca's Stoic writings differ from those of his Greek authorities (and, for that matter, from the philosophical writings of his Roman predecessor, Cicero). To begin with, and most crucially, both in his *Moral Essays* (the twelve books of "Dialogues," including the three works meant to "console" someone on some grievous loss, plus *On Mercy* and *On Favors*) and in his 124 *Moral Letters to Lucilius,* Seneca writes to specific, named addressees as their spiritual adviser or guide.[2] He writes as himself a deeply committed adherent of Stoicism, but his purpose is not primarily to expound and defend Stoic doctrines, with appeal to the philosophical arguments on which the Stoic philosophers rested them. Rather, he means to offer advice and assistance to his addressee (and, by implication, his readers in general) in their own efforts to heal their spiritual disorders and discomforts either in general or in particular respects and circumstances. Moreover, he writes explictly in his *Letters to Lucilius,* and implicitly or explicitly in each of his Stoic essays, as someone who is working to improve himself and the character of his life through his increasing grasp of the truths of Stoic theory.[3] On that basis he offers to aid others (Lucilius, his own brother Novatus—later Gallio—, Serenus, the Emperor Nero, Aebutius Liberalis, his mother Helvia, other friends) in their own efforts (sometimes only presumed) to improve themselves and their lives through grasping the truths of Stoicism to whatever imperfect degree, and making them their life's guide so far as they can manage to do that. In Stoic terms, he counts himself as a προκόπτων or *progrediens* who may have gotten further in the long effort to win through to a secure grasp on the true basis for living a good human life, but who, like his addressees, has still much more work to do before he could conceivably claim to have attained this goal. In this, of course (except for his explicitness), he does not differ from the earlier Greek thinkers. However, he does not write as an expert philosopher or an expert in philosophical truth. He is a philosophical fellow struggler—a

---

[2] The essential work on this aspect of Seneca's writing is Ilsetraut Hadot, *Seneca und die Griechisch-Römische Tradition der Seelenleitung.*

[3] See, e.g., *Letters* 6 (paragraphs 1, 3–4), 8.2, 27.1, 45.4, 61.1–2, 68.8–9, 71.36–37, 87.4–5.

seeker after the truth who, like his addressees, is a philosophical amateur, not an official Stoic teacher presenting and defending the school's dogmas.[4] He writes as a Roman, for other Romans of the upper classes, seeking to grasp, and help others grasp, the way of life propounded in and by the Stoic philosophical tradition, and to shape their own lives so far as possible in accordance with it.

One finds, in fact, not just with Seneca, but with our other main authors in the history of Stoicism under the Roman Imperial regime, Epictetus and Marcus Aurelius, an almost *impassioned* interest in curing one's own spiritual ills, in moral self-improvement, and in helping others to cure and improve themselves. This has always been a major source of their appeal. More strictly philosophical authors who were also sources in later times for Stoic theory, such as Cicero or Sextus Empiricus or Plutarch, have not played nearly so large a role in the survival and continued appeal of Stoic ideas in the Renaissance and since as these Stoics of the Imperial period.[5] However, all three of these authors—as Stoics—are committed to regarding spiritual cures and self-improvement as depending, in the last analysis, on a person's own improved and deepened *understanding* of certain philosophical truths. These truths, according to Stoics, provide the crucial grounding and support for the Stoic way of life as the best one for a human being. Moreover, understanding these truths and accepting them *for* these philosophical reasons—the ones put forward in Stoic theory as proving their truth—is the only secure basis on which to live a Stoic life at all. For Stoics, life is not improved simply by improved choices and behavior, however welcome that might be in other respects, but only by behavior to the extent that it reflects and derives from an improved state of mind. And according to Stoic conceptions, only an improvement in one's grasp of the *reasons* that make the Stoic doctrines true can constitute such an improved state of mind. Thus, for the Stoics only people's beliefs about practical matters, only the state of their minds (their power of reasoning) in relation to these, affect how their lives go, for better or for worse, and whether or not they are good lives. For the Stoics, for whom a mind just *is* a power of thought—there are no nonrational aspects of the human mind on their view, as there are, for example, for Plato and Aristotle—the only way, ultimately, to improve a person's beliefs is to give them better reasons, and to help them appreciate,

---

[4] See, e.g., *Letter* 45.4.

[5] I think here especially of Justus Lipsius, who devoted many years of work to editing Seneca's works, and to propagating their salutary message for the improvement of individual and political life in early modern Europe. See John M. Cooper, "Justus Lipsius and the Revival of Stoicism in Late Sixteenth-Century Europe," in *New Essays on the History of Autonomy*, ed. Natalie Brender and Larry Krasnoff.

in purely rational and philosophical terms, the implications and power of those reasons for transforming oneself and one's way of life.

A Stoic spiritual adviser or guide, such as Seneca wants to be, is therefore in quite a delicate position. By contrast with the Stoic conception of the human good and a well-lived human life, the Epicurean does not make any sort of improvement of one's mind and in one's understanding any part of the goal: for Epicureans, a constant pleasurable state of feeling constitutes the good and is the goal of a well-lived life. So an Epicurean could happily rely in his own spiritual guidance simply on getting his patients vividly to see the world through Epicurus's eyes—as a place made up of atoms and void swirling eternally, with no divine powers of any sort controlling anything that happens, and in which only a pleasurable state of mind is worth striving for. He could limit himself to getting his patients to memorize various basic precepts as guides to achieving and maintaining that state of mind, and to train themselves to keep them in mind as they face adversities and make their choices. For an Epicurean, it does not matter at all on what grounds one holds to this general view, indeed whether one holds to it on any grounds (that is, philosophical reasons) at all: all that matters is that one *does* keep it and the relevant precepts in mind, and holds to them with a feeling of conviction. But for a Stoic, whose ultimate goal is precisely to improve his own and others' minds—their grasp of philosophical truths on the basis of the reasons that in fact make them true—matters can never be so simple.[6]

Writing, as he does, in the ancient tradition of the spiritual director, Seneca adopts a style of writing, and a whole series of rhetorical devices, aimed at winning his addressee over to the Stoic worldview and to feeling its uplifting power, and the sublimity and grandeur of life led in accordance with it. By living this way, Seneca repeatedly makes us feel, we make ourselves partners of the cosmic god, Jupiter or Zeus, in world government, by regarding all external conditions and events, and even ones in one's body, as strictly indifferent from the point of view of one's personal good as a rational mind. Speaking, as he does, to persons who are still quite deeply engrossed in bad and harmful ways of life, or constantly apt to fall back into them, this literary style and these rhetorical presentations of the Stoic view are, in themselves, entirely appropriate. Indeed, some might argue that it is only through writing of that inspirational sort that any author has any chance at all of actually affecting the way people live their life: what is needed is a fundamental reform or conversion, and only emotion-stirring appeals to one's deepest feelings can effect that. Both Plato's and Aristotle's theories of moral character, in their different

[6] For a discussion of Seneca's engagement with Epicurus and the Epicurean outlook on life, see below, chap. 13, sect. II.

ways, support some such view. Because, for them, human beings have three independent sources of motivation that can and do affect not just how they feel but how they choose and how they act, it can make excellent sense to suppose that appeals, through inspiring writing, to our deepest feelings (seated in parts of the soul other than reason) are the crucial and most fundamental requirement if one is to work any permanent improvement in another's life orientation. Indeed, it has been argued that, for Aristotle, reasoned conviction about moral truth is nothing more than the thought content of such emotionally induced states of feeling.[7]

Seneca, however, is, and wishes to write as, a Stoic—not a Peripatetic, or a Platonist—however much, along with others at his time, he admires these ancient thinkers and regards them, along with Zeno and Chrysippus, as among the most authoritative of philosophers. There is a danger—and I will argue that Seneca does fall victim to it—that in relying so heavily on these devices of the spiritual director, a Stoic writer will tend to forget or neglect the fact that the ultimate goal (for himself as well as for his addressees) is to improve one's own philosophical understanding of the reasons why the truths of Stoicism really are true. For a Stoic, as I have said, a mere feeling of conviction—such as might well be imbued by these rhetorical means—is not good enough. It might well help at early stages of the process, and might even have some salutary effects at much later ones, in helping people to get through rough spots in their life or bolster them against momentary temptations or other stresses that could lead one to slide back. But it is crucial for any Stoic to keep in mind that on Stoic views such feelings of commitment can never be more than an ancillary aid to—they cannot provide the substance of—improvement.[8] As

---

[7] I take this to be John McDowell's view. See "Virtue and Reason" and "Some Issues in Aristotle's Moral Psychology" in his *Mind, Value and Reality*.

[8] Ilsetraut Hadot, in her account of Seneca's methods as spiritual adviser, marks a distinction between a first stage, where patients come to know the basic theoretical views that support the Stoic way of life, and a second, in which these views become ingrained in their soul, plus a third, in which, through further practice as well as further encouragements of the same sort as at the second stage, they come to be active and effective always in their life (*Seneca*, pp. 103–26). Thus, on her account, the rhetorical encouragements, which take place at the second and third stages, are preceded by a stage at which the patient first learns the philosophical theories in a purely intellectual way. Here she speaks in terms of their coming to *know* them: "Erst muß man sich die Elemente des Wissens aneignen, . . . was ein rein intellektueller Vorgang ist, sodann muß man sich das Wissen so einprägen, daß man es immer parat hat," p. 105). For Hadot, therefore, rhetorical presentations do not compete with philosophical explanations, or replace them in Seneca's practice: they are a useful, indeed much needed, supplement applied subsequently to an intellectual, presumably philosophical, training. However, on examination it becomes clear that at the first stage all that happens, for her, is that the doctrines are laid out for patients so that they now know what views or opinions they are expected to hold; here to know the doctrines is simply to know

I will argue, however much Seneca himself does show a detailed and excellent knowledge of Stoic philosophical doctrine and the philosophical grounds that Stoic philosophers put forward in order to establish it, he often evinces a harmfully dismissive attitude to the value, for the good life itself, of knowledge of these matters. The result is a Stoicism, however orthodox and however precisely rendered as theory, that is nonetheless a very different thing in practice and application from the Stoicism of the founders, Zeno and Chrysippus, and their Greek successors. The ideas remain the same, in principle, but as ideas they no longer have the same practical meaning. They no longer play the same role in a person's life.

II

We can begin by taking note of Seneca's frequent disparagement of Stoic philosophical argumentation—that is, reason giving—of certain prominent sorts.[9] In a large group of his *Letters to Lucilius* Seneca complains contemptuously about the syllogisms of "dialecticians" (*dialectici*), including Stoic ones, whether on ethical topics or not.[10] He declares them as *worse* than useless. He rails against people who, he says, debase philosophy by spending all their time on such "logical" pursuits instead of taking hold of the real problems of life by directly ridding themselves or others of the fear of death, bondage to external objects and events, and the like, through other uses of language than the logically deductive. Thus in *Letter* 111 Seneca advises Lucilius to devote himself to true philosophy—to effect his own cure by becoming great-souled, fully self-confident, invincible as he faces the vicissitudes of life, and by showing these qualities through his *actions*. If he does that, he will have no need of logical games, as if expertise in those showed any high accomplishments in philosophy:

---

what they are, and be inclined to believe them—not at all, necessarily, to understand them, to know they are true, because one understands the reasons of theory that make them true. For the first stage she refers, in the first instance (p. 118 n. 95), to *Letters* 66 and 67, where Seneca sets out the Stoic theory of the good. There Seneca uses rhetorical modes of presentation, and avoids relying heavily on philosophical argumentation, just as much as he does when he moves on to Hadot's second and third stages. In fact, Hadot quite systematically underrates the value (indeed necessity, for a Stoic) of philosophical argument as providing the basis of belief—just as her author, Seneca, does, as I argue below.

[9] See *Letters* 45, 48, 49, 82, 83, 87, 111; also the harsh remarks in 71.6 and 85.1. The remarks in 102.20 are different: they speak in some exasperation about the relative waste of time that has to go into a Stoic response to caviling counterarguments of non-Stoic "dialecticians" out to upset the Stoics' moral applecart (see 102.5); Seneca has just spent some pages dutifully responding.

[10] In this he follows Cicero. See Cicero, *Tusc. Disp.* 2.29–30.

to parade one's superiority in those would be like walking on tiptoe to deceive others about one's height (111.3). No: you do not become braver, or more temperate, or loftier by these means (111.2). Again, it may be proper, Seneca concedes, to learn about logical puzzles and come to a proper appreciation of them (102.5, cf. 49.6), but a mind can only be permanently at play and not a serious one if it keeps on dealing with Greek σοφίσματα (logical paradoxes, roughly)—things, he says, that have no established name in Latin, because Romans have no use for them, but that Cicero has well dubbed *cavillationes* (railleries, jests). To devote oneself overseriously and overmuch to logical paradoxes is simply to drag philosophy down from its proper heights and onto the flat ground.[11] Such devotion to logic does not profit one in the least and is no proof of adeptness at philosophy—quite to the contrary.

Seneca objects particularly (in several *Letters* numbered in the 40s) to overfascination with logical paradoxes and fallacies, such as that of the liar or the "horned one" (see 45.8, 45.10, 49.8), to which Chrysippus and other Stoics had given so very extensive attention. Now, I think we should certainly agree that one can become *too* occupied with these things. This may apply especially to young persons getting attracted to philosophy for the first time—just as they also are often overimpressed with skeptical arguments about the existence of the external world, and so forth. So Seneca's warnings are surely not out of place. But in his polemic against such abuses he is led also to express doubts about the value of knowing anything about these arguments at all. He goes so far as to say that "not to know them does no harm, nor does the one who does know them benefit from the knowledge" (45.8). In fact, he goes yet farther: the games of logic played in worrying over such conundrums and figuring out how to resist the inferences are not merely of no profit, they

[11] J. Barnes (*Logic and the Imperial Stoa*, 12–23) discusses some of these passages in examining Seneca's attitude to the study of logic, its place and value as one part of philosophy itself. He argues, persuasively to my mind, that Seneca is objecting (a) to an obsessive and pointless fascination with the famous sophisms and conundra of the Liar et al., with which Chrysippus had already dealt adequately, a fascination sustained beyond the point where anything of value can come from attention to them, and at the expense of more serious and more important moral inquiry; and (b) to any other study of logic that has no payoff for the overriding ethical purposes and ambitions of philosophy itself. Thus he is not rejecting the study of logic. Indeed, he commends it—when it is conducted with due regard to its utility for ethical concerns. My concern in what follows is not with Seneca's attitude to the study of logic as a part of the overall study of philosophy, but rather with his failure sometimes to see clearly enough just how extensive, in fact, the implications for ethics actually are of certain studies in logic broadly conceived (i.e., in "dialectic" in the Stoic sense) and certain ones in physics—and, more generally, for the mental formation needed by anyone who is to live a good and happy life according to the Stoic understanding of what that consists in.

are actually harmful (48.9), since they crush and weaken the spirit of anyone who takes them seriously. Surely, he says, no one, asked whether he has lost his horns, who replies no, is so foolish as actually to feel around on his head, when it is suggested that since he has not lost them he must still have them (45.8). So what does it matter if he doesn't grasp the basis of the fallacy sufficiently to object that his answer did not have that implication (or to see how to answer more carefully, so as explicitly to deny in his answer that he has ever had horns)? Or again, take the problem posed by this syllogism (48.6): Mouse is a syllable;[12] but a mouse eats cheese; so a syllable eats cheese. Suppose, says Seneca in mock horror, I cannot solve this problem: what danger looms for me? What harm do I face? Here, in his concern to disabuse Lucilius of any overfascination with such logical puzzles or fallacies, Seneca comes very close to, if he does not actually espouse, simply rejecting all claim to value in the logical studies concerned with them.[13]

Actually, of course—and this is why the Stoics make knowledge of "dialectic" (skill in arguing) a full virtue, just as much as justice or temperance or wisdom itself[14]—the original Stoics thought on very good grounds that you *would* be in serious danger if you did not know precisely what the fallacy is in these and all other such cases. There are, after all, other risks here besides that of getting persuaded that you do have horns or that some syllables eat cheese, and the like. These fallacies are in fact of very general application. If you are not alert to the fallacy of many questions (which the horned fallacy rests upon), or to the difference between using a word to talk about itself rather than about what it normally refers to (as in the "mouse" syllogism), or to the other fallacies the Stoics spent so much time studying, then you will be open in more complicated cases of the same form to not seeing immediately what is wrong with the argument. So even if you would never infer that some syllables eat cheese, you might very well draw an erroneous inference in a more complicated case and then even act upon it. Thus you might in some circumstance get confused and so decide and act wrongly.

Furthermore, someone who wishes to live his life by perfecting so far as possible his own mind, his own reason, as the needed basis for a "smooth" and happy life, as any Stoic must wholeheartedly do, really cannot allow

[12] Anyhow, it is in Greek and Latin: μῦς, *mus*, both of which strings appear as syllables in quite a few other Greek or Latin words.
[13] Barnes (*Logic and the Imperial Stoa*, 13–14) intriguingly speculates that Seneca's repeated polemic against playing around with these arguments may be evidence that in first-century Rome the study of logic might actually have been all the rage—contrary to the usual inference scholars have drawn from Seneca's and other evidence about first-century philosophy.
[14] See Diogenes Laertius, *Lives of Eminent Philosophers*, 7.46–48, and Cicero, *De Finibus* 3.72.

MORAL THEORY AND IMPROVEMENT: SENECA   317

any haughty Roman disdain of Greekish *subtilitas* (see 113.1) to lead
him simply to dismiss the study of logic, and logical fallacies, as beneath
one's Roman upper-class dignity. He should realize that something is
wrong with anyone's mind, with their moral and practical understanding, who cannot solve such paradoxes. People like that should worry
about themselves. To be sure, Seneca could be right to insist that the
study of logic (or at least of these recherché fallacies) is not the *first* prerequisite, that there are more important matters that come first. Philosophy certainly offers to humankind something much more important than
mere logical facility (48.8): it offers counsel on urgent matters of daily
life, it offers true relief from the burdens of life as it is led by all of us who
do not have philosophy as our certain guide. So no doubt close and nar-
row or exclusive attention to logic could be a harmful distortion of
proper philosophical values. But (despite his disparagements) Seneca
himself brings out, in the course of developing this line of thought, that
one cannot do without a full facility at logic if one is to attain (anyhow
ultimately) the goal that philosophy puts before itself. Philosophy promises,
he says (48.11), to make me equal to god—that is why I have come to
philosophy, it is that promise that I want to hold philosophy to. Yes. But
certainly god knows all the logic there is to know, including a perfect understanding of all the logical fallacies, so if I am to be his equal, I had better learn all that, too.

In these *Letters* (45, 48, 49), then, Seneca's willingness to blur the line
between overfascination with logic, or logical fallacies, and any proper
study of them, seems clearly to reveal an inadequate and weak grasp of
the real value for the moral life of the study of logic. In several connected
Letters (82, 83, 85, 87) Seneca ridicules as foolishness (*ineptiae*) all those
famous snappy Stoic syllogisms on moral subjects for which Zeno was so
famous (or infamous). For example, the following one (82.9): No bad thing
is glorious, but death is [that is, is sometimes] glorious; therefore death is
not a bad thing. Wonderful, says Seneca! So, having learned this, I've
now been freed from fear of death? How foolish! Is that how a general
leading his men into battle, to meet death in defending their wives and
children, would ever address his troops (82.20–22)? Obviously not. So,
Seneca concludes, that is not how a philosopher should seek to improve
himself or others listening to him, either. Instead of answering the question whether to fear death by, as Seneca sees it, such fruitless and foolish
dialecticians' subtleties that do not persuade anyone, one ought to weigh
and solve it with a view to actual persuasion. You ought not to merely
force someone by logical necessity to grant the conclusion that death is
not to be feared, because it is nothing bad for you—when despite accepting
the premises and seeing the logical necessity of the inference, his true opinion was, and remains, to the contrary. But Seneca's reference to forcing,

by contrast with persuading, is a short-sighted characterization of Zeno's intentions in propounding such syllogisms. In fact, you have to carefully reflect on these little arguments in order finally to see the meaning of the premises, and finally to appreciate their truth—and so, finally, to *understand* why you really do have to accept the conclusion as true, if you accept the premises. There really is, or can be, *persuasion* through them—when they are properly reflected upon.

Ironically, despite his disparagement, Seneca himself explains and defends this particular argument of Zeno's pretty well. He considers the following counterargument to the opposite conclusion (presumably one from a Peripatetic opponent): Nothing indifferent is glorious, but death is glorious; so death is not indifferent (82.10). This shares the same minor premise with the Zenonian one—that death is glorious—but has a different major. Seneca crisply points out the error in the major premise: certainly nothing indifferent is *per se* glorious, but that does not mean that some indifferent things are not sometimes contingently so—namely, when they have been made glorious by virtue's approach to and handling of them (82.12). For example, a death might be glorious because of its circumstances and the way it came about or was accepted by the one who died. So the Peripatetic major premise is false, and the syllogism is unsound: it gives no good reason to hold death not to be the indifferent which the Stoics hold it to be. By contrast, as however Seneca does not point out, Zeno's major premise, that nothing bad is ever glorious, is true. It depends upon the deep truth, on Stoic principles, that anything by its *nature* bad (as anything bad at all must be) must be bad in all its instances (and never mind any special contingencies). And, clearly, something bad in that way could never be a source of true glory: having any instance of something in itself bad can never be a mark of any great accomplishment on your part, it cannot be a legitimate mark of distinction as a person. And there is no doubt that sometimes death can be such a mark. Its manner can be a great accomplishment—if it comes and is borne with a fully virtuous disposition. If you ponder all this, which is involved in Zeno's syllogism, and truly reflect on it, you really might, it seems to me, come to be persuaded that no death is ever a bad thing for the person whose death it is. You would not at all simply feel compelled by the necessities of logical argument to grant the conclusion, having granted the premises—without however believing it. (And the fact that a general addressing his troops would never use such an argument is neither here nor there so far as true persuasion—persuasion on solid grounds of reason—is concerned.) Yet, after refuting the Peripatetic counterargument, Seneca still has nothing good to say about Zeno's argument. He refuses to agree with Stoics who say that Zeno's syllogism is valid and sound (*veram*), whereas the opponent's is not: he says that *all* this sort of argumentation should be banished forthwith (*totum genus istuc exturbandum iudico*, 82.19). There are other, better ways of showing that no one's death is ever bad for them—and only those can win conviction, he insists.

In *Letter* 83.9 ff. Seneca treats in a similar way another Zenonian syllogism: No one entrusts a secret to a drunk man, but one will entrust a secret to a good man; so a good man will not get drunk. In parallel, Seneca contemptuously says, you might as well argue as follows: No one entrusts a secret to a sleeping man, but one will entrust a secret to a good man; so a good man will not go to sleep. So, there must be something wrong with Zeno's argument: the second conclusion is plainly false and unacceptable, and that means that in both cases (since they are of the same form) either at least one premise must be false or else the conclusion does not actually follow. Seneca rightly rejects one proposed way of defending Zeno's syllogism against this alleged parallel; he says this stems from Posidonius, and that it is the only way of defending it (83.10).[15] But again he does not reveal the deeper aspects of Zeno's argument, or show, as he does in the previous case, why the alleged parallel is not a sound argument and not a true parallel at all. He thinks Zeno's syllogism is simply a failure even as an argument—as well, of course, as a piece of moral persuasion aimed at getting people not to drink to excess. Instead, Seneca says, you should explain why the good and wise person will not get drunk by pointing to the facts, not by such verbiage (83.27): you need to show the hideousness and oppressiveness of the drunken state, and highlight the awful harms that have resulted from it. However that may be, in accepting the alleged parallel about the sleeping man as a true one, Seneca actually misses Zeno's point. It is a fundamental fact about fully good persons that they will keep someone's secret entrusted to them. That means that, because they do take with full seriousness the duty not to divulge a secret, they will never put themselves in a situation, such as that

---

[15] Posidonius's defense turns on exploiting the possibility that by "a drunk man" in the major premise Zeno might have meant a habitual drunkard, not a person, whether a drunkard or not, who *is* drunk. In fact, as Seneca correctly says (¶11), the Greek μεθύων (see H. von Arnim, *Stoicorum Veterum Fragmenta* (hereafter *SVF*), 1.229) and Seneca's Latin *ebrius* really do not mean "drunkard" but only "drunk," so Zeno surely did not mean what Posidonius says he did. Seneca also (dubiously) objects that on Posidonius's preferred understanding of the first premise (that no one entrusts a secret to a drunkard) it is in fact false (¶¶12–17). Characteristically, however, he does not observe that with this understanding all that follows is that the good man will not be a drunkard, and that truism is surely not what Zeno intended to establish: his presumably desired conclusion was that the good man will not get drunk. See *SVF* 3.643 (Stobaeus), 644 (Diogenes Laertius), 712 (Philo), on the Stoic doctrine (presumably to be traced back to Zeno) that the wise person will not become drunk.

of being drunk, where they know they cannot be sure they will not divulge it. More to the point, they will also not put themselves in a position where, if someone should tell them a secret then, they could not count on being able to keep it. But, of course, going to sleep is not one of those situations: while asleep one can neither receive nor divulge a secret. Involuntary sleep-talk is an unavoidable hazard; and if it happens, it is no moral fault. So Seneca's allegedly parallel syllogism is no true parallel at all. If no one entrusts a secret to a sleeping man, that is because it is actually impossible to do that, and so nothing follows about whether the good man will ever go to sleep.

In *Letters* 85 and 87.11 ff. Seneca delivers himself of, and explains, a whole series of Stoic syllogisms on virtue as the only good and as sufficient by itself for happiness, setting them alongside ones of other schools (Peripatetic, Epicurean) designed to undermine these Stoic views. But here again, he does so with the declaration that he takes no pleasure in this sort of argumentation, and that he is only giving these syllogisms at Lucilius's repeated request (85.1).

Seneca's treatment of all these Zenonian syllogisms betrays a serious undervaluation not just, as before with the analysis of logical fallacies, of the study of logic but of philosophical reasoning itself. As I have shown, there is a good point in each of Zeno's syllogisms discussed in 82 and 83, one of direct relevance to how to lead your life—provided that you attend to them in the right, philosophical way. This is true of the others too. Seneca is presumably correct that no one will make these arguments the sole or even the most important ground of his acceptance of their conclusions. Other philosophical considerations are available too. But his own preference for "pointing to the facts" by, for example, graphically and movingly describing the oppressiveness and hideousness of the drunken state, is a preference for rhetorical appeals to a person's feelings, over solid reasons why the conclusions really are true. The original Stoics were firm and clear about the far greater value of sound and solid reasoning for establishing such conclusions. In this discussion Seneca shows himself neither clear nor firm about this. Had he been so, he could not have dismissed these syllogisms as simply beside the point—that is, of no use for moral improvement.

III

Next, I want to discuss a late series of *Letters* (106, 113, 117) in which Seneca struggles with three interconnected, strange-sounding Stoic doctrines: (1) that the virtues are corporeal entities (that is, bodies), (2) that the virtues are actually living beings (animals), and (3) that though a virtue such as wisdom (for example) is a good thing, being wise or being just is not good.[16] All three are doctrines to know which, he tells Lucilius, is of *no* profit: to concern oneself with such questions is to waste time on superfluities; these are matters for the schoolroom, not for living one's life (106.11–12). Nonetheless, in the case of the first of these three doctrines, concerning the corporeality of the virtues, Seneca is quite willing to explain to Lucilius why, however surprising, or even outrageous, the idea might seem at first presentation, it is nonetheless true, and to endorse on his own behalf the Stoic reasoning which establishes it (106.4–10). The other two doctrines he rejects as too offensive to common ways of thinking to be tolerated, however much they might be part of the panoply of that Greek Stoicism with which in general he aligns himself.

That the virtues must be corporeal follows from the fact, strongly insisted on by the Stoics, that anything that has effects, that causes anything, has to be something robust and bodily. Virtues such as bravery, or temperance, to mention just two of them, plainly do have effects, since they lead us to act in certain ways and prevent us from acting in others. So there is no possibility of doubt about their actually being bodily conditions, conditions in fact of our minds or souls, which for the same reason must themselves be bodies. Still, while explaining and defending this—to the common consciousness—very surprising Stoic view, Seneca does insist that it is *of no use* to know that virtues are bodies; for him, this is a purely theoretical question of no practical moment.

However (to turn to the second of these three Stoic doctrines), Seneca holds that there is no good reason to follow the effete, white-sandal-wearing Greeks and hold that the virtues are living beings (113.1), even as a matter of mere and pure theory. Here, just as Chrysippus himself refused to follow his teacher Cleanthes in the latter's view of the being of

---

[16] At 106.2 Seneca pretends that Lucilius had requested to be told whether the good is a body, but that he had delayed responding because this was one of the questions that he was writing on in some books he was then composing in which he would give a systematic account of the whole of moral philosophy, dealing with all its problems; in 108.1 and 109.17 he mentions this proposed work again. In 106.2, because it would be rude to keep him waiting, Seneca agrees to take Lucilius's question out of the proper order in which it would be taken up in that work; he will answer it now, and proceed to tell him whatever has to do with questions "of the same sort," without waiting to be asked. He defines this "sort" vaguely, as questions to know about which is pleasant rather than useful (*magis iuvat quam prodest*). It is clear that not all the immediately following letters are part of the series thus promised (107 and 110 clearly are not, but 108 and 109 clearly are), and it is not clear for how long after 106 we should look for successors in the projected series. However, because Seneca emphasizes that the questions discussed in both 113 and 117 do belong to the class of things to know which is of no profit to us (113.1: *disputationibus nihil profuturis otium terere*; 117.20: *quid mihi profiturum est scire?*), I am inclined to think they are intended as further installments.

the act of walking (what in physical reality that act *is*), Seneca claims for himself the freedom to declare as absurd that the virtues should be so many animals (113.23).[17] Nonetheless, Seneca sets out quite perspicuously the reasons why orthodox Stoics did think that virtues are animals—given the corporeality of all qualities, and so of virtues as well, which, as we have just seen, Seneca accepts. Seneca's own objections against this conclusion are, however, extraordinarily weak. If you think the matter through, it is soon very clear that Seneca is wrong, and Stoic orthodoxy right—or, rather, that on their shared views about the corporeal nature of the virtues, it does pretty well follow that they are animals. Rather than decrying this conclusion because to ordinary ways of thinking it sounds altogether bizarre, Seneca ought to have joined with Chrysippus in helping non-Stoics to appreciate why, in this matter as in so many others, ordinary ways of thinking are really inadequate and should not be allowed to determine a serious person's beliefs. As he himself explains the Stoic view (113.2–5), a virtue is just the mind or soul disposed in a certain specific way (a different way for each virtue). The soul or mind is a bodily substance spread through the remainder of a person's body, a substance which *itself* is able to perform all the functions of thinking, reacting to impressions received, deciding, and acting (which, however, does not mean that it could perform these if or when it was not so spread through a living organism). So, the Stoics argue, the soul satisfies all the conditions for being an animal: *it* thinks, decides, acts, and performs all the other functions of a living thing. Hence the same is true of a virtue (or a vice)—that is, for the soul under some certain conditions of its own disposition *in* thinking, deciding, etc.

Now, one certainly might question whether it is right to hold that the soul all by itself does perform these functions. One might develop instead a view along the lines of Aristotle's, according to which the (rest of the) body performs them, but *in virtue of* being ensouled—not that the soul itself thinks, decides, and so on.[18] Seneca, however, leaves all such legitimate questions aside. After briefly stating the Stoic view, he instead sets out a series of arguments (113.6–22) that he thinks raise insuperable difficulties for the idea that virtues are living beings (without questioning whether souls all by themselves perform all the life functions of animals). One alleged difficulty to which he keeps returning is this: if the orthodox

---

[17] Seneca not infrequently elsewhere (and perfectly reasonably) insists on his own right and privilege, even though a committed Stoic, to have and defend his own philosophical opinions, even where they may be in opposition or conflict with those of the school's founders and orthodox spokesmen. See *Letters* 45.4 and *On Favors* I 3.8 ff., and my discussion of his stance in *On the Private Life* in chap. 13 below, last three paragraphs of sect. II.

[18] See *De Anima* 1.1.403a3 ff., 1.4.408b11–18.

view is true, then emotions such as anger, fear, or grief—indeed all opinions and thoughts, and, beyond that, all the virtuous acts a virtuous person does—are additional living beings, additional animals (see 113.6, 20), over and above the virtues themselves. But that, he says, is inadmissible: *quod nullo modo recipiendum est.* For we would then have on our hands a virtual infinity of living things all sojourning in some one soul, one person (113.8), if not at some single time then at any rate over a person's lifetime. In fact, says Seneca in supposed refutation of the orthodox view, it is not the case that whatever a person does *is* that person (*non enim quicquid ab homine fit, homo est*). That of course is true (and the Stoics by no means disagree): a person's (or a mind's) thoughts, words, impulses, assents, full-blown actions, are not that person or mind, or even that person or mind disposed in some way. These are things it does, not the mind itself or anything that it is. However, a virtue (or a vice) differs crucially from these other psychic phenomena: it *is* that person or mind disposed in some specific, continuing way. So the orthodox view about virtue and vice being animals does not commit Stoics to holding that every thought or action of any person is itself an animal, as Seneca says it does. On the orthodox view only persons (or their mind), qualified by those qualities that affect the way they (or it) think or decide or perceive, counts, case by case, as an animal. Thus each virtue, and each vice, must be counted an animal, but there is no threat of any virtual infinity of different animals residing in any given human soul. So Seneca's first objection is a gross failure.

A second objection (113.13–16) is no more effective. Contrary to what Seneca says, the way in which a person's soul, or their soul qua disposed in some relevant specific way, is an animal does not entail (objectionably) that these animals are distinct substances, distinct either from one another or from the person. The soul, and the soul disposed in each of the ways that its virtues or vices dispose it, is an integral part of the single substance that is that person. Altogether, we have just one animal there, namely a human being, even though each of these specific parts of it also counts as "*an* animal." Distinguishability in this case does not imply distinctness—that is, separate physical identity. Seneca is certainly entitled as a Stoic and a philosopher to think his own thoughts and reach his own conclusions (as Chrysippus did in rejecting his teacher Cleanthes' view about the physical reality of acts like walking). But in this instance he has not thought well, and his own conclusions are not philosophically defensible. If he goes forward living his life on the basis of these views, he will quite certainly be living in a confused and inadequate state of mind—precisely on a question about virtue itself, about how one must conceive and understand its nature, as the supremely good thing it is. Living on the basis of the orthodox views that he rejects would undoubtedly be better, given his other philosophical commitments. In fact, he should have taken more seriously than he does the disparaged "subtle" question whether virtues are living things or not. The orthodox Stoic answer is not the absurd and ridiculous thing, once you really understand it, that Seneca represents it as being.

It is true that, like the more basic question of whether the virtues are bodies, this is a theoretical question, one rather remote from any direct effects on one's way of life or one's commitment to it. But if you are really going to be devoted to virtue above all else, and indeed regard it as the sole good thing in life, you surely ought to want to know, if possible, what this thing is that you value so highly. The more you understand about it—both the fact that it is a bodily condition, and not for example some airy Platonic or Aristotelian immaterial something or other, and the fact that it is actually a living thing all on its own—the more secure your own commitment to it and its overwhelming value ought to be. Correspondingly, the less you know about what it is, and the more indifferent you are to knowing about this in the first place, the less secure is your commitment, the less well-grounded in your total set of conceptions about virtue and its value. This, at any rate, is what anyone should think who, like Seneca as well as Zeno and Chrysippus, holds that it is only one's reasoned understanding of how things in fact stand, as regards their value, that can provide the direction for our lives that we so direly need.

Seneca is on no better ground—indeed, I think, conspicuously worse—in his rejection (*Letter* 117) of the third Stoic doctrine I referred to, that while wisdom and other virtues are good things, having them is not a good thing. In this instance, however, Seneca does not so much maintain for himself that having wisdom or being wise *is* just as much a good as wisdom is as declare that one can flip a coin on this point—it doesn't matter whether being wise is a good or not; you can, if you like, hold either that it is or that it is not, or, in fact, you can hold no opinion at all on the question. Seneca does raise many objections against the Stoic view, and he also makes clear his acceptance of them. He argues, in fact, that being wise really is a good, a second good alongside wisdom itself. But he does not insist on the point. His chief contention (in the end) is that it does not matter whether one knows the answer to this question or not, or which answer one gives (117.33).[19] It won't make you wise to know the

[19] As usual with Seneca the organization of this *Letter* is fluid at best, so any declaration about his contentions (main or secondary) is somewhat problematic. A review of the whole *Letter* will enable me to explain my understanding of Seneca's contentions here. He begins, in response to Lucilius's query whether the Stoic doctrine is true, that being wise is not a good thing, by stating (§1) that he disagrees with his fellow Stoics on this point, and declaring that he will first set out the Stoic view and then be bold enough to state his own

difference between wisdom and being wise, if indeed there is any, so it is completely useless to fuss over such a matter, or to hold an opinion one way or the other.

Though he does so in a disparaging tone of voice pretty much throughout, Seneca works into his discussion a fairly clear explanation of the Stoics' reasons for denying that such entities as being wise or being just, and so on, are good things (117.2–5, 12–13). Anything good must be a bodily thing, since it must *do* good; it must have good effects (as Seneca has already explained in *Letter* 106). The virtues, then, are physical conditions of bodily entities, namely of minds or souls. These do, obviously, have good effects, namely, the virtuous person's good actions. As Seneca states the view at 117.12, wisdom, for example, is "the mind perfected or developed to the highest and best degree." Being wise, on the other hand, is an incorporeal entity, something that functions only in relation to language and conceptual thought—in fact a predicate: it is what *holds good* or *is true* of any bodily thing that has wisdom, precisely because it does have it. As such, it is not a body, or a condition or arrangement of a body, at all; it is what one (truly) *says of* a thing that has wisdom in it, indicating that

---

opinion. He sets out the Stoic view in §§2–5, where he includes in his exposition two connected objections of other philosophers (perhaps Peripatetics), together with the Stoics' way of accommodating their position to these objections. In introducing these objections, in §4, Seneca alerts us again that this is a preliminary exercise—preliminary to his taking steps to "withdraw [from orthodoxy] and take up a different position" (*secedere et in alia parte considere*). At the beginning of §6, he reiterates his disagreement (*ego non idem sentio*), clearly implying that he holds that being wise *is* a good thing: he says the orthodox have only been led to assert the contrary because they have been caught by a "first link" in a chain of argument, which prevents them logically from saying anything else. (He does not make explicit what link he has in mind.) He then presents arguments in favor of his own position on this question, §§6–17, beginning (§6) with some methodological considerations. In the course of explaining his own view (i.e., that being wise *is* a good thing) he takes care to distinguish his position on one crucial point from that of the Peripatetics, and in the course of doing that he says again (§14) that he is not yet stating how things seem to him (*nondum enim quid mihi videatur pronuntio*). I take this second warning to indicate that his full and true position, which he only gets to much later, §§18–20, is that it does not matter which view you adopt. Your life, your moral understanding, is not affected one iota one way or the other; this is a purely theoretical question devoid of moral or practical significance. (After that, §§21–33, Seneca elaborates on this point, decking it out with high-minded fluff and adding exhortations to true wisdom, which consists in actions and not in worrying about philosophical niceties; but his statement of his position and his argument is concluded in §20.) Thus Seneca's position is a bit complex. On the one hand, he really does disagree with orthodoxy on the theoretical question whether being wise is a good thing; on the other hand, and more important, he insists that this *is* a theoretical question, and a theoretical disagreement. There is no good point in embroiling oneself in such controversies. In that sense, he can say at the end (§20) that since it does not profit anyone to know which view is true, he will take a chance on holding the one view, while Lucilius can go for the other. It won't matter.

it does have it. It is, according to Stoic terminology, an incorporeal "sayable" (λεκτόν; *dictum*, §13). Hence, being wise cannot do anything, cannot have any effects all its own, and so cannot be good (or bad, either—or indifferent, for that matter, neither good nor bad). What does things, what makes a difference, is the bodily condition itself of wisdom, to which being wise is related as the (nonphysical) attribute belonging to the object which has wisdom in it. Similarly, being happy (the predicate or sayable that holds good of a person whose life is being happily led) is not a good thing, because in the relevant sense it is no *thing* at all. The thing that is good is happiness itself, or the happy life, and these of course are bodily entities that have effects in the world.[20] You can certainly say indifferently, in Greek and Latin as well as in English, that you want happiness or that you want to be happy; the Stoics' point is that it is important to see clearly that, however closely related these two ways of speaking are and however indifferent in practice the choice between them may be, they are not equivalent in meaning or equally acceptable for all purposes. The first thing wanted (happiness) is, once achieved, a physically existing thing; the other (to be happy) is an incorporeal something-or-other true of the person who has that physical thing.

Seneca, however, does not want to accept the conclusion that being wise, being happy (*et alia*) are not good things: that flies in the face of common sense, as well as common ways of speaking. So he attempts to develop an account of their "metaphysical" status that will make them

---

[20] Seneca reports "other philosophers" (117.4) as raising as an absurd consequence of the orthodox view something that Stoics themselves actually insisted on maintaining: that though happiness or the happy life (*beata vita*, Greek εὐδαίμων βίος) is a good, being happy or living happily (*beate vivere*, εὐδαιμονεῖν) is not. As we have seen, the latter is a predicate, so plainly it cannot be a good; the former is a real, physically existing thing (a whole integrated series of actions produced by a virtuous soul) which can therefore be a good. One can see the Stoics maintaining that being happy is not a good thing by juxtaposing two passages of Arius Didymus's *Outline of Stoic Ethics* (in Stobaeus, *Eclogae* 2.77, 16–27 and 2.97, 15–98, 6 Wachsmuth [*SVF* 3.16, 3.91]; also in Anthony Long and David Sedley, *The Hellenistic Philosophers*, texts 63A and 33J, respectively). Seneca's immediately following objection (117.5), and the Stoic response, also mirror closely what we find in the second of these two Arius passages. Seneca's distinction in Latin between something *expetendum* (chosen) and something only *expetibile* (to be chosen) (which in his text is very hard to understand) is simply his rendering of the Greek αἱρετόν and αἱρετέον respectively, as the Arius passage makes clear. The Stoics' point is that any act of choosing (likewise, mutatis mutandis, for wishing, or welcoming, or desiring) is directed at some physical object or condition that one chooses (i.e., chooses to *have*)—according to the regimented terminology of Stoicism, this is the *expetendum* or αἱρετόν. But there is also in that same act something, namely a predicate, that is being chosen to be *true of* something, e.g., yourself. This is part of the content of the act, namely what is (again, in Stoic regimented language) *expetibile* or αἱρετέον, "to be chosen." Choices or wishes, etc., are *of* these predicates (what you wish is *to be happy*). This you will be, if you come to *possess* happiness.

not incorporeal predicates, not sayables at all, but rather robust bodily existents. The reason he gives for not accepting the Stoics' conclusion is that, according to him (117.6), there is *no one* who does not hold that wisdom (*sapientia*) is a good, and that being wise (*sapere*) is also. Now, no doubt this is so, if one is counting only people, whether actual Stoics or not, who have not had the Stoic theory, and its grounds, explained to them; but how about those to whom these have been explained? Surely the latter do not hold this. Why does Seneca not align himself with them (the educated minority), rather than the rest, however more numerous? Why not simply explain the relevant Stoic distinctions, apply them to the current case, and draw the conclusion that, indeed, as a matter of correct philosophical theory, being wise is not a good thing? Seneca could, as a concession to common ways of thinking (and speaking), emphasize that this is only intended as a theoretical truth, that one certainly does not need to insist on it in contexts of common life. In common life one is justifiably not in the habit of distinguishing between predicates and the physical conditions in virtue of which they hold true of things. So in common life one can perfectly well say and indeed mean that being wise is a good thing. Because one is not distinguishing between predicates and physical conditions (or thinking in any determinate way at all about either), there is no reason not to take this simply to mean that wisdom is a good thing.[21] Seneca, however, prefers, as, he thinks, a matter of proper philosophical methodology (indeed a Stoic methodology), to insist on going along with the general opinion of mankind in this matter: what "everyone" holds must be true, he says (in a misleadingly Aristotelian-sounding tone of voice).[22] On that principle, he is committed to holding,

---

[21] In fact, Seneca has already said in effect, at the end of §3, that precisely this is what the orthodox Stoics do. He says that they *do* say that being wise is a good thing, all the while referring "being wise" to that on which it depends, namely wisdom. This concession is not the same as the one Plutarch quotes from Chrysippus's *On Goods* (*On Stoic Self-Contradictions* 30, 1048a; Long and Sedley, *Hellenistic Philosophers*, 58H), but it is related to it. Chrysippus grants that someone who speaks of "preferred indifferents" (such as health) as good things to possess need not be making any mistake, so long as the sense he attaches to the word "good" in that context is not in error (ἐν μὲν τοῖς σημαινομένοις οὐ διαπίπτοντος αὐτοῦ)—i.e., so long as he does not mean (e.g.) that health, etc., actually make a life better, or truly "benefit" one. And he seems to commend such a practice as being in accordance with the ordinary use of words. I think Chrysippus is entirely right to grant this, and that there is no philosophical, or other, danger in doing so. I also think the other concession, the one Seneca takes note of, is again entirely acceptable.

[22] One might connect this methodological principle with Aristotle's frequent appeals to "reputable opinion," including especially matters of common opinion or common linguistic usage, as one reference point that philosophical analysis must be responsible to. However, Aristotle's practice is subtle and nuanced, as Seneca's principle is not: Aristotle never holds that common opinion must be true, only that there has to be something to be said for

against orthodoxy, that being wise and being just, and so on, are good things, just as wisdom and justice themselves are.

How then does Seneca intend to argue that such entities are not after all incorporeal somethings-or-other? He clearly agrees that if that is their status, they cannot in fact be good things at all. One way of achieving this objective would be to adopt the Peripatetic position that wisdom and being wise (and so on) are in each case actually just one and the same thing (for a Stoic, that same thing would be the relevant aspect of the physical condition of the wise mind). But Seneca rejects this solution (§8), stating as his opinion that although, as the Stoics insist, wisdom and being wise are two different entities, nonetheless both of them can be and are good things. His first argument (or the first part of his exposition of the reasons for his view) is extraordinarily weak, since it turns on a gross misuse of an agreed Stoic principle.[23] His central contention, to which he comes in §§14–15 (with reference back to §12), is more interesting. For orthodox Stoicism, an incorporeal entity such as being wise is but one example of a vast range of other exactly similar entities (viz., attributes, which Seneca calls in Latin *accidentia,* §§3, 10). Using these (and only by using them) you can say of anything that it has some quality: being red, being round, being wet, being alluring, being tall—right across the whole range of qualitative alterations that any bodily thing can undergo. Against this, anyhow for the special case with which we are concerned, Seneca objects in the following way.

In his own exposition of the Stoic doctrine in §12, it was the example of a field and the evident difference between the field itself and owning it

---

it and that the ultimately correct philosophical account of things must preserve this. It might be true only if interpreted in a certain way, but not in others—and that way might, in truth, not really conform to what ordinary people mean in asserting it. On Aristotle see John M. Cooper, "Aristotle on the Authority of 'Appearances'" in *Reason and Emotion* 281–91.

[23] Seneca states at the beginning of §7 that in defending the commonsense view he is going to use "our weapons" (*nostris armis*), i.e., he is going to draw on accepted Stoic principles in order to undermine the orthodox view and establish his own. His argument in §9, however, grossly misconstrues the orthodox principle from which it starts out: that "all things are either good, bad, or indifferent." This applies only to *things* in the strong sense of physical objects, or physical conditions of such objects. It does not apply to incorporeal entities, such as orthodox analysis shows being wise to be. Ignoring this exclusion, Seneca argues that if, as the orthodox would have it, being wise is not good, then, since it would be agreed by all not to be bad, it must be something indifferent; but, he says correctly, it conflicts with Stoic doctrine to say that being wise is indifferent, since indifferent things can be possessed both by good and by bad persons, but being wise (whatever it may be, metaphysically speaking) can only belong to a good person. So, he concludes, being wise must be good, after all: if it is not indifferent, it is also certainly not bad; but then the only alternative left is for it to be good.

that was supposed to establish the distinction needed to show the rationale for recognizing, with the Stoics, incorporeal predicates—and, in particular, for not just recognizing a difference between wisdom and having wisdom (as it were, owning it), but for regarding the latter as something incorporeal. In §14 Seneca returns to the alleged analogy between a field and owning it, on the one hand, and wisdom and having it (that is, being wise), on the other. Now he denies that these cases are really similar at all (*non est quod compares inter se dissimilia,* §15). Owning a field can, he seems to say, perfectly well be regarded as an incorporeal attribute belonging to the person who owns the field. But we should not regard having wisdom (that is, being wise) in the same way: in this case what is possessed is not some external thing, like a field, but something that pervades and structures the very nature or being of the thing that, as it were, "owns" it. Admitted. But how does that matter to the analysis? Seneca is not very clear. Perhaps his thought is that the thing that is wise, the person's mind, is so fused with the wisdom that it "possesses" that we can no longer satisfactorily mark off a separate subject (the mind) that bears any relevant predicate (as we can with the person who owns a field). What *is wise* is, to be sure, a different entity from the wisdom that it possesses, just as the field's owner is from the field, but in this case we cannot mark any bodily thing off as that which has some *other* bodily thing, in virtue of which it comes also to possess some (incorporeal) predicate, that of being wise. (Its) being wise ought rather to be considered part of the mind's very substance, somehow. And in that case, as Seneca then concludes, being wise will in fact be something bodily, namely, in effect, it appears, the wise mind itself—that is, the mind *taken together with* its wisdom. Hence being wise can, and indeed must, be a good thing, just as much so as the wisdom that that mind possesses.

I am not sure, however, that I have understood Seneca's thought here. For one thing, having as he thinks established that being wise is something good and so something bodily, he continues in §16–17 by telling a different story about exactly which bodily thing it is. Now he says that being wise is to be equated with the good actions that the wise person does on the basis of his wisdom.[24] For another, my interpretation leaves in place the Stoic theory of incorporeal predicates in cases other than those, like that of the moral predicates we are discussing, where the quality fuses with and transforms the very nature of the thing so qualified— owning a field, for example, and a limitless range of others such as being

[24] For the Stoics these actions, which of course are bodily existents with effects, are additional goods, over and above the virtuous qualities possessed by the mind that does them. See, e.g., Sextus Empiricus, *Against the Theoreticians* (*Adv. Mathematicos*) XI 22–26 (Long and Sedley, *Hellenistic Philosophers*, 60G 1–2).

red or cold. But some of what Seneca says might be thought to indicate that he is really committed, on the basis of his analysis of being wise and wisdom, to denying altogether, for all cases, that there are any incorporeal predicates.[25] However, if at all, Seneca might be minded to resolve these unclarities (and there is no indication at all that he ever published any more extended discussion of these issues than what we find in *Letter* 117), he faces a formidable task if he really intends to adopt for ethical purposes, even at the level of "theory" that he is here disparaging, any account of predicates along any of these lines. If he joins the Peripatetics in abolishing incorporeal predicates altogether (holding instead that what words express are not incorporeal senses but rather "thoughts in the mind"), what is he going to do with the Stoic claim that we have many good reasons for accepting into our ontology a whole level of (incorporeal) states of affairs, in addition to the bodies and bodily qualities that "ground" them (for example, the state of affairs consisting in Socrates' being wise)? For if we do countenance incorporeal states of affairs, we are surely thereby committed to accepting, as incorporeal parts of them, the predicates of Stoic theory. Is Seneca prepared to get along without states of affairs? How? Alternatively, if he only abolishes a restricted range of incorporeal predicates in favor of some material counterpart in those cases, how is he going to justify treating the semantics of linguistic predicates like "is wise" so radically differently from other cases apparently of quite the same kind ("is hot" or "owns a field")? It would seem that this analysis should be offered either for all of them or for none.

Of course, as we have seen, Seneca does not really care, for purposes of moral philosophy and for spiritual guidance—that is, his current purposes—whether his own or the orthodox Stoic account of the value of such things as being wise is accepted as correct. Hence, for current purposes, he has no need to clarify his position on what exactly these entities *are*. That, we can charitably conclude, is why he does not clarify it. His

[25] See the end of §7 and §8: even in the case of heat and being hot, Seneca here says, we should not think of these two things, admittedly two different entities, as being "of different sorts" (*sortis alterius*). On that view, to take another of his examples, being healthy, since it is of the same sort as health itself, is a good thing if the latter is. But that implies that being healthy is not an incorporeal predicate, any more than being wise is on Seneca's sketched account. This passage does seem clearly to suggest that the same analysis will be offered for all of what the Stoics put forward as incorporeal predicates, at least for ones that are connected to a thing's inherent qualities (health, redness, roundness, etc., as well as wisdom and its ilk), if not also for cases like owning a field. If being hot is to be taken as something bodily, that is because it is being somehow assimilated to the hot *thing*; so any application to owning a field and all such other examples would have to be by assimilating owning a field to the *owner*. The distinction, of which Seneca makes so much in §§12 and 14, between the field and owning it, is another matter altogether, and would still stand even if owning a field were declared, like being hot, to be something bodily.

main point (§§20, 33) is precisely that it doesn't matter whether you be-lieve that being wise is, or is not, a good. He is led into developing his novel account of being wise et alia, whatever exactly it comes to, only through his rather reckless acceptance of the methodological principle I referred to, that what everyone holds must be true. However, it seems to me that Seneca's main point is clearly mistaken—and that, therefore, it does matter what view you hold on the nature of such entities as being wise. It is, of course, true enough that someone who has never given any thought at all to predicates and senses and states of affairs, and has never heard of disputes between Stoics, Peripatetics, and other philosophers over the "metaphysical" status of such entities, can without ill effects continue to think as well as to speak with ordinary folk about the good-ness of being wise or being just, and so on. But can he count on continu-ing to live in that fool's paradise? If not, had he not better learn at least a smattering about this subject, sooner rather than later, so as to avoid the disturbance that might affect him if, in an unguarded moment long after beginning to live a Stoic life, someone should explain to him that being just cannot be a good thing after all, because it is something incorporeal? In any event, this is not the situation of Seneca's actual addressees, Lucil-ius and us readers. Seneca is busy in this *Letter* telling us about the Stoic doctrine, as well as presenting a novel doctrine of his own—all the while declaring that it does not matter which, if either, we accept. And now—at least, again, for a Stoic, who holds that the only sure basis on which to live our lives is through our understanding of the reasons *why* living ac-cording to the Stoic doctrine is required if we are to achieve our ultimate goal in life of happiness—we cannot avoid coming to some decision for ourselves about these matters. If being just or wise is *not* something cor-poreal, then (we realize) it cannot be good; hence we *must* stop holding it to be good, or we will henceforth be living in a seriously confused, in-coherent, state of mind, precisely as regards crucial practical questions about the value of the virtues. And, contrariwise, if we are to continue to think of being just as something good, then—in the face of the Stoics' ar-guments to the contrary—we had better take the trouble to assure our-selves that there is an acceptable alternative theory of predicates, and the rest, which makes them corporeal. If we do not do this, then, as on the other alternative, we will live in a state of confusion and incoherence in our thoughts about virtue and its value. Our commitment to virtuous liv-ing will be badly compromised.

Thus, once we become aware of these subtle questions about the status of such entities as being wise or being just, we cannot remain indifferent about their answers. Even if we do not choose to enter into the debates our-selves, we must hold that being wise et alia are either not good (because in-corporeal) or good (and corporeal)—and obtain assurances somehow that these are philosophically defensible positions. Because of the admittedly distant connection to the question whether being wise is a good thing, the philosophical theory of predicates—are they incorporeal entities or not?—turns out actually to matter for ethical philosophy and for the moral life. If, despite all this, Seneca persists in holding that it does not matter what you think about the value status of being wise, he must somehow think that one can lead the life of virtue the Stoic way on some basis other than as full an understanding as possible of the philosophical theories that, taken together, establish its correctness—including these ones, that all predicates are incorporeal and that no incorporeal entity can be a good thing.

We should bear in mind, of course, that Seneca writes for readers who are not philosophers themselves and are not expected to become philosophers; they are, and will remain, at best nonphilosopher *progredientes*. He is offering, as their spiritual adviser, to help to convince them of the basic truths of Stoic moral philosophy, and to strengthen their capacity and commitment to live in accordance with the moral and more generally practical principles of Stoicism. He is not urging anyone to take a complete course in Stoic philosophy but rather simply to listen to him, to take his explications to heart, and to live according to them.[26] It is unreasonable to criticize him for not telling his readers that if they do not become complete philosophers, with the fullest possible command of the whole of Stoic physical and logical theory, its grounds, and its implications for and other connections with Stoic ethical philosophy, they cannot hope to live a perfectly and completely happy life, according to the Stoic understanding of what that requires. That is not my criticism. My complaint is that sometimes, as in the *Letter* we have been considering, Seneca so completely cuts off the basis on which he is encouraging his addressee to live from the reasons provided by Stoic philosophical theory for living that way that it becomes highly questionable whether they *can* be making real progress toward virtue and the fully happy life if they follow him. If—and, as a Stoic, Seneca certainly does think this—virtue is a matter of rational, indeed intellectual, understanding of a whole system of reasons that support deciding, acting, and living in a certain way, then those who are making progress toward that goal, and wish to make further progress, must never lose sight of the fact that the only way to do so is to increase their *understanding* of just why those ways of deciding, acting, and living are the right and best ones. It is this fact that Seneca—objectionably, from the original Stoics' point of view—obscures.

---

[26] It is even open to him, as he explains at a number of places, especially in the first thirty *Letters*, to quote, draw on, and incorporate many Epicurean dicta and theses into his own Stoic advice about, and encouragement for, the moral life. See my discussion in chap. 13 below, sect. II.

IV

Through this *Letter,* as through all the *Letters* discussed in the two preceding sections, there runs a common thread: the uselessness of attending to or knowing about certain matters of philosophical theory that have no palpable and immediate ethical consequences. What then does Seneca think it would be useful to attend to? As I just mentioned, in his *Letters* to Lucilius, Seneca's aim is to help those who are not going to become full-fledged philosophers to make progress in improving themselves through the adoption of the Stoic outlook on human life and on its place in the world at large. When (in Seneca's authorial conceit) Lucilius asks him for the Stoic arguments, Seneca gives them (even if, as we have seen, he sometimes disparages and even disagrees with them). And often enough he gives the arguments unprovoked, especially where these are closely connected to ethical concerns. He certainly knows them, both the arguments in "dialectic" and physics and those in ethics proper. But very often, as we saw with his criticisms of Zeno's attempt to prove that the virtuous person will never get drunk, he prefers to rely on graphic, rhetorically elaborated descriptions of the evils consequent on holding other views than the Stoic ones, or in general on engaging in Stoically disapproved conduct or attitudes. Indeed, my impression is that, taking the *Letters* together with the *Moral Essays,* Seneca relies for his persuasiveness much more often on the rhetorical rather than the logical or philosophical aspects of his presentations.[27]

There is no doubt that such argumentative styles have their appeal, and their real and important uses. Arguments aimed at arousing the reader's feelings are surely effective up to a point, and perhaps especially so with persons like Seneca's addressees, who are struggling at relatively early

---

[27] *On Anger,* for example, begins with a purple passage describing in graphic, even lurid detail, the effects of "this most hideous and frenzied of all the emotions," and regularly after that great care is taken to leaven the exposition of various points of Stoic doctrine about anger with frequent inspirational illustrations drawn from Roman history, or contemporary events, or features of daily life, all described with impressive fullness and intended to evoke in his readers a lively recognition, from their personal experience and general knowledge, of the fundamental soundness of Stoic positions on the questions under review. When at the beginning of book II he needs to address a point of philosophical theory (whether being angry requires having decided to be) he apologizes for this descent onto "barer ground," promising that soon his discourse will rise to "loftier" topics (2.1)—as, in fact, it does beginning only a few pages later, at chapter 5. Even on the "bare" ground of §§1–4 there occur lively reminders of our states of mind when reading about Clodius driving Cicero into exile, or Marius's capture of Rome with his army and Sulla's proscriptions, and of the effects on Alexander of his musician Xenophantus's playing. See *On Anger* in *Seneca: Moral and Political Essays,* ed. J. M. Cooper and J. F. Procopé.

stages to make headway in their moral self-improvement. As a literary artist Seneca has had many detractors over the centuries, to be sure, but he has also been read and admired by many others for the forcefulness and inspiration of his writing.[28] Seneca's father saw to it that he was well trained in his youth, before he turned to philosophy, in the rhetorical schools of Rome, and the skills he learned then (and practiced for a time before the courts) are evident on every page of his philosophical works. Armed with those skills, however, and writing in the ancient tradition of the spiritual adviser, Seneca loses sight of what he officially recognizes as the goal of moral improvement: an improved mind, an improved understanding, on the basis of which then to conduct one's life. He allows his preference for rhetorical styles of argumentation to occlude all interest in many of the more abstruse philosophical questions that anyone must pursue if they are actually to make progress toward this goal, and he also places rhetorical argumentation at the front of his stage even in his presentation of the more narrowly ethical parts of Stoic philosophy. The result is a Stoicism that plays down the philosophical argumentation lying behind and supporting the ethical conclusions that he so treasures. Instead, he promotes those conclusions to a large extent solely through rhetorically induced feelings in favor of them. This is certainly Stoicism of a sort, but no longer quite what Zeno and Chrysippus had in mind.[29]

---

[28] See Cooper and Procopé, *Seneca*, xxvi–xxxii. He was, of course, the principal author for Justus Lipsius in the sixteenth-century revival of Stoicism.

[29] The first draft of this chapter was prepared for a conference on Roman Stoicism held in April 2000 at Northwestern University, the University of Chicago, and the University of Illinois at Chicago. I read parts of it as the keynote address at a graduate student conference sponsored by the departments of Classics, Philosophy, and History and Philosophy of Science at the University of Pittsburgh in February 2000. I thank the organizers of the Chicago conference for the stimulus to work on this topic, and the organizers and participants in both conferences for the stimulating and helpful discussions that took place on both occasions. I want to thank particularly Brad Inwood not only for his incisive questions in Chicago but also for the extensive written comments on my complete text that he sent me shortly afterward. My efforts to respond to them led to many improvements in this revision.

CHAPTER 13

MORAL THEORY AND MORAL IMPROVEMENT:

MARCUS AURELIUS

I

LIKE HIS STOIC PREDECESSOR SENECA, Marcus Aurelius writes in his *Meditations* in the ancient tradition of the spiritual adviser or spiritual guide.[1] But since he addresses himself to himself, and not to some counterpart of Seneca's Lucilius or to any envisaged general readership, his self-guidance takes on the character (to adopt Pierre Hadot's characterization of the *Meditations*) of *spiritual exercises*.[2] Thus, for Marcus, the act of writing serves not just to lay down for himself precepts or other guidance on ways of improving one's life through adherence to a philosophical, and more specifically the Stoic, world view. His writing is itself practice in adopting that outlook, in embedding it in his consciousness, with a view to making it, so far as possible, effective in his daily life. Informed and inspired by the frank encouragements for leading the philosophical life that Epictetus provided to his students in his *Discourses* as reported by Arrian, Marcus in his *Meditations* gives varied, repeated, vivid, heartfelt representations of the main directives for leading a good life that we find expounded in Epictetus. He makes vivid and attractive to himself, in varied ways, the general outlook on life and the world contained in traditional Stoic philosophical doctrine from the time of Chrysippus, apparently conveyed to him in significant part through Epictetus.[3]

---

[1] See above, chap. 12, "Moral Theory and Moral Improvement: Seneca," sect. I.

[2] See P. Hadot, *The Inner Citadel*, trans. Michael Chase (a translation of *La Citadelle Intérieure: Introduction aux "Pensées" de Marc Aurèle*), chap. 3. Even if one may suppose that by the time of his death Marcus had himself conceived the idea of publication for his work and had arranged and otherwise prepared it with a reader in mind other than himself, these notes' self-address is no mere artifice of authorship.

[3] In recording his moral debts in book I, Marcus tells us (chap. 7) that it was Iunius Rusticus, a Stoic senator and later city prefect under Marcus as emperor, who had wakened in him (this would have been around 145–46, when Marcus was about twenty-four years old) a sense of his own spiritual defects and turned him toward philosophy—including introducing him to some "notes" of Epictetus from Rusticus's own library. This may have been our *Discourses* of Arrian (but could be a separate set of notes taken by Rusticus himself while a student of Epictetus, about 120; see A.S.L. Farquharson, ed. and trans., *The Meditations of the Emperor M. Aurelius*, 2:446); in any event, the frequent quotations in the

Though, like Marcus, he writes as a spiritual adviser and not as a teacher of Stoic theory, Seneca shows ample evidence of precise and extensive knowledge of Stoic philosophical doctrine and the arguments and other philosophical considerations on which, as philosophical theory, it rested. The same is true of Epictetus, whose *Discourses* present informal discussions on the moral and the philosophical life with pupils who attended the formal instruction in Stoic philosophy (with detailed close reading of treatises of Chrysippus, among other traditional Stoic authors) that constituted the actual curriculum of his school.[4] By contrast with these other two—for us—leading Stoics of the Imperial period, Marcus is a novice at philosophy,[5] though he is clear and decisive in his commitment to Stoicism as the guide to life that he is training himself to follow. He knows and accepts that our minds, our reason, are our most important and valuable possessions, and that it is only through cultivating and strengthening our minds—and relating them properly to the reason of Zeus, which governs the universe—that we can improve ourselves and our lives.[6] Marcus's greater distance from, and reduced interest in, technical philosophical theory raises much more clearly and acutely than (as I have argued in chapter 12) Seneca's works do the question of the relevance of moral theory to moral improvement, in Marcus's version of Stoicism. I will argue that Marcus's predilection for the sort of rhetorical presentation of Stoic ideas that we see also in Seneca—a predilection de-

---

Meditations from the *Discourses* make it plain how thoroughly Marcus read the latter, and how extensively he relied on Epictetus's *Discourses* and their spiritual message in his own self-addresses. On quotations by Marcus of Epictetus, see Hadot, *Inner Citadel*, 66–70.

[4] On the character of the *Discourses* and their relation to Epictetus's formal teaching, see John M. Cooper, "The Relevance of Moral Theory to Moral Improvement in Epictetus," forthcoming in Mason and Hatzistavrou, *Zeno and His Legacy*.

[5] P. Hadot denies that Marcus and other public men such as Cato the Younger or Rogatianus were "amateur philosophers" (*Inner Citadel*, p. 4). They lived according to Stoic ideas, on the basis of a personal formulation of the "fundamental principles of the school in favor of which they had made their choice of life," and that is all it meant in antiquity to be a philosopher. That is an exaggeration, and an oversimplification. Hadot is right to emphasize that philosophy in antiquity was a way of life, but the philosophical life (as led by a Stoic, or a Platonist, at any rate) traditionally required philosophical study, attention to theory and argument, as well as living day to day in a certain way. Ironically, Hadot puts his finger on what this extra is when he glosses (p. 10) a passage of Epictetus (4.8.12) as follows: "the goal of philosophy is not to wear a cloak but to reason correctly." Correct reasoning, on Stoic views anyhow, requires wide attention to philosophical argumentation and a steady grasp of the actual philosophical reasons that make the "fundamental principles" of the Stoic way of life true. Marcus certainly did wish to live in accordance with Stoic principles, but as he himself remarks at the end of book I (1.17), he did not pay a lot of attention to theoretical writings of philosophy.

[6] See, e.g., *Meditations* 3.9, 4.4, 4.39, 5.9, 5.21, 6.16 (end), 6.32, 8.35, 12.3. See also below, sect. V.

riving from his approach to philosophy as spiritual adviser, not as philosophical theorist—leads him to ignore, or deny, as Seneca does too, but much more starkly, the crucial and central place in moral improvement, as the Stoic philosophers themselves conceive it, of improvement in one's philosophical grasp of the underlying philosophical theory of morality and the good life that the Stoics taught.

II

Like Seneca, especially in the first twenty-nine or so of his *Letters to Lucilius* (but, notably, unlike Epictetus), Marcus often cites, and adopts for his own edification, Epicurean dicta and Epicurean doctrines. Both authors have often been found, as a result, to be no true Stoics (if that is defined as adherence to the orthodox ideas of Chrysippus)—but "eclectics" or "syncretics" instead.[7] With Seneca, this criticism is entirely mistaken. With Marcus Aurelius, the evidence is divided. I want to concentrate my attention in what follows on this one aspect of Marcus's *Meditations*. In doing so I can, I believe, bring out most effectively the essential character, as I see it, of Marcus's conception of what it takes to improve oneself morally—and of his Stoicism overall.

Let me begin with Marcus's appeals to Epicurean moral dicta and to the example of Epicurus himself, in order to strengthen his commitment to the life of philosophy. Here is a quick list. On the topic of bodily pain, Marcus cites the Epicurean tag that pain if intense will be short (because it will do away with us), if prolonged then it will be mild.[8] Again, in 7.64 he quotes Epicurus as saying that pain is neither unbearable nor long-lasting if we remember its limitations and don't make it more stressful and harder to bear through our own objections to it. Further, at 11.26 he has been taken to be citing Epicurean advice to have constantly in one's mind some great figure from the past who lived virtuously.[9] If so, he may

---

[7] See J. M. Dillon and A. A. Long, eds., *The Question of "Eclecticism": Studies in Later Greek Philosophy* (Berkeley: University of California Press, 1988), esp. "Introduction" and chap. 1.

[8] 7.33; cf. Plutarch, *De audiendis poetis* 36b, which more or less quotes Epicurus to precisely this effect; and compare Epicurus, *Principal Doctrines* 4, which does not however say quite this same thing.

[9] However, the manuscripts in 11.26 read ἐν τοῖς τῶν Ἐφεσίων γράμμασι, not τῶν Ἐπικουρείων which, e.g., Grube translates (*The Meditations of Marcus Aurelius*). It does seem from a comparison with Plutarch, *Table-talk* 7.5, to which Haines refers ad loc. (C. R. Haines, *The Communings with Himself of Marcus Aurelius Antoninus*, rev. text and Eng. trans., Loeb Classical Library) that some "Ephesians' writings," which seem to have been some text containing magical formulae, may have associated or compared the recitation of

be recalling, whether from Seneca's own account or not, the advice of
Epicurus himself that Seneca reports in *Letter* 11.8: "Cherish some man
of high character, and keep him ever before your eyes, living as if he were
watching you, and ordering all your actions as if he beheld them."[10] Elsewhere (9.41), Marcus does hold Epicurus himself up as a model of the
philosopher resolutely leading a good, philosophical life, without allowing his own illness to distract him from his normal philosophical work;
he cites some lines of Epicurus on this subject not preserved elsewhere,
and draws from them the moral that we should always be concerned
solely with the action of the moment, and the means whereby to accom-
plish it.

In these first appeals to Epicurus we see much the same sort of practice
that we also find in Seneca. It is instructive to pause, before returning to
Marcus in section III, to examine in detail Seneca's practice. That is the
task of the remainder of this section. Seneca regularly concludes the first
twenty-nine *Letters to Lucilius* with a salutary dictum (a "useful pre-
cept," *praeceptum utile*, 24.22)—something, as Seneca says (*Letters* 2.4),
to fortify Lucilius against poverty, or death, or other potential annoy-
ances. He does so more often than not with something from Epicurus. In
both authors this partly reflects the fact that, as I noted above, they are
not writing as official Stoic philosophers and teachers, simply expounding Stoic doctrine. A Stoic philosophical treatise, or even a Stoic teacher's
more informal discussion of the sort we find in the *Discourses* of Epictetus, would not permit this. But the genres of moral and spiritual advice
giving and exhortation that Seneca and Marcus adopt in their writings,
even if marked as coming from a committed Stoic, do permit an author
to look where he pleases for useful admonition. The perspective of
philosophers whose basic views are diametrically opposed to the ("true")

---

some magical words with recalling to mind fine models from the past—at any rate, Plutarch
himself does make this association. So the Plutarch passage gives support for retaining the
manuscript reading. Moreover, the expression "the writings of the Epicureans" in this connection would be somewhat odd: which Epicureans would these be (other than Epicurus
himself), and why does Marcus not say straight out that it is Epicurus, if he was recalling
the passage Seneca translates (see n. 10), or Seneca's translation of it? Had he forgotten who
the precise author was? So it must remain doubtful whether there is a citation of Epicurean
advice in 11.26, after all.

[10] Seneca, *Epistulae Morales*, trans. R. M. Gummere, Loeb Classical Library, Cambridge:
vol. 1. If Marcus is recalling Epicurus's prescription here, it could well be that Marcus's intended advice (which he leaves implicit) is different from Seneca's. For Seneca, we should
picture a great man of the past as a witness to one's own possible wrongdoing, or an approving mentor if one acts well, so as to use pleasing, or not offending, him as a monitory
incentive for better behavior. For Marcus the thought might rather be to hold him up simply as a model for emulation as one goes about one's daily tasks. That is the burden of such
further reflections as 4.38.

Stoic ones can nonetheless have force and effect, especially at early stages of the philosophical enterprise of reorienting one's life. But there is more to be said. As Seneca quite reasonably explains in *Letter* 21,[11] it is just a mistake—in fact, a misunderstanding of how philosophy works—to think that a true Stoic must not cite approvingly anything a philosopher says whose basic philosophical principles are not the Stoic ones. In that context, he cites, from a letter of Epicurus to Idomeneus, this sentence: "If you wish to make Pythocles rich, do not add to his store of money, but subtract from his desires" (21.7). Sentences like these give moral advice, and it should be obvious to everyone that such advice might be supported by reasons drawn from distinct and even quite incompatible philosophical theories of morality or the human good. So, as Seneca quite appropriately says, dicta like the ones he quotes, which he reasonably thinks *can* be supported on a Stoic basis, as well as on some different Epicurean one, must be regarded as public property, just as much as uplifting bits of poetry are that were written on the basis of no philosophical argumentation or view at all. They are not the special preserve of someone writing from the perspective of Epicurean theory.[12]

Of course, when Epicurus speaks of "subtracting from [Pythocles'] desires," he is succinctly drawing on his own theory that desires are of three kinds: natural and necessary, unnecessary but natural nonetheless, and "empty" or vain desires that depend on the false belief that one needs some specially delicious food or needs to engage in some other pleasurable activity that, however nice, is in fact naturally optional.[13] So for Epicurus, the way to make Pythocles rich—that is, fully supplied with what he needs so as to achieve and maintain the highest level of pleasure—is to help him get rid of ("subtract") all such empty desires. Assuming that to be fully supplied is what it is to be rich, Epicurus's point is that you cannot make anyone rich by getting them a vast amount of money to use in procuring the means for satisfying a full array of desires, including some that are empty. No amount of money can possibly be sufficient to prevent someone infected with empty desires from frequently suffering severe pains of want, or fear, or other anxieties inevitably associated with that kind of desire—and so from falling back from the highest level of pleasure. A "full supply" for happiness necessarily includes, first of all, a mind bent on limiting the desires solely to ones that are not empty or

---

[11] *Letters* 21.9–10; cf. *Letters* 8.7–8.

[12] *Publicae sunt*, he says at 21.9; so also 8.8 and 33.2. In the last of these passages he adds, perfectly correctly in my opinion, that they are *maxime nostrae*, i.e., *Stoicae*, however much they are the words of an Epicurean.

[13] See *Principal Doctrines* 29–30, and cf. 26. For discussion, see John M. Cooper "Pleasure and Desire in Epicurus," in *Reason and Emotion*, 485–514.

vain. Natural desires, but only these, can be sustained without opening the door to such self-inflicted distress. At *Letters* 16.7–9, after quoting another Epicurean sentence about what constitute true riches, Seneca cites explicitly and discusses approvingly this distinction between empty desires and natural ones and, following Epicurus, he again urges Lucilius to avoid the empty ones altogether.

Now in doing this, as I have said, Seneca need not be assuming the whole burden of Epicurus's theory of the nature of pleasure and the natural means of achieving it at its highest level, much less Epicurus's theory that the human good is constituted by living securely in the experience of pleasure at that level. Seneca says himself at 21.9–10 that in quoting Epicurus he is doing what Roman senators do when they ask someone proposing some action to make the motion in two parts, so that they can vote for the part they approve of, and not be forced to vote for a part that they do not, or else against the part they do approve. He adds that he is all the more glad to quote Epicurus's words about riches in that he can thereby address even a person with a vicious precommitment to pleasure as his chief concern in life, who might hope to go to Epicurus for reassurance in his pursuits—and to learn from Epicurus how to indulge his vices more consistently and satisfyingly. Seneca's quotation can show such a person that, on the contrary, if he really follows Epicurus's advice he will perforce be driven to live virtuously (*honeste vivere*).

Here we must bear in mind that Seneca is speaking to Lucilius (and the rest of his readers) as someone who has made a basic commitment to redirect his own life on the basis of Stoic philosophy, but still falls far short of consistency and completeness in doing so. At this early stage in his *Letters,* Seneca is giving advice about how to get going, and keep going, in this process, to those not far along in such self-improvement. He is not suggesting that if you followed Epicurus's advice to the letter you would then already be "living virtuously," that is, on the strict and proper Stoic understanding of what that entails. For the Stoics, "living virtuously" means living in accordance with principles that recognize nothing but virtue itself as a good, and that deny more than conditional value or disvalue to anything except virtue and vice respectively—to bodily pleasure and pain, to everything external to the inherent condition of one's own mind and its exercise. His point is rather (see 21.10) that Epicurus's theory, like Stoic principles, does speak against *inflamed* appetite. It demands the restriction of one's appetites—pleasures being the natural object of all appetites, as such—merely to the pleasures that nature itself demands for the preservation of life, and, when circumstances might permit this, to harmless, free, and appetitively unpressured choice of "optional" extra pleasures. There is nothing overtly vicious in such a program for life—no vile, driven self-indulgence. In that limited but significant sense, living according to it would amount to "living virtuously," and in speaking so strongly against inflamed appetites Epicurus takes with the Stoics what Seneca can consider a first crucial step toward full virtue. Having taken that first step, the committed hedonist would then be in a good position to move one step beyond and recognize the truth of the full Stoic view that those same pleasurable objects should be pursued not with an *appetite* for their pleasures (even a mild, unpressured one), but instead with a reasoned desire for them as recommended to us by universal nature itself, and by our nature as rational human beings.

Thus Seneca rejects the specific sort of attachment to the objects of the Epicurean natural desires that Epicurus recommends, since Epicurean natural desires impel us toward external objects of satisfaction with the idea that the pleasure they give is actually good. According to Stoic theory, this way of being impelled is seriously in error. In fact, the objects of Epicurean natural desires, and their pleasure, are strictly indifferent as to goodness or badness, though they are definitely worth pursuing for their own sakes, because in some suitable way they are "in accordance with nature." Thus Seneca and the other Stoics agree with the Epicureans in approving *an* attachment to those very same objects. So, having learned from Epicurus to limit oneself to Epicurean "natural" desires, one might go on to learn from the Stoics to attach oneself to their objects also only as "natural," not as good. In this way one can see the appositeness of Seneca's comparison with the practices of Roman senators: he "votes" with the Epicureans on what they reject and on what they accept, but he gives different reasons for the acceptance and the rejection, and he recommends a different way of impelling oneself toward the objects of pursuit that Epicureans and Stoics accept in common.

Similarly, in commenting on another Epicurean dictum at *Letters* 8.7 ("If you would enjoy real freedom, you must be the slave of philosophy"), Seneca says that the person who submits and surrenders himself to philosophy is immediately "turned round" and does not have to wait to find his life truly a free one, that is, one under the direction of his own mind. So if one begins to live philosophically even by taking to heart Epicurean doctrines about pleasure, one's essential freedom is already won, even though much work remains before the full value of that freedom can be realized. The word Seneca uses here for "turning round" is *circumagere*, the precise equivalent of the one that Plato's Socrates uses in the well-known passage of *Republic* VII in stating his view that education does not put knowledge into people's heads but gets them to redirect the vision of their mind's eye (cf. 518c8–9: περιακτέον; d4: περιαγωγῆς).[14]

---

[14] It is surely that passage that Seneca's choice of words here recalls, and Gummere (n. ad loc. in the Loeb edition) must be mistaken to rely on a passage of Persius to suggest that

Even turning to philosophy in its Epicurean version does reorient one's life away from sensuous self-indulgence and toward the use of reason in determining one's manner of life. So Epicurus stands with the Stoics on the correct side of one very important gap between good and bad living, and deserves our respect and regard for that reason.

Bolder is Seneca's treatment in *Letter 97* of Epicurean doctrine about justice and the reasons that exist for not acting unjustly. Epicurus notoriously held that rules of justice resulted from an agreement human beings reached in the distant past to leave each other in peace, and that universal nature and human nature itself did not in any way dictate these rules. Until the practices of justice were developed by voluntary human agreement, there was no "natural" basis for anyone's wanting to act in those ways, or not wanting to violate them.[15] And he held that, though everyone manifestly benefits from the general observance of that overall system of rules, nonetheless people might sometimes find themselves in a position to violate them to their benefit because they could expect not to be found out. Still, he held, they would never have sufficient reason to violate them. That is because—and, according to him, this is the sole reason for this forbearance—if they ever did violate the rules of justice in effect in their community, they could never really be sure they would not be discovered and punished.[16] This lack of assurance would have the effect that they would suffer from fear and anxiety more or less continuously thereafter—thus negating any increase in the level of pleasure they might otherwise have attained through the benefits brought by the violation. Seneca approvingly quotes (97.13) Epicurus's central claim about the anxious and unhappy state of mind of anyone who does injustice. But in the course of defending his right as a Stoic to do this (97.14–16), he ingeniously exploits that claim to show that, contrary to Epicurus's view, in fact the rules of justice *do* rest on a natural foundation—that every human being is by *nature* averse from doing injustice, and not merely through the effects of human conventions. As usual Seneca's writing at this point is succinct, but I understand his argument as follows.

The first and worst penalty for having acted wrongly is simply to have done it, as Stoic theory clearly demonstrates: virtuous action is good in itself for one who acts that way, vicious action is correspondingly bad in itself, and that means that anyone who acts unjustly has necessarily harmed himself (his mind, his consciousness, his essential self), and so his life, by so acting. However, it is also true that secondary penalties press

---

Seneca is just employing here a special usage of the verb in Latin to mean "emancipate" a slave by "spinning him round" and dismissing him to freedom.

[15] See *Principal Doctrines* 31, 33, 36.

[16] See *Principal Doctrines* 34–35.

close upon these first ones, in the form, as indeed Epicurus says, of constant fear, terror, and distrust of one's own security. But, Seneca asks, why
do people always experience these further penalties, if, as Epicurus
thinks, they always do? It is surely not always and necessarily reasonable
(on Epicurean grounds) to have these anxieties. Surely sometimes, if you
could just forget about having done it (simply put it altogether out of
your mind) and not give yourself away in your effort to keep it secret, no
one could ever find out you had done the thing. In fact, what makes
people nonetheless always distrust their future security is that their own
consciences reveal them to themselves as deserving punishment. Even
they recognize somehow that they have violated principles established by
nature itself for mutual relations among human beings. This retrospective natural aversion from acting as they have nonetheless done shows itself in guilty feelings, which take the form of possibly quite irrational fear
that others will find out. As Seneca says (97.15), "the very proof that we
are by nature averse to crime is that even in circumstances of safety there
is no one who does not feel fear." Thus the very fear that results from doing
injustice, the sure expectation of which Epicurus had held out as the only
true reason not to do injustice when one might get away with it, itself reflects the fact that we all willy-nilly recognize that there is another and
better reason not to do it: by nature and in itself an unjust action is a bad
thing for the one who does it. Hence, in this case too, Seneca can say
(97.15) that we (Stoics) can agree with Epicurus on one point, that unjust
actions are followed always by unending anxiety about being found out
and punished—that is in itself one serious mark against doing injustice—
while disagreeing with him on the conventional versus natural basis of
the rules of justice and on the most fundamental reasons why crime should
be avoided.

A similar account could be given for the other Epicurean dicta that
Seneca cites as "daily lessons" in the early *Letters,* as well as for the other
places in the *Letters* where he enlists Epicurus in aid of his project of self-
and other-reformation.[17] Leaving those aside, however, I want to draw

---

[17] It is curious and noteworthy that only in the passage in *Letter* 97 discussed just above
does Epicurus figure in any of the *Letters* after 85, and that much the largest number of citations of Epicurus come in the first thirty *Letters:* exactly what accounts for this distribution is, to me anyhow, unclear. Several of the "daily lessons" deal with poverty (meaning
lack of money and material resources) as not to be feared or lamented in any way—these
are of course closely related to the account of true riches relied upon in the citation at 21.7
from the letter to Idomeneus discussed above. In addition to that, remarks about poverty
and riches are found at *Letters* 1.5–6, 4.10, 9.20, 14.17, 16.7, 17.11, 27.9. Additional
"lessons" consider the importance of ignoring what the many may think about you
(whether in praise or blame) and paying attention only to oneself and to others similarly devoted to philosophical truth (7.11, 25.6, 29.10); the legitimacy of making oneself the slave

attention to one last passage from Seneca, this time in one of his *Moral Essays,* the fragment *de Otio* ("On the Private Life"). Seneca's thesis in this work is that one ought in fact not to lead an active life of public service (as he has himself mostly been doing, as an adviser to Nero)—but instead live in "retirement," devoting oneself to one's own reading and writing. He notices (1.4) that this thesis sounds very much like an Epicurean one. Epicurus famously advised his followers to "Live unnoticed,"[18] because living in the social or political foreground of the community and working for the common good would inevitably put you in the position where you could not possibly maintain your own undisturbed, fully pleasurable state of consciousness. Only by living a sheltered private life with a bunch of like-minded friends could this, the goal of life, be achieved. Furthermore, Seneca's thesis seems to contrast sharply with what we always thought the Stoics stood for, who tell us re-

---

of philosophy, in which true freedom is alone to be found (8.7, discussed above); that the self-sufficiency of the wise man does not mean that he will not want friends (9.1); the value of constantly picturing some good man of the past as observer of one's own actions (11.8, 25.5); various thoughts about death (that death always lies open, if one's circumstances make continued life unbearable; that one goes out from life as one came in, empty-handed; that it is absurd to seek death if one is oneself responsible for what is unsatisfactory about one's life; that one need not fear death because of any pain one may experience as one dies) (12.10, 22.14, 23.22–23, 26.8); the folly of always busying oneself to arrange one's affairs so that one can live as one prefers and ought, but using that busyness as an excuse for never actually doing it (13.16, 23.9); the importance of fixing limits to one's desires so that one can live in the present and not always in the future (15.9); the evils of anger (18.14); that one's choice of congenial company at meals is more important than the menu (19.10); the importance of not just holding and stating philosophical opinions but living according to them (20.9); the need to act promptly and vigorously to do what one has decided to do, when the time comes, and not make excuses (22.6); that the beginning of salvation is the knowledge that one is in error (28.9); that Epicurus distinguishes among those who need no guidance from a teacher to find their own way to philosophical truth, those like his pupil Metrodorus who, given some direction, will follow on their own, and a third sort like Hermarchus (Epicurus's successor in the leadership of the school) who need actual encouragement and forceful application on the teacher's part to bring them along to that end (52.3–4); how even one being burned in Phalaris's bull (or being wrung with the pain of strangury on one's deathbed, as Epicurus himself was) can find their condition pleasant (66.18, 67.15, 92.25); that Epicurus agrees with Seneca's Stoic distinction between things you would prefer to have and things that, though you would prefer not to have them, you accept and approve and treat as "goods" just because they have come your way and you know how to handle them (66.47–48); Epicurus's late-won, posthumous fame (79.15); that Epicurus says just what the Stoics do, that only the wise man knows how to return a favor (81.11); that Epicurus is wrong to say that virtue makes you happy, but is not sufficient for happiness: his distinction between virtue and its pleasures is a futile one, if as he thinks it is not a contingent connection (85.18).

[18] See Plutarch's little essay "Is It Well Said, to 'Live Unnoticed'?" ed. and trans. B. Einarson and P. H. DeLacy, Loeb Classical Library, *Plutarch's Moralia* vol. 14, esp. 1128f–1129a.

peatedly in their works that (in Seneca's words) we ought to ceaselessly "devote ourselves to the good of the community, to aid the individual, to raise an aged hand to assist even our enemies."[19] Is not Seneca then, he asks, in maintaining this thesis, defecting to the Epicureans and abandoning, even if only selectively, his Stoic principles in exchange for Epicurean ones?

Seneca responds by insisting first that Zeno and Chrysippus themselves did not live lives of public service, but of scholarly retirement. Surely a Stoic ought to do what they have done, not what they tell us to do. They must have done what they did from Stoic philosophical conviction; so the Stoic philosophy, when properly understood, must support this choice. And he adds (6.4–5) that in fact Zeno and Chrysippus did vastly more good for the community (anyhow, the larger community of mankind as a whole) through their philosophical discoveries and their arguments for them—and, of course, through their writings—than they could ever have done by taking active part in the political life of their local communities instead. So when they say in their writings, as they often do, that the best life is one actively devoted to the public good, and certainly seem to mean by that the "political life" as ordinarily understood, we must hear that with a certain qualification. On deeper reflection, we can see, precisely on the ground of basic Stoic principles, that the best active life will not be a "political" one, but one of retirement—provided that one's reading and writing are aimed at establishing the philosophical bases needed by others for the improvement of their own lives. Here, as occasionally elsewhere,[20] Seneca quite appropriately, and precisely as a Stoic, insists that he is not at all obligated to follow blindly the philosophers who are the founders, or later authorities, for Stoic theory. Precisely because our self-improvement consists, according to the Stoics, in coming to our own reasoned conclusions it must be up to each of us (in full seriousness, of

---

[19] *De Otio* 1.4, trans. John M. Cooper and J. F. Procopé, in *Seneca: Moral and Political Essays*, 173.

[20] See *On Favors* I 3.8–4.6 (Cooper and Procopé, *Seneca*, 198–200), where Seneca takes Chrysippus to task for an oversubtle and in the end unacceptably frivolous discussion of the details of Greek mythology of the Graces (i.e., the "Favors"): Seneca is not obligated just unthinkingly to approve of and accept in his own thought any and every thing Chrysippus or other Stoic authorities may have said. See also II 21.4 and the discussion (III 18 ff.) of the favors that Seneca insists (contrary to the Stoic Hecaton's stated view) that slaves can do their masters. In the *Letters*, see 45.4: "I have made myself over to no one; I bear no one's name. I give much credit to the judgment of great men, but I claim some also for my own. These men, too, have left us not positive discoveries but problems needing to be solved"; and 113.23–24. Finally, there is Seneca's emphatic rejection in *Investigations into Nature* (*Naturales Quaestiones*), 7.22.1, of the Stoic theory that a comet is just a sudden fire and not an eternal body like the others in the heavens: *ego nostris non assentior*, he says. (I thank Brad Inwood for the reference.)

course, and after full and careful consideration) to make up our own minds about what the fundamental principles of the school do imply on practical questions.

III

A number of Marcus's citations of Epicurus (those noted above, at the beginning of section II) are like these of Seneca. The preceding review of Seneca's practice, and his defense of it, helps to place these citations in the right light. They indicate overlaps between Epicurus and the Stoics in advice or opinion on specific points of detail about the good life, though of course the theoretical grounding will differ significantly between the two philosophical systems. "Syncretism" or "eclecticism" of this kind—if one might wish to call it that—is no ground for thinking that with Marcus (or Seneca) the philosophical principles of Stoicism have undergone any weakening or compromise, or any dilution with Epicurean or other ideas that do not really fit properly into a Stoic context. So, in exercising in this way the freedom granted them in their choice of literary genres, they are to be neither credited nor blamed for making innovations in Stoic philosophical theory, or for attaching less weight to any fundamental point of that theory than a full Stoic philosopher would do.

Marcus does however have a whole series of references to Epicurean physics, rather than ethics, where the same thing cannot be said. These do, I think, indicate a serious, and potentially quite damaging, falling away from the integrity of Stoic thought—not, however, on any of the core points of Stoic ethical doctrine, which are of course Marcus's dominant concern. Here I have in mind Marcus's frequent references to the atomic physical theory.[21] This theory relied on the movements of atoms falling and colliding helter-skelter to produce the existing (apparent) world order. It denied any intentional imposition of principles of order by the sort of divine mind that the Stoics regarded as responsible both for the world itself and indeed for every event within it. In some of these passages Marcus's immediate topic is the actual or possible consequences of atomic physics itself—for example, the question what we should think about our own deaths if the world is just atoms moving in the void. In others, the focus is on the associated denial that gods have anything to do with the initiation, organization, or functioning of the physical universe. The striking thing about many of these passages is that in them Marcus

---

[21] The passages I have in mind include ones in the following chapters: *Meditations* 2.11, 4.3.2, 4.27, 6.4, 6.10, 6.24, 7.32, 7.50, 8.17, 8.25, 9.28.1, 9.39, 9.40, 10.6, 10.7.2, 11.18.1, 12.14.

speaks, for the moment, as if the atomic theory might actually be true, and the Stoic theory of a single world-animal of which all individual substances, including each human being, are integral parts, might be false. In these passages he contrasts the two cosmological theories as co-equal, alternative possibilities to be taken seriously and contended with. Consider, for example, 6.4: "All existing things will very soon change, either by being burned off in vapor [i.e., in the Stoic ecpyrosis at the end of the current world order], if in fact being is unified, or by being dispersed [into their constituent atoms]."[22] Or 9.39: "Either all things spring from one intellect, occurring as in one body, and then the part must not complain about what comes about for the sake of the whole. Or all is atoms and nothing but a hodgepodge[23] and dispersal: why then be perturbed?—say to your mind, to what governs you, 'You have died, decayed, are reduced to a beast; you are just playing a role, in a herd, grazing.'"[24]

Marcus's point in these remarks and others like them is to drive home the thought that even if the Epicurean worldview is correct, he can and ought still to maintain the attitude of unperturbed personal integrity and

---

[22] πάντα τὰ ὑποκείμενα τάχιστα μεταβαλεῖ, καὶ ἤτοι ἐκθυμιαθήσεται, εἴπερ ἥνωται ἡ οὐσία, ἢ σκεδασθήσεται. The same alternatives occur in two further remarks of book VI, and each time the second alternative involves σκεδασμός, dispersal: 6.10, 6.24. At 6.24 this is specified as a dispersal into things' constituent atoms (both Alexander the Great and his lowliest muleteer ended equally in death, either by being taken up into the same seminal reasons of the cosmos or by being dispersed apart into atoms, ἢ διεσκεδάσθησαν εἰς τὰς ἀτόμους). This shows that at the other two places, too, the dispersal envisaged is into atoms, and not merely into material constituents of some sort or other (perhaps, instead, the elements earth, air, fire and water, for example). See also 7.32: "About death: either a dispersal (σκεδασμός) if atoms or, if a unity, either a quenching (σβέσις) or a relocation (μετάστασις)." The alternative of relocation, according to 10.7.2, would be the change of the *pneuma* or spirit animating one's body into fiery air (i.e., the vaporization referred to in 6.4) and its reunion therein with the reason of the world itself, from which it came (see 4.4, 12.26)—i.e., its resumption into the seminal reasons as referred to in 6.24. These two passages (together with 9.39, cited in the main text just below) make it virtually certain that elsewhere when Marcus refers to the "dispersal" of a thing without mentioning atoms (6.10 bis, 8.25, 10.7, 11.3) he is thinking of the atomic theory (presumably not, however, at 8.51 and 10.18, where the contexts make that inference inappropriate).

[23] The Greek κυκεών, which I translate here and in other passages to be quoted below as "hodgepodge," refers to a "posset," some sort of hot blended drink. (Webster's *New Collegiate Dictionary* says it consists of sweetened and spiced milk curdled with ale or wine.) There seems no doubt that Marcus's choice of this word in this context reflects Heraclitus's use of it in a famous saying (Heraclitus B125 DK), where Heraclitus points out that even a posset will come apart if it is not kept moving (so that the world order too depends on constant movement and change).

[24] ἤτοι ἀπὸ μιᾶς πηγῆς νοερᾶς πάντα ὡς ἑνὶ σώματι ἐπισυμβαίνει, καὶ οὐ δεῖ τὸ μέρος τοῖς ὑπὲρ τοῦ ὅλου γινομένοις μέμφεσθαι· ἢ ἄτομοι καὶ οὐδὲν ἄλλο ἢ κυκεὼν καὶ σκεδασμός. τί οὖν ταράσσῃ; τῷ ἡγεμονικῷ λέγε· τέθνηκας, ἔφθαρσαι, τεθηρίωσαι, ὑποκρίνῃ, συναγελάζῃ, βόσκῃ.

the self-protecting withdrawal into his own mind that he is pressing upon himself throughout as the essence of true happiness—usually, of course, on the basis of Stoic doctrine. In the second of the two passages I have quoted he clearly recognizes that he would have to give up much else that he obviously prizes in the Stoic philosophy, and that he wishes to incorporate into the way he thinks of and conducts his life. He could not truthfully maintain that by having minds we are marked off metaphysically from the rest of the world's animal life and from all merely physical processes. He could not maintain that in having minds we possess something of enormous intrinsic value, something with the ability to structure itself in a firm and lasting way through the adoption of self-authorized rational principles that are also principles for the permanent organization of the world itself. He could not claim that, because of this, we transcend the ephemeral character of everything else in the world that is not a mind. Nonetheless—he seems to be telling himself—he could hang on to his inner Stoic happiness by recognizing and accepting the fact of his own reduced status as a temporary compound of atoms, with a mind like a cow's, propelled by the necessitated movements of its constituents to mouth the words and form the thoughts of some mere actor in a play. By not rebelling and objecting or lamenting, he would, he thinks, retain his Stoic integrity and withdrawal into himself, and so his happiness, even if the Epicurean atomic theory should turn out to be true.

Or, more radically, he could just give up living—but do so serenely, without ill effect on his own happiness. Thus 6.10: "Either a hodgepodge and mutual entanglement and dispersal, or a unity and organization and providence. If the former, why am I so eager to spend time in a haphazard mixture and mess of this sort? Why have any other concern than how ever to 'return to dust'? Why be perturbed? The dispersal will get to me, whatever I do."[25] Here, he rejects the advice of the passage previously cited, of docilely accepting the fact that he and everything else is just atoms and void (nothing but a "mess") but living on with the recognition that he is not a rational mind, according to the lofty Stoic conception of what that means, but in fact no better than any cow in a pasture. Now he suggests, instead, opting for suicide as his last Stoically rational act, an act of refusal—allegedly serene and unperturbed, quite undefiant—to live in a messy, disordered Epicurean world, from which such minds are ab-

---

[25] ἤτοι κυκεὼν καὶ ἀντεμπλοκὴ καὶ σκεδασμός· ἢ ἕνωσις καὶ τάξις καὶ πρόνοια. εἰ μὲν οὖν τὰ πρότερα, τί καὶ ἐπιθυμῶ εἰκαίῳ συγκρίματι καὶ φυρμῷ τοιούτῳ ἐνδιατρίβειν; τί δέ μοι καὶ μέλει ἄλλου τινὸς ἢ τοῦ ὅπως ποτὲ "αἶα γίνεσθαι"; τί δὲ καὶ ταράσσομαι; ἥξει γὰρ ἐπ' ἐμὲ ὁ σκεδασμός, ὅ τι ἂν ποιῶ.

sent.[26] He ought not, and, he implies, would be able not to, become in the least perturbed at the knowledge of the disordered character of reality; he would simply exercise, right away, the Stoic's established right to "take himself out" upon recognizing the unsuitability of continued life under these circumstances.

Thus in these first three passages we find Marcus giving two quite different pieces of advice to himself about how to react in case the Epicurean physical theory is true. On the one hand (9.39), he tells himself that he could go on living, with his happiness intact. On the other (6.10), he supposes this would not be possible, but that one could nonetheless retain one's happiness long enough to commit suicide. Either way, there is nothing to fear from the prospect that Epicurean, not Stoic, physical theory might contain the essential truth of things. The knowledge that it did would give no good ground for departing from the Stoic ideal of withdrawal into oneself and unperturbed personal integrity. Sometimes, however, Marcus goes even further toward reconciling himself to life in a godless atomic world than he does in 9.39. In 12.14 he insists (on what ground, he does not say) that even in an Epicurean world the Stoic mind will actually remain intact: now, he would not have to say to himself, to his mind, as in 9.39, "You have died, decayed, are reduced to a beast. . . ." Here, he gives three alternatives as to how the world of nature might be conducted, in place of the two we have met so far. The first of these is the Stoic view, and the third is again the Epicurean one (for our purposes, we need not take the second into account). He says: "Either the necessity of fate and an inviolable organization of events, or a propitiable providence, or a haphazard mess with no one in charge. . . . If an ungoverned mess, be content that in such an inundation *you* have within yourself an intellect that *does* govern. And if the inundation is to sweep you away, let it sweep away your flesh, your vital breath, all the rest; but your intellect it will *not* sweep away."[27]

Having thus boldly exempted the internal world from any effects of the "haphazard mess," in 4.27 Marcus turns to redeem the external one, too,

---

[26] See also 2.11. Always bear in mind, he tells himself here, whenever you do anything, that you can depart from life at any moment. Nothing holds you to live among other men, whether there *are* gods as the Stoics believe, or there are not, or they don't concern themselves with human affairs, as the Epicureans hold. What could life mean to *him* in a world empty of gods or empty of providence, as in the latter two cases?

[27] I translate the Loeb text: ἤτοι ἀνάγκη εἱμαρμένη ⟨καὶ⟩ ἀπαράβατος τάξις, ἢ πρόνοια ἱλάσιμος, ἢ φυρμὸς εἰκαιότητος ἀπροστάτητος. . . . εἰ δὲ φυρμὸς ἀνηγεμόνευτος, ἀσμένιζε, ὅτι ἐν τοιούτῳ κλύδωνι αὐτὸς ἔχεις ἐν σαυτῷ τινα νοῦν ἡγεμονικόν. κἂν παραφέρῃ σε ὁ κλύδων, παραφερέτω τὸ σαρκίδιον, τὸ πνευμάτιον, τἄλλα· τὸν γὰρ νοῦν οὐ παροίσει.

in consequence. "Either a thoroughly organized world order or a hodgepodge thrown together indeed, but still a world order. Or can there exist
within yourself a sort of ordered world, while in the All there is disorder—especially when all things are so distinct from one another yet fused
together and mutually affecting?"[28] And in 10.6 he argues, on the basis
of this presumed order even in a hodgepodge world, that in an Epicurean
universe he would have to recognize himself as "part of the whole," just
as much as on the Stoic understanding of that whole as a "thoroughly
organized world order." As a result, in an Epicurean world, just as on
the Stoic theory, he says, he would "not be displeased with anything
assigned to me from the whole; for nothing is harmful to the part if it
benefits the whole."[29] Further, he would regard himself as "somehow
closely (οἰκείως) related to parts of the same kind" as himself, so that he
"will do no action contrary to community, but rather will make those of
my same kind my concern, and direct my every impulse to the common
advantage, and away from the opposite. When that is achieved, life will
necessarily flow smoothly (εὐροεῖν)."[30] Thus, in this further set of passages, Marcus claims not only that the self-governing Stoic mind survives,
but that the whole of Stoic moral theory will retain its applicability, in a
world that is recognized not to be constructed by a divine mind and regulated by it for the good of the world as a whole, but to be the random
and temporary outcome of the collocation and entanglement of atoms
moving solely according to the laws of motion that apply to such invisible material particles. Hence, Marcus says, in such a world one should
recognize good reason not to object to, but rather to welcome with joy,
anything that happened to oneself in the course of natural events, and
should recognize good reason to work sedulously for the natural advantage of human beings in their communal associations and not merely for
one's own narrowly personal advantage. And in living that way one

---

[28] ἤτοι κόσμος διατεταγμένος ἢ κυκεὼν συμπεφορημένος μέν, ἀλλὰ κόσμος. ἢ ἐν σοὶ μέν
τις κόσμος ὑφίστασθαι δύναται, ἐν δὲ τῷ παντὶ ἀκοσμία, καὶ ταῦτα οὕτως πάντων δι-
ακεκριμένων καὶ διακεχυμένων καὶ συμπαθῶν; I translate the manuscripts' text, which I
believe does make sense, even if the sense might be found surprising. See A.S.L. Farquharson ad loc.: The Meditations of the Emperor Marcus Antoninus 2:614–15, who rightly
points out that even on Epicurus's theory the actual world we live in does have principles of
order, however contingent or epiphenomenal.

[29] οὐδενὶ δυσαρεστήσω τῶν ἐκ τοῦ ὅλου ἀπονεμομένων· οὐδὲν γὰρ βλαβερὸν τῷ
μέρει, ὃ τῷ ὅλῳ συμφέρει.

[30] καθόσον δὲ ἔχω πως οἰκείως πρὸς τὰ ὁμογενῆ μέρη, οὐδὲν πράξω ἀκοινώνητον,
μᾶλλον δὲ στοχάσομαι τῶν ὁμογενῶν καὶ πρὸς τὸ κοινῇ συμφέρον πᾶσαν ὁρμὴν
ἐμαυτοῦ ἄξω καὶ ἀπὸ τοὐναντίου ἀπάξω. τούτων δὲ οὕτω περαινομένων ἀνάγκη
τὸν βίον εὐροεῖν.

would achieve the very condition (εὔροια βίου, a smooth flow of life) in terms of which the Stoics beginning with Zeno had always defined happiness (εὐδαιμονία).[31]

IV

In these passages, then, taken together, there are two claims deserving separate treatment: a weaker and then a much stronger one. The weaker claim is Marcus's assurance to himself that even in an Epicurean universe that he came to recognize as such he could continue to live happily (maybe only long enough to die happily in it)—with no disturbed or upset feelings caused by that knowledge, or by any of its implications. Secondly and much more strongly, he assures himself that even under the conditions of an Epicurean universe, he would continue to regard himself as a self-governing mind and to have the same reasons that, as a Stoic, he has all along recognized for living for others and achieving happiness through the moral life—the life of justice, temperance, and courage, all grounded in a wise understanding of what is and what is not good or bad for a person, but merely indifferent, though possibly worth assigning some positive or negative intrinsic value in a human life.

First, then, let us consider the weaker claim. Would good reasons survive for Marcus to maintain his Stoic attitude of unperturbed indifference to external events, perhaps only long enough to commit suicide, if he knew he lived in an Epicurean universe? I should emphasize that in speaking of "an Epicurean universe" here I am not saddling Marcus with the task of living happily while accepting the Epicurean account of the nature of pleasure and of human happiness as consisting in the highest level of continuing pleasure. The Stoics hold with considerable plausibility (and there is no reason to doubt that Marcus saw and agreed with this point, though he seems nowhere to touch on it) that anyone who accepted bodily pleasure as a good at all, let alone (in some version) the highest good or goal of life, could never reasonably have the confidence about his condition and its prospects that anyone must have who is to be counted as living happily. They could not be confident that the same pleasure they are experiencing at some one moment will continue indefinitely for the future; that they do not control.[32]

---

[31] See Arius Didymus in Stobaeus, *Selections* II (77, 20 Wachsmuth), and Sextus Empiricus, *Against the Theoreticians* (*Adversus Mathematicos*) XI 30 (and cf. Diogenes Laertius, *Lives of Eminent Philosophers*, trans. R. D. Hicks, Loeb Classical Library, 7.88).

[32] See Plutarch's treatise *That It Is Impossible to Live Pleasantly According to Epicurus's Doctrines*, (trans. B. Einarson and P. DeLacy, Loeb Classical Library), 1086c–1107c, esp. chap. 6 (1090c–91a). The Epicureans hold that the goal of life, this highest level of pleasure,

Marcus's claim is only that even in an Epicurean world he could retain his happiness where happiness is understood according to the Stoic account, not the Epicurean. Stoics rely for their happiness on the demonstrated strength of their own mind in holding resolutely to their conviction that nothing outside their mind and its activities, which they do control, is either good or bad for them personally. On this view, in order to achieve happiness, and confidently retain it, one need only continue in a particular set of firm beliefs about what is good and bad for oneself. The celebrated "smooth flow of life" that Zeno and Marcus, too, talk about as constituting happiness simply consists in the smooth flow of the actions one performs, the practical thoughts one smoothly has, and one's smooth reactions to events, when and precisely because one is in the state of mind constituted by believing these things so firmly and unwaveringly. And, of course, one's own reasoning powers give one control over what one believes, on the basis of what considerations (or what arguments). Since those beliefs (according to plausible Stoic arguments) determine all one's actions, practical thoughts, and reactions to things that happen, it follows that one controls through one's own reasoning power whether or not one is happy. It is this state of belief that we must take Marcus to be claiming he could retain even if he knew that his universe was an Epicurean one.

Now if one imposes a low enough standard for what counts as one's beliefs and for what counts as subjectively strong enough grounds for holding them, it might seem obvious that Marcus very well might succeed. In particular (I will return to this in my conclusion), one might have the sort of belief and conviction that we associate nowadays with religious faith—not resting on reasons to any important extent, but on some attitude of acceptance of some other sort. But for a Stoic, a belief is to be

---

is a state of feeling or consciousness that, given various presumed natural facts about human bodies and souls, and certain of their mental abilities, simply follows causally upon a person's maintaining certain mental attitudes no matter what is happening to or around them. (They can recall past pleasures, etc., if any part of the body is giving pain; they can bear in mind that pain if severe is typically short-lived, and so on.) How can one be sure that these exercises *will* always suffice to achieve this result? Everyone knows how precarious any such causal judgment is. The awareness of this precariousness would have to affect the state of mind of anyone who, for the moment, was in fact in pleasure at a very high level: if they were honest with themselves, they would have to have a nagging doubt about the future, which, when added to their current state of mind, would prevent them from actually attaining the absolutely highest level of pleasure, even for that moment. And if they were dishonest or somehow managed to prevent such doubts from affecting their peace of mind for that moment, the inherent unattainability of the needed rational confidence in the future would disqualify them from counting as *happy* even then. One is only happy at any moment, the Greek philosophers all agree, if that condition can rationally be projected also into the future. In placing happiness thus outside any agent's strict control, Epicurus makes it even in principle unavailable to any human being. Or so Stoics argue.

understood as something that rests upon reasons that give it, in one's opinion, rational support—that reveal it as true, on the ground of those reasons. However, it does not count as believing something, as Epictetus never tires of stressing, that you assert some Stoic proposition and recite correctly some arguments held in the Stoic school to be sound bases on which to conclude that it is true. You have to take it to heart, you have to assert it (and any grounds on which you hold to it) as something you personally are convinced of. It may not be completely clear just what the psychological condition of conviction here referred to actually consists of, but I take it that some such requirement is a reasonable constraint on what is to count as someone's belief. Certainly, mere assertion does not. Now in the passages cited, Marcus does show clearly that he accepts this constraint. It is clearly a heartfelt revulsion against the idea of living in a "hodgepodge" world that leads him to say, in 6.10, that if it were revealed that that was what the world actually was like, there could be nothing in it to attract him to stay. The right thing to do would simply be, calmly and quietly, though disdainfully, to find a way out through death. Better death than living on and suffering disappointment and distress at having to put up with that fact about how the world is—as Marcus seems to envisage here he inevitably would suffer. Similarly, when in a more optimistic mood, he says at 9.39 that he could actually live on unperturbed, simply by telling himself plainly and straightout that his mind is nothing but some mechanically manipulated atomic construct, going through the motions of thinking but without really doing so—so that he had better stop striving to be anything else. Here too he speaks with heartfelt conviction about what one ought to think and how one ought to act. Likewise when at 12.14 he defiantly insists that even in a "haphazard mess" of a world he would in fact *retain* his full Stoic mind, so that he would not have to tell himself such things in order to preserve his equanimity and live on happily. Here too he is clearly speaking with personal conviction: presumably, he relies on his own well-entrenched experience of himself as an agent as a solid ground for holding that his mind really is the real Stoic McCoy, not an Epicurean pseudo-mind playing at mentality.

Perhaps we can think that Marcus might be able to generate within himself a sufficiently strong, heartfelt conviction to count as a belief that (even in an Epicurean world) he would remain a self-governing Stoic mind, in total control of the only source of anything good or bad for himself. (As I mentioned, Marcus does not tell us on what grounds he might hold that to be true; it might instead seem that Epicurean physics would in fact decisively rule out all possibility that we are such minds. I will return below to this question shortly.) Or perhaps he could truly believe that although he would not be a self-governing mind, nonetheless one need not and should not allow that to be of concern—that one should calmly accept our lot to be like that of cows grazing in a field, and yet live on calmly under that conception. Or perhaps he could believe that, if that proved too difficult, one could and should just commit suicide, placid and unconcerned. The trouble, however, is that these three responses are inconsistent with one another: Marcus cannot hold at the same time that the right thing to do is to kill himself, *and* to live on knowing he's not a Stoic mind, *and* to live on knowing he is one. Indeed, he cannot consistently hold that he is and that he is not a Stoic mind in the first place. The evidence I have cited therefore, if charitably interpreted, really seems to show that Marcus is simply dithering on this question. Either he holds different views at different times, or at each moment when he considers the matter he dithers then, being unable to make up his mind which view is correct.

Nor is this a matter on which, as he himself seems clearly to conceive it, he can afford to live on in such a state of indecision. Marcus plainly does think it might actually turn out that Epicurean physics is *true*. Plainly, he prefers if possible to believe Stoic physics, but he seems quite serious in supposing that, rationally, one might have to conclude that it was not true. So he really does need to reach some firm point of view from which to act, in the light of this (as he sees it) real possibility. How is he to think of himself, how is he to regard his mode of life, if Epicurean physics is true? So long as he remains uncertain, or divided in his opinions, Stoic orthodoxy, at any rate, will say that he cannot be living smoothly and so not happily, either now when he writes these things or in the imagined future when he comes to recognize that the world really is an Epicurean one. Marcus is having trouble making up his mind just what to think; until he does make up his mind, and stick to some single account, he is living unhappily and unsmoothly. Presumably, in fact, he needs to apply himself all the more sedulously to Stoic theory, or to *some* theory, so as to achieve the required consistency of view. Without such theoretical work, he cannot live with the firmness and consistency of belief required, according to Stoic theory, to sustain the claim to be living smoothly and happily. This, at any rate, is what Stoic orthodoxy would say.[33] Given his continued uncertainty about what response is rationally

---

[33] As I have just indicated, Stoic orthodoxy held that belief is ideally an all-or-nothing affair: for example, either you should believe that it is right to kill yourself under the circumstances we have been envisaging or you should believe you should go on living (either, again, with the view that you are a Stoic mind or with the view that you are not one—but not both). One might object, however, that belief, even ideally, is really not like that. Really, belief in a proposition is always something a person holds with some implicit *degree of belief*—and rarely if ever is anyone's degree of belief in anything to be set at 100 percent. Indeed, it might be said (though the Stoics would dispute this), it is not reasonably to be insisted on

left open to him, then, there is good reason to think that Marcus has not in fact put himself in a position from which to retain his happiness when he supposes that there genuinely is a possibility that Epicurean physics, not the Stoic theory of nature, contains the truth.

What reasons, however, might Marcus think he has for retaining his Stoic equanimity, on any of the three competing responses he envisages, even while recognizing that the world is an Epicurean one? As I mentioned, he does not explain at all what these might be, but we can illuminatingly address this question to ourselves on his behalf.

One should distinguish between two components of the Stoic happy state of mind. First there is the bottom-line set of beliefs about what is good and bad for a human being, and what has positive and what negative value of the lesser sort I referred to earlier. Then there are the grounds on which one holds these beliefs. On Marcus's supposition of an Epicurean universe, of course, all of Stoic natural theory about a world mind and a providential order of events within the world would be false.

---

that even ideally one should reach the position in which one could set the degree of their belief in any proposition at 100 percent. This might provide a defense for Marcus. Perhaps he is entitled to believe, to different degrees, all three of the propositions we have been discussing. Believing them all at once would not necessarily be the sort of inconsistency Stoic orthodoxy would claim it is—that would depend on the degrees of belief assigned. Accordingly, his holding these conflicting beliefs would not necessarily show that he is not living smoothly and happily already, or that he would not continue to do so while holding the same views after discovering that the world is a hodgepodge. In fact, there are possible antecedents in earlier Greek philosophy (especially with Carneades, about whom Marcus might have read in Cicero's *Academica,* who drew on aspects of Stoic theory itself) that might have permitted someone of Marcus's time to develop such a view of belief as always coming in degrees (though, so far as we know, no major theorist did). But such sophistication is presumably beyond Marcus's capacities, and beyond his intentions in devoting himself to philosophy in the first place; in any event, nothing in the *Meditations* suggests he had any such new thoughts about such a technically philosophical matter as the nature of belief and its degrees. More relevant to present concerns, there is strong reason to fear that this alternative view would not have helped Marcus in dealing with the issues I have raised, in any case. He is looking for tranquillity despite knowing the world is Epicurean, and for grounds adequate to sustain his commitment to social service as what his happiness consists in. If on all the relevant matters he holds differing and conflicting opinions, even only to different degrees, it seems very doubtful that he could really attain the "smooth flow of life" that, as a Stoic, he is aiming at. Uncertainty about where the truth lies (conjoined to the conviction that it *does* lie somewhere, and in only one place) would presumably leave him in a state of some distress and turmoil, whatever view he held with the highest degree of belief and so whatever action he might take in any instance. If what you are after is tranquillity and smoothness of life, you had better adopt the all-or-nothing view of belief characteristic of Stoic orthodoxy, and so aim at holding just one belief among any set of differing ones. Holding three on some one question, with differing degrees of belief, must leave you in much anxiety as to which of them is actually true, and so which one it would be best to act upon.

Further, these are crucial points in the Stoic argument for their view of what happiness is—and for why it cannot matter for our happiness how external events turn out, whether in accordance with our wishes or contrary to them. So he cannot be claiming that Stoics would retain their happiness by continuing to retain such background beliefs of natural philosophy or metaphysics that support these bottom-line value judgments. The most he can be claiming is that even in what was recognized as an Epicurean world, one could continue to maintain Stoicism's central claims about what is of value to a human being (and what does not matter, ultimately), without basing them at all on these grounds. But on what grounds would one then maintain them? Remember, as I explained, it (reasonably) does not count for the Stoics as believing these central claims about human values if one just stubbornly insists on holding they are true (say, because you see you can retain your imperturbability and inviolability if you do hold to them): you have to think you have good reason for asserting them, independent of the desirable effects for you *if* they are true. After all, in the ideal case these beliefs have to be so firmly and well entrenched that nothing that might happen to you could cause you to doubt them, much less to give any of them up.[34] You have to rely on the strength of the reasons you have for believing them if you are to retain the requisite confidence, as you look to the future, that you will always continue to believe and rely on them: otherwise these beliefs would not begin to give you the touted "smooth flow of life." What would those good reasons be, in an Epicurean world?

We can agree with Marcus, I think, that, even on Epicurean physical theory, among the real *parts* of the world are all the individual animals and plants. Their natures as members of their species are really existent forces within the world: on Epicurean theory these are not simply eliminated in favor of atoms and their movements in the void.[35] So one can ask what, given our specific natures as human beings, with our linguistic

---

[34] See Diogenes Laertius's explanation of knowledge (ἐπιστήμη) for the Stoics as "a standing condition in the reception of impressions that is unchangeable by argument (λόγος)" (*Lives*, 7.47) (also Sextus Empiricus, *Against the Theoreticians* [*Adversus Mathematicos*] 7.151: "knowledge is a cognitive grasp that is secure and firm and unalterable by argument"). Knowledge may not be what Marcus is realistically aspiring to, since he may well regard it as beyond his powers; but any condition that he can attain, which will give him some approximation to the secure happiness that knowledge would provide, must itself be conceived as an approximation to that condition of firmness and unchangeability, grounded in the depth of one's understanding of the relevant truths and the reasons that show them to be such.

[35] See *Letter to Herodotus* 68–71, with D. Sedley "Epicurean Anti-reductionism" in *Matter and Metaphysics*, eds. J. Barnes and M. Mignucci, 295–327.

and other reasoning abilities, is good for *us*. What constitutes *our* specific good (parallel to the specific goods of the members of the other animal and plant species)? Familiar Stoic arguments might now be invoked to show that this must be or include centrally the perfection of our defining natural powers, and in particular those that constitute our rationality. But what is to show that an Epicurean ideal of the mind—one structured through the acceptance of hedonist assumptions about the importance of pleasure in any animal life—does not in fact constitute that natural perfection? What is to show that, furthermore, our final good is not a perfection that centrally includes the actual experience of pleasure at the highest level, as a sort of copestone to that (preliminary) perfection of our minds themselves in seeking it? Having this pleasure would be a crucial indication of the natural smooth functioning of our whole organism. On the assumption of the truth of Epicurean physics, Marcus cannot rely here on Stoic ideas about the special character of rationality as linking us to the governing reason of the whole world in order to enforce the conclusion that only the state of the mind itself counts as good or bad for us, and that externals like pleasure are necessarily indifferent (though under normal conditions preferable to their opposites). On Epicurean physics, there is no such thing as a governing reason of the world anyhow. The result is that Marcus could not be sure, under the assumption of the truth of Epicurean physics, that pleasure was not the highest good, instead of one's own self-directed rationally correct thoughts and choices. Thus I cannot see that Marcus could have any good basis for claiming, given Epicurean physics, that his happiness consists in holding firmly to the view that nothing outside his mind's own actions counts as good or bad for him, or that he can control by his mind's voluntary acts whether he is happy or not. That means he could not live in an Epicurean world with any rational assurance that he could continue to live happily, and he could not rationally decide to commit suicide at once, while still retaining the unperturbed existence that as a Stoic he had attained. The news that the world was an Epicurean one would rationally have horrifying effects on him—even if they lasted only for as much time as he needed to do away with himself.

I conclude, then, that Marcus fails to substantiate his weaker claim, the claim that if he knew he lived in an Epicurean universe he would continue to have good reason to maintain his Stoic attitude of unperturbed indifference to external events. One would expect that a fortiori he must fail to establish the stronger one—that even in an Epicurean world, recognized as such, he would retain all the usual Stoic reasons not just for living on unperturbed, but for living so as to achieve happiness through the moral life of service to others. Still, there are things to be learned about Marcus's Stoicism from considering this second claim as well.

V

In 10.6, quoted above, Marcus says that he would still recognize himself as most "closely related to parts [of the world] of the same kind" as himself, that is, human beings. In consequence, he would regard himself as naturally directed toward communal goods and would find his own natural fulfillment in such work. But what could give him this idea? He cannot claim that the study of the rest of the animal world, and nature's intentions as revealed there for the other animals, shows us nature's intentions in regard to how human life should be conducted—with the conclusion that the perfectly structured, naturally most successful, mind (the one structured most fully in accordance with nature's intentions in creating our species) must be one that recognizes obligations to other humans, or one that embodies others of the traditional virtues, such as courage and temperance.[36] In the Epicurean world, nature does not have any intentions at all. But if we rule out considerations drawn from ideas about nature's own intentions, how can Marcus defend this claim? On Epicurean physical assumptions (and simple observation), I suppose he could still say we humans do just naturally feel drawn to one another, in a way we are not drawn to other animals. On such evidence, he could say that we are most "closely related to parts of the same kind" as ourselves. We do intuitively (and so, we could say, "naturally") take an interest in other people and their lives, in a way that we do not (all of us, or people in general) in the lives of other species. We have a natural sympathy for and empathy with other human beings, but not with the world's other animal life. One might then understand why someone, even in an Epicurean world, might be drawn to desire for himself a life of devotion to human interests overall—as with Marcus, for example, who at age seventeen was already marked out, as the Emperor Antoninus's adopted son, for the career of a top imperial administrator and eventual emperor himself. That would be an understandable, "natural" development from this basic natural sense of connection with other human beings, as such. But Marcus needs something stronger, if he is to sustain his Stoic commitments, as such—that is, as ones (still) imposed by reason itself—in response to the news that the world was an Epicurean one. He needs to argue that, as a basic and central requirement (however much people may sometimes or even often manage to ignore or deny it), reason requires us to devote ourselves substantially to the common good, and to prefer that over our own personal advantage. It is this further step that I cannot see that Marcus has any reason to take, if (he supposes) he lives

---

[36] See Cooper and Procopé, *Seneca*, xx–xxiii.

in an Epicurean world. From knowledge of how things go in life, one might reach the conclusion, with Epicurus, that one has strong and well-entrenched reasons to cooperate and coordinate with other people, but that would not be to say, as Marcus as a Stoic needs to say, that acting constantly for the common good is a ground-level, central, and basic requirement of reason itself.

Now, in the foregoing I have assumed that Marcus shares the orthodox Stoic conception of what it means for human nature to be rational. I have also assumed that he understands the claims (and vulnerabilities) that follow from the fact that, as Stoics think we do, we consist essentially of our minds, that is, our ability to reason things out and to govern our lives in accordance with our own understanding of the relevant facts. For the Greek Stoics, it is because we are essentially rational minds, and nothing else, that we cannot be harmed by anything but our own rationally controlled mental acts (something that Marcus very frequently tells himself).[37] It is in the strongest possible sense entirely up to us whether we live smoothly and happily or not. Such success in life depends only on whether we reach a situation in our rational reflections from which all our rationally controlled mental acts do, and we can be sure that they will continue to, conform with one another smoothly and without causing us any self-inflicted distress.

It is clear that Marcus accepts that he can retain his happiness in an Epicurean world (or as much happiness as he has yet attained) only if and to the extent that he can hold fast to these fundamental Stoic doctrines about human nature and about what, in consequence, is good and what bad for us. I said above (p. 354) that for orthodox Stoicism the only way to do that is to embed those views in your mind as deeply as possible, on the basis of as clear and comprehensive an understanding as you can manage of reasons that really do support their truth. That is because of the essential rationality of a mind. This means, to begin with, that minds, just as such and inherently, function on the basis of reasons (whether good, bad, or indifferent, to be sure). Whenever any person thinks that things are so-and-so (holds them to be that way, I mean), they do so on the basis of some reason—even if it is a ridiculously inadequate reason, even if in a way they themselves know that it is ridiculously inadequate and would not attempt to deny it, or even if they could not articulate any intelligible reason at all for believing what they do, and loftily refuse to try. The very act of believing something includes the thought that there is sufficient reason to believe it. This being so, any belief is potentially open to being destabilized by the person's coming to think that there is *not*

---

[37] See, among other passages, 2.9, 4.39, 5.19, 5.21, 6.32, 6.41, 8.29, 8.47, 9.42.2, 11.16, 12.3, 12.8, 12.22.

sufficient reason to believe whatever it may be, or that there is better reason to believe something else instead. To think either of these things is automatically to be disposed to cease holding the original belief. To be sure, someone can refuse to listen to counterarguments, and insist on holding fast to their original belief by just dismissing or blocking out counter-thoughts; reason can be misused, in this as in other ways. Still, the fact that minds are rational means that, unless interfered with, they do follow (what they think is) the better reason. Furthermore, being rational gives minds the ability, and the tendency, to find (or recognize when it is presented to them) and follow what in fact *is* the better reason. Universal standards for rational belief, and the tendency to use and follow them, are part of the inherent equipment of any mind.[38] So the only completely secure method of rendering a belief truly stable is to rest it on sufficient reasons, reasons adequate to rationally withstand all possible counter-considerations and counterarguments. In this way and to this extent, what is true (or what is rationally best supported) has the greatest power to influence minds. You do not have to explain why a mind believes what is true or best supported by reason; that follows of itself, if nothing interferes.[39] You only have to explain why a mind believes something else, that is, what it might be that has *mis*led it.

We need to ask, however, whether Marcus accepts this particular orthodox Stoic view. Or does he hold a different philosophical position about what does or might render someone's acceptance of the Stoic outlook on life secure, so that they might retain it in an Epicurean world where one was forced to give up believing the principal reasons which on Stoic theory establish it as the truth, and where, as I have argued, no sufficient new reasons would be available to reestablish them?

In reading and thinking about Marcus, as I began by emphasizing, one ought always to bear in mind that he is writing to himself, not for an audience (even if it is possible that he expected, or came to expect, to have other readers after his death). He does not write as a Stoic philosopher, explaining Stoic philosophical theory and defending Stoic views against those of other philosophers or against philosophical objections that had been or might be directed against them.[40] Writing as a private person

---

[38] On this see "Stoic Autonomy," chap. 9 above, sect. II.

[39] That is why for orthodox Stoicism the first and dominant rule of the art of persuasion (rhetoric) is to speak the truth. Rhetoric is counted by Stoics as an "art of speaking well" (see Diogenes Laertius *Lives*, 7.42), differing in essentials from dialectic only in its scope and the contexts of its application (see Sextus Empiricus, *Against the Theoreticians* [*Adv. Math.*] 2.6–7, citing Zeno). And (see Alexander of Aphrodisias, *On Aristotle's* Topics, I. 11–12) speaking well, according to them, consists in saying what is true and appropriate.

[40] In *Meditations* 1.17.8, he gives thanks that once he became attracted to philosophy as a youth he did not fall in with any "sophist" (the word would indicate a teacher, normally of

(even though the Roman Emperor), who was taught philosophy by Stoic teachers at Rome in his youth and later through his own reading of Epictetus, he discusses simply the topics that are of practical significance for him in leading his own life. Such theoretical questions are not among them. Nonetheless, a number of things he does say strongly suggest that, in theory, he accepts the orthodox Stoic view about reason that I have adumbrated in the preceding section.

He refers frequently to his ἡγεμονικόν or the "ruling part" of his soul—his mind or reason, λόγος—as the superior element in a human being's make up and as something that must stand apart from, and above, all that happens in the body as well as what happens outside oneself, making use of the latter but not being made use of by them. Everything, he says (12.33), depends upon how one's "ruling part" treats or uses itself—that is, whether it structures itself and activates itself and the rest of the organism in voluntary action in the right way. The rest is smoke and corpses, as he picturesquely puts it. In 10.24, in asking himself how he is using his "ruling part" at the moment, his first question is whether he is making it full of νοῦς—understanding or intelligence. Likewise, in 9.22 he directs himself to rush to his own "ruling part" and make it into a *just* intelligence or understanding. Not infrequently, he refers to our "ruling part" directly as νοῦς in us, as at 12.14 with the expression νοῦς ἡγεμονικός, "ruling intelligence." He frequently (as in 9.22, just referred to) speaks of this part of ourselves as itself part also of the reason of the whole world (that is, Zeus). In 5.27 he speaks of Zeus as having given a fragment of himself (ἀπόσπασμα) to each person, namely each person's "intelligence and reason," to be their leader and ruler (προστάτην καὶ ἡγεμόνα). In 12.26, each person's intelligence is god and flows from the nature of the Whole. Reason is something that gods and human beings have in common (7.53). Now, Marcus does not speak often about how Zeus, that is, the mind or "ruling part" of the Whole,

---

rhetoric, but in this context it appears that he means a teacher of philosophy), or turn to books (to writing them, if we read ἐπὶ τὸ συγγράφειν with Reiske; or, if we retain the manuscript reading, ἀποκαθίσαι ἐπὶ τοὺς συγγραφεῖς, to reading the books of "commentators"; or, if with Farquharson we read ἐπὶ τοῦ συγγραφᾶς . . . ἀναλύειν, to analyzing written books), or to analyzing technical philosophical arguments or studying the philosophy of nature. Instead he had a Stoic teacher like Apollonius and got advice from people such as the Roman nobleman and personal mentor, Q. Iunius Rusticus (who got him to read Epictetus), and Claudius Maximus, all three of whom he pays homage to in *Meditations* I and all of whom seem to have emphasized the practical, not the theoretical or dialectical aspects of Stoic theory and indeed of philosophy itself. In 8.1 he says frankly that he is "very far from philosophy," i.e., from being a philosopher and living the way a philosopher does, in whole days spent reading, thinking, arguing about philosophical matters. His station in life, to speak of nothing else, has been against this.

functions, but he does once (7.75) refer to everything that happens as following in accordance with nature's impulse in creating the cosmos, so that everything happens for some intelligible reason (and is not ἀλόγιστον). Thus Zeus's perfect mind, with its perfect understanding, does whatever it does precisely on the basis of the completely sufficient reasons why just that is to *be* done: Marcus never tires of repeating that everything that happens in the world at large happens for the good of the Whole. As to human beings, again, he does not discuss the details of how human action is generated, but in 5.14 he explains perfect actions (κατορθώσεις), the actions of morally virtuous people, as ones that result from a process of reasoning starting from the premise that suits the case and advancing straight on to the end standing before the actions. So he does consider both Zeus's mind and the human mind as, basically, faculties for understanding, ones that naturally do follow reason and are inherently guided by reason's own standards in their movements and actions. Zeus's is guided without fail and completely, human beings' only if not malfunctioning. On this conception of human reason, it should not be possible to reach a secure—unalterable and impregnable—commitment to Stoic moral views except on the basis of deeply entrenched, correct reasoning.[41]

But then, what are we to make of Marcus's willingness to claim, as we have seen he does, the independence of his Stoic moral principles from the basis in philosophical analysis on which they ultimately rested for the original Stoics of the third century B.C.? When in 12.14 (quoted above, sect. III) Marcus intimates that he would refuse to be perturbed if he knew he lived in an Epicurean universe, because his essential self, his intellect, would remain his own possession, exempt from the Epicurean flow of atoms, he seems to mean, as I have said, that he would not have to allow the knowledge that all was atoms and void to undermine his own self-possession. As he puts it elsewhere,[42] apparently quoting the Cynic Monimus, "everything is in what we think" (ὅτι πᾶν [or: πάντα] ὑπόληψις). Nothing can force us to think that such "external" matters as whether there are gods in the universe, or transcendent minds, or a teleological system of nature, make any difference to us—our *own* minds remain our own possession. If we do not let these things make a difference,

---

[41] See *Meditations* 8.48: we know from experience that reason (the ἡγεμονικόν) when it holds some view unreasonably can nonetheless be invincible in its acceptance and implementation of that view; all the more, then, must it be so when it judges *with* reason (μετὰ λόγου). A mind free from passion (and so judging truly) is totally invincible, an acropolis.

[42] The words appear in 2.15 and 12.8; cf. also 3.9. See also 9.32, "You can rid yourself of many superfluous troubles, for they depend wholly on your thoughts . . ." (πολλὰ περισσὰ περιελεῖν τῶν ἐνοχλούντων σοι δύνασαι, ὅλα ἐπὶ τῇ ὑπολήψει σου κείμενα . . .).

then they do not; the Stoics tell us that we are masters of our own state of mind, so far as happiness and its reverse are concerned. Now, we can grant Marcus that we would be able to live happily if we do not think that these things matter—nothing outside us can force us to think they do. But what can even enable us to think that they do not? On the Stoic view that Marcus seems to accept, what we believe is what we think we have sufficient reason to believe. What could make him think he has sufficient reason, in an Epicurean world where there are no transcendent minds, no gods, no teleological system of nature, to believe that he is a self-possessed mind exempt from the flow of atoms? I have argued that, in fact, it is extremely doubtful that he actually does (could) have sufficient reason to believe this. Still, as I have emphasized, it is possible to believe things in the face of better reason not to; so perhaps after all he might be right that he could retain this first belief. (I will say more in a moment about how he might be envisaging that possibility.) But, even so, on Marcus's own view, retaining our equanimity, our "smooth flow of life"—which is what he is laying claim to (see εὑροεῖν, 10.6)—requires more than just believing these things at some specific moment or for some short period, in a fit of enthusiastic endorsement; it requires believing them with consistency and firmness, without wavering or serious doubt.[43]

---

[43] Admittedly, Marcus is not maintaining that he already is perfectly happy, or that he (or anyone) could remain so upon learning that the world is just atoms and the void. Perhaps that really would be impossible, since such a state of mind does depend upon a full understanding of a whole series of truths which, on this hypothesis, one would have to deny. He is only "making progress." All he is claiming is that the distance he has advanced toward the goal of final happiness through his (prior) belief in Stoic moral theory, and in his own self-governing mind, could be maintained even under the conditions of his thought experiment. As a "progressor," perhaps he has not been relying on any real understanding of the philosophical reasons for these Stoic views anyhow; so maybe he could continue to rely even in an Epicurean world on whatever the alternative basis has been for being a Stoic in the first place. But here lies the central difficulty, as I see it. If Marcus has been relying for the alleged (relatively) smooth flow of his life on some commitment to Stoic views other than one that centrally involves an understanding of the actual reasons that support their truth, then in what sense can we say that he has even been making progress toward happiness? Progress toward a state of full understanding (a prerequisite for happiness) surely depends on a gradually increased partial understanding. So, in Marcus's case, if he really has been relying on something other than good reasons for holding his Stoic views, he has simply been deluding himself in thinking that he has been living smoothly and happily to any significant degree at all.

VI

If it is so unclear how Marcus could rationally retain, in an Epicurean world, his first belief, in the fact that he possesses a mind that governs itself, it must be even more doubtful that he could find reasons to retain his hold on Stoic moral principles and his consequent commitment to a life of service to humanity. What, then, does Marcus rely on, in persuading himself that he could? If you look again at the passages I have quoted, it emerges clearly enough that in place of philosophical grounds for belief we find rhetorical images and flourishes playing at least a significant role in Marcus's self-persuasions. Thus his recurrent term for the Epicurean hypothesis, that the world is a κυκεών or hodgepodge, vividly invites disbelief in it. The suggestion conveyed by the term is clearly that such a view of the beautiful world we behold is simply unworthy of its majesty. In 6.10 the disgust at that idea, so invoked, is turned to support Marcus's conclusion that nothing in such a world (unlike a divinely ordered world) could hold any attraction for *him*. Someone of his refined moral sensibilities, and commitment to order in his own life, should disdain all attachment to anything such a world might bring him. In 12.15, in a passage that may have been written as a continuation of 12.14 (referred to in the previous paragraph), he invokes the image of a lamp that keeps its radiance until actually extinguished, in order to incite himself to hold on, in the face of the Epicurean hypothesis, to his conviction in his own mind's inviolability. He must not allow the "truth, justice, and temperance" in himself to be extinguished so long as his own life lasts. He is to regard his own mind as like such a lamp of truth and justice!

These and other rhetorical appeals to be cited below both have considerable charm and certainly can have effects on one's beliefs. But they appeal, in the first instance, to one's settled dispositions and feelings: Marcus already places a high value on moral action, and on the thought of his own mind's inviolability. From that basis they evoke a sort of conviction in (alleged) moral or other practical truths. Those attitudes are or provide the reasons proposed for believing them. But these are not *good* reasons for them—reasons that would stand up to philosophical scrutiny. However pretty and inspiring the thought may be that one ought to imitate a lamp, or that nothing in a world devoid of divinity and divinely directed order can have any attraction at all for a rightly brought-up person, it is child's play to undermine such thoughts as reasons for believing or disbelieving the things in question, or for acting in accord with such ideas. And, as I have emphasized, Marcus is claiming in these passages that he could retain such beliefs not just for a brief moment in reaction to the presentation of the appeal, but firmly and consistently. One cannot, of course, rule out the possibility that Marcus might have such a ready store of uplifting images and flourishes to present to himself that he could expect to be able to produce a fresh application of pleasing rhetoric whenever, under the burden of the recognition that the world really is an Epicurean one, he might begin to waver or to lose touch with his Stoic commitments. But if the Stoics are right, his mind, like all minds, really is subject to be moved by better reasons where they exist, and as we have seen it seems clear that the better reasons in that case go against such conclusions. Marcus cannot immunize himself against their inevitable effects. If he ignores or gives a distant second place to philosophical examination and argument, if he relies wholly or principally on rhetorical images and flourishes to maintain his beliefs, he cannot expect to have any secure basis at all for living a Stoic life, whether under the Epicurean hypothesis or in general.

In fact, throughout the *Meditations,* rhetorical appeals to Marcus's (and the reader's) feelings play a conspicuous role.[44] In one passage, for example, Marcus tries to shame himself with graphic, pithy second-century rhetoric into accepting Stoic ideas:

> [Go ahead and] keep on doing yourself outrage, my soul! You won't much longer have time to hold yourself in honor; each person has only one life, and yours is almost finished while you do not respect yourself, but put your happiness in charge of the souls of others.[45]

(He seems to mean, by letting the good opinions of others count for too much in your own way of living.) In another passage, he impresses upon himself the inviolateness of the human mind and its elevation above all that concerns or interests it:

> Things themselves cannot by any means touch the soul, they do not have any entry into the soul, they cannot turn the soul or move it. Only the soul itself turns and moves itself, and whatever judgments it deems itself worthy to make of them, it makes the things that submit themselves to it conform to those.[46]

We also find numerous graphic comments expressing the transitoriness and (so) basic worthlessness, in themselves, of all those objects. Thus 6.15:

---

[44] On these aspects of the *Meditations,* see R. B. Rutherford, *The* Meditations *of Marcus Aurelius: A Study* (Oxford: Clarendon Press, 1989), 8–21.

[45] ὕβριζε, ὕβριζε αὐτήν, ὦ ψυχή· τοῦ δὲ τιμῆσαι σεαυτὴν οὐκέτι καιρὸν ἕξεις· εἰς γὰρ ὁ βίος ἑκάστῳ· οὗτος δέ σοι σχεδὸν διήνυσται μὴ αἰδουμένῃ σεαυτήν, ἀλλ' ἐν ταῖς ἄλλων ψυχαῖς τιθεμένη τὴν σὴν εὐμοιρίαν (2.6).

[46] τὰ πράγματα αὐτὰ οὐδ' ὁπωστιοῦν ψυχῆς ἅπτεται, οὐδὲ ἔχει εἴσοδον πρὸς ψυχήν, οὐδὲ τρέψαι οὐδὲ κινῆσαι ψυχὴν δύναται· τρέπει δὲ καὶ κινεῖ αὐτὴ ἑαυτὴν μόνη, καὶ οἵων ἂν κριμάτων καταξιώσῃ ἑαυτήν, τοιαῦτα ἑαυτῇ ποιεῖ τὰ προσυφεστῶτα (5.19).

Some things are hastening to come to be, others are hastening to have been, and some part of what is coming to be is already extinct. Flowings and changes renew the world order continually, just as the incessant passage of time ever makes new the infinity of ages. So what can anyone hold in high honor among the things that rush past in this river, where there is nowhere to take a stand? It is as if one set out to love some particular sparrow flying past—it's already gone out of sight.[47]

Sometimes this denigration of everything but our own personalities is mingled with the pride appropriately felt by someone who has grasped clearly the significance of this superior position, when many people do not, but debase themselves by being enthralled by some object of their transitory interest: "Next, consider the things themselves, how short-lived they are, how unimportant, how they can be had by a catamite or whore or robber."[48] And how could an aristocrat like Marcus be willing to let himself get classed with people like *that*? On the positive side, to encourage himself to accept the Stoic view of beneficial acts as their own reward, he tells himself (5.6) about a vine that produces its grapes year after year without even being conscious of its own benefits—so he too should not dwell on what he may have done for others, as if that were something to his credit or deserved some reward. Or consider this about squealing pigs: "Picture to yourself everyone who is pained or dissatisfied with anything as being like a pig kicking and squealing when sacrificed":[49] we are like those pigs if we lament our own fate.

We should recall here that in addition to Stoic teachers (and other teachers of philosophy, including at least one Platonist: Sextus of Chaeronea)[50] Marcus was for a long time under the tutelage of the

[47] τὰ μὲν σπεύδει γίνεσθαι, τὰ δὲ σπεύδει γεγονέναι, καὶ τοῦ γινομένου δὲ ἤδη τι ἀπέσβει· ῥύσεις καὶ ἀλλοιώσεις ἀνανεοῦσι τὸν κόσμον διηνεκῶς, ὥσπερ τὸν ἄπειρον αἰῶνα ἡ τοῦ χρόνου ἀδιάλειπτος φορὰ νέον ἀεὶ παρέχεται. ἐν δὴ τούτῳ τῷ ποταμῷ τί ἄν τις τούτων τῶν παραθεόντων ἐκτιμήσειεν, ἐφ' οὗ στῆναι οὐκ ἔξεστιν; ὥσπερ εἴ τίς τι τῶν παραπετομένων στρουθαρίων φιλεῖν ἄρχοιτο· τὸ δ' ἤδη ἐξ ὀφθαλμῶν ἀπελήλυθεν (6.15). See also 4.43, 5.33, 7.48, 9.14, 9.30, 10.11.
[48] μέτιθι τοίνυν ἐπ' αὐτὰ τὰ ὑποκείμενα, ὡς ὀλιγόχρονα καὶ εὐτελῆ καὶ δυνάμενα ἐν κτήσει κιναίδου ἢ πόρνης ἢ λῃστοῦ εἶναι (5.10). See also 6.34.
[49] φαντάζου πάντα τὸν ἐφ' ὡτινιοῦν λυπούμενον ἢ δυσαρεστοῦντα ὅμοιον τῷ θυομένῳ χοιριδίῳ καὶ ἀπολακτίζοντι καὶ κεκραγότι (10.28).
[50] In acknowledging his debtors in *Meditations* I, Marcus mentions with appreciation an "Alexander the Platonist" (1.12, presumably referring to him thus in order to distinguish him from "Alexander the Grammarian," i.e., of Cotiaeum, listed shortly before). It seems that this was not one of his teachers, however; we are told in Philostratus's account of Alexander (*Lives of the Sophists* 2.5; p. 571 in the ed. of Olearius, whose pagination is given in the margins of the Loeb ed.) that he was appointed by Marcus in 174 as his Greek secretary, and what Marcus says in appreciation of him seems clearly to relate to the latter

rhetorician Fronto. Fronto trained him in the rhetoric of the second so-
phistic, and it seems apposite to say that in his reliance on rhetorical
means of persuasion to the neglect of philosophical reasons, Marcus
shows more the influence of Fronto than he does that of his later Stoic
teachers (or his reading of Epictetus).[51] Moreover, of course, in following
in his writing, along with Seneca and Epictetus in his *Discourses,* the ancient tradition of the spritiual adviser, Marcus adopts a genre that depends fundamentally on moving his reader (and himself) through such
means. In one stirring passage he sums up the human situation as follows: "all the things of the body are a river, the things of the soul are a
dream and puffed-up vanity, life is a battle and sojourn in a foreign place,
posthumous fame is forgetfulness." He continues, in an impressive exhortation to "philosophy" as the only guide, the only salvation: "What
then can we have by us to send us along our way? One thing only, philosophy."[52] But if Marcus pays no serious heed to philosophical argument, not just in physical and dialectical theory but even in ethics itself,

---

function, and not to anything philosophical. In any case, Philostratus's account rather
counts against Alexander's having had any philosophical interests or responsibilities: it suggests that his nickname "Clay-Plato" (p. 570) might relate solely to his declamatory style
(see Sceptus of Corinth's witticism, p. 573). Earlier in book I (at 1.9) Marcus expresses appreciation for good example and edifying instruction from Sextus, Plutarch's nephew, a Platonist philosopher whose lectures in Rome Marcus is said to have attended even as emperor
(Cassius Dio, *Roman History* 71.1.2). Marcus's curious espousal of one doctrine not part
of standard Stoic teaching but rather, at least later on, characteristically Platonist could reflect these lectures: that humans share a single "intellectual soul" (νοερὰ ψυχή) and "reason" (λόγος), even if this appears to be divided, each having his own individual one (see
4.4, 7.9, 9.8, 12.30). (Oddly, however, the Life of Marcus in the *Historia Augusta* lists [2.7]
Sextus among his Stoic teachers, along with Apollonius of Chalcedon, apparently principal
among them, Iunius Rusticus, Claudius Maximus, and Cinna Catulus: all five of these
philosophers are named by Marcus among his benefactors in *Meditations* I. *Historia Augusta* adds the name of one Peripatetic as a further teacher of philosophy, Claudius Severus:
this is presumably the Severus to whom Marcus gives particularly fulsome recognition in
1.14.)

[51] I don't mean to say that one detects in his own writing to any noticeable degree application of Frontonian theories about or preferences among rhetorical means of persuasion. I
am speaking here simply of the background in his own education and culture of rhetoric as
something prestigious, something to be relied on as an independent and self-sufficient
source for the conduct of one's life. The most convenient access to Fronto's literary remains
is in C. R. Haines's edition and translation of *The Correspondence of Marcus Cornelius
Fronto with Marcus Aurelius Antoninus, Lucius Verus, Antoninus Pius, and Various
Friends,* 2 vols., Loeb Classical Library.

[52] συνελόντι δὲ εἰπεῖν, πάντα τὰ μὲν τοῦ σώματος ποταμός, τὰ δὲ τῆς ψυχῆς ὄνειρος
καὶ τῦφος· ὁ δὲ βίος πόλεμος καὶ ξένου ἐπιδημία· ἡ δὲ ὑστεροφημία λήθη. τί οὖν τὸ
παραπέμψαι δυνάμενον; ἓν καὶ μόνον φιλοσοφία (2.17). He continues: "This consists in
keeping the divinity within free from outrage and undamaged . . ." (τοῦτο δὲ ἐν τῷ τηρεῖν
τὸν ἔνδον δαίμονα ἀνύβριστον καὶ ἀσινῆ. . . .)

he can hardly mean by "philosophy" much more than just the leading bottom-line moral doctrines of Stoicism (even if accurately rendered). Those, as here, he supports most often simply from rhetorical motifs, not philosophical analysis and argument, even purely "ethical" in character (whatever that might be for a Stoic).

Marcus's heavy reliance on rhetorical, not philosophically argumentative, modes of self-persuasion may be among the reasons that readers, and some scholars, have thought of Marcus's Stoicism as a sort of religion, or a philosophy taking the place of a religion, rather than simply a philosophy (even one that was being thought of as a way of life).[53] Christians, for example, in praying to God and in their own meditations on Christ's life and death, may attempt to induce in themselves feelings (and, for them, the reality) of purity of heart, so as to win God's favor and his grace, and thereby become converted permanently to a Christian way of life. Although there is no analogue of Christian grace in Marcus's Stoic outlook, it does often seem that his reliance on affecting his own feelings, as the way to establish or reinforce commitments to Stoic doctrines, is not very different from such religious practices. It is as if Marcus was striving to induce in himself a sort of religious faith in the basic propositions of Stoic philosophy—one that did not rely on, or need, support from philosophical reasons and reasoning. This is certainly Stoicism of a sort, but it is no longer what Zeno and Chrysippus had in mind.

---

[53] See J. M. Rist, "Are You a Stoic? The Case of Marcus Aurelius," in *Jewish and Christian Self-Definition*, ed. E. P. Sanders, 3:23–45. Rist writes, in conclusion, "For Marcus, in modern terms, if we are to call him a Stoic, then Stoicism is not a philosophy, but a religion or 'philosophy of life' . . . a rather unphilosophical religion. . . . Marcus . . . is left with the almost unsupported dogmas of Providence . . . and the necessity to cling to what is right and do it" (p. 43).

BIBLIOGRAPHY

Ackrill, J. L. "Aristotle on *Eudaimonia.*" *Proceedings of the British Academy* 60 (1974): 3–23.

———. *Aristotle's Ethics.* London: Faber, 1973.

Aelian. *On the Characteristics of Animals.* Text with English translation by A. L. Scholfield. Loeb Classical Library. Cambridge, Mass.: Harvard University Press, 1959.

Aesop. *Corpus Fabularum Aesopicarum.* Edited by A. Hausrath and H. Hunger. 1 vol. in 2 pts. Leipzig: Teubner, 1940–59; vol. 1, pt. 1, 2nd ed., 1970.

Alexander of Aphrodisias. *De Mixtione* (On mixture). *CAG, Supplementum Aristotelicum,* vol. 2, pt. 2, edited by Ivo Bruns, 1892. Translated by Robert B. Todd, q.v.

———. *De Fato* (On Fate). Text and translation by Robert W. Sharples, q.v.

———. *In Topicorum libros octo commentaria. CAG,* vol. 2, pt. 2, edited by M. Wallies, 1891. Translated in part in J. M. van Ophuijsen, *Alexander of Aphrodisias on Aristotle's "Topics 1."* London: Duckworth, 2001.

Allen, James. *Inference from Signs.* Oxford and New York: Oxford University Press, 2001.

Allen, R. E., ed. *Studies in Plato's Metaphysics.* London: Routledge & Kegan Paul; New York: Humanities Press, 1965.

Antisthenes. *Antisthenis Fragmenta,* edited by F. D. Caizzi. Milan: Istituto editoriale cisalpino, 1966.

Aristotle. *The Complete Works of Aristotle.* Edited by J. Barnes, 2 vols. Princeton: Princeton University Press, 1984.

———. *The Works of Aristotle.* Edited by Sir David Ross. 12 vols. The Oxford Aristotle. Oxford: Oxford University Press, 1908–52.

Arius Didymus. *Epitome of Stoic Ethics.* Edited and translated by A. J. Pomeroy. Atlanta: Society of Biblical Literature, 1999.

Arnim, Hans von, ed. *Stoicorum Veterum Fragmenta [SVF],* 4 vols. Leipzig: Teubner, 1904–20.

Aspasius. *In "Ethica Nicomachea" Commentaria. CAG,* vol. 19, pt.1, edited by G. Heylbut, 1889. Translated in part in David Konstan, *Aspasius, Anonymous, Michael of Ephesus on Aristotle's "Nicomachean Ethics 8 and 9."* London: Duckworth, 2001.

Aurelius, Marcus. *The Communings with Himself of Marcus Aurelius Antoninus.* Text with English translation by C. R. Haines. Loeb Classical Library. Cambridge, Mass.: Harvard University Press, 1916.

———. *The Meditations of Marcus Aurelius.* Translated by George M. A. Grube. Indianapolis: Hackett, 1983.

———. *The Meditations of the Emperor Marcus Antoninus.* Text with translation and commentary by A.S.L. Farquharson. 2 vols. Oxford: Oxford University Press, 1944; reprinted 1968.

Balme, David M. "Aristotle's Biology Was Not Essentialist." *Archiv für Geschichte der Philosophie* 62 (1980): 1–12.

———. *Aristotle's "De partibus animalium" I and "De generatione animalium" I (with passages from II. 1–3).* Translated with notes. Oxford: Clarendon, 1972.

———. "The Snub." *Ancient Philosophy* 4 (1984): 1–8. Revised and reprinted in Gotthelf and Lennox, *Philosophical Issues,* 291–312.

———. "Teleology and Necessity." In Gotthelf and Lennox, *Philosophical Issues,* 275–85.

Bambrough, Renford, ed. *New Essays on Plato and Aristotle.* London: Routledge & Kegan Paul; New York: Humanities Press, 1965.

Barnes, Jonathan. *Logic and the Imperial Stoa.* Leiden and New York: Brill, 1997.

Basore, John W., ed. and trans. *Seneca, Moral Essays.* 3 vols. Loeb Classical Library. Cambridge Mass.: Harvard University Press, 1928–35.

Bett, Richard. *Pyrrho: His Antecedents and His Legacy.* Oxford and New York: Oxford University Press, 2000.

Bickerman, Elias J. "Autonomia: Sur un passage de Thucydide (1,144,2)." *Revue Internationale des Droits de l'Antiquité* 5 (1958): 313–44.

Bobonich, Christopher. *Plato's Utopia Recast.* Oxford and New York: Oxford University Press, 2002.

Brittain, Charles. *Philo of Larissa.* Oxford and New York: Oxford University Press, 2001.

Brittain, Charles, and John Palmer. "The New Academy's Appeals to the Presocratics." *Phronesis* 46 (2001): 38–72.

Broadie, Sarah. *Ethics with Aristotle.* New York: Oxford University Press, 1991.

Brunschwig, Jacques. "Le Fragment DK 70 B 1 de Métrodore de Chio." In *Polyhistor,* edited by K. A. Algra, P. W. van der Horst, and D. T. Runia, 21–38. Leiden and New York: Brill, 1996.

Burnyeat, Myles F. "Antipater and Self Refutation." In *Assent and Argument,* edited by B. Inwood and J. Mansfeld, 277–310. Brill: Leiden and New York, 1997.

———. "Can the Sceptic Live His Scepticism?" In Schofield et al., eds., *Doubt and Dogmatism,* 20–53. Reprinted in Burnyeat and Frede, eds., *Original Sceptics,* 25–57.

———. "Enthymeme: Aristotle on the Logic of Persuasion." In *Aristotle's "Rhetoric,"* edited by D. J. Furley and A. Nehamas, 3–55. Princeton: Princeton University Press, 1994.

———. "The Origins of Non-deductive Inference." In *Science and Speculation,* edited by J. Barnes, J. Brunschwig, M. F. Burnyeat, and M. Schofield, 193–238. Cambridge and New York: Cambridge University Press, 1982.

———. "The Sceptic in His Place and Time." In *Philosophy in History,* edited by R. Rorty, J. B. Schneewind, and Q. Skinner, 225–54. Cambridge and New York: Cambridge University Press, 1984. Reprinted in Burnyeat and Frede, eds., *Original Sceptics,* 92–126.

Burnyeat, M., and M. Frede, eds. *The Original Sceptics*. Indianapolis: Hackett, 1997.

Campbell, Lewis, ed. *The "Theaetetus" of Plato*. Oxford: Oxford University Press, 1861; 2nd ed., 1883.

Chadwick, J., and W. N. Mann, trans. *Tradition in Medicine* ("On Ancient Medicine"). In Lloyd, ed., *Hippocratic Writings*.

Charlton, William. *Aristotle's "Physics" Books I and II*. Translated, with introduction and commentary. Oxford: Clarendon Press, 1970.

Cherniss, Harold F. *Aristotle's Criticism of Plato and the Academy*. Baltimore: Johns Hopkins Press, 1944.

——. "The Relation of the *Timaeus* to Plato's Later Dialogues." *American Journal of Philology* 78 (1957): 225–66. Reprinted in R. E. Allen, ed., *Studies*, 339–78.

——, ed. and trans. *On Stoic Self-Contradictions* and *On Common Conceptions*. In Plutarch, *Moralia*, vol. 13, pt. 2, 1976.

Cicero. *De fato* (On fate) *and Stoicorum paradoxa* (Stoic paradoxes). Text with English translation by H. Rackham. Loeb Classical Library. Cambridge, Mass.: Harvard University Press, 1942.

——. *De finibus bonorum et malorum* (On ends). Text with English translation by H. Rackham. Loeb Classical Library. 2nd ed. Cambridge, Mass.: Harvard University Press, 1931.

——. *De legibus* (On laws). Text with English translation by C. W. Keyes. Loeb Classical Library. Cambridge, Mass.: Harvard University Press, 1928.

——. *De natura deorum and Academica*. Text with English translation by H. Rackham. Loeb Classical Library. Cambridge, Mass.: Harvard University Press, 1933.

——. *De officiis* (On duties). Text with English translation by W. Miller. Loeb Classical Library. Cambridge, Mass.: Harvard University Press, 1913.

——. *Tusculan Disputations*. Text with English translation by J. E. King. Rev. ed. Loeb Classical Library. Cambridge, Mass.: Harvard University Press, 1945.

Clement of Alexandria. *Le Protreptique*. Text and French translation by Claude Mondésert. 2nd ed., augmented. Paris: Éditions du Cerf, 1949.

Commentaria in Aristotelem Graeca [CAG]. 23 vols. Berlin: Reimer, 1882–1909.

Cooper, John M. "Aristotle on the Authority of 'Appearances.'" In Cooper, *Reason and Emotion*, 281–91.

——. "Contemplation and Happiness: A Reconsideration." In Cooper, *Reason and Emotion*, 212–36.

——. "Justus Lipsius and the Revival of Stoicism in Late Sixteenth Century Europe." In *New Essays on the History of Autonomy*, edited by N. Brender and L. Krasnoff. New York: Cambridge University Press, 2004, 7–29.

——. "Pleasure and Desire in Epicurus." In Cooper, *Reason and Emotion*, 485–514.

——. *Reason and Emotion*. Princeton: Princeton University Press, 1999.

——. *Reason and Human Good in Aristotle*. Cambridge, Mass.: Harvard University Press 1975; Indianapolis and Cambridge, Mass.: Hackett, 1986.

———. "The Relevance of Moral Theory to Moral Improvement in Epictetus." Forthcoming in *Zeno and His Legacy: The Philosophy of Epictetus,* edited by Andrew S. Mason and Antony Hatzistavrou (Larnaca, Cyprus: Municipality of Larnaca, 2004).

Cornford, Francis M. *Plato's Theory of Knowledge.* London: Kegan Paul, 1935.

Corpus Medicorum Graecorum [CMG]. Berlin: Akademie-Verlag, various dates.

Crombie, I. M. *An Examination of Plato's Doctrines.* 2 vols. London: Routledge & Kegan Paul, 1962–63.

de Haas, Frans A. J. "Mixture in Philoponus: An Encounter with a Third Kind of Potentiality." In *The Commentary Tradition on De generatione et corruptione: Ancient, Medieval and Early Modern,* edited by J.M.M.H. Thijssen and H.A.G. Braakhuis, 21–46. Turnhout, Belgium: Brepols, 1999.

———. "Recollection and Potentiality in Philoponus." In *The Winged Chariot: Collected Essays on Plato and Platonism in Honour of L. M. de Rijk,* edited by M. Kardaun and J. Spruijt, 165–84. Leiden: Brill, 2000.

Deichgräber, Karl. *Die Griechische Empirikerschule.* Reprint of original edition of 1930, with supplements. Berlin and Zürich: Weidmann, 1965.

———, ed. and trans. *Hippocrates, Über Entstehung und Aufbau des menschlichen Körpers (περὶ σαρκῶν),* Berlin and Leipzig: Teubner, 1935.

Denniston, J. D. *The Greek Particles.* 2nd ed. Oxford: Clarendon Press, 1954.

Diels, Hermann. *Doxographi Graeci.* Berlin: Reimer, 1979.

———. "Hippokratische Forschungen V." *Hermes* 53 (1918): 57–87.

Diels, Hermann, and Walther Kranz, eds. and trans. *Die Fragmente der Vorsokratiker (DK).* 7th ed. Berlin: Weidmann, 1952. Translated in part in J. Barnes, *Early Greek Philosophy.* Harmondsworth and New York: Penguin, 1987.

Diès, Auguste, ed. and trans. *Platon: "Théétète." Oevres Complètes,* vol. 8, pt. 2. Budé text. 2nd ed. Paris: Les Belles Lettres, 1950.

Dihle, Albrecht. "Kritisch-exegetische Bemerkungen zur Schrift Über die Alte Heilkunst." *Museum Helveticum* 20 (1963): 135–50.

Diller, Hans, trans. *Hippokrates Schriften.* Reinbek bei Hamburg: Rohwolt, 1962.

———. "Hippokratische Medizin und attische Philosophie." *Hermes* 80 (1952): 385–409. Reprinted in his *Kleine Schriften zur antiken Medizin,* edited by G. Baader and H. Grensemann, 46–70. Berlin: de Gruyter, 1973.

Dillon, John M., and Anthony A. Long, eds. *The Question of "Eclecticism": Studies in Later Greek Philosophy.* Berkeley: University of California Press, 1988.

Dio Cassius. *Roman History.* Text with English translation by E. Cary and H. B. Foster. 9 vols. Loeb Classical Library. Cambridge, Mass.: Harvard University Press, 1914–27.

Dio Chrysostom. *On Freedom.* Text with English translation by H. Lamar Crosby. Loeb Classical Library. *Discourses,* vol. 5. Cambridge, Mass.: Harvard University Press, 1951.

Diogenes Laertius. *Lives of Eminent Philosophers.* Text with English translation by R. D. Hicks. 2 vols. Loeb Classical Library. Cambridge, Mass.: Harvard University Press, 1925.

Dirlmeier, Franz, trans. *Aristoteles, "Nikomachische Ethik."* 1956. 5th edition, Berlin: Akademie Verlag, 1969.

Drossaart Lulofs, H. J., ed. *Aristotelis "De generatione animalium."* Oxford Classical Texts. Oxford: Clarendon Press, 1965.

Einarson, B., and P. DeLacy, eds. and trans. *That It Is Impossible to Live Pleasantly according to Epicurus' Doctrines.* In Plutarch, *Moralia,* vol. 14, 1967.

Epictetus. *The Discourses, as Reported by Arrian, the Manual and Fragments.* Text with an English translation by W. A. Oldfather. 2 vols. Loeb Classical Library. Cambridge, Mass.: Harvard University Press, 1928.

Eusebius. *La préparation évangélique.* Text with French translation by Jean Sirinelli and others. Paris: Éditions du Cerf, 1974–.

Falcon, Andrea. *Corpi e Movimenti.* Naples: Bibliopolis, 2001.

———. *Unity without Uniformity: Aristotle and the Science of Nature* (provisional title), forthcoming 2005.

Farquharson, A.S.L. ed. *The Meditations of the Emperor Marcus Antoninus.* Translated with commentary. 2 vols. Oxford: Oxford University Press, 1944; reprinted 1968.

Festugière, André Jean, ed. and trans. *L'Ancienne médecine. Hippocrate,* vol. 2, pt. 1. Paris: Klincksieck, 1948.

Fine, Kit. "The Problem of Mixture." *Pacific Philosophical Quarterly* 76 (1995): 266–369.

Frede, Michael. "The Ancient Empiricists." In his *Essays,* 243–60.

———. *Essays in Ancient Philosophy.* Minneapolis: University of Minnesota Press, 1987.

———. *Galen: Three Treatises on the Nature of Science.* Indianapolis and Cambridge, Mass.: Hackett, 1985.

———. "The Sceptic's Two Kinds of Assent and the Question of the Possibility of Knowledge." In *Philosophy in History,* edited by R. Rorty, J. B. Schneewind, and Q. Skinner, 255–78. Cambridge: Cambridge University Press, 1984. Reprinted in his *Essays,* 201–222; and in Burnyeat and Frede, eds., *Original Sceptics,* 127–51.

———. "The Stoic Conception of Reason." In *Hellenistic Philosophy,* vol. 2, edited by K. J. Boudouris, 50–63. Athens: International Association for Greek Philosophy, 1994.

———. "Substance in Aristotle's *Metaphysics.*" In his *Essays,* 72–80.

Frede, Michael, and Günther Patzig, eds. and trans. *Aristoteles, "Metaphysik Z."* 2 vols. Munich: Beck, 1988.

Fronto. *The Correspondence of Marcus Cornelius Fronto with Marcus Aurelius Antoninus, Lucius Verus, Antoninus Pius, and Various Friends.* Text with English translation by C. R. Haines. 2 vols. Loeb Classical Library. Cambridge, Mass: Harvard University Press, 1919.

Furth, Montgomery. *Substance, Form and Psyche.* Cambridge and New York: Cambridge University Press, 1988.

Galen. *On the Doctrines of Hippocrates and Plato.* Text with translation and commentary by Phillip DeLacy, 3 vols. CMG 4.1.2, 1978–84.

———. *Three Treatises on the Nature of Science.* Translated by Michael Frede, q.v.

Gauthier, René Antoine, and Jean Yves Jolif, eds. and trans. *Aristote, "L'Éthique à Nicomaque."* 2nd ed., Louvain: Nauwelaerts, 1970.

Gellius, Aulus. *Attic Nights.* Text with English translation by John C. Rolfe. 3 vols. Loeb Classical Library. Cambridge, Mass.: Harvard University Press, 1927.

Gotthelf, A., and J. G. Lennox, eds. *Philosophical Issues in Aristotle's Biology.* Cambridge: Cambridge University Press, 1987.

Gregory of Nyssa. *De dominica orationes v.* In *Gregory von Nyssa,* vol. 3, edited by F. Oehler. Leipzig: Engelmann, 1859.

Grube, George M. A., trans. *The Meditations of Marcus Aurelius.* Indianapolis: Hackett, 1983.

Hadot, Ilsetraut. *Seneca und die Griechisch-Römische Tradition der Seelenleitung.* Berlin: de Gruyter, 1969.

Hadot, Pierre. *La Citadelle intérieure.* Paris: Librairie Arthème Fayard, 1992. Translated by Michael Chase as *The Inner Citadel.* Cambridge, Mass.: Harvard University Press, 2002.

Haines, C. R., ed. and trans. *The Communings with Himself of Marcus Aurelius Antoninus.* Loeb Classical Library. Cambridge, Mass.: Harvard University Press, 1916.

Hardie, R. P., and R. K. Gaye, trans. *Aristotle: Physica.* In *The Works of Aristotle,* ed. Ross, vol. 2, 1930.

Heiberg, I. L., ed. and trans. *Hippocratis Opera.* CMG, vol. 1, pt. 1. Leipzig and Berlin: Teubner, 1927.

Helmbold, W. C., ed. and trans. *On Moral Virtue.* In Plutarch, *Moralia,* vol. 6, 1939.

Himerius. *Himerii Declamationes et orationes cum deperditarum fragmentis,* edited by A. Colonna. Rome: Officina Polygraphica, 1951.

Hippocrates. Text with English translation by W.H.S Jones et al. 8 vols. Loeb Classical Library. Cambridge, Mass.: Harvard University Press, 1923–95.

———. *Ancient Medicine.* Text with English translation by W.H.S. Jones. Loeb, Classical Library. Cambridge, Mass.: Harvard University Press, 1923.

Historia Augusta. Text with English translation by D. Magie. 3 vols. Loeb Classical Library. Cambridge, Mass.: Harvard University Press, 1921–32.

Huffman, Carl A. *Philolaus of Croton.* Cambridge and New York: Cambridge University Press, 1993.

Hull, David. "Philosophy and Biology." In *Contemporary Philosophy,* vol. 2, edited by G. Fløistad, 281–316. The Hague and Boston: M. Nijhoff, 1981.

Irwin, Terence H. "The Monism of Practical Reason." Paper read to the Eastern Division meeting of the American Philosophical Association, December 1999.

———, trans. *Aristotle: Nicomachean Ethics.* Indianapolis and Cambridge, Mass.: Hackett, 1st edition, 1985; 2nd edition, 1999.

Isocrates. Text with English translation by L. van Hook, and G. Norlin. 3 vols. Loeb Classical Library. Cambridge, Mass.: Harvard University Press, 1945.

Joachim, H. H., trans. *Aristotle: De generatione et corruptione.* In *The Works of Aristotle,* ed. Ross, vol. 2, 1930.

————. *Aristotle on "Coming-to-be and Passing-away."* Revised text with introduction and commentary. Oxford: Clarendon Press, 1922.

Joly, Robert, ed. and trans. *Des chairs.* In his *Hippocrate,* vol. 13. Budé text. Paris: Les Belles Lettres, 1978.

Jones, W.H.S. "Philosophy and Medicine in Ancient Greece." *Supplements to the Bulletin of the History of Medicine,* no. 8. Baltimore: Johns Hopkins Press, 1946.

Jouanna, Jacques, ed. and trans. *De L'Ancienne médicine. Hippocrate,* vol. 2, pt. 1. Budé text. Paris: Les Belles Lettres, 1990.

————, ed. and trans. *Des vents* and *De L'art. Hippocrate,* vol. 5, pt. 1. Budé text. Paris: Les Belles Lettres, 1988.

Kahn, Charles H. "The Greek Verb 'To Be' and the Concept of Being." *Foundations of Language* 2 (1966): 245–65.

Kant, Immanuel. *Groundwork of the Metaphysics of Morals.* In his *Practical Philosophy,* translated and edited by Mary J. Gregor, with a general introduction by Allen Wood. Cambridge Edition of the Works of Immanuel Kant. New York: Cambridge University Press, 1996.

Kassel, Rudolf, ed. *Aristotelis "Ars Rhetorica."* Berlin: de Gruyter, 1976.

Kühlewein, Hugo, ed. *Hippocratis Opera.* 2 vols. Leipzig: Teubner, 1892–1902.

Kühn, Carolus Gottlob, ed. and trans. *Galen: Opera Omnia.* 20 vols. Leipzig: C. Cnobloch, 1821–33; Hildesheim: Olms, 1964–65.

Laroche, Emmanuel. *Histoire de la racine NEM-en grec ancien.* Paris: Klincksieck, 1949.

Lawrence, Gavin. "Nonaggregatability, Inclusiveness, and the Theory of Focal Value," *Phronesis* 43 (1997): 32–76.

Liddell, H. G., R. S. Scott, and H. S. Jones. *A Greek-English Lexicon [LSJ].* 9th ed. Oxford: Clarendon Press, 1940; with a new supplement, 1996.

Littré, Emile. *Oeuvres complètes d'Hippocrate.* 10 vols. Paris: J. B. Baillière, 1839–1961.

Lloyd, G.E.R., ed. *Hippocratic Writings.* Harmondsworth and New York: Penguin, 1978.

————. "Who Is Attacked in *On Ancient Medicine?*" *Phronesis* 8 (1963): 108–26.

Lloyd-Jones, Hugh, and Peter Parsons, eds. *Supplementum Hellenisticum.* Berlin and New York: de Gruyter, 1983.

Long, A. A. "Freedom and Determinism in the Stoic Theory of Human Action." In his *Problems in Stoicism,* 173–99. London: Athlone Press, 1971.

Long, A. A., and D. N. Sedley, eds. and trans. *The Hellenistic Philosophers.* 2 vols. Cambridge and New York: Cambridge University Press, 1987.

Louis, Pierre, ed. and trans. *Aristotle, "De la génération des animaux."* Budé text. Paris: Les Belles Lettres, 1961.

Marco, Massimo di. *Timone di Fliunte Silli.* Rome: Edizioni dell'Ateneo, 1989.

Marcus Aurelius, *see* Aurelius, Marcus.

Martin, Alain, and Oliver Primavesi. *L'Empédocle de Strasbourg.* Berlin: de Gruyter, 1999.

McDowell, John H. *Mind, Value and Reality.* Cambridge, Mass.: Harvard University Press, 1998.

———. "Some Issues in Aristotle's Moral Psychology." In his *Mind, Value, and Reality*, 23–49.

———. "Virtue and Reason." In his *Mind, Value, and Reality*, 50–73.

Merkelbach, Reinhold. "Un petit αἴνιγμα dans le prologue du *Protreptique* de Clément d'Alexandrie." In ΑΛΕΞΑΝΔΡΙΝΑ: *Mélanges offerts à Claude Mondésert*, 191–94. Paris: Cerf 1987.

Molina, Luis de. *On Divine Foreknowledge: Part Four of the Concordia by Luis de Molina*. Translated with an introduction and notes by A. J. Freddoso. Ithaca: Cornell University Press, 1988.

Mullach, F.W.A., ed. *Fragmenta philosophorum Graecorum*. 3 vols. Paris: Didot, 1883.

Nachmanson, Ernst, ed. *Erotiani vocum Hippocraticarum collectio cum fragmentis*. Göteborg: Eranos, 1918.

Nussbaum, Martha. *Aristotle's "De Motu Animalium."* Text with translation, commentary, and interpretive essays. Princeton: Princeton University Press, 1978.

Ober, Josh. *Political Dissent in Democratic Athens*. Princeton: Princeton University Press, 1998.

Olympiodorus. *In Aristotelis "Meteora." CAG*, vol. 12, pt. 2, edited by G. Stüve, 1900.

Osborne, Catherine. *Rethinking Early Greek Philosophy*. Ithaca: Cornell University Press, 1987.

Ostwald, Martin. *Autonomia: Its Genesis and Early History*. American Classical Studies, no. 11. American Philological Association. Chico, Calif.: Scholars Press, 1982.

Owen, Gwilym E. L. "Aristotle on the Snares of Ontology." In *New Essays on Plato and Aristotle*, edited by R. Bambrough, 69–95. Reprinted in his *Logic, Science, and Dialectic*, 259–78.

———. *Logic, Science, and Dialectic*. Ithaca: Cornell University Press, 1986.

———. "The Place of the *Timaeus* in Plato's Dialogues." *Classical Quarterly*, n.s., 3 (1953): 79–95. Reprinted in his *Logic, Science, and Dialectic*, 65–84.

Peck, A. L. *Aristotle, "Parts of Animals."* Loeb Classical Library. Cambridge, Mass.: Harvard University Press, 1937; last revision, 1961.

Pfaff, Franz, ed. and trans. *In Hippocratis Epidemiarum Librum II Commentaria ex Versione Arabica*. In *CMG*, vol. 5.10.1, along with *In Hippocratis Epidemiarum Librum I Commentaria*, edited by Ernst Wenkebach. Leipzig and Berlin: Teubner, 1934.

Philo Judaeus. *Works*. Text with English translation by F. H. Colson et al., 10 vols. and 2 suppls. Loeb Classical Library. Cambridge, Mass.: Harvard University Press, 1929–62.

———. *Every Good Man Is Free*, translated by F. H. Colson. Loeb Classical Library, vol. 9. Cambridge, Mass.: Harvard University Press, 1941.

Philoponus, John. *In Aristotelis Libros "de Generatione et Corruptione" Commentaria. CAG*, vol. 14, pt. 2, edited by H. Vitelli, 1897. Translated in part by C.J.F. Williams as *Philoponus on Aristotle's "On Coming-to-Be and Perishing."* 2 vols. London: Duckworth, 1999.

————. *In Aristotelis "Physica" Commentaria. CAG*, vols. 16 and 17, edited by H. Vitelli, 1887–88. Translated in part by A. R. Lacey in *Philoponus on Aristotle's "Physics 2*,*"* London: Duckworth, 1993; and by M. J. Edwards in *Philoponus on Aristotle's "Physics 3*,*"* London: Duckworth, 1994.

Philostratus. *Lives of the Sophists.* Text with English translation by W. C. Wright. Loeb Classical Library. Cambridge, Mass.: Harvard University Press, 1921.

Photius. *Bibliothèque.* Edited and French translation by René Henry. Paris: Les Belles Lettres, 1959. Translated in part by N. G. Wilson in *The Bibliotheca: A Selection.* London: Duckworth, 1994.

Plato. *Complete Works.* Edited by John M. Cooper, associate editor D. S. Hutchinson. Indianapolis and Cambridge, Mass.: Hackett, 1997.

————. *Philebus.* Translated by Dorothea Frede. In *Plato: Complete Works.*

————. *Platonis Opera.* Edited by John Burnet. 5 vols. Oxford: Clarendon Press, 1900–1907.

Plutarch. *Moralia.* 17 vols. Loeb Classical Library. Cambridge, Mass.: Harvard University Press, 1927–76.

————. *Is It Well Said, to "Live Unnoticed"?* Edited and translated by B. Einarson and P. DeLacy. In *Plutarch: Moralia*, vol. 14, 1967.

————. *On Moral Virtue*, ed. and trans. by W. C. Helmbold. In *Plutarch: Moralia*, vol. 6, 1939.

————. *On Stoic Self-Contradictions and On Common Conceptions.* Edited and trans. by H. Cherniss. In *Plutarch: Moralia*, vol. 13, pt. 2, 1976.

————. *Progress in Virtue.* Edited and translated by Babbitt. In *Plutarch: Moralia*, vol. 1, 1927.

Pohlenz, Max. "Das zwanzigste Kapitel von Hippokrates *de Prisca Medicina.*" *Hermes* 53 (1918): 396–421.

Pohlmann, R. "Autonomie." In *Historisches Wörterbuch der Philosophie*, vol. 1, edited by J. Ritter, 701–19. Basel: Schwabe, 1971.

Richardson, Gabriel. *Happy Lives and the Highest Good: Aristotle's "Nicomachean Ethics."* Princeton: Princeton University Press, 2004.

Rist, John M. "Are You a Stoic? The Case of Marcus Aurelius." In *Jewish and Christian Self-Definition*, vol. 3, edited by E. P. Sanders, 23–45. Philadelphia: Fortress Press, 1980–83.

Ross, William David, trans. *Aristotle, "Ethica Nicomachea."* In *The Works of Aristotle*, ed. Ross, vol. 9, 1925.

————. *Aristotle, "Metaphysics."* 2 vols. Revised text with introduction and commentary. Oxford: Clarendon Press, 1924.

————. *Aristotle's "Physics."* Revised text with introduction and commentary. Oxford: Clarendon Press, 1936.

Runciman, W. G. *Plato's Later Epistemology.* Cambridge and New York: Cambridge University Press, 1962.

Rutherford, R. B. *"The Meditations" of Marcus Aurelius: A Study.* Oxford: Clarendon Press, 1989.

Ryle, Gilbert. "Plato's *Parmenides.*" *Mind* 48 (1939): 129–151, 302–325. Reprinted in Allen, ed., *Studies in Plato's Metaphysics*, 97–147.

Schiefsky, Mark J. "*Technê* and Method in the Hippocratic Treatise *On Ancient Medicine.*" Ph.D. diss., Harvard University, 1999.

Schneewind, J. B. *The Invention of Autonomy.* Cambridge and New York: Cambridge University Press, 1998.

Schofield, Malcolm. "Academic Epistemology." In *The Cambridge History of Hellenistic Philosophy,* edited by K. Algra, J. Barnes, J. Mansfeld, and M. Schofield, 323–51. Cambridge: Cambridge University Press, 1999.

Schofield, M., M. F. Burnyeat, and J. Barnes, eds. *Doubt and Dogmatism.* Oxford: Oxford University Press, 1980.

Sedley, David N. "Epicurean Anti-reductionism" In *Matter and Metaphysics,* edited by J. Barnes and M. Mignucci. Naples: Bibliopolis, 1988.

———. "The Motivation of Greek Skepticism." In *The Skeptical Tradition,* edited by Myles Burnyeat, 9–29. Berkeley and Los Angeles: University of California Press, 1983.

Seneca. *Ad Lucilium "Epistulae Morales"* (Letters). Text with English translation by R. M. Gummere. 3 vols. Loeb Classical Library. Cambridge, Mass.: Harvard University Press, 1917–25.

———. *Moral and Political Essays,* edited and translated by John M. Cooper and J. F. Procopé. Cambridge and New York: Cambridge University Press, 1995.

———. *Moral Essays.* Edited with an English translation by John W. Basore. 3 vols. Loeb Classical Library. Cambridge, Mass.: Harvard University Press, 1928–35.

———. "On Anger." In *Moral and Political Essays,* 17–116.

———. "On Favours I–IV." In *Moral and Political Essays,* 193–308.

———. "On the Private Life." In *Moral and Political Essays,* 172–80.

Sextus Empiricus. *Works,* 4 vols. Text with an English translation by R. G. Bury. Loeb Classical Library. Cambridge, Mass.: Harvard University Press, 1933–49.

Sharples, Robert W. *Alexander of Aphrodisias on Fate.* Text with English translation and commentary. London: Duckworth, 1983.

Simplicius. *In "Categorias" commentarium. CAG,* vol. 8, edited by K. Kalbfleisch, 1907. Translated in part by F. J. de Haas and B. Fleet in *Simplicius on Aristotle's "Categories 5–6";* B. Fleet, in *Simplicius on Aristotle's "Categories 7–8";* and R. Gaskin in *Simplicius on Aristotle's "Categories 9–15."* London: Duckworth, 2000–02.

———. *In Physicorum libros quattuor priores commentaria. CAG,* vol. 9, edited by H. Diels, 1882. Translated in part by J. O. Urmson in *Simplicius on Aristotle's "Physics 4.1–5."* London: Duckworth, 1992.

Smith, Wesley D., ed. and trans. *Epidemics 2, 4–6. Hippocrates,* vol. 7. Loeb, 1994.

———, *The Hippocratic Tradition.* Ithaca: Cornell University Press, 1979.

Smyth, Herbert W. *Greek Grammar.* Cambridge, Mass.: Harvard University Press, 1920.

Sorabji, Richard. *Matter, Space, and Motion.* Ithaca: Cornell University Press, 1988.

———. *Necessity, Cause, and Blame.* Ithaca: Cornell University Press, 1980.

Stewart, J. A. *Notes on the "Nicomachean Ethics" of Aristotle.* Oxford: Clarendon Press, 1892.

Stobaeus. *Eclogae* (Selections). Edited by C. Wachsmuth and O. Hense. 5 vols. Berlin: Weidmann, 1884–1923.

Striker, Gisela. *Essays on Hellenistic Epistemology and Ethics.* Cambridge and New York: Cambridge University Press, 1996.

———. "On the Difference between the Pyrrhonists and the Academics." In her *Essays,* 135–49.

———. "Sceptical Strategies." In Schofield et al., *Doubt and Dogmatism,* 54–83. Reprinted in her *Essays,* 92–115.

Tarrant, Harold. *Scepticism or Platonism?* Cambridge and New York: Cambridge University Press, 1985.

Thucydides. Text with English translation by C. F. Smith et al. 4 vols. Loeb Classical Library. Cambridge, Mass.: Harvard University Press, 1923–30.

Todd, Robert B. *Alexander of Aphrodisias on Stoic Physics.* Leiden: Brill, 1976.

Westerink, Leendert Gerrit, ed. *Anonymous Prolegomena to Platonic Philosophy.* Amsterdam: North Holland, 1962.

Williams, C.J.F. *Aristotle's "De Generatione et Corruptione."* Translated, with introduction and commentary. Oxford: Oxford University Press, 1982.

Woodfield, Andrew. *Teleology.* Cambridge and New York: Cambridge University Press, 1976.

Wright, M. R. *Empedocles: The Extant Fragments.* Edited with an introduction, commentary, and concordance. New Haven: Yale University Press, 1981.

Xenophon. *Scripta Minora (Hiero, Agesilaus, Constitution of the Lacedaemonians, Ways and Means, The Cavalry Commander, On the Art of Horsemanship, On Hunting).* Edited with English translation by E. C. Marchant. Loeb Classical Library. Cambridge, Mass.: Harvard University Press, 1925.

INDEX OF PASSAGES

GENERAL INDEX

abstract natural powers vs. observed facts, 8–10, 16–17, 33–35, 35n.42

Academica (Cicero), 84–90, 86–88nn.10–12, 91–92, 91n, 94–95, 355n

Academics vs. dogmatists, 79. *See also* Academic vs. Pyrrhonian skepticism

Academic vs. Pyrrhonian skepticism, 78–79, 81–103; Academics described as skeptics, 83–84, 83n; Aenesidemus, 82n.3, 84–85n.7; as ancient/classical vs. Renaissance/modern skepticism, 82, 82n.4; aporetics, 83n, 85n; Arcesilaus, 82n.3, 83n, 84–90, 86–88nn.10–12, 89–91nn.16–18, 91–95, 92n.22, 94n; Arcesilaus on assent without knowledge, 95–98, 96–99nn, 102; Arcesilaus vs. Sextus, 82n.4, 98–103, 99–101nn.28–30; Carneades, 81, 82n.3, 83n, 85–86, 99, 100; Cicero on, 81–82n.2, 83, 85, 90n.18; Cicero on Arcesilaus's skepticism, 84–90, 86–88nn.10–12, 89n.16, 91–98, 91n, 92n.22, 94n, 97–98nn; Clitomachus, 81–82nn.2–3, 99; ephectics, 83n, 85n; Gellius on, 83n; Plato, 85, 91–92, 92–93nn.22–24; Pyrrhoneans described as skeptics, 83, 83n, 84–85n.7; Pyrrho, 81–82n.2, 84n.7, 90n.18; Sextus, 82–83nn.3–5, 83–84, 98–103, 99–102nn.28–31; Socrates, 85, 86–88, 90–91n.18, 90–98, 93nn.23–24, 96–97n; Stoics, 81–82nn.2–3, 85, 96–97n, 99n; and unperturbedness, 99n, 101–2, 101–2n.31; zetetics, 85n

Ackrill, J. L., 294n.39

actions/choice, 326n, 329n

Adeimantus, on justice. *See* justice, Plato on

Aelian: *On the Characteristics of Animals,* 207n.5

Aenesidemus, 81–82, 81–82nn.2–3, 84–85n.7

Aesop: *Fabulae Aphthonii Rhetoris,* 207n.5

Aëtius, 220n.32, 222n

Against the Sophists (Isocrates), 76

air (element). *See* earth, air, fire, and water

Alexander of Aphrodisias, 151n.4, 156n.12; on liberty of indifference, 239; on light, 221n; *On Fate,* 238n.51; *On Mixture,* 173, 173n.30, 219n; on responsibility, 238n.51; on Zeus, 219n

Alexander the Platonist ("Clay-Plato"), 366–67n.50

Ammonius, 155n.10

Anaxagoras, 35, 88

animals, Aristotle on. *See* teleology, natural

Anonymous Prolegomena to Platonic Philosophy, 83n

Antidosis (Isocrates), 71–77

Antigone (Sophocles), 204n

Antiochus of Ascalon, 78, 85

Antipater Sidonius, 207n.5

Antisthenes, 66, 73

apathy, 81n.2

Aphorisms (Hippocratic Corpus), 4n.6

Apollonius of Chalcedon, 361n, 367n.50

aporetics, 83n, 85n

Arcesilaus: on assent without knowledge, 95–98, 96–99nn, 102; Platonic dogmatism of, 100n.29; skepticism of, 82n.3, 83n, 84–90, 86–88nn.10–12, 89–91nn.16–18, 91–95, 92n.22, 94n; skepticism of, vs. Sextus's skepticism, 82n.4, 98–103, 99–101nn.28–30

Aristo, 81–82n.2

Aristocles of Messene, 221n; *On Philosophy,* 90n.18

Aristotle: as an Academic, 85; as Alexander's tutor, 73; on autonomy, 207n.5; on common opinion, methodology of conceding to, 327–28n.22; on Democritus, on explanation and origins, 112–13n, 117; on embryology (*see* embryology/reproduction); on Forms, 47n, 174–75, 202–3; on hypothetical necessity (*see* hypothetical necessity); Isocrates on, 73; on living a life of justice, 77; on mixture (*see* mixture); on moral character, 312–13; on motivation, 313; on promoting

rationality/thought: and autonomy
(*continued*)
eudaimonia as excellent contemplation,
296–98, 297n.43, 300–308, 305–
8nn.57–61; and free will/responsibility,
240 (*see also under* autonomy, Stoic);
goodness as rational order, 262–63,
265–66, 268; Kant on, 236; Marcus
Aurelius on, 361–63, 362nn, 367n.50;
misuse of, 241n; pleasure/reason in
beautiful/harmonious/truthful mixture,
278, 299–300; Socrates rules out pleasure/
reason as the good, 271, 271n.2, 272–
78, 273–75nn, 277nn, 279, 279n, 284–
85, 287–88; and the soul, 262–63;
standards of, 218, 225; Stoics on, 213–
14n.17, 213–18, 214–15nn.20–21,
217n.26, 224–25, 228, 240–41n, 359;
and virtue, 234–35. *See also* autonomy,
Stoic
reason. *See* rationality/thought
reduction, methodological/theory vs.
ontological, 123n.10
Regimen in Acute Diseases (Hippocratic
Corpus), 3n.2
reproduction. *See* embryology/reproduc-
tion
Republic (Plato): Cherniss on, 45–46,
64n.26; Cornford on, 64n.26; on education, 341; on foundations/underlying
principles, 19, 20n.22, 22; on necessary
pleasures, 298, 298n.45; on philosophy,
72; on sensation, 45–46; on Socratic
dialectic, 74; *Theaetetus* 184–186 vs.
Republic 522–525, 45–47, 63–64,
64n.26. *See also* justice, Plato on
resemblance. *See* embryology/reproduction
rhetoric: oratory vs. philosophy, 65–80;
Plato on, 69–71; Stoics on, 360n.39
Rhetoric (Aristotle), 66–67, 281–82
rightness/wrongness, 69–70, 74
Rist, J. M., 368n
Rogatianus, 336n.5
Ross, William David, 138n, 280n.14

Sameness/Similarity, 44, 46, 54–55
Schofield, Malcolm, 81n.1, 91n, 94n
seasons/meteorological regularities, 125–
26, 125n.12
Sedley, David, 99n, 102

self-sufficiency. *See* finality/self-sufficiency,
Plato and Aristotle on
semen. *See* embryology/reproduction
Seneca, 309–14; on bodily movement,
229n.42; and Chrysippus, 313, 314, 345,
345n.20; on common opinion, methodology of conceding to, 327–28, 327–28n.22;
on defense of philosophical (even non-
Stoic) opinions, 322n.17, 338–39, 345,
345n.20; on human minds as disjointed
portions of Zeus's mind, 239n; influence
of, 311–12, 311n, 334, 334n.28; on moral
improvement via philosophical truths,
311; on public service vs. private living,
344–46; rhetorical presentation vs. philosophical argumentation by, 313–14n.8,
333–34, 333n; Stoic commitment of, 337,
339, 339n.12, 346; Stoic goals of, 309–
14; Stoic philosophical doctrine, knowledge of, 336; and Zeno, 313, 314, 345.
Works (see also *Moral Letters to Lucilius*):
De Otio, 344–46; *Moral Essays*, 310,
333; *On Anger*, 333n
sense-perception, 43n.1, 47. See also
Theaetetus 184–186
Serapion, 28n
Sextus Empiricus, 81–82; on body, 219n;
Pyrrhonian Sketches, 82n.3, 98–100,
219n; on skepticism, 97; skepticism of,
82–83nn.3–5, 83–84, 98–103, 99–
102nn.28–31; Stoic influence of, 311; on
the Stoics on knowledge, 96
Sextus of Chaeronea (Platonist philosopher), 366–67
Simonides, 93nn.23–24
simple bodies: as elements, 161–62, 161n,
169–71, 170–71nn; perceptible qualities
of, 156–57nn.12–13, 156–60, 159n.16
Simplicius, 132n.4
skepticism, 78–79, 97. *See also* Academic
vs. Pyrrhonian skepticism
Smith, Wesley, 4–5n.6
Socrates: on finality/self-sufficiency (*see*
finality/self-sufficiency, Plato and Aristotle on); on justice (*see* justice, Plato on);
on reason's ideal of knowledge, 95–96;
skepticism of, 85, 86–88, 90–91n.18,
90–98, 93nn.23–24, 96–97n; on sperm
movement, 181
Socratic dialectic, 73–76, 77–78